FREEDOM IN CONTEMPORARY CULTURE

CATHOLIC UNIVERSITY OF LUBLIN

WORLD UNION OF THE CATHOLIC PHILOSOPHICAL SOCIETIES

REDACTION COMMITTEE

s. Zofia J. Zdybicka
Józef Herbut
Andrzej Maryniarczyk
Alicja Łyskawka
Natasza Szutta

FREEDOM IN CONTEMPORARY CULTURE

Acts
of the V World Congress
of Christian Philosophy
Catholic University of Lublin
20–25 August 1996

Volume I

The University Press
of the Catholic University of Lublin
Lublin 1998

Cover design
JERZY DURAKIEWICZ

Technical editor
EWA ŁUPINA

Sponsors
KONRAD ADENAUER STIFTUNG
KOMITET BADAŃ NAUKOWYCH
MINISTERSTWO EDUKACJI NARODOWEJ

© Copyright by Redakcja Wydawnictw KUL, Lublin 1998

ISBN 83-228-0721-X (Vol. I-II)
Vol. I   83-228-0729-5
Vol. II 83-228-0737-6

REDAKCJA WYDAWNICTW
KATOLICKIEGO UNIWERSYTETU LUBELSKIEGO
ul. Konstantynów 1, 20-708 Lublin
tel. 524-18-09 (centrala), 525-71-66 (kolportaż)

Wydanie I. Zam. 157/97

Zakład Małej Poligrafii KUL

mory and hearts of the Participants. The numerous letters we received er the Congress have encouraged us to entertain such hopes.

The unique atmosphere of scientific reflection and debate was complemented by such related events as: the Holy Mass marking the opening of conference in the presence of Their Eminences: Joseph Cardinal Glemp, Primate of Poland; Henryk Cardinal Gulbinowicz; Arbishop Józef Kowzyk, the Apostolic Nuntio for Poland; everyday Eucharist, an exhibition icons, concerts, a meeting with the authorities of Lublin at the Crown stice Court at the Old City of Lublin, sight-seeing trips to Kazimierz, mość, Częstochowa and Kraków.

An unforgettable impression was left in the hearts of the Participants by visit to the Majdanek Concentration Camp and the common prayer in s place of the death of hundreds of thousands of innocent people from ny nations and various religious denominations. The Majdanek Camp is a gic testimony of the consequences of misconceiving freedom and subjugan of man by his fellow human being. It constitutes an unceasing call for a ly human freedom.

The Congress took place four years before the end of the twentieth centy, which will pass to history as a period of inhuman forms of slavery as ll as excesses of exorbitant freedom – totalitarianism and extreme liberal1. The idea behind the Congress and its materialisation referred to the tiative of the Conference of the Rectors of Polish Universities dating to 91. Thus the Congress was a unit in a chain of events which aim at preting us, through a reflection upon important problems of man, to the eat Jubilee of Christianity and at ushering us, endowed with new hopes, o the Third Millennium.

It is our heart-felt wish that this volume may become a lasting testimony our gratitude to all the Participants for their contribution into the reflecn on the problem of freedom, for presented papers, discussion, and, ove all, for their invaluable presence.

On behalf of the Organising Committee
Zofia J. Zdybicka

F

This volume contains the proceedings of the World Cor
tian Philosophy, which was held at the Catholic University
land), from the 20th to the 26th of August, 1996. The purpc
gress was to reflect together on the question of 'Freedom in
Culture'. More than 300 people from 30 countries of the wo1
the conference. Pope John Paul II addressed a special mess:
ticipants of the Congress and gave his own reflection concer1

Many distinguished professors from well-known universiti
well as all over the world discussed diverse aspects of the p1
dom. They gave 18 plenary presentations and over 150 pape1
groups. These concerned the following topics: conceptions of
and contemporary; problems related to freedom; freedom –
freedom – society – politics; freedom and science; freedom –
cation; freedom and religion. These presentations provided 1
for discussion among eminent specialists.

The volume we present contains the papers given at ple1
shop sessions delivered in English, German, French, Italiar
They are published in the order they were presented at the C
papers and Polish translations of plenary papers will form a
ond) volume. We publish the papers as they were sent in b
who alone should be held responsible for their content. We di
with the texts save for the minor grammatical and technical i

The Congress was an event rich in impressions and philos
tion. Naturally, the proceedings alone cannot convey the in
phere of scholarly debate, reflection and exchange, which c
been recorded in writing. All we can do here is trust, that bo
ing atmosphere and the exchanges at the debates were re

AVANT – PROPOS

Le présent volume contient les actes du Congrès Mondial de la Philosophie Chrétienne, qui s'est tenu à l'Université Catholique de Lublin, du 20 au 26 août 1996. Ce Congrès s'est assigné pour but une réflexion sur le problème de la liberté dans la culture contemporaine. Plus de 300 personnes de 30 pays du monde ont pris part à cette rencontre. Jean-Paul II a bien voulu s'adresser aux Participants en leur faisant parvenir sa propre réflexion sur la liberté.

D'éminents Professeurs de célèbres Universités, étrangères et polonaises, se sont penchés sur divers aspects du problème de la liberté. Dix-huit conférences ont été prononcées en séances plénières et plus de 150 conférences et communications dans des groupes thématiques. Elles étaient centrées sur les problèmes suivants: conceptions de la liberté, anciennes et contemporaines, questions en rapport avec la liberté; liberté – morale – droit; liberté – société – politique; liberté – science; liberté – culture – éducation; liberté – religion. Les conférences, plénières aussi bien que celles faites dans les sections, ont donné lieu à des discussions animées entre spécialistes.

Le volume présenté (I-II) comporte les textes des conférences plénières et de celles faites dans les sections, prononcées en anglais, allemand, français, italien et espagnol. Ils sont publiés en conformité avec la structure du Congrès. Les textes présentés en polonais ainsi que les traductions en polonais des conférences prononcées en séances plénières paraîtront dans un volume à part. Nous publions les textes tels qu'ils ont été fournis par les Auteurs; qui sont les seuls responsables de leur contenu. Nous ne sommes aucunement intervenus dans la teneur; notre "ingérence" s'est bornée à opérer de menues corrections de nature grammaticale et technique.

Le Congrès a constitué un événement plein de richesses. Les actes publiés ne sauraient évidemment pas communiquer toute l'atmosphère de la concentration scientifique, l'ambiance des discussions fougueuses, qui n'ont pas pu être retenues par écrit. Nous espérons que le climat du Congrès tout comme l'échange de vues lors des séances et pendant les rencontres amicales resteront dans la mémoire et dans le coeur des Participants. Les nombreuses lettres qui nous sont parvenues après la clôture du Congrès, nous autorisent à nourrir l'espoir qu'il en sera ainsi.

Le climat ardent de la recherche, climat unique en son genre, a trouvé un complément précieux dans tout ce qui entourait le Congrès: célébration commune de l'Eucharistie au départ, avec la participation de Son Eminence le Cardinal Józef Glemp, Primat de la Pologne, de Son Eminence le Cardinal Henryk Gulbinowicz, de Son Excellence l'Archevêque Józef Kowalczyk, nonce apostolique en Pologne, – la messe quotidienne, une exposition d'icônes, des concerts, des rencontres avec les Autorités de la ville de Lublin dans le bâtiment historique du Tribunal au centre de la Vieille Ville, les flâneries à travers Lublin, des excursions à Kazimierz-sur-Vistule, à Zamość, à Częstochowa et à Cracovie.

Une trace inoubliable dans le coeur des Participants a laissé la visite commune du Camp d'Extermination à Maïdanek et la prière oecuménique là ou des centaines de miliers de personnes innocentes de différentes nationalités et confessions ont trouvé la mort. Maïdanek constitue un signe tragique des conséquences d'une liberté mal comprise et de l'oppression de l'homme par l'homme. C'est aussi un cri incessant appelant une liberté authentiquement humaine.

Le Congrès a eu lieu quatre ans avant la fin du XXe siècle, qui passe dans l'histoire comme une époque de formes inhumaines d'esclavage et de manifestations d'une liberté dégénérée – du totalitarisme et du libéralisme extrême. L'idée du Congrès et sa réalisation se sont situées dans le sillage de l'initiative de la Conférence des Recteurs des Universités Polonaises (KRUP) prise en 1991. C'est donc là un des maillons dans la chaîne des événements qui, par la réflexion sur d'importants problèmes de l'homme, doivent nous préparer au Grand Jubilé du Christianisme et au franchissement du seuil du IIIe Millénaire avec une espérance nouvelle.

Notre voeu est que ce volume soit aussi une expression durable de notre reconnaissance qui va à tous les Participants, reconnaissance pour leur apport à la réflexion sur le problème de la liberté, pour les conférences données, pour les discussions, pour leur présence enrichissante.

Pour le Comité d'Organisation

Zofia J. Zdybicka

Droga Siostro Profesor,

z prawdziwą radością przyjąłem wiadomość, jaką przekazała mi Siostra Profesor w liście z dnia 11 kwietnia br., że Wydział Filozofii Katolickiego Uniwersytetu Lubelskiego wraz z World Union of Catholic Philosophical Societies organizują V Światowy Kongres Filozofii Chrześcijańskiej na temat «Wolność w kulturze współczesnej».

Dobrze się stało, że tak bardzo aktualny dla naszej epoki problem wolności, stał się tematem tego Kongresu. Żyjemy bowiem w czasach szczególnie wrażliwych na kwestię wolności i wyróżniających się bardzo silnym dążeniem do wolności osobistej i społecznej. Równocześnie jednak rozumienie wolności jest zróżnicowane do tego stopnia, że urasta do największego problemu współczesnego człowieka i współczesnej kultury, obok problemu prawdy o człowieku.

Intelektualiści, zwłaszcza filozofowie, są powołani w szczególny sposób do tego, by zgłębiać prawdę o ludzkiej wolności i przez to przyczyniać się do odpowiedzialnego korzystania z niej i budowania «kultury wolności». Wszystkim Uczestnikom V Kongresu Filozofii Chrześcijańskiej, odbywającego się w dniach 20 - 25 sierpnia w Katolickim Uniwersytecie Lubelskim przesyłam wyrazy duchowej łączności. Cieszę się, że na obrady tego Kongresu wybrano Lublin, miejsce krzyżowania się dróg i kultur, a także Katolicki Uniwersytet Lubelski, Uczelnię, z którą jestem bardzo ściśle związany poprzez długie lata mego nauczania, także dotyczącego problematyki wolności. Serdecznie pozdrawiam Was wszystkich przybyłych tak licznie z różnych krajów świata.

Wielebna Siostra
Prof. dr hab. Zofia ZDYBICKA
Dziekan Wydziału Filozofii
Katolickiego Uniwersytetu Lubelskiego
Lublin

W Encyklice *Veritatis splendor* i w Przemówieniu do Zgromadzenia Ogólnego ONZ z 5 października 1995 roku poświęciłem tej problematyce szczególnie wiele miejsca. We wspomnianym już Przemówieniu zwróciłem między innymi uwagę na istotną sprawę, jaką jest związek wolności z prawdą: «Wolność jest miarą godności i wielkości człowieka. Życie w warunkach wolności, do której dążą jednostki i narody, jest wielką szansą rozwoju duchowego człowieka i moralnego ożywienia narodów. Podstawowy problem, jaki dzisiaj musimy podjąć, to problem odpowiedzialnego korzystania z wolności, zarówno w jej wymiarze osobistym, jak i społecznym. (...) Wolność ma swoją wewnętrzną "logikę", która ją określa i uszlachetnia: jest podporządkowana prawdzie i urzeczywistnia się w poszukiwaniu i w czynieniu prawdy. Oderwana od prawdy o człowieku, wolność wyradza się w życiu indywidualnym w samowolę, a w życiu politycznym w przemoc silniejszego i w arogancję władzy» (n. 12). W kulturze współczesnej nastąpiło wyeksponowanie roli wolności przy jednoczesnym umniejszaniu roli prawdy, zwłaszcza prawdy obiektywnej na korzyść prawdy, której twórcą jest człowiek, aż do odmówienia prawdzie jakiegokolwiek znaczenia, a nawet uznania jej roli za ograniczającą człowieka. W dziedzinie niezmiernie ważnych relacji między wolnością i prawdą oraz wolnością i dobrem istnieje w myśli współczesnej zakłócenie, które może mieć katastrofalne skutki dla obecnej i przyszłej kultury. Oderwana od prawdy i dobra wolność staje się bowiem zagrożeniem dla człowieka, bytu osobowego, a więc zdolnego do poznania prawdy i w sposób świadomy i wolny spełniającego się poprzez dobre czyny. Wolność człowieka jest wolnością ku dobru. Natomiast dobro, by było dobrem człowieka musi być poznane, chodzi o dobro prawdziwe. Istnieje bowiem fundamentalny związek ludzkiej wolności z prawdą i dobrem.

Rodzi się stąd potrzeba przywrócenia przekonania o wzajemnej harmonii w człowieku między wolnością i prawdą, właściwego rozumienia roli i charakteru sumienia oraz wolności ludzkich decyzji. W Encyklice *Veritatis splendor* napisałem, że «sumienie wyraża się poprzez akty "sądu", odzwierciedlające prawdę o dobru, a nie poprzez arbitralne "decyzje". Zaś miarą dojrzałości i odpowiedzialności tych sądów - a ostatecznie samego człowieka jako ich podmiotu - nie jest wyzwolenie sumienia od obiektywnej prawdy, prowadzące do rzekomej autonomii jego decyzji, ale przeciwnie - intensywne poszukiwanie prawdy oraz kierowanie się nią w działaniu» (n. 61). W akcie wolności człowiek spełnia się jako osoba. Dzięki wolności posiada on zdolność kierowania swoim życiem i może otwierać się na dobro, stając się coraz bardziej człowiekiem.

Wolność ludzka jest wolnością rzeczywistą, jest sposobem istnienia człowieka jako osoby. Nie jest to jednak wolność absolutna, lecz ograniczona. Ma rozpoznawalne przez człowieka granice: «Jest to wolność istoty stworzonej, a więc wolność dana, którą trzeba przyjąć niczym kiełkującą dopiero roślinę i troszczyć się odpowiedzialnie o jej wzrost. Stanowi konstytutywny składnik owego wizerunku istoty stworzonej, który leży u podstaw godności osoby ... Wolność jest zatem zakorzeniona w prawdzie człowieka i skierowana ku wspólnocie» (n. 86). Posiada swe źródło i fundament w Jezusie Chrystusie, który jest prawdziwym wyzwolicielem człowieka. To On «wyswobodził nas ku wolności» (por. Ga 5, 1), to On objawił, że warunkiem autentycznej wolności jest szczere i otwarte uznanie prawdy, to On objawił, że wolność urzeczywistnia się przez miłość, to znaczy przez dar z siebie w służbie Bogu i braciom (por. *Veritatis splendor*, n. 87). Tak rozumiana i tak kontemplowana wolność rzutuje na pozostałe dziedziny kultury, na naukę i sztukę, które także obowiązane są budować na prawdzie i wolności.

Dzielę się z Wami tymi refleksjami, pragnąc w jakiś sposób włączyć się w prace Kongresu i życzę Wam, by wspólne obrady, dyskusje i filozoficzny dialog przyczyniły się do rozjaśnienia prawdy o ludzkiej wolności. We wspomnianym już Przemówieniu na forum ONZ powiedziałem, że «poszukiwanie wolności jest niepowstrzymanym dążeniem, które ma swoje źródło w uznaniu godności i nieocenionej wartości ludzkiej osoby i musi się wiązać z działaniem dla jej dobra» (n.3). Zwracam się do Was, miłośników mądrości, byście nie ustawali w poszukiwaniu wolności i pomogli innym odnaleźć jej pełnię w prawdzie, przyczyniając się w ten sposób do budowania kultury wolności, która jest duszą cywilizacji. Niech ten Kongres przyczyni się do uświadomienia, że nosimy w sobie zdolność do osiągnięcia mądrości i cnoty. «Dzięki tym darom i z pomocą łaski Bożej możemy zbudować w nadchodzącym stuleciu i dla dobra przyszłego tysiąclecia cywilizację godną człowieka, prawdziwą kulturę wolności» (tamże, n.18).

Wszystkim przesyłam moje Apostolskie Błogosławieństwo.

Watykan, 1 sierpnia 1996 r.

Jan Paweł II

HIS HOLINESS POPE JOHN PAUL II

(Translation)

Dear Sister Professor,

It was with profound joy that I received the news you communicated to me in your letter of this past 11th of April that the Faculty of Philosophy of the Catholic University of Lublin and the World Union of Catholic Philosophical Societies are organizing the Fifth World Congress of Christian Philosophy on the theme "Freedom in Contemporary Culture".

It is good that the problem of freedom which is so relevant to our epoch has become the subject of this Congress. We live in times which are particularly sensitive to the question of freedom and which are distinguished by a strong aspiration to personal and social liberty. Yet at the same time the understanding of freedom is diversified to such a degree that it has grown to become the greatest problem facing contemporary man and contemporary culture beside the problem of the truth about the human person.

Intellectuals, and especially philosophers, are in particular called upon to probe into the truth about human freedom and thereby to contribute to its being used in a responsible way and for the building of the "culture of freedom". To all the participants of the Fith Congress of Christian Philosophy taking place on the 20 to the 25th of August at the Catholic University of Lublin, I send expressions of spiritual communion. I am glad that Lublin, a crossroads of routes and cultures, has been chosen for the venue of the Congress. I am also glad the Catholic University of Lublin, a University with which I am very closely connected through years of teaching there, teaching concerning freedom, has been chosen. I extend my heartfelt greetings to all of you who have come in such a great number from diverse countries of the world.

In my Encyclical Letter *Veritatis Splendor* and in my Address to the General Assembly of the UNO on the 5th of October, 1995, I devoted particularly much time to problems of freedom. In the above mentioned Address, I pointed to the essential issue of the connection of freedom with truth: "Freedom is the measure of man's dignity and greatness. Living the freedom sought by individuals and peoples is a great challenge to man's spiritual growth and to the moral vitality of nations. The basic question which we must all face today is the responsible use of freedom, in both personal and social dimensions. [...] Freedom has an inner logic" which distinguishes it and ennobles it: freedom is ordered to the truth, and is fulfilled in man's quest for truth and in man's living in the truth. Detached from the truth about the human person, freedom deteriorates into license in the lives of individuals, and, in political life, it becomes the caprice of the most powerful and the arrogance of power" (no. 12). In contemporary culture more emphasis has been put on the role of freedom, with simultaneous disparagement of the role of truth, in particular objective truth, which is belittled in favour of the truth whose creator is man, to the point of denying truth any meaning, or even regarding its role as a limitation for man. In the area of the extremely important relationships between freedom and truth and between freedom and the good, there exists a disturbance in the contemporary thought which may have disastrous consequences for both the present and future culture. Detached from truth and the good, freedom becomes a threat to man, to the human person as a being that is capable of knowing the truth and that fulfils himself in a conscious and free way through his good acts. The freedom of man is a freedom directed to the good. And the good, in order to become the good of man, has to be known, it has to be truly good, for there exists a fundamental connection between human freedom, truth and good.

Hence the need arises of restoring the belief in the mutual harmony between freedom and the truth in the human being, and also of restoring the correct understanding of the role and nature of conscience and the freedom of human decisions. In the Encyclical Letter *Veritatis Splendor* I wrote that "[...] conscience expresses itself in acts of 'judgment' which reflect the truth about the good, and not in arbitrary 'decisions'. The maturity and responsibility of these judgments – and, when all is said and done, of the individual who is their subject – are not measured by the liberation of the conscience from objective truth, in favour of an alleged autonomy in personal decisions, but, on the contrary, by an insistent search for truth and by allowing oneself to be guided by that truth in one's actions" (no. 61). In a free act an individual fulfils himself as a person. It is owing to freedom that the human being has the capacity to direct his life and is able to open himself to the good, thus more and more becoming man. Human freedom is a real freedom, it is the mode of the existence of an individual as a person. However, it is not an absolute freedom, but a limited one. It has its limits which are discernible to man: "Human freedom belongs to us as creatures; it is a freedom which is given as a gift, one to be received like a seed and to be cultivated responsibly. It is an essential of that creaturely image which is the basis of the dignity of the person. [...] Freedom, then, is rooted in the truth about man, and it is ultimately directed towards communion" (no. 86). It has its source and foundation in Jesus Christ who is the true liberator of man. It is He who "has set us free for freedom" (cf.Gal 5:1), who revealed that the frank and open acceptance of truth is the condition for authentic freedom, who revealed that freedom is acquired in *love*, that is in the gift of self in *service to God and one's brethren* (cf. *Veritatis Splendor*, no. 87). Freedom understood and contemplated in this way projects itself on the remaining areas of culture, on science and art, which are also bound to build upon truth and freedom.

I share these reflections with with the intention to join in the work of the Congress in some way and I wish that your common debates, discussions and philosophical dialogues may contribute to the clarification of the truth about human freedom. In the above mentioned Address to the United Nations I said that "the quest for freedom cannot be suppressed. It arises from a recognition of the inestimable dignity and value of the human person, and it cannot fail to be accompanied by a commitment on behalf of the human person" (no.4). I appeal to you, lovers of wisdom, never to stop in your search of freedom and to help others to find the fullness of freedom in truth, thus contributing to the building of the culture of freedom, which is the soul of civilization. Let this Congress help us realize that we all carry in ourselves the ability to attain wisdom and virtue. "With these gifts, and with the help of God's grace, we can build in the next century and the next millenium a civilization worthy of the human person, a true culture of freedom" (ibid, no. 18).

To all of you I extend my Apostolic Blessing.

Vatican, 1 August 1996

STANISŁAW WIELGUS
Rector of the Catholic University of Lublin

The Opening Address for the V World Congress of Christian Philosophy at the Catholic University of Lublin
FREEDOM CONFRONTING OLD AND NEW TOTALITARIANISM

Your Eminencies,
Excellencies,
Voivode of Lublin,
President of Lublin,
Ladies and Gentelmen,

I am deeply honoured to welcome so many eminent Guests and distinguished Scholars, who will participate in the Fifth World Congress of Christian Philosophy, which will take place here, at the Catholic University of Lublin, on the occasion of the Fifth Anniversary of the Faculty of Philosophy.

First of all, I would like to welcome His Eminence Cardinal Józef Glemp, the Primate of Poland, our tried and tested Friend.
Let me cordially welcome:

– His Excellency Archbishop Józef Kowalczyk, the Apostolic Nuncio to Poland;

– His Eminence Cardinal Henryk Gulbinowicz, Archbishop of Wrocław.

– His Excellency Bolesław Pylak, Archbishop of Lublin and the Grand Chancellor of the Catholic University of Lublin;

– His Excellency Julio Teran Dutari, The President of the International Federation of Catholic Universities.

– His Excellency Angelo Scola, The Rector of Pontificia Universita Lateranense.

– His Excellency Prof. Bohdan Bejze, Bishop of Łódź.

- His Excellency Dr Kazimierz Górny, Bishop of Rzeszów

Let me also welcome the Host of this region, Voivode of Lublin, Mr. Wiesław Brodowski.

- The Secretary of State in the Ministry of National Education, Prof. Zbigniew Olesiński.
- The President of Lublin, Dr. Krzysztof Stefaniuk;
- The most cordial welcome to the President of the Polish Academy of Sciences, Prof. Leszek Kuźnicki.
- The most cordial welcome to the President of the Committee of Philosophical Sciences of the Polish Academy of Science, Prof. Jerzy Pelc.
- To the President of the World Union of Catholic Philosophical Societies – Prof. Jean Ladrière;
- To the President of the Polish Philosophical Society, Prof. Władysław Stróżewski.
- To the General Secretary of the World Union of Catholic Philosophical Societies – Prof. George Mc Lean;
- To the Secretary of "Christiani Democratici Uniti", the Doctor honoris causa of our University – Prof. Rocco Buttiglione.
- To the Senator of the Republic of Poland, Prof. Alicja Grześkowiak.
- To the General Superior of Grey Ursuline Sisters, Mather Jolanta Olech.
- To the Chiev Commander of the Lublin Voivodship Police Force, Mr. Damazy Herman.
- To the Second Secretary of German Embassy, Dr. Anke Konrad.

I am very happy to greet all the Rectors, Deans and other Representatives of the Universities.

First of all let me cordially welcome:

- the Rector of the University of Łódź and the President of the Conference of the Polish Universities – Prof. Michał Seweryński;
- the Rector of the Universidad Metropolitana de Ciencias de la Education Santiago de Chile, and at the same time the General Secretary of the Associacion Catholica Interamericana de Filosofia – Prof. Gonzalez Lopez Jesus.
- the Rector of the Maria Curie-Skłodowska University in Lublin – Prof. Kazimierz Goebel;
- the Rector of the Agriculture University of Lublin – Prof. Józef Nurzyński;
- the Rector of the Technical University of Lublin – Prof. Iwo Pollo;
- the Rector of the Internationale Akademie für Philosophie – Lichtenstein Prof. Joseph Seifert.
- the Rector of the World Phenomenology Institute – Prof. Anna Teresa Tymieniecka.

– the Vice-rector of the Catholic University of Leuven – Prof. Herman de Dijn.
– the Vice-rector of the Pontificia Universita Urbaniana – Prof. Battista Mondin.
– the Vice-rector of the Arkhangelsk State Medical Academy – Prof. Andrej Sołowiew.
– the Vice-rector of the Medical University of Lublin – Prof. Leszek Szewczyk
– the Vice-Commander of Academy of Air Forces in Dęblin – Collonel Dr. Stanisław Kurek.

It is my great honour and pleasure to welcome all to the Fifth World Congress of Christian Philosophy from all over the world; from Europe, South and North America, Asia and Africa.

In particular, let me welcome the eminent and distinguished scholars from: Argentina, Austria, Belgium, Brazil, Canada, Chile, China, Czech Republic, Ecuador, France, Germany, Great Britain, Ireland, Italy, Japan, Lichtenstein, Lithuania, Mexico, Netherlands, Peru, Poland, Romania, Russia, Slovak Republic, South Africa, Spain, Switzerland, Uganda, United States of America, and – last but not least – from Vatican City.

Ladies and Gentelmen,

According to some historiosophers, the 20th century has already ended. It was exceptionally short. It began with the outbreak of the 1st World War and ended with the fall of communism in Europe. And still it was the century exceptionally abundant in good and evil. It was the time of an unbelievable development of technology and extraordinary achievements of the human mind in every field of science. But it was also the time of terrible suffering for hundreds of millions of people who had to survive exceptionally cruel wars and long lasting totalitarian rule. Many nations apprehended well the bitter taste of enslavement and humiliation, therefore regaining independence and freedom after the fall of communism was met with euphoria. For many millions of people, born and brought up in enslaved countries, freedom was associated with something ideal. It seemed to them that once it came, it would bring along welfare, common happiness, harmony and social unity. When it actually did, it brought about disappointment for many of them. For some it even became the synonym for their lives' disaster. It turned out that freedom alone does not solve automatically the painful economic and social problems which had grown over the past decades; what is more it creates additional, previously unknown obstacles and threats, difficult to handle for a man brought up in an enslaved country.

It turned out, too, that people who were formerly united in their struggle against totalitarianism now cannot find a common language, cannot reconcile their views, their ideologies and visions of their country's development, that they start hating one another or even fight ruthlessly. Mythological and idealistic dreams of freedom disappeared like soap-bubbles, leaving the feeling of disappointment and wrong doing in many minds. Only after a few years did the liberated nations begin to realise that freedom brings the dream of welfare, stabilisation, development and harmony only when it is founded on moral law, when it is inseparably connected with taking the responsibility for oneself and for others and, as a consequence, with the sense of duty; when it is inseparably connected with love, truth and moral good, as the Holy Father said in front of the Branderburger Tor in Berlin this year. Only after years of doubts and disappointment do people thrown into the new reality begin to realise that freedom is beautiful as well as difficult; that it requires a great effort and activity; that freedom left to itself will not survive; that without fair law it will become a new tyranny; that it will become a hollow sound everywhere the strong do not have to obey the law.

The constation that freedom must be built on law poses, however, numerous questions. Namely, on which law? Is the human law sufficient? Is it the man – weak, erroneous, sometimes egoistic and vicious who is to be the ultimate point of reference for moral good and evil, for truth and falseness? Should we not look for more profound points of reference, transcending man and reaching out for something Eternal and Permanent?

These questions are faced today by the societies liberated from old totalitarianisms, but threatened by the new ones, perhaps even more dangerous for our civilisation than the previous ones, more and more often called – "the totalitarianism of the lack of idea", extreme individualism, moral relativism and consumerism". These totalitarianisms, just like the former ones, having in view power and money and now controlling the powerful mass media, greatly influence today the consciousness of hundreds of millions of people and impose on them myths and orders created often with premeditation which appeal to the basic instincts and which, this time, function beyond the sphere of good and evil; beyond the sphere of truth and lie; which give orders without giving rational arguments; which never say: "Do so because it is good, because it is true", but they formulate their orders in an entirely different way: "Do so because everyone else does so, because in is the human condition, because such is the logic of history, because such is the call of your nature and your sexuality, because you have it in your blood, because only in this way will you succeed, and get to the depth of your life and pleasure.

These myths are hardly discussed. They are not codified. They are not even named as were the old ones created by the propagandists of the old totalitarian ideologies. The effectiveness of the myths of the new totalitarianisms depends on their anonymity. Uncovered, they become powerless.

It is true that the creators of the myths giving birth to totalitarianisms have always been, first of all, intellectuals. But it is also true that it is only intellectuals that are able to overcome the myths dangerous for man which enslave him and make him doubtful about the sense of existence. It seems that Christian intellectuals are able to do that because it is them who have inherited the great humanistic tradition shaped by Christianity, which has been the religion of freedom and equality from the very beginning; which has always been universalistic and pluralistic in its forms, dialogic and personalistic; which has always taught the responsibility for the gift of freedom; which has co-created the idea of democracy, the vision of the law-abiding state of law and the vision of human rights. But Christian intellectuals cannot live on the past. Remembering the past they should look into the future. They should become the protagonists of changes which would lead to the creation of the new world – peaceful, cooperative, foregrounding order and democracy, respecting human rights, truly tolerant. These goals seem to be a utopia when confronted with the brutal reality of the contemporary world characterised by serious political, social and economic problems, manifesting themselves in old and new wars, in growing unemployment, in increasing economic polarisation of the world making the poor countries receive less and less, and the rich ones more and more; in still growing technological hiatus between the countries influencing considerably the living standards of different societies, in growing frustration and psychological depression of millions of people; in rapidly increasing crime rates and terrorism; and, finally, in still present mental contamination of societies, manifesting itself in xenophobia, nationalism, fanaticism, terrifying ignorance and the massive manipulation of social consciousness performed by the new totalitarianisms, consumerism, relativism and the lack of idea – using lies and dishonesty on a large scale.

Unfortunately humanity is still possessed by new or brought back to life demons that poison human hearts and minds and which are the actual source of wars, terrosim and all kinds of savagery. The contamination of human minds by lie, sinister ideas, irrationalism and surrealistic ways of building the world as well as anti-values is more dangerous than the pollution of the environment. It is the intellectuals who should find an antidote to this aberration. Such an antidote, that – for sake of our civilisation – may and should be used in the process of counterpoisoning human consciousness is, undoubtedly, Christian philosophical thought. Its task is, among others, to uncover falseness, bad intentions, ignorance and distribution of criminal theories but also to shape the consciousness open to freedom, truth, democracy, good and tolerance; to provide objective knowledge about man and his function in the world; to regenerate the world of social and civil values; to awaken in people the conscience and responsibility for their own and others' lives; to teach thinking about global problems; finally, to make an attempt to draw a new vision of the intellectually and morally reborn world, a truly free world.

The V World Congress of Christian Philosophy dedicated to freedom in contemporary culture takes place in Poland, the country in which, for the past 200 years, freedom has been treated as a value more precious not only than bread but than life. I am very happy to host the Congress at the Catholic University of Lublin which does appreciate the price of freedom and the threat to freedom since, in its 80 years' history, it had to contend with two totalitarianisms – Hitler's and Stalin's – and which, over decades, was the only intellectually free university in the huge area under communist rule. Finally, I want to thank all the Participants in this Fifth World Congress of Christian Philosophy for having accepted our invitation and coming here, to the Catholic University of Lublin.

I would like to thank the scholars who have prepared and will deliver lectures at this Congress.

In a very special way I would like to express my gratitude to Professor Stanislaus Ladusans, who died – unfortunatelly – in 1992. It is he, who as the president of the Associatio Catolica Interamericana de Filosofia, inspired us to organize this Congress.

I appreciate all the efforts done by the Faculty of Philosophy in order to prepare this Congress.

Special credit I want to address to the Dean of that Faculty, Prosessor Zofia Zdybicka for her exceptionally great job.

Let me express my gratitude also to the sponsors for their generous financial support, which made this congress possible, first of all to:
Komitet Badań Naukowych,
Ministerstwo Edukacji Narodowej,
Urząd Miejski w Lublinie, Wydział Kultury i Spraw Społecznych,
Joseph Van de Wiele Foundation, Belgium,
Konrad Adenauer Stiftung, Deutschland,
Fundacja „Galeria na Prowincji", Lublin,
Bank Depozytowo-Kredytowy S.A., Lublin,
Bank Polska Kasa Opieki S.A., Lublin,
Bank Przemysłowo-Handlowy S.A., Lublin,
Pierwszy Bank Komercyjny S.A., Lublin,
Polski Bank Inwestycyjny S.A., Lublin,
Wschodni Bank Cukrownictwa S.A., Lublin,
Cukrownia Lublin S.A.,

Gospodarstwo Szklarniowe „Leonów",
Spółka z o.o. „Nałęczowianka",
Zakłady Mięsne w Lublinie „Lubmeat",
Zakłady Przemysłu Owocowo-Warzywnego „Milejów",
Spółka Akcyjna „Ruch",
Fundacja „Sacrum Paideia".

Thank You very much.

I wish all the Participants of the Fifth World Congress of Christian Philosophy a very fruitful meeting, creative debates as well as a pleasant stay at our University and in our city.

God bless You all!

The Fifth World Congress of Christian Philosophy on "Freedom in Contemporary Culture" is open.

Thank You for your attention.

Card. JÓZEF GLEMP
Primat de Pologne

HOMÉLIE D'OUVERTURE DU CONGRÈS

Mesdames et Messieurs les Professeurs,
Participants au Congrès Philosophique
de Lublin,

Ressemblés à l'église de l'Université catholique de Lublin, c'est par la prière, par la prière eucharistique, que nous inaugurons nos débats philosophiques sur les problèmes de la liberté dans la culture contemporaine. En principe le fait de limiter le thème de la liberté à la culture contemporaine paraîtrer très intéressant et en même temps évident, car il serait difficile et presque impossible de traiter, au cours d'un congrès, le problème de la liberté à travers diverses époques et cultures.

Indépendamment du cadre limitant le sujet, dans le domaine de la foi, et en particulier dans les enseignements de la Bible, nous percevons que la notion de liberté est profondément enracinée dans l'ensemble de l'enseignement de Dieu. Dieu, en tant que plénitude de la liberté appelle l'homme à co-participer à sa liberté. Il délivre ceux qui demeuraient dans les ténèbres du péché et à l'ombre de la mort pour les faire entrer dans l'espace de la liberté absolue qui n'est accessible qu'en Dieu. Il est évident qu'en parlant de la liberté qui est en Dieu et que l'homme ne peut obtenir qu'en Dieu, nous nous trouvons dans le domaine de la théologie. Mais le philosophe ne reste pas indifférent à ce que l'homme sait de la liberté par expérience propre et à ce que les sciences ont à dire à son sujet.

"C'est pour que nous restions libres que le Christ nous a libérés" (Ga 5,1), ces paroles que saint Paul a adressées aux Galates constituent la définition fondamentale de la liberté dans la Bible. En nous penchant sur les fragments des textes que nous venons d'entendre aujourd'hui, ceux du prophète Ezéchiel et de l'Évangile selon saint Mathieu, nous pouvons maintenant essayer d'élargir notre savoir à propos de l'enseignement biblique au sujet de la liberté.

Les paroles du prophète Ezéchiel, adressées contre le roi de Tyr, ne touchent pas directement le problème de la liberté. Mais la conséquence des actes du roi, qui par adresse et malice a amassé une grande fortune, est la limitation de la liberté de ses sujets et de sa liberté personnelle. Voici comment le prophète caractérise ce roi: "[...] tu as dit: »Je suis un Dieu, j'habite une demeure divine, au coeur de la mer« (Ez 28, 2). En se situant à la place de Dieu, il limite la liberté de ses sujets, en conséquence de cette omission de la vérité. Le roi n'est qu'un homme. Il l'éprouvera très douloureusement au moment où les nations barbares envahiront Tyr, lui apportant la mort. La vie en dehors de la vérité provoque des perturbations dans le domaine de la liberté. Il serait juste de citer ici les paroles que Jean-Paul II a prononcées à Berlin devant la Porte de Brandebourg, paroles qui confirment cette vérité: "[...] l'homme n'est pas maître de sa propre vie, ni de celle d'autrui; s'il veut être un homme dans la vérité, il doit entendre et écouter. Sa libre créativité ne se développe de façon efficace et durable que si elle repose sur la vérité, qui est son fondement [...] il n'y a pas de liberté sans vérité".

Noua trouvons un enseignement similaire dans le message de l'Évangile selon saint Mathieu qui nous rapporte les paroles du Christ ayant trait aux difficultés que les riches rencontrent, voulant entrer dans le Royaume des Cieux. La richesse, conçue comme possession et attachement aux biens matériels, limite la liberté de l'homme à atteindre le bonheur éternel. Le Christ se sert ici d'une comparaison très imagée: "[...] il est plus facile à un chameau de passer par un trou d'aiguille qu'à un riche d'entrer dans le Royaume des Cieux" (Mt 19,24). Les apôtres pour suivre Jésus ont tout laissé. Ils étaient capables de faire un sacrifice et de renoncer. Ainsi ils sont devenus libres pour choisir le Christ. Pour être libre comme un enfant de Dieu, il faut savoir sacrifier aussi bien sa richesse que sa misère. Jean-Paul II le constate clairement dans l'allocution précitée: "Animés par un esprit de sacrifice, de nombreux hommes sont naturellement prêts au renoncement, dans la vie de tous les jours [...] ils se sacrifient pour la liberté, pour la défendre des menaces intérieures ou extérieures [...]. Personne ne peut être exempt de sa responsabilité personnelle à l'égard de la liberté. Il n'y a pas de liberté sans sacrifice".

L'Église en Pologne a parcouru un long chemin d'épreuves dans sa lutte pour la liberté. Au cours des dernières dix années, nous nous sommes rendus compte que l'on ne peut pas atteindre la liberté sans se fonder sur la vérité et les renoncements. Tout simplement, la liberté coûte. Parfois on nous demandait pourquoi l'Épiscopat luttait-il si fermement pour la liberté de religion et de l'Église, on nous disait – la foi, on peut la pratiquer en privé, sans rumeur, et les libertés civiques sont bien plus importantes. Mais une telle constatation n'est pas vraie, car la liberté de professer librement sa foi est la plus fondamentale des libertés civiques. En gagnant sa liberté, l'Église frayait la voie aux libertés civiques de tous. Car on ne peut pas dire que les libertés civiques sont assurées si en même temps la liberté de conscience et de confession est soumise à des restrictions.

Prions le Christ qui ne cesse de nous libérer pour la liberté véritable, que les débats de ce Congrès philosophique de Lublin nous permettent de comprendre les problèmes actuels de la liberté et de savoir les incorporer dans notre vie en enrichissant ainsi la culture contemporaine. Ainsi soit-il.

BOLESŁAW PYLAK
Erzbischof von Lublin
Poland

Exzellenz! Sehr verehrter Herr Apostolischer Nuntius!
Eminenzen!
Exzellenzen!
Verehrter Herr Rector Magnificus!
Sehr verehrte Damen und Herren!

Als Bischof der Erzdiözese Lublin und zugleich Großkanzler der Katholischen Universität heiße ich alle Gäste, die zum 5. Kongreß der christlichen Philosophie gekommen sind, herzlich willkommen! Ich freue mich sehr, daß Sie als Ort Ihrer Tagung gerade Lublin gewählt haben, was für unsere Universität sicher eine Ehre ist, besonders aber für die Philosophische Fakultät, die eben das 50jährige Jubiläum ihres Bestehens feiert. Lublin als Ort Ihres Kongresses verstehe ich als eine Anerkennung für die Katholische Universität Lublin für ihre Verdienste innerhalb der Länder Mittel- und Osteuropas. Unsere Universität war in der kommunistischen Zeit wohl das einzige Zentrum des freien christlichen Denkens. Aber auch heute, in der neuen politischen Wirklichkeit, hat unsere Nochschule besondere Aufgaben zu erfüllen. Zwar haben wir in unserem Land verschiedene katholische Hochschulen; sie sind aber hauptsächlich kirchliche Fakultäten. Die Katholische Universität Lublin hingegen ist eine humanistische Universität mit allen Rechten und Pflichten, an der die meisten Professoren und Stutenten Laien sind. Unsere Lubliner Nochschule hat also in bezug auf die erwähnten Fakultäten eine führende Rolle. Sie hat weiterhin eine besondere Aufgabe zu erfüllen in bezug auf die Nachbarländer, die nun ihre wissenschaftliche Zentren einrichten bzw. von neuem aufbauen. Auch Ihr Kongreß hat eine besondere Bedeutung für unsere Nachbarländer.

Der zweite Gedanke meiner Begrüßung nimmt Bezug auf das Kongreßthema: Die Freiheit in der gegenwärtigen Kultur. Ich glaube, daß der Hauptgrund, warum Sie dieses Thema gewählt haben, darin liegt, daß wir mit der Freiheit nach der schweren kommunistischen Erbe in dem politischen, sozialen und ekonomischen Bereich noch nicht richtig umgehen können. Das ist ein echtes Problem im Leben unseres Landes.

Aber die Freiheit als solche besitzt ein viel breiteres Ausmaß. Es geht dabei um die Wirkung des Menschen als Person, die verantwortlich für ihre Taten ist. Die so verstandene Freiheit gehört – wie das Wesen des Menschen – zum Hauptthema verschiedener wissenschaftlicher Disziplinen wie Philosophie, Theologie, Soziologie und Pädagogik, daher stößt die Problematik Ihres Kongresses auf das hohe Interesse verschiedener Wissenschaftler. Besonders denke ich hier an die Theologen, für die die Relation der Freiheit und der Gnade seit Jahrhunderten ein Hauptdisskusionsthema bildet.

Die Sozialwissenschaftler interessiert die Freiheit im sozialen Bereich, darunter die Manipulation in bezug auf den einzelnen Menschen und die ganze Gesellschaft. Wir wissen, daß die Manipulation – ein Einfluß auf die menschliche Psyche, zusammen mit seiner Freiheit – häufig zur Hauptaufgabe der Medien gehört, da die Medien eine immer größere Rolle im sozialen Bereich spielen.

Das Problem der Freiheit interessiert auch die Pädagogik, da die Erziehung des Menschen eine Heranbildung zum Wirken in Freiheit bedeutet.

So bin ich der festen Überzeugung, daß der Kongreß nicht nur ein Beitrag zur Weiterentwicklung der Wissenschaft innerhalb der Antropologie als solcher ist, sondern auch eine praktische Bedeutung aufweist. Die Freiheit des Menschen und sein Wirken bildet ein Schlüsselproblem für den Menschen als einzelnen und auch die ganze Gesellschaft.

So wünsche ich Ihnen allen – sehr verehrte Damen und Herren – einen guten Verlauf Ihrer Tagung. Wir möchten, daß Sie sich alle hier an der Katholischen Universität Lublin wohlfühlen. Das ist auch mein Wunsch an Sie alle!

Haben Sie bitte Verständnis, wenn manche Schwierigkeiten – besonders Probleme mit Ihrer Unterbringung – auftauchen. Gott begleite all Ihr Tun!

ZOFIA J. ZDYBICKA
Université Catholique de Lublin
Pologne

Vos Eminences,
Vos Excellences,
Monseigneur le Recteur
Chers Collègues et Amis,
Mesdames et Messieurs,

Au nom de la Faculté de philosophie, qui fête cette année ses cinquante ans (1946-1996), je voudrais vous exprimer toute notre joie, notre émotion et notre gratitude. Nous sommes très heureux d'avoir parmi nous tant d'excellents maîtres de philosophie venus du monde entier.

Merci beaucoup pour votre présence. Je vous souhaite que durant ce Congrès notre Faculté devienne votre Faculté.

Nous ne pouvons pas commencer nos travaux sans évoquer le nom du Professeur Stanislas Ladusans, de Rio de Janeiro (Brésil), le Président de l'Associação Catolica Interamericana de Filosofia (ACIF), initiateur et organisateur des quatre Congrès de Philosophie Chrétienne ayant eu lieu jusqu'à présent: 1979 en Argentine, 1986 au Mexique, 1989 en Equateur, 1992 au Pérou.

Le Professeur Stanislas Ladusans a aussi été l'initiateur du présent Congrès. C'est lui qui a choisi la Pologne, Lublin, l'Université Catholique de cette ville comme lieu du Ve Congrès. Lors de son séjour chez nous, en 1992, nous avons ensemble fixé le sujet du Congrès: la Liberté dans la culture contemporaine. La mort inopinée du Professeur Stanislas Ladusans, en 1993, ne lui a pas permis de participer activement aux préparatifs du présent Congrès. Le choix du sujet n'est pas dû au hasard. La soif de liberté – qui est aujourd'hui comme le signe d'un "nouveau printemps des peuples", en Europe et en Asie tout comme en Afrique et en Amérique du Sud et en Amérique Centrale – amène nombre de guerres et devient une menace pour la liberté, vu qu'elle engendre des nationalismes extrémistes. Il en est de même de la vie personnelle de l'homme. La liberté mal interprétée dégénère en anarchie et en individualisme, qui, poussé à l'extrême, devient pernicieux. Il en résulte une déformation de la vie sociale et culturelle. Ces problèmes sont un défi pour les philosophes, pour les philosophes chrétiens en particulier : il leur incombe de défendre la "bonne" liberté humaine contre les altérations, contre son bradage, de montrer aussi à l'homme du troisième millénaire les perspectives d'une civilisation d'amour et de paix.

La Pologne a été choisie comme lieu de ce Congrès pour cette raison qu'avec la naissance de "Solidarność" les peuples d'Europe centrale et orientale ont commencé leur marche vers la liberté. Lublin, lui, est le lieu où coexistent et s'interpénètrent, dans le respect mutuel, deux civilisations: la civilisation occidentale, latine, et la civilisation orientale, byzantine. A Lublin se trouve Maïdanek, le camp de concentration où quelque 350 000 êtres innocents ont été assassinés par les hitlériens et qui est un témoignage éloquent d'une "liberté dégénérée". L'Université Catholique enfin a été choisi pour accueillir le Congrès car c'est elle qui pendant toute la période du totalitarisme communiste (1944-1989), seule entre l'Elbe et Vladivostok, a été le centre de la pensée libre et indépendante, centre où était préservée et proclamée la vérité de la liberté humaine, la vérité du droit inaliénable à la liberté, droit qui revient aussi bien à l'individu qu'aux sociétés entières.

Nous espérons que le professeur Stanislas Ladusans spirituellement restera avec nous et qu'il nous aidera à travailler d'une manière fructueuse.

Nous avons reçu beaucoup de télégrammes de différentes personnes et institutions. Puisqu'ils sont très nombreux et parfois très longs, je vais citer seulement les noms de ceux qui nous les ont adressés :

– Monseigneur le cardinal Franciszek Macharski,
– Monseigneur l'archevêque Henryk Muszyński,
– Monseigneur l'évêque Alfons Nossol,
– Monseigneur l'évêque Jan Szlaga;
– le Professeur Jerzy Osiowski,
– le Professeur Jerzy Wyrozumski,
– le Professeur Jerzy Zdrada.

Maintenant, nous pouvons commencer. J'invite à prendre place à la table d'honneur

– Son Excellence le Professeur Julio Teran Dutari de l'Equateur,
– le Professeur George Mc Lean des Etats-Unis,
– le Professeur Urbain Dhondt de Belgique,
– le Professeur Andrius Valevicius du Canada et
– le Professeur Andrzej Szostek de notre Faculté, qui va présider cette séance.

Plenary Sessions

MIECZYSŁAW A. KRĄPIEC
Catholic University of Lublin
Poland

THE NATURE OF HUMAN FREEDOM

Man's freedom is manifest in various realms of human life. There is freedom of the socio-political kind, the negation of which is a state of constraint. There is freedom in choosing and professing a religion; there is freedom in scientific and cognitive works; another sort is freedom in the domain of human moral action; there is freedom in artistic creativity; there is freedom from coercion and terror; there is freedom to choose one's own profession and to choose a suitable way of life.

The freedoms mentioned and others not mentioned presuppose some prior understanding of the nature of man's freedom. Consequently, insofar as it is possible, we must try to trace out what man's freedom is. In what acts of human activity does our human freedom, which takes such varied forms and which gives form to human activities, reach fulfillment?

In order to answer this question, we must consider the following: first, the awareness of freedom in our human activity; second, how the experiential fact of freedom may be explained. This fact may be explained in philosophical terms by "separating" freedom as such from both indeterminism and determinism, and then by setting forth the structure of man as a personal being, the structure manifest in specifically human activity – activity which is *free*. This activity is realized through acts of decision, acts which are a synthesis of human cognition and love. Acts of decision cannot be separated from man's activity as a person. At the same time, these acts are indispensable or inalienable, for by them we effect our self-determination and constitute ourselves as real sources of activity – each of us becomes an efficient cause that realizes a good. This involves a freedom to the good, not a freedom to evil.

1. The first thing to consider in our internal experience of freedom is our awareness of freedom. We are aware that we act freely and not out of external compulsion. In acting, we know that we can carry out precisely that action, that we are not *compelled* to carry out the action. We experience that we will to act in just this way. The experience that *I can*, that *I don't have to*, that *I will* to act is given to me while I am actually involved in the living experience of action. Of course, we are speaking here of activity on the personal level, which is usually referred to as free and conscious activity. Our biological acts, those determined by our biological nature, are actions "of man", only to a lesser extent are they "human" activities, activities at a personal level. Biological activities occur "within me". I am their subject, but they do not depend upon my cognition or volition. On the other hand, "human activities" are those that I carry out as a consequence of knowing and willing them. Only the act that is mine, that is personal, that which is called the "human act", is recognized as free activity, as flowing from self-determination, from an act of decision.

The awareness of freedom, manifested in ordinary cognitive experience, is not an abstract cognition characterized by necessity. It cannot be reduced to any sort of scientific cognition. Max Scheler noted this, though he was mistaken in reducing this cognition to an emotional stream of consciousness that shines through a creative process being played out in the present. The awareness of our free activity is a reflection that is constantly concomitant to us, said to be *"in actu exercito"*, as distinct from *"in actu signato"*. It is not some sort of objective cognition, a cognition that possesses a defined or determined object, but a cognition that continually accompanies our processes of cognition and action. This "registration" of our cognition and the activity that comes forth from our cognitive acts is constantly occurring within us. This "concomitant reflection" is an authentic witness to the freedom of our acts of decision, and thereby, a witness to our human freedom.

For many modern and contemporary thinkers, the argument based on the awareness of human freedom would appear to lack any grounds in man's real freedom. They would point out that the mere awareness of freedom may at times be the unawareness of a determination.

2. For this reason, the awareness of the fact of freedom needs to be explained in philosophical terms. First, we must show that human freedom cannot be reduced either to indeterminisim or to some unconscious determinism. Indeterminism, the absence of any kind of determination in activity, is not freedom, but it describes a merely accidental mode of activity, if in fact there is any such a state as indeterminism. The absence of any determinant source of activity is the same as the absence of any activity at all. There is no defined or real source of activity. If, then, some activity is acknowledged as indeterminate, that activity presupposes the existence of

a variety of sources of activity that come together without any determination. This is an "accident" and a coincidence of activies in relation to some result or process. Indeterminism thus involves the invocation of an accident: it is not by itself a rational explanation of activity, but rather it implies the lack of any explanation of the fact of activity. The various forms of determinism, among which we may include physico-biological, psychological and theological determinism, are incapable of unifying man in a necessary manner in his free action that involves decision.

First of all, physico-biological determinism in the form of the operation of the defined laws of nature, without doubt exerts some influence upon human activity. This influence, however, affects facts preparatory to the act of decision. This influence bears upon various organic predispositions that precede and enable the performance of an act of decision by the higher factors of the intellect and the will, whose acts carry out free activity. There can be no doubt that man's activity involves his entire ontic structure, which manifests itself in activity. Activities or processes in the human organism at the atomic, molecular and biological levels together form the "underpinning" for the emergence of the cognitive acts of the intellect and the acts of volition of our will. However, the underpinning or material aspect of these acts, though determined in itself, has no bearing upon the activity of the higher faculties of the intellect and will. The latter are simply of another nature, even though they function on top of the material, determinate foundation of our body, as our body makes possible the emergence of higher, spiritual acts, free acts.

The question arises, whether the physico-biological determination of our organism is not indeed the cause of some kind of psychic determinism. After all, we are a psycho-physical unity, and everything that occurs in our organism in the form of determined biological processes has some influence on the operation of our psyche, the human psyche, a psyche rooted in biological material. Of course, in our life we experience biological and psychic determinisms in various forms of dependence upon assorted pharmaceuticals, tobacco, alcohol, psychotropic drugs, and people even speak of dependence upon television, rock music and other stimuli, all of which without doubt limit our freedom of decision. In extreme cases, they appear to deprive man altogether of any freedom to decide on the proprietary, independent and personal character of his activity. Yet, despite the fact of dependence, man is constantly faced with the opportunity to rid himself of dependence and to return to a "normal" state. Physicians and psychologists collaborate in this. Their experience shows that freedom exists, that it is possible to rid oneself of dependence acquired by long practice, that it is possible to return to the normal state, the state of free decisions.

Thus the state of dependence is treated as a pathological state, not as the normal human state. This is universally held to be true, and it is the reason underlying organized therapeutic projects that make it possible for individuals to recover the state of "freedom in activities". People, who have been subjects of various kinds of psychic determinims, have had the natural and direct living experience of regaining the state of freedom. When someone begins to work upon himself, he knows that, despite the difficulty, he is capable of liberating himself from psychic determinants. The widespread conviction and the internal experience of man's volition, along with the very nature of cognition and volition or love, indicate that human freedom is not eliminated by various psychic determinants, that this freedom can be strengthened by rational and volitional acts. This freedom can also be lost to a large extent by acts that are irrational and deliberately crippling to oneself.

Certain philosophers, such as N. Hartmann, thought that human freedom stands in contradiction to God's providential action. They would argue that if God exists and "predestines" man to eternal salvation, then by the same token God is depriving man of freedom. Moreover, morality itself depends on human freedom, but it would preclude God's acting upon man, for if God were to act upon man, we would have a "theological determinism", and in a certain way, man would be enslaved by the overpowering influence of God's action, which man is not capable of resisting.

This way of presenting the problem lacks any grounds in being or cognition. God transcends all nature, and he transcends man both in the act of being and in cognition. Not all the relations existing in man and in creation reach God. Certain relations pertain only to certain groups of beings, and this is true of the relations involved in human acts of volition and decision. Human freedom is not an ontic phenomenon proper to "being as that which exists", but only to man. Human freedom is a categorical state of being, not a transcendental state. In the analysis of being, we have no grounds for extrapolating from our human freedom to God, who absolutely transcends all modes (categorical and created modes) of human existence and activity. Thus we cannot rationally predicate anything of the modes of God's activity, since it would be necessary first to have "seen" God immediately, in order to establish the "mode" of God's activity.

In the best case, then, we *do not know* how to reconcile God's providential action with free human activities. This much is certain that God transcends all categorical modes of activity. Freedom and determination are given to us in human living experience. We cannot impose the human experience of freedom and determination upon God, for God's transcendence comprehends both freedom and determination, and it cannot be confused with the categories of human existence and knowledge. Thus any objection from a position of "theological determinism" in human activity is not based on rational premises. A proper response to the objections against human freedom calls for a fuller explanation of what the act of man's freedom as the act of a material-spiritual being is. The structure of the human being, besides purely material and biological acts on the one hand, and psychic acts involving self-awareness on the other hand, is also endowed with sensory sources of cognitive and appetitive activity. What we are concerned with here is sensory cognition, which reaches its apex in mental representation, in cognitive acts involving representation, and in acts involving our appetites or affectivities. Sensory life, thus understood, is organically linked with material-biological processes. Consequently, sensory life may at times intensify our intellectual-cognitive and volitional life. The processes of sensory cognition and the emotional-appetitive acts involving our emotions can affect our human freedom in various ways, as our freedom is realized in acts of conscious and deliberate decision. They can fortify and intensify our freedom, but they can also debilitate and greatly limit our acts of freedom. Hence, in understanding the nature of human freedom, it is important to turn attention to our sensory life and to the life of our appetites, to both concupiscible and irascible appetites. Human freedom is not absolute, but it is dependent upon and involved in the gestalt of our sensory life, especially the life of our emotions and appetites, which contain material-organic moments and moments of sense-cognition. The appetites as drives to a good that can be known at a sensory level, or to flight from an impending evil, are usually inseparably joined with our acts of decision, as human and free acts. Never is the connection of appetite and freedom neutral. On the contrary, our appetites may either weaken our freedom, as when they are not under the direction and control of our reason, or they may strengthen this freedom, as when they cooperate with man's rational life. Hence the education of the emotions or appetites is simultaneously intensification of our human freedom. Whenever one puts the appetites outside the rational sphere, or treats the purely appetitive or affective life as autonomous, freedom is limited and diminished because the human decision has deteriorated it.

Human freedom is revealed in the decision acts of man's reason and will. These acts are legible to us, and we are conscious of them, since they are acts of our spirit, which binds into one and creates a synthesis of our acts of reason and will, our acts of cognition and volition. If the human freedom that is realized in acts of decision can be compared to an iceberg, the acts of decision that are marked by freedom are only the visible tip, and the other bio-physical factors are not accessible to us in immediate cognition. Yet the acts of decision that are decisive for freedom are not concealed. They can be described in cognitive terms and can be explained in terms of causes, wherein we must consider both the conscious acts of decision itself, and refer to the determining psycho-physical structure, namely to our appetites, our sense-cognition and our inherited genetic code. Each of these in its own measure affects our freedom in its specifically human aspect, the freedom which ultimately "proclaims itself" in acts of decision.

4. The activities of intellectual cognition and of the act of free choice performed by our will contribute to the human decision, to the human free choice that is the source of man's activity. The mechanism of free choice was analyzed in detail by Saint Thomas Aquinas in the *Summa Theologica, Prima Secunda, questions twelve to fifteen*. There he examined the activity of the intellect and relation to an end and in relation to the means that lead to the end. He emphasized the freedom of the will. The activity of the will concerns only internal decisions, the choice of a judgement about the good. The will has dominion over its acts in relation to all the goods that are presented in judgements, as long as these are not infinite goods. This means that our will, and we ourselves, are incapable of not wanting the good as good, if the good is the formal object of the will. No active power can be neutral in relation to its formal object. Consequently, if we affirm the existence of the will as the appetitive power of the intellect, then it possesses its own formal object, an object that imposes a certain necessity, and this is the good as the analogically conceived good. In relation to the good as good, thus understood, we do not possess any freedom of the will, for all the acts of the will aim at their object under the angle of and in the perspective of the good, even when we are bringing about what is objectively evil. The will, however, in the acts it deliberately elicits, is not subject to coercion, since these acts flow from the will itself and remain within it. If, then, the will in this way elicits its own acts, it can do so only in accord with its own formal object and with its own internal structure. Consequently, no one can command from outside the deliberate internal acts of the will. This is not the case in external acts of the will, those which are concerned with the external execution of a decision. The external executions of acts of the will may be and sometimes are compelled as a result of coercion and violence. Thus our freedom in activity, what we call freedom of the will, concerns only the immanent acts of the will, those immediately elicited by the will itself in relation to the volition of all sorts of concrete goods, those which are not the necessary good, the good *qua* good. Freedom so understood is revealed in the form of what is called "freedom of choice" (*libertas specificationis*) and "freedom of activity" (*libertas exercitii*). By virtue of the first one, of the freedom of choice, the will is not determined by necessity to will this and not some other good, since every concrete good is limited and can be presented to the will as an "incomplete" good, a good that as such does not necessitate a choice for it. By virtue of the second type, namely the freedom of activity, however, we are able either to execute or not to execute acts of the will for some good. As a consequence of the freedom of the will, I can

choose between the goods "A" and "B", and with respect to one and the same good, "A", I may want it on one occasion, and not want it on another.

Human activity, which we call the human act, is present to our consciousness through cognition, and it is carried with a feeling of freedom, to a greater or lesser degree. The free act is an act that binds together the intellect and will as the ultimate factors that constitute the decision. The acts of the intellect and the acts of the will are intertwined and they remain connected dialectically, creating one act of decision. Whenever the intellect indicates something in a practical judgement with specific contents, there is – on the part of the will – a corresponding act of choice or permission. The indication of the content of the good in practical judgements on the part of the intellect is of particular importance, for the good presented in this way becomes the motive on account of which the action comes into existence.

5. The essential drama of freedom (of free choice) occurs not in the phase of theoretical cognition, where there may be only some general intention to act, but in the *practical* phase, where cognition is concretely ordered to the attainment, in the decision act, of some good that is presented to us (to our will) by a practical judgement concerning this good. I (or my will) do not choose a good immediately, but I choose one practical judgement from among many concerning the concrete good. At the moment of choice, the intellect is presenting a series of practical judgements concerning a concrete good and concerning the possibility of its realization. From among many practical judgements (at times just one practical judgement is sufficient), through my will I *choose* one concrete judgement concerning the good, and at this moment I determine myself to activity. *The act of my decision is an act of choosing one practical judgement concerning the good, the judgement which I wish to attain or realize.* Consequently, I do not immediately choose a good that is external to me, I only choose a judgement concerning the good. By choosing this judgement I determine myself to further activity. I order myself to "set in motion" my motor powers and – by physical activity – to attain the good presented in my practical judgement. I have made my choice deliberately and without coercion. Consequently, man's freedom is internal to him, for man *determines himself* by the free choice of the practical judgement concerning a concrete good which he is to attain in further activity. Following this is the moment of self-determination to activity: by the free choice of some judgement concerning the good I am to attain, I have determined myself, I have constituted myself as the efficient cause and the real source of activity. This is what the act of decision is. By the act of decision (by the free choice of the practical judgement concerning a good), I have constituted myself as an acting being. Karol Wojtyła called the moment of the act of decision the moment of self-constitution as the author of an act, as the author of human moral activity. The self-constitution that takes

place in the act of decision is conditioned as well by the cognitive process in which I cognitively interiorize things and the contents of the good, and by the interiorized cognition of things, I experience that I possess myself, and subsequently experience that by my will I am master of my own acts of volition and non-volition. Thus I experience "self-mastery." The experience of "self-possession" through the cognitive interiorization of the contents of goods, and then the experience of "self-mastery" by the will over one's own acts in relation to the good (we are not speaking here of the infinite good, the good *qua* good) characterizes well the interdependence of our acts of practical intellectual cognition and our acts of the will that lead to a new state of being: the constitution of oneself – self-constitution – in an act of decision, of a new source of activity, and thereby of a source of a moral act. Every conscious and deliberate human activity (every moral act) is thereby a moral activity. No human activity is entirely amoral.

Thus, through the act of decision, we are free in a human way. The will chooses for itself a practical judgement and decides that this judgement is that whereby I ultimately determine myself to activity. Autodetermination, which is an act of decision constitutive of man's freedom, takes place in a man who is about to act in a real manner.

6. What is the ultimate justification for the fact of freedom? It is our structure as a being, and this structure ultimately finds expression in the very nature of our intellect and will. If the intellect has being as its object of cognition, then man is not limited in his cognition. Man is capable of having knowledge of anything, so long as it presents itself to him in the form of a being that can in some way be conceived. As man's intellect has an unbounded range in cognition, at the same time it bears a necessary order to the good as good. Being and good are the same thing. Every concrete being-good can be presented to the reason as a being-good with some shortcoming, as a limited being-good, one which does not by any necessity of its own attract man to itself, one from which man is capable of distancing himself both cognitively and emotionally (or volitionally). For real activity to exist, there first must exist real and necessary conditions. A man decides these conditions when he makes a concrete practical judgement concerning the good, a judgement that is recognized by the will or volition as the ultimate judgement determining him to activity. This freedom of activity and choice enters into the very structure of human activity. If one negates freedom in acting, at the same time one negates human nature as active.

The human nature, as we have traced it out and understood it here, can increase or diminish in man depending on his upbringing and self-development. Our freedom increases to the extent to which we increase our abilities in our acts of decision, these acts being acts of the free choice of a practical judgement concerning a good to be realized in our conduct. Human freedom is always a freedom in the choice of a practical judgement concerning a good, never concerning an evil as such, though what is evil may present itself as an apparent good. Man has the ability to come to some understanding of the true good. Thereby he has the ability to choose a good that is simultaneously a truth, a real good.

Perhaps the foregoing considerations on human freedom and its limits will permit us better to understand man in his essentially human act of freedom, which is the act of decision that unifies the life of the reason and the will, and thus all that is cognition and love or volition. It is only in the act of decision that man declares himself as man. Cognition taken by itself and love taken by itself as such are exceptionally value-laden acts of man. Yet not every man is called to the same specific processes of cognition, nor is every man supposed to bring to realization the same concrete acts of volition or love. Every man, however, as he is a man, must perform acts that realize his humanity. Our acts of decision are such acts in which we ourselves select in acts of volition or love those concrete practical judgements, and these are acts of the reason, that concern the good we are to realize.

The deliberate choice of a practical judgement is our act of human freedom; in our freedom we bring about autodetermination that transcends both indeterminism and determinism. We constitute ourselves as free sources of activity, sources that are determined, but determined deliberately. We create an unrepeatable and personal face for ourselves. Hence the freedom realized by our acts of decision "sculpts" our personal humanity. Acts of decision rely upon a knowledge of the truth about the good. We can "read out" the true content of the good, distinguish it from that which has been falsified, and we can realize this good. Every falsification of the truth about the human good is essentially a limitation of human freedom. The falsification of the truth about the human good in the areas of religion, science, morality, law, or property, is especially dangerous for man's personal development, for it makes human freedom difficult or even impossible, and thereby makes it difficult or impossible for man to realize his humanity. Man's truth and good are inseparably joined in man's free acts of decision that realize the real good. The good is always the motor or motive of every human activity of decision. When one fails to consider or rejects the good as the motive or end of human activity, one dehumanizes man, reducing him to the role of a useful tool or a mere thing. The real and true good that man chooses as the motive and end of human activity ultimately justifies human freedom as it is manifest in acts of freedom. Freedom is always *a freedom to realize a good*, not an evil, in every domain of life.

PETER VAN INWAGEN
University of Notre Dame
United States

THE MYSTERY OF METAPHYSICAL FREEDOM

There are many kinds of freedom – or, as I prefer to say, the word 'freedom' has many senses. In one sense of the word, an agent is "free" to the extent that his actions are not subject to control by the state. It is, however, obvious that an agent may be free in this sense but unfree in other senses. However little the state may interfere with my actions, I may be unfree because I am paralyzed from the waist down or because I am subject to a neurotic fear of open spaces that makes it impossible for me to venture out of doors or because I am so poor that I am unable to afford the necessary means to what I want to do. These examples suggest that freedom is a merely negative concept – that freedom is freedom from constraint, that freedom consists in the mere absence of constraint. If freedom is in this sense a negative concept, this explains why there are many kinds of freedom: there are many kinds of freedom because there are many kinds of constraint. Because there are political constraints, there is political freedom, which exists in their absence; because there are internal psychological constraints (such as neurosis), there is psychological freedom, which exists in their absence; because there are economic constraints, there is economic freedom, which exists in their absence – and so on.

When we turn from politics and psychology and economics to metaphysics, however, we encounter discussions of freedom – discussions involving words like 'freedom', 'free', and 'freely' – that it is hard to account for if freedom is no more than a negative concept. Consider, for example, the following words of Holbach:

> Man's life is a line that nature commands him to describe upon the surface of the earth, without his ever being able to swerve from it, even for an

instant [...] Nevertheless, in spite of the shackles by which he is bound, it is pretended he is a free agent [...].

Or consider the ancient problem of future contingents, which would seem to depend on considerations different from those adduced by Holbach, for it has only to do with whether statements about future events must be either true or false, and has nothing to do with causation and physical law. Consider, again, the problem of divine knowledge of future human action. Consider, finally, the problem of evil and the attempts to solve that problem that appeal to the freedom of creatures and the alleged impossibility of a free creature that is certain to do no evil.

I think it is fairly evident that the concept of freedom that figures in the discussions raised by these metaphysical problems is the same concept. I think it is not easy to see how this concept could be understood as a merely negative concept, as a concept that applies to any agent just in the case that that agent's acts are not subject to some sort of constraint.

Consider, for example, the problem of free will and determinism, the problem that is raised by the above quotation from Holbach. Although my present actions may be determined by the laws of nature and the state of the world before my birth (indeed, millions of years ago), it does not follow that this state of affairs places me under any sort of constraint. A constraint on one's behavior is an impediment to the exercise of one's will. If the state places me in chains, then my will to be elsewhere, if I attempt to exercise it, will soon come into conflict with the length and solidity of my chain. If I am an extreme agoraphobe, then my will to go about the ordinary business of life will come into conflict with sensations of panic and dislocation the moment I step out of doors. If I am very poor, my will to own a warm overcoat will come into conflict with my lack of the price of the coat. It is things of these sorts that are meant by 'constraint'. And it is evident that determinism places me under no constraints. It is true that in a deterministic world, *what my will is on a given occasion* will be a consequence of the way the world was millions of years ago and the laws of nature. It is true that in a deterministic world, *whether my will happens to encounter an obstacle on a given occasion* will be a consequence of the way the world was millions of years ago and the laws of nature. But it is certainly not inevitable that my will encounter an obstacle on any given occasion in a deterministic world, and even in an indeterministic world, my will must encounter obstacles on many occasions. Indeed, there is no reason to suppose that my will will encounter obstacles more frequently in a deterministic world than in an indeterministic world. Anyone who believes that freedom is a negative concept will therefore conclude that the so-called problem of free will and determinism is founded on confusion. (So Hobbes, Hume, Mill, and many other philosophers have concluded.)

The situation is similar with the problem of divine knowledge of future human actions. We are often told that there really is no problem about this, since the fact that God knows that one is going to tell a lie (for example) in no way forces one to lie. Since God's knowledge does interfere with the exercise of one's will, since the false words that issue from one's mouth are the words that it was one's will to speak, God's knowledge that one was going to lie is consistent with the lie's being a free act.

All this can sound very sensible. And yet one is left with the feeling that the freedom this leaves us with is, in Kant's words, a "wretched subterfuge." This feeling can be embodied in an argument. The argument is, to my mind, a rather powerful one. If the argument is correct, then freedom is not a merely negative concept. Or, at any rate, there is a concept of freedom that is not a merely negative concept, and this concept is a very important one. It is this concept, I believe, that figures in the metaphysical problems I have cited. I will call it metaphysical freedom. In calling it metaphysical freedom, however, I do not mean to imply that it is of interest only to the metaphysician. I believe that this concept is also of importance in everyday life, and that the concept that metaphysicians employ is just this everyday concept, or perhaps a refinement of it. (I should be willing to argue that all concepts that we employ in philosophy or science or any other area of inquiry are either everyday concepts or explicable in terms of everyday concepts.)

In ordinary English, the concept of metaphysical freedom finds its primary expression in simple, common words and phrases, and not in the grand, abstract terms of philosophical art that one is apt to associate with metaphysics. (The situation is similar in French, German, and Latin. I should be surprised to learn of a language in which the concept I am calling "metaphysical freedom" could not be expressed in simple, common words and phrases.) It is true that philosophical analysis is needed to distinguish those uses of these simple words and phrases on which they express this concept from other uses on which they express other concepts. Nevertheless, in particular, concrete contexts, these simple words express that very concept of freedom (not, as we shall see, a negative concept), that figures in metaphysical problems like the problem of freedom and determinism. But perhaps the meaning of these abstract remarks will not be clear without an example.

One of the simple words that expresses the concept of metaphysical freedom in English is 'can'. What are we asking when we ask whether I am free to tell the truth tomorrow if it has been determined by events in the remote past and the laws of nature that when, tomorrow, I confront a choice between lying and telling the truth, I shall lie? Only this: 'I am free to tell the truth' means 'I *can* tell the truth', and 'I am not free to tell the truth' means 'I *cannot* tell the truth'. Metaphysical freedom, therefore, is simply what is expressed by 'can'. If we accept this thesis, however, we must take care to understand it properly. We must take care to avoid two possible sources of confusion: the ambiguity of the word 'can' and false philosophical theories about what is expressed by certain sentences in which it occurs.

As to the first point, the word 'can' is extremely versatile, and can be used to express many ideas other than the idea of metaphysical freedom (a fact illustrated by this sentence). One example must suffice. In negative constructions, 'can' sometimes expresses an idea that might be called 'moral impossibility'. One might say to a hard-hearted son, "You can't refuse to take your own mother into your house" – even though one knows perfectly well that in the sense of 'can' we have been discussing he certainly *can* refuse to take his own mother into his house because he has already done so. We must take care that if we propose to use the simple word 'can' as our means to an understanding of metaphysical freedom, we do not allow our understanding of metaphysical freedom to be influenced by any of the many other concepts this simple word can be used to express. The best way to avoid such influence is not to rely on the word 'can' alone in our attempt to understand metaphysical freedom, but to examine also as many as possible of the other simple, ordinary words and phrases that can be used to express the concept of metaphysical freedom (or unfreedom). To illustrate what I mean, here are three sentences in which idioms of ordinary speech other that do not involve 'can' are used to express the concepts of metaphysical freedom and unfreedom:

– He will *be able* to be there in time for the meeting.

– You must not blame her for missing the meeting; she *had no choice* about that.

– It was simply *not within my power* to attend the meeting.

(Oddly enough, the phrase 'of his own free will' does not express the concept of metaphysical freedom, despite the fact that 'free will', as a philosophical term of art, means just exactly what I mean by 'metaphysical freedom'. To say that someone attended a meeting of his own free will is simply to say that no one forced him to attend the meeting. The phase 'of his own free will' thus expresses a merely negative concept, the concept of the absence of coercion.)

False theories about the meanings of philosophically important words and phrases abound, and the philosophically important word 'can' is no exception to this generalization. There are those who, recognizing the importance of idioms like 'I can do X' for the metaphysical problems of freedom, have simply insisted that this word means something that supports their favorite philosophical theories. An example of such a theory would be: 'I can do X' means 'There exists no impediment, obstacle, or barrier to my doing X; nothing prevents my doing X'. I will not argue specifically for the conclusion that this theory is false; the argument I will later present for the incompatibility of metaphysical freedom and determinism, however, will have the consequence that this theory about the meaning of 'I can' is false – since, if the theory were true, metaphysical freedom would be compatible with determinism. At this point, I wish merely to call attention to the fact that there do exist tendentious theories about the meaning of 'I can do X'.

If we consider carefully the meaning of 'I can do X' ('I am able to do X'; 'It is within my power to do X') do we find that the idea expressed by this form or words is a merely negative one, the idea of the absence of some constraint or barrier or obstacle to action? It would seem not. It is true that the presence of an obstacle to the performance of an action can be sufficient for one's being unable to perform that action. But it does not follow that the absence of all obstacles to the performance of an action is sufficient for one's being *able* to perform that action. And the idea that ability could consist in the absence of obstacles does seem, on consideration, to be a very puzzling idea indeed. To see this, let us examine carefully the relation between the concept of ability and the concept of an obstacle. We should note that not just any obstacle to one's performance of an action is such that its presence renders one unable to perform that action – for some obstacles can be surmounted or eliminated or bypassed (for short: some obstacles can be overcome). Let us ask a simple question: *which* obstacles to the performance of an action are such that their presence renders one unable to perform that action? Why, just those obstacles that one is *unable* to overcome, of course. And it seems fairly obvious that the concept of an obstacle that one is unable to overcome cannot be analyzed or explained in terms of the concept of an obstacle *simpliciter*. (Is the concept of an obstacle that one cannot overcome the concept of an obstacle such that there is some "decisive" obstacle to one's overcoming it? – No, not unless a "decisive" obstacle is understood as an obstacle that one is unable to overcome ...) These reflections suggest very strongly that the concept expressed by the words 'I can do X' or 'I am able to do X' cannot be a merely negative concept, the concept of the absence of some sort of obstacle or barrier or impediment to action. But let us turn now to the question of the compatibility of determinism and metaphysical freedom. I shall present an argument for the conclusion that determinism is incompatible with metaphysical freedom. Since, as we have seen, determinism and metaphysical freedom are compatible if metaphysical freedom (the concept expressed by 'I can do X') is a merely negative concept, this argument will be in effect an argument for the conclusion that metaphysical freedom is not a merely negative concept.

As Carl Ginet has said, our freedom can only be the freedom to add to the actual past – for the past is unalterable; it is what we *find ourselves with* in any situation in which we are contemplating some course of action. (Or to put this point in the terms I have been recommending, all we *can* do, all we are *able to do,* is add to the actual past.) And, unless we are bona fide miracle workers, we can make only such additions to the actual past as conform to the laws of nature. But the only additions to the actual past that conform to a deterministic set of laws are the additions that are actually made, the additions that collectively make up the actual present and the actual future. This is simply a statement of what is meant by determinism, which is the thesis that the law of nature and the past together determine a unique future. Therefore, if the laws of nature are deterministic, we are free to do only what we in fact do – that is, we are unable to act otherwise than we do and are ipso facto not free in the sense in which the term 'free' is properly used in metaphysics.

This little argument has great persuasive power, and it is probably no more than an articulation of the reasons that lead, almost without exception, the undergraduates to whom I lecture to join Kant in regarding the merely negative freedom of Hobbes and Hume as a wretched subterfuge. If the argument is correct, as I have said, it refutes the idea that metaphysical freedom is a merely negative concept, for the past and the laws of nature are not impediments to the exercise of one's will. But, more generally, we may well ask what we are to say of this argument and its consequences, for these consequences go far beyond establishing that metaphysical freedom is not a negative concept. One possible reaction to the argument would be to say, with Holbach, that, because determinism is true, we therefore do not possess metaphysical freedom. (An epistemologically more modest reaction would be to say that, because we do not know whether determinism is true, we do not know whether we possess metaphysical freedom.) I shall return to the possibility that we lack freedom (or that we do not know whether we have freedom). For the moment, let us see where the argument leaves those of us who would like to say that we are free and that we know this. Many philosophers have regarded it as evident that we are free, and have accepted something like our argument for the incompatibility of determinism and metaphysical freedom. These philosophers, therefore, have denied that the world is deterministic, have denied that the laws of nature and the past together determine a unique future.

These philosophers (among whom I count myself) face a difficult problem. They assert or postulate that the laws of nature are indeterministic. One might ask how they know this, or what gives them the right to this postulate. These are good questions, but I will not consider them. I want to consider instead another question that these philosophers must answer: does postulating or asserting that the laws of nature are indeterministic provide any comfort to those who would like to believe in metaphysical freedom? If the laws are indeterministic, then more than one future is indeed consistent with those laws and the actual past and present – but how can anyone have any choice about which of these futures becomes actual? Isn't it just a matter of chance which becomes actual? If God were to "return" an indeterministic world to precisely its state at some time in the past, and then let the world go forward again, things might indeed happen differently the "second" time. But then, if the world is indeterministic, isn't it just a matter of chance how things *did* happen in the one, actual course of events? And if what we do is just a matter of chance – well, who would want to call that freedom?

It seems, therefore, that, in addition to our argument for the incompatibility of metaphysical freedom and determinism, we have an argument for the incompatibility of metaphysical freedom and indeteminism. But the world must be either deterministic or indeterministic. It follows that, unless one of the two arguments contains some logical error or proceeds from a false premise, metaphysical freedom must be a contradiction in terms, as much an impossibility as a round square or a liquid wine bottle. We may in fact *define* the problem of metaphysical freedom as the problem of discovering whether either of the two arguments is defective, and (if so) of locating the defect or defects.

The problem of metaphysical freedom, so conceived, is a very *abstract* problem. Although, for historical reasons, it is natural to think of the problem as essentially involving reference to the physical world and its supposedly intransigent laws ("man's life is a line that nature commands him to describe on the surface of the earth ..."), it does not. For suppose that man's life is in fact *not* a line that nature commands him to describe on the surface of the earth. Suppose that nature presents us with two or seventeen or ten thousand lines inscribed on the surface of the earth, and says to us (in effect), "Choose whichever one of them you like". How could it be that we really had any choice about which "line" we followed, when any deliberations we might undertake would themselves have to be segments of the lines that nature has offered us? Imagine that two of the lines that nature offers me diverge at some point – that is, imagine that the lines present the aspect of a fork in a road or a river. The common part of the two lines, the segment that immediately precedes their divergence, represents the course of my deliberations; their divergence from a common origin represents diagrammatically the fact that *either* of two futures is a possible outcome of my deliberations. My deliberations, therefore, do not determine which future I shall choose. But then what *does* determine which future I shall choose? Only chance, it would seem, and if only chance determines which of two paths into the future I follow, then how can it be that I have a choice about which of them I follow?

The problem of metaphysical freedom is so abstract, so very nearly independent of the features of the world in which agents happen to find themselves, that it could – it would; it must – arise in essentially the same form in a world inhabited only by immaterial intelligences, a world whose only inhabitants were, let us say, angels.

Let us consider such a world. It is true that if there were only angels, there would be no physical laws – or at any rate there would be nothing for the laws to apply to, so we might as well say there would be none. But if we assume the angels make choices, we have to assume that time (somehow) exists in this non-physical world, and that the agents are in different "states" at different times. And what is responsible for the way an angel changes its states with the passage of time? One possibility is that it is something structurally analogous to the laws of physics – something that stands to angels as our laws of physics stand to electrons and quarks. (I'm assuming, by the way, that these angels are metaphysical simples, that they are not composed of smaller immaterial things. If they were, we could conduct the argument in terms of the smallest immaterial things, the "elementary particles" of this imaginary immaterial world.) This "something" takes the properties of the angels at any time (and the relations they bear to one another at that time: the analogue, whatever it may be, of spatial relations in a material world) as "input", and delivers as output a sheaf of possible futures and histories of the world. In other words, given the "state of the world" at any time, it tells you what temporal sequences of states could have preceded the world's being in that state at that time, and it tells you what temporal sequences of states could follow the world's being in that state at that time. Maybe it couldn't be written as a set of differential equations (since nothing I have said implies that the properties of and relations among angels are quantifiable) as the laws of our physical world presumably can, but I don't think that affects the point. And the point is: either "the sheaf of possible futures" relative to each moment has only one member or it has more than one. If it has only one, the world of angels is deterministic. And then where is their free will? (Their freedom is the freedom to add to the actual past. And they can only add to the actual past in accordance with the laws that govern the way angels change their properties and their relations to one another with time.) If it has more than one, then the fact that one possible future rather than another, equally possible, future becomes actual seems to be simply a matter of chance. And then where is their free will?

I said above that this way of looking at a postulated "world of angels" was one possibility. But are there really any others? We have to think of the angels as being temporal and as changing their properties with the passage of time if we are to think of them as making choices. And we have to think of them as bearing various relations to one another if we are to think of them as belonging to the same world. And we have to think of them as having natures if we are to think of them as being real things. Every real thing that is in time must have a nature that puts some kinds of constraints on how it can change its states with the passage of time. Or so, at any rate, it seems to me. But if we grant this much, it seems that, insofar as we can imagine a world of non-physical things (angels or any others) we must imagine the inhabitants of this world as being subject to something analogous to the laws of physics. If this "something" is deterministic, then (it seems) we can't think of the inhabitants of our imaginary world as having free will. And if this "something" is *in*deterministic, then (it seems) we can't think of the inhabitants of our imaginary world as having free will. Thus, the "problem of metaphysical freedom" is a problem so abstract and general that it arises in any imaginable world in which there are beings who make choices. The problem, in fact, arises in exactly the same way in relation to God. God, the theologians tell us, although He did in fact create a world, was free not to. (That is, He was *able* not to create a world.) But God has His own nature, which even He cannot violate and cannot change. (He cannot, for example, make Himself less than omnipotent; He cannot break a promise He has made; He cannot command immoral behavior.) And either this nature determines that He shall create a world or it does not. If he does, He was not free not to create. If it does not, then, it would seem, the fact that He *did* create a world was merely a matter of chance. For what, other than chance, could be responsible for the fact that He created a world? His choice or His will? But what determined that he should make *that* choice when the choice not to make a world was also consistent with His nature? What determined that His will should be set on making a world, when a will set on *not* making a world was also consistent with His nature? We should not be surprised that our dilemma concerning metaphysical freedom applies even to God, for the dilemma does not depend on the nature of the agent to whom the concept of metaphysical freedom is applied. The dilemma arises from the concept of metaphysical freedom itself, and its conclusion is that metaphysical freedom is a contradictory concept. And a contradictory concept can no more apply to God than it can apply to anything else.

The concept of metaphysical freedom seems, then, to be contradictory. One way to react to the seeming contradiction in this concept would be to conclude that it was real: metaphysical freedom seems contradictory because it is contradictory. (This was the conclusion reached by C. D. Broad.)

But none of us really believes this. A philosopher may argue that consciousness does not exist or that knowledge is impossible or that there is no right or wrong. But no one really believes that he himself is not conscious or that no one knows whether there is such a city as Warsaw; and only interested parties believe that there is nothing morally objectionable about child brothels or slavery or the employment of poison gas against civilians. And everyone really believes in metaphysical freedom, whether or not he would call it by that name. Dr Johnson famously said, "Sir, we know our will's free, and there's an end on't." Perhaps he was wrong, but he was saying something we all believe. Whether or not we are all, as the existentialists said, condemned to freedom, we are certainly all condemned to *believe in* freedom – and, in fact, condemned to believe that we *know* that we are free. (I am not disputing the sincerity of those philosophers who, like Holbach, have denied in their writings the reality of metaphysical freedom. I am saying rather that their beliefs are contradictory. Perhaps, as they say, they believe that there is no freedom – but, being human beings, they also believe that there is. In my book on freedom, I compared them to the Japanese astronomer who was said to have believed, in the 1930s, that the sun was an astronomically distant ball of hot gas vastly larger than the earth, and also to have believed that the sun was the ancestress of the Japanese imperial dynasty.)

I would ask you to try a simple experiment. Consider some important choice that confronts you. You must, perhaps, decide whether to marry a certain person, or whether to undergo a dangerous but promising course of medical treatment, or whether to report to a superior a colleague you suspect of embezzling money. (Tailor the example to your own life.) Consider the two courses of action that confront you; since I don't know what you have chosen, I'll call them simply A and B. Do you really not believe that you are *able* to do A and *able* to do B? If you do not, then how can it be that you are trying to decide which of them to do? It seems clear to me that when I am trying to decide which of two things to do, I commit myself, by the very act of attempting to decide between the two, to the thesis that I am able to do each of them. If I am trying to decide whether to report my colleague, then, by the very act of trying to reach a decision about this matter, I commit myself both to the thesis that I am able to report him and to the thesis that I am able to refrain from reporting him: although I obviously cannot do *both* these things, I can (I believe) do *either*. In sum: whether we are free or not, we believe that we are – and I think we believe, too, that we *know* this. We believe that we know this even if, like Holbach, we *also* believe that we are not free, and, therefore, that we do not know that we are free.

But if we know that we are free – indeed, if we are free and do not know it – , there is some defect in one or both of our two arguments. Either there is something wrong with our argument for the conclusion that metaphysical freedom is incompatible with determinism or there is something wrong with our argument for the conclusion that metaphysical freedom is incompatible with *in*determinism – or there is something wrong with both arguments. But which argument is wrong, and why? (Or are they both wrong?) I do not know. I think no one knows. That is why my title is, "The *Mystery* of Metaphysical Freedom". I believe I know, as surely as I know anything, that at least one of the two arguments contains a mistake. And yet, having thought very hard about the two arguments for almost thirty years, I confess myself unable to identify even a possible candidate for such a mistake. My opinion is that the first argument (the argument for the incompatibility of freedom and determinism) is essentially sound, and that there is, therefore, something wrong with the second argument (the argument for the incompatibility of freedom and indeterminism). But if you ask me *what* it is, I have to say that I am, as current American slang has it, absolutely clueless. Indeed the problem seems to me to be so evidently impossible of solution that I find very attractive a suggestion that has been made by Noam Chomsky (and which was developed by Colin McGinn in his recent book *The Problems of Philosophy*) that there is something about our biology, something about the ways of thinking that are "hardwired" into our brains, that renders it impossible for us human beings to dispel the mystery of metaphysical freedom. However this may be, I am certain that I cannot dispel the mystery, and I am certain that no one else has in fact done so.

BATTISTA MONDIN
Pontificia Università Urbaniana
Italy

FREEDOM, AN ESSENTIAL AND PRIMARY CONSTITUENT OF THE HUMAN PERSON

That freedom is an essential and primary constituent of the human person is such a truth that today very few people would put it in doubt. As a matter of fact, in the list of human rights and absolute values, freedom is always given the first place. But it has not always been so.

In a famous paragraph of his *Encyclopedia of the Philosophical Sciences* (n. 482) Hegel declares that the truth that freedom is the proper essence of the spirit was obtained for the first time by Christianity. "Entire parts of the world, Africa and the Orient, had never had this idea, and still do not have it; the Greeks and the Romans, Plato and Aristotle and the Stoics did not have it: they knew only the contrary, that man is free only thanks to birth (as an Athenian, a Spartan, etc. citizen) or thanks to the strength of character or culture, thanks to philosophy (the slave, even if he is in chains, is free). This idea came into the world through Christianity, for which the individual as such has an infinite value, and, being the object and the scope of God's love, is destined to have absolute relations with God as spirit, and makes it so that this spirit dwells in him: that is, man is himself destined to total freedom".

Greek people had certainly a deep appreciation for freedom, but to them freedom meant especially exterior, political freedom. Psychological, interior freedom was not yet envisioned by them. Historians recognize that freedom of the will rarely became an object of philosophical investigation in ancient times. "Taking the history of philosophy in its totality" – writes H. Daudin in his excellent work *La liberté de la volonté*[1] – "we see that

---

[1] H. Daudin, *La liberté de la volonté*, PUF, Paris 1950, pp. 2-3.

certain themes are present from the beginning and in every time to the study of philosophical minds; such is the case of the truth of sensory knowledge, source of the philosophy of the concept; the orientation of human life (Gorgias), source of ethics. But this is not the case with regard to the theme of the freedom of the will is absent from the philosophies of pagan antiquity, even from the greatest and most complete. Whereas this theme gains an extraordinary importance in the Christian philosophies of the end of antiquity and in all mediaeval thought. And in modern era, the place that it occupies does not cease to enlarge itself, while the attempts to find a solution diversify themselves and oppose each other more, all the times".

Those who are familiar with the patristic and scholastic ages know that the *De Libero arbitrio* written during those periods are countless. They start with Origen and Augustin and end with Erasmus and Luther.

Among other things St Augustin is responsible of the voluntaristic turn of the Christian anthropology, which up to him was still an anthropology based on the *logos*, and therefore with a clear intellectualistic character.

Augustin himself before his conversion had a very high idea of philosophy, gained through the reading of the *Hortensius* of Cicero and was a strong advocate of the rights of reason. Reason was the only authority that he was willing to recognize; he rejected the authority of the Church and embraced that sort of philosophical and very rationalistic religion that was manicheism. Later on, disappointed by the manicheans, he discovered the utility of believing, *De utilitate credendi*, he acpepted the authority of the Catholic church and returned to the faith of his mother. At the same time he found in the *liberum arbitrium* the key for the solution of the problem of evil, which for so many years had caused to him all kinds of difficulties and troubles: "(Haec quaestio) (unde male facimus) me admodum adolescentem vehementer exercuit, et fatigatum in haereticos impulit, atque dejecit"[2]. His long and tough fight against the heresy of Pelagius contributed during the last years of his life to strength even more his voluntaristic position.

Augustin, as we all know, is not only the main figure of the Latin Fathers, but also the Doctor of the Church who contributed more than anybody else in the shaping of Christian culture of the Middle Ages and partly even of modern culture. After Jesus Christ and St Paul no other single person has exercised such a great and deep influence on the Latin Church and on the Christian culture as St Augustin. His religious philosophy and his theological doctrines had a decisive influence on the development of Christian thought especially in the Middle Ages, but also during the Renaissance and the Reformation period. In the *Protestantische Real-Enzyklopädie*

---

[2] Augustin, *De libero arbitrio* I, 2, 4.

we can read the following statement: "There is no dogma of the Roman church that can be understood without turning to St Augustin. But it is not only on the dogma of the Latin Church that he has impressed his mark more than anybody else, but also on the hierarchical development of the same dogma, so that the science of its development is based on him"[3].

The voluntaristic trend of the Augustinian anthropology was not only preserved during the middle Ages through St Bernard, Alexander of Hales, Bonaventure and Duns Scotus, but it was further reinforced and pushed to its extreme consequences by Ockham, Luther, Baius and Giansenius.

Although freedom, as Hegel says, is a conquest of Christianity, and the history of ideas proves that the deepest studies of freedom, in all its main aspects, have been made by the Christian thinkers of the Middle Ages (St Thomas and Scotus first of all), it is a dogma of modern secular historians that freedom has gained citizenship only through the revolutionary efforts of modernity. What is true and can be easily recognized is that modern civilization has provided new means and new spaces for human freedom, and many more individuals can profit of them, but at the same time it has also increased the number and the power of the chains that prevent the person of making use of his own freedom.

During the last two centuries the philosophical problem of freedom of the will has not made any progress, and its solutions have not made any fruther step in clarity. The problem of freedom is strictly tied with the problem of man, since as we know freedom is an essential and primary quality of human nature. But the anthropologies presented by the leaders of modernity and post-modernity have become more and more agnostic and nihilistic, since the "death of God" has also caused the "death of man". So the problem of freedom has become more difficult and taxing than ever.

At first sight, it seems that freedom of choice (free will) is an arbitrary claim, even absurd, inasmuch as it would contrast with the laws of nature, which have a rigorously deterministic character. Now, if man is a product of nature, as the theory of evolution states, it is clear that, notwithstanding the testimonial of consciousness, which gives us the impression of being free, it is necessary to conclude that freedom is an illusion. For this reason, on the philosophical plane, the problem of freedom will always remain open, even when on the practical level (political, social, economic) every form of oppression disappears. William James is correct when he writes: "A common opinion prevails that the juice has of ages ago been pressed out of the free will controversy, and that no new champion could do more than warm up stale arguments which every one has heard. This is a radical mistake. I know of no subject less worn out in which an inventive genius has a better

---

[3] Loofs, *Augustinus, Protestantische Real-Enzyklopädie*, 3 ed., II, p. 277.

chance of breaking new ground, of deepening our sens of what the issue between the two parties really is, of what the ideas of fate and free will imply"[4].

The problem of freedom has many sides. In this lecture I shall stick to my theme: freedom as the most fundamental constituent of the human person. I will try to show:

1. Without freedom there is no human person, since the human person is a cultural being;

2. Freedom is the great gift with which man is endowed in order to increase in his humanity;

3. Not whatever exercise of freedom is apt to the "making" of the human person;

4. In the exercise of his freedom man needs the help of God, of society and of the physical nature;

5. In order to increase in his humanity and to become fully human man needs to take care of and educate his freedom.

I. WITHOUT FREEDOM THERE IS NO HUMAN PERSON, SINCE THE HUMAN PERSON IS A CULTURAL BEING

In order to qualify a human being we do not find any other better name than *person*. According to St Thomas this word designates what is most perfect in the universe: "Persona significat id quod est perfectissimum in tota natura, scilicet subsistens in natura rationali"[5]. This is a name that we never use for plants or animals, but only for man (and for all the beings that belong to the world of the spirit: God and angels). And when we wish to give a comprehensive name to man's being, a name expressing his entire reality in a precise and unequivocal way, we say that he is a person.

The Boethian and thomistic definition of man as a *rationalis natura individua substantia* is an excellent one. But concretely what does it mean? Actually what is the specific character of the human person as distinct, on one side, from the sub-human beings, and on the other side, from the angelic and the divine persons?

If we take a look at the history of philosophy we find two opposite views of man: the naturalistic view of the Greeks and the historical view of the moderns.

---

[4] W. James, *The Dilemma of Determinism*, cit. by C. Lamont, *Freedom of Choice affirmed*, Boston 1969, p. 15.

[5] Aquinas, *S. Theol.* I, 23, 3.

Classical philosophy (Plato, Aristotle, Zenon, Plotinus, etc.) considered man as a natural being: a being constituted of an immutable essence that is given from nature, from which he derives not only the biological laws but also moral precepts: "Act according to nature" was the categorical imperative of Greek philosophy. This was clearly a static concept of man, founded on the primacy of the intellect over the will, contemplation over action, nature over history.

Modern philosophy has performed a radical turn. It no longer sees man as a part of nature, but rather as a product of himself. Man is the artificer of himself, the *causa sui*. This is the thesis of Nietzsche, Hegel, Sartre, Heidegger, and the majority of the moderns. This is a "historical" concept of man, based on the primacy of the will and freedom over knowledge, praxis over theory, existence over essence, history over nature. On the moral plane there exists no imperative other than to translate his own possibilities (his own potency!) into act.

There is, however, a middle road between these two opposite views: to consider man as neither a natural being nor a simply historical being, but rather a cultural being. This means that not all of man is a product of nature, nor a product of history, but partly of nature and partly of history, and that this fusion between history and nature is called culture.

The whole of man is not the work of culture. Much of what exists in him comes from nature. His entire somatic and biological dimension is directly produced by natural forces. That small human being which comes to light after nine months of gestation in the womb of the mother is the fruit of genetic laws that nature has inscribed in the bodies of the parents. The organisms and faculties of which are nourished the baby and the adult proceed from nature. Also, a great number of somatic and psychic activities which we perform depend on the laws of nature.

Still, a great part of that which we possess and do, already from when we are one-year-olds, is not the fruit of nature, but rather of culture. This is the most remarkable characteristic that immediately distinguishes man from animals and plants. Differently from other living entities whose being is entirely produced and prefabricated by nature, man is in large measure the builder of himself. While plants and animals endure the natural environment that surrounds them, man is capable of cultivating nature and profoundly transforming it, adapting it to meet his own needs. Culture is not something accidental for man, a pastime, but makes up part of his nature, and it is a constitutive element of his essence. In the past philosophical anthropology based itself on reason, freedom and language in order to distinguish man from other beings. Contemporary philosophy has discovered that culture is not less important for the definition of the human person. Culture, in fact, characterizes man and distinguishes him from animals no less clearly than reason, freedom, and language. In effect, animals do not have culture, they are not creators of culture: at the most, they are passive receivers of cultural initiatives carried out by man. To grow and survive the animals are provided with certain instincts and certain assistance, be it with the aim of defense or of protection; instead, "man, in place of all these things, possesses the reason and the hands, which are the organs of organs, in that with their help man can procure for himself instruments of infinite styles for infinite aims"[6].

Man is a cultural being in two senses: first of all in that he is the artificer of culture, but also, as we haveseen, in that it is he himself who is the prime receiver and the greatest effect of culture. Culture, in its two principal accepted meanings – of formation of the individual (subjective sense) and of society's spiritual form (objective sense) – has the goal of realizing the individual in all his dimensions, in all his capacities. The primary aim of culture (and John Paul II correctly insists on this) is to cultivate man inasmuch as he is an individual – that is, the single man – as a unique and unrepeatable example of the human species. The objective of culture – in the anthropological sense – has always been that of making man a person, a fully developed spirit, able to bring to complete and perfect realization that project which Providence has consigned to him. Man as a cultural being is not prefabricated: he must construct himself with his own hands. "Culture – according to the beautiful words of John Paul II to the representatives of the UNESCO – is that by which man, as man, becomes more human, he "is" more, he draws closer to "being". It is also what founds the very important distinction between what man is and that which he has, between being and having. All having of man is not important for culture, it is not a creative factor of culture, excepting in the measure in which man, with the mediation of his 'having', can at the same time more fully 'be' as man in all the dimensions of his existence, in all that characterizes his humanity".

II. FREEDOM IS THE GREAT GIFT WITH WHICH MAN IS ENDOWED IN ORDER TO INCREASE IN HIS HUMANITY

That man is free it may be easily granted. According to Descartes, "of the liberty and the indifference which is in us, we are so conscious, that there is nothing in us that we comprehend more evidently and more perfectly"[7]. But why is man endowed with such a precious gift?

One of the most frequent arguments that we find in the history of philosophy in support of the existence of free will, is that it is the *conditio*

---

[6] Thomas of Aquinas, *Summa Theologiae* I, 76, 5 ad 4m.
[7] Descartes, *Principia philosophiae*, n. 41.

essendi moralitatis. Without free choice there is no responsibility, no moral action. "Male facimus ex libero voluntatis arbitrio", writes St Augustin, and he goes on to show that if human activity were not free, then it could neither be approved or disapproved. On the same line St Thomas Aquinas declares that "if we move ourselves to action necessarily, then deliberation, exhortation, command, praise and blame are destroyed, which are the things for which moral philosophy exist"[8]. Therefore, according to St Thomas the denial of free will "is an opinion extraneous (*extranea*) to philosophy, because it is not only contrary to faith, but also overthrows the principles of moral philosophy"[9].

This is all very true. But to the human person freedom means much more.

Theology teaches us that the pure spirits gained their final status, namely the achievement of their being: their happiness or unhappiness, with an act of choice alone: for God (the angels) or against God (the demons). This is not the case of man, whose progress or regress in humanity is, on the contrary, the result of a very long chain of free choices.

Through the DNA man is only physically entirely defined and qualified. He belongs to the human species. But whatever belongs to the spiritual nature of the human person remains entirely open and undetermined and it is going to be the result of many choices. In the early years of life of the choices of the parents and teachers, of the friends and even of enemies; but later one's own spiritual, cultural and moral growth will depend exclusively on his personal choices.

Therefore freedom of the will is not only the *conditio essendi moralitatis*, but also the *conditio essendi humanitatis*. According to Tertullian *homo est qui futurus est*[10]. And John S. Mill, in his *Essay on Liberty* writes: „Among the many works that life rightly tries to achieve and to make more perspicuous, the first in order of importance is surely man himself"[11].

III. NOT WHATEVER EXERCISE OF FREEDOM IS APT TO THE "MAKING" OF THE HUMAN PERSON

That not whatever use of freedom contributes to the full achievement of the human person seems to be an obvious truth, supported by everyday experience. To use freedom to lie, to steal, to cheat, to drink, to sell drugs,

---

[8] Aquinas, *De malo*, c. 6.
[9] *Ibid.*
[10] Tertullian, *De anima*, c. 53.
[11] J. S. Mill, *Saggio sulla libertà*, Milano 1981, p. 88.

to kill people etc. is certainly a possibility, but it does not help the person to increase in his humanity.

According to Nietzsche, Sartre, Camus and many other contemporary philosophers freedom is lawless, since nothing is above it. Freedom is not simply a fundamental constituent of the human being but the very essence of the human person. "It is impossible – Sartre declares – to find other limits to my freedom than freedom itself; or, if one prefers, this means that we are not free to cease being free"[12].

On this ground Nietzsche, Sartre, Camus etc. have claimed for man an unrestricted use of freedom. But this view is as false as its opposite: the denial of its existence.

Man is neither totally deprived of freedom, as determinists claim, nor absolutely free as many libertarians proclaim.

Freedom does not coincide with the essence of man, since man is not a pure spirit, but is a power given to him in order to grow in humanity and to reach his highest fulfilment, through the control of his natural impulses, instincts and passions.

On the other hand, if freedom is lawless everything becomes allowed: abortion and euthanasia, homsexuality and masturbation, *lager* and *gulag*. Man is placed beyond good and evil; as matter of fact all distinction between good and evil disappears. The only criterion for judging the value of an action is its beauty or its power: the power of the will that performs it. And the degree of freedom corresponds to the degree of power. Freedom is no longer a faculty given to man in order to grow in humanity but simply to express his power of being, his *conatus essendi*, according to Spinoza's famous expression. It is the freedom of the lion or of the elephant over the other animals of the forest.

But this is not true: man cannot claim this sort of freedom. Man's freedom is neither limitless nor lawless as Nietzsche and Sartre have claimed to be. And this can be easily seen. 1) Freedom is not identical with the essence of the human person: it is one of its fundamental properties together with life, thought, language, culture etc. Therefore freedom is also subject to the same limits to which life, thought, speech, work etc. are subject[13]. 2) Man is not free from being corporeal, social, sexual, etc. Before starting to make use of his freedom man is already placed within a physical, social, and cultural environment, and has already being guided in his life by primordial instincts. Man is not free to use language to his pleasure, otherwise language would no longer attain its aim, which is that of communicating with others. To attain this result, language must be used according to the rules and

---

[12] J. P. Sartre, *L'être et le néant*, Paris 1943, p. 515.

[13] "Intelligere et velle creaturae non est eius esse" (Aquinas, *De potentia*, 9, 9).

meanings which have being imposed on it. 3) Man is not free in tending towards good; this would be the suicide of the will, because just as the intellect tends naturally towards truth, the will tends naturally towards good. The tendency of the will towards good is necessary, but natural not coerced. With this regard St Thomas makes the following remark: "As the intellect of necessity adheres to the first principles, the will must of necessity adhere to the last end, which is happiness: since the end is in practical matters what the principle is in speculative matters"[14]. Freedom exercises itself within the horizon of the natural tendency towards good. On this point St Thomas is correct when he states: "Voluntas nihil facit nisi secundum quod est mota per suum obiectum quod est bonum appetibile" (Will does nothing if not that which it is moved to doing by its own object, which is the desirable good"[15]. 4) Man cannot remove himself from a certain dependence on the world, society and history. The weight of the world, society and history on single individuals is so obvious and so grave that philosophers of every tendency are today more inclined to denounce the state of profound slavery in which human will operates than to exalt freedom as Sartre and Camus have done. 5) Finally, human freedom is conditioned by passions. The influence of the passions on the will cannot be disguised, because we are speaking about a fact which we experience in ourselves every day, and it has been registered in famous sayings such as: "Video bona proboque, deteriora autem sequor" (I see and feel the good, but I follow the evil) (Ovid); "non enim quod volo bonum, hoc ago; sed quod odi malum, illud facio" (Not the good that I wish, I do; but the evil that I hate, I pursue) (St Paul). As we will see, one of the fundamental tasks of man in order to increase in his humanity is that of gaining control over his passions. Such is the objective of moral virtues as has been taught by philosophers of all ages: from Socrates, Plato, Aristotle, Zeno up to Descartes, Spinoza, Leibniz and Kant.

So, it is quite clear that man is neither endowed with an infinite freedom nor is he allowed to make a lawless use of his freedom if he cares to grow in humanity and to enrich his being, which is the being of an incarnate spirit.

IV. IN THE EXERCISE OF HIS FREEDOM MAN NEEDS THE HELP OF GOD, SOCIETY AND THE PHYSICAL NATURE

As we have seen freedom has not just an ethical and juridical function but also, and first of all, an anthropological and ontological function: freedom is given to man in order that he may achieve himself, his own being.

---

[14] Aquinas, *S. Theol.* I, 82, 1.
[15] Aquinas, *De veritate*, 14, 3.

Nature has endowed man with freedom in order that he may shape his person according to virtue. To be truly man is a matter of vocation not of necessity; it is a matter of choice not of necessity; a matter of virtue and art not of chance. There is a special virtuosity in the art of being a man. Freedom of choice is really a radical freedom; it concerns one own's being.

At this point the person has to face a very serious question: who is the perfect man? Which is the best model of humanity that one should keep constantly before his eyes in order to build up a nice monument of humanity? Artists in their work make use of models: a beautiful woman for the Gioconda, a strong athlete for Moses.

The Fathers of the Church and philosophical christology provide a good answer to this question. They speak of an ideal man, the *archegethes anthropos*. But to whom is to be assigned this title of *archegethes anthropos*, of ideal man, of model of humanity for every human being? According to the *Genesis*: „God made man in his own image" (1, 27). This means that man's model is God himself. But which God is the model of man? The God of power and justice of the Old Testament or the God of mercy and love of the New Testament?

The final revelation of God is Jesus Christ; he is the incarnation of God's love; he is the *via, veritas et vita* (Jo 14, 6). The one who sees him, sees the Father. Jesus Christ is therefore the *archegethes anthropos*. One becomes a true man in the measure he is capable to imitate Jesus Christ. The *imitatio Christi* is the true way for becoming truly human. "Deus factus est homo ut homo fieret Deus". This famous statement of the Greek Fathers is the best synthesis of Christian anthropology and ethics.

Cultural anthropology shows that models are essential in human life. And, actually, each culture exhibits its own model of humanity. Christian anthoropology presents the person of Jesus Christ as the only adequate model that reveals to man his full humanity.

Let's see, now, how a human being should use his freedom in the definition and the achievement of the project of the ideal man.

Just roughly sketched by nature, the human person, during its infancy, still reamins a project open to many interpretatons and definitions. In this stage of life the exercise of freedom must be very careful, since a wrong choice with regard to the project will bear very serious consequences.

Speaking of the object of the human will St Thomas says that there are two ways of considering the final end, abstractly and concretely. "We can speak of the last end in two ways: first, considering only the aspect of last end; secondly, considering the thing in which the aspect of last end is realized. So, then, as to the aspect of last end, all agree in desiring the last end: since all desire the fulfilment of their perfection, and it is precisely this fulfilment in which the last end consists. But as to the thing in which this aspect is realized, all men do not agree as to their last end: since some desire riches, as their consummate good; some, pleasure; other something else"[16].

The human will tends to the good and the final end in general by necessity. The exercise of freedom takes place in the definition and in the choice of the concrete final end, namely in the choice of the ideal man, the project of humanity that a person admires and seeks to imitate in order to become perfect and to reach complete happiness.

Although, at first sight, the freedom that man enjoys seems to be so wide as to exclude every restriction in the choice of his project of humanity; actually a more accurate exam and our psychological experience reveal that not every human project correponds to the requirement of the *capacitas infiniti* (the infinite openness, *Offenheit*) that is proper of the human person. Each one of us is aware of the contrast between what we are and what we want to be; between the real I and the ideal I; the Ego and the Id, the project already achieved and the project that we would like to achieve.

This proves that there are rules that freedom should follow – as in every work of art – in order, first, to define its project of humanity, and secondly, to bring it into reality. The main rules are three. 1) The first is that man is not the supreme being, but just a possibility tending towards the infinite; this means that in the human project is alread inscribed the possibility of ascending up to God. 2) The second is that man is not an isolated being, self-sufficient by himself: he is neither an angel nor a monad, without doors and windows, according to Leibniz famous definition; man is, in his very nature, a social being: he must live, grow, realize himself in society, in communion with other human beings. More than a *Dasein* man is a *Mitsein*. To live, in giving and receiving, from the Thou (Buber) or the Other (Levinas) belongs to the very nature of man. So the exercise of freedom and the definition of the human project must be done paying attention to the Thou, the Other. 3) The third rule is that man is an incarnate spirit. The person belongs by its very essere to the reign of the spirit. But man is not a pure spirit. The human person is an embodied spirit: to be in the body and, through the body, in the world is an essential condition for him. This means that the human project cannot be defined nor achieved outside or against nature. Nature is not an enemy of man, but rather it is his most important handmaid. Therefore man's freedom cannot be turned against nature, in the same way as it should not be turned against God and his neighbour.

---

[16] Aquinas, *S. Theol.* I/II, 1, 7. „Quamvis autem ex naturali inclinatione voluntas habeat ut in beatitudinem feratur secundum communem rationem, tamen quod feratur in beatitudinem talem vel talem, hoc non est ex inclinatione naturae sed per discretionem rationis" (*In IV Sent.* 1, 3).

These three rules prove that man's project, in order to be a good one, in conformity with the needs of the ideal man, should be defined and built in harmony with God, the neighbor and the cosmos (nature). Therefore a human project, to be valid, should not sin against God, the neighbour and nature.

But these general rules are meant more to set boundaries to freedom than to provide it with means for the realization of the ideal man, the *archegethes anthropos*. The basic means that may assist freedom in achieving its project of humanity are law and virtue (and also grace, if one speaks as a Christian anthropologist). We reach here the final point of our lecture.

V. IN ORDER TO GROW IN HIS HUMANITY AND TO BECOME FULLY HUMAN MAN NEEDS TO TAKE CARE OF HIS FREEDOM AND TO EDUCATE IT

Man's project and its achievement depend on culture and on freedom. Culture and freedom are distinct but not separate activities. Culture is the result of free creativity of man; vice versa freedom is guided by culture.

Freedom needs culture, it needs *consilium*, discipline, cultivation, otherwise it acts blindly and perversely.

The realization of the ideal man, the *imago Dei*, is a work of man (and, for a Christian, also of God). The art that helps man to cultivate and guide his freedom is ethics.

Today there is a tendency to contrast ethics and freedom and to see in ethics the chains of freedom. But this is a very serious distortion of the facts, since ethics is nothing else than the guide of freedom. It does this in two ways: law and virtue. With law ethics provides freedom with rules for its conduct; with virtue it gives freedom the power to act in conformity with the project of the ideal man.

1. LAW AND FREEDOM

Man needs discipline in order to bring his person to full achievement; for this reason he needs the help of the law. Let's hear the opinion of St Thomas on this point. In a celebrated article of the *Summa* he writes:

Man has a natural aptitude for virtue; but the perfection of virtue must be acquired by man by means of some kind of training. Thus we observe that man is helped by industry in his necessities, for instance, in food and clothing. Certain beginnings of these he has from nature, viz., his reason and his hands; but he has not the full complement, as other animal have, to whom nature has given sufficiency of clothing and food.

Now it is difficult to see how man could suffice for himself in the matter of his training: since the perfection of virtue consists chiefly in withdrawing man from undue pleasures, to which above all man is inclined, and especially the young, who are more capable of being trained. Consequently a man needs to receive this training from another, whereby to arrive at the perfection of virtue.

As to those young people who are inclined to acts of virtue, by their good natural dispositions or by custom, or rather by the gift of God, paternal training suffices, which is by admonitions. But since some are found to be depraved and prone to vice, and not easily amendable through words, it was necessary for such to be reastrained from evil by force and fear, in order that, at least, they might desist from evil-doing, and leave others in peace, and that they themselves, by being habituated in this way, might be brought to do willingly what hitherto they did from fear, and thus become virtuous. Now this kind of training, which compels through fear of punishment, is the discipline of laws. Therefore, in order that man might have peace and virtue, it was necessary for laws to be framed[17].

The function of the law (divine and human, natural and positive) is essentially that of helping the person to find and to know what ought to be done in order to be fully and authentically human, especially in the social dimension, which leads man to achieve his project of humanity with the help of his neighbour and at the same time prescribe to him to contribute to the achievement of the projects of humanity of his neighbour. The law helps the single person to discover principles and criteria of action that otherwise, left alone, very likely would not be able to know.

With regard to its origin, in its general dictates, the law cannot have any other foundation than the nature of man himself. Addressed to man's freedom, to be its guide, it is from the depth of his being that the law draws its first origin. This is the only plausible explanation of the fact that on the first moral principles there is a so wide consensus among the civil legislations of any time and place.

Only when the fundamental truths of anthropology (the absolute value of the human person and its projectuality directed towards the *archegethes anthropos*) are denied, also the origin and function of the law become obscure. It is then easy to distort the meaning of the law, by giving to it the character of an arbitrary imposition, and making of it a more or less democratic convention in view of the common good, rather than seeing in the law a very important help for the good of the person.

Actually, eradicated from its natural origin, the law has lost its authority in the forum of conscience, and is systematically ignored and violated. Even laws that in the past were considered sacred and inviolable (as not to kill, respect your father and mother, do not steal etc.) today vacillate not only in the consciences but even in civil codes.

---

[17] Aquinas, *S. Theol.* I/II 95, 1.

In order that law may recover in the forum of conscience its dignity of fundamental value and its function of providing a guide to freedom, it is necessary to bring it back to its natural and divine origin. Let's listen again St Thomas Aquinas on this subject.

Since all things subject to Divine providence are ruled and measured by the eternal law, it is evident that all things partake somewhat of the eternal law, in so far as, namely, from its being imprinted on them, they derive their respective inclinations to their proper acts and ends. Now among all others, the rational creature is subject to Divine providence in the most excellent way, in so far as it partakes of a share of providence, by being provident both for itself and for others. Wherefore it has a share of the Eternal Reason, whereby it has a natural inclination to its proper act and end: and this participation of the eternal law in the rational creature is called the natural law (...) The light of natural reason, whereby we discern what is good and what is evil, which is the function of the natural law, is nothing else than an imprint on us of the divine light. It is therefore evident that the natural law is nothing else than the rational creature's participation of the eternal law[18].

2. FREEDOM AND VIRTUE

The second and even more decisive help to freedom in the shaping of the form of the ideal man comes from virtue. As a matter of fact virtue is nothing else than the habitual good use of freedom in doing something: "Virtus humana, quae est habitus operativus, est bonus habitus et boni operativus" (Human virtue which is an operative habit, is a good habit, productive of good works)[19].

Virtue, as law, in many environments, today, does not enjoy good reputation. By many people it is mocked and despised. This holds for the virtue of chastity as for the virtue of conjugal fidelity, for the virtue of obedience as for the virtue of sincerity etc. And this is a clear sign of the level of corruption in which our society and its culture are fallen. But the dispise and the loss of virtue are severely payed. Without it man does not become a good person but a wild animal. It cannot be otherwise, since when somebody rejects the sweet yoke of virtue, he falls necessarily under the heavy and malign yoke of vice. Either one reiterates good actions and in such a way his freedom becomes virtuous; or he reiterates bad actions and his freedom becomes wicked.

To dispise virtue and to consider it as an enemy of freedom is not only a sign of wickedness but also of ignorance. It means to refuse to recognise which is the authentic reality of man: that man is essentially a cultural being,

---

[18] Aquinas, *S. Theol.* I/II, 91, 2.
[19] Aquinas, *S. Theol.* I/II, 55, 3.

a being which is going to be shaped according to an ideal project, the *archegethes anthropos*. The achievement of the project of the human person as the achievement of any other project needs virtue and art. Virtue is the good disposition of the soul, it is the health of the soul, in the same way as health is the good disposition of the body. "Virtue itself – St Thomas says – is an ordered disposition of the soul, in so far as the powers of the soul are in some way ordered to one another, and to that which is outside. Hence virtue, inasmuch as it is a suitable disposition of the soul, is like health and beauty, which are suitable dispositions of the body"[20].

As we know, freedom is a child of both the intellect and the will. Therefore the education of freedom demands an education of both intellect and will.

Firstly of the intellect, and this is done through the acquisition of the intellectual virtues, especially of wisdom, *caput scientiarum*, the head of sciences. "It belongs to wisdom, that is an intellectual virtue, to pronounce right judgments about divine things"[21]. But it pertains also to wisdom to shed light on conscience and to provide it with the fundamental criteria and laws of morality. Wisdom dispels the darkness of ignorance and shows to the intellect the ultimate truths about God and man, about the ideal man and about man's final end.

Secondly of the will, through the acquisition of the four cardinal virtues: prudence, justice, fortitude and temperance. The leading moral virtue is prudence: *prudentia est auriga virtutum*. Prudence is the *recta ratio agibilium*: the right reason about things to be done. It is directly rooted in reason: it is an habit of practical reason, but its function is to provide a good direction to the will in its acts of choice. According to St Thomas, "moral virtue cannot be without prudence, because it is a habit of choosing, i.e., making us choosing well. Now in order that a choice be good, two things are required. First, that the intention be directed to a due end; and this is done by moral virtue, which inclines the appetitive faculty to the good [...] which is a due end. Secondly that man take rightly those things which have reference to the end: and this he cannot do unless his reason counsel, judge and command aright, which is the function of prudence. Therefore there cannot be any moral virtue without prudence"[22]. Therefore "prudence is a virtue most necessary for human life. For a good life consists in good deeds. Now in order to do good deeds, it matters not only what a man does, but also how he does it; to wit, that he do it from right choice and not merely from impulse or passion. And since choice is about things in

---

[20] *Ibid.*, 55, 2 ad 1.
[21] Aquinas, *S. Theol.* II/II, 45, 2.
[22] Aquinas, *S. Theol.* I/II, 58, 4.

reference to the end, rectitude of choice requires two things; namely, the due end, and something suitably ordained to the due end. Now man is suitably directed to his due end by a virtue which perfects the soul in the appetitive part, the object of which is the good and the end. But to that which is suitably ordained to the due end man needs to be rightly disposed by a habit of his reason because counsel and choice, which are about things ordained to the end, are acts of the reason. Consequently an intellectual virtue is needed in reason, to perfect the reason, and make it suitably affected towards things ordained to the end; and this virtue is prudence. Consequently prudence is a virtue necessary to lead a good life"[23].

CONCLUSION

We have seen that freedom is not only an essential constituent of man, but it is the power given to him by God that enables the human person to choose between many possible projects of humanity and to achieve a project of humanity that is a good imitation of the ideal man, the *archegethes anthropos*.

In order to become truly man, one needs to cultivate first and above all his freedom, with the help of law and virtue. As Maritain beautifully writes: "L'homme véritablement et pleinement *naturel*, ce n'est pas l'homme de la nature, la terre inculte, c'est l'homme des vertus, la terre humaine cultivée par la droite raison, l'homme formé par la culture intérieure des vertus intellectuelles et morales. Lui seul a une consistance, une personalité"[24]. And St Thomas Aquinas: "Solus ille dicitur bonus homo simpliciter qui habet bonam voluntatem"[25].

Therefore, to educate man to make good use of his freedom is the best way to make him a good man, a good imitation of the *archegethes anthropos* and to help him to reach the final goal of his life, which consists in sharing in the life of God, whose life, as we know, is love, since *Deus caritas est*.

Therefore in the participation of the love of God, which is the *pericoresis* of the *agape* of the blessed Trinity, there is the consummation, namely the complete fulfilment, of human freedom and of human life of each one of us.

---

[23] Aquinas, *S. Theol.* I/II, 57, 5.
[24] J. Maritain, *Religion et culture*, in *Oeuvres 1912-1939*, Paris 1975, p. 558.
[25] Aquinas, *De virtut. incommuni* 7, ad 2m.

GIOVANNI REALE
Università Cattolica di Milano
Italy

MESSAGGIO FILOSOFICO MEDIANTE IL MITO E CONCETTO DI LIBERTÀ IN PLATONE

1. LE DIFFICOLTÀ DI LETTURA E DI INTERPRETAZIONE CHE PLATONE PRESENTA

Platone è certamente uno di quei filosofi apparentemente facili da leggere, ma, in realtà, assai difficili da comprendere. Le ragioni di queste difficoltà sono soprattutto due.

In primo luogo, nei suoi dialoghi si intrecciano messaggi incrociati: da un lato, alcuni messaggi vengono presentati con linguaggio che espone concetti in modo esteso e dettagliato; e dall'altro, certi messaggi vengono presentati invece con linguaggio brachilogico e fortemente allusivo, che comunica solo ai discepoli dell'Accedemia cose che fanno riferimento per cenni a ciò che veniva sviluppato nelle lezioni (ossia alle cosidette "dottrine non scritte").

In secondo luogo, nello stesso linguaggio chiaro ed esteso si intrecciano, in varie maniere, due differenti modi di affrontare e di trattare la questione in oggetto: quello del *logos dialettico* e quello del *mito poetico*.

Molte interpretazioni di Platone sono state e continuano ad essere errate, e in ogni caso assai parziali (e di conseguenza inadeguate), proprio per il motivo che non si è preso coscienza in via preliminare di tali problemi, e non si è cercato di risolverli in maniera corretta.

Il primo problema è certamente quello più complesso, e la sua soluzione risulta decisiva per la comprensione di tutta una serie di questioni metafisiche, gnoseologiche e assiologiche. Tuttavia esso non condiziona in maniera determinante la comprensione del concetto di libertà, di cui qui parliamo e perciò non ne tratteremo[1].

---

[1] Da nessuna testimonianza pervenutaci risulta infatti che Platone trattasse la questione concernente la libertà in connessione con temi trattatti esclusivamente nelle sue lezioni acca-

Invece per il nostro tema risulta essere veramente essenziale la presa di coscienza e la soluzione del secondo problema, in quanto Platone ha espresso il suo pensiero sulla libertà – e proprio nei suoi punti culminanti – avvalendosi, in modo preminente, di immagini e di miti[2]. Proprio di questo problema, di conseguenza, dobbiamo trattare in via preliminare.

II. "LOGOS" E "MYTHOS" IN PLATONE

A partire dall'età moderna, soprattutto in conseguenza della "rivoluzione scientifica", si è interpretato la filosofia come passaggio dal "mito" al "logos", e quindi si è inteso la filosofia nel suo sviluppo come progressiva *evoluzione del logos*.

Pertanto, si è considerato il mito come un linguaggio "pre-filosofico", ossia come una forma di rappresentazione priva di valore conoscitivo, ossia priva di carattere scientifico. Di conseguenza, i miti platonici sono stati considerati come qualcosa che interessa i letterati ben più che i filosofi[3]. E così si spiegano le ragioni per cui *Il Fedone* è stato in larga misura trascurato dai filosofi in tutta la parte mitica, che invece è essenziale.

Una notevole responsabilità nella diffusione di questa convinzione ebbe lo Hegel, questa volta con una motivazione non di carattere "scientifico", ma strettamente "speculativo".

Hegel nelle sue *Vorlesungen über die Geschichte der Philosophie* ha fatto alcuni rilievi che vanno attentamente considerati.

L'esposizione dei filosofemi in forma di miti che fa Platone costituisce, a suo giudizio, certamente una attrattiva nella lettura dei suoi dialoghi, ma essa costituisce una fonte di malintesi. Pertanto, afferma Hegel, sbaglia chi giudica i miti platonici una cosa eccellente[4].

Ecco le parole stesse di Hegel: "Il mito è una forma di esposizione che, in quanto più antica, suscita sempre immagini sensibili che sono adatte per la rappresentazione, non per il pensiero; ma questo attesta impotenza del pensiero, che non sa ancora reggersi di per sé, e quindi non è ancora pen-

---

demiche, ossia sulle sue "dottrine non scritte", anche se, ovviamente, ci sono rapporti fra le prime e le seconde.

[2] Come è noto, Platone ha parlato nei suoi dialoghi dei problemi ultimativi dell'uomo e della sua sorte in larga misura con i miti. Si pensi per esempio al *Fedone*, che procede, proprio in maniera programmatica, per metà mediante concetti e per l'altra metà per miti.

[3] Questo è avvenuto specialmente nel nostro secolo, condizionato dalle varie forme della mentalità "scientistico-tecnologica".

[4] Hegel, naturalmente, non era condizionato in questo giudizio da una mentalità "scientistica", ma da presupposti "teoreticestici", o meglio ancora, di carattere "speculativo".

siero libero. Il mito fa parte della pedagogia del genere umano, poiché eccita ed attrae ad occuparsi del contenuto; ma siccome in esso il pensiero è contaminato da forme sensibili, il mito non può esprimere ciò che vuole esprimere il pensiero. Quando il concetto si è fatto maturo non ha più bisogno di miti"[5].

Le conclusioni che Hegel crede di dover trarre sono categoriche: "Per trarre dai dialoghi di Platone l'intelligenza della sua filosofia è dunque necessario sceverare dall'idea filosofica ciò che appartiene alla rappresentazione, particolarmente quando egli per esporre un'idea filosofica ricorre ai miti: soltanto così può riconoscersi che tutto ciò che appartiene soltanto alla rappresentazione come rappresentazione, non è di pertinenza del pensiero, ma è l'essenziale. Ma se non si conosce per sè ciò che è concetto, ciò che è speculativo, non si può evitare il pericolo di essere indotti da questi miti a dedurre dai dialoghi tutta una serie di proposizioni e di teoremi, presentandoli come filosofemi platonici, mentre essi non lo sono affatto, e appartengono soltanto alla rappresentazione e non al concetto[6].

Ma da qualche tempo è invece in atto, in senso contrario a quanto dice Hegel, proprio una rivalutazione del valore conoscitivo del mito in generale, e in particolare del mito in Platone[7].

Walter Hirsch, un seguace di Heidegger, ha riportato questa questione in primo piano[8]. Conviene qui ricordare la sua tesi, che rappresenta un efficace correttivo, anche se, almeno in parte, rischia di cadere in errori opposti a quelli in cui è caduto Hegel.

Il mito platonico, non è un residuo di riflessione pre-filosofica, né una formulazione provvisoria di problemi successivamente trattati a livello di logos; ma non è neppure una forma trans-concettuale, di tipo intuitivo mistico e quindi irrazionale.

Che cos'è, allora, il mito platonico?

È un metodo di intendere e di esprimere certi aspetti del reale che, per loro stessa natura, non sono coglibili ed esprimibili con il puro logos. Il mito, precisamente, è strettamente connesso con i problemi della vita.

Più precisamente: il pensiero mediante il logos spiega l'essere e il mondo delle Idee. Ma confrontandosi con le Idee (peraltro indispensabili), il pensiero si scopre *vivente*. Proprio in quanto "vivente" il pensiero compren-

---

[5] Hegel, *Vorlesungen über die Geschichte der Philosophie*, in *Sämtliche Werke*, herausgegeben von H. Glockner, Stuttgart 1964[4], vol. 18, pp. 188 sg.

[6] Ibidem.

[7] Sui miti di Platone si è sempre scritto molto; ma solo di recente si è cercato di giungere al fondo dei problemi, in parallelo con l'inizio della crisi dello scientismo.

[8] W. Hirsch, *Platons Weg zum Mythos,* De Gruyter, Berlin-New York 1971.

de l'impossibilità di concepire un'Idea di anima, in quanto l'Idea è un essere immobile, mentre l'anima è *mobilità* e *vita*. Il mito, di conseguenza, si impone come "una storia dell'esserci dell'anima (storia che per il logos rimane paradossale) nella unità delle sue origini e del suo fine, unità che dura al di là del tempo e oltrepassa ogni divenire"[9].

Dunque, non il logos può comprendere ed esprimere la vita e la sua problematica, ma appunto il "mito", che, in questo ambito, supera il logos e diventa mito-*logia*, ossia una forma di logos che si esprime mediante il mito. Così inteso, il mito si impone addirittura come espressione più alta della metafisica platonica.

Senza dubbio Hirsch rende giustizia a ciò che Hegel aveva negato, ma eccede; e, in larga misura, finisce per sopravvalutare il mito stesso a danno del logos.

III. IL "LOGOS" E IL "MYTOS" COME SISTOLE E DIASTOLE DEL CUORE DELLA FILOSOFIA PLATONICA

Insisto su questo problema per due motivi ben precisi.

In primo luogo, per il motivo che Platone, come ho detto già all'inizio, esprime il suo concetto di libertà prevalentemente mediante miti. E si tratta di un concetto espresso per immagini, di per sé non solo molto bello, ma – a mio giudizio – di uno dei più bei concetti espressi non solo nell'ambito della cultura antica, ma in tutti i tempi, a livello razionale.

In secondo luogo, insisto sul problema per il motivo che, mentre alcuni grandi interpreti (come Stenzel[10], Jaeger[11], Pohlenz[12], Mondolfo[13]) si sono accorti della portata di tale dottrina platonica, la comune opinione non l'ha recepita, in quanto condizionata da vari pregiudizi sul mito, soprattutto provenienti dalla mentalità "scientistica", positivistica e neopositivistica e comunque razionalistica all'eccesso.

Cerchiamo allora di comprendere il modo in cui va inteso il "mito" di Platone.

In primo luogo, va ricordato che il termine "mythos" viene usato dal nostro filosofo in vari sensi, e quindi ricopre un'area semantica assai ampia.

---

[9] Ibidem, p. X.
[10] J. Stenzel, *Platon der Erzieher*, Leipzig 1928.
[11] W. Jaeger, *Paideia. Die Formung des griechischen Menschen,* I, Berlin 1954².
[12] M. Pohlenz, *Der hellenischen Mensch*, Göttingen 1947.
[13] R. Mondolfo, *La comprensione del soggetto umano nell'antichità classica,* Firenze 1958, La Nuova Italia.

Platone considera, nel senso più generale, i suoi stessi dialoghi come miti (addirittura considera "mito" la sua stessa *Repubblica*, ossia la sua opera filosoficamente più ricca e impegnata[14]), in quanto egli ritiene che la chiarezza, il rigore e la fondatezza ultimativa appartengono solamente all'oralità dialettica[15].

Inoltre, egli tende a considerare oggetto di un discorso "mitico" tutta la realtà in qualche modo legata al divenire (quindi il cosmo e l'anima)[16], perché la pura *noesis* è possibile solo in riferimento all'essere immobile ed eterno, e dunque al mondo ideale[17].

Bisogna ricordare che Platone collega il "mythos" anche con il "discorso che incanta", che esercita forza persuasiva, quasi con una magica forza[18].

In ogni caso, va rilevato quanto segue.

Così come c'è un *logos buono* e uno *cattivo* (quello sofistico ed eristico)[19], analogamente c'è anche un *mythos buono* e uno *cattivo* (quello di molti poeti, che andrebbe addirittura bandito dallo Stato ideale)[20]. E come il logos buono è quello che mira alla Verità, così analogamente, anche il *mythos* valido è quello che mira alla Verità stessa, mediante la *rappresentazione per immagini*[21].

Quale è, allora, il rapporto che sussiste fra queste due vie alla Verità, ossia fra il buon *logos* e il buon *mythos*?

Abbiamo visto le opposte posizioni assunte da Hegel e da Hirsch, e abbiamo già indicato quale sia la via corretta da battere, che media gli opposti: "mythos" e "logos" sono *vie parallele*, indispensabili all'uomo per accedere alla Verità.

Konrad Geiser ha precisato in maniera corretta quanto segue: "Questo parallelismo fra mito e logos va dunque spiegato come necessaria conseguenza dell'insufficienza della nostra umana facoltà del conoscere. Non possiamo cogliere la verità afferrandola immediatamente, dobbiamo piuttosto

---

[14] Cfr. W. Luther, *Die Schwäche des geschriebenen Logos. Ein Beispiel humanistischer Interpretation, versucht am sogenannten Schriftmythos in Platons Pheidros (274 B 6 ff.)*, "Gymnasium" 68(1961) p. 526-548.

[15] Cfr. *Fedro*, 274 B-278 E.

[16] Cfr. *Timeo*, passim.

[17] Cfr. *Repubblica*, libri VI e VII, passim.

[18] Così, ad esempio, nel *Fedone*.

[19] Si veda, per esempio, l'*Eutidemo*, passim.

[20] Così Platone si esprime soprattutto nella *Repubblica*.

[21] Nel *Fedone* Platone dice espressamente quanto segue: "... è la cosa più conveniente di tutto che, chi è sul punto di intraprendere il viaggio verso l'altro mondo, *rifletta con la ragione e mediti attraverso i miti* su questo viaggio verso l'altro mondo e dica come immagina che essa sia; se no, che altro si potrebbe fare in tutto questo tempo che ci separa dal tramonto del sole?" (61 E).

cercare di avvicinarla per differenti vie: da una parte per immagini e globalmente, attraverso il mito, dall'altra attraverso le analisi e le sintesi del logos, dunque attraverso i concetti del linguaggio, della matematica e della dialettica. Se questa concezione è corretta, è allora lecito ritenere che mito e logos per Platone assolvono una funzione complementare e che nessuna delle due forme è in grado di sostituire l'altra. Nella misura in cui è possibile rendere il contenuto di verità del mito nella forma di logos, nella stessa misura va presa la forza particolare del linguaggio mitico. Il lettore accorto non tenterà dunque di «demitizzare» con il logos i miti di Platone, cercherà semmai di ampliare e di integrare le loro asserzioni con i metodi del logos"[22].

Tutto questo è vero, ma sono necessarie alcune integrazioni e ulteriori approfondimenti.

La posizione assunta da Platone nei confronti del mito trascende il suo preciso significato storico, in quanto, oggi, torna a reimporsi dal punto di vista teoretico.

L'uomo contemporaneo, ormai da alcuni decenni, si sta rendendo ben conto che la scienza è ben lontana dal pervenire a verità ultimative in modo incontrovertibile, e che, in particolare, i metodi della "scienza", per quanto validi nel loro ambito, non possono affatto essere assunti come metodi esclusivi di accesso alla Verità[23]. Ed è addirittura in atto una rivalutazione teoretica del mito come via alla Verità[24].

Questo spiega in larga misura il grande successo che Platone torna ad avere in Occidente, a partire dagli anni ottanta. I suoi scritti si vendono a decine di migliaia di copie, molto più dei libri dei filosofi moderni e contemporanei.

Io sono convinto che una delle cause di questo successo è dovuta, in larga misura, proprio ai messaggi veritativi di Platone in forma di mito, che parlano a tutti gli uomini di cultura, ben al di là degli specialisti e delle chiusure delle varie scuole[25].

---

[22] K. Geiser, *Platone come scrittore filosofico. Saggi sull'ermeneutica dei dialoghi platonici*. Con una premessa di M. Gigante, Napoli 1984, Bibliopolis (opera pubblicata solo in lingua italiana), pp. 134-135.

[23] È, questa, l'idea che sta ormai nascendo e diffondendosi in seguito alla crisi dello scientismo e del tecnicismo ad oltranza.

[24] Si veda: K. K. Hübner, *Die Wahrheit des Mythos,* München 1985 (cfr. anche: H. Pietschmann, *Das Ende des naturwissenschaftlichen Zeitalters*, Wien-Hamburg 1980 e E. Chargaff, *Unbegreifliches Geheimnis*, Stuttgart 1981).

[25] Si tenga presente che Platone, in questi anni, è un *best seller* nella vendita di opere filosofiche.

Per concludere su questo punto, vorrei citare un significativo passo del maggiore esponente italiano della pittura metafisica, Giorgio de Chirico, in cui viene espresso il concetto-chiave che qui ci interessa: "Da lungo tempo ormai mi sono reso perfettamente conto che *io penso per immagini o raffigurazioni. Dopo lungo riflettere ho costatato che, in fondo, è l'immagine la principale espressione del pensiero umano*, e gli altri fattori, per mezzo dei quali si esprime il pensiero, come, ad esempio, le parole, i gesti e le espressioni, non sono che espressioni secondarie che accompagnano l'immagine"[26].

Dunque, la conclusione con la quale termino la prima parte di questa mia relazione è la seguente: il "mythos" platonico è "un pensare per immagini", e, dunque, come il pensare per concetti, esso pure ha di mira la verità. Ma ha il vantaggio di essere più comunicativo, e soprattutto più persuasivo (ha maggiore efficacia psicagogica), presentato in funzione dello strumento della grande arte platonica (una delle più grandi di tutti tempi). E, in ogni caso, il "mythos" non agisce mai a danno del logos, ma sempre e solo in sinergia con esso.

Ecco la simbolica affermazione che Platone mette in bocca a Socrate, che si accinge a discutere dell'immortalità, poco prima della morte: "è la cosa più conveniente di tutte per colui che è sul punto di intraprendere il viaggio verso l'altro mondo, riflettere con la ragione (*diaskopein*) e meditare attraverso i miti (*mythologein*) su questo viaggio verso l'altro mondo e dire come immagini che esso sia"[27].

Dunque, il filosofare platonico è un far ricerca con la ragione e un pensare per miti in strutturale simbiosi. Logos e mythos sono come "sistole" e "diastole" del cuore del pensiero filosofico platonico.

VI. LA CONTEMPLAZIONE DELLA VERITÀ COME FACITRICE DI UOMINI

Il concetto di "libertà" cui qui io farò riferimento non è quello specifico e ristretto di carattere politico, ma quello che riguarda l'uomo di fronte alle supreme scelte ultimative, che lo fanno "uomo" prima ancora che "cittadino".

"La verità vi farà liberi", dice il Vangelo[28]. Ma è proprio questo il concetto di fondo cui Platone mira, soprattutto nel grandioso mito dell'Iperuranio e della "Pianura della Verità" che si trova nell'Iperuranio stesso[29].

---

[26] Cfr. *L'Opera completa di de Chirico 1908-1924*. Presentazione e apparati critici e filologici di M. Fagiolo Dell'Arco (?), Milano 1994, Rizzoli Editore, p. 5.
[27] *Fedone*, 62 E.
[28] Giovanni 8, 32. Card. Glemp: Non c'è libertà senza Verità.
[29] *Fedro*, 248 B.

Platone vuole mettere in piena evidenza il rapporto ontologico strutturale che sussiste fra "l'essere uomo" e la "Verità". Le anime, prima della nascita, cercano di vedere e contemplare quanto più è possibile ciò che sta nella "Pianura della Verità", per il seguente motivo: "il nutrimento adatto alla parte migliore dell'anima proviene dal Prato che è là, e la natura dell'ala con cui l'anima può volare si nutre proprio di questo"[30].

Ebbene, al differente grado di Verità che l'anima ha visto corrisponde il differente "spessore" etico umano che l'anima assume. Al più alto grado di visione di Verità corrisponde l'essere filosofo, al più basso grado di visione di Verità corrisponde il più basso grado di vita umana, che è quella del tiranno[31].

Il concetto di fondo espresso da Platone è dunque il seguente: solamente per la Verità tu sei un uomo, e senza la Verità non puoi essere un uomo.

Ecco le sue sferzanti parole: "In effetti, l'anima che non ha contemplato la Verità non potrà mai giungere alla forma di uomo"[32].

Alfred Taylor è stato uno dei pochi studiosi che ha saputo dare il giusto peso al mito della "Pianura della Verità": "È in virtù di tale pura contemplazione che gli dèi e gli uomini eseguono il compito pratico di stabilire e mantenere l'ordine naturale nel regno della mutabilità e del divenire. Come Mosè, essi fanno ogni cosa secondo il modello che hanno visto «sul monte»"[33].

Ma prima di passare al punto-chiave del mito di Er del libro decimo della *Repubblica*, che è quello che qui maggiormente ci interessa, c'è ancora un concetto da mettere in rilievo, ossia il nesso strutturale di questa dottrina con quella di Socrate.

Si ricordi che Socrate riduceva tutte quante le virtù a una sola, e che identificava l'essenza della virtù con la *conoscenza*. La Virtù è *conoscenza*, evidentemente, del Bene e del Bello, che coincidono con il Vero nel grado supremo[34].

Dunque, la virtù, che è un esplicarsi della libertà umana al suo più elevato grado, *ossia come scelta del meglio*, per il Greco coincide con *la conoscenza stessa del meglio*, e quindi con la visione e fruizione del Bene con cui coincide la Verità.

---

[30] *Fedro*, 248 B-C.
[31] Cfr. *Fedro*, 248 D-E.
[32] *Fedro*, 749 B.
[33] A. E. Taylor, *Plato. The Man and His Work*, London 1974[4], p. 307.
[34] Cfr. G. Reale, *Storia della filosofia antica* (*Historia filozofii starożytnej*), przeł. E. I. Zieliński, t. I, s. 326 nn.).

Ma veniamo al mito di Er in cui Platone esprime nel modo migliore il suo pensiero su questo punto.

V. UOMO, VIRTÙ E LIBERTÀ NEL MITO DI ER

Sul mito di Er[35] ci sarebbe molto da dire; ma, in questa sede, ci interessa solamente il suo nucleo centrale, che consiste nella presentazione dell'*atto della libera scelta della vita dell'uomo*.

La questione di fondo che emerge assai bene è quella della "scelta del destino", con la connessa strutturale relazione dinamica fra "libertà" e "necessità" nella costituzione della persona umana. Si potrebbe anche dire che il mito di Er rappresenta per immagini l'*atto metafisico di quella libera scelta dalla quale dipende l'essere-uomo*.

Ecco alcuni tratti essenzaili del mito.

Le anime che devono reincarnarsi giungono nel luogo in cui ha sede la Necessità e le sue figlie, ossia le Moire: Lachesi che presiede nel passato, Cloto che è sovrana del presente, Atropo da cui dipende il futuro. Qui un ministro, prendendo dal grembo di Lachesi tutti i "modelli" di possibili vite, dice quanto segue: "Parola della Vergine Lachesi, figlia di Necessità. Anime caduche, eccovi giunte all'inizio di un altro ciclo di vita di genere mortale, in quanto esso si conclude con la morte. *Non sarà il dèmone a scegliere voi, ma voi il dèmone*. Il primo estratto sceglierà per primo la vita alla quale sarà tenuto per necessità. *La virtù non ha padroni; quanto più ciascuno di voi l'onora, tanto più ne avrà; quanto meno l'onora, tanto meno ne avrà*. La responsabilità, pertanto, è di chi sceglie; il dio ne ha colpa[36].

Il passo contiene due idee rivoluzionarie, preparate certamente dai Presocratici e da Socrate, ma che Platone porta al loro vertice.

In primo luogo, viene capovolto il rapporto fra l'uomo e il dèmone in cui il Greco aveva creduto. L'uomo non viene scelto dal dèmone, rimanendogli soggetto come a fatale necessità; è l'uomo stesso a scegliere il proprio dèmone, ossia *a decidere la propria sorte*. In altri termini: è l'uomo stesso che sceglie ciò che vuole moralmente essere, con tutte le conseguenze che questo comporta (eudaimonia = eu daimon echein).

In secondo luogo, viene scolpita in maniera indelebile, come su una tavola di bronzo, l'eterna massima: "La virtù na ha padroni: quanto più ciascuno l'onora, tanto più ne avrà; quanto meno l'onora, tanto meno ne avrà"[37].

---

[35] Cfr. *Repubblica*, X 614 A-621 D.
[36] *Repubblica*, X 617 D-E.
[37] *Repubblica*, 618 E.

Si noti che, come qualcuno ha ben rilevato, la scelta e l'onore che vien tributato alla virtù si riferisce certamente "alla libertà dell'uomo di guadagnarsi entro il corso fissato della vita nell'al-di-qua una parte maggiore o minore di virtù" e non solo e non tanto quella originaria pre-natale: questa è conseguenza di quella[38].

Ancora alcuni punti meritano di essere messi qui in rilievo.

Le anime ricevono in sorte l'ordine con cui dovranno recarsi a scegliere, fra i modelli di vita, quello desiderato. Le prime ne hanno quindi a disposizione un gran numero, le successive sempre di meno; e tuttavia anche le ultime hanno a disposizione tanti modelli di vita quanti bastano per operare una conveniente scelta[39].

Ma la grande sorpresa che il mito riserba è quella dell'"anamnesi" capovolta. Infatti, come, venendo sulla terra, l'anima, mediante la conoscenza filosofica, "ricorda" qualcosa che ha contemplato nella Pianura della Verità, così, nella scelta di una nuova vita nell'al-di-là per il ritorno nell'al-di-qua, ricorda ciò che di essenziale ha imparato quando era nell'al-di-qua[40].

In primo luogo, ricorda ciò che gli ha insegnato *l'esperienza del dolore e della sofferenza*, che sono collegati a certe scelte di vita[41].

In modo emblematico, Platone dice che mentre la prima delle anime, senza conoscenza, sceglie quella che in apparenza sembra la migliore mentre in realtà è la peggiore delle vite, ossia quella del tiranno (con le spaventose conseguenze e sofferenze che comporta), l'anima cui toccò l'ultimo posto nella scelta fu Ulisse, che, per l'insegnamento che gli aveva dato il dolore nella precedente vita, rinunciò alla vita di avventure e scelse la vita più semplice[42].

Scrive Platone: "L'anima di Ulisse, a cui la sorte aveva riservato proprio l'ultimo posto fra tutti, si avviò alla scelta, lasciando da parte ogni desiderio di gloria, *memore della sofferenza della vita precedente*; si aggirò pertanto a lungo, alla ricerca della vita di un uomo qualunque, privo di preoccupazioni, e la trovò a fatica, relegata in un angolo, trascurata dagli altri. Non appena la scorse, la prese di buon grado, dicendo che non avrebbe fatto altra scelta neppure se fosse stato sorteggiato per primo"[43]. Il grande Ulisse reso saggio dalle esperienze della sofferenza e del dolore sceglie la vita semplice di un uomo qualunque.

---

[38] J. Stenzel; cfr. sopra, nota 10.
[39] Cfr. *Repubblica*, X 618 E ss.
[40] Glemp: la libertà comporta sacrificio, rinuncia.
[41] Cfr. *Repubblica*, X 618 C e 619 D.
[42] *Repubblica*, 620 C.
[43] *Repubblica*, 620 C-D.

In secondo luogo, l'anima ricorda, perché diventa indelebile – la suprema conoscenza del Bene: una volta guadagnata, infatti, tale conoscenza rimane per sempre sia nell'al-di-qua sia nell'al-di-là.

Ecco le belle conclusioni di Platone: "Ebbene, caro Glaucone, proprio qui si annida *ogni rischio per l'uomo*, e qui bisogna concentrare ogni impegno (... nella realtà della vita). Piuttosto, trascuriamo tutte le altre conoscenze per farci ricercatori e cultori solo di quella che metta in grado di riconoscere e di scovare l'uomo che sappia conferire la capacità, pratica e teorica, di *scegliere sempre e in ogni caso la migliore vita possibile*, dopo un attento discernimento di ciò che è utile e dannoso. [...] In tal modo, un uomo, traendo le debite conclusioni da tutto ciò e non perdendo di vista la natura dell'anima, sarà in grado di fare *una scelta fra la vita migliore e la peggiore*, ritenendo la peggiore quella che lo porterebbe al risultato di essere più *ingiusto*, e, viceversa, come migliore quella che lo porterebbe verso comportamenti più *giusti*. E tutto il resto lo lascerà salutandolo, dato che *questa è la scelta vincente, sia per la vita terrena che per l'altra*"[44].

E poiché ho concentrato il mio discorso in prevalenza sul "mythos" platonico inteso come un "pensare per immagini", non meno importante del logos dialettico, e anzi come necessario complemento di esso, voglio concludere con il messaggio con cui Platone consegna il mito di Er nelle nostre mani.

Si tratta di un messaggio di chiusura veramente emblematico: "Ecco, caro Glaucone, in quale modo si è salvato questo mito, e non è andato perduto. Ed esso, in verità, può, a sua volta, salvare anche noi, se gli prestiamo fede".

Il discorso sulla Verità (fatto per via di logos e per via di immagini) è quello che fa liberi e che salva, perché è la Verità e solo la Verità che fa liberi e salva.

---

[44] *Repubblica*, X 618 B-E.

JULIO TERÁN DUTARI
Pontificia Universidad Católica
Ecuador

ANALOGIE DER FREIHEIT
ALS KERN EINER CHRISTLICHEN PHILOSOPHIE
nach dem Werk Erich Przywaras

Henri de Lubac hat einmal dem Lebenswerk H. U. von Balthasars dieses Lob gezollt: Sein Ausmaß ist derart unüberschaubar tief, daß die Kirche kein ähnliches in unserer Zeit kennt[1]. Lange zuvor hatte sich derselbe Balthasar, gerne im Verhältnis des Schülers zum Meister stehend, ein gleiches Urteil über das Werk Erich Przywaras [*1889 Katowice – †1972 Murnau] gebildet. Daher wollte er dessen vielfältiges, uferloses, ja gigantisches Schrifttum vor der Zerstreuung retten. Denn rein äußerlich gesehen, mag es wenig Greifbares zu bieten scheinen, was der Nachwelt als immerwährendes Erbe vermacht werden könnte. Aus der ungeheurer Menge dieser Veröffentlichungen – über 800 Titel, davon etwa 50 Bücher[2] – hat Balthasar eine Reihe von Schriften in Auswahl herausgegeben. Drei Bände sind 1962 (10 Jahre vor Przywaras Tod) erschienen[3], die wohl der beste bibliographische Fundort für Interessenten bleiben werden. Der dritte umfaßt unter dem Namen *Analogia Entis* zwei Hauptteile: zunächst das berühmte und wenig verstandene Buch gleichen Namens von 1932 und dann eine Sammlung späterer Aufsätze um das Grundanliegen der Analogie. Außerhalb die-

---

[1] Vgl. H. de Lubac: *Paradosso e mistero della Chiesa*. Brescia 1986, s. 127. – Im Gegensatz dazu vgl. H. U. von Balthasars Wort: „Erich Przywaras ungeheuerer theologischer Auftrag – am Tiefgang und Breite mit keinem anderen dieser Zeit vergleichbar". In: „Tendenzen der Theologie, Eine Geschichte in Porträts". Hrsg. von H. J. Schultz (Stuttgart-Olten 1966), s. 357.

[2] Vgl. L. Zimny: *Erich Przywara. Sein Schrifttum 1912-1962* (Einsiedeln 1963). – 19 de agosto de 1996ie Ergänzungen bis 1968 bietet ders. Verf. in: Erich Przywara 1989-1969. Eine Festgabe. Patmos-Verlag (Düsseldorf 1969) 37-39.

[3] E. Przywara: *Schriften I-III* (Einsiedeln 1962).

ser Schriften stehen jedoch eine ganze Reihe tiefschürfender, sorgsam verfaßter Werke, die der Auswahl Balthasars entkamen oder allzu spät hinzukamen[4].

Dieses ganze Schrifttum Przywaras dreht sich, vorab in der gedrägten Ausgabe Balthasars, um ein einziges, klares, alles durchwirkendes Thema: *Analogia entis*, Seinsanalogie. Dieser Titel eignet sich ohne Zweifel dazu, in die Archive der Geschichte einzutreten. Ist er aber in sich selbst handgreiflich genug und leicht verständlich? Wer könnte dies behaupten! Mußte er nicht seinerzeit vom Verfasser immer wieder erläutert, gegen allerlei Mißdeutungen geschützt und neuen Fragestellungen unterworfen werden?

Es gibt in der Tat nicht unwichtige Fakten, welche das Werk Przywaras von innen her bedrohen und weiteren, breiten Kreisen zu versperren scheinen. Weil dies bekannt und sogar in kritischen Besprechungen notiert worden ist, genügt es im Moment, nüchtern auf drei Stichworte zu verweisen. Erstens die Sprache: schwierig, eigenartig, gequält; in ihrer Formelfreudigkeit grenzenlos; selbst den deutschen Leser abschreckend; vielleicht nur manch einen fleißigen Ausländer verlockend. Zweitens der Denkstil: überall von flammenden Gegensätzen durchkreuzt, vom Bann nie endender Teilungen und Unterteilungen getrieben, von einer „universalen Klassifikatorik"[5] verfolgt und am Ende nur in der Schwebe frei schwingend. Drittens die Willenshaudlung: unaufhaltsamer Drang, dies und jedes zu verspüren, alles unter die eigene Kompetenz zu ziehen, hinter die Versuche anderer zu kommen, um das „Letzte", „Eigentliche", „Entscheidende" zu enthüllen und vor den Inbegriff seiner eigenen Konzeption zu bringen und zur Rechenschaft zu verpflichten.

---

[4] Es geht nicht nur um die beachtenswerte zweibändige Artikelsammlung aus den Anfägen „Ringen der Gegenwart. Gesammelte Aufsätze 1922-1927, I-II" (Augsburg 1929) und um eine ganze Reihe dichterischer bzw. „spiritueller" Werke minderen Umfangs, alle monographischen Autorenstudien – u.a. Newman, Scheler, Kierkegaard, Kant, Augustinussowie viele, meist aus Rezensionen enstandene Essais, oder gar sämtliche dicke Collage-Arbeiten wie „Humanitas. Der Mensch gestern und morgen" (Nürnberg 1952); sondern auch um so wichtige spätere Deutungssynthesen wie die große „Deus Semper Maior. Theologie der Exerzitien. Mit Beigabe: Theologumenon und Philosophumenon der Gesellschaft Jesu. I-II" (Wien-München 1964), das kleine wertvolle Werk „Was ist Gott. Eine Summula" (Nürnberg 1953), die Ausweitung der Analogieperspektiven in „Mensch. Typologische Anthropologie I" (Nürnberg 1959) und die theologischen Versuche der Exegese „Christentum gemäß Johannes" (Nürnberg 1954), „Alter und Neuer Bund. Theologie der Stunde" (Wien-München 1956), oder der Geschichtstheologie: „Logos. Logos-Abendland-Reich-Commercium" (Düsseldorf 1964). „Katholische Krise" (In Zusammenarbeit mit dem Verfasser herausgegeben und mit einem Nachwort versehen von B. Gertz, Düsseldorf 1967).

[5] Vgl. H. U. von Balthasar: *Erich Przywara. In: Tendenzen der Theologie im 20. Jahrhundert*. (Siehe Fußnote 2) s. 359.

Ohne auf diese Bedenken im einzelnen näher einzugehen, könnte man fragen, ob diese formalen Aspekte der Gestalt, in der uns Przywaras Werk begegnet, vielleicht doch auch das inhaltliche Anliegen der Analogie bedrohen. Es drängt sich hier in präziserer Weise die beunruhigende Frage auf: Ist die Analogieauffassung Przywaras von diesen formalne Unzulänglichkeiten innerlich betroffen? Ist sie nicht als ganze hinfällig?

Nichtsdestoweniger glauben wir jetzt, einen beständigen, fortdauernden Wert des Werkes Przywaras gerade in seinem Grundanliegen der Analogie retten zu können. Dieser besteht in einer dialogischen Freiheitsauffassung, die den Kern seines (als christliche Philosophie von uns verstandenen) Uranliegens ausmacht. Wir versuchen es im folgenden durch eben dieselben drei Pisten zu zeigen, die von den zuletzt erwähnten Vorwürfen herrühren: a) Unausweichliche Vielfalt der sprachlichen Annäherung (in der Metaphysik) an einen letzten Kern aller Dinge, b) Denkerische Einbindung der ganzen geschöpflichen Wirklichketi in gegensätzliche Verhältnisse dem Geheimnis Gottes gegenüber, c) Willentliche Annahme des steten Geschehens einer unverfügbaren Freiheit Gottes und der Menschen. – Die sich darin artikulierende Lehre verdient den Namen „Analogie" beizubehalten, und zwar „Analogie der Freiheit". Diese betrachten wir als das Herz einer christlichen Philosophie.

I. METAPHYSISCHE ANNÄHERUNG ZUM ENTSCHEIDENDEN

Wir haben hier mit dem zu tun, was in der Sprache Przywaras Metyphysik heißt und deshalb ein unverzichtbares Anliegen des Denkens ist, weil damit die konstitutive Struktur der menschlichen Wirklichkeit und ihre restlose Begründung durch das Göttliche gemeint wird. Eben diese zentrale Aufgabe jedes menschlichen Tuns, zum entscheidenden Kern aller Dinge zu kommen, wird auch im Denken nur frei wahrgenommen und kann dort nicht in einförmiger Weise sich vollziehen. Es gibt einen unaufgebbaren Pluralismus jener tiefen Reflexion, in der eine letzte Dichte des Selbst- und Weltverständnisses aufgeht. Ihre Grundformen haben sich als Philosophie und Theologie geschichtlich gebildet und wurden von Przywara durch langes Umgehen präzis und nuanciert gesichtet, geübt und aufeinander bezogen.

Für ihn konnte Metaphysik nicht allein philosophisch geschehen. Schon dieser Aspekt seines Anliegens muß gegenüber der immer wiederkehrenden Versuchung von Rationalismus, Säkularismus, Entmythologisierung usw. als bleibend verstanden werden. Faktisch trägt Philosophie heute noch die Spuren des Theologischen auf vielfache Weise mit sich, wie Przywara durch unermüdliche Analysen gezeigt hat: rein evolutiv gesehen, ist heutiges Philosphieren untrennbar vom griechischen Bezug auf den religiösen Mythos, vom frühchristlichen und mittelalterlichen Integrationsdrang mit Glaubensdenken, von der neuzeitlichen Emanzipation gegenüber Theologie und sogar von der neueren Inbezugnahme alter religiösen Traditionen im außereuropäischen Denken. In ihrem Inhalt als Weisheitsliebe oder Liebesweisheit verstanden, birgt die Philosophie – soweit sie dem Empirismus und Positivismus nicht ganz verfällt – einen heimlichen, aber unverkennbaren Hinweis auf die vielfältigen Weisen der göttlichen Offenbarung, insofern diese der religiösen Erfahrung aller Weltkulturen verschiedentlich zugrunde liegen und als solche von den entsprechenden Religionen, bzw. von der christlichen und katholischen Theologie, zumindest wie sie Przywara und die meisten Theologen heutzutage verstehen, ausgewiesen werden. Mit Vorliebe hat Przywara im westlichen Philosophieren die christlichen Wurzeln und in der philosophischen Weisheit des Ostens die religiösen Motive außerbiblischer Offenbarung aufgezeigt.

Er hat auch in ähnlicher Weise nachgewisen, daß prinzipiell und de iure eine Beziehung der Philosophie zur Theologie besteht, etwa durch folgende Leitlinien: Die unmögliche Selbstgenügsamkeit der Denkprinzipien; die wesentliche Offenheit und Transzendenz des Denkens auf „je Größeres" in Geschichte und inhaltlicher Tragweite; der freie Charakter des Philosophierens (vornehmlich in der Bejahung der scheinbar rein logischen Notwendigkeit) und somit – wenigstens implizit – der transzendent dialogische Zug jeder Philosophie gegenüber einer geheimnisvoll sich offenbarenden, über unser Denken verfügenden Freiheit; infolgedessen die Heilsbedürftigkeit allen Denkens, das nur auf den innermenschlichen Dialog baut. So weit reicht für Przywara der augustinische Spruch von „intellectus quaerens fidem".

Öffnet sich heute das metaphysische Denken auf derartige Offenbarungen, so begegnet es den geschichtlichen Formen von Theologien christlicher und sogar außerchristlicher Prägung. Aber gegen die ständigen Versuchungen des Fideismus, des Irrationalismus oder auch eines rein äußerlichen theologischen Aggiornamento muß andererseits bekräftigt werden, daß keine Theologie sich selbst unter Ausschluß eines Mindestmaßes von Philosophie genügen kann. Faktisch kann man wieder feststellen, wie oft der Pluralismus der Theologien, auch im Katholischen, aus den jeweils begleitenden Philosophien entsteht, was die prinzipielle Notwendigkeit eines breiteren philosophisch-theologischen Horizonts erklärt. Weiterhin ist Offenbarungsdenken prinzipiell einer Selbstrechtfertigung bedürftig, die aber Philosophie impliziert, nicht nur als Begriffsinstrumentar, sondern als Mensch-, Welt- und Offenbarungsverständnis im Glauben der Offenbarung selbst („fides quaerens intellectum"). Darüber hinaus weist die Offenbarung dem Philosophieren neue Ziele zu, nicht nur als Bewährungen des Glaubens, sondern auch als echt philosophische Antworten auf die fragende Weisheitsliebe menschlicher Traditionen. Ohne diese „Philosophie treibende" Funktion wäre die

Theologie nicht der Offenbarung treu. So bleibt theologisches Denken auf das philosophische stets rückbezogen.

Welcher Art ist nun für Przywara diese Hin- und Rückbezogenheit von Philosophie und Theologie innerhalb dessen, was er metaphysisches Denken nennt und was – mit welchem Namen auch immer – eine ständige Aufgabe reflex menschlichen Tuns bleiben wird? Wir wissen es schon, er bezeichnet sie als Analogie; das philosophisch-theologische Verhältnis ist eine der wichtigsten Formen seiner „analogia entis". Von dieser mag nur eingehend behauptet werden: Erstens, sie ist eine Entsprechung von zwei geschichtlichen Gestalten jenes gründlichen Sprechens, das aufs Entscheidende in der Wirklichkeit geht: Philosophie (immer mehr als Anthropologie verstanden) ist ein Sprechen, in dem sich das göttliche Geheimnis dem Menschen mitteilt und sich selbst aussprechen will. – Zweitens, die Entsprechung dieser beiden Gestalten des Sprechens ist keinem rätselhaften Prinzip und keiner verschlüsselten Formel unterworfen, sie besteht in der „reductio in Mysterium" (Rückführung beider ins Geheimnis des je größeren Gottes), wobei alles darauf ankommt, wie eine Begegnung eben dieses souveränen Gottes und des selbständig gemeinschaftlichen Menschen im freien dialogischen Sprechen miteinander ausgesagt werden kann. – Drittens, das Sich-Entsprechen von („metaphysischer") Philosophie und Theologie, als geheimnisvolles Geschehen, auf das wir frei Sprechenden eingehen dürfen und bis zu einem gewissen Grad müssen, enthält nicht nur das Paradoxon von Notwendigkeit und Freiheit, Logik und Ethik in sich; es zeugt vielmehr von der wunderbar unverzichtbaren Verbindung zwischen natürlich Gesetzmäßigem und gnadenhaft Angebotenem und Empfangenem (das thomasische „gratia non destruit sed supponit et perficit naturam").

II. DAS GEGENSÄTZLICHE GEFÜGE DER WIRKLICHKEIT IM VERHÄLTNIS ZUM JE GRÖSSEREN GOTT

Weil wir Menschen in der Welt stehen (darin kann Przywara mit Heidegger übereinstimmen), haben wir die unabweisbare Aufgabe, durch all unser Tun das Entscheidende aller Dinge zu erreichen. Dafür ist uns (wenigstens anfänglich) tiefgehend reflexes Denken notwendig, in der unvermeidlichen Pluralität seiner Grundformen, vorab der religiös-theologischen und der philosophischen Gestalt. Dieses so verstandene „metaphysische" Denken geschieht in der komplexen Vielfalt menschlichen Sprechens und Sich-Entsprechens; also in einer „Analogie", welche vermutlich die einzig echte Weise ist, ein Gefüge der ganzen Wirklichkeit im Denken zusammenzustellen. Wie sieht nun dieses Gefüge in seiner Struktur aus? Im folgenden versuchen wir, die Hauptzüge eines integrierenden Denkens im Sinne Przywaras vorwiegend philosophisch zu skizzieren, obwohl er selbst diese konkrete Systematisierung nicht bietet, im Gegenteil, sein Mißtrauen gegen alle endgültige Systematik in Philosophie und in Theologie nie verheimlicht und erst recht eine fertige philosophisch-theologische Metaphysik oder auch eine alles umfassende Weisheitssynthese nicht unter seinem Namen dulden würde. Trotzdem hat er sich vor der Notwendigkeit gebeugt, in unabschließbar begrenzten Versuchen diesen Zusammenhalt des Ganzen von Gott her und auf Gott hin auszusprechen. Nichts anderes kann ich hier bieten als meine schematische Rekonstruktion dessen, was ich als den logischen Vorgang Przywaras zu interpretieren wage. Für eine auf den Texten bauende Rechtfertigung derselben muß ich auf meine anderen Studien hinweisen[6].

Die Welt wird als ein Gewebe von sich entsprechenden, verbindenden und übersteigenden „analogischen" Beziehungen verstanden. Beziehung meint hier Gegensatz. Es drückt sich auf diese Weise eine uralte Ahnung der Menschheit aus, die in der Philosophie seit Heraklit bis Hegel und Marx (und weiter noch) zu belegen ist und vielerlei Gestalten – nicht nur des Kampfes, auch der Liebesbande – annimmt. In einer ersten Etappe hieß es bei Przywara, mit einem berühmten Begriff deutscher Geistesgeschichte, Polarität. Die Gegensätzlichkeit wurde bei ihm zuerst auf ontologische Elemente (hauptsächlich Sosein – Dasein) zurückgeführt, dann aber auf bewußtseinsphänomenologische, was ihn zum Menschlichen führte. Also hat er immer mehr die Wirklichkeit vom gegensätzlichen Menschen her gesehen. Kein Wunder, daß wir als Ergebnis seiner Entwicklung feststellen: in der Metaphysik wird der analogische Gegensatz zu einer vom Mitmenschlichen her gedachten Entgegnung und Begegnung aller Dinge im Kosmos und in der Geschichte.

---

[6] Durch folgende Arbeiten habe ich zur Forschung des philosophisch-theologischen Werkes Przywaras beigetragen: „Erich Przywaras Deutung des religionsphilosophischen Anliegens Newmans". In: Newman-Studien, Nürnberg, 7. Folge (1967) 247-260. – „Wissenschaftliche Literatur über Erich Przywara". In: Erich Przywara 1889-1969. Eine Festgabe. Patmos-Verlag. Düsseldorf 1969, 40-47. – „Die Geschichte des Terminus „analogia entis" und das Werk Erich Przywaras". In: Philosophisches Jahrbuch 77 (1969/1970) 163-179. – „Christentum und Metraphysik. Das Verhältnis beider nach der Analogielehre Erich Przywaras". München 1973. Pullacher Philosophische Forschung, Band IX, 647 s. – „Analogía de la Libertad. Un tributo al pensamiento de Erich Przywara". – Pontificia Universidad Católica del Ecuador. Serie Teológica Ecuatoriana N. 12. – Quito 1989, XI + 231 S. ERs handelt sich hier um eine Sammlung von Studien, die zu verschiedenen Anlässen teils neu konzipiert und redigiert, teils aus den früheren Untersuchungen heraus den gegenwärtigen Themen angepaßt wurden. – „Notas para una analogía de la libertad". In: P. Hünermann, D. J. Michelini, C. Cullen, H. D. Mandrioni, J. Terán Dutari (Hrsg.): Pensar América Latina. Homenaje a Juan Carlos Scannone. Buenos Aires, 1991, 85-91.

Wichtigstes Faktum dieser – wenn man will, anthropozentrischen – Feststellung aber ist dies: Nur die dialogische Freiheitsbegegnung zwischen den Menschen (wie sie im Gegenüber der Geschlechter und der Generationen, in erzieherischen und gemeinschaftsbildenden Vorgängen usw. sich gibt) erscheint als ursprünglicher Ort, an dem wir jene vielfältige, universelle Verhältnisentsprechung erfassen, die im geschichtlichen Kosmos herrscht.

Von diesen zwischenmenschlichen Beziehungen werden also primo et per se die Merkmale der Analogie ausgesagt. Es sind Merkmale der dialogischen Freiheit. So kann man Przywaras abstrusen Formeln (wie „in-über", „ähnlich-unähnlicher") einen tieferen Sinn abgewinnen, die auf das Abgründige eines mitmenschlichen Freiheitsgeschehens verweisen. Bei diesen Ausdrücken und ihren Verbindungen kommt gerade das Unabschließbare der Freiheitsbeziehungen zur Sprache: es sind gewiß wechselseitige Beziehungen; jeder Terminus der Beziehung ist „in" und „über" dem anderen; aber dieser Komplex schwingt nicht in sich selbst, er weist vielmehr von sich weg, sowohl nach oben, über sich hinaus auf ein unsagbares göttliches Geheimnis, als auch nach unten auf die untermenschliche Unendlichkeit gegensätzlicher Verhältnisse, die den zwischenmenschlichen Dialog stützen und auf ihre Weise ermöglichen.

Damit ist gesagt, daß dieses zwischenmenschliche Freiheitsverhältnis nicht nur das Denkmodell ist, durch das alle Verhältnisse der kosmischen Dinge miteinander und mit dem Menschen ontologisch oder phänomenologisch schon je immer erfaßt wurden, sondern auch Anlaß gibt, das Grundverhältnis des Menschen auf das Göttliche in seinem Wesen als eine Freiheitsentsprechung zu begreifen, und zwar als eine solche, die das Geheimnis göttlicher Freiheit als gründendes, universelles und dauerndes Geschehen im menschlichen Kosmos der Geschichte sehen läßt.

So erscheint für Przywara das Bild dieser ganzen Wirklichkeit als stete Schöpfung. Und diese heißt nun ein Gefüge von unzähligen, sich entgegensetzenden Verhältnissen, die trotz ihrer „Eigenwirklichkeit" sich nicht genügen, nicht in sich ruhen, sondern sich um den Menschen kreisend verschränken und überbieten. Diese ganzen Verhältnisse aber – wie auch die gesamte Menschheit und jeder einzelne Mensch – sind wesentlich auf ein je Höheres angelegt und verhalten sich schließlich, sei es einzeln, sei es von ihrem Kern im Menschlichen her, sei es auch zusammen im Ganzen des Kosmos, unmittelbar zu jenem ursprünglichen Freiheitsgrund, den Przywara als göttliches Geheimnis der Welt angesprochen hat und das „Allwirkliche" in und über der „eigenwirklichen" Schöpfung nennt.

III. DAS WILLENTLICH ANZUNEHMENDE GOTT-GESCHÖPF-VERHÄLTNIS ALS GRÜNDENDES FREIHEITSGESCHEHEN

Aus dem Dargelegten erhellt, daß jedes Verhältnis zwischen Gott und Geschöpft nur in analoger Entsprechung zum Freiheitsverhältnis zwischen Gott und Mesnch zu denken ist. Anschließend wird dieses letzte folgendermaßen auseinandergelegt: Freiheit meint primär das personale Verhältnis einer Selbstverfügung und -schenkung, innerhalb dessen eine verfügt geschenkte Freiheit (die der Mensch ist) und eine verfügend schenkende Freiheit (die Gott heißt) bezeichnet werden. Menschliche Freiheit begegnet dabei als Offenheit im doppelten Sinne von Ohnmacht und Mächtigkeit: Ohnmacht zunächst, weil etwas von jeder inneren Notwendigkeit und Geschlossenheit Entbundenes; es hat ja letztlich nicht von sich selbst her Vollendung, Sinn und Glück. Jedoch Mächtigkeit, weil etwas im mitmenschlichen Selbstvollzug, was zu einer schenkenden Selbstverfügung befähigt ist, einem letzten Ziel von Vollendung, Sinn und Glück über sich hinaus zustrebt und ihm sogar widerstreben kann. Gott wird wesentlich als befreiende Freiheit gedacht, indem er menschliche Freiheit befreit und „offen" macht, diese Offenheit des Menschen dauernd trägt und sich selbst auf diese Weise „offenbart" und schenkt. Es ist aber eine freie Offenbarung und Schenkung, die sich selbst entziehen kann: ein von jeder berechnenden Notwendigkeit der Logik und der bloß menschlichen Liebe entferntes Geheimnis – nach einem Augustinuswort abgründiger Gott im abgründigen Geschöpf durch das Grundverhältnis der Freiheitsbegegnung.

Freiheit ist also die einzige Weise, in der Gott und Geschöpf zu einem echten – wenn auch undurchdringlichen – Verhältnis bezogen werden können. Nur als eine sich frei bindende kann die Immanenz Gottes im Geschöpf mit seiner unverlierbaren Transzendenz zusammengehen; nur als eine sich frei absetzende kann die Transzendenz Gottes über dem Geschöpf seine wesentliche Immanenz behalten. Auf die Problematik des Wirkens übertragen, erscheint wiederum als einzig mögliche Antwort diese Auffassung eines Freiheitsverhältnisses, das Gott und Mensch (bzw. Geschöpf) nicht von außen her nachträglich verbindet, sondern ein göttliches Allwirken und ein menschliches (bzw. geschöpfliches) Eigenwirken in ihrer sozusagen „dialogischen" Begegnung als der geheimnisvoll eine Ursprungsgrund jedes weltlichen Wirkens (des freien, determinierten, undeterminierten oder wie auch immer) erscheinen läßt.

Diese denkerische (vorwiegend philosophische) Zusammenfassung des analogen Gott-Geschöpf-Verhältnisses kann nun, zumal bei ihrem besagten „Geheimnis", nicht vom reinen Denken ergründet werden. Sie wird willentlich frei in der geschichtlichen Begegnung mit dem freien Gott angenommen. Nun gehört aber solche Freiheitsbegegnung mit Gott in die Sphäre des Religiösen, dessen reflektiertes Denken ein primär theologisches ist. Darum muß ich hier auf meine anderweitige Rekonstruktion dessen verweisen, was gemäß Przywaras Lehre ein analog philosophischer Ausdruck dieser strukturellen theologischen Einsichten wäre[7]. Die Analogie der befreienden Freiheit Gottes mit der befreiten Freiheit des Menschen ist vollendet und endgültig in Jesus Christus als Einheit in der Person selbst geschehen. Von diesem einzigartigen Faktum her, das nur im christlichen Glauben angenommen und in seiner Theologie verstanden wird, nimmt jenes geschichtlich erscheinende, konstituve und gründende Freiheitsverhältnis zwischen Gott und Geschöpf sein letztes Maß und seine wesentliche Struktur her, was dann als dessen innere und doch frei gegebene Notwendigkeit in der Philosophie durchleuchtet und entfaltet werden kann. Deshalb kann dieser letzte Sinn der „Seinsanalogie" (die eine wahre Kreuzesstruktur in sich trägt) nur erfahren werden, indem sich die eigene Freiheit, sich in die Unberechenbarkeit des geschichtlich mitmenschlichen Freiheitsspiels einlassend, der göttlichen Freiheit anvertraut. Verstehen kann man die Analogie der Freiheit nur so weit, als man sie vollzieht.

IV. ANALOGIE DER FREIHEIT ALS KERN CHRISTLICHER PHILOSOPHIE

Mit welchem Recht kann bei dieser Freiheitsentsprechung noch von einer „Analogielehre" die Rede sein? Bekanntlich faßte Przywara sein Anliegen in das tradierte Wort „Seinsanalogie". Hier wäre zu zeigen, daß im Zuge einer legitimen philosophiegeschichtlichen Entwicklung die Verwendung des Begriffs der Analogie für diesen neuen Freiheitszusammenhang so kohärent ist, daß von einer „Freiheitsanalogie" mit Recht gesprochen werden darf. Dazu jetzt nur folgendes: Przywara hat den Analogiebegriff auf allen Hauptlinien der historischen Entwicklung übernommen und weitergeführt. Alle gegen sein diesbezügliches Vorgehen erhobenen Einwände lassen sich ohne Schwierigkeit entkräften. Denn er baut nicht nur auf Thomas von Aquin auf; die ganze Geistesgeschichte von den Vorsokratikern bis zur Phänomenologie und Existenzphilosophie behält er im Auge. Mag Przywara vielleicht in der Behandlung all dieser Quellen manche Interpretationsfehler historischer Art gemacht haben, er gelangt doch immer trefflich zu den Hauptzielen des geschichtlichen Verlaufs. Insbesondere muß ihm zugegeben

---

[7] Vgl. J. Terán Dutari: Zur philosophisch-theologischen Auffassung der Freiheit bei K. Rahner und E. Przywara. In: H. Vorgrimler (Hrsg), „Wagnis Theologie. Erfahrungen mit der Theologie Karl Rahners". Freiburg-Basel-Wien 1979, s. 284-298.

werden, folgender wichtiger Unterscheidung der Analogiekritiker viel Wert beigemessen zu haben: Analogie könne einerseits als Eigenschaft eines Begriffs (wie des Seins) verstanden werden, welcher dann zum strukturellen und möglicherweise universellen Ordnungsprinzip gemacht wird; dies lehnt er gegenüber jeder verbreiteten thomistischen Interpretation entschieden ab, die Karl Barth zu seiner Empörung vor dem alles nivellierenwollenden analogischen Seinsbegriff Anlaß gibt. Analogie könne man aber andereseits auch, und zwar richtiger, verstehen als Entsprechungsweise der Prädikation, des Aussagens und Zuschreibens eines und desselben Begriffes in bezug auf verschiedene Adressaten, hauptsächlich auf Gott und Mensch (bzw. Geschöpf).

In der Tat ist Przywara in dieser letzten Richtung so weit gegangen, daß er mit innerer Kohärenz eine dritte Ebene erreicht hat, die der Analogie als wesentliches Merkmal dialogischen Sprechens. Somit wird dem alten Namen „Entsprechung" (*correspondentia*) als passendste Übersetzung der griechschen „ἀναλογία" eine tiefere Bedeutung zuerkannt. Dabei geht es aber im Sinne Przywaras nicht so sehr um den Dialogismus, sondern vielmehr um die in einer christlichen Philosophie enthaltenen Impulse jener in Christus geschehenden „recapitulatio" aller Dinge durch die Freiheitsbegegnung Gottes und des Menschen, die das Herz seiner Analogielehre als Analogie des Kreuzes darstellt.

Przywara hat keine Uminterpretation des Seins als Freiheit vorgenommen, wenn er auch gleich am Anfang von einer „*Analogia entis* der ungeschaffenen und geschaffenen Liebe" als wahrem Gesicht der Seinsanalogie spricht[8] und immer wieder Ähnliches insinuiert. Strukturell hat er aber die zwischenmenschliche Freiheitsbeziehung als sichtbare Entsprechung unserer freien Gottesbeziehung bergründet. So sehen wir hier die philosophisch höchste und bleibende Leistung seiner Lehre, die damit zur Preisgabe jener verführerischen Parole der Neuzeit führt: „etsi Deus non daretur". An deren Stelle hat er in herrlich befreiender Freigebigkeit das unaufgebbare und uns heute dringend notwendige Wort Augustins vom je größeren, ewigen Gott der Geschichte ertönen lassen: „Deus semper maior".

---

[8] E. Przywara: Religionsbegründung. Max Scheler – J. H. Newman (Freiburg 1923), s. 181. – Der Satz beginnt mit den bemerkenswerten Worten: „Darum ist Liebe ... das Sein".

ROCCO BUTTIGLIONE
Internationale Akademie für Philosophie Fürstentum Liechtenstein
University of Teramo, Italia

PERSON AND SOCIETY

We shall approach our topics through three different and interrelated questions: what is the person? what is society? what is the relation obtained between these two concepts?

1. What is the person? The concept of the person does not belong to the initial philosophical heritage that we have received from the Greeks. Although we may recognize here and there some hints of an insight into the nature of the person in some Greek authors (interestingly enough more among the tragic poets than among the philosophers), the concept enters into the history of culture in a post-classical age and belongs initially more to the domain of theology than to that of philosophy. It is in the fourth and fifth century that some theologians start making use of this concept. Christian theologians have been concerned since the beginning with some paradoxical assertions contained in the Gospels and expecially in the Gospel of St. John chapter 14[1]. Jesus proclaims that he is the Son of God. This may be a scandal to the Jews but does not create the least difficulty to the Greeks, whose gods used to have sons and daughters, and whose offspring were so abundantly diffused on earth that to call a powerful lord "son of a god" was hardly more than a sign of courtesy. The sons of God in the Greek world were not however gods. They were men. Men of a particular quality or excellence, heroes or demigods at most but not gods. What is rather disturbing to the Greeks is the unclarity on the proper relationship obtaining between the Father and the Son. Jesus is not just a man who

---

[1] Ch. 14, 8-11.

pretends that he is the son of a god. He is God himself, and not one of the many gods of the Greeks but God in the same sense in which the God of the Jews is God. The God of the Jews is one God. He is the only God of his people and pretends to be also the only God of the Universe. To the Jews it was a blasphemy that any man could pretend to be God. To the Greeks it was a nonsense that the Son could at the same time be his own Father and that two could be one[2].

We spare our reader the additional complications deriving from the presence, in the same text of St. John, of the Holy Spirit[3] because they do not change anything essential in the nature of the problem: how can one (THE ONE) be two. Until our own days the criticism of the dogma of the Trinity belongs to the usual and easiest performances of all adversaries of the Christian churces who maintain this belief. It seems to be a clear example of an irreducible opposition between faith and reason.

The theologians of the fourth century had to find an answer to the rationalists of their times and they did it through a profound meditation on the nature of the relationship obtaining between the Father and the Son[4]. As a rule a relation is somehow added to a substance in such a way that the substance is only accidentally modified through the relation[5]. A man who rides a horse stands of course in a relation to his horse, he remains however a man and the horse remains a horse and when he alights from the horse the two are divided and nothing essential was changed in any of them. In the case of the divine Father and Son quite the opposite is true[6]. Each one of them exists in the love of the other and through the love of the other so that they could never subsist, nay, could never be thought of, apart from this relation. Here the relation is not an accident, something added to a substance already existing in itself. Here the relation is in the substance and modifies the substance. What is essential in God is the reciprocal love of the Father, the Son and the Holy Spirit[7]. Each one of the persons of the Trinity exists through the others, experiences himself as gift coming from the other and the self-giving of the other to himself. If we really understand what this means, then it becomes less illogical the idea that two (or three) may be one. This being that exists in the relation and through the relation to the other is called, in the language of theology, the person. We stand

---

[2] St Paul I Cor. 1, 22 and ff.

[3] Ch. 14. 15 and ff.

[4] C. Andresen, *Zur Entstehung und Geschichte des trinitarischen Personbegriffs*, in: „Zeitschrift für die neutestamentliche Wissenschaft", 52 (1961).

[5] St Thomas Aquinas, S. Th. I. q. 28. 1. 2. c.

[6] S. th. I. q. 40. 2 ad 4. See also for a general background J. Ratzinger, *Il significato di persona nella teologia*, in *Dogma e Predicazione*, Brescia 1974.

[7] St Augustine, *De Trinitate* 15, 6, 10.

here in the inner core of the Christian faith, in the center of the trinitarian doctrine that so sharply differentiates the Christian idea of God from the Jewish or the Islamic one.

Since the beginning it was, however, clear that the concept of the person does not apply to God alone. In the Gospel of St. John chapter 15[8], the Evangelist considers the relation of Christ to his disciples and compares this relation to that of the vine and the branches. To be inserted into the vine is not an accident for the branches. They could never be branches if they were not branches of the vine. The relation to the vine pertains to their very essence, this relation constitutes them as branches. Through the love of Jesus and the assistance of the Holy Spirit the disciples become one with Jesus, they recognize his presence in themselves as their own true self and because of this they also become one with each other. The love of Jesus creates the *communio* among themselves and, at the same time, introduces them into the inner life of the Father and of the Holy Spirit: they become God through the participation to the love of God, by adoption. In order for this to be possible we must accept that the disciples also are persons, that is beings whose essence is affected from within through the relation to another being of the same kind. It is not difficult to draw the further conclusion that if the disciples are persons, then all men are. We could have jumped to this conclusion from the very beginning. As a matter of fact it is evident that the relation obtaining between a father and a son is absolutely different from that obtaining between a rider and a horse. Without the horse the rider would not be a rider any more, but he would still be a man. Without the father the son would not be at all. A man is a man even if he does not ride any horse, but no man is a man if he is not the son of somebody. Here the relation constitutes the subject. It goes without saying that the same holds true, and is even more evident, in the case of a mother. A pregnant woman gives us the natural model of a substantial relation in which one being inhabits in the other in such a way that no clear-cut dividing border can be traced separating the two. The child is in the mother but also the mother can be said to be in the child in the sense that the event of pregnancy and birth modifies her existence in such a way that she will never be the same any more, she has been changed in her very essence[9]. Another meaningful example of the personal participation in the life of the other is the relation of husband and wife, in which the two become one flesh. Each one of the spouses becomes what he/she is in the relation to the other and through the

---

[8] Ch. 15, 1-17.

[9] St Thomas Aquinas would perhaps observe that here we have an event that changes the subject (an actio or a passio) and the relation is a consequence of the event. See S. Th. I. q. 41. 1 ad 2.

assistence of the other. It is in the experience of the spousal love and more broadly in that of the family that we have the first intuition of the fact that two may be (or become) one through love[10].

I hope that now to my reader it will not seem any more so odd the idea that one may live in the other so that one plus one are still one. What seemed to be the irrational core of a contemptible superstition, through a more detailed analysis has resulted to be a presentation of an important truth on God and on man. Both God and man are persons, and a person is a subject who subsists in the other and through the other.

We must now set aside the theological and also the metaphysical side of the question. We will not argue in favour of the Trinity because it is a matter of faith and therefore all we can do is to explain – against possible caricatures or misrepresentations – what it is all about. We will rather concentrate our attention on the anthropological concept of the person. Even if the concept arises on the basis of the christological controversies of the IV century the arguments purporting its extension to humans seem to be thoroughly rational and philosophical, so much so that it may be accepted by many who would question both the theology of the Trinity and the existence of God.

In the Middle Ages a definition of the person came to be known affirming that the person is an individual substance of an intellectual nature[11]. This definition is not bad but needs to be explained on the background of the historical genesis of the concept. The definition stresses the fact that the person is not just a relation. The person is a substance that, being intellectual, is not concerned primarily with itself and with the satisfaction of its instinctual drives but is rather directed outwardly towards the world, capable of recognizing the good in itself and of identifying itself and its particular good with the general good[12]. So the definition of the person as a substance of an intellectual nature goes one step beyond the idea of the person as a being constituted through the relation to another. It tells us that the person transcends (can transcend) the immediate and emotional relation of sexual or parental love to accept being constituted by all other personal relations selected and experienced according to the truth on the human person. The reason of the openness of the person to the other, the cause of the capacity of not identifying himself with the immediate interest of his body but with

---

[10] See K. Wojtyła, *Rodzina jako communio personarum. Próba interpretacji teologicznej*, "Atheneum Kapłańskie", 1974, a. 66, v. 83, n. 3.

[11] S. th. I. q. 29. 1. The definition is of Boethius.

[12] It seems to me that just for this reason the person lies beyond the limits of any eudaemonistic ethics. The "appetitum proprium" of the person qua person does not regard his particular bonum but the bonum in se.

the relation to the other, lies in the intellectual character of the human person. We must also observe that the definition we are commenting stresses also the substantiality of the person and defends us therefore against the possible error of thinking that the person is only relation so that the two elements of the relation have no real identity and are just parts of a whole that only can claim properly substantiality. On the contrary, each subject of the personal relation is a whole in itself that opens itself to the other through an act of freedom and comes to constitute a new whole that is always kept in life through the free self-giving and the love of its members. None of these subjects loses its individuality in the whole or is possessed by the others in the same way in which they possess themselves[13].

If the medieval definiton may be more complete and precise it should however be recognized that it lacks the flavour of the original discovery of the relation in which two may be or become one. It should be kept in mind that the first definition arose in the context of theology and regards more directly the way in which God is the person, while the second definition regards more the way in which man is the person and the unity of the divine persons, their reciprocal inhabitation, is of course much more complete and perfect than the way in which humans are present one in the other and constitute a community[14].

In order to complete our understanding of the person we may now compare this concept with two other different ways of understanding the nature of the human being. We do not want to contrast absolutely these different understandings of the human being and do not even want to investigate which one of them is true or in what form they may be combined in a more differentiated explanation of what man is. It is enough here to sketch these two possible alternative forms of comprehension of the human phenomenon.

We may understand man simply as an isolated subject, that is a subject of such a nature that the relation to others is just, always and in all cases, a mere accident in the aristotelian sense of the word[15]. A similar understanding of man as an isolated individual stands at the beginning of one possible interpretation of Descartes philosophy and of modernity in general. Here the subject is so isolated from others and their real existence is so inessential to him that he may even doubt that they are and that he lives in a world in which he is the only existing subject[16]. If we absolutize this attitude then

---

[13] K. Wojtyła, *Osoba i czyn oraz inne studia antropologiczne*, TN KUL, Lublin 1994, p. 120 and ff.

[14] S. Th. I. q. 29. 3.

[15] *Metaphysics* E 3 1027 a 29 and ff.

[16] This is of course only one possible interpretation of Descartes. Del Noce has differentiated four different possible interpretations, according to the priority given to

man may retreat in the castle of his individuality and regard any relation to others as an obstacle or a threat to himself. He does not stand in need of others in order to reach his fulfillment. Between the I and the other stands a barrier that may be overcome only through acts of the will that create a provisional encounter of the two sovereign subjects. It is, on the other hand, always possible that one subject tries to become master of the other, transforming the other into a slave, a mere object or an instrument for the realization of his particular will. The relation between such subjects will be then a relation of mutual distrust and the general attitude of men to one another will be one of self-defense that may easily be turned into a kind of pre-emptive aggression against the other. Thomas Hobbes has described a world of mere individuals and some theorists of an unbridled liberalism suggesting a political theory that concretizes this anthropology[17].

A third way we have to approach the human phenomenon is that of the mass and the undifferentiated community. Here man is considered only as a member of the social group and he lives so plunged into the group that he is hardly aware of having an autonomous personality and of being the carrier of a personal moral responsibility. In most ancient civilizations this dimension of the collective personality of the group is absolutely dominant. The individual is thoroughly dependent upon the group. Penal responsibility is considered to pertain mainly to the group and this explains the phenomenon, so utterly disgusting to the civilized mind but so obious to many pre-Christian civilizations, of crossed revenge, that is of the revenge taken upon one member of a group for the actions of other members of the same group. The same conception of *Sippenhaft* (collective responsability of the family or of relatives) reappears in the law doctrines of the Third Reich and, in a different form, in the communist regimes. The underlaying idea is that the individual is just a manifestation of something that is more substantial, i.e. the species or the aggregates in which the species presents itself, family, race or class.

In the collectivist ideologies the substance is attributed only to the species or to the social group, and the individual is considered only an accident[18]. It would be too easy to imagine that this way of conceiving of the human responsibility belongs only to the past and that it has disappeared in our own times. Even after the collapse of the collectivist doctrines of the XX century this approach persists and may even be growing in scope in the

---

the methodological doubt, to the doctrine of the substance, to the theory of freedom or to the ontological proof of the existence of God.

[17] See F. Toennies, *Thomas Hobbes, der Mann und der Denker*, 2 Stuttgart 1922.

[18] A typical example is given by K. Marx in his *Sixth Thesis on Feuerbach*, where he proclaims that man is just a sum or an aggregate of social relations.

near future. Terrorist groups very often share this mentality. In underdeveloped countries this approach may even mobilize a large consent, because it corresponds to a deep-seated conviction that rules most aspects of the everyday life of the individuals. This explains why any group who disagrees, for instance, with the politics of the US government and is convinced of having been wronged through this government feels justified in taking innocent US citizens as hostages or in revenging upon them the real or supposed wrong suffered. On the other hand, this may become true also in our own "civilized" countries. Fanatical religious or political groups once and again pretend to act on the basis of collective responsibilities and attack individuals who are only guilty of belonging to a social group considered to be the author of some evil deeds. These ideas may gain mass support also in our countries. Take for instance the prejudice spreading against minority groups when some of their members commit illegal actions. Measures restricting the rights of all the members of the group are often viewed with favour by large masses who feel this to be an adequate and justifiable retaliation.

2. What is community? I think it has already become evident that the way in which we consider the human community is thoroughly determined through the way in which we consider the human person.

A first meaning of society may be detected when we consider the interaction of mere individuals. Here society is a mere accident to its members. Each one of them remains in the action thoroughly foreign to the others. For some reasons each member of society thinks that he can profit from the action of the others and therefore they establish what each of them should do, so that the result of the common action may be approved of by each one of the subjects of the action. The fundamental instrument determining the formation of the artificial will of the society is then the contract. Through the contract two or more independent wills unite and become, in a certain sense, one will. The basis of society is here the exchange of equivalents, that is each subject accepts that what he receives through the cooperation is equivalent to what he gives. Here we have the free will of the individuals but no inner participation to the common action. The relation of exchange may be fair, and nevertheless the participating subjects remain foreign to each other, the action does not engage their inner self. This is what the German sociologist F. Toennies named "Gesellschaft", sharply distinguishing it from "Gemeinschaft" or community. In this kind of society we have a system of interacting social roles. We expect the other to act in a certain way that we can easily foresee not because we know his interiority but because we know the role he is supposed to perform. So for instance when we ask a policeman for defence against an aggression we know he will help us even if we do not know whether he likes us or not or whether he today feels like acting or not. We know he will do what he is supposed to do according to his social role. In this perspective life in society may be a necessity, but it remains an exterior necessity. All men may stand in need of the support of other men, and may be therefore obliged to participate in a society. It would however be better for them if they could be sufficient in themselves and one is all the more free the less he stands in need of the support of others.

A second model of society may arise if we consider man as just a member of the group not possessing a real individual substance. While in the first model a lot of attention must be given to a clearly and carefully established system of social roles, and to the rights and duties pertaining to each subject on the basis of his roles and of the related obligations, in the second model a detailed legal system is superfluous and may even be cumbersome. Much more important is the capacity to interpret the spirit of the community and to voice the unconscious beliefs that keep together the social body. What is needed here is charismatic leadership, personal affiliations and political myths. We have already pointed out that this is rather the original state of all societies. This origin is repeated in every new generation in the experience of the family. The child in the family is not originally conscious of his separate individuality and responsibility. In the very beginning the baby conceives of himself just as a part of the body of the mother (or of the mother as a part of his body). Only slowly he separates himself from the mother and the process of education is a kind of psychological and cultural being born that stretches itself well within the adolescence. This process is not always completed. One may remain psychologically dependent upon the family even in his mature years, may never succeed in "growing up". In some traditional societies the mature individuality may be the exception rather than the rule. One of the many important meanings of the philosphical drama of Socrates is just the struggle of the individual against the collective powers of mores and tradition to establish the rights of his individual personality[19]. It is worth remembering that the first way in which these rights are affirmed has the form of the right to obey truth rather than the acquired convictions of the social group. Since the beginning the idea of truth and of obedience to truth is linked to the idea of the free and independent personality. We can name this more original form of society "community". In the community the action is not the result of a contract, of a formal obligation. It stems from within and the unity among the members engages directly their own interiority. It may even be wrong to speak of "interiority" as opposed to "exteriority". Here interiority and exteriority are still mingled and undifferentiated. They arise only through the struggle

---

[19] See for instance the dialogue of Socrates with the Laws in the *Cryto*.

of the individual to assert himself and to acquire control over his own interiority separating and opposing it to the common interiority of the group. S. Freud has described this process and named it the Oedipus complex[20]. A naive philosophy of history has considered the "community" a model confined to the past and considered the occurrence of the individual an event that has changed once and forever our approach to the human phenomenon. The Enlightenment is considered the definitive emancipation of the individual and the beginning of a new age. It is not difficult to point out that contemporary history has shown more than one dreadful coming back to the past. The Enlightenment proceeded breaking all traditional societies one after the other. It seems, however, that man does not tolerate an excessive amount of individualism. The inner self expands itself only in a non-utilitarian relation to others and the perception of many fundamental values is made more difficult or even impossible in a world in which only individuals exist. It may even be contended that in order to be born and educated and to reach full human maturity humans need an environment of community in which they can progressively differentiate themselves and acquire consciousness of themselves. A thoroughly individualistic society destroys the cribs in which human values and human individuality are formed. Hence comes the phenomenon of a massive coming back to community after society and after Enlightenment had developed all its potentialities. This may be a key to explain the totalitarian phenomena between the two World Wars, but his may also be a key to understand what is taking place now in our societies. Young people seek refuge in communities against the alienation of a society in which all genuine experience of togetherness seems to have become impossible and are ready to alienate their precious freedom in a mass culture that offers at least some hints of protection and shelter, however precarious and false this offer may be. We must add that it would be false to pretend that traditional societies do not recognize the phenomenon of human individuality. We already mentioned Socrates who is, in one sense, the great discoverer of individuality in the Western tradition. It would not be difficult to find similar examples also in other civilizations.

Of course, also to the third model of understanding of the nature of man corresponds a model of social organization. It is the model of the Church as a place in which free human beings choose to belong in love and truth to one another. This is a society based on freedom. One is not born in it but enters into it through a free act of choice. Through this act, however, one engages his freedom so that he will never be the same any more and he will never be able to enjoy fully his own humanity out of the society he has entered into. His act of choice shares his humanity with others.

---

[20] S. Freud, *Das Ich und das Es*, Vienna 1923.

We have said that the model of this community is the Church because the origin of the corresponding idea of the person is in the Christian theology, in the Christian idea of the Trinity. Of course, also non-ecclesiastical communities may be thought of according to the model of the Church. Another fitting example for this idea of society is that of the family, considered not from the point of view of the relation of parents to children but from that of the relation between bridegroom and bride. Here again we have a relationship grounded upon an act of freedom and freedom is the needed presupposition for the very existence of the act. The nature of the act is however such that no further act of the will can change what has come to being through the self-giving of the person in spousal love. Here we have a community based on freedom.

3. What is the relation obtained between a person and society? We have presented three different metaphysical models of the person and shown the way in which to each model of the person corresponds an idea of society. Plato in the *State* has written that society is man "written large" and our investigation shows that he is, at least up to a certain point, right. The idea of society we have is thoroughly dependent upon the idea of man we have. Up to now we have just presented models. We did not try to attribute more truth to one of them rather than to the others. We have bracketed their claims to be true and have concentrated our attention on their characteristics and on their inner logics. In this last section of our contribution we shall not try to answer the question "which one of these models is true?" We shall not do this in part because we lack the time needed to disentangle the correct answer from the intricacies that envelope it and make so difficult its access, and in part because no single answer can be said to be absolutely true in itself. Man is a subject who, in a certain sense, creates himself. On the basis of an original gift of God man completes his own essence through his own action. He may therefore choose to be just an individual, who has no essential relations to any human beings. We can meet in our everyday life human subjects who have made this choice and who incorporate this model. The same holds true as what regards the model that ascribes substantiality only to the human society and not to the individual. The choice to live according to one or another model of the person is a choice of each human being. It is however influenced through the whole culture one lives in as well as each individual choice influences the whole culture. It would be wrong to imagine that each human being creates a social environment of his own according to his existential choice and it would be wrong to pretend that each human being is determined in his existential choice through the objective spirit of the environment he lives in. Each human subject makes his choice and gives to his environment the form of his choice; and so also

each different smaller society, encompassed in the society at large, lives according to a certain idea of man. It would be false to imagine that in a given civilization all smaller societies participate in the same spirit. Sometimes different societies and communities have conflicting ethoses and the balance of society at large can be kept only through the conflict of these different ethoses. In our Western societies we have (or we used to have) a communitarian ethos of the family contrasted with the individualistic ethos of the civil society and of the market place. For all these reasons we must be very cautious in saying that a certain model is true and another false. If true means to have a measure of empirical existence, all models are true, to a certain extent, and each one of them may have a certain function in allowing a given community to exist.

If we nevertheless ascribe a certain superiority to the model of the person as individual and as community at the same time, this occurs for two reasons[21]. The first is that is seems to be evident that the first two models must sacrifice and repress some potentialities that essentially pertain to man on the basis of the original gift of being given by God. To be just an individual or just a member of a community implies a kind of castration for the human person, a fundamental dimension of what the person is must be repressed or cut out, a portion of his being must remain undeveloped and, under circumstances, this betrayal of the full vocation of the person must come to the fore and become conscious. The second reason is that it seems that our civilization has been moving for centuries from the model of the member of a community towards the model of the individual. Now on the one hand this model seems to have won with modern democratic societies and, on the other hand, seems to have entered into a deep crisis with modern mass societies. It is odd, and worth some reflection, that our societies may be characterized at the same time as individualistic and as mass societies. We experience at the same time the triumph of individualism and the reaction against individualism. Will this reaction lead us back to a pre-individualistic, pre-enlightment society? It is quite possible that the future will not belong to our proud Western nations but that some traditional societies, that succeeded in incorporating the advantages of our technology without the absolute individualism that is so deeply connected with it in our life styles, will take the lead bringing us back to a kind of technological barbarism. This evolution is commonplace in the latest fashion of sociological science fiction, and this seems to be taking place in countries like Japan, China, India and the whole magical South-East Asia. European societies stand in front of long ranging transformations. The simple defense of our

---

[21] See K. Wojtyła, *Osoba: podmiot i wspólnota*, in: *Osoba i czyn oraz inne studia antropologiczne*, op. cit., pp. 373 and ff.

individualistic model does not seem to have any chances. It is also hard for us to imagine that we could feel at home in a pre-enlightnment civilization. If we want to look forward we have to reconsider the model of the coexistence of the individualistic and the communitarian dimension in the unity of the human person. We must rethink the possiblity of a societal cohesion brought about not through the denial of the substantial value of the individual but through the free self-giving of each member of the society in a conscious act of love. This is the challange of our civilization. I strongly suspect that the call of John Paul II to rediscover the Christian roots of Europe has something to do with the spiritual development I have been trying to explain. The Christian root of the European civlization is the idea of the person as an individual and as a community. This idea appears in the realm of history with Christianity, with the Christian idea of the Trinity. It is however an anthropological and a philosophical idea. It is so human that men of different civilizations and cultures may understand it and accept it. We cannot define Europe without the idea of modernity and without enlightenment, without the discovery of the individual and the defense of his rights. It is however impossible to define Europe only through the concepts of enlightenment, of individualism and of modernity. These cencepts, that have been also powerful spiritual forces in the development of our civilization, seem today to have entered into the path of dialectics of self-destruction. No society can exist without a certain amount of communitarian thought and feeling, no human being can survive if his demands for a fundamental feeling of security, of being accepted and sheltered, are not met. The self-destruction of enlightenment and of Europe can only be avoided if we go beyond individualism and communitarianism, towards a new and more perfect understanding of the Christian idea of *communio*.

HERMAN DE DIJN
Katholieke Universiteit Leuven
Belgium

FREEDOM IN CONTEMPORARY CULTURE

I. INTRODUCTION

Discussions about freedom often concentrate on questions about free will and action, and problems such as freedom, determinism and weakness of the will. A disadvantage of many of these discussions is what could be called a kind of quasi-physicalistic conception of freedom and of the human being. Man's behaviour is considered here as an effect, more or less strictly determined by external and/or internal causes. Insufficient attention is given to the special nature of the concept of freedom as originating in the context of moral and juridical talk and activity. Many of the philosophical problems relating to freedom may be due to insufficient attention to the *kind* of language-game(s) in which such a concept is operating[1].

A concept such as freedom or free will does not primarily belong to one particular theory. It is a concept coming from our ordinary or common sense conception of things. It is a concept belonging to what some have called *the human world*[2] or *the human condition*[3], which is a world or a condition primarily of meanings, not of (pure) objective causation[4]. It is a concept which cannot be understood apart from other "strange" concepts, such as the concept of person or self. Understanding these concepts presupposes a familiarity with a human way of live, a *Lebenswelt* in which one partici-

---

[1] Cf. Gabriel Marcel, *Foi et réalité*, Paris, Aubier-Montaigne, 1967, p. 135.

[2] Cf. Roger Scruton, *Modern Philosophy. An Introduction and Survey*, London, Sinclair-Stevenson, 1994, chap. 18: "The Human World".

[3] Cf. Helmuth Plessner, *Conditio humana*, Pfullingen, Günther Neske Verlag, 1964.

[4] See also: William Desmond, *Perplexity and Ultimacy*, New York, SUNY, 1995, p. 78: "there is an idiocy to freedom as beyond the intelligible structures of univocal, causal determination".

pates. This *Lebenswelt* is a world which is dominated by "the priority of appearance"[5], in the sense that the participants implicitly understand that no explanation in terms of so-called "real essences" can replace this world. This "priority of appearance" is due not to a lack of intellectual daring, to a giving in to illusion. It is due to the inescapability of taking ourselves and others seriously and to the inevitability to adopt an intentional and even moral stance towards ourselves and others (which does not mean that taking an external point of view may not – *at times* – be required and/or allowed)[6]. "As agents we belong to the surface of the world, and enter into immediate relation with it"[7]. Probing into the depth of things in order to come to "the real thing" may render the surface unintelligible and may lead to serious distortions which undermine the human way of acting[8]. To try exclusively to explain (rather than describe) the surface on which we live in terms of something "neutral and objective" in order to be able to leave the surface behind, is therefore a serious mistake, not only philosophically, but even humanly speaking[9]. It is a kind of superstition with respect to the human world. *Especially* after we have discovered the path of scientific and critical thinking, it is necessary not to forswear "the priority of appearance", and to resist the extremist pursuit of an unobtainable theoretical and practical objectivity[10]. Otherwise, instead of justifying our participation in the human world, we will only undermine it.

This does not mean that the human world is a world where the (always hypothetical) laws of nature are suspended. It is rather a world where the supposed "real essences" are seen as infused with *meanings*: as when we immediately understand a smile not as flesh and bones, but "as spirit, freely revealed"[11]. The human soul is not the ghost in the machine. It is what we are in direct contact with when we see a human face[12]. The human face is a mystery: it can strike us with wonder. But it is not a mystery to be explained in the way a problem is to be explained[13]. It is an unmysterious mystery in

---

[5] Term borrowed from: Roger Scruton, "Modern Philosophy and the Neglect of Aesthetics", in: Idem, *The Philosopher on Dover Beach. Essays*, Manchester, Carcanet, 1990, p. 108.

[6] For a comparable position, see: Peter Strawson, "Freedom and Resentment", in: Idem, *Freedom and Resentment and Other Essays*, London, Methuen, 1974, p. 1-25.

[7] Roger Scruton, "Modern Philosophy and the Neglect of Aesthetics", p. 108.

[8] Scruton refers here (p. 110) to punishment.

[9] Cf. Roger Scruton, *Modern Philosophy*, p. 240.

[10] Cf. Roger Scruton, "Modern Philosophy and the Neglect of Aesthetics", p. 98-112.

[11] Cf. Roger Scruton, "The Philosopher on Dover Beach", in: Idem, *The Philosopher on Dover Beach*, p. 9.

[12] Ibidem.

[13] I borrow this opposition between mystery and problem from Gabriel Marcel, *De la dignité humaine*, Paris, Aubier-Montaigne, 1964, p. 111 ff.

the sense that it is accessible to everybody on condition that certain ways of seeing and reacting are preserved and participated in.

My contention is that a discussion of the notion of freedom today cannot escape a confrontation with the changes brought about in the lifeworld by the predominance of the scientific point of view and the technological-instrumentalist attitude usually associated with it. There is not only the threat of a rejection of the notion of freedom due to scientific and reductionist illusions. There is not only the threat of a quasi-physicalist *philosophical* understanding of the notion of freedom mentioned at the beginning. There is the further problem of an "infection" of this common sense-notion due to the general climate we are living in: a lifeworld itself affected by modern or postmodern illusions which influence the understanding of people even concerning the surface-meanings themselves. It can be argued that these illusions are at least partly the result of the penetration of instrumentalist and objectifying attitudes and insights related to the predominance of science and technology in contemporary culture. However, there must be something in common sense itself which has allowed these attitudes to affect and distort it.

My way to approach the notion of freedom will combine two moves. One is to relate this notion to other notions which are essentially linked to it, like the notions of self and of happiness (understood as that fundamental end the self is geared to in free activity)[14]. The other is to confront different conceptions of this cluster of concepts so as to be able to track certain distortions brought about in common sense itself by the modern and postmodern situation we are living in. Not only is it not possible to discuss the problem of freedom in isolation from other notions surrounding it in real life, it is equally impossible not to take into account the fundamental cultural-historical changes that have taken place in the human life-world.

II. THE POSTMODERN SEARCH FOR HAPPINESS

Modern, as well as postmodern man, thinks happiness to be an end which can be obtained by his own effort. Of course, postmodern man has lost the belief in the inevitable progress towards the enlightened ideal of individual and collective happiness on the basis of Reason (science and technology, with or without the direction of the party of the people). But

---

[14] One could, of course, add other crucial notions such as rationality (or, better perhaps, reasonableness). For a discussion of this notion in relation to the pursuit of happiness, see: Arnold Burms en Herman De Dijn, *De rationaliteit en haar grenzen*, Leuven, Universitaire Pers Leuven; Assen, Van Gorcum, 19954.

postmodern man still believes in the possibility he can *produce* happiness through his own efforts. The modern ideals of freedom and equality have been transformed in the postmodern principles of tolerance and of equal rights of individuals. Negative freedom (freedom from all hindrances by tradition and from unsollicited interference by others) and the equal right to organize one's own life according to one's own plans are, of course, only the conditions for happiness. Positive freedom consists in the active production of happiness in a perfectly controlled way. Happiness is no longer projected into an afterlife or into a glorious future; it is something to be obtained immediately using the machines for happiness provided so abundantly by the postmodern market. The only problem is obtaining these machines.

Basically, there are two sorts of machines for happiness, depending on the conception one has of it. Machines of the first kind produce happiness in the form of the absence of painful and the presence of agreeable experiences. The market provides many versions of such machines, some mechanical, some chemical, and of varying degrees of sophistication. At first sight, it is surprising that many more people do not organize their lives using these machines which efficiently produce a pleasurable life. Undoubtedly, this has to do with the fact that most people do not believe this sort of life constitutes real happiness. On the contrary, they consider those who organize their lives in this way to be a kind of failure. It is a well-known fact that people who are deeply dissatisfied with themselves organize their lives around these machines. A figure in one of the novels of Philip Roth expresses it like this: "Nobody wants to feel that good if they aren't in deep despair"[15]. People who organize their lives in function of these machines of the first kind are not considered free, but rather slaves, slaves of their need for continual gratification or satisfaction. They are considered unfree, even though they can do what they want, and even though they seem to be able to want what they want. Although they may claim to be happy, their happiness is "uninteresting". It is uninteresting for two reasons: it is divorced from important forms of life, and it is a solipsistic happiness divorced from the recognition of others. In their search for satisfactions, these individuals are characterized by a self-forgetfulness which betrays an incapacity to engage as a self in really significant activity with others. The kind of freedom which is present at this level looks rather like a slavery betraying an incapacity to real freedom.

Real happiness then must have something to do with being related to, or engaging in what is significant, and with the recognition by others of being in such a state. Indeed, it seems essential for happiness that others recognize oneself or could recognize oneself as leading the sort of life in which

---

[15] Philip Roth, *The Counterlife*, London, Penguin, 1988, p. 44.

true happiness consists. Typical for the postmodern situation is the belief that this sort of happiness can also be produced at will, using machines for happiness of the second kind, available on the postmodern, postindustrial market. To be related to, or to engage in what is important, also in the eyes of others, is ultimately to be marked by certain signs or distinctions, to be recognizable as somebody interesting. What is needed is the acquisition of symbolic goods, i.e., non-natural goods that provide one with recognition as somebody interesting or important[16]. To be really happy depends on "meaning something" for others. Machines for happiness of the second kind are machines which produce us as "meaningful" in the eyes of the others: i.e., they must be of such a kind that using them gives us *a guarantee* of our being interesting for others. The postmodern market is effectively a market where one can buy the signs, symbolic goods or values which provide recognition. This is the case not only with clothing, cars, houses, etc., but also with more "spiritual" values such as manners, travelling, literature and film, intellectual and aesthetic values, and even with very personal values such as one's character, body, sexuality. There is – in principle – nothing, no symbolic good, which is not the object of intervention, modelling, marketing, etc. There is, in other words, no value whatsoever, which escapes becoming the object of fashion. Since values are more or less interdependent, it is inevitable that people try to obtain happiness by taking great care to produce for themselves a certain *lifestyle* (i.e., a way of life consisting of an interrelated set of activities having to do with interrelated symbolic goods) which should give them the desired recognition. In this endeavour people are supported by special sources of information (e.g., lifestyle-magazines) and *ad hoc*-technicians (lifestyle experts[17]).

Since symbolic goods or values require differentiation or distinction, and since no distinctions are considered as escaping intervention, the law of fashion dominates the search for recognition and, therefore, also of happiness. The only way to really differentiate oneself from others and to appear as interesting to others, is to compose a lifestyle which is in the frontline of what is "in fashion". As a consequence, the postmodern way of seeking rec-

---

[16] The notion of non-natural goods is borrowed from: K. Britton, "Hume on some non-natural distinctions", in: C.P. Morice(ed.), *D. Hume. The Bi-centenary Papers. Edinburgh*, Edinburgh Univ. Press, 1977, p. 205-209. Non-natural goods are goods which are not means sought for the fulfilment of a natural need. Their significance in our lives can only be understood in function of the symbolic order dominating human living; this is why I also call them symbolic goods. MacIntyre speaks here of "goods internal to a practice"; see Alisdair MacIntyre, *After Virtue. A Study of Moral Theory*, London, Duckworth, 1981, p. 171 (and elsewhere).

[17] Even the medical profession has changed its nature: it no longer provides experts of healing, but experts helping to manage our general health in function of our life-style.

ognition and happiness is characterized by *activism*. The continuous attempt to be "in fashion" requires a constant remodelling of oneself and of one's lifestyle. Typical is also the abhorrence of anything "natural" or "pre-given", unless it can be manipulated and changed (cf., the present-day interest in manipulating one's own body and sexuality). The individual should be free and even has to be free to adopt that lifestyle which brings recognition and happiness. Like modern man, the postmodern individual is "doomed to freedom" (Sartre); it is the Promethean freedom to manipulate oneself and one's values, the symbolic goods through which one obtains recognition. In this light, it is quite comprehensible that individuals characterized by signs they cannot (easily) change into "interesting" characteristics, are claiming that they too have an equal right of recognition, and that therefore *any* difference which someone is adopting or is identified with, should be recognized as equally important. (Consequently all non-recognition is undeserved and unjustified rejection[18]). If, *per impossibile* this demand would be successful, it would mean the end of recognition: trying to implement this demand leads inevitably to indifference and insincerity.

The happiness provided by these machines for happiness of the second kind seems at first sight to be ideal happiness: it is happiness related to being associated with something valuable or important, *and* recognized as such by others. At the same time, it is a sort of happiness which one can produce oneself, in which one is "one's own master". There are, however, certain drawbacks. The happy life, as depicted here, is a life characterized by activism and unrest: it is necessary to worry continuosly about changing fashions of lifestyle. Furthermore, the happiness seems hollow, since in its pursuit the distinctions or values with which the self is associated are not really important or interesting *in themselves*, but only insofar as they prove to be means for the self to obtain recognition.

The self which searches for happiness in this second way, can properly be called *a narcissistic self*. Like narcissistic people, postmodern individuals, although capable of finding certain signs or distinctions interesting or valuable, cannot really identify with these values because at any moment these may have to be given up and exchanged for new signs or distinctions. What these individuals are ultimately interested in is the affirmation of the pure self – an affirmation they know they cannot give to themselves directly: so they strive to obtain it with certainty through their guaranteed positive reflection in the eyes of others. The narcissistic, postmodern self is caught in a catch 22: because it wants to play it safe and to guarantee self-recognition, it

---

[18] For an interesting discussion of this point, see: Charles Taylor, *Multiculturalism: Examining the Politics of Recognition*, Princeton, Princeton Univ. Press, 1994.

cannot relate to values or distinctions in such a way that these can be considered as really important; if, as a self, it would get really interested, it could no longer be safe. All this is obscurely felt in the postmodern mentality: people only go through certain motions; nothing is really important in itself. But why then should the self itself be important ? The end of history (i.e. of the transcendence of values vis-à-vis the human self) is the end of the self or subject itself. Only the forgetfulness present in activism can provisionally hide this truth from the postmodern self[19].

The real problem is not that of determinism; it is rather that of self-realization and recognition (as Hegel clearly saw). Unfortunately, the attempt, as in the postmodern mentality, to control self-realization and the recognition by others leads to a fundamental doubt both with respect to what is really valuable and with respect to the value of the self itself. The only solution seems to be to get in touch with what is really valuable in itself (or "by nature", as Aristotle would say) and to find real recognition by others, i.e., recognition of oneself as identified with what is really valuable.

III. HAPPINESS AND RESPONSIBILITY

From the foregoing, we can learn what is required for real happiness: it is the more or less implicit awareness of leading a worthwhile life, which supposes 1) that one is linked to symbolic values which are truly interesting and 2) that one is prepared to "verify" this link in asking for real recognition from others. The link with symbolic values should not be narcissistic, which means that our relationship with them should be a relationship of genuine identification, a relationship where they are not considered only as means to obtain recognition. But such a relationship cannot be perfectly controlled. If we are genuinely interested in certain values with which we identify ourselves in our search for happiness, then we inevitably run the risk of unhappiness, of self-loss, in case it turns out that we are identified with something which is not of real value or in case we don't succeed in obtaining recognition. This is, of course, why the postmodern self tries to control the recognition of others by controlling his lifestyle, i.e., his relation to symbolic values. The ideal of freedom of the postmodern self is basically no different from the modern one: it is the ideal of total control, which ends in activism or – for the lucid ones – in indifference and cynicism or even despair.

---

[19] See also: Herman Lübbe, *Fortschrittsreaktionen. Über konservative und destruktive Modernität*, Graz, Styria, 1987, p. 123-129.

Apart from the happiness produced by the machines for happiness of the first and second kind, there is another kind of happiness in which people feel the deep satisfaction of self-realization precisely because what happens in their life and to their life is experienced as something which is not purely of their own making, yet deeply fulfils their desire for *personal* meaning or significance. Real happiness is related to a sense of wonder and gratitude for something which exceeds what one deserves or obtains through one's own efforts. It is this sense of unexpected gift which is expressed in the very word "happiness" (or "good luck"): something which happens to us as a kind of grace. The recognition by others of the significance of what the happy person is or does is part of happiness and equally experienced as a wonderful gift, even when one thinks it is deserved.

There is nobody who does not want happiness or meaningfulness. In the same way in which a player in a game wants to win, a person wants happiness. The analogy is very fruitful (probably more than an analogy). The cardplayer has to play with the cards given to him, using all the intelligence and the astuteness he possesses. He cannot win, if he is not prepared to run the risk of losing. If he cheats so as to make sure he will win, he makes it impossible to really win. The happiness of winning has to do with running the risk, and with the surprise of good luck. The obtainment of real happiness has the same "logic". Using the talents and bearing the distinctions one is endowed with, one has to run the risk of being or becoming important or significant and of being recognized in one's being or actions as significant. The pleasure of happiness has to do with running this risk and with the surprise of good luck[20]. Any attempt to avoid the risk and "to play it safe" or "to master the game completely", changes winning into something else. It is no wonder that some writers, like the famous Dutch historian Johan Huizinga, define man not as *homo sapiens*, but *homo ludens*[21]. One could add that *sapientia*, true wisdom, can perhaps only be present in a playful mind open for the wonder to happen. The postmodern culture could be characterized as a culture which foolishly tells people they can win happiness by cheating, by controlling the game.

---

[20] Cf. Gilbert K. Chesterton, *Orthodoxy*, New York, Doubleday (Image Books), 1959, p. 113: "The perfect happiness of men on earth [...] will not be a flat and solid thing, like the satisfaction of animals. It will be an exact and perilous balance; like that of a desperate romance"; p. 31: "By asking for pleasure, he lost the chief pleasure; for the chief pleasure is surprise".

[21] Cf. Johan Huizinga, *Homo ludens. Proeve ener bepaling van het spelelement der cultuur*, Groningen, Wolters-Noordhoff, 1985.

[22] The notion "state that is essentially a by-product" is borrowed from: Jon Elster, *Sour Grapes. Studies in the Subversion of Rationality*, Cambridge, Cambridge Univ. Press, paperback 1985, p. 43 ff.

Real happiness implies that neither it, nor the recognition to which it is related, can ever be guaranteed or manufactured. Although we cannot refrain from looking for happiness, we should *not* look for it as the *direct* result of our endeavour. Happiness requires a fundamental passivity. Happiness is a state which is essentially a *by-product* of our activity[22]. Happiness can only be obtained in a kind of forgetfulness of itself: in a concentration on something else (as in the case of the game of cards, where we concentrate not on our desire to win, but on the game *of cards*). And yet, it is through or in this something else that *our* happiness is found: through or in a meaningfulness or value which as it were reflects upon ourselves, makes ourselves meaningful or valuable, thus constituting *our* happiness. *Example*: when a person seeks happiness in life as a writer, he has as it were to forget about himself and engage in an activity (literature) which existed before him, in an attempt to create work which is really valid as a good piece of literature. The literature he produces has to be considered (by himself and others) as something valuable in itself and not simply as a means to obtain gratification. And yet it is in producing this piece of work that the writer seeks *his* own self-realization and happiness. Even if a person would seek happiness by cultivating his own life (as a kind of work of art), it is still because this can somehow be considered as not-purely subjective value; even then one might ask why he should seek *his own* happiness in this cultivation of a certain style or way of living.

If real happiness can only be obtained as a by-product of being in touch with what is significant or valuable in itself, then it cannot be sought as a premeditated end (state) which one tries to obtain as economically as possible using certain independent means. This implies that real happiness requires a peculiar relationship between ourselves and those signs, distinctions or values through which we seek happiness. If the "objects" related to the pursuit of happiness are not means used in function of an independent end, then they cannot be sought because of some quality they have which guarantees success. The objects or values related to happiness must as it were contain an aspect by which they transcend their being reducible to bearers of interesting qualities. What makes them really interesting and valuable is their irreducible concreteness. Their value is intrinsically tied up with their particularity. The non-natural or symbolic goods or values which are suitable candidates for our search for happiness are necessarily "incarnated" in concrete things. This particularity or incarnation makes them somehow irreplaceable and at the same time intrinsically vulnerable[23]. Human happiness

---

[23] About values in general, and their vulnerability in particular, see: Herman De Dijn, "Waarden en normen; idealen en principes", in *Tijdschrift voor Filosofie* 58 (juni 1996), p. 261-276.

is always related to being in touch with concrete, incarnated value. As Oakeshott has put it beautifully: "I cannot *want* happiness; what I want is to idle in Avignon or to hear Caruso sing"[24].

Our relationship with these concrete objects or activities must be a relationship of *personal* involvement. These objects somehow define our lot or destiny in a way we cannot perfectly control. Even when we *choose* to search for happiness in relation to certain sorts of objects or activities (like having children, or becoming a writer), this choice should be as much a *being chosen or bound* by the other as a binding of the other to us. In other words, the objects or activities through which we try to realize ourselves should have an *appeal* for us which we cannot completely recuperate. The relation of involvement we are discussing is a relation of *identification* which is such that in the end we do not choose in an independent and neutral way that with which we identify ourselves. Just as we cannot *decide* to love ourselves, we cannot, strictly speaking, decide to be identified with something. The objects through which we reach happiness are therefore inevitably characterized by a certain transcendence vis-à-vis our choices and decisions. Yet, at the same time, they may not be so alien to us as to have nothing to do with us: they are the objects through which we realize *ourselves*. Their transcendence must be capable of becoming some sort of immanence: although they are always somehow escaping our choice and decisions, yet it is through and in them that our own destiny is at stake, and that we somehow reach fulfilment.

The desire for happiness is in a way a desire for truth: the truth of being linked to objects/values which are really valuable, and the truth of being linked to them in an adequate way. Therefore the desire for happiness is also a desire for recognition by others, especially by others who are *connoisseurs* in the matter, by masters. To obtain such recognition is part of happiness as genuine happiness. Again, this recognition cannot be guaranteed: it depends on the other, and any attempt to enforce it takes away its capacity to add to our happiness. It not only is unenforcable, it is necessarily somehow inaccessible to us. And it is precisely this character of inaccessibility which allows it to add to our happiness: as the unmasterable and inaccessible, yet wonderful gift of recognition by the other. The standpoint which the other takes towards us is a standpoint we can never take vis-à-vis ourselves: it is non-transparent and asymetrical[25]. A writer cannot take the standpoint of the reader vis-à-vis his own work (and vis-à-vis himself). And yet, as a writer, one is necessarily geared towards this irrecuperable standpoint of the

---

[24] Michael Oakshott, *On Human Conduct*, Oxford, Clarendon Press, 1975, p. 53.

[25] For a more detailed account of this, see: Herman De Dijn, *Kan kennis troosten?* Kapellen, Pelckmans – Kampen, Kok Agora, 1994, p. 94-98.

other. The eventual recognition by the reader is precisely what the writer wants: as a gift one could not possibly give to oneself, and which yet is a recognition of oneself. Therefore, the other should give recognition, but not for the sake of easing the desire of the one asking for recognition: if the writer would discover that this is behind the recognition of the reader, he would be very disappointed. The recognition should be genuine recognition, recognition for that *through* which the person asks personal recognition.

Both the desire for happiness and the desire for recognition, which is an essential part of it, are desires which can only be successful if one somehow manages to ignore them, if one concentrates on something else (i.e., the value which must be present and through which one finds personal happiness and recognition). Even the person who gives recognition must ignore his desire to give recognition: his recognition can only be genuine, and therefore acceptable, if it is given indirectly, *via* his applause for whatever it is which is valuable in itself[26].

The concept of "real" happiness is clearly *logically* related to a certain concept of the self and of freedom, just as this was the case with the hedonistic and narcissistic concept of happiness. This new concept of the self displays a self which is never pure, which cannot distance itself completely from all distinctions and values. On the contrary, it presupposes a system of differences and values which are there *before* the self, and in which the self experiences itself as a self with a personal destiny which it receives as a gift. This self is the opposite of a self which controls everything in function of ends which it chooses absolutely: it is characterized by a fundamental passivity. There is a concern for ourselves before all decision; this is shown clearly, for example, in experiences of anxiety. The notion of freedom must here necessarily be very different from that associated with absolute choice or decision: much more central than free choice is, as we will see, the notion of a responsibility "which precedes freedom"[27].

It is commonly accepted that freedom presupposes more than being able to do what one wants. The question is whether these wants are not imposed upon me by others or by the pressure of circumstances. Maybe they are wants which although they are clearly my wants, are felt as alien to my real self, producing a kind of inner division or disruption, as in the person disliking certain tendencies within himself. Real freedom then seems to suppose

---

[26] Arnold Burms, "Helping and Appreciating", in S. Griffioen (ed.), *What Right Does Ethics Have Public Philosophy in a Pluralistic Culture*, Amsterdam, VU Univ. Press, 1990, p. 72.

[27] Emmanuel Levinas, *Autrement qu'être ou au-delà de l'essence*, Dordrecht, Kluwer, 1988, p. 163.

that I can accept my desires or wants from a higher perspective, a second-order perspective, as H. Frankfurt puts it: in a reflective self-evaluation I have to be able to identify with my first order desires, I must be able to want my wants, to accept my wants within the picture I have of my (ideal) self. Only then can we talk of autonomy[28]. A well-known problem with these considerations is why we should stop at the second level: maybe these desires are again somehow alien to my real self? According to Frankfurt this danger of regression is eliminated because I can autonomously *decide* to allow my desires to really be my desires[29]. It is in and through personal decision-making of this kind that I am really autonomous. But now another danger is lurking: is this kind of autonomy present in pure decision not the same as arbitrariness or perhaps even the subconscious operation of motives unknown to us?[30] Furthermore, pure self-determination seems nonsensical[31]: it would mean to create value out of a situation where there is no value, to create desire *ex nihilo*. (This is as nonsensical as the idea that one could *decide* to love oneself). A decision not triggered by any preceding distinction or value could not get off the ground. It is an abstraction in Hegel's sense of the word. Only if we can experience ourselves as already having importance and if we are able to see other things as already desirable in themselves, can there be desire of a self.

Paradoxically, Frankfurt himself seems to understand this when he talks about a fundamental sort of *passivity* in certain desires the self can have and with which it most deeply identifies itself. We are not free not to care about ourselves, and yet in this caring we seem to be most ourselves: it is not the person who doesn't (any longer) seem to care about himself who is considered most autonomous. When we really care about certain people or certain things, our caring seems to be characterized by what Frankfurt calls *volitional necessity*[32]. Volitional necessity is present whenever someone says, or could say: "Here I stand; I cannot do otherwise"[33]. We are characterized here by a sort of passivity which we do not at all feel as a hindrance to our

---

[28] Harry Frankfurt, *The Importance of What We Care About. Philosophical Essays*, Cambridge, Cambridge University Press, 1988, Chap. II.

[29] Harry Frankfurt, o. c., p. 170 ff.

[30] Cf. Stefaan Cuypers, *Persoonlijke aangelegenheden. Schets van een analytische antropologie*, Leuven, Universitaire Pers – Assen, Van Gorcum, 1994, p. 114-5.

[31] Cf. William Desmond, o. c., p. 78: "If there is any self-production, it is not a creation from nothing. The self must *already be* for it to produce. The self is a creation, but not first a self-creation. If it were the latter, you would have the absurdity of its lack of itself being the original of itself. The lack would be the original, and hence nothing would be the original source".

[32] Harry Frankfurt, o. c., p. 86-88.

[33] Reference to Luther's saying in Harry Frankfurt, o. c., p. 86.

freedom. On the contrary, we endorse it, we would not and could not bring ourselves to cut ourselves off from this caring. Willing to perform such action is *unthinkable* for us[34]. It is in this volitional necessity that we feel most ourselves. It is the capacity to lead a life of caring dominated by a calling or a vocation of which we are not the origin, which frees our lives from arbitrariness. And yet, this caring for ourselves or for the other is not the result of an absolute decision, of free choice *ex nihilo*[35]. On the contrary, it is this identification with ourselves and with the other in us, which is the origin of our freedom. It is the responsibility to the value(s) we already have, that makes us capable of acting in a free and meaningful way. Of importance here, says Oakeshott, is not willing, but response[36]. Real freedom, as Spinoza puts it, is not the capacity to do what one wants, nor even to want what one wants. Real freedom is *power* to act[37]. However, this power can only originate in responsibility: responsibility with respect to our own value and to the valuable other who or which is in our care. The dedication to ourselves and the dedication to the other through which we *indirectly* realize ourselves could not get off the ground but for this volitional necessity which characterizes our self-identity.

Because freedom is rooted in and conditioned by responsibility, it is not to be confused with the insignificance of the act which I could do or could as well not do. Freedom cannot be ascribed to actions except retrospectively: whether or not they can be seen as fitting into a meaningful response to values as related to the person's self-identity[38]. This is not to say that coherence is all important: a life characterized by responsibility is a life which is of course not chaotic, but it is essentially characterized by the surprise of meaningful encounters[39].

The ordinary idea of autonomy is tied to a view on values (including one's own value) as acceptable only if one could step back from them and then, in a moment of critical appraisal and pure decision, could adopt these values as one's own. It is as if values could not become our values unless we could adopt or recreate them as ours. Far from this being real autonomy, it

---

[34] About the unthinkable, see: Harry Frankfurt, o. c., Chap. 13 "Rationality and the Unthinkable".

[35] Harry Frankfurt, o. c., p. 87: "[...] it may seem appropriate to regard situations which involve volitional necessity as providing instances of passivity".

[36] Michael Oakeshott, o. c., p. 39. See also: Gilbert K. Chesterton, o. c., p. 39: "The worship of will is the negation of will"; and Gabriel Marcel, o.c., p. 137: "il faut rompre une fois pour toutes avec cette idée que la liberté est essentiellement liberté de choix".

[37] B. Spinoza, *Tractatus Politicus*, Chap. II § 7.

[38] Gabriel Marcel, o.c., p. 139.

[39] Ibidem.

is the impossible ideal of the narcissistic self. Real autonomy does not presuppose a recuperation of oneself as valuable and of other values through a moment of criticism and radical doubt in which one, as it were, would recreate the world of value. "The game cannot begin with doubting"[40] or with the doubting subject, certainly not in the real world of self-realization. Things begin with *trust*: the trust present in the self-esteem which is there at the moment the self is there; the trust present in caring about valuable things entrusted to me and appealing to me *before* any choice[41].

The phenomenon of volitional necessity, which is the possible condition of freedom as a powerful responsibility, presupposes a self which is radically different from the self as it appears in the ideological conception of autonomy so closely related to modern and postmodern narcissism. Real freedom presupposes that one has always been identified as someone valuable, important, lovable and that one has adopted this standpoint of the other as one's own standpoint in one's self-love or self-esteem. Self-esteem is internalized esteem of others. Self-identity requires the adoption of the standpoint of the other vis-à-vis oneself as part of one's own standpoint. This adoption is not the work of the constituted self; it is presupposed by the constituted self. The constitution of the self implies that one somehow becomes sensible to the attraction of the others towards oneself and that one internalizes this attraction, thus coming to love oneself and becoming capable of responsibility vis-à-vis oneself. Of course this implies that one's own attitude towards oneself will be co-determined by the "quality" of the attraction of the other towards us. This may lead to all sorts of existential problems not only in one's relation to oneself, but also in one's relation to others and to other values[42]. I cannot elaborate on this complication here.

To be a self presupposes the ability to be attracted by a certain picture of oneself which is reflected in the attitudes of others towards us, but which is always the result of an internalization of our attractiviness towards others. In this relation to ourselves, we necessarily appear to ourselves as a kind of mystery. We take over an attraction which we cannot completely recuperate because this attraction of the other towards us is not something which can

---

[40] Cf. Ludwig Wittgenstein, "Cause and Effect: Intuitive Awareness" (transl. R. Rhees), in "Philosophia" 6(1976), p. 414.

[41] This is a central idea in C. S. Lewis, *The Abolition of Man*, Glasgow, Collins-Fount Paperbacks, reprint 1990. For an analysis of the notion of trust, see: Lars Hertzberg, "On the Attitude of Trust", in "Inquiry" 31(1988), p. 307-322.

[42] Cf. Stanley Cavell, *The Claim of Reason: Wittgenstein, Skepticism, Morality, and Tragedy*, New York and London, Oxford Univ. Press, 1979, p. 177: "That [what you do] will be love in the child's world; and if it is mixed with resentment and intimidation, then love is a mixture of resentment and intimidation, and when love is sought *that* will be sought".

be explained or understood from a neutral position which could be occupied by an external spectator. The standpoint of the other vis-à-vis ourselves is non-transparent and a-symmetrical[43]. We are as it were more attracted by the attraction of the other, than by any specific quality which attracts him. Nevertheless, our attractiviness to others is linked to the attractiviness of certain meaningful signs or distinctions ("characters" in the Greek sense). To internalize the attraction of others is to internalize to a certain extent the attractiviness of certain signs and distinctions (which form a system in which we occupy a specific position).

Although we already have a significance, this significance is not given objectively, once and for all or *in toto*. It is a significance which has to be reflected again and again in our encounters with others. Furthermore, this significance is a gift which is at the same time a responsibility: a *Gabe* which is at the same time *Aufgabe*; a care and loyalty with respect to what we are supposed to be, which engages us in meaningful, human activity. The significance which we have requires us to some degree to develop this significance according to the "laws" which link meanings together (e.g., to be a boy or a girl requires one, as one grows up, to develop certain, diversified relations with male and female persons). This is the origin of our *own* attempt at self-realization in relation to the pursuit of further specific identifications with values. It is in this pursuit that one runs the risk of happiness or unhappiness. Our responsibility vis-à-vis ourselves becomes a responsibility vis-à-vis other values which we recognize and accept as playing a role in our personal destiny. Again this requires an attraction towards distinctions whose appeal precedes all decisions from the standpoint of a neutral spectator.

But how can an identity which is given to us, or which is revealed to us, really be *our* identity? How can self-realization be a realization of *self* if it happens through distinctions or signs which are given or which happen to befall us? In real life there doesn't seem to be a serious problem here. Whom do we consider as people who are most "themselves"? It is people who don't seem to bother much about themselves. They seem to act from a deeper source. They are not constantly trying "to be themselves". They are *responsible* people whose life is in the service of something bigger, or people who simply "are there" instead of constantly trying "to be somebody". It is precisely because they are not desiring to be free, that they seem *really* free. It is in simply living, or doing what they have to do, that they are really themselves. They are bound to what they are, to that which they are responsible for, but this bondage is not slavery, not self-loss, but real freedom[44]. It

---

[43] See note 25.
[44] Cf. Gilbert K. Chesterton, o. c., p. 71: "Love is bound; and the more it is bound the less it is blind".

is precisely egocentric or narcissistic people who don't succeed in "losing themselves" in a cause, activity or value, who do not seem to be able to "forget themselves", who seem least of all real selves. It is an idea, present even in common sense, that when a person's will is determined too strongly by the emotions, by the heart, then this will is of necessity pathological. The opposite is rather the case[45].

Self-identity and self-esteem are not based on an act of self-constitution and self-appreciation, not even in a retrospective way. They require that one accepts oneself as valuable even though one cannot completely or perfectly penetrate or recuperate this value. There is a real existential problem here: it is to live with this insecurity without anxiety. One's relation to oneself has to be characterized by a spontaneous *trust* as to one's own worthiness: one has to love oneself and care for oneself even though one cannot fully penetrate or comprehend what is so "shining" about oneself. Self-esteem must as it were operate spontaneously, unreflectively (as the Chinese thinker Lao-Tzu puts it: "He who looks at himself, does not shine"[46]). It is the presence of this basic trust which allows one to further realize oneself in a non-narcissistic, non-activistic way. To the degree this trust is lacking, the self-forgetfulness and the spontaneity needed for real self-realization will be impossible or difficult as well. Again there is a real difficulty in this self-realization: one does run real risks here both in one's relation to what is valuable and in one's desire for recognition by others. This may lead to a frantic search for self-realization in which anxiety and the desire for certainty takes the upperhand. A cramped self-consciousness hinders responsible activity. It becomes almost impossible to "forget oneself" in one's activity, to transcend the egocentric desire for certainty and complete self-determination.

It may seem paradoxical that self-realization requires self-forgetfulness and self-transcendence. This is because one does not sufficiently attend to the special nature of the self which is such that its self-realization must take on a special form as well. Just as the self cannot constitute itself in a direct relationship to itself, it cannot realize itself except by making a detour in which it must as it were first forget itself so as to be able to find itself. Just as the self cannot be a gift given to oneself, it cannot directly realize itself as something "shining". What is required for a successful self-realization is the *happy* coincidence between a self-forgetful activity *and* the recognition by others of the bond between the responding self and what is "shining" or

---

[45] Harry Frankfurt, o. c., p. 189; see also Gilbert K. Chesterton, o. c., p. 19: "The madman is not the man who has lost his reason. The madman is the man who has lost everything except his reason".

[46] Quoted in Josef Pieper, *Musse und Kult*, München, Kösel Verlag, 19585, p. 57 note 46.

valuable. It is in this recognition that the self is reflected for itself in an unexpected and therefore wonderful way. In this reflection, one can recognize oneself as related to a value which one can never master and which nevertheless somehow belongs to oneself.

That the self is able to recognize itself somehow in the reflection of the other must mean, of course, that in self-transcendence the self is not completely absent, that the concern for oneself is still there, be it obliquely. But are self-care and self-transcendence not altogether incompatible? That this is not so, is brought out by the following consideration: "When we feel admiration, we usually want to convey this admiration to the person to whom it is directed. We miss our aim if the communication of our admiration would raise a conceited feeling in the person to whom it is destined. This cannot be our aim: it would mean that we would make the person whom we admire conceited and therefôre less admirable. If we nevertheless do convey our admiration, this undoubtedly implies the idea that someone can be struck agreeably by the sense of being admired without becoming conceited"[47]. In other words, in admiring someone, we clearly think that it is possible for self-transcendence and concern for self-realization to go together in a non-contradictory way. This requires that the person is capable in his desire for self-realization to seek this self-realization in an oblique way, thus running the risk of happiness.

Some might say that the real danger appearing in the view on the free self and its happiness put forward here is not self-loss, but fanaticism: the fanaticism involved in the sort of responsibility described. How can one be certain that in one's loyalty and caring one is not fanatic, one is not under the spell of what is ultimately destructive of the self and of what is really valuable? In the first place, there is the check of the recognition of others with whom one has to confront oneself in one's identification (as well as in the quality of one's identifications: whether one is not over-anxious, over-ambitious, etc.). Secondly, one has to attend to the nature of values which requires a peculiar attitude towards them. Values are transcendent and at the same time necessarily incarnated in symbols which are intrinsically vulnerable[48]. Therefore, our loyalty to values should always go together with an awareness of their vulnerability and of the possibility that others (or even we at other moments) cannot see them as we see them at this moment. This does not mean that our loyalty is only provisional; it means that we know

---

[47] Cf. Arnold Burms, "Rationaliteit, zelftranscendentie en zelfbetrokkenheid", in: Stefaan E. Cuypers (ed.), *Indirecte rede: Jon Elster over rationaliteit en irrationaliteit*, Leuven, Acco, 1994, p. 203-4.

[48] See note 23.

that we cannot penetrate the light of our values and demonstrate it to ourselves and others in such a way that it cannot be escaped. What is most dear and holy to us always somehow escapes us (and escapes us in different ways: in its impenetrability and in its vulnerability). But this transcendence of what is valuable makes it the more dear and holy to us and heightens our responsibility. All this explains why loyalty can be different from fanaticism (which supposes either that all values are really only provisional and accidental means for the overriding ideal, or that everybody can and should agree with what we find valuable). It also explains why loyalty can demand us in certain circumstances to endure in the *tragic* situation in which we, in full awareness of the impossibility of others to see as valuable what we feel responsible for, hold on to our values in opposition to the judgment of others as to what constitutes real value. It also explains why loyalty can require us to hold on to what we are responsible for even *beyond* the line where it appears as "shining" to us. (This is the case when we mourn that which we most cared about: in an holding on, which is at the same time a forgetting in which the fanaticism of our holding on is deflected). It is the greatness of religion – but not its only greatness – to help us not to despair in such tragic or ultimate situations.

CONCLUSION

Real freedom is not autonomy in the sense in which this is usually understood. Real freedom presupposes responsibility. It is grounded in a fundamental passivity which is the source of all activity (including even activistic and narcissistic activity). Freedom then paradoxically requires *volitional necessity* as in caring, dedication and loyalty to oneself and to whatever it is that one *finds* oneself responsible for. Even though in volitional necessity the will is bound or necessitated, this necessity is different from being constrained either externally or internally. Volitional necessity, as in self-esteem and in the caring for the other, has to do with the attraction of what is already valuable in itself, before we decide it is so. It is an attraction in us of which we are not the origin, but which is nevertheless *our* attraction rooted in the unreachable depth of our being, an attraction which we do not experience as alien, but which we implicitly (and sometimes explicitly) endorse or affirm in an *amor necessitatis*. Through the attraction of what is a transcendent value, one is prepared and capable of foregoing what is useful or immediately pleasurable and one is capable of forgetting oneself (one's concern for the certainty of direct gratification).

It should be clear that a culture, like the postmodern culture, in which values are conceived and treated as commodities available for the narcissistic self-affirmation of individuals, does not make it easy for these individuals to realize themselves in accordance with the real nature of the self and in accordance with the real nature of freedom as presupposing responsibility vis-à-vis transcendent, but necessarily incarnated values. It is also not surprising that in such a culture, characterized by activism, individuals have a hard time finding real happiness. It is true that the postmodern attitude to values and to self-realization may help people to escape fanaticism and the possible excessiveness of the demands of responsibility. But this possibility of escape has a price: a growing indifference and/or the absurdity of the claim that any difference whatsoever is to be respected simply because it is someone's or some group's adopted difference.

Must this lead us to despair concerning present culture and society? Fortunately, contemporary culture is not monolithic[49]. It contains strong tendencies towards narcissism and activism which erode customary ways to seek happiness. But this does not mean that all individuals or groups are under the spell of these attitudes. A lot will depend on the capacity of survival of groups and individuals who live in the midst of postmodern society and who are capable to somehow conserve their transcendent values and transmit the right attitudes towards them. The very dissatisfaction of so many individuals with the postmodern way of life and the formation of ghettos or networks of groups of people who to some degree escape the influence of postmodern society or resist it, show that the tendencies present in postmodern culture are not necessarily all-pervasive, let alone all-powerful. But the last word is given to the poet[50]:

> A more heartening fact about the cultures of men
> Is their appalling stubborness. The sea
> Is always calm ten fathoms down. The gigantic
> anthropological circus riotously holds open all its boots.

---

[49] We are not yet in the situation described in Huxley's *Brave New World* where "the savage" is a total outsider of society.

[50] William Empson, *Collected Poems*, London, Chatto and Windus, 1969, p. 83.

ANGELO SCOLA
Pontificia Università Lateranense
Vatican

LIBERTÀ GRAZIA DESTINO[1]

In un contesto di filosofia cristiana – insisto volutamente sull'aggettivo "cristiana", perché non si potrebbe procedere in modo del tutto simile in un congresso che non esplicitasse tale qualificazione della filosofia – vi sono almeno due ragioni che spingono a riflettere sul tema della libertà, prendendo spunto dalla celebre opera guardiniana *Libertà, grazia, destino*[2]. Entrambe, già presenti nell'intento guardiniano, mantengono, e forse vedono addirittura accresciuta, la loro urgente attualità, anche se il quadro generale di riferimento si presenta oggi assai diverso – non però senza importanti elementi di continuità – rispetto a quello cui Guardini, peraltro osservatore profetico della parabola culturale della modernità, faceva riferimento.

La prima ragione è, per così dire, strettamente antropologica. Senza rinunciare al portato della grande tradizione del pensiero cristiano, la riflessione sulla libertà è chiamata, a partire dalla modernità, a farsi carico di un dato basilare: l'uomo può interrogarsi sulla sua essenza solo dall'interno della sua esistenza. Ciò non coincide affatto con l'affermazione di Sartre che l'«esistenza precede l'essenza», da cui il filosofo francese deduce la negazione della libertà. Significa piuttosto prendere sul serio, come fa il Balthasar, la natura drammatica dell'antropologia: quando riflette su di sé il singolo uomo si trova già in azione sulla scena "del gran teatro del mondo"[3]. Da

---

[1] Relazione tenuta durante The Fifth World Congress of Christian Philosophy *Freedom in contemporany culture,* Lublino 21 agosto 1996

[2] Il grande pensatore, geniale educatore di svariate generazioni di giovani, scrisse questo testo nel 1948: *Freiheit, Gnade, Schicksal. Drei Kapitel zur Deutung des Daseins*, München, 1948 (tr. it. *Libertà, grazia, destino*, Brescia 1968).

[3] Cfr H. U. Von Balthasar, *Teodrammatica*, Milano 1982, vol II, 317: *"Noi possiamo interrogarci sull'«essenza» dell'uomo soltanto nel vivo atto della sua esistenza"*. Cfr. anche ID., *Teo-*

questo consegue che un'indagine adeguata sulla sua essenza, la quale non può alla fine essere elusa, riceve piena luce dalla considerazione di tutti gli elementi costitutivi della sua esistenza. Ciò è ancor più esigito dalla natura della libertà alla quale appartiene, nel suo nucleo costitutivo, anche un "autoporsi di sé" che implica, strutturalmente, l'io in azione. Analizzare la natura e i dinamismi della libertà richiede allora un attento esame di tutti gli elementi costitutivi dell'esistenza dell'uomo come individuo e come persona.

Ora, ci si può legittimamente chiedere se, in questo esame, convenga a dei filosofi cristiani mettere tra parentesi il peso della grazia (che alla fine è l'evento di Gesù Cristo stesso). Certo è possibile! Tanti dibattiti sulla natura della filosofia cristiana, sulla sua stessa possibilità o addirittura sulla sua pertinenza teorica lo dimostrano[4]. Sono però sempre meno i filosofi convinti dell'efficacia di una scelta antropologica che parta da una sorta di *epoché* circa il nesso tra l'evento di Cristo e l'uomo. Non foss'altro perché alla sensibilità culturale odierna appare assai più problematico un concetto di "natura", inteso come terreno neutro di incontro tra le varie *Weltanschauungen*, che non il proporre la ragionevolezza scandalosa dell'evento di Gesù Cristo. Egli è l'autentica *"silhouette"* dell'uomo (come affermava Przywara), che non annulla, peraltro, una oggettiva, autonoma dimensione di natura e di legge naturale[5]. Ora, guadagnare i tratti costitutivi della libertà dall'interno di una riflessione sull'uomo, così come effettualmente è dato (cioè in Cristo), impone considerarla nel nesso con gli altri fattori che *formano il tessuto fondamentale dell'esistenza*[6]. Da qui l'intreccio proposto dal Guardini, tra libertà, grazia e destino.

Partendo da questa prima ragione antropologica si indovina anche la seconda ragione che sembra avvalorare ulteriormente la bontà della scelta di analizzare la libertà in connessione con la grazia e il destino. Essa è di natura metodologica. Romano Guardini, nell'«avvertenza iniziale» alla sua celebre opera, sottolineava come la comprensione della fede nell'epoca moderna sia segnata dalla scissura occorsa nel tardo medioevo tra la filosofia e la teologia, ossia dalla perdita del «tutto» che solo consente all'esistenza cristiana di essere compresa nella sua interezza. La scissione nata, tra l'altro, dalla giusta preoccupazione di salvare la gratuità della grazia, ha implicato la perdita dell'idea di natura come creazione e quindi l'«unità» del «prestabilito disegno» del Padre[7]. La conseguenza non è stata di poco conto se il nostro

---

drammatica, Milano 1980, vol. I, dove l'autore rende conto largamente della sua proposta di uso delle categorie teatrali.
[4] Cfr AA.VV., *La filosofia cristiana nei secoli XIX e XX*, Roma 1994, 2 vol.
[5] *Gaudium et spes* 36.
[6] Cfr R. Guardini, *Libertà...*, op. cit. 193.
[7] Ibid. 7-11.

autore ha potuto affermare che *"il credente non sta più con la sua fede nella realtà del mondo, né ritrova la realtà del mondo nella sua fede"* [8]. Anche perché *"la ricchezza della rivelazione è inesauribile, ma essa deve essere interrogata e gli interrogativi muovono dalla realtà del mondo. Incalcolabili sono del pari le possibilità di azione raccolte nella figura e nella forza del Cristo, ma esse devono venir scoperte e ciò si compie quando la vita reale giunge a Cristo"*[9].

La presente riflessione sulla libertà, dunque, vorrebbe prendere le mosse, oltre che dalla natura drammatica dell'antropologia, dal principio del "pensare al tutto partendo dal tutto". Senza estrinsecismi tra filosofia e teologia, tra natura e grazia, tra *ratio* e *fides*, si vorrebbe adottare, metodologicamente, la scelta di cogliere la realtà dell'uomo nella sua esistenza, ove si rivela anche la sua essenza[10].

In questo orizzonte integrale, per il legame ontologico dell'uomo con la persona di Cristo, la libertà con tutta la sua autonomia è posta e sostenuta dalla *grazia*. Nell'economia di grazia e libertà si compie il *destino* dell'uomo[11]. Il Destino, per cui il cuore umano è fatto, viene così sperimentato come buono nel tempo e capace di aprire gli spazi della vita definitiva (eterna) in Dio. Una visione radicalmente diversa dalla concezione pagana del *fatum*, la cui tragica necessità finiva per minare la libertà.

Si procederà in due tempi: anzitutto, partendo dal basso, si farà emergere l'intreccio fra libertà, realtà ed intuizione del destino; in secondo luogo si cercherà di decifrare il destino dell'umana libertà nell'orizzonte della grazia, cioè di Gesù Cristo.

---

[8] Ibid. 8.

[9] Ibid. 9.

[10] Questi due aspetti (drammaticità e principio di totalità) sono, secondo Heidegger, già propri della metafisica come tale: *"Da qui si ricava il precetto: ogni questione metafisica deve essere posta nella sua totalità e, sempre dalla posizione essenziale di quell'esistente che muove la questione"*: M. Heidegger, *Che cosa è la metafisica*. A cura di A.Carlini, Firenze 1985¹, 4.

[11] Anche se la categoria di destino (*Schicksal*) è sviluppata da Guardini in chiave antropologica prima (*Libertà...*, op. cit., 193-241) e teologica poi (cit. 241-322) in sé e per sé – e in ogni caso nella presnte trattazione che si ispira solo rapsodicamente all'opera guardiniana, essa mantiene un obiettivo riferimento al tema ontologico nel senso dell'essere come *Geschick* da cui *Geschehen, Geschichte*: proprio degli *Holzwege*. Si veda la precisa definizione che ne dà Pietro Chiodi nella traduzione autorizzata dagli *Holzwege*: *"In questo termine tedesco Geschick risuonano i seguenti significati: forma conveniente, struttura necessaria, destino. L'essere ha una tal Geschick – cioè all'opera si addice una tale struttura necessaria – per cui mentre si rivela, ad un tempo si nasconde, si sospende... Questo epoché fa sì che l'essere si riveli per epoche. L'epocalità costituisce la storicità originaria e costitutiva – il destino – dell'essere. L'essere geschichlich dell'essere è il il fondamento e l'origine del suo essere geschichtlich, cioè storico*: M. Heidegger, *Sentieri interrotti*. A cura di P. Chiodi, Firenze, 1986², VI.

I. LIBERTÀ, REALTÀ E INTUIZIONE DEL DESTINO

1. Nella cultura contemporanea il tema della libertà occupa un posto del tutto privilegiato, ma, per certi aspetti, questa centralità assume i tratti di un'invadenza ipertrofica, che tende ad alterare la libertà giungendo alla sua negazione[12].

Se è vero che essa oggi assume la stessa decisività che la ragione aveva al tempo dei lumi, è anche onesto rilevare come manifesti sintomi di crisi non trascurabili. L'enfasi sulla libertà, posta dai contemporanei, ha portato a sottolinearne solo aspetti parziali che ora la costringono ad una sorta di vertiginosa autosospensione.

La situazione della libertà appare così paradossale: da una parte è facile cogliere, nel vissuto, come la libertà venga affermata in modo semplicemente assoluto, come abbattimento di ogni limitazione. Ogni barriera posta alla libertà, ogni dipendenza di qualsiasi natura è sentita dal soggetto umano come insostenibile e degna di riprovazione. Questo è particolarmente documentabile nel processo formativo: la stessa idea di «educazione» è considerata spesso illiberale per se stessa. L'educatore (e i genitori), già nel comunicare un certo valore, sperimentano uno scetticismo che finisce per caratterizzare la loro stessa impresa[13].

Dall'altra parte lo stesso soggetto, che così insistentemente rifiuta ogni legame, si trova a non sapere cosa fare di quella libertà così strenuamente difesa. La paura di perderla si manifesta paradossalmente come paura ad esercitarla. La libertà diviene incapace di rischio – inteso in senso oggettivo come lo sporgersi consapevole dell'io verso il reale – e genera così una sorta di paralisi interna all'io.

In che cosa identificare la causa di questa *impasse* mortale per la libertà? In sintesi estrema potremmo affermare che la crisi attraverso cui la libertà sta passando dipende dalla sua pretesa di mantenersi priva di oggetto. Ciò non solo nel senso del "non volere radicale" di Schopenhauer[14], teso ad evitare quella che sarebbe un'illusoria libertà di scelta equivalente, di fatto, alla schiavitù delle determinazioni del mondo apparente, ma anche nel senso di non volersi legare al particolare come condizione per preservarsi indefinitamente disponibili al tutto. Il riferimento in proposito è agli influssi delle filosofie e religioni orientali (fra tutte il Buddismo)[15]. Potremmo, in altro

---

[12] Sintetiche osservazioni sulla parabola della libertà e sulla libertà negata a partire dalla modernità in: P. Gilbert, *Libertà e impegno*, La Civiltà Cattolica 3505 (1996) 147, 17-20.

[13] Profonde osservazioni in proposito già in R. Guardini, *Grundlegung der Bildungslehre*, in *Vom stilleren Leben, Welt und Erziehung* 16, Würzburg 1956.

[14] Cfr A. Schopenhauer, *Il mondo come volontà e rappresentazione*, Bari 1928, 383.

[15] Per inciso giova ricordare il peso che esse ebbero sullo stesso Schopenhauer. Esso, dovuto all'orientalista Majer conosciuto nell'ambiente di Göthe, è evidente fin dalla prima

modo, dire che la libertà langue in una crisi di astrattezza. Ci troviamo in una cultura che ha reso astratta la libertà, ossia l'ha privata della sua relazione costituiva con la realtà. La libertà, intesa secondo i canoni moderni come emblema dell'io, si presenta come inceppata nel suo incontro con il reale. Così l'uomo smarrisce la verità già nel suo livello elementare, quello definito dal sempre valido principio classico come dell'*adaequatio intellectus et rei*. Dove la *res* è ciò che il soggetto spirituale innanzitutto incontra e che sola ha la capacità di mettere in moto l'io mediante la sua provocazione.

Ci sovviene a questo proposito ancora una lezione interessante dell'autore di *Libertà, grazia, destino*. Romano Guardini, infatti, ha sempre descritto l'esistenza come «vivente concreto», ossia come realtà che per essere tale va colta nelle sue opposizioni costitutive, non risolvibili in sintesi[16]. Così potremmo dire che la libertà, compresa come costitutivo dell'esistenza del concreto vivente, è tale solo nella sua polarità con la realtà. La libertà «concreta» è dunque messa in moto dall'impatto con il reale.

È a partire dal reale che è rintracciabile nel soggetto spirituale il destarsi della esperienza elementare della libertà. Definiamo qui il reale – ad un tempo mondo[17] e storia[18] – come quella trama spazio-temporale in cui l'uomo si imbatte – come individuo e persona perciò per se stesso ed in costitutiva relazione con le altre persone e con le cose – con avvenimenti, situazioni e circostanze inevitabili ed evitabili[19].

2. Nel rapporto con la realtà la libertà dell'uomo rivela una natura complessa, articolata in tre fattori che ora conviene esaminare più da vicino.

a) Il primo aspetto della libertà, che emerge dall'impatto con il reale, può trovare una più valida spiegazione nella prospettiva di quel realismo

---

edizione de: *Il mondo come volontà e rappresentazione* (1818). Importanti notazioni di metodo sul nostro problema sono indirettamente ricavabili da Congregazione Dottrina della Fede, *Orationis formas* (15.X.1989), nn. 1-3.

[16] Ci riferiamo al celebre *Der Gegensatz-Versuche zu einer Philosophie des Lebendig-Konkreten*, Mainz 1925.

[17] R. Guardini, *Mondo e persona*, in *Scritti filosofici*, Milano 1964, vol II.

[18] R. Guardini, *Libertà...*, op. cit. 116-120 e 154. Meritano di essere qui riprese due affermazioni: "*Il mondo come natura è ordinato al mondo come storia*" (117). "*Perciò in definitiva il mondo non porta il carattere di* natura, *ma quello di* storia. *Entro il mondo v'è natura... ma nella sua totalità non può essere pensato mediante il concetto di natura*"(154).

[19] In un certo senso "reale" è qui inteso come è il mondo del *Dasein* di Heidegger. Il *Dasein* è sempre un *essere – nel – mondo* dove però *l'essere – nel – mondo* cui in ogni suo atto il *Dasein* si rapporta quando trascende l'esistente onticamente inteso verso la totalità dell'essente (*das Ganze des Seienden*) non pregiudica per noi la questione di Dio. Puntuali osservazioni im questa direzione sono fatte da Armando Carlini in M. Heidegger, *Che cos'è la metafisica* cit, V-XI, 14-15 (n. 9), 35-40, 58-59.

cristiano che ha la sua fonte più classica in Tommaso d'Aquino. Egli, nel *"De passionibus"* un trattato della Summa Teologica che mantiene tutta la sua attualità anche in confronto con le scienze psicologiche moderne[20], descrive come primo esito del rapporto uomo-realtà la nascita di una attrattiva originaria, in un certo senso preconscia[21], che polarizza il successivo muoversi della volontà umana guidata dalla *ratio*.

L'io sta di fronte alla *res* non neutralmente, non con un'indifferenza, ma con un *amor naturalis*, ossia mosso da una *passione* che spinge e indirizza l'azione del soggetto inevitabilmente verso il compimento di sé.

"Passio est effectus agentis in patiente... ipsum appetibile dat appetitui, primo quidem, quandam coaptationem ad ipsum, quae est complacentia appetibilis; ex qua sequitur motus ad appetibile... Prima ergo immutatio appetitus ab appetibili vocatur amor, *qui nihil est aliud quam complacentia appetibilis; et ex hac complacentia sequitur motus in appetibile qui est* desiderium..."[22].

Il soggetto che si imbatte nella realtà assume da questa in qualche modo una *forma*, una intima impronta che lo rende ad essa affine (*amor*). Da qui scaturisce, conseguentemente, il *moto* (*desiderium*) verso la stessa realtà informante.

Da ciò si evince, inoltre, che tale *amor naturalis* ha un carattere ontologico, ossia costitutivo del rapporto del soggetto con il reale e non aggiunto estrinsecamente ad esso.

L'esperienza della libertà ha quindi il suo *incipit* non in una indifferenza, ma in una polarizzazione verso il compimento del soggetto. Questa può essere definita come *desiderio ontologico* che spalanca la libertà dell'uomo alla realtà in forza della amabilità stessa del reale[23]. Tale desiderio possiede il carattere di apertura alla realtà totale, anche se, a causa dell'umana natura, deve sempre determinarsi, come desiderio di questo o quell'essente.

Ora, a questo proposito, è importante osservare come la cultura attuale sottolinei ampiamente il fattore del desiderio, al contrario dell'epoca a noi precedente, concentrata sul «dovere» come principio informativo della libertà. Tuttavia essa lo fa estenuandolo, ossia non lo coglie più nella dimensione di apertura alla realtà totale, ma lo lascia in balìa di una serie indefinita di oggetti «finiti», cioè lo riduce al susseguirsi delle sue inevitabili deter-

---

[20] *De passionibus* (S. Th. I-II, qq. 22-48).

[21] Il termine è preso dal Maritain. Sempre attuali notazioni su questa questione in J. Martain, *Freudisme et psychanalyse*, in *Quatre essais sur l'esprit dans la condition charnelle*, Paris 1939. Cfr A. Scola, *L'alba della dignità umana*, Milano 1982.

[22] I-II, q.26.9.3,CO.

[23] Tale desiderio è preconscio, precede, in un certo senso, l'atto libero vero e proprio e tuttavia ne costituisce l'indispensabile sostrato. È superfluo notare che il vocabolo preconscio non intende precludere la considerazione dell'inconscio freudianamente inteso. Cfr A. Scola, *L'alba...*, op. cit. 143.152.

minazioni. In tal modo, l'*amor naturalis* disperde la sua energia e perde la capacità di riconoscere e seguire tutta intera la parabola implicata dalla libertà provocata dal reale.

Perché il desiderio, l'*amor naturalis*, viene come barattato con indefiniti desideri finiti? Il desiderio si infrange a partire da una opzione per la quale l'io non accoglie la realtà in tutta la sua provocazione. Per finire è una mancanza di *realismo* ciò che frantuma il desiderio originario.

L'opzione di cui parliamo crediamo possa, a diverso titolo, essere iscritta all'interno dell'orizzonte nichilista, ossia di quella forma di pensiero, «debole», che stenta a reperire nella realtà segni inequivocabili del suo esserci[24]. Ma se il *reale non è*, per così dire, *reale* e l'uomo non può farne esperienza, allora non esiste ultimamente verità e la libertà stessa, resa incapace di apertura alla totalità del reale rimane sospesa come una sorta di *capacitas* senza oggetto adeguato (al di là della sua inevitabile determinazione nella direzione di questo o quell'essente).

A causa di ciò, il passaggio che si impone ora alla nostra riflessione è la considerazione, per forza di cose sintetica, dell'intero percorso dell'esperienza elementare di incontro e di comprensione della realtà che l'uomo compie per vivere. E' necessario precisare che in questo contesto, esperienza non designa un modo di conoscenza tra gli altri, ma indica piuttosto l'essenza ed il processo del conoscere con la struttura dell'evidenza che le è propria[25].

La conoscenza umana, lanciata e sostenuta dalla energia della libertà, si stupisce davanti al mistero di ciò che in linguaggio tomistico chiamiamo *distinctio realis*[26]. La ragione coglie nel cuore stesso dell'essere, una differenza tra la cosa concreta e l'essere totale. Questa differenza ontologica fonda e

---

[24] Riprendo volentieri un'affermazione assai nota e geniale del compianto filosofo Augusto Del Noce: *Il nichilismo oggi corrente è il nichilismo gaio, nei due sensi, che è senza inquietudine (forse si potrebbe addirittura definirlo per la soppressione dell'*inquietum cor meum *agostiniano) e che ha il suo simbolo nell'omosessualità (si può infatti dire che intende sempre l'amore omosessualmente, anche quando mantiene il rapporto uomo-donna)*: in A. Del Noce, *Lettera a Rodolfo Quadrelli*, Inedito 1984. Importanti studi sul nichilismo in: A. Molinaro(a cura di), *Interpretazione del nichilismo*, Herder -Pontificia Università Lateranense, Roma 1986.

[25] Per la rigorosa fondazione del concetto di esperienza con le sue radici storiche (da Aristotele fino a Hegel e ad Heidegger), nonché per l'esame del suo nesso con la teologia contemporanea che, insistentemente vi fa riferimento, si veda. A. Bertuletti, *Il concetto di esperienza*, in AA.VV., *L'evidenza e la fede*, Milano 1988, 112-181.

[26] Tommaso non si è occupato *ex professo* del problema della *distinctio realis*, ma dopo lunghe discussioni oggi è fuori dubbio che sostiene la reale distinzione fra essenza e essere. L'espressione *distinctio realis* non si trova come tale in lui, che invece ha usato qualche volta il termine *compositio realis* (cfr De Ver. q.27 a.1 ad 8). Fra Tommaso e Heidegger c'è in comune l'affermazione della differenza fra essere e ente, ma le interpretazioni della differenza sono diverse sin dal primo momento. Per Tommaso è espressione della contingenza mentre Heidegger l'assolutizza chiudendola su di sé (cfr Perez de Haro, *El Misterio del ser*, Barcelona

manifesta il mistero dell'essere che sorprende incessantemente la nostra ragione perché l'essere si dà sempre e soltanto come sussistente in ogni singolo ente che, tuttavia, non lo può mai esaurire. L'ente è manifestazione dell'essere e questo è il fondamento che rimanda all'ente come a sua manifestazione[27]. Essere ed ente si offrono simultaneamente nella struttura originaria all'evidenza che possiede un carattere simbolico. Questo tipo di "linguaggio" procede senza separare l'originario dall'immediato ma designando la referenza immediata in modo da rinviare spontaneamente alla referenza seconda. Ciò dipende dalla duplice proprietà del rapporto ontologico: la *differenza* tra l'essere e l'ente e la *inseparabilità* dell'essere dall'ente. L'atto di apprensione dell'essere in cui si manifesta la struttura originaria del rapporto della coscienza alla verità e dell'evidenza che misura questo rapporto è complesso perché implica sempre due differenti modalità di intellezione: una *antipredicativa* (conoscenza virtuale dell'essere connaturale al pensiero), una *predicativa* (si esprime nel giudizio e conosce l'essere a partire dall'esistente concreto). Questa seconda ha un carattere apodittico ma solo negativo, mentre la prima ha un carattere positivo ma indeterminato. E non è possibile assorbire questa dialettica in una sintesi di carattere superiore[28].

1994, 152-162). Non sono pochi gli autori che hanno confrontato Tommaso e Heidegger sul problema della metafisica e in particolare della concezione dell'*esse*. Rimandiamo a C. Fabro, *Tomismo e pensiero moderno*, Roma 1966, 21-45.

[27] Si può parlare allora di una polarità, di una oscillazione nella quale ciascuno dei due poli (ente o essere) rimanda all'altro, in cui essere e ente si rapportano come fondamento e manifestazione: l'essere è la profondità e il fondamento degli enti, i quali sono manifestazione dell'essere; fondamento e manifestazione sono inseparabili e si richiamano a vicenda. Lo stupore è l'inizio ma anche elemento permanente di ogni pensiero filosofico vero. L'uomo infatti è l'unico ente capace di interessarsi all'essere, di cogliere la sua ricchezza e di comprendere la sua differenza ontologica con gli enti. L'uomo è aperto non solo agli enti ma all'essere che in essi si manifesta, è attraversato da una curiosità illimitata, per cui non gli bastano gli enti e neanche la somma di tutti essi. L'uomo riconosce la realtà sensibile come adeguata, come corrispondente alla sua ragione, e simultaneamente si accorge che il reale esperimentato, porta sempre con sé un punto di fuga che impedisce ogni possesso esauriente. Il dinamismo della ragione umana non si appaga con la conoscenza degli enti particolari e neanche dell'essere degli enti. Inoltre se gli enti *sono* in quanto partecipano dell'attualità dell'essere, questa attualità però non impone di per sé che l'ente abbia una determinata forma essenziale, non essendo dello stesso ordine delle essenze. Non si può inferire la necessità di una qualsiasi forma essenziale dalla ricchezza dell'atto di essere. La differenza ontologica rivela quindi un duplice paradosso contenuto nel rinviarsi reciproco tra enti e essere. Da una parte, l'essere è superiore agli enti poiché è pienezza infinita, mentre gli enti sono sempre determinati, limitati dalla loro essenza. Ma, dall'altra parte, gli enti sono superiori in quanto effettivamente sussistono, gli enti "sono" reali, mentre l'essere è \piuttosto quello che fa che gli enti siano e non è, in se stesso, una cosa che esiste. Lo esprime icasticamente l'affermazione tomana: "*Esse significat aliquid completum et simplex, sed non subsistens*" (*De Pot.* 1,1).

[28] Questa esposizione della struttura originale è dovuta a A. Bertuletti, *Il concetto di ..*, cit, 166-171.

Tuttavia è impossibile far oscillare heideggerianamente la differenza tra essere ed ente come fosse un mistero ultimo che tace su di sé. Questa differenza rinvia imperiosamente oltre se stessa, verso un'ulteriore differenza fra il mondo e l'unico fondamento sufficiente sia per l'essere degli enti che per gli enti nella loro forma concreta. È quello che la filosofia cristiana ha sempre chiamato *Ipsum esse Subsistens*: l'essere stesso rimanda verso un Mistero abissale che non ha altro fondamento che se stesso, verso una libertà ultima[29]. La differenza diventa allora il luogo della manifestazione dell'essere non come necessità ma come evento gratuito che ha il suo fondamento in una libertà infinita[30]. Può essere utile notare per inciso che il tema della

---

[29] In polemica con Heidegger scrive É. Gilson: *La trascendenza assoluta dell'essere sull'ente appare pienamente, nella metafisica dell'esse, solo nel momento in cui, teologizzando a fondo la nozione di essere, la si identifica con la nozione filosofica di Dio* (E. Gilson, *Constantes philosophiques de l'être*, Paris 1983, 206). Sul rapporto fra Dio e Essere la letteratura è sterminata, sia da prospettive per le quali Dio è l'Essere, sia da tentativi recenti che provano a ridire Dio senza assimilarlo all'Essere. All'origine di questo rinnovato interesse si trova senz'altro la critica heideggeriana alla costituzione onto-teo-logica della metafisica, con il corrispondente oblio dell'essere (cfr M. Heidegger, *Identität und Differenz*, Pfullingen 1957) e le successive repliche che rivendicano comunque la necessità di una ontologia. Gilson aveva sostenuto fermamente "*che non c'è che un Dio e questo Dio è l'essere, ecco la pietra angolare di tutta la filosofia cristiana*" (E. Gilson, *L'esprit de la philosophie médiévale*. Paris 1989², 51). Evidentemente questo passaggio dall'essere agli enti all'*Ipsum Esse* non è transitabile se non rispettando rigorosamente la legge della analogia, passando attraverso una negazione che metta bene in luce i limiti del nostro linguaggio per parlare del Mistero dell'Essere (cfr Tommaso, *Contra gentes* I,5). Balthasar è stato sempre sensibile ai limiti della nostra conoscenza naturale di Dio, ripetendo spesso gli assiomi di Agostino: *si comprehendis non est Deum* e di Anselmo: *Deus semper maior*. Nell'*Epilogo* della Trilogia respinge eventuali rimproveri di ontoteologia nei confronti della sua riflessione sull'essere e su Dio (cfr la seconda parte di *Epilog*, intitolata *Schwelle*, in particolare 40-41).

[30] E' soltanto la scoperta di questa ulteriore differenza teologica che permette di chiarire la questione dell'origine delle essenze. Aprendo la differenza ontologica alla differenza teologica, non si è più costretti a far derivare le essenze dall'essere, ma la loro origine si trova piuttosto nella Intelligenza divina che liberamente le pone in essere facendole partecipare del suo Essere sussistente. La differenza ontologica diventa il luogo della manifestazione, della gloria della metafisica, a condizione che nella sua profonda affermazione dell'essere non venga ridotta a necessità ma rimanga come evento (*Geschehen*) di assoluta libertà e perciò sempre aperta (cfr H.U. von Balthasar, *Theologik*, II, 226, 231; ID., *Epilog*, 65) . In questo senso, la differenza è un segno di creaturalità e l'essere mostra la sua condizione di manifestazione della gloria di Dio. Il tema fondamentale della metafisica resterà sempre il ripensamento continuo e stupito di questo "miracolo" dell'essere, così come si esprime nella celeberrima domanda: *Perché l'essere piuttosto che il nulla?* (Sulla ammirazione si vedano: Aristotele, *Metafisica* A, 982b. 12f; Platone, *Teeteto*, 115d; M. Heidegger, *Che cos'è la Metafisica*, op. cit.; R. Vignolo, *H. U. von Balthasar: estetica e singolarità*, Milano 1982, 168-190). Si potrebbe tracciare un panorama sintetico delle risposte filosofiche a queste domande, di cui Parmenide ed Eraclito, con i loro epigoni (anche attuali) sono i due estremi insoddisfacenti.

libertà fa qui la sua apparizione in connessione con l'ontologia. L'adeguata considerazione della struttura simbolica all'umana esperienza mostrerebbe anche come il fondamento ontologico implichi l'autocompimento della libertà stessa, la quale appare così quale dimensione propria della struttura originaria[31]. Il tema della libertà rivela allora l'intima correlazione tra ontologia e antropologia. Nel contesto della struttura simbolica dell'esperienza che implica l'antropologia in sé drammatica, riceve chiara luce la condizione esistenziale enigmatica dell'uomo (*Dasein*). Infatti, il soggetto umano esperisce se stesso come un essere in tutto e per tutto finito e contingente, ma allo stesso tempo aperto all'infinito[32].

Il fatto che l'uomo sia limitato (che è e potrebbe non essere), che la sua essenza possieda una modalità d'esistenza limitata, la quale procede dall'essere infinito e unitotale senza consumarlo, rappresenta la radice dell'interrogazione sul senso di sé e delle cose. Se l'uomo non facesse questa esperienza del limite e di questa apertura all'illimitato non si porrebbe interrogativi come «chi sono?», «da dove vengo?», «dove vado?», «da dove e verso dove tutto ciò che esiste?»[33] Da qui nasce sia il pensiero religioso che quello filosofico dell'umanità. Il senso religioso non è altro rispetto alla natura razionale dell'uomo, è, anzi, il momento in cui la ragione si inoltra nel mistero e si interroga sul senso ultimo delle cose, del destino.

Può essere suggestivo ricordare in questa circostanza che anche Romano Guardini, nel suo saggio *Fenomenologia e teoria della religione*, aveva parlato di un *carattere simbolico delle cose*, mediante il quale l'assoluto pone nella

---

[31] Lo sviluppo del tema in A. Bertuletti, *Sapere e libertà*, in AA.VV, *L'evidenza e la fede*, op. cit, 444-465

[32] Cfr le già classiche riflessioni di H. De Lubac in: H. de Lubac, *Il Mistero del soprannaturale*, Milano 1978, 161-230.

[33] Filosoficamente o precristianamente non si riesce a dare risposta adeguata al problema nella sua radice ultima: *Perché esiste il mondo se Dio non ne ha in alcun modo bisogno?*. Il vertice a cui giunge il filosofo è la struggente domanda di rivelazione proposta nel celeberrimo passaggio del *Fedone* (XXXV) di Platone (Cfr A. Scola, *Hans Urs von Balthasar: uno stile teologico*, Milano 1991, 35-36). L'oscillazione fra ente e essere rimanda verso un Mistero abissale che non ha altro fondamento che se stesso, che è una libertà ultima. Nel culmine della risalita metafisica scopriamo che l'origine ultima di tutti gli enti non è la pienezza non-sussistente e impersonale dell'essere degli enti, ma la pienezza sussistente di un Essere personale, di un Tu. Da questo punto di vista sono pertinenti le critiche che Lévinas ha indirizzato a Heidegger. Per il filosofo tedesco il mistero dell'essere si riduce a un evento impersonale, il puro c'è (*es gibt*) dell'ente, la pura donazione anonima dell'ente. Lévinas denuncia giustamente l'insufficienza di questo aspetto del pensiero heideggeriano, dove manca assolutamente l'alterità vivente della persona, assorbita dalla totalità neutra dell'*Ereignis* dell'essere come tale (cfr A. Léonard, *Pensée des hommes et foi en Jésus Christ*, Paris 1980, 292). Il Magistero della Chiesa ha definito che la ragione umana con la sua luce naturale può conoscere veramente e certamente un Dio personale (cfr. *DS* 3875).

struttura della differenza ontologica una traccia ineludibile di sé: *Tutte le cose attestano se stesse come direttamente reali ed essenziali: ma fanno subito presentire che non solo l'ultima realtà, bensì punto di passaggio, attraverso cui emerge ciò che è davvero ultimo e autentico: forme espressive che lo manifestano*[34].

Se ciò che abbiamo ora descritto brevemente indica la traiettoria del realismo, quando invece la libertà finita viene inibita dalla rinuncia metodica alla domanda ontologica fondamentale – rinuncia fatta propria dal positivismo e dallo scetticismo nichilista di carattere nietzschiano e heideggeriano – allora la dinamica del desiderio si frantuma (anche quando la libertà non fosse teoreticamente negata) nella ricerca estenuante di una soddisfazione che ha già rinunciato a seguire tutto il percorso, cui la struttura del reale comunque inesorabilmente invita.

b) Questa «crisi del desiderio» emerge chiaramente anche nel secondo fattore costitutivo della libertà: esso è comunemente denominato «libero arbitrio». L'economia globale della presente riflessione induce a non entrare nello specifico di questo aspetto del tema che implicherebbe un'analisi dell'atto di libertà nella sua relazione costitutiva col soggetto di tale atto[35]. Vorremmo invece limitarci a rilevare un fenomeno proprio della nostra epoca e, poi, a compiere qualche considerazione essenziale sul fondamento della libertà di scelta.

Non è un caso che uno dei pericoli più comuni del nostro tempo sia quello di voler far coincidere l'intera dinamica della libertà con la possibilità di scelta, mentre questa non è che un suo momento, sia pur essenziale.

Da una parte qui assistiamo all'esito, raggiunto anche da un certo filone di pensiero cattolico che ha rimosso la dimensione dell'*amor naturalis* (desiderio originario) nella dottrina della libertà, definendola come indifferenza di fronte alle diverse possibilità di scelta[36]. Dall'altra invece rileviamo, da parte di un filone molto più popolare, una riduzione della libertà a possibilità continuata di scelte, guidate ultimamente da un desiderio nel suo stato di crisi, cioè nella sua frantumazione indefinita. In entrambi i casi va poi notato che per potersi mantenere sempre disponibile verso il soddisfacimento di desideri limitati questa libertà ridotta a libertà di scelta deve, in un certo senso, rendersi indisponibile ad una scelta che implichi un legame stabile e

---

[34] R. Guardini, *Fenomenologia e teoria della religione*, in *Scritti filosofici*, Milano 1964, II, 207.

[35] R. Guardini, *Libertà...*, op. cit. 74-82.

[36] Cfr il saggio di S. Pinckaers, *Les sources de la morale chrétienne*, Fribourg 1985, 244-257.

quindi un cammino verso il compimento ultimo dell'io[37]. Così, la libertà scelta perviene ad una decurtazione, diviene una libertà del «non legame una esclusiva libertà «da».

Il realismo cristiano, così come lo abbiamo brevemente abbozzato [sopra, ci invita invece a cogliere la libertà dell'uomo rispettandone la com lessità originaria.

A questo punto ci sembra opportuno riprendere la terminologia di v Balthasar nella prospettiva della sua antropologia drammatica, per fonda all'interno della natura complessa della libertà, la dimensione della scel L'illustre teologo di Basilea, infatti, parla della libertà finita dell'uomo cor costituita in una polarità irriducibile ed inseparabile: essa è libertà come *a tomovimento* e quindi certamente capacità di scelta a partire da un cent proprio non rinunciabile ma essa è anche, nello stesso tempo, libertà con *assenso*[38]. La stessa capacità di scelta, a partire dall'autopossesso, implica momento di autoapertura e trascendimento, e ultimamente, di obbedienz La libertà di scelta, dunque, non è compresa fino in fondo se non quanc arriva ad implicare anche la necessità della decisione come adesione[39].] questo ultimo pilastro è bene infatti riconoscere una duplicità di aspett essa è riconoscimento della propria strutturale apertura nei confronti del realtà, ma anche di necessità intrinseca di adesione.

---

[37] Prova di esso è come oggi è vissuto il rapporto padre-figlio. Nella tradizione del pen ero occidentale vi è una pagina molto significativa in questo senso.È la *parabola del Figl prodigo*. I tre fattori del nesso paternità/libertà sono simultaneamente in gioco: desiderio-ori ine, scelta-compagnia nel cammino, adesione-verità del destino. Nell'esperienza della mise cordia del padre verso il figliol prodigo si vede cosa deve essere paternità e cosa deve esse figliolanza. Come dice *Efesini* 4,6: la paternità di Dio opera in tutti ed è sempre presente tutti nella libertà. Quando il figlio gli dice: «Dammi la mia parte, io vado per conto mio», padre, colui che è all'origine, dà. Quello va e sperpera, gioca la sua libertà, cioè crede che suo desiderio si attui attraverso un certo tipo di scelta: rompere i legami per prendere propria strada. Poi viene la crisi. Torna indietro. E la passione paterna al destino del figlio così grande che riaccoglie lo sciagurato che lo aveva vilipeso ed offeso; lo perdona perché n padre più potente di ogni altra cosa è il reimmettere il figlio sulla strada del destino, cic liberare la sua libertà. Si vede qui, in un certo senso, come nella paternità si possa raggiunge il vertice della tenerezza. Cfr A. Scola, *Paternità e libertà*. Prolusione al *Master in Pastora matrimoniale e politica familiare*. Fano 3 luglio 1996.

[38] Lo stesso Guardini parla acutamente di libertà come *"appartenere a se stessi nel domi io sopra la propria azione"* ma subito aggiunge che la libertà in definitiva *"si realizza solo da anti a Dio poiché l'uomo è un essere finito e un essere finito significa essere davanti a Dio"*: F Guardini, *Libertà...*, op. cit. 100.

[39] *"Il primo pilastro della libertà è chiaramente «posto» o «dato», il secondo è sia «posto» ch «imposto»; posta è la necessità («Geworfenheit») di uscire da sé per decidersi e fare buona prov nel coessere con gli altri uomini e cose, dove il modo e il grado dell' autorealizzazione restan aperti"*: H.U. von Balthasar, *Teodrammatica* II, op. cit., 204.

Si potrebbe affermare che tale tensione tra i due poli costitutivi della libertà finita – che implica l'esclusività del proprio io rispetto ad altri soggetti (individualità) e contemporaneamente il riconoscimento di infinite possibilità di altre libertà finite (personalità)[40] – è l'attestarsi antropologico della distinzione emergente dall'indagine sulla struttura ontologica del reale[41].

Proprio in questa esperienza di uscita da sé della libertà finita e quindi nell'esercizio del co-essere con altre libertà finite, l'io si accorge che nessuna delle altre libertà incontrate può colmare la sua capacità di adesione totale, poiché nulla della realtà del "mondo" può essere suo fondamento e destino.

L'assenso, allora, significa riconoscimento che l'uscita verso l'altro, segno ad un tempo di un bisogno e di una ricchezza, è l'uscita verso esseri essi pure dotati di un centro di libertà capace di autopossesso. Ed alla fine, se questa apertura all'altro come condizione della propria verità deve essere possibile, allora essa implicherà il riconoscimento di una libertà infinita, quella del Mistero, dell'Essere in dipendenza dal quale la libertà finita esiste come finita. Come un bimbo in braccio a sua madre, la libertà finita è avvolta da ogni lato dalla libertà amante dell'infinito.

Questo è il motivo per cui *"la libertà finita in quanto* autexousion, *adesione a se stessa nella libertà dell'autopossesso, non si aliena affatto ma intimamente si adempie mediante l'adesione e l'assenso a quell'Essere che si è ormai scoperto come liberamente fondante tutte le cose, come fondante in particolare la libertà finita dentro libertà infinita"*[42].

c) Con quanto detto mi sembra che si possa affermare che la libertà di scelta, se è colta in unità con la struttura integrale del desiderio ontologico che la precede, non può che concepirsi come in cammino verso un punto ultimo, un *telos*, che il pensiero classico ha chiamato Dio. Anche la teologia contemporanea quando si fa carico con rigore delle complesse vicende teoretiche del pensiero moderno, giunge alla fine ad affermare il Dio Unitrino come quell'evento in cui nell'evidenza simbolica della fede, si rivela il fondamento che contiene in sé la differenza nella perfetta eguaglianza e "spiega" così la differenza ontologica senza sottrarre alla libertà il compito della decisione. In questo senso occorre riconoscere il terzo fattore che spiega la libertà dell'uomo che è l'unico suo oggetto adeguato: il Mistero stesso del Dio Unitrino. È questo il vero motore della nostra libertà; anche il nostro desiderio senza questa prospettiva ultima rimarrebbe incompiuto e si perderebbe in se stesso. L'unico scopo adeguato alla nostra natura è l'infinito.

Riassuntivamente si può dire, ancora con Balthasar, che la libertà finita, nella sua autoesperienza, si accorge irriducibilmente di essere un «da dove»

---

[40] Ibid. 199-201.
[41] A. Scola, *Hans Urs von Balthasar...*, op. cit. 101ss.
[42] H. U. von Balthasar, *Teodrammatica* II, op. cit., 230.

(*woher*), di essere realmente donata a se stessa, mentre il suo movimento di autoapertura le fa cogliere la propria esistenza come un «verso dove» (*wohin*)[43]. La libertà finita, dunque, è compresa nella sua struttura fondamentale solo nel riconoscimento di una libertà infinita, autofondantesi in modo assoluto e perciò capace di fondare illimitate libertà finite, dotate in se stesse di autopossesso e di capacità di assenso attraverso il rapporto con il reale[44].

Siamo così ampiamente entrati nella seconda parte della nostra relazione: la dinamica stessa della libertà umana, drammaticamente polarizzata verso il suo compimento, implica il problema di un fine ultimo, di uno scopo, di un destino che si presenti al cuore dell'uomo come la meta adeguata della propria azione e della propria adesione. Tutto ciò è stato intuito, in un certo senso, nel pensiero greco, in modo particolare da Platone e Plotino. Il suo inveramento ultimo rimane, però, impedito dalla strutturale inconoscibilità del mistero a partire dal basso e dalla fragilità ambivalente che caratterizza il movimento della libertà finita. Essa sperimenta così una sorta di reduplicazione del proprio dramma a causa di una debolezza congenita per la quale tende a trattare il Mistero come una *res* fra le altre (idolatria).

Particolare attestazione di tutto questo è l'esperienza contraddittoria che l'uomo fa della propria creaturalità come irrimediabile finitezza, ossia come «essere per la morte», che sembra di fatto contraddire il desiderio che la realtà suscita nell'uomo[45]. La libertà sembra trovare nell'essere per la morte, l'insormontabile ostacolo a raggiungere il destino. L'emergere quotidiano della morte come immanente alla libertà finita si rivela in quelle che Balthasar chiama le tre polarità in cui l'uomo esperisce la propria condizione drammatica: spirito-corpo; uomo-donna ed individuo e comunità. A partire dalla prima e fondamentale polarità, spirito-corpo, l'essere umano non riesce a trovare un equilibrio tra i due poli. Essi sono in definitiva continuamente minacciati proprio dalla finitezza del soggetto la cui morte coincide con la separazione dello spirito dal corpo. La stessa relazione uomo donna rimane così irretita nel «circolo vizioso» morte-generazione, ed anche l'individuo sembra scomparire nel collettivo a causa della sua irrimediabile brevità.

Tutto ciò fa intuire come il problema di un destino buono per la libertà finita sia sperimentabile ed assicurabile solo là dove il Mistero ultimo si riveli egli stesso, mostrandosi, coinvolgendosi e dicendosi definitivamente. Se la dinamica dell'incontro tra la libertà finita dell'uomo e la realtà porta ad intu-

---

[43] Ibid. 199ss.

[44] Fin dal rapporto primordiale con il tu destante la propria autocoscienza, il sorriso della madre per il bambino in cui l'essere stesso si rivela bello, buono, vero e uno, il soggetto umano è spalancato verso una libertà infinita che sola può rendere ragione dell'enigma dell'uomo: cfr H.U. von Balthasar, *Uno sguardo d'insieme...*, op. cit., 41.

[45] Al riguardo cfr H.U. von Balthasar, *Teodrammatica IV*, Milano 1986, 109ss.

ire il fondamento ed il destino ultimo in un mistero libero autofondantesi, il nome di tale destino e il suo volgersi verso la libertà umana è sperimentabile solo per grazia, per la gratuità di un evento che sorge nella storia, assolutamente indeducibile e singolare. In Gesù Cristo si dà nella storia una presenza che solleva la "pretesa" di portare il Nome definitivo di questo mistero che sta all'origine delle cose. In Gesù Cristo incontriamo inoltre un soggetto pienamente umano e finalmente consapevole del proprio «da dove» e «verso dove» e che perciò si rivela come Colui che compie il destino dell'uomo.

Si tratterà ora di vedere quale dottrina cristiana in particolare illumini il mistero dell'uomo verso il suo destino: in quale senso Gesù Cristo stesso, via verità e vita, dia volto e assicuri il destino per il quale l'uomo percepisce di essere fatto e come, partendo da questo avvenimento di Cristo, sia possibile vedere la stessa libertà umana, scoprendola da sempre progettata all'interno di quel disegno di grazia che può assicurarne il compimento.

II. LA LIBERTÀ NELLA GRAZIA: IL DESTINO DI DIVENTARE FIGLI NEL FIGLIO

Se ora noi ci poniamo esplicitamente all'interno della rivelazione ci accorgiamo che il darsi grazioso di Dio all'uomo accade esattamente affinché quest'ultimo raggiunga la sua pienezza e venga introdotto nella vita stessa di Dio[46]. Nell'avvenimento singolare di Cristo noi contempliamo il realizzarsi totale ed infallibile della reciprocità tra Dio e l'uomo e l'attuarsi così del disegno originario di Dio sulla creazione. In Cristo l'uomo riconosce la possibilità di raggiungere il compimento di sé: essere introdotto nell'esperienza della figliolanza divina (cfr Ef 1, 5-11).

In tal senso il centro della riflessione diviene obiettivamente Gesù Cristo stesso, il figlio di Dio incarnato, morto e risorto *propter nos* nel quale si compie definitivamente la reciprocità tra libertà finita ed infinita. In questa visione Gesù Cristo, nella sua singolarità[47], è visto come l'attuarsi infallibile del disegno del Padre. In modo particolare nel mistero pasquale si compie definitivamente l'Alleanza tra Dio e l'uomo (patto di reciprocità tra la lib-

---

[46] Cfr *Dei verbum* 4. Sarebbe di grande interesse fornire le basi teoretiche e metodologiche capaci di mostrare come questo passaggio debba compiersi superando definitivamente ogni estrinsecismo tra ragione e fede, nella convinzione che "fede e ragione si generano insieme nel farsi critico della fede". E' il risultato della ricerca teologica di Giuseppe Colombo (cfr G. Colombo, *La ragione teologica*, Milano 1985) così come è sintetizzato dal Bertuletti (cfr A. Bertuletti, *La "ragione teoligica" di Giuseppe Colombo. Il significato storico-teoretico di una proposta teologica*, in Teologia XXI (1996) 1, 18-36).

[47] Per la questione della singolarità di Gesù Cristo cfr A. Scola, *Questioni di antropologia teologica*, Milano 1996, 9ss.

ertà finita ed infinita) che ha avuto la sua preistoria nella elezione veterotestamentaria di Israele ad essere l'alleato di Dio.

Nella morte e risurrezione di Cristo si compie il disegno di salvezza di Dio, indipendentemente dalla risposta dei singoli uomini[48]. Cristo vive la sua missione e la compie *pro nobis*[49] senza il previo consenso delle libertà finite. «*Quando eravamo ancora peccatori Cristo morì per noi*» (cfr *Rm* 5, 6-10).

Nel mistero pasquale contempliamo come il figlio di Dio fatto carne, assumendo una natura umana, in tutto simile alla nostra, si fa carico per obbedienza al Padre di tutti i peccati degli uomini, attuando così ciò che i padri hanno felicemente chiamato un *admirabile commercium*.

Il suo eterno, filiale ed eucaristico «sì» al mistero della sua generazione dal Padre, iscritto, mediante la Sua missione, nel tempo, può farsi carico di tutto il «no» pronunciato, antieucaristicamente, dalla libertà finita che perverte, nel peccato, la sua struttura originaria definita da un «da dove» e «verso dove» in un «da sé» e «verso sé».

Avviene così uno scambio che riscatta la libertà finita, la strappa dalla sua autochiusura, e mediante il dono dello Spirito Santo, che il Cristo risorto dona alla chiesa, la introduce nella vita trinitaria. In tal modo la libertà finita di ogni singolo uomo è chiamata a ratificare personalmente l'evento di grazia che Cristo realizza infallibilmente per tutti.

La grazia di Dio, che coincide essenzialmente con la persona di Gesù Cristo, attua il piano universale di salvezza. Ad ogni uomo in Cristo è data oggettivamente e gratuitamente la possibilità di raggiungere il proprio destino. In Cristo Dio ha realizzato il suo progetto di avere figli nell'unico figlio. Lo Spirito Santo è quel dono che scaturisce dal mistero pasquale e che abilita la libertà finita ad aderire a ciò che in Cristo è stato realizzato una volta per tutte. Il mistero tremendo della libertà finita consiste nella possibilità di rifiutare la grazia che pure la avvolge da ogni parte e di "mancare" così il suo proprio destino[50].

Da quanto abbiamo osservato è ora possibile trarre qualche conclusione per il nostro tema.

L'impostazione proposta porta a considerare la libertà finita, nella sua dinamica integrale, non come una realtà chiusa e compiuta in se stessa, a cui si aggiungerebbe, come un *superadditum*, la grazia. In realtà la struttura stessa della libertà finita è costitutivamente aperta alla grazia, che è Cristo stes-

---

[48] Il ritorno alla "figura" storica di Gesù di Nazaret è oggi di viva attualità nella letteratura teologica: cfr E.P. Sanders, *Gesù la verità storica*, Milano 1993; R. Penna, *I ritratti originali di Gesù il Cristo*, Roma 1996.

[49] Cfr M. Hengel, *Crocifissione ed espiazione*, Brescia 1988, 178ss.

[50] In questo senso è d'interesse S. Ubbiali, *Il peccato originale. L'esistenza dell'uomo e l'aporia del male*, in AA.VV., *Questioni sul peccato originale*, Padova 1996, 9-60.

so, in quanto essa stessa è stata pensata in vista di Cristo morto e risorto. Allora, guardando all'unità del piano salvifico in Cristo, la stessa libertà creaturale sembra potersi considerare in un certo senso come una dimensione (ingrediente) del Soprannaturale, pur restando permanentemente dotata di una sua autonomia.

Tutto ciò ci costringe ulteriormente a riflettere sul fatto che unico è l'ordine ed il fine di tutta la creazione[51]. Si supera così, cristocentricamente[52], ogni considerazione della realtà creata all'interno di una antropologia del duplice fine: *"Dio ha realizzato quella prima trasmissione dell'essere mediante cui vennero creati esseri finiti, coscienti e liberi, nell'intenzione di introdurli, mediante un secondo atto di libertà, nei suoi misteri di vita divina (elevazione) e di compiere liberamente così la promessa nascosta nell'atto in-finito dell'essere. Non è necessario distinguere quanto al tempo questo atto secondo dal primo, poiché la causa finale alberga in se stessa, come causa prima ed universale, tutte le articolazioni della causa efficiente (del divenire del mondo e dell'uomo)"*[53].

Cristo, che redimendo l'uomo lo abilita al suo destino, appare anche come colui nel quale la creazione stessa è fatta ed ha la sua consistenza: *la creazione è dunque «in Cristo»*[54] ed avviene nella sua originaria mediazione.

Inoltre, parlare di creazione in Cristo e non solo nel *Logos*, vuol dire partire dalla missione onnicomprensiva di Gesù di Nazareth, che, coincidendo perfettamente ed imprepensabilmente con la sua persona, si rivela essere preesistente alla creazione stessa. Tale nozione, che non deve tanto far pensare ad una vita prenatale di Gesù quanto ad una implicazione della sua missione universalmente valida, è contemplata al fine di cogliere la dimensione cristologica dell'intera creazione. Essa è dunque, fin dal principio, l'attuarsi dell'alleanza tra Dio e l'uomo in Cristo.

Arriviamo così infine a parlare di *creazione dalla Trinità*[55], cui fa esplicito riferimento Bonaventura e, in parte, anche Tommaso. Solo un Dio Trinitario può essere creatore di libertà finite distinte ontologicamente da sé, ove esse non risultano essere né create per una necessità da parte del soggetto divino (per avere qualcuno da amare o per sondare le sue possibilità), essendo questi già in se stesso amore nella vicendevole dedizioni delle ipostasi, e nemmeno il risultato di una caduta primordiale di uscita dal divino.

---

[51] Cfr A. Scola, *Questioni...*, op. cit. 135ss.
[52] Sulla questioni del cristocentrismo si veda: G. Moioli, *Cristologia. Proposta sistematica*, Milano 1978, 43-56.
[53] H. U. von Balthasar, *TeoDrammatica* II, op. cit., 376.
[54] Cfr A. Scola, *Hans Urs von Balthasar...*, op. cit. 144.
[55] Cfr. G. Marengo, *Trinità e creazione*, Roma 1990.

La creazione di libertà finite risulta invece essere la creazione di una immagine del Dio trinitario, un dono che la Santissima Trinità fa di sé. La differenza e la relazione tra la libertà finita ed infinita è dunque immagine della differenza santa ed infinita, presente nel mistero stesso di Dio, tra l'Ipostasi paterna ed il Figlio, tenuta aperta e sigillata dalla fecondità dello Spirito Santo, che da entrambi procede.

Nel mistero di grazia della incarnazione, della morte e risurrezione di Gesù di Nazareth accade dunque che colui che è archetipo (*Urbild*) e tel-etipo della libertà creata si unisce all'immagine derivata (*Abbild*), la purifica e la introduce negli infiniti spazi di libertà propri del mistero santo di Dio.

In conclusione, se la dinamica intera della libertà umana, mediante l'impatto con la realtà e l'attrattiva dell'*amor naturalis* che ne risulta, rivela che l'uomo è posto costitutivamente nella ricerca del proprio compimento, allora possiamo affermare che l'uomo è veramente libero quando sa affermare la propria libertà non come autonomia assoluta, ma quando arriva a concepirla come capacità di adesione al Dio Unitrino.

In tal senso l'uomo incontra la suprema possibilità di essere libero, cioè di raggiungere il proprio destino, solo quando incontra Cristo, colui che essendo il Figlio eterno di Dio nella carne, offrendosi una volta per sempre, ci ha dato la possibilità di essere noi pure figli in lui.

L'atteggiamento filiale di obbedienza nei confronti di Dio compie così, senza superarle, le polarità della libertà finita. Nella *sequela Christi*[56], l'uomo sperimenta che la morte è stata vinta e la sua esistenza, continuamente perdonata, è già risorta, ponendo in definitiva armonia la tensione spirito-corpo. Il rapporto uomo-donna, nella nuzialità fondata sul sacramento, si presenta come strada in cui si è introdotti alla relazione individuo-comunità, di cui la *communio* ecclesiale rappresenta la forma matura.

Libero è dunque, ultimamente, colui che è figlio, che riconosce la paternità di Dio stesso su di sé come grazia. Qui trovano il loro senso finale tutte le dinamiche proprie della libertà finita. La Chiesa, che nasce dal fianco aperto di Cristo e che vive dello Spirito di libertà che il suo Signore ha in comune con il Padre, si rivela così il luogo della libertà e della liberazione per ogni uomo perché luogo della figliolanza.

La più grande carità di cui l'uomo di oggi, come quello di ieri, ha bisogno, è quella di incontrare Cristo. Ciò accade concretamente mediante l'inserimento nella *communio ecclesiale*[57], dove si può sperimentare che, per grazia, la libertà è accompagnata al suo vero destino dove, in una parola, si scopre di non essere più schiavi, ma figli (cfr *Gal* 4, 7).

---

[56] Cfr. A. Scola, *Questioni...*, op. cit. 71-102.
[57] Cfr. A. Scola, *Hans Urs von Balthasar...*, op. cit. 116.

JOSEF SEIFERT
International Academy of Philosophy
in the Principality Liechtenstein

TO BE A PERSON – TO BE FREE

It seems to be indispensable to achieve four things in order to bring to evidence that "to be a person is to be free": 1) A number of important metaphysical and epistemological insights need to be gained and argued for in order to understand that the real existence of freedom in the ultimate, metaphysical sense is possible in itself (non-contradictory) and absolutely inseparable from the personhood of *any* person, whether human or divine; 2) The moral drama of freedom and the fact that free choice extends to the final goals of free acts needs to be explained; 3) The bearers and spheres of freedom in the subject, and their unity, need to be elucidated in order to overcome a false separation between external moral actions which realize states of affairs in the world and fundamental moral attitudes. Freedom must also not be conceived too narrowly so as to situate it in external actions only and not in the core of the being and attitudes of the human person; and 4) The highest act of human freedom, in which also the full being and meaning of what it means to be a person is actualized, needs to be shown not to consist in a creation, and not even in volitional actions, but in a *co-operative* dimension of freedom.

The reader alone can be judge whether I will succeed in the following to accomplish these four difficult tasks, at least in form of an outline.

I. TOWARDS A METAPHYSICS AND EPISTEMOLOGY OF FREEDOM

1. FREEDOM IN THE STRONG METAPHYSICAL SENSE IS ABSOLUTELY INSEPARABLE FROM PERSONHOOD – HUMAN FREEDOM CAN BE KNOWN TO EXIST WITH INDUBITABLE CERTITUDE

The title of this paper suggests at least this: that to be a person and to be free are inseparable. Freedom belongs so essentially to personhood that no being can be called a person if he or she is determined from without, by physical forces, other persons, or even by his or her own nature – rather than by the free center of the person, by the person himself. Certainly, the *actual ability to use freedom* is not inseparable from personhood and not given to embryos and new-born babies, unconscious or comatose patients, and is absent in all human beings during sleep and in certain types of grave mental retardation. But to be a person entails the fundamental metaphysical *faculty*, a *capacity in principle,* to perform free acts[1]. *As faculty,* freedom resides on the level of the substantial being of the person or, more precisely, is inseparable from the substantial spiritual being of the person, but this faculty of freedom is ordained to be exercised in conscious actualization in which alone we encounter and experience it, and from whence alone we gain the metaphysical insight into its bearer, the person, and the existence of the free *power* and free *potentialities* which must exist prior to the actualizations of free acts. Freedom is one of the arch-data which cannot be defined in terms of something else or reduced to something besides itself. It includes, however, many dimensions and traits which can be analyzed and some of which we will discuss: It is not only a *freedom from* determining causes, an "I can but I do not need," as Karol Wojtyła describes it, but also the power of *self-determination* that makes free acts utterly different from chance-events (which, if they existed, would also not be determined from without)[2]. Freedom also involves a special possession of one's being, which

---

[1] The notion of *faculties (powers)* was very well developed by the scholastic philosophers, especially by Saint Thomas Aquinas. See also John Crosby, "Evolutionism and the Ontology of the Human Person", *Review of Politics,* 38 (April, 1976), S. 208-243. On the notion of the substantial being of the person cf. also my *Essere e persona. Verso una fondazione fenomenologica di una metafisica classica e personalistica.* (Milano: Vita e Pensiero, 1989), ch. 8-9.

[2] See the interesting discussion of many meanings of "chance" in Aristotle's *Physics.* In the discussion of Professor Peter van Inwagen's paper (who held that if determinism is false "then one's acts are a result of chance," as he puts it in his Abstract), Dr. Marek Piechowiak argued rightly that the alternative between either determinism or human acts being the result of chance, and the ensuing logical argument that from the falsity of determinism it

is only possible in and through the free agent's capacity of self-governance and self-determination. Also the person's being governed and determined by himself corresponds to the free determining and governing oneself. Freedom also entails the power to engender from oneself acts of responding and taking stances towards objects and other persons, of fulfilling oughts and obligations, as well as the capacity of serving goods and other persons[3], and of self-donation[4], and in this consideration it is a *freedom for*. Freedom is also intimately connected with the life of the intellect and involves the capacity of opening one's mind in knowledge to receive information, of loving the truth, of cooperating freely with the process of knowledge, and of consenting freely to that which is known[5], as well as the capacity of accepting gifts. Freedom includes likewise the power to start a causal chain of events and to initiate activities and actions which lead to the realization of states of affairs. Moreover, free agents alone can relate to moral oughts and realize moral values.

For all of these manifestations of freedom to be actually what they present themselves to be in our experience and knowledge of freedom, freedom in the metaphysical sense must exist. Any being the content of all of whose acts would be determined by fate, or by any conceivable cause outside the given free person himself, even by God, would be deprived of freedom and therefore also lack personhood. We would have before us a complicated marionette or at best an animal, but not a person[6]. To be a person,

---

would follow that all acts are the product of chance, is not only logically incorrect (because there are other possibilities), but it is also false precisely because free *self-determination* differs totally from chance in the sense of uncaused events.

[3] See Professor William Desmond's paper "Freedom Beyond Autonomy" in the Proceedings of this Congress.

[4] On the concept of self-donation see especially Karol Wojtyła, Karol Wojtyła, *Liebe und Verantwortung* (München: Kösel-Verlag, 1979); and Dietrich von Hildebrand, *Das Wesen der Liebe*; *Dietrich von Hildebrand. Gesammelte Werke* III (Regensburg, 1971), ch. 1-7, 9, 11. See also the papers of Rev. Andrzej Szostek and Professor Damian Fedoryka read at this Congress and included in the Proceedings.

[5] I distinguished in Josef Seifert, *Erkenntnis objektiver Wahrheit. Die Transzendenz des Menschen in der Erkenntnis* (Salzburg: A. Pustet, ²1976), I, ch. 3, a conviction and assent which are the inevitable consequence of knowledge and an assent which is a free act and which plays a great role in Tadeusz Styczeń's ethics. See on this also the idea of *real assent* in John Henry Cardinal Newman's *The Grammar of Assent* as well as the notion of *"freie Anerkennung"* in Rev. Professor Tadeusz Styczeń's paper delivered during this Congress.

[6] To P. Inwagen's objection that also determined persons would deserve respect and belong to "the kingdom of ends," I would reply a) that the other essential attributes of a person's being (for example intellect) would also become impossible without freedom because they are held together objectively with freedom in the necessary essence of personhood, and b) that if, *per impossibile*, human beings would retain their intellect, feelings, etc.,

whether finite or infinite, whether human, angelic, or divine, necessarily entails freedom. To say this is not a mere matter of definition but the formulation of a synthetic a priori truth founded ontologically, namely on the essence of personhood which possesses a necessary link to freedom[7]. Of course, *human* freedom does not *have to exist in actu* all the time nor does it exclude many dependencies on conditions, situations, etc. It does not exclude either that certain external and irrational moments of action (for example the question at which exact time we decide to go to town, etc.) may be due to unconscious causes such as commands given to a person under hypnosis. But the elementary fact of freedom remains intact and is presupposed in all dependencies of our will on other conditions and partial causes, and is clearly given to our experience and knowledge. That person and freedom are inseparable is one of those innumerable "eternal truths" intended by Augustine's term *"rationes aeternae"*[8]. A being who would not be free, and who could not, at least potentially, use his freedom, could not possibly be a person, for in a being deprived of freedom also the other essential marks of personhood would collapse. Freedom in the strong metaphysical sense of real and ultimate freedom, and not only some subjective experience of freedom, belongs even to the very core of the essence of personhood[9].

To say this implies one of the crucial discoveries of metaphysics: *freedom (as well as personhood) is a pure perfection* and thus not an essentially limited "categorial" attribute[10] valid only for the world or for human persons. In other words, the 'transcendental' character of an attribute can also, but not

---

without freedom, while they would still deserve respect, they would not be persons because personhood is inseparable from the vocation to free acts and love which constitute the *raison d'être* of personhood and without which the perfection, vocation and drama of being a person and many other attributes of the person remain impossible.

[7] See on this epistemology Adolf Reinach, "Über Phänomenologie", in: Adolf Reinach, *Sämtliche Werke*, Bd. I, *ebd.*, S. 531-550; Max Scheler, *Der Formalismus in der Ethik und die materiale Wertethik*, 5. Aufl. (Bern und München: Francke, 1966). Dietrich von Hildebrand, *What is Philosophy?*, 3rd edn, with a New Introductory Essay by Josef Seifert (London: Routledge, 1991); Josef Seifert, *Erkenntnis objektiver Wahrheit. Die Transzendenz des Menschen in der Erkenntnis* (Salzburg: A. Pustet, 2nd edition, 1976); Fritz Wenisch, *Die Philosophie und ihre Methode* (Salzburg: A. Pustet, 1976)

[8] For example, in his *De libero arbitrio,* II, or in his famous Quaestio "De Ideis" (contained in the *83 Questions on Diverse Subjects*).

[9] See on this notion of the "core of the essence" some works by Roman Ingarden, Jean Hering and others on "Essences" as well as my *Sein und Wesen* (Heidelberg: Universitätsverlag C. Winter, 1996), ch. 1, where I discuss at length these works as well as the issue of essence.

[10] I use this common term although also some so-called "categories," for example substance, are likewise "pure perfections" and therefore this use of "categorial" in contradistinction to "transcendental" is misleading.

only, be constituted by the fact that no entity can be without it, as it is the case with the traditional so-called 'transcendentals' (being, essence, something, unity, truth, goodness, beauty). These are absolutely universal properties of finite and infinite beings, and of entities of all categories and ontological regions, precisely in virtue of being properties which belong analogously to *everything that is*. For this reason, these "transcendentals" in the traditional sense, i.e., those properties which are coextensive with being, are the objects of extremely abstract concepts in which one prescinds from all the differences between stones, frogs, human persons, angels, works of art, God – all of which possess these "transcendental properties." Consequently, the content of these transcendental properties of being (if one does not consider them in view of their higher, archetypal, or absolute embodiment, but *in their transcendental character coextensive with being*), is very minute – in order to remain applicable to stones, cows, persons, and God. Of course, this abstractness of the transcendental notions of 'being,' 'unity,' 'truth,' etc. its never real *in its abstractness* as correlate to the logical content of the transcendental concepts. Rather, these transcendental properties can only be realized in concrete entities and on different levels of being but when we consider them in the specific form of *moral goodness,* etc., we *no longer consider them in their transcendental character that is coextensive with being.*

But what is most significant about these transcendental properties is *not the fact that they are coextensive with being* but *rather the fact that they are free from the limitations and finitudes that belong to certain religions of being only.* What accounts for the really significant 'transcendental' character of an attribute is the fact that is a *"pure perfection"* (either because of its absolutely universal character of the traditional transcendentals *or for other reasons*). This all-decisive character of "pure perfections" is the only point of view which Duns Scotus' revolutionary doctrine of the transcendentals accepts as the criterion for transcendentality, which gives rise to a new concept of "transcendentality" which identifies at the same time the *chief reason for the significance of the traditional "transcendentals":* namely, that they are free from the inherent ontological and axiological *limits* of regional, *purely* categorial or limited attributes of being.

This all-decisive character of the traditional transcendentals, and of other attributes, as pure perfections can be characterized in the following way: a) that it is absolutely better to possess them than not to possess them, for whatever the reason[11]; b) that all these attributes (pure perfections), in logi-

---

[11] On this whole topic of the pure perfections and for the reasons, discovered by Scotus, why this addition is necessary, cf. Wolter, Allan, *The Transcendentals and their Function in the Metaphysics of Duns Scotus* (St. Bonaventure, New York: Franciscan Institute Publications, 1946). Cf. also my *Essere e persona,* cit.

cal consequence of their first and evident characteristic, must be compatible with each other (for otherwise a contradiction would follow: Pure perfection A, for example being, would be both absolutely better to possess, because it is a pure perfection, and absolutely better not to possess, because it would be incompatible with the possession of pure perfection B, for example wisdom); and that c) they, and only they, admit of absolute infinity, nay, are even only themselves when they are infinite (each finite form and limit taking away from the fullness of what formally constitutes them, from their *ratio formalis*). For our purposes here we may prescind from other marks of the pure perfections[12].

In all of this the pure perfections which Anselm of Canterbury formulated for the first time quite clearly[13] but which the Presocratic Xenophanes had for the first time identified as a crucial topic for metaphysics and philosophy of God, differ from the "mixed perfections" or the *essentially limited beings and natures*. These (such as being gold or having any other specific character of animals, plants or creatures) are only good from a certain point of view, they are often incompatible with each other, and they do not admit of absolute infinity.

Precisely for this reason only the pure perfections, and *all of them*, are truly transcendental, i.e. they transcend all limits of the single spheres and limiting categories of being, *in virtue of their character as pure perfections*. Now, while *all transcendentals in the traditional sense are also pure perfections*, because their being in all spheres of being *guarantees* their character as pure perfections, *not all pure perfections are transcendentals in the traditional sense*. Life and all essential characteristics of personhood are *not transcendental in the traditional sense* but are also pure perfections and thus *free of the inherent limitations* of finite beings, a fact which constitutes the most essential feature also of the traditional transcendentals, in fact their very *transcendentality consists chiefly in this very fact*. Not above all because of their character as "universal properties of all beings", but because of their nature as *pure perfections*, the traditional transcendentals (those co-extensive with being in Scotus' terms) are without any limits and can *therefore* be truly attributed to God. Again: This character of being free of all inherent and essential limitations and therefore attributable to God constitutes *the most significant reason for their transcendentality*, so much so that we could follow Scotus and define transcendentality solely in these terms.

---

[12] Such as their "simply simple" (*simpliciter simplex*) character and their participatability to more than one single subject or *hypostasis*. Cf. on this also my "Essere Persona Come Perfezione Pura. Il Beato Duns Scoto e una nuova metafisica personalistica," *De Homine, Dialogo di Filosofia* 11 (Rom: Herder/Università Lateranense, 1994), pp. 57-75.

[13] In his *Monologion,* ch. 15.

This great revolutionary discovery of Anselm, in the refinements added by Duns Scotus' teaching on the transcendentals (which are only implicit in Saint Thomas' treatment of the divine names, where, however, some other refinements of Anselm's discovery, touching the *id quod* and *id quo* distinction, are found) is the *condition of the possibility* of a *personalist metaphysics*. For only a metaphysics of the pure perfections, *and their clear distinction from the transcendentals which are coextensive with being,* allows us to attribute to God not only the most universally shared properties of being, goodness, etc., but also life (which is not shared by all beings) and above all personhood, freedom, knowledge, wisdom, justice and love (which exclusively persons possess). While these higher attributes of life and personhood, including freedom, are *not common to all things,* they are nevertheless absolutely better to possess than not to possess, as the great Anselmus put it[14], and therefore they are just as attributable to the absolute being and to the divine persons as the transcendental properties that are coextensive with being. A metaphysics which would regard personhood and freedom only as categorial inner-worldly properties would destroy the foundations of a personalist metaphysics and imply an agnosticism regarding the absolute being, and at any rate provide no metaphysical justification for the fact that the human *person,* and not abstract being or goodness as such, is the *imago Dei.*

All of this can only be understood and accepted in its truth on the basis of an implicit or explicit metaphysical intuition of the following content: The pure perfections whose possession is absolutely speaking better than their non-possession for whatever reason, include – besides such transcendentals which are common to *all beings* – others which belong only to *some innerwordly* beings and to God (such as life or freedom), and still others which are exclusively divine perfections such as omniscience or necessary real existence. And these are not less 'transcendental' than those which are coextensive with being but are, on the contrary, the *noblest kinds of the transcendentals,* namely the ones in which the universal "co-extensive" transcendentals (of goodness, being, etc.) find a much higher embodiment and which are nevertheless in their own nature (of justice, life, personhood) *irreducible* to the more universal "co-extensive" ones. And for this reason for *their nobility, not because of an inherent limitation,* the intrinsically highest and noblest pure perfections cannot be shared or possessed in a limited form by *all beings* but only by the higher ones which alone can possess those pure perfections which lower beings cannot even participate in. In other words, personhood and freedom are not categorial contractions and limitations of being but are pure perfections which are fully themselves only in their infinite

---

[14] *Ibid.,* ch. 15.

divine *gestalt* and belong for this very reason much more fully and literally to God than to us, whether they are co-extensive with being or not: God alone Is HE WHO IS, Being in the purest sense, but also He alone knows, and is wise and just in the fullest sense. The absolute fulfillment of the *ratio formalis* of all of these attributes which are pure perfections is only found in God. They are not intrinsically limited as are all species of plants and animals, or as human and angelic nature.

Only this rational metaphysical intuition, when it is applied to the highest pure perfections found in the world, namely to personhood and personal attributes such as freedom, allows us to attribute these to God and to grasp, with Julio Terán Dutari and Father Erich Przywara[15] the relation of the human person to the supreme being as a *Freiheitsentsprechung* (as a dialogical interrelation of free subjects).

But not only God, also the human person is free, even though in a more limited mode. In fact, *every person is free and would not be a person without being free,* an insight the full metaphysical weight of which only our metaphysics of pure perfections could show. And this freedom allows the person – in actuality or at least in principle – to elicit free acts, to determine himself in different ways and on different levels of his being, and to respond in different manners to objects and persons. Above all, only freedom permits the realization of the highest objective values in the universe which cannot exist, not even in God, except through freedom[16]. Moral values and the divine justice whose essential link to freedom Anselm expresses clearly in his magnificent formulation of justice as *rectitudo voluntatis propter se ipsam servata* (rightness of the will preserved for its own sake) that the moral perfection of justice (which he defines in terms of its Biblical meaning where it is equivalent to moral goodness as such) also in God requires necessarily freedom and cannot exist except through freedom, : "One has [...] to know that justice cannot exist except in the will if justice is rectitude preserved for its own sake"[17]. The highest morally good acts, justice, love, mercy, and countless others, though they are also dependent on many factors which are

---

[15] See the contribution of the Most Rev. J. Terán Dutari to the Proceedings of this World Congress.

[16] These various rational insights into the pure perfections and their relation to God constitute also the basis of a truly personalistic interpretation of the ontological argument and of the content of *id quo maius nihil cogitari possit,* which I tried to present in my *Gott als Gottesbeweis* (Heidelberg: Universitätsverlag C. Winter, 1996), ch. 11.

[17] Cf. Anselm von Canterbury, *De veritate,* I, and the same author, *De conceptu ...,* III; ii, 143, 16-17, where he says: (*Sciendum [...] est quia iustitia non potest esse nisi in voluntate, si iustitia est rectitudo voluntatis propter se servata*).

not within our free power[18], cannot exist without the free acts or free cooperation of persons.

Moreover, neither the intelligible essence of freedom, nor its real existence in us, is a mere hypothesis or assumption. No, we understand what constitutes freedom and know indubitably the truth that we are free. Augustine[19] – as René Descartes[20] or Hans Urs von Balthasar[21] after him – asserts the truth that nothing is more evident to us than our freedom: Our very existence and conscious life are not more indubitably given, though perhaps more easily understood, than our freedom. And indeed we know of our freedom with the same type of immediate and reflective evidence with which we know of our own existence[22]. The awareness of our own free will – a knowledge which is so evident that it cannot be deception – is part of the evidence of the *Cogito* as unfolded by Augustine[23]. And the existence of free will in us is so evident that its evidence in a certain sense is more primary and indubitable than that of all other evident truths given in the *Cogito*[24].

---

[18] Such as human models which inspire us or divine grace.

[19] Augustine, *De libero arbitrio*, 2; *De civitate Dei*, V.

[20] René Descartes, *Discours de la Methode*, in: *Oeuvres de Descartes*, ed. by Charles Adam & Paul Tannery, VI, 1-78; *Meditationes de Prima Philosophia*, *Oeuvres de Descartes*, ed. by. Charles Adam & Paul Tannery, Bd. VII (Paris: J. Vrin, 1983), 1-561.

[21] See Hans Urs von Balthasar, *Theodramatik II: Die Personen des Spiels*, 1: *Der Mensch in Gott*, (Einsiedeln: Johannes Verlag, 1976), pp. 186 ff. See also Balthasar, *TheoLogik, Wahrheit der Welt* (Einsiedeln: Johannes Verlag, 1985), II, A. Wahrheit als Freiheit, 1. In the Italian translation of this work by Guido Sommavilla: *Verità del Mondo. TeoLogica*, vol I (Milan: Jaka Book, 1987), see pp. 96 ff. See also Hans-Eduard Hengstenberg, *Grundlegung der Ethik* (Stuttgart: Kohlhammer, 1969), pp. 11 ff., where he analyzes a similar ineluctable givenness of moral good and evil, a sort of cogito-argument for the givenness of good and evil.

[22] Investigating this matter more closely, we could distinguish between the evident givenness of freedom on different levels: a) in the immediate inner conscious living of our acts, b) in what Karol Wojtyła calls "reflective consciousness" (which precedes the fully conscious self-knowledge), and c) in explicit reflection and self-knowledge properly speaking in which we make our personal freedom the explicit object of reflection, d) in the insight into the nature of freedom, an insight which grasps the necessary and intelligible essence of personhood, which is realized in each and every person, and e) in the clear and indubitable recognition of our personal individual freedom, an evident knowledge which depends, on the one hand, on the immediate and reflected experience of our being and freedom, and, on the other hand, on the essential insight into the eternal and evident truth of the connection between freedom and personhood.

[23] See Ludger Hölscher, *The Reality of the Mind. St. Augustine's Arguments for the Human Soul as Spiritual Substance* (London: Routledge and Kegan Paul, 1986). See also the discussion of this in Josef Seifert, *Back to Things in Themselves. A Phenomenological Foundation for Classical Realism* (London: Routledge, 1987), ch. 4-5.

[24] Of course, this priority is not to be understood absolutely: for without the evidence of our existence and thinking activity also our freedom and will could not be given. Neverthe-

For even if we could be in error about all things, which is impossible, Augustine says, it would still remain true that we do not want to be in error and of this free will we can have certain knowledge:

> Item si quispiam dicat, errare nolo; nonne sive erret sive non erret, errare tamen eum nolle verum erit? Quis est qui huic non impudentissime dicat, Forsitan falleris? cum profecto ubicumque fallatur, falli se tamen nolle non fallitur. Et si hoc scire se dicat, addit quantum vult rerum numerum cognitarum, et numerum esse perspicit infinitum. Qui enim dicit, Nolo me falli et hoc me nolle scio, et hoc me scire scio; jam et si non commoda elocutione, potest hinc infinitum numerum ostendere. (Augustine, *De Trinitate* XV, xii, 21)

> Likewise if someone were to say: «I do not will to err,» will it not be true that whether he errs or does not err, yet he does not will to err? Would it not be the height of impudence of anyone to say to this man: «Perhaps you are deceived,» since no matter in what he may be deceived, he is certainly not deceived in not willing to be deceived? And if he says that he knows this, he adds as many known things as he pleases, and perceives it to be an infinite number. For he who says, «I do not will to be deceived, and I know that I do not will this, and I know that I know this,» can also continue from here towards an indefinite number, however awkward this manner of expressing it may be. (Translated by McKenna, *ibid.*, pp. 480-2)

> Vivere se tamen et meminisse, et intelligere, et velle, et cogitare, et scire, et judicare quis dubitet? Quandoquidem etiam si dubitat, vivit; si dubitat, unde dubitet, meminit; si dubitat, dubitare se intelligit; si dubitat, certus esse vult; si dubitat, cogitat; si dubitat, scit se nescire; si dubitat, judicat non se temere consentire oportere. Quisquis igitur aliunde dubitat, de his omnibus dubitare non debet: quae si non essent, de ulla re dubitare non posset.

> On the other hand who would doubt that he lives, remembers, understands, wills, thinks, knows, and judges? For even if he doubts, he lives; if he doubts, he remembers why he doubts; if he doubts, he understands that he doubts; if he doubts, he wants (*wills*) to be certain; if he doubts, he thinks; if he doubts, he knows that he does not know; if he doubts, he judges that he ought not to consent rashly. Whoever then doubts about anything else ought never to doubt about all of these; for if they were not,

---

less, Augustine's remark is valid *secundum quid,* in the following sense: that if we assumed, *per impossibile,* that all other truths given in the *Cogito* would be doubtful, we could still be certain that we would freely *want* and *wish* to avoid error and to reach the truth.

he would be unable to doubt about anything at all. (St Augustine, *The Trinity*, translated by Stephen McKenna, Washington, DC: The Catholic University of America Press, 1970)

The evidence of this knowledge cannot even be refuted by any or all possible forms of self-deception because these imply or presuppose already the evidence of free will[25]. It is not possible in this context to discuss all the possible objections against the evidence of this thesis and thereby bring more fully to evidence the indubitable knowledge we can gain regarding our freedom.

2. DEFENSE OF THE THESIS "TO BE A PERSON IS TO BE FREE" IN VIEW OF THE METAPHYSICAL APORIES POSED BY HUMAN FREEDOM: DOES THE ASSERTION OF HUMAN FREEDOM IMPLY A CONTRADICTION OR TURN MAN INTO GOD?

Evident as the actual existence of freedom in us and the nature of freedom is, however, human freedom, i.e., a freedom that necessarily includes the capacity for free self-determination, poses profound metaphysical riddles precisely because it appears in a finite person. Human freedom is one of those amazing miracles of being which, the longer you think about them and marvel at them, the more incomprehensible they become. By the astonishing traits of human freedom numerous and insoluble apories are raised which appear to put into question that to be a person is to be free, and even challenge the very existence and non-contradictoriness of freedom.

Aristotle formulates one of those absolutely astonishing features of freedom when he says that due to our freedom we are "the lords over the being and the non-being of our actions"[26]. Is it not a prerogative of God to be Lord over the being and the non-being of a thing? Does being lord over being and non-being not imply some – exclusively divine – creation from nothing, some absolute *fiat* (there shall be...) which brings forth the being of something from nothing? Does Aristotle attribute to the human will then the bringing forth of an act by a simple inner word of a *fiat*, without the

---

[25] Cf. D. von Hildebrand, "Das Cogito und die Erkenntnis der realen Welt. Teilveröffentlichung der Salzburger Vorlesungen Hildebrands: 'Wesen und Wert menschlicher Erkenntnis'", *Aletheia* 6/1993-1994 (1994), 2-27. Josef Seifert, *Back to Things in Themselves*, cit.

[26] Aristotle, *Eudemian Ethics*, II.vi.8-9; 1223 a 3 ff.: *"hoon ge kurios esti tou einai kai tou mee einai"* ("and he is lord of their [his actions'] being and non-being.") See also Aristotle, *Nichomachean Ethics*, III; and *Magna Moralia*, 87 b 31 ff., especially 89 b 6 ff. Aristotle could hardly be more explicit on freedom as he is in these texts, calling the free agent the first principle, cause, lord, master of the action.

person being determined to such a *fiat* by any cause other than his or her free center itself? Is there such a god-like quality in any finite person as to be the lord over the being and non-being of something? The answer imposes itself on us: While we cannot create from nothing and received both our being and our free will, freedom as becoming the absolute beginning of free acts of the person is linked to a god-like attribute of man which can be described in terms of St. Augustine's remarks on the free will: "for if we will, it *is*; if we will not, it *is not*..."[27] Kant, too, when he expresses the profound puzzle of such an absolute beginning of causality in freedom, refers to this relationship – mentioned by Plato – between the essence of freedom and the first mover[28]. But it certainly does not constitute a valid objection against freedom that it has a character truly analogous to God's creating entities from nothing, at least as long as the essential distinction between limited human and infinite divine freedom is maintained.

Another and real metaphysical difficulty posed by freedom regards its relationship to causality. Does not every change require a cause? But if this is true, the free act which involves a change, also requires a cause – which in turn contradicts freedom. Does not a real *beginning* of causality in the free agent contradict the principle of causality which states that "every contingent being and every change must have an efficient cause through the power by which it comes to be"? This absolute beginning of causality in the free agent only apparently contradicts the principle of causality[29]: In reality,

---

[27] (Emphasis mine). The full text reads: "for we do many things which, if we were not willing, we should certainly not do. This is primarily true of the act of willing itself – for if we will, it *is*; if we will not, it *is* not..."

Augustine continues a little further down: "...Our wills, therefore, *exist* as *wills*, and do themselves whatever we do by willing, and which would not be done if we were unwilling." Augustine, *The City of God*, transl. M. Dods (New York: The Modern Library, 1950); (Book V by Rev. J.J. Smith), Book V, 10, pp. 156-157.

[28] Kant, *Critique of Pure Reason* B 478.

[29] Kant is so puzzled by this apparent contradiction that he thinks that we are led to an antinomy here, having both to assume freedom and to deny it at the same time. He writes on this enigma of freedom:

"We must therefore admit [...] an *absolute spontaneity* of causes, by which a series of phenomena [...] begins by itself; The transcendental idea of freedom is [...] that of the absolute spontaneity of action, as the real ground of imputability; it is, however, the real stone of offence in the eyes of philosophy, which finds its insurmountable difficulties in admitting this kind of unconditioned causality [...] a faculty of *spontaneously* originating a series of successive things or states [...]".

I. Kant, *Critique of Pure Reason*, B 472, 474, 476. Transl. F.M. Müller. See on the solution of the Third antinomy Josef Seifert, *Widerspruchsfreiheit: Das Antinomienproblem als ein Grundproblem der 'Kritik der reinen Vernunft' und der Philosophie überhaupt* (In Vorbereitung, 1997?); see also ders., "Das Antinomienproblem als ein Grundproblem aller Metaphysik: Kritik der Kritik der reinen Vernunft" in *Prima Philosophia*, Bd. 2, H 2, 1989.

there is absolutely no contradiction here; on the contrary, free action is an archetypal case of efficient causality and the only type of cause which can provide a beginning and absolute explanation of efficient causality because it does not refer to another more primary cause which produces it. Thus it certainly does not refute freedom in that it fulfills the principle of efficient causality in an exemplary way and constitutes a prime example of efficient causality without which all other efficient causes remain unintelligible because they send us eternally back to another cause that causes them and can never explain any beginning and principle of efficient causality[30].

But while the above and, I take it, correct statement of the principle of causality in no wise contradicts freedom, the false Kantian formulation of it, which leads Kant to the construction of an opposition between causality and freedom in the *Third Antinomy* of the *Critique of Pure Reason,* does. For the alleged principle that "every change follows upon another change according to a necessary law" applies perhaps to physical and chemical reality but certainly not universally and not to persons. If it were to apply to persons and human acts, it would indeed contradict freedom.

The extent to which this self-engendering of acts, this being the principle of actions and of causality is god-like, becomes apparent when we consider that it is almost unthinkable that man be both a creature and free. This leads us to a real and profound objection against freedom which does not touch the relationship between freedom and the principle of causality but between freedom and the total dependence of the human person on divine creativity. How can a radically dependent creature be free? Must not omnipotence, if it creates us, completely cause our being and everything that is in us? Is not such a creaturely dependence on God, then, a contradiction to freedom? Is not even the foreknowledge of free acts incompatible with free-

---

[30] The self-moving of free acts and free subjects, this having the source of motion within the subject-person of action himself, truly makes free acts stand within one's own power, instead of being moved from the outside, caused by another cause, impressed also Plato in the *Phaedrus* so much that he said that such a self-moving soul must be beginningless, not deriving its motion from another source but being its absolute origin. And he goes on to describe the soul as if it were a beginningless, eternal, absolute source of movement which is divine. Platon, *Phaedrus* 245 c 5 ff. Nevertheless, in the semi-creationism proposed by Plato in the *Timaeus,* Plato holds that also the human soul is created by the demiurg. See the justification of the demiurg as an important element of Plato's metaphysics (and not a myth as most interpreters thought) in the second volume of Reale's *Storia della filosofia antica* (now also in Polish), and in Giovanni Reale, *Verso una nuova interpretazione die Platone,* 16. Edition (Milan: Jaka Book, 1996); and Giovanni Reale, *Zu einer neuen Interpretation Platons. Eine Auslegung der Metaphysik der großen Dialoge im Lichte der "ungeschriebenen Lehren",* transl. by L. Hölscher, mit einer Einleitung von H. Krämer, ed. by J. Seifert (Paderborn: Schöningh, 1993).

dom, as Cicero holds in *De Natura Deorum*? Again and again in the history of philosophy, atheism or at least the denial of fundamental properties of the divine being went hand in hand with the acknowledgment of freedom – precisely because freedom is so god-like and appears to be impossible in a creature[31].

Augustine is profoundly concerned as well with the problem of atheism as consequence of freedom. He has to introduce many distinctions between different kinds of necessity and to develop his fine philosophy of the "order of causes" in order to explain this puzzle how freedom can exist in a creature whose acts are foreknown by God and who is nonetheless free[32]. Soeren Kierkegaard likewise struggles in his philosophical diaries with this problem of how God can give freedom to that which he creates. Kierkegaard solves this enormous difficulty, which we could truly call a (philosophically given) "mystery of metaphysical freedom," in a beautiful way by saying that omnipotence does not extinguish human freedom. On the contrary, precisely this – the creation of freedom – requires omnipotence. No finite power could create a free being. Only all-powerful causality can produce something so tremendous, something so incredible – a free being:

> [...] all finite power makes dependent; only omnipotence can make independent, can create from nothing that which subsists in itself, by omnipotence taking itself constantly back again [...] without abandoning the slightest part of its power [...] this is the incomprehensible thing that omnipotence cannot only bring into being the most imposing thing, the world's visible totality, but also the most fragile thing of all, a being that is independent vis-à-vis omnipotence. Hence that omnipotence which can lie so heavily on the world, can also render itself so light that that which became (through it) receives independence[33].

Another metaphysical puzzle and something that even seems to be a contradiction, appears to follow from freedom: that the free agent both determines himself and does not determine himself but is instead determined by himself. In being the lord over the being and the non-being of his actions, the free agent has also the equally amazing power of self-determination, of being in a sense the *causa sui*. For in engendering acts, in saying a

---

[31] Thus the radical skeptic Carneades and the atheist Epicurus were great philosophers of freedom, insisting on man's sovereignty and independence from the gods. They were atheists in part, precisely in order to save freedom. Something similar could be said of one motive of Sartre's atheism.

[32] Augustine, *The City of God*, V, 8-11, especially V, 9. See also Augustine, *De libero arbitrio*, II.

[33] Soeren Kierkegaard, *Papirer* VII, I, 141. See also a similar text in R. Descartes, *Principia Philosophiae*, I, 40 ff.

"fiat", which is preceded by a causal nothing (i.e., which is not caused or determined by a preceding cause), man both determines himself and is determined by himself, "creates himself (his own act)" and is turned good or evil by himself[34], dominates himself and is being dominated by himself. He becomes as it were subject and object at once, being he who determines and also he who is determined, he who governs and he who is governed, as Karol Wojtyła so clearly expounds[35]. This most amazing fact would involve a contradiction indeed were it not clear that it cannot be in one and the same sense that man determines himself and does not determine himself (but is determined). But this double aspect of freedom is not a contradiction if the person both determines himself and does not determine himself (*being* determined by himself) – but *in different senses*.

One could also raise another objection against freedom in terms of the principle of sufficient reason. In effect, the first conscious discovery of the principle of sufficient reason by Leibniz led him to formulate it in a faulty way which indeed contradicts freedom, at least the freedom of choice. Correctly stated, however, this principle of sufficient reason states that "every being (not only contingent ones and changes, as in the case of the principle of [efficient] causality) [or change] must have a sufficient reason – either within our outside itself – which adequately explains the existence and essence of that being [or change] in all its aspects." This principle, which in its correct statement does not contain the idea of a perfectly good or necessary cause (as Leibniz's interpretation of this principle in the light of the "best possible world" thesis) does not contradict freedom because the being of the person and his free power and will is precisely the sufficient explanation of free action, or at least – in finite persons – a significant *part of the sufficient reason* of free acts[36]. Yet this does not dissolve the apories and astonishing characteristics of freedom. For who can penetrate the admirable nature of this free engendering and this independence and self-dependence of man as free agent?

Another metaphysical problem and apparent impossibility and contradiction touching freedom relates to the seeming impossibility that *human be-*

---

[34] Of course, the positive and the negative cases are very different here: while we can attribute the evil solely to our own will (and to other evil wills and factors which influence us), any good will (at least in a supernatural sense) cannot be solely attributed to the human will but is also the work of God and his grace. Nevertheless, there is a specifically creative dimension of our freedom also and exclusively in the positive use of the will for the good which in a true sense is the cause of the goodness of the person.

[35] Karol Wojtyła, *The Acting Person (Boston: Reidel, 1979)*; cf. also the corrected text, authorized by the author (unpublished), (official copy), Library of the *International Academy of Philosophy in the Principality Liechtenstein*, Schaan.

[36] Free acts in finite persons require of course also the action of the infinite divine being.

ings, who depend on physical events in their brains, could be free. For in the physical and biological world all changes do seem to be dependent on preceding events which determine them. If one delves into these features of freedom, one will find no evidence for the non-existence of human freedom but the clear evidence of man's spiritual and substantial soul as a necessary condition of human freedom. For it is absolutely impossible that any material tissue of the brain, any product of natural or evolutionary processes could be free. A free act can only proceed from an indivisible, spiritual person, from man's soul as a spiritual and subsisting (substantial) reality. No neurons in the brain or epiphenomena of brain processes can explain freedom[37].

3. IS FREEDOM SELF-CREATION?
FREEDOM AND ITS CONDITIONS: BEING, COGNITION, AND VALUE

When we seek to conceive – with J.-P. Sartre – man's freedom in terms of self-creation, we might be led to the idea of a free spontaneous positing by which man determines things and himself completely, entirely, creating his own essence and that of things. To be free would signify to be autonomous in such an absolute way that one neither has ontological presuppositions nor an essence which would not depend on human freedom.

Yet such a self-creating freedom is not only in itself absurd but *human* freedom obviously presupposes many things which do not depend on our freedom, both in the subject and in the object of a free act. The very existence of the subject of conscious acts as an "individual substance of rational nature" precedes any free act. Never could an epiphenomenon or accident of another thing or a material substance which consists of a multiplicity of non-identical parts be the subject of free acts. In order to be possible, any free act presupposes ontologically the existence of its subject as a spiritual entity that stands in itself. In that sense of freely engendering its own existence no entity can be *causa sui*[38]. Moreover, the essences of things are also pregiven, especially with respect to their dependence on necessary and eternal "essential plans" (*eide*) but also with respect to the contingent natures which contain meaningful elements that need to be investigated empirically because they lack absolute necessity: also these empirical sides of nature,

---

[37] See on this Josef Seifert, *Leib und Seele. Ein Beitrag zur philosophischen Anthropologie* (Salzburg: A. Pustet, 1973); see also my *Das Leib-Seele Problem und die gegenwärtige philosophische Diskussion. Eine kritisch-systematische Analyse* (Darmstadt: Wissenschaftliche Buchgesellschaft, 2nd edition, 1989).

[38] Fichte's idea of a free self-creation of the subject of free acts, of a free self-constitution and self-positing to which the I owes its own being, proves absurd when we contemplate the intelligible structure of free acts.

which are created by *some* free act, are in no way the product of *human* freedom[39].

A legitimate sense of self-creation, however, can refer to acts themselves and to the determination which they bestow on their subject. His existence, however, is experienced by man as a given, as a gift which is entirely independent of his freedom and which is presupposed by it. Moreover, he recognizes that his nature – of being free and of having many other attributes, such as the ability to know or to perceive, such as the value he possesses and his being faced with objective goods – is independent of his free self-determination.

Among the pregiven conditions of freedom is also the uniqueness of each person. There is something unique, irreplaceable and unsubstitutable in the free subject. Yes, man can have twins and conceivably even countless "clones," other human beings who are just like him in all gifts and in appearance[40]. But in his own freedom, each man possesses, in the very bottom of his being, something which is inalienably his, which nobody else can ever actualize for him, and which he can use in such ways as to determine himself in radically different fashions, by becoming good or evil.

Thus the experience of freedom and of the abyss of concrete, individual life of the spirit, refutes any averroist or transcendental idealist system which regards the free subject as some universal spirit, as some logical synthesis or unity, as *one* ego common to all. No, the individual thisness, the *haecceitas* of the person, appears most deeply in his freedom and in the *Tua res agitur* freedom involves. Therefore it is not by chance that one of the greatest philosophers of freedom, Duns Scotus, was also one of the most profound philosophers of *individual thisness*[41].

Yet not only the subject is presupposed for freedom, but also some object. We arrive here at two essentially necessary truths which link freedom to consciousness and to knowledge of objects which are not constituted by freedom. "Nothing is willed that is not first conceived"[42] – this scholastic principle speaks of what Husserl and Brentano would call the *intentionality*

---

[39] On the decisive difference between necessary and contingent essences see Dietrich von Hildebrand, *What is Philosophy?*, 3rd edn, with a New Introductory Essay by Josef Seifert (London: Routledge, 1991); see also Josef Seifert, *Sein und Wesen*, cit., ch. 1-2.

[40] In reality, I know from very close friendships with various "identical twins" that they are profoundly different in appearance and personality, which becomes clear when one knows them well; and this would just as well apply to "human clones."

[41] On *individuality* see also Francisco Suarez, *Metaphysical Investigations*, V (On Individuality). On this and other metaphysical aspects of freedom see likewise Josef Seifert, *Essere e persona*, cit, ch. 9.

[42] *"Nil volitum nisi cogitatum"*.

of the free act, its directedness to some object in the way of thinking. I cannot just will as I can feel a headache or be drowsy, i.e., as a subjective non-intentional state which is not directed to anything over against itself. Just as I cannot perceive without perceiving *something*, know without knowing *something*, so I cannot will without my act being *directed at something* which stands over against myself or, being in me, still appears as object of my free acts: for example working at improving my behavior.

In formulating the fundamental dependence of will on knowledge and thought, the Medievals sometimes use another proposition, namely "nothing is willed that is not first known"[43]. In so speaking, the medieval philosophers indicated more than that each act of volition presupposes some awareness of an object, however erroneous. They implied that volition presupposes knowledge, cognition of that which is. And it proves indeed impossible that our relation to an object in a free act, however much prey to deception we are, consists of nothing but illusion and error. For in each error and deception we know something and know some truth – for example, that we exist or that those things at which our will is directed possess some true value or that we should look for truth. But also all concrete rational human actions and commitments presuppose, in different degrees, some knowledge of being and value. For instance, when we defend a slave from being sold or mistreated, we have some understanding of the true dignity of the person in contradistinction to the lower value of a lifeless thing or that of an animal. Even in evil and largely irrational human acts some true knowledge is presupposed. Willing presupposes the subject's relation to an object, but also to at least some truth and value.

Nevertheless, man actualizes certain aspects of his own being and of his own essence (of how he is) only through freedom[44]. The deepest dignity of the person lies in a vocation[45] that needs to be responded to, and in a value that needs to be conquered and is not simply a possession[46]. Man's dignity does not consist solely in the inalienable value which he possesses as person who is endowed with freedom but also in those values which can accrue to him only through the good use of his freedom. This dignity which lies in man's searching for the truth, in his obeying his conscience, doing justice, etc. can be lost by man. Its gain depends on man's freedom. In this sense, then,

---

[43] *"Nil volitum nisi praecognitum"*.

[44] On the distinction between *what-being* (*ti einai*) and *how-being* (*poion einai*) see my "Essence and Existence", cit., ch. 1; and my *Sein und Wesen*, cit., ch. 1.

[45] This concept of "vocation" plays a central role in Urs von Balthasar's conception of the person.

[46] This reminds of Gabriel Marcel's statement: *"être une personne n'est pas une possession, mais une conquête."* (To be a person is not a possession but a conquest).

man "creates himself to be evil or good" or is himself accountable for being good or evil, depending on the free stance he takes towards truth and goodness[47].

II. ETHICS, FREEDOM AND MOTIVATION: THE DRAMA OF HUMAN FREEDOM CAN ONLY BE UNDERSTOOD IN THE LIGHT OF THE FREE CHOICE OF THE END AND NOT ONLY OF THE MEANS

1. CATEGORIES OF THE "GOOD"

Someone could think that truth enslaves the human person, as well as any value in the object. Truth and value constitute limits to human freedom and thus appear to threaten the person's autonomy. This is a radical misunderstanding of freedom, however. Far from destroying human freedom, truth liberates it. Each rational action presupposes a certain state of the world, the existence of certain bonds or the absence thereof, certain values etc. Thus each human action by its nature has a connection to truth. Truth is, as Karol Wojtyła the philosopher says, "the internal principle of human action"[48].

Truth does not destroy or threaten freedom and neither do values Kant's idea that freedom is only autonomous if its entire source proceeds from the subject and if it does not depend on any object, is profoundly wrong. He fails to see that not all influences from values and objects threaten freedom or are like mere causes exerted on the subject. There are indeed such influences which are hostile to freedom, such as drug-addiction or psycho-terror. But truth and true values liberate freedom. We do not create but discover them, and they are not dependent on our freedom. They are to be found and are pregiven to the subject in the world and in the nature of things. But when we find them, they do not oppress us or deprive us of our freedom, but renew and liberate us. They give a "purpose" and end to human actions; they liberate freedom to itself and render possible the deepest dimensions of it. For only in response to truth and to true goods can freedom be fully freedom, can freedom be meaningful rather than senseless arbitrariness. Only in response to the good can free acts embody value, can

---

[47] In the case of goodness, man does not simply create himself or his goodness, as we shall see. He partakes of goodness and there are many aspects of morally good acts which involve gifts, too. Therefore, even with respect to moral goodness we can speak of "self-creation" in a very restricted sense only.

[48] Karol Wojtyła, *The Acting Person* (Boston: Reidel, 1979), ch. 1 ff.

freedom have a why for the sake of which we act. And such a why cannot derive from a mere arbitrary decree or decision of the free will but must stem from the nature of reality. Only truth and true values will make us free.

This axiological dimension of freedom – its link to knowledge and to value – forces us to consider a new essentially necessary truth about freedom: the object of a free act does not stand in front of us as totally neutral, indifferent, but as "important," i.e., it is raised out of the sphere of the wholly indifferent[49]. Otherwise there would be no reason to will it. This importance can be positive or negative. Purely negative importance as such, however, cannot motivate our affirming will but only our rejecting or some other form of "negative willing," i.e., of saying in some way "no" to something. If we call therefore *any* positive importance 'good,' an object attracts our will always *sub specie boni*, under some aspect of the good, as Saint Thomas and Professor Mieczysław A. Krąpiec say. We *always* want something which stands before us either as positively important – this is a necessary condition in order for us to will it affirmingly – or as negatively important, which is required for us to reject it, to will that it not be, or to flee from it.

Yet if we follow Aristotle's and Thomas Aquinas' teaching that all men desire the good in the sense of something that stands before us as *positively important*, and if we then interpret this good which "all men desire" as their happiness, do we then not lose freedom? Does the knowledge of the good not determine freedom by necessity? If our will wants the good, which is identified with happiness, by necessity, freedom can only have the role of executing what the intellect shows us to be good. Morally evil choices are then simply based on error and ignorance and Socrates is right in asserting that no man commits injustice or another evil willingly.

2. THE DRAMA OF HUMAN FREEDOM CAN ONLY BE UNDERSTOOD IN THE LIGHT OF THE FREE CHOICE OF THE END AND NOT ONLY OF THE MEANS: CATEGORIES OF THE "GOOD"

Even if it is true that we will necessarily *some* good, the drama of freedom definitely presupposes at least two entirely different points of view of motivation between which we can choose and which are irreducible to each other. If all men wanted necessarily the same end and could choose only the means which they deem best for this end, freedom or at least the drama of

---

[49] Cf. Dietrich von Hildebrand, *Ethics* (Chicago: Franciscan Herald Press, ²1978); *Ethik*, Gesammelte Werke, vol. II (Stuttgart: Kohlhammer, ²1973), ch. i.

freedom would be impossible. Also some followers of Aristotle (who had asserted such a thing) admit this, for example Cornelio Fabro, who attributes also to Thomas Aquinas the view that the will can choose between ultimate ends, specifically between a perverse and a good end[50]. And the older distinction common to many scholastics between the *bonum utile,* the *bonum commodum* and the *bonum honestum,* among which we can choose, goes in a similar direction. Kant, in his distinction between acting from inclination (*Neigung*) and *from duty* (*Pflicht*) formulates for the first time quite clearly two radically and incommensurably distinct points of view of human motivation, a truly epochal ethical discovery. Yet in my opinion, there are so many confusions regarding this matter in Kant, that one can say that a viable distinction between fundamentally different categories of the good (of importance), between which the drama of human freedom unfolds, is owed to Dietrich von Hildebrand[51]. He identifies three types or categories of importance. First, Hildebrand distinguishes between the objective value and the merely subjectively satisfying. There is an abysmal distinction between them which shows that the 'good' which all men desire is not univocally and not even truly analogically 'good.' What are those distinctive marks between the intrinsically good – to which Hildebrand's notion of 'value' refers – and the merely subjectively satisfying?

1) First, value-importance is objective and intrinsic, the merely subjectively satisfying is relative to the subject. What possesses objective value is precious in and of itself. The dignity of man is such a value which does not derive from any relationship to our inclinations, drives, instincts, appetitus – but belongs to the person by his own nature. Value in this sense is, above all, preciousness in itself which does not consist in the ability of an object to satisfy or to fulfill us but is an intrinsic positive importance that raises a being out of the neutral, of the indifferent. We express linguistically this character of *bonum in se*, which already Duns Scotus has contrasted with the Thomist understanding of *bonum ad aliud* (good as relational to *appetitus*) in that our language does not allow us to say of such values as the dignity of the person or justice that they are *dignity for me,* or *justice related to my desires*. No, they are dignity and justice as intrinsic values, as intrinsic preciousness of things.

On the contrary, the merely subjectively satisfying of the cigarette depends on our likes or dislikes. For a non-smoker, the smoke of a cigarette

---

[50] Cf. Cornelio Fabro, *Riflessioni sulla Libertà* (Rimini: Magggioli, 1983), S. i-xi, 13-132.

[51] In thinking about the Socratic problem and the Aristotelian-Thomistic thesis that all men desire the good, as well as on Max Scheler's theory which holds that each evil act consists in a preferring the lower good to the higher, Dietrich von Hildebrand arrived at one of his most stunning discoveries, that of the three categories of importance.

may be disagreeable, something negatively important. For the smoker it is subjectively satisfying. This positive or negative quality depends on the pleasure or displeasure it gives to a subject.

Whereas the quality of the subjectively satisfying or of the subjectively dissatisfying may be grounded in the nature of the object – such as in the case of the good taste of some Marzipan of Toledo or a warm bath when one is cold – it can also be entirely divorced from the true nature of the object, such as when the torture and blood of his victim fill the sadist with intense satisfaction.

2) Objects endowed with the two mentioned kinds of importance address themselves quite differently to the subject. The good insofar as it is endowed with intrinsic value addresses a call to us. It appeals to our freedom to conform to it, to give it a due response. In fact, this call addressed to us by beings endowed with intrinsic value reveals the innermost meaning of freedom. For example, we ought to respect a human person in virtue of his or her dignity. When we treat him like a thing or as a slave, we contradict this call. Objective values do not leave us in our arbitrariness but call us to conform our hearts and actions to them.

At the same time, they address themselves specifically to our freedom because no machine and no animal governed by instincts but only a free subject can say yes to values, can properly relate to goods endowed with intrinsic preciousness.

On the contrary, the merely subjectively satisfying addresses itself to us not with a call to give it a due response, but with an enticement; if it is illegitimate, it seduces us. As long as it remains legitimate, we are entirely free to follow its invitation or not to follow it. We cannot speak here of a call. While not demanding a response from the person and not addressing a call to him, however, the merely subjectively satisfying has a tendency to dethrone our freedom, to enslave us. Just think how a passion for gambling, for sexual satisfaction, for money or power can dominate and enslave a man or a woman. Thus the true meaning and possession of freedom in the moral sense becomes first possible through the response to goods endowed with intrinsic value.

3) Thirdly, the subject relates quite differently to the object in the case of a good endowed with intrinsic value as opposed to a merely subjectively satisfying object.

The intrinsic good is object of a certain self-donation, of a certain conforming ourselves to it, of our giving it its due response. We subordinate ourselves to an object endowed with intrinsic value in love, in admiration, in the concern for truth and justice, or in the adoration of the infinitely holy God.

On the contrary, any such giving of oneself is missing in the case of the merely subjectively satisfying. There we appropriate the object to us, we consume it, we use it, as the French expression "je me rejouis de" shows, which means both 'to use' and 'to take pleasure in,' a fact on which Karol Wojtyła has put his finger in an admirable way[52].

4) Fourthly, the two kinds of importance show a radically different type of gradation. Objective and intrinsic values are graded according to a principle of hierarchy. They rank higher or lower in the axiological sense.

The merely subjectively satisfying, however, possesses only degrees of intensity. Aristipp saw this when he distinguished in his hedonism only a) the intensity of pleasure b) its duration c) the ease to obtain it; d) the question of negative effects. All of these criteria remain within the category of the merely subjectively satisfying, as Hildebrand shows[53]. Only when Aristipp attributes wisdom to the man who follows these criteria, he presupposes intrinsic value – but thereby he contradicts himself.

5) While both values and the merely subjectively satisfying have a relation to joy and happiness, their relationship to happiness is quite different.

What possesses intrinsic value can render us happy only when we give ourselves to it. The true happiness bestowed on us by values presupposes that we participate in the intrinsic value of a thing or of a person. This happiness is the joy which only a thing of objective value can bring about. It is the radiance of value in the soul that perceives it. We can gain this happiness and win our soul only when we give ourselves, when we lose our souls. Happiness is a superabundant gift.

On the contrary, merely subjectively satisfying objects are used by us for our satisfaction. They are means to our pleasure. Moreover, our subjective satisfaction is quite compatible with the knowledge that the importance of the object depends on its capacity to please us.

We thus see, there are profoundly distinct senses of positive importance which address themselves to quite different centers in us. What is more, they can be pursued in indifference to each other and in independence of each other: someone can pursue what satisfies his concupiscence or pleases his pride *entirely without any concern whatsoever whether his acts are in harmony with what is good in itself.*

---

[52] See Karol Wojtyła, *The Acting Person* (Boston: Reidel, 1979), where an outstanding critique of hedonism explains this linguistic peculiarity of the French and Polish language. See also my "Karol Cardinal Wojtyła (Pope John Paul II) as Philosopher and the Cracow/Lublin School of Philosophy" in *Aletheia* II (1981). See likewise the discussion of this paper through Georges Kalinowski and Tadeusz Styczeń in *Aletheia* IV (1987).

[53] Hildebrand, *Ethics, ibid.*, ch. iii.

Hildebrand proceeds to show a third category of importance which is indispensable for understanding such acts as gratitude, forgiveness, or love, as well as for understanding happiness. This third sense of the good is described by Hildebrand as the "objective good *for* the person." It shares with the subjectively satisfying that it is essentially a good *for* someone; it addresses itself to a person and is a good *for* him or her. It shares with value the objectivity, however. It lies objectively in the true interest of a person, constitutes an objective "pro" for the person, serves his or her true happiness and fulfillment, is verily a gift for him or her. In desiring happiness, as distinct from mere subjective pleasure, we truly desire the objective goods for us. In gratitude, we respond to such gifts for us, and in the *intentio benevolentiae* of love we desire the objective good for the beloved person. The objective good for the person is not divorced from intrinsic value. On the contrary, each value, when it is profoundly understood or when the person embodies it, also addresses itself to him as his gift and source of happiness. The justice of Socrates is of intrinsic value but also a great objective good for him. The beloved person is precious in himself but also a source of happiness for those who love him, etc.[54]

Understanding the irreducible diversity of these three categories of importance, we also understand the drama of human freedom. Human freedom does not unfold just in relationship to the means for the good or to practical judgments, while we would have to will the end, the good, by necessity.

No, given the profound difference of the three categories of importance, given the three fundamentally different meanings of the 'good,' we understand now the depth and drama of man's freedom in deciding between these different kinds of importance. Man can choose his own satisfaction in indifference to the intrinsically valuable. He can rob a man, wanting to enjoy his wealth and the pleasure going along with his possessions, without even asking himself whether his action is intrinsically better or not. He can rape a girl because this satisfies his lust or his sadistic desire for power and humiliation of others, without having to believe that his action is in itself better than not raping the girl. He can even lead warfare against the good because he sees it obscuring his own power and greatness. In so doing, he does not pay a bit of attention to the question whether or not his action is good in itself.

Thus man can do the evil, clearly seeing that it is evil, as Ovid put it: "*Video meliora proboque; deteriora sequor.*" (I see the better and approve of it; but I do what is worse). Man can, contrary to Socrates' view, knowingly

---

[54] See Hildebrand, *Das Wesen der Liebe*, cit., ch. vi-x.

do injustice. In fact, he can resent and hate justice and all that is intrinsically good.

Man cannot only be indifferent to what is intrinsically good but also – and most amazingly – towards the objective good for himself. Man can gamble or give himself to his lust, knowing well that this leads to his sickness, to his moral destruction, or even to his damnation. Yet he can choose the road to his evil or to his pernicion because he can pursue that which satisfies him subjectively now and fulfills his will to power in indifference not only to intrinsic value but even to his own objective good. Thus also this objective good *for ourselves* is not necessarily willed by us. On the contrary, we can very well engage in alcohol, in drugs, in adultery and rape, in deceit and lies, *knowing perfectly well that this does not lead us to true happiness*. Therefore, the self-love which consists in desiring our *true happiness,* our salvation in God, is a rare and very meritorious and difficult moral act.

This presupposes, apart from the three categories of importance, also the ability of isolating them from one another, the capacity of absolutizing the merely subjectively satisfying and of taking it outside of its legitimate place which it possesses only as long as it is integrated in the right order of goods. Socrates' famous thesis is thus proven wrong.

In order to understand the drama of human freedom, we must not only consider objective values such as aesthetic values of beauty in nature and art or intellectual values such as the thorough knowledge of a language. These demand a due response – but they frequently do not impose moral obligations on us. Only when we are faced with such goods which do not only address a general call to respond to them adequately but which issue a moral call, are we faced with the whole depth and the drama of human freedom. The dignity of the person, his life, the elementary objective goods for him, such as his clothing and food, or the basic intellectual development of the person, truth, etc. – are not themselves moral values. Nobody is in the moral sense good or evil for having or not having them. Nevertheless, these values and goods are morally relevant. They issue moral calls and obligations to us and for this reason are called by Hildebrand "morally relevant" goods or evils[55]. They involve directedness to our conscience, they issue quite another serious call than aesthetic values do, or even an obligation to respond to our freedom. And most morally relevant goods are related to the person or some aspect of the person's being. In view of the centrality of the morally relevant good of the person, who is endowed with intrinsic dignity, it becomes understandable why some formulations of the fundamental moral norm refer only to the person, such as Kant's various personalistic formula-

---

[55] *Ibid.*, ch. 19.

tions of the categorical imperative[56] and the personalistic principle of Polish personalist ethics: *"persona est affirmanda propter seipsam"* (the person ought to be affirmed for his or her own sake), or *"persona est amanda propter seipsam"* (the person ought to be loved for his own sake)[57].

If we respond adequately to morally relevant goods[58], we realize moral values. These involve quite another unconditional sense of 'goodness,' as Kant says. Moral values presuppose necessarily human freedom. Without it, they cannot possibly exist. Yet while this bond is evident, it is not analytically but synthetically true that it exists. Theologians such as Calvin admitted guilt and sin without admitting freedom. It follows from the essence, not from the mere definition, of moral values that they presuppose freedom[59]. Also this is an absolutely necessary truth, a *veritas aeterna*. Moral values are therefore linked to responsibility; we are accountable for our moral goodness or evilness. They appeal to moral conscience and deserve punishment or reward. All moral val-

---

[56] See especially the fourth one of the following eight versions of the "categorical imperative":

1. "Act only according to that maxim by which you can at the same time will that it should become a moral law" (1. Form., Immanuel Kant, *Foundations of a Metaphysics of Morals*, p. 44; *Grundlegung zur Metaphysik der Sitten*, II. Teil).

2. "Act as though the maxim of your action were by your will to become a universal law of nature" (2. Form., *ibid.*, p. 45).

3. Formulation "Handle so, daß die Maxime deines Willens Grundlage jederzeit zugleich als Prinzip einer allgemeinen Gesetzgebung gelten könne" (Kant, *Kritik der praktischen Vernunft*, § 7.).

4. Formulation: "Act so that you treat humanity, whether in your own person or in another, always as an end and never as means only" (*Foundation*, cit., p. 54).

5. In the third formulation of the principle, i.e., Kant expresses the idea of "the will of every rational being as a will giving universal law" (ibid., p. 57).

6. "The principle of every human will as giving universal laws in all its maxims" (ibid., 57).

7. "Act with reference to every rational being (whether yourself or another) so that it is an end in itself in your maxim" (ibid, p. 64).

8. "Act by a maxim which involves its own universal validity for every rational being" (ibid., p. 64).

[57] See Karol Wojtyła, *Liebe und Verantwortung* (München: Kösel-Verlag, 1979), Tadeusz Styczeń, Andrzej Szostek, Karol Wojtyła, *Der Streit um den Menschen. Personaler Anspruch des Sittlichen* (Kevelaer 1979).

[58] I cannot deal here with many other types of morally relevant importance. See on this Hildebrand, *Moralia, Gesammelte Werke* vol. IX (Regensburg: Habbel, 1980).

[59] See Aristotle, *Magna Moralia* 87 b 33 ff: "For this is the most important condition for virtue, freedom. To put it simply, free is that which we do without being forced to do it." Cicero, Augustine, and most philosophers recognized the necessary link between freedom and morality.

ues, at least all obligatory ones[60], should be realized by every person; the partial value-realization and specialization which is natural in other spheres of value, such as aesthetic or intellectual values, is here inappropriate. Moral values have a higher rank than other values and are the highest objective goods for the person. Moral values most properly are *the* good of the soul, moral evil is most radically opposed to the good of the soul, as Plato states[61]. In morality in its highest perfection lies the ultimate existential calling of man and the only ultimate fulfillment of the being of the person qua person. For this reason all moral values are also morally relevant, i.e., we ought to strive for their realization above all in ourselves but also in others. Moral values also imply the most direct relationship to God and to religious values. None of these features belong to the other values[62].

We now see that the drama of human freedom lies precisely in choosing either pride and concupiscence in contempt of the call of moral values – or in choosing to conform our lives to the call of moral and morally relevant goods[63]. In criticizing sharply the idea that "the good is what all men desire"

---

[60] This addition is to exclude two things: a) an ethical rigorism which does not allow for a sphere of "optional" moral goodness or of heroism which is not required from all; b) the opinion that finite persons can absolutely speaking realize *all* moral values (whereas the *absolute perfection* of justice, mercy, etc. can only be found in God).

[61] Plato, *Politeia*, X.

[62] Kant calls moral values the only values that are 'good without qualification.' What does this mean?

(a) 'Good' in the context of moral goodness is understood first as 'good without qualification' in the sense of intrinsic goodness (See I, Kant, *Foundations of a Metaphysics of Morals*, 48 f.)

(b) 'Good without qualification' can also be interpreted in the sense that moral values are values in a higher sense.

(c) Good without qualification can also be understood in the sense that moral goodness cannot be 'abused' like other talents which turn terrible when abused.

(d) Moral goodness is likewise 'good without qualification' in the sense that moral goodness makes the *person as such* good; it is not just something good *in him* but touches his very being.

(e) Another sense in which moral goodness alone is 'good without qualification' is: Moral values are the ultimate objective good *for* persons.

Plato gives in the *Gorgias* as main argument why it is better *for man* to suffer injustice than to commit it: that the moral value itself is higher and more beautiful than freedom from suffering, and that the ugliness of moral evil is far greater than that of suffering injustice.

(f) Morally good qualities are "good without qualification" also in the sense that moral values are 'pure perfections'.

[63] St. Augustine sees this when he speaks, in *The City of God*, of the two ultimate principles of good and bad acts and of the Two Cities: "amor Dei usque ad contemptum sui" (love of God even to the point of contempting oneself) and "amor sui usque ad contemptum Dei" (love of self even to the contempt of God).

as if the intrinsic good or even the objective good for our person, let alone that for other persons, were desired and willed by necessity, we do not deny that there is both a natural ordination to intrinsic goodness and to the objective good for the person, and even a natural tendency in man driving him towards them. And this thirst for the good and for happiness as an ineradicable inclination which is the condition even for suffering from its privation is indeed a "necessary directedness of will and desire" to their ends (when the end of the will is understood not as the object of rational choice but as the end of the will's "natural inclination.") But at the level of our personal and free relationship to reality, we need to choose these goods freely and can choose perverse ones, an insight of which Cornelio Fabro shows that we can find it also in Saint Thomas[64].

III. BEING FREE IS NOT RESTRICTED TO THE SPHERE OF ACTION BUT ENCOMPASSES MANY SPHERES OF HUMAN WILLING

1. DIFFERENT LEVELS OF HUMAN FREEDOM – ACTUAL AND SUPER-ACTUAL, DIRECT AND INDIRECT FREEDOM, AFFECTIVE RESPONSES, OTHER "GIFTS" AND COOPERATIVE FREEDOM

In order to understand the nature of freedom and the different kinds of acts which it renders possible, we must first distinguish, with Hildebrand, two quite different dimensions or perfections of freedom[65]. The first one unfolds in relation to the important object; it involves a free 'yes' or a free 'no' spoken to it. It is the freedom to respond, to take a stance, affirming or rejecting an object or state of affairs.

The second dimension of freedom consists in the will being able to engender free acts, and to initiate new causal chains, thereby also becoming the lord over our external actions and being able to initiate activities which then might lead to the realization of states of affairs which we realize in the outside world, after "affirming" (willing) them freely in an inner response. The second dimension of freedom may also lead to the making or creating of objects, works of art, etc., which are not reducible to states of affairs.

The first perfection of our will is deeper and has a much wider scope than the second. It encompasses also all purely inner responses, including

---

[64] Fabro, Cf. Cornelio Fabro, *Riflessioni sulla Libertà* (Rimini: Magggioli, 1983), S. i-xi, 13-132.

[65] See Hildebrand, *Ethics*, ch. 20 ff.

those directed to objects which we can in no way change[66], such as God or our neighbor, perhaps a more gifted person than we are, whom we can freely respect, affirm in love, or reject in hate and envy[67], or a cross or illness, which we can freely and humbly accept or against which we can rebel.

The second dimension of human freedom chiefly refers to free actions in the strict sense, i.e., to acts which aim at the realization of states of affairs which are not yet real but can be realized through me (the object-sphere of *prattein,* of acting in the narrower sense of this term) or to objects which we can make or produce *(poiein)*. In such actions and productive acts which are geared to the real world outside of ourselves, we initiate those activities which bring about the intended states of affairs or objects of making.

Both dimensions of freedom involve the mysterious inner power to engender acts without any preceding cause or our nature forcing us to act. This essence of freedom is common to all free acts and actions.

The first perfection of the will, the responding one, involves not only choice because it can freely affirm a good without choosing properly speaking, but it also includes the freedom of choice. Free choice is not restricted to the choice of the proper means to achieve the good as final end, as we have already seen: we do not want with necessity – as the final end – the intrinsic good or the happy life or the realization of moral values and the adequate response to the truth, and especially to morally relevant goods. Hence, we can fail to will the first and most important objective goal of our freedom – to conform our life to the truth and to true goods. For we can choose a life of subjective satisfaction in indifference towards intrinsic values and morally relevant goods, and even in indifference towards our own objective good. Thus we can choose between ultimate ends, between good and evil, between the love of God up to the neglect of self (*amor Dei usque ad contemptum sui*) and the self-love up to the contempt of God (*amor sui usque ad contemptum Dei*), as Augustine puts it in *De civitate Dei*. This choice between the ultimate ends is the drama of human freedom.

---

[66] Hildebrand, in his *Ethics*, failed to see clearly the independence of this first perfection of human freedom of the second and the central and all-encompassing role of free responses not only with respect to non-realized states of affairs which can be realized through me, but with respect to all kinds of morally relevant goods. Cf. Josef Seifert, *Was ist und was motiviert eine sittliche Handlung?* (Salzburg: Univ.Verlag A. Pustet, 1976). In his later work, Hildebrand corrected this mistake of his *Ethics*. Hildebrand, *Moralia, Gesammelte Werke* Bd IX (Regensburg: Habbel, 1980).

[67] We do not refer here to the affective response of love, envy or hatred, which we cannot freely engender. But there is also free affirmation of the person as a whole which we can call a volitional dimension or form of love. The full reality of love requires both the free response to the person and the affective response of love, which in turn can be sanctioned by the free will.

In order to understand human freedom, we must understand the further truth that freedom has many dimensions above and beyond its role in external action. There is first the impossibility of reducing the first dimension of freedom, its responding character, to that free response of *willing* which is an integral part of external action only and which presupposes something that is not yet real but can be realized through me. Also when I read a book or watch a movie, or become witness of crimes or suffer events which I cannot change, I can take purely inner stances, freely affirming the good, rejecting the evil, praising God or cursing him. These are not external actions but free inner responses possible even when I am perhaps unable to respond in any external action. I can direct such inner free responses to individual goods or evils, such as to a person to whom I forgive a wrong, or to a scene of torture which I have to witness in a concentration camp, or to whole general spheres of values, such as to moral values as such, to the dignity of the human body, to all human rights, etc.

Besides such actual free responses, which I experience here and now and direct to an object, there are also superactual free responses in the person. These continue to exist in us even when we do not actually experience them or think of them. As we know many things superactually even when we do not think of them, we find also that concretely lived free acts and responses do not exhaust themselves in our actually experiencing them. Both our responses to individual beings (such as our love for our wife or child) and to general types and whole spheres of value, such as attitudes of reverence, the virtues of justice, of purity, etc. can last in the form of *superactual* acts. They manifest themselves in our emotions, feelings, concrete responses and actions, etc. All virtues and vices are superactual acts. They profoundly influence the concrete actual consciousness of a person and are as it were a *basso continuo* which accompanies the actual melodies of our daily life.

Finally, there is the so-called fundamental moral option for or against all morally relevant goods, for or against God and the whole world of values. This response has the most universal scope of objects at which it is directed. This attitude may also be called the *general moral attitude*. This most general attitude, however, is not called so because in itself it would be an abstract entity but it is 'general' in at least three distinct ways: (1) It is really or potentially present in all other morally good or evil acts; and (2) it has the most general morally relevant good as its object: both in the sense of *all* morally relevant goods to which it responds and the supremely concrete and yet all-encompassing good: God. Moreover, (3) it is called to become superactually real in the person, and thus receives the character of lasting foundation of a person's moral life, which is a condition for fulfilling its character of underlying the entirety of a person's individual responses and moral acts.

Certainly, the general moral response to the world of morally relevant goods can also exist in us merely momentarily as a stance we take at a certain moment towards the whole world of values. But it is intended to achieve a superactual reality in our soul and deserves the name *attitude* (rather than momentary stance) only when it has become superactual. It also can and should have a special depth in different senses, and not only in that of the superactual life of the person. It can be more or less firmly rooted in the person, it can qualitatively be more or less deep, play a greater or lesser role in our lives, last more or less long in its identity throughout time, as opposed to fast-changing attitudes, etc. The fundamental moral attitude, especially when it is freely sanctioned, constitutes in a sense the backbone of our moral life, and is the fountain of concrete actions. Being also strengthened and formed by them, it possesses utmost significance in any adequate philosophy of virtue and ethics. It must not be regarded as unconscious, however, though it is more hidden to our reflection than concrete intentions.

The fundamental moral attitude (option)[68] does have both a content and an object, though its content can be extremely 'thin' and formal such as when the generally good moral attitude of an atheist or skeptic has only the form of not wanting to do anything in truth forbidden him, and if he is ready to obey all moral obligations if they exist and if he knows them, submitting in this formal and abstract way to the truth (while leaving open the content and knowability of truth and feeling unsure whether perhaps *in truth* everything is permitted, as Nietzsche thought). Yet the will to submit to truth in thought and action remains always a decisive element of the person's fundamental morally good attitude. For all moral imperatives bind in the name of truth; and judgments which make a claim to truth are presupposed everywhere in our moral life. And nothing is permitted except if it is permitted in truth.

The good fundamental moral attitude may take on much more content, however. It may be based on a clear recognition of the truth and its basic contents, and refer specifically to morally relevant goods which are under-

---

[68] This notion is of fundamental moral option, apart from being interpreted in many false transcendental idealist senses as unconscious, free of content, formal, never experienced, etc., is today also frequently divorced from an understanding of its foundational role for the sphere of action. It is chiefly because of this "teleological" (consequentialist) misunderstanding that we avoid this term in relation to the fundamental moral attitude. Also this term refers only to one of the elements related the fundamental moral attitude, which Hildebrand called "the fundamental moral intention." It is not possible here to distinguish all these elements and acts. *Sittlichkeit und ethische Werterkenntnis. Eine Untersuchung über ethische Strukturprobleme*, 3rd edition (Vallendar-Schönstatt: Patris Verlag, 1982).

stood to exist. It may thus take the essentially different form of a clear general will to respond adequately to the morally relevant goods and also of the general will to *be* morally good.

This general will to *be good* constitutes a new and very important element of the fundamental moral attitude which is another value-responding attitude towards the unique and specifically *moral value* to be realized by me[69].

---

[69] The fundamental moral attitude as the 'general will to be good' refers to the 'bonum est faciendum' in the sense of the sphere of moral values and disvalues in the person him- or herself. The acceptance of the call to realize moral values in our own person was thought by Max Scheler to be impossible or at least to involve phariseism: To be interested in my own moral goodness would, according to this philosopher, fail to accept the principle that the moral value "rides on the back of my actions." It would be a self-centered attitude and involve a turning away from the morally relevant object of the good of our neighbor. But this is not true although it is true that the genuine interest in the other's good, in the morally relevant good, is indeed a condition of authentic morality. A careful phenomenology of the fundamental moral attitude forces us to recognize a two-fold directedness of the *Grundhaltung* – to all morally relevant goods and to the realization of moral values in us.

It would be unobjective not to want to be good ourselves if it is recognized that moral values are higher than even all morally relevant ones which are not themselves moral values.

First we recognize here the fact that moral values are also morally relevant values, whether they exist in us or in other persons. Parents have to be interested also and primarily in the moral goodness of their children, Socrates is committed to further the moral virtue of his fellow-citizens. To show disinterest in the moral goodness in others is such a bad attitude that it becomes questionable whether any moral goodness can be in a person who fails to give this response.

But if we respond to moral values, we should respond to them in all subjects and in all their forms which we recognize as such. But as it would be morally wrong to be disinterested in moral values as such, it would be most illogical not to be interested in their realization *in us*. That this interest as such has nothing to do with phariseism or egocentricity in morality is seen when we understand that the general response to moral values in us and in others must be first of all a value-response, not just a response to the objective good for us, i.e., in order to be "saved" or to attain highest happiness and objective good *for us*. The general response to moral values is first of all a value response which falls into the second kind of general morally good response to all morally relevant goods, among which moral values occupy the first place. The deeper the essence of moral goodness is understood and responded to (as embodied in God, as participation in his goodness, in its supernatural essence, as glorification of God), the more pure and sublime is the general moral attitude.

Thus it would be illogical in the highest degree not to be interested in our own moral goodness as if that were any less important than the moral values in others. We must distinguish the egocentric or pharisaic interest 'only in *our* salvation' or even in a purely subjectively satisfying aspect of glorifying ourselves and of enjoying our superiority through moral values from the value-response to moral values. Only the latter is phariseism while the form is an integral part of the fundamental good moral attitude.

But it is in the 'general will to be good' that we find a second and radically new moment, namely the awareness that moral values cannot be realized by us primarily in the

By saying that this will to be good, too, has to have a value responding character, we do not exclude that it should involve also an interest in our own (or anybody else's) *objective good for the person*. On the contrary, the objective good for persons including our own constitutes a dimension of morally relevant goods that *must* be responded to in order for our attitude to be truly morally good. It is more problematic to determine whether a general moral attitude would still be good if we were interested *only* in our own salvation and if the will to be morally good did not include *any* response to the intrinsic value of morality. Imagine that someone were to say, for example: "I do not care a bit for moral goodness as such but I know: I shall be damned if I am not good. Therefore, and therefore alone (to win my salvation and to avoid punishment), I shall be good. Otherwise I would not give a damn for justice and goodness". Would this still be morally good? It appears to be so only in the most rudimentary way, and even this only by involving still a certain unconscious response to the value of one's own person and possibly even to moral goodness because of its intrinsic value[70].

This leads us to a further insight into the true nature of the fundamental moral attitude in his sense: it ought to preserve the hierarchy within the motives of moral acts, and the hierarchical relationship between morally relevant goods and moral values, intending the realization of justice and other morally good acts first of all because of their intrinsic moral goodness.

The element of the fundamental moral attitude directed to all morally relevant goods and moral obligations differs from the more general commitment to truth in being one step more concrete by being based on the recognition that there are some morally obligatory and morally relevant things besides 'whatever truly binds us' as such. It concretizes the *Grundhaltung*

---

world or in other persons but only in ourselves. Only over ourselves can we have this kind of control which permits us to realize moral values directly. Therefore the general 'will to be good' refers not to the moral goodness of others but to our own. It also accepts the irreplaceable character of our own person and the primary way in which their call is directed to our own self, in the sense of a special absoluteness of the moral obligations being addressed to us in such a way which forbids us ever to say that "we should commit a moral evil so that another one avoids an even greater one." Such a moral weighing of goods is excluded from this self-directedness of the 'general will to be good' which recognizes the unique insubstitutable *"Tua res agitur"* in the moral imperative.

[70] If someone is not at least implicitly motivated by the inherent preciousness of moral values but excludes this in the form of a radical disinterest or even hatred for them, the interest in his own objective good is either not even possible any longer or – if it is possible – is deprived of any moral value. One could express this also in terms of the traditional distinction in theology between repentance out of love and out of fear. Repentance out of fear with the total exclusion of any love would seem to be not only imperfect but no repentance at all. Repentance motivated by fear but not rejecting all love is imperfect.

towards truth also by going one step further beyond the moral relevance of truth itself and by recognizing some other morally relevant goods.

We could further distinguish the morally required and obligatory *Grundhaltung*[71] to submit to all morally *obligatory* goods, and the 'optional' *Grundhaltung* which lies in the determination to follow also moral invitations.

Born from the encounter of subject and morally relevant object, besides "moral invitations" to perform free sacrifices or heroic acts such as Maximilian Kolbe's giving his life for a family father, also moral obligations arise which possess another moment of absoluteness and make a direct appeal to our conscience which is evident in cases in which the same morally relevant good (a human life) is at stake without any obligation for us entering into the picture (for example when we see human persons as shoppers in a supermarket where their lives do not impose special or actual moral obligations on us). The universality of the object of the fundamental moral attitude reveals itself also in the response to *all* obligations as new moments compared with the morally relevant goods (for example a human person or life). For this moral obligation and law requires, as Kant saw (though he falsified the object of this insight profoundly by claiming that pure reason gives this law to itself), a new and unconditional respect (*Achtung*), possessing itself a new absoluteness that calls quite logically for a new moment of obedience in the fundamental moral attitude. This element within the fundamental moral attitude is not explicable through the commitment to objective goods such as human life that are morally relevant but do not deserve in themselves this absolute subordination and obedience owed to the moral obligation itself[72]. Inasmuch as the objective moral obligations are always mediated through our knowledge and conscience, and bind us in this form of being recognized and acknowledged by the subject, one could also describe the fundamental moral attitude as the determination to always follow one's conscience.

Also the fundamental openness to non-obligatory moral calls can exist on many levels of qualitative depth and purity: a) it can exist to some more or less limited degree as in most morally good human persons; b) it can also exist in the form of a heroic and in a certain sense unlimited morally good attitude to respond as far as possible not only to *all morally obligatory goods but also to all non-obligatory goods* and indeed to choose the more perfect goods before the lower ones. Such an "unlimitedly morally good attitude"

---

[71] Strictly speaking obligatory is the fundamental moral *intention* to respect all morally obligatory goods and to acquire this *Grundhaltung*, but since the general superactual *attitude* is not within our direct free power (but only the indirect one), it cannot directly be morally obligatory to have it.

[72] See Josef Seifert, *Was ist und was motiviert eine sittliche Handlung?*, cit.

towards non-obligatory goods is found in St. Theresa of Avila, who reports in her *Life* (Autobiography) having vowed to do always what appeared to her morally more perfect.

The fundamental moral attitude can be differentiated also according to the underlying ethical knowledge (the purity and depth of ethical knowledge, its closeness to the moral data, etc.) as well as in accordance with the different degrees of the depth of the will and the volitional affirmation of the morally relevant goods. There are also many degrees of moral consciousness informing and characterizing the fundamental moral attitude. Its scope is still immensely universal but with each specific understanding of concrete morally relevant goods it becomes more conscious and is enriched and expanded with respect to its content and object.

If a person accepts the existence of God as an infinite personal being most worthy of love (as an *id quo maius nihil cogitari possit*), the good fundamental moral attitude may assume much more content still and exist in the form of the unambiguous love of God and love of neighbor. When the truth about the world and God revealed by Christ is accepted, a completely new quality of the fundamental moral attitude and of the virtues informed by *caritas* comes to exist[73].

The fundamental moral attitude is also one of obedience and of surrender to God. Socrates already expressed this by saying in the *Apology*: "I respect you, Athenians, but I have to obey God more than you." This obedience to God constitutes a new personal reference point discovered quite naturally in the very nature of the moral ought but much more clearly present and grasped when the existence of God is known and consciously responded to. The "thou shalt..." of the moral ought involves in its essence and at its root a moment which finds explicit expression in the *Old Testament*: "For I am the LORD your God: [...] and ye shall be holy; for I am holy"[74]: The reference to the absolute divine personal being is not only found in the Bible but discovered in other essential marks of morality: in responsibility, punishment, etc. Cardinal Newman thought in his *Grammar of Assent* that this *datum* prior to all religion is the "creative principle of all religion." So much did he recognize that it precedes all positive religion.

---

[73] See on this the phenomenological analyses of Dietrich von Hildebrand in his *Transformation in Christ. On the Christian Attitude of Mind*, last edition with a new sub-title: *Transformation in Christ. Our Path to Holiness*. Reprint of 1948 (New Hampshire: Sophia Institute Press. 1989), and by the same author, *Ethics*, cit., as well as by the same author, *Das Wesen der Liebe*, cit., ch. 11.

[74] The full text is: "44 For I am the LORD your God: ye shall therefore sanctify yourselves, and ye shall be holy; for I am holy:", *Lev.* 11:44. See also *Lev.* 11:45; 19:2; 20:26; 21:8, and also 1 *Peter* 1:16: "16 Because it is written, Be ye holy; for I am holy."

There are countless degrees and forms of this fundamental moral attitude directed to God: obedience to God, desire that His will be done, the solemn affirmation of his holiness in adoration, etc. The climax of this gesture in the general morally good attitude lies in the explicit religious acts of the love and of the glorification of God.

Is then an atheistic morally good attitude possible? I think that it is. An atheist can very well have the general morally good attitude related to truth: "If truth exists, I will accept it; if God exists, I will glorify him." But the good general attitude of the atheist is morally good only if the atheist is *open in principle, i.e. if God does exist and were to be known to him,* to this motivating ground of morality. If the atheist rejected God explicitly *and in principle* (even if he were to find that he exists) or if he were to set up his moral goodness against God, all his acts would lose any moral value for the reason of embodying diabolical pride and revolt against God. Any moral attitude such as described by Nietzsche : "if there were a God, how could I stand not to be one. Therefore there is no God", could only be evil. But on the other hand, the fundamental morally good attitude towards truth and the good might even demand atheism, not objectively but subjectively, if someone had an image of God according to which God, if He corresponded to this image, truly would deserve to be rejected in the name of an eternal moral order and in the name of evident moral values. Such a conception of God which would justify the rejection of God includes the widespread deterministic Calvinist image of a God who would condemn angels and men to eternal punishment for their sins although these sins and the fact that they do evil would solely depend on God's own will against whose decree the creatures could in no way act. An acceptance of such a God would be morally evil, at least if one understands properly what one believes in such a determinist interpretation of sin and hell. Therefore, a rejection of such a God who would correspond to this false image, is morally demanded. It is also clear that, when we presuppose the objective goodness of God, this moment of the morally good attitude, the response to God, differs very much depending on the vagueness or clarity of someone's metaphysical conception of God. This element of the morally good attitude towards God reaches from a vague "openness to God" as the atheist or agnostic can even possess it, to the fervent and unconditioned love of God.

Many authors thought that the fundamental morally good attitude is restricted to a very formal abstract level, or even is a-thematic in the sense of having no object at all[75], but in reality, as we now easily see, it can have very rich and concrete objects, embracing them all in their wealth of content and

---

[75] This is the "transcendental" conception of the "fundamental option" found in Karl Rahner and other authors, which is, in my opinion, in contradiction to the nature of inten-

branching off into the different concrete virtues which respond to single spheres of morally relevant goods such as rights (justice) or property (honesty), or the dignity and 'sacredness' of the body and human sexuality (chastity and purity), and giving rise to responses to still more individual goods. Also the morally good attitude towards God is, if we understand God as supreme embodiment of all pure perfections, directed to an extremely *concrete* and *living* reality, the archetype of all individual *thisness* and qualitative *concreteness* as the perfect justice, love, goodness, wisdom, and all-encompassing perfection.

At least to receive its full meaning, the general free moral attitude must also exist superactually, i.e. to say its reality in us cannot be restricted to the times when we consciously live it, think of it. This attitude is not meant to endure merely a few moments but to become a lasting and formative basis of our moral life. A person's rational life, his knowing and willing, can extend far beyond the limits of the moment and of the short islands of the present. It can last, without being subconscious. The superactual attitudes are rather *supraconscious* and constitute the background and form of conscious human life. Not all human experiences allow for such a superactual existence. But to many, such as to "knowing some object" and "knowing that" (which refers to states of affairs), or to love, it belongs essentially that they exist only really if they are superactual and not restricted to short islands of time. Both general moral attitudes and responses to individual persons, such as the love of our child or spouse, can be superactual. Thus, starting from the most general fundamental moral option for or against the morally relevant goods as such, for or against God, for or against truth, the life and formative influence of superactual free acts extend to concrete attitudes towards individual persons. Our moral life is deeply formed by such superactual responses and attitudes. Such attitudes can also open our intellect and contribute much to our value-perception or lead to value-blindness[76]. Thus they exert an enormous influence on our moral life.

---

tional consciousness which must have an object, reducing the fundamental option to an irrational state of consciousness. Of course, if *a-thematic* were to mean the superactual character of this attitude which continues to exist even when I do not actually perform and live it, it would be quite corrrect to attribute this to the fundamental moral attitude. If the term meant that this attitude *can never be actualized in consciousness,* it would again be a false assertion because all superactual attitudes can and should become actually conscious from time to time. The same would apply to the thesis that the fundamental moral attitude can never become the theme or object of reflection. Superactual realities differ wholly from the sphere of the subconscious. See the discussion of the superactuality of virtues in Dietrich von Hildebrand, *Ethics*, cit.

[76] See on all of this the important work of Dietrich von Hildebrand, *Sittlichkeit und ethische Werterkenntnis*, cit.

Drawing the conclusion for our topic, we see that to be free is not restricted to external actions directed towards realizing not-yet-existing states of affairs in the world, nor to free responses to individual beings. Freedom entails also general virtues (or vices) to whole spheres of morally relevant goods and the most fundamental moral attitude. Thus freedom is situated at the level of the very core of the being of the person which can be actualized only through freedom.

IV. COOPERATIVE FREEDOM AND THE GIFT OF SELF AS SUPREME FULFILLMENT OF PERSONS

It is clear that we cannot directly realize superactual attitudes by a simple *fiat*. We can engender freely general moral intentions, yes, but they neither immediately take root in the person nor acquire instantaneously the personal depth proper to superactual acts. Similarly, we cannot, by a simple fiat of our will, bring about affective responses such as grief or love, joy, compassion, or repentance, however appropriate also these affective and spiritual affections are to their objects[77]. Yet this does not imply that we have no freedom or responsibility with respect to our superactual attitudes or to our spiritual affective responses such as love, repentance or grief. We come to recognize two further important manifestations of freedom here: (1) the *indirect* role of our free acts, and (2) cooperative freedom.

(1) A single free action of helping someone lies within the power of our immediate freedom (in spite of the difficulties and limitations we may experience with respect to its actualization), and has an immediate and direct effect in the world and on our conscious life. Yet each action has also indirect effects on the person; it will influence and gradually change our superactual attitudes and the kind of emotional responses (love or hatred, warmth or envy and bitterness) we give to others. This applies to good as well as to bad actions. There are many other forms of indirect influence of our freedom. When we meditate on our lives, for example, instead of acting thoughtlessly and without the necessary reflection, we will influence our lives indirectly. Yet this act of meditation itself can be commanded, we can take time to think about the purpose of our lives or hunt from pleasure to pleasure, from noise to noise and divert ourselves in the negative sense de-

---

[77] On the spiritual forms of affectivity see Dietrich von Hildebrand, *The Sacred Heart. An analysis of human and divine affectivity.* (Baltimore/Dublin: Helicon Press, 1965), 2nd ed.: *The Heart* (Chicago: Franciscan Herald Press. 1977); *Über das Herz. Zur menschlichen und gottmenschlichen Affektivität,* (Regensburg: Josef Habbel, 1967).

scribed by Pascal[78]. Thus we come to understand that our freedom has an enormous indirect influence distinct from direct freedom by which we bring about free acts.

(2) Even more amazing is what Hildebrand terms "cooperative freedom." We cannot directly bring about with our freedom attitudes towards persons or values which result indirectly from many free actions, nor can we immediately evoke affective responses of repentance, compassion, or love, which arise in our nature without participation of our freedom and which are morally and humanly speaking adequate to their human or divine object. But besides indirect freedom exerting great influence on such data of the moral life as virtues and vices, we also have another important capacity: namely that for cooperative freedom, for relating freely and in a particularly intimate way to those realities in us that arise without freedom. We can conspire freely with the tears of repentance that arise in us or suppress them, we can disavow feelings of hatred freely or identify ourselves with them. We can cooperate with emotions of love and form them freely from within by sanctioning them. Hildebrand calls this cooperative freedom. With this concept, we touch upon what constitutes the very heart of human freedom. Recognition of cooperative freedom even modifies what we have said about freedom at the beginning of this paper, describing freedom in terms of being "the lords over the being and the non-being of our acts." This characterization of freedom in terms of autonomy does not describe adequately many aspects of freedom such as the freedom in the grateful receiving of gifts, in gratitude as such, and in cooperative freedom[79].

---

[78] Blaise Pascal, *Pensées*, nr 139 (136). See also Seifert, *Schachphilosophie* (Darmstadt: Wissenschaftliche Buchgesellschaft, 1989), pp. 90-105.

[79] See W. Desmond's paper read at this Fifth World Congress of Christian Philosophy. See also Balduin Schwarz, "Über die Dankbarkeit." In: Tenzler, J. (Ed): *Wirklichkeit der Mitte. Beiträge zu einer Strukturanthropologie. Festgabe für August Vetter zum 80. Geburtstag.* Freiburg-München 1968, pp. 677-704; "Del agradecimiento." (Spanish translation of this paper by Juan Miguel Palacios) In: *Ediciones del Departamento de Etica y Sociologia de la Universidad Complutense en omenaje a su catedratico director R.P. José Todolí Duque O.P. con ocasion de su jubilacion.* Madrid 27 de Mayo de 1985; the same author, "Der Dank als Gesinnung und Tat". In: J. Seifert (Ed.) *Danken und Dankbarkeit. Eine universale Dimension des Menschseins.* (Heidelberg: Carl Winter-Universitätsverlag, 1992), pp. S. 15-26; "Some reflections on gratitude," in: B. Schwarz, (Ed.): *The human person and the world of values. A tribute to Dietrich von Hildebrand by his friends in philosophy* (=C.1) (New York, 1960), pp. 168-191; "Réflexions sur la gratitude et l'admiration," in: *Entretiens autour de Gabriel Marcel* (Neuchâtel, 1976), pp. 229-248 (also *ibid.*, pp. 242-248, Diskussion). See also Balduin Schwarz (Ed.), *Dankbarkeit ist das Gedächtnis des Herzens. Aphorismen* (München: Don Bosco Verlag, 1992).

In many cases, of which the highest involve divine grace, we find in our soul gifts and experiences of joy or love which arise in us without depending on our freedom. Yet inasmuch as such movements of our soul are adequate or inadequate to their object, good or bad, we must not let them arise in us without involvement of our freedom. When they are bad, we ought to disavow them, thereby not immediately eradicating them but "decapitating" them, as it were. We can freely say 'no' to our feeling of intense envy, when we realize its evilness and inappropriateness. This is not an act of repression but, on the contrary, an act of conscious confrontation with ourselves. By disavowing feelings of envy, the person disassociates himself from them. Thus they become movements of the soul for which we are no longer responsible in the way in which we are responsible when we let envy grow in us without taking such a free stance.

Much more profound is the interpenetration of freedom and affective responses – or other non-free experiences and gifts in us – in the positive case. When deep love or a feeling of repentance is granted to us – a feeling or movement of our soul which we never could have given to ourselves – our freedom is not condemned to remain outside such gifts. It can join in with the gift. We can freely sanction our affective response or an attitude of our will of which we recognize that it has gift-character and does not stand simply in our power. By such a free *sanctioning* of these acts, we integrate them into our free life. Analogously, we can appropriate and accept into our freedom all intentional and good acts which arise in our soul, including our acceptance and conviction of the truth. Also in the sphere of the intellect we can integrate by a free sanction, and affirm from within, convictions which arise organically and without being free acts from our cognition. Given the rationality of the conviction and its character as a theoretical and adequate response to reality (states of affairs), we can also sanction it or add to convictions resulting simply from knowledge (*being convinced by the object known*) convictions which have the character of *free real assent*[80]. We can say a free yes to truth, a response which takes on a new role when it is not merely based on evident knowledge but on probable knowledge or on faith[81]. We can turn what is given to us as a gift into a free act, by freely sanctioning such gifts. Gift and freedom interpenetrate each other here. We might speak, with Dietrich von Hildebrand[82], following a great and original discovery of his, anticipated by other thinkers, in particular by Saint Francis

---

[80] This played a great role in Stoic philosophy of the judgment.
[81] Dietrich von Hildebrand did not discuss the role of freedom in theoretical responses such as convictions, which he regarded as not free in his *Ethics*, cit., ch. 17.
[82] See Dietrich von Hildebrand, *Ethics*, cit., ch. 25, pp. 316-337.

de Sales[83], of a spiritual wedding of our will with our affections and with other noble movements or acts in us, including the free assent to truth. By affections which well up in us as gifts, such as deep emotions of love, our will is enriched and allowed to partake as it were of the wealth of those affections and of other movements of the soul which possess gift character. Thus the deepest dimensions of freedom do not actualize themselves simply by the free center of the person alone. They are even not only formed by, but also dependent on the value of the object which gives purpose and meaning to our freedom.

Rather, the deepest dimension of human freedom requires a gift which precedes it and in cooperation with which can freedom alone attain its supreme dignity[84]. This is true – in a special way – of the deepest act of freedom realized only in love and in the gift of Self, in which we give to the other not only a response or *something* in ourselves, in which we not only perform acts, but give our very self to the other. This self-donation in love requires, in its fullness, on the human level, also the gift of the affective response to the beloved person.

This fact, which is evident on the level of affective experiences and general attitudes and convictions, is much more evident on the level of Christian faith, where we understand the supreme act of freedom to lie in a free acceptance of, and cooperation with, divine grace. Faith is a free act of "faith in," and submission to, God and a consequent "belief that" what He reveals to us is true. Even more profoundly, the supernatural love of *caritas*, without which we cannot say a *"Totus Tuus,"* requires the gift of grace. In this ultimate sense, then, "to be free" means to cooperate with gifts in the natural and supernatural order, and without using our freedom in cooperation with such gifts we can never attain the highest perfection to which the person is called, nor fulfill what it means "to be a person."

---

[83] See Andreas Laun, "Die mitwirkende Freiheit bei Dietrich von Hildebrand und die geistliche Lehre des hl. Franz von Sales," in: *Truth and Value. The Philosophy of Dietrich von Hildebrand*. Aletheia Vol. V. Bern: Peter Lang Verlag. 1991, pp. 258-264. Also in: the same author: *Fragen der Moraltheologie heute*. Freiburg-Basel-Wien: Herder. 1992, pp. 216-220. See likewise A. Laun, *Der salesianische Liebesbegriff – Nächstenliebe – heilige Freundschaft – eheliche Liebe* (Eichstätt: Franz-Sales-Verlag, 1993), pp. 91 ff.

[84] While this is a purely philosophical distinction based on the data of affective experiences, it is clear that this philosophical distinction is of the highest importance for an understanding of the Catholic theological teaching on justification.

MICHEL SCHOOYANS
L'Université Catholique de Louvain,
Belgium

LIBERTÉ HUMAINE ET PARTICIPATION POLITIQUE

L'histoire contemporaine – celle dont nous avons tous été témoins – révèle que tous les malheurs qui ont affligé l'humanité procèdent d'aberrations provenant, toutes, du mépris des principes fondamentaux d'une philosophie politique d'inspiration personnaliste.

Nous diviserons donc cet exposé en trois grandes parties. Nous commencerons par évoquer les grandes idéologies qui, à partir de principes néfastes, ont inspiré des régimes méconnaissant les requêtes fondamentales d'une philosophie politique digne de l'homme. Nous examinerons ensuite les sources métaphysiques d'où jaillit cette philosophie sociale. Enfin nous réexposerons les principes fondamentaux qui sous-tendent une philosophie sociale personnaliste.

I. TROIS IDÉOLOGIES CONTEMPORAINES: LEURS PRINCIPES FONDAMENTAUX

Notre siècle a vu fleurir trois grandes idéologies qui portent toutes trois la marque d'une forte influence hégélienne. Ces idéologies ont pour nom le *nazisme* (auquel, pour simplifier, nous rattachons ici le fascisme), le *communisme* et, plus récemment, le *néolibéralisme*. Sauf dans certains pays, les deux premières idéologies sont généralement entrées dans une phase de latence, alors que l'idéologie néolibéraliste est en franche expansion.

1. LE NAZISME

L'idéologie nazie a conduit à l'exaltation du corps social, de ce que Feuerbach appelait *l'humanité générique*. Sous ce rapport, la parenté est fondamentale entre le nazisme et le fascisme: tous deux sont des *organicismes* considérant que les hommes ne sont que des membres d'un corps social qui les dépasse et même les transcende. Seul le corps social existe vraiment.

Alors que le fascisme exalte *l'État*, le nazisme précise que la seule chose qui importe, en définitive, c'est la *race*, entendez la race aryenne, dont la pureté doit être préservée et même améliorée à tout prix. Cette idéologie entraîne donc une sélection des procréateurs, une médecine du corps social, le permis de procréer, la "solution finale" pour les êtres considérés comme inutiles ou nuisibles.

L'essor de cette idéologie, et sa concrétisation dans les régimes hitlérien et mussolien, ont été largement favorisés par la philosophie du droit développée par Binding et par Kelsen dès les années 20. À ce moment, sous l'influence de ces deux auteurs, triomphait en Allemagne le *positivisme juridique*. C'est ce triomphe qui a mis le droit dans l'impossibilité de s'opposer au nazisme et qui en a même favorisé l'essor.

2. LE COMMUNISME SOVIÉTIQUE

L'idéologie communiste n'insiste pas sur la pureté de la race mais plutôt sur pureté idéologique, sur *l'orthodoxie*. Le dissident est fou, aliéné. L'unidimensionalisation de la pensée est la règle générale.

On retrouve ici le thème de l'humanité générique, évoquée par Lénine sous deux présentations imagées: la société est un *orchestre*, où chaque instrumentiste pris individuellement exerce une simple fonction dans l'ensemble; la société est une immense *machine*, dont chaque individu n'est qu'un rouage voué à être remplacé par un autre rouage.

C'est dans ce contexte qu'apparaît le rôle de la psychiatrie: il faut détruire la personnalité pour détruire les défenses personnelles face au mensonge. Il faut déprogrammer-reprogrammer les dissidents.

En somme, le nazisme et le communisme ont voulu imposer une police des corps et une police des esprits. Actuellement, ces idéologies n'ont plus la vigueur maléfique qu'on leur a connue, mais la vigilance reste de mise face à leur résurgence possible et même à la vitalité qu'elles ont conservée dans certains milieux.

3. LE NÉOLIBÉRALISME

L'idéologie néolibéraliste mérite un examen plus détaillé en raison de son actualité et de sa vitalité.

a) *Historiquement*, le libéralisme présente diverses caractéristiques: totale *liberté* dans le domaine économique, selon l'esprit d'Adam Smith; vision *utilitariste* de l'homme: Bentham recommande le calcul des intérêts; vision *hédoniste* de l'homme: égoïste, libertin et calculant ses plaisirs. L'homme par excellence, c'est celui qui est à la fois producteur, consommateur et jouisseur. L'enfant, le vieillard, le malade, le handicapé, le pauvre n'ont guère de valeur.

De là la place du *contrat* dans la tradition libérale: le contrat est un équilibre d'intérêts calculés entre individus.

Le seul élément *modérateur* qui apparaît, c'est la référence à la divinité. Plusieurs grands documents commencent par des expressions comme "Au nom du Dieu Tout Puissant" ou "Au nom de l'Être Suprême".

b) *Actuellement*, le néolibéralisme reprend et radicalise ces caractéristiques. Il affirme la totale liberté, la totale autonomie individuelle dans tous les domaines. L'individu est *seul* à définir ses normes morales; il agit en référence à sa seule conscience. Il se prend pour *législateur*. S'il en a la force, l'individu définit la valeur qu'il accorde aux autres. Il se prend pour *juge*. L'individu s'érige en maître absolu de son existence et de celle des autres. Il se prend pour *créateur*.

Le néolibéralisme pousse au paroxysme les autres traits du libéralisme classique; il les exacerbe. *L'utilitarisme*: l'homme n'est plus seulement producteur et consommateur; il est un produit, c'est-à-dire qu'il est appelé à l'existence selon certains critères et dans les limites de certains quotas. *L'hédonisme*: l'homme cède à la recherche effrénée du plaisir, jusqu'au "don" de la mort", aux autres et à soi-même.

Le *consensus* prend la succession du contrat. En l'absence de toute référence à une réalité transcendante, de toute référence au vrai, au bien, au juste, tout devient négociable. Il n'y a plus de normes qui surplombent les individus, dès lors que les normes elles-mêmes sont toujours négociables.

La règle de la majorité fournit le critère pragmatique de la norme juridique. Celle-ci découle exclusivement de décisions volontaires, toujours modifiables. Cette mentalité donne lieu à une éthique "procédurale", dont la théorie a été faite par Rawls, et qui est courante dans la plupart des comités d'éthique.

c) Les *droits de l'homme* les plus fondamentaux sont ainsi mis en péril. On assiste notamment à des alliances nouvelles entre juristes et médecins, qui veulent arriver à un "consensus" portant sur des pratiques nouvelles que le droit positif légalise. Une difficulté majeure surgit parfois ici du fait de la survivance de quelque article constitutionnel garantissant le droit à la vie. Cette difficulté est cependant régulièrement contournée par la *tactique de la dérogation*. Cette tactique apparaît en France dès l'article 1 de la loi Veil sur l'avortement, et elle se rencontre dans toutes les lois qui traitent des *manipulations génétiques*. Dans ce cas, la tactique de la dérogation consiste, par exemple, à ergoter pour définir les conditions dans lesquelles l'embryon échappera à la protection que la constitution lui garantit. Le droit de l'être humain à la vie, depuis ses commencements les plus secrets, dépend de plus en plus d'une décision "procédurale", c'est-à-dire d'un simple consensus.

Il en résulte, comme l'a relevé Sojénitsyne, que l'idéologie néolibérale conduit le droit à dévorer la morale et à se substituer à elle. Comme cela s'est passé en Allemagne dans les années 20, nous assistons à l'affirmation d'un nouveau *positivisme juridique* qui donne force de loi aux décisions issues de la volonté des plus forts. La morale est donc phagocytée par le droit positif; elle devient par le fait même *relative* aux intérêts des individus qui ont assez de puissance pour faire de la loi le reflet de leurs intérêts.

d) Enfin, non content de relativiser radicalement la morale à partir de *l'individu*, le même néolibéralisme la relativise également à partir des *cultures*. Chaque culture a son éthique, sa morale. Nous sommes donc ramenés ici à Spencer, Durkheim et Levi-Bruhl.

e) De cette brève analyse de l'idéologie néolibérale se dégagent diverses conclusions.

1) Cette idéologie incline les individus à *rejeter toute dépendance* face à un être supérieur ou face aux autres. De fait, à force de n'obéir qu'à nous-mêmes, nous rejetons les autres. Toute dépendance est intolérable; toute fidélité est conditionnelle et conditionnel est l'amour lui-même.

2) Imaginer qu'il soit possible d'arriver à un consensus par voie "procédurale" est totalement *utopique*, puisque, par définition, le consensus procède de la subjectivité d'hommes qui se réservent le droit strictement individuel de définir leur vérité et leur conception de la justice.

3) L'affirmation individualiste du moi, conduite jusqu'à ses ultimes conséquences, requiert une maîtrise totale de la vie et de la mort. L'idéologie libérale est héritière directe de la tradition *nihiliste et nietzschéenne*. Elle débouche nécessairement sur la *"culture de la mort"*.

C'est ce qui explique l'obstination à légaliser l'avortement et l'euthanasie, à banaliser la stérilisation de masse, à faire du prosélytisme pour le suicide – de préférence médicalement assisté. L'expansion du sida trouve là une de ses explications les plus profondes et les plus évidentes. Les hommes *donnent* la mort et même *se donnent* la mort parce qu'ils croient qu'il est impossible de combler le désir d'un au-delà, qui est pourtant gravé à la fine pointe de leur âme. Alors ils croient se libérer de ce désir moyennant le plaisir souverain et dérisoire qu'ils recherchent dans la mort.

II. LA RÉFÉRENCE FONDATRICE À DIEU

1. AUTORITÉ ET OBÉISSANCE

Face à ces idéologies et aux modèles de sociétés qui s'en réclament, nous pouvons nous rattacher à des principes d'action sociale et politique enracinant l'engagement temporel dans la référence à Dieu.

Quelle qu'en soit la modalité – politique, économique, social, intellectuel – *tout* pouvoir, pour se justifier, doit être référé à Dieu. Si en effet Dieu a doté l'homme d'une *constitution sociale*, cet être raisonnable et libre qu'est l'homme, il entre dans le dessein de Dieu que les hommes se dotent d'instances de pouvoir appropriées pour organiser leur vie ensemble, en particulier dans le domaine politique. Du coup, le pouvoir est *relativisé* et *modéré*. En effet, la référence à Dieu éclaire cette réalité *sui generis* qu'est le pouvoir. Au niveau spécifiquement politique, le pouvoir met en relation des hommes qui ont tous reçu du même Dieu la même constitution sociale. Cela implique immédiatement qu'aucun homme n'est fondé à exercer sur autrui une autorité qui ne soit raisonnable, librement consentie, justifiée et légitime. Cela implique aussi que, sous peine de s'aliéner, *aucun homme n'est fondé à obéir si ce n'est par un constentement libre et éclairé à celui qui commande légitimement.*

2. ABSOLUTISME ET ANARCHIE

Ce que n'ont pas vu beaucoup de théoriciens modernes, et ce qu'ignorent les idéologies contemporaines, c'est que ni le prince, ni le peuple, en raison même de leur finitude, n'étaient fondés à se poser en instance *ultime* de pouvoir. *L'absolutisme* du prince a son pendant exact dans *l'anarchie* révolutionnaire du peuple. Le rejet par le prince et/ou par le peuple de la *référence fondatrice commune* à Dieu, avec la relation constituante qu'elle implique, entraîne le rejet de la relation de sociabilité inscrite dans le chef du prince comme dans celui de tous les autres membres du corps politique.

L'athéisme politique ne provient pas seulement de l'athéisme métaphysique ou de la sécularisation ambiante, ou d'une "profanation" de Dieu. Il résulte aussi d'une réduction du pouvoir à la volonté de puissance, d'une perversion du pouvoir en "hybris", d'une mort de la relation constitutive du pouvoir. Rappelons Machiavel: "Tout État où la crainte de l'Être suprême n'existe pas, doit périr s'il n'est maintenu par la crainte du prince même qui supplée au défaut de religion" (*Discours*, 1, 11).

Tous les totalitarismes contemporains dérivent des conceptions purement *immanentistes* du pouvoir qui ont fleuri à l'époque moderne, et dont Hobbes est le prototype. L'histoire moderne et contemporaine le confirme:

l'agnosticisme de principe, en politique, et à fortiori l'athéisme, engendrent automatiquement une nouvelle forme d'idolâtrie qu'est la religion civile, dont la charte est exposée dans l'avant-dernier chapitre du *Contrat social* de Rousseau. Une fois chassée la référence à Dieu, *rien*, hormis des conventions, ne peut plus modérer le pouvoir *dans sa nature intime*. Bien plus, lorsque Dieu est chassé de l'horizon politique, le pouvoir finit par se transmuter en puissance pure, *démesurée*: celle du prince ou celle du peuple – vite antagoniques. En ce sens, *le choix politique est un choix pour ou contre Dieu*.

La société humaine est constituée par des êtres complémentaires, ayant des talents divers, des capacités différentes, mais dotés, tous, de raison et de volonté libre. Le but vers lequel tend la société, c'est le bonheur de ses membres. Chaque membre est donc invité à contribuer, selon sa personnalité propre, à la réalisation du *bien commun*, dont dépend le bonheur de chacun. À chaque homme échoit un rôle irremplaçable au bénéfice de la communauté, et cette fonction, protégée par le *principe de subsidiarité*, est *service*. L'ouvrier, l'agriculteur, le technicien, le commerçant, etc. exercent des fonctions au service de la société, au service du bien commun. Mais il en va de même du prince: il coordonne, harmonise l'activité des membres de la société, il gouverne celle-ci, c'est-à-dire l'oriente, à son niveau propre, vers le bien commun. C'est pourquoi le prince ne peut exercer l'autorité en marge du corps politique, composé d'êtres raisonnables, libres et contribuant – eux aussi – au bien commun. De ce point de vue, l'exercice du pouvoir et de l'autorité apparaît comme un service d'une communauté d'êtres raisonnables et libres.

3. LE POUVOIR EST DÉLÉGUÉ

La référence à Dieu introduit en effet heureusement dans la réflexion sur le pouvoir, et par là dans la vie politique, un élément de *rationalité*. Cet élément est trop souvent gommé de la réflexion contemporaine, où le positivisme juridique fait excellent ménage avec les théories de la politique pure et du pouvoir nu. Les théories fondant le pouvoir en Dieu s'inscrivent souvent, quant à elles, dans le prolongement d'une *métaphysique de la participation existentielle*. Le monde, fait par Dieu – y explique-t-on – n'est pas le lieu de l'incohérence, de l'arbitraire, de l'inconnaissable, de l'absurde; il obéit à un dessein divin, que l'homme peut connaître et grâce auquel il peut agir. La justification du pouvoir ne doit donc pas être cherchée dans un pessimisme radical, mais dans la *nécessité naturelle*, pour les hommes, d'un *gouvernement* qui conduise la société vers le bonheur.

Cette référence à Dieu explique qu'en dernière analyse tout pouvoir humain soit *délégué*. Dieu délègue aux hommes la responsabilité de se gouverner, comme par ailleurs il leur délègue de *procréer*. Dieu donne *procuration* aux hommes: il leur donne tout ce qui leur est nécessaire pour prendre en mains la direction de leur existence. C'est pourquoi la conduite de la société n'est pas soustraite à la loi morale. D'une certaine façon, l'homme est pour lui-même sa propre providence. Dans la gestion de la société comme dans la gestion du monde naturel, l'homme jouit d'une autonomie, fondée dans sa relation *existentielle* à son créateur, et qui pour ce même motif déploie l'inventivité et la responsabilité de l'être fini.

III. LES PRINCIPES DÉRIVÉS

De la référence fondatrice à Dieu, qui vient d'être rappelée, découlent des principes qui nous sont familiers mais qu'il n'est pas inutile d'évoquer rapidement.

1. Le *bien commun* demande que l'on tienne compte des requêtes de la justice sous toutes ses modalités: sociale, distributive, commutative. Les requêtes de la justice distributive, en particulier, donnent lieu à une *option préférentielle* pour les pauvres, les handicapés, les plus faibles.

2. Le *principe de subsidiarité* nous alerte sur les formes innombrables d'abus de pouvoir, dans tous les domaines. Il est aussi le point focal de tout l'enseignement social de l'Église sur la démocratie. Dès qu'on parle, par exemple, de *participation* à la vie politique ou économique, on met en oeuvre ce principe. L'homme a non seulement quelque chose à *apporter* aux autres, mais est aussi en droit de *recevoir* des autres quelque chose de leur richesse. Jean-Paul II a fréquemment étendu le champ d'application de ce principe, et du principe suivant, aux *relations Nord-Sud*.

3. Autre principe qui nous est familier: la *destination universelle des biens*. Il nous rappelle que nous sommes *gestionnaires* responsables d'un monde mis à notre disposition, à celle d'autrui, à celle des générations futures. C'est à la lumière de ce principe que se comprend la portée et les limites du droit de *propriété privée*. Même si celle-ci est garantie par l'exercice de la liberté individuelle, je ne dois pas moins en faire un *usage social*. La réflexion sur ce thème devrait déboucher sur une discussion concernant la destination universelle des biens *intellectuels*, si souvent occultés aux populations du Tiers-Monde.

4. *L'homme au travail*. Le quatrième principe de référence porte sur le *travail*. Avec Heidegger, la philosophie contemporaine a souvent souligné que l'homme était un "être ouvrier", capable d'humaniser la nature, d'y inscrire ses projets. L'activité de l'homme n'est pas préprogrammée; son avenir doit être *inventé*. Nous pourrions creuser ce thème en dégageant la corrélation entre le travail comme *devoir* et comme *droit*. Cela nous permettrait de creuser le thème du *chômage*, tant au Nord qu'au Sud.

5. *La personne humaine*. Cependant, la référence qui domine les autres nous renvoie à la centralité de la *personne humaine*. C'est effet en tant que personne raisonnable et dotée de volonté libre, que l'homme est image de Dieu. Comme le souligne souvent Jean-Paul II, tel est le point d'ancrage des *droits de l'homme*, du droit à la *vie*, du droit à la *liberté religieuse*, du droit à la *famille*, etc. *L'égale dignité* de tous les hommes est le nouveau nom de l'égalité et il offre à la *fraternité* son fondement essentiel. Contre des idéologies qui prétendent fonder une fraternité sans père, nous avons la mission de dire au monde que tous, nous avons reçu de Dieu la vie en partage. En plus de tout cela, comme chrétiens, nous avons le privilège d'annoncer au monde que ce Dieu est Amour et que ce Dieu est Père. Tel est le fondement chrétien de la *solidarité*.

6. Tel est le défi majeur auquel nous sommes confrontés au seuil du XXIe siècle. Face au parti pris de rejet de principes, central dans le néolibéralisme pur et dur, face au nouvel *an-archisme*, nous sommes invités à une tâche particulièrement exaltante et infiniment joyeuse: celle qui consiste à proclamer sans restriction ni dérogation, l'égale dignité de tout homme, et celle qui consiste à être témoins actifs de ce qui manque le plus aux hommes d'aujourd'hui: *la tendresse et l'espérance*.

TADEUSZ STYCZEŃ, SDS
Catholic University of Lublin
Poland

FREEDOM AND LAW. FOR OR AGAINST LIFE? THE ETHICIAN CONFRONTING THE "INEFFICIENCY" OF TRUTH

Homo homini res sacra
– *Seneca*
Hominum causa omne ius constitutum est
– *Iustiniani Corpus Iuris Civilis*

I. STATUS QUAESTIONIS. DOES FREEDOM REMAIN ITSELF WHEN IT AGREES TO THE ABSURDITY OF A "LAW AGAINST LIFE"?

Answering the question suggested by the subject of my presentation, as an ethician, I am supposed to make a statement concerning a "law against life". However, the formulation a "law against life" itself raises our spontaneous objection. Is this not an objection on the part of our reason, an advocate of truth? Trying to save his rationality, when put in front of the provocation of a "law against life", man is simply made to ask himself the question about the origin and basis of the thing that seems "one of the strangest aberrations which have ever entered the human mind"[1]. How could it ever happen that the three words: a "law against life" were joined together in

---
[1] Cf. Clarence Irving Lewis, *An Analysis of Knowledge and Valuation*, La Salle 1946. Part of this book, entitled *Poznanie, działanie i wartościowanie* (Recognition, Action, Valuation), is included in the volume: J. Krzywicki (ed.), *Filozofia amerykańska. Wybór rozpraw i szkiców historycznych*, Boston University Press, 1958, p. 213. The author of the above statement continues by saying: "Odmówienie wszelkim ocenom wartościującym prawdziwości i fałszywości oraz charakteru poznawczego musiałoby prowadzić do moralnego i praktycznego cynizmu" (The denial of the truthfulness or falsity, or of the cognitive character, of moral valuations would have to result in moral and practical cynicism. All action would then become senseless).

such contradictory a way? And how can one ever try to justify their logical conjunction? Is a "law against life" simply possible, is it at all conceivable? Or maybe it has only been a result of the time when people happened to take "a day off" from using their reason? But would it not mean that it was the time when they took a day off from being themselves; that they have lost themselves?

Indeed. This formulation is shocking due to the falseness inherent in it, due to the most extreme form of falseness, namely absurdity. A "law against life" is nothing but a *contradictio in adiecto*, just like squaring of the circle is! Hence man raises a radical objection here. By this he defends truth and – simultaneously – himself: his own rationality and freedom. He directly notices that he would stop being himself, that he would renounce his independence, and so enslave himself, if he accepted, with a free decision making act, something in which he has recognized falseness, and which he has himself already considered as false[2]. Is this not where the spontaneous objection to a "law against life" arises? This objection is simply an expression of man's respect for truth that he has himself recognized. It is simultaneously manifestation of his respect for his rationality and freedom, and ultimately, of his respect for the truth about himself as a rationally free being.

Hence also an ethician – an advocate of ethos, and so an advocate of "truth governed freedom"[3] – asks if man – a rationally free being – is allowed to agree to the absurdity of a "law against life"? Does man not decompose his identity when he agrees to this absurdity, when he violates his rationality, and hence his freedom, in a suicidal way [4]; even if he does it by

---

[2] "Ktokolwiek głosi coś sprzecznego z postawą, którą sam zajmuje, ten albo żartuje, albo też sprowadza swe własne stanowisko do niedorzeczności" (Whoever proclaims something contradictory to what he himself believes, is either joking or reducing his own position to absurdity), op. cit., p. 221.

[3] This concise description of ethos as "truth-governed freedom" (included in John Paul II's address to the creators of culture, in the Church of the Holy Cross in Warsaw, on June 13th 1987), constitutes the very heart of the "moral structure of the freedom of man", as well as of his moral culture, which is the spirit of all culture. This issue was elaborated on by John Paul II, and lately raised by him even twice in his significant addresses: in his message to the UNO of October 5th 1995, on the occasion of the 50 years of the existence of this organization; and in his speech delivered in front of Brandenburger Gate in Berlin, on June 23rd 1996.

Cf. also T. Styczeń, *"Dlaczego 'Ethos'?"* (*Why Ethos?*), in: "Ethos" 1 (1988), pp. 3-7; cf. also Bishop J. Herranz, *La struttura morale della libertà* (Introduzione al Simposio Internazionale *Evangelium vitae* e diritto, Roma 23rd-25th May 1996), and also V. Possenti, *Le società liberali al bivio*, Genova 1991, p. 335 and next.

[4] The point here is what John Paul II describes – also in the address to the World Congress: "Freedom in the Contemporary Culture" in Lublin – as "moral structure of free-

the power of his own dynamism? Can he use his freedom against truth, if such a use of freedom ultimately turns it against itself?

This is why, whenever ethicians speak about what constitutes the essence of law and its basis, they try – for centuries now – to direct our attention to what constitutes the essence of man's humanity. The result of their reflection has been expressed in the probably most concise a way by the well-known statement from the Justinian's Codex: *Hominum causa omne ius constitutum est*[5]. The reason for the existence of the law is to protect the good that man is. Hence a legal act, *lex*, is supposed to give expression of what belongs to every human person – *suum cuique*[6] – by the power of his being human. This *suum cuique* is nothing but *ius, ius naturale*, a right, that is *iustum*, a right deriving from nature, where also *iustitia*, justice, comes from. Therefore authentic law-making, legis-lation is nothing but juris-prudence, the reason's reading and translating into the language of a legal act (*ordinatio rationis*)[7] of what belongs to man by the power of his being what he is, by the power of the essence of his nature, and what – on these grounds – serves the good of all people, and of each particular person *(bonum commune, "res publica")*.

It requires – in the first instance – protection of man's life. One cannot say "yes" for man as man without a "yes" for his life. The one who by means of the law says "no" for the life of man, says – by means of this law

---

dom". This structure directly reveals the inseparable bond between the categorical duty to affirm the truth recognized by the subject, and the essence of his freedom. What I have personally recog-nized as truth having stated it myself, must not categorically be denied by me – even if I am in the position to do so – on the grounds of the absolute nature of the axiological dimension of truth, even if I may do so. This problem was one of the main topics of discussion during the Congress. The discussion was provoked by the lectures delivered by Fr A. M. Krąpiec, OP, Fr G. Cottier, OP, Prof. L. Elders, Prof. V. Possenti, Prof. J. Seifert, Prof. D. Fedoryka, Prof. A. Szostek, MIC, Dr. W. Chudy, and Dr. A. Wierzbicki. It is probably worth recalling that the discussion concerned primarily what the Author of the encyclical *Veritatis splendor* stressed, especially in No 50, while presenting the personalistic interpretation of the morally binding power of the natural law.

[5] Cf. *Corpus Iuris Civilis*, vol. primum, Digesta 1.5.2., P. Krueger – Th. Mommsen (ed), Berolini (apud Weidmannos) MCMXI (p. 35). CF. B. Łapicki, *Prawo rzymskie (Roman Law)*, Warsaw 1948, pp. 31-32, where the author presents Cicero's and Seneca's views on the tasks of the state, at the same time stressing the ideas of Hermogenianus, the author of the formula: hominum causa omne ius constitutum sit. Cf. also W. Waldstein, *Ist das suum cuique eine Leerformel?* "Studia et Documenta Historiae et Iuris", LXI (1995), Romae, Pontificia Universitas Lateranensis, pp. 179-215.

[6] Cf. Wolfgang Waldstein, *Ist das suum quique eine Leeformel?* "Studia et Documenta Historiae et Iuris" LXI (1995) Romae, Pontificia Universitas Lateranensis, and – by the same author: *Legislation (LEX) as an Expression of Jurisprudence (IUS)*, "Ethos", Special Edition, No 2 (1996), pp. 143-153.

[7] Cf. endnote no 6.

– "no" for man as man[8]. Man is who he is, if he at all is, which means – in the conditions imposed by this world: if he is alive. Hence St. Thomas Aquinas will say: *Viventibus vivere est esse*. From there derives the fundamental significance of the affirmation of the existence of man – of the fact that he is – for the affirmation of the essence of man – of who he is[9]. It will suffice to refer to the law of contraposition taken from logic: $(p \rightarrow q) \rightarrow (\sim q \rightarrow \sim p)$ in order to explain the matter definitely, and thus to conclude it. Any law against the life of man is an anti-law which is only considered to be the law; it manifests lawlessness identified with law, which is called contradiction: $(p \wedge \sim p)$ – in the language of the logic, and absurdity in every day language. Hence everyone who finds truth in the classical statement taken from the Corpus Iuris Civilis, which says: *Hominum causa omne ius constitutum est*, and which hence makes the good that man is the reason for which the law is the law, must be shocked by the very choice of words in the formula: "a law against life"[10].

Will it then bear any sense – and is it at all needed – to carry on any further ethical analysis of the case of a "law against life"? It might seem that it does not and that it is not. Does anti-truth not annihilate itself? It seems not to need any help. Sed contra ...

1. THE ABSURDITY OF A "LAW AGAINST LIFE" HAS BECOME A FACT OF ... CULTURE

It turns out – unfortunately – that such an analysis not only bears sense, but is also badly needed. It is so, firstly, because it is the object of investigation and its aim that determine the method of investigation; and secondly, which is the most important factor here, the mentioned object, namely, a

---

[8] Cf. T. Styczeń, *Etyka a polityka, czyli czym jest – i czym musi być państwo i prawo, o ile człowiek ma pozostać człowiekiem* (*Ethics and Politics – What is and what must the state and the law be if man is to remain human*), in: T. Styczeń, *Solidarność wyzwala* (Solidarity Liberates), Lublin TN KUL 1993, pp. 162-163.

[9] As man's existence is ultimately a gift from his Personal Creator, the affirmation of the Creator of man is impossible without the affirmation of the life of man as a divine gift *par excellance*. St. John, the Evangelist will say: "Anyone who says 'I love God' and hates his brother is a liar, since no one who fails to love the brother whom he can see can love God whom he has not seen" (1 J, 20); while St. Ireneus will continue by saying: Homo vivens – gloria Dei – the living man is the Glory of God. Cf. T. Styczeń, *Nienarodzony miarą i szansą demokracji* (*The Unborn as the Measure and Chance of Democracy*), in: T. Styczeń (ed): *Nienarodzony miarą demokracji* (*The Unborn as the Measure of Democracy*), Lublin RW KUL 1991, p. 22-23.

[10] It is also worth referring here to St. Thomas's definition of *lex* as *ordinatio rationis ad bonum commune ab eo qui curam communitatis habet promulgata*.

"law against life", does exist in spite of its bearing marks of logical, ethical and juridical absurdity. This absurdity has become a fact. It has become a fact and it remains a fact in many democratic states all over the world in the form actual lawlessness appearing under the guise of the actual institution of the law.

A significant manifestation of this situation – which would be treated as an "argument from an example" by logic[11] – is the fact of legalization of abortion. Firstly, it was made a fact in parliaments, or by means of plebiscites, by the will of the majority of citizens, the "holders" of their states. Then, through the system of international organizations, this absurdity managed to reach the top of the cultural and political scene of the world, so that it could now shape its cultural face from this height[12]. In this way, the fact bearing this absurdity, and essentially a fact of anti-culture, managed to find its place in the world as a product of people, and so as a fact of their pecu-

---

Protection of the common good of all, within a given society, assumes firstly, the effort to guarantee everyone legal protection of their lives – *ab eo qui curam communitatis habet*. The state – as a law-maker supposed to protect already by means of legal acts (*lex*) any other good of its citizens (the so-called good for the person) – cannot – without falling into contradiction with the principle of the protection of these goods – legally exclude some lives from this protection, if life is the good fundamental for the person in relation to all the other goods, including the major one of being a person. The state as a law-maker cannot do it, especially to the citizens who fall within the category of the completely helpless (incapable of aggression) and hence completely innocent ones? The state cannot do it without falling into a contradiction with the principle that it has itself accepted. Cf. *Evangelium vitae*, 72.

Moreover, the principle of justice imposes a particular duty on the law-maker, namely the duty to exercise special care, which results from the principle of the preferential treatment of the poor (cf. encyclical *Sollicitudo rei socialis*). A precise expression of this formula can be found in Wincenty Kadłubek's formula: *Iustitia est quae maxime prodest ei qui minime potest* ("Monumenta Poloniae Historica", vol. I. Lvov 1872, p. 255), known today as the max-min principle; cf. also John Rawls: *A Theory of Justice*, Oxford 1972. While formulating the *max-min* principle as the criterion for the recognition of any public institution as a just one, Rawls clearly refers to the intuition to which the mediaeval canonist of Cracow gave a verbal expression that is ingenious in its simplicity.

[11] Cf. T. Czeżowski, *Logika. Podręcznik dla studiujących nauki filozoficzne* (*Logic. A Handbook for Students of Philosophical Sciences*), Warszawa 1968.

[12] Cf. Pope John Paul II's letter of March 18th 1994 to Ms Nafis Sadik, General Secretary to the UN International Conference on Population and Development in Cairo in 1994. "L'Osservatore Romano", sabbato 19 marzo 1994, where on page 7 we read: *For example, the international consensus of the 1984 Mexico City International Conference on Population that "in no case should abortion be promoted as a method of family planning" is completely ignored in the draft document. Indeed, there is a tendency to promote an internationally recognized right to access to abortion on demand, without any restriction, with no regard to the rights of the unborn, in a manner which goes beyond what even now is unfortunately accepted by the laws of some nations.*

liar culture. What gives this culture this horrifying peculiarity if not people's consensus to an action that brings absurdity into effect?

Probably nothing else shows so sharply and so bitterly the destructive powers of the revolt made by people's act of consensus on something that is an evident absurdity, as the fact that the object of this revolt is such a respected institution of the human culture as the one of the law. Indeed, the institution which for thousands of years constituted the foundation and the basic manifestation of people's moral and political culture, suddenly – in a certain historical moment – became its own contradiction by the act of their free decision. What would Seneca – the author of the words: Homo homini res sacra!, say to it were he able to stand among us today?

An ethician – deeply disturbed by this act – concludes its ethical and cultural diagnosis.

2. THE CULTURE OF ABSURDITY – THE CULTURE OF DEATH
THE CULTURE OF DEATH – THE DEATH OF CULTURE

Here are the three component parts of this diagnosis. By making a legal act which excludes from any legal protection those who being completely innocent are being killed, and by protecting – or even assisting those who kill them, by means of the very same law-making act(!), the subject of this law, that is the state as the law-giver, not only extremely harms people, but it also deeply distorts the essential sense of the law, changing it into **lawlessness under the misleading name of the law**[13].

There is something more to it. In the very same act of legalizing lawlessness, **the state** – a law-making subject – **distorts its own identity, and thus makes a suicidal coup d'etat**. It changes its role, which consists in minister-

---

[13] "[...] these attacks tend no longer to be considered as "crimes"; paradoxically they assume the nature of "rights", to the point that the State is called upon to give them *legal recognition and to make them available through the free services of health-care personnel. Such attacks strike human life at the time of its greatest frailty, when it lacks any means of selfdefence)."* EV. No. 11. – and further: "[...] *the "right" ceases to be such, because it is no longer firmly founded on the inviolable dignity of the person, but is made subject to the will of the stronger part"* EV. No. 20. Between No. 68 and No. 70 we find a deep analysis of the contradiction which introduces a split into the contemporary democratic society, as it on the one hand proclaims that recognition of the equality of the dignity that belongs to each human person lies at its foundation (Cf. *The Proclamation of Human Rights* of 1948), while on the other hand, excludes from any legal protection – by means of legal acts – the value which is fundamental to every human person, namely the value of life; and it does so in relation to the category of the weakest and utterly helpless human persons. Is man not who he is, if he at all is, which – in the conditions imposed by this world means: if he is alive.

ing to all for the sake of their common good, into the one of the executor of the majority will, of the will of the majority constituted by the strong who use violence against the helpless, which actually marks the essence of totalitarianism. Thus, the principle of the equality of all before the law is violated, and ultimately, the very principle of justice – the inviolable foundation of the order of any law-abiding state -is undermined at its very root[14].

Hence we have to do here with – secondly – with **an act of distortion of the essence of the state.**

Finally, the **self-destructive** power of this absurdity is deepened and escalated by constant reference to freedom and to the principle of majority rule, which is the formal structure of democracy. The right to freedom is identified here with the right to arbitrary exercise of power over others, which deprives them of the right to live, and thus of all other rights; and which results in the fact that those who participate in this act – due to the self destruction of their freedom – themselves become the first and the main (morally suicidal!) victims of the violence that they do. This self-destruction reaches the very depth of the human subject. The reason is that the first and the most tragic victim of violence done in the name of the law and the state is not the one who is its subject, but the one who is using it. *Happier is the victim of the wrong than the wrong-doer*, as Socrates will say. Hence **any form of participation** in depriving innocent human beings from the legal protection of their right to live, by means of a legal act made by the state, turns out to be an act of a suicidal moral death for the one who does it. It results in a split in the inner structure of the human subject, which reaches the very root of the rationally free "ego"[15]. Anyparticipation in carrying out this absurdity means moral self-annihilation[16].

---

[14] *The "right" ceases to be such, because it is no longer firmly founded on the inviolable dignity of the person, but is made subject to the will of the stronger part. In this way democracy, contradicting its own principles, effectively moves towards a form of totalitarianism. The State is no longer the "common home", where all can live together on the basis of principles of fundamental equality, but is transformed into a tyrant State, which arrogates to itself the right to dispose of the life of the weakest and the most defenseless members, from the unborn child to the elderly, in the name of a public interest which is really nothing but the interest of one part. EV 20;* cf. Card. J. Ratzinger, *Kirche, Ökumene und Politik*, Einsiedeln 1988, esp. pp. 183-198 and pp. 198-211; cf. also R. Buttiglione, *Ku prawdziwej demokracji. Osoba, społeczeństwo i państwo w encyklice Jana Pawła II Centesimus Annus (Towards True Democracy. The Person, the Society and the State in John Paul II's encyclical Centesimus Annus)*, "Ethos" 6(1993) No 2-3, pp. 93-47.

[15] Here we face the drama of man, which is the drama of freedom in the "trap" of the truth recognized by him (cf. note 2). By recognizing, with his own cognitive act, what he has recognized, man observes that he has the power to deny what he has himself recognized, and that he must not deny it. He is forbidden to do it both by the truth about what he has recognized, which he has himself recognized, and by the truth about who has recognized it, namely by the truth about himself as a witness of truth, and as one to whom truth has been

entrusted. He realizes that he is capable of doing a thing that he must not do on any condition: of denying the truth that he has himself recognized. Thus his freedom is freedom in the trap of the recognized truth. And even if recognized and ignored by man, truth will remain itself anyway. Instantly, an essentially rhetorical questions appears here: will he, man, remain himself if he, as the subject of a free act, denies the truth which he still considers true, as the subject of his own cognitive act?

Hence man's freedom shows itself in the form of his power to decide about himself by means of the power to choose affirmation or negation of the recognized truth: it is either the power of self-fulfillment or the power of self-destruction. The choice of what and who he chooses belongs to man as to the subject of freedom. It depends entirely on him whether he will choose the truth, and himself – his self-fulfillment – together with it, or whether he will deny the truth, and himself together with it, whether he will deny himself and decompose his own identity, the inner coherence of his personal subjectivity. (This problem was discussed during the Congress by A. Szostek, MIC, who referred to the author of *The Acting Person*).

Moreover, has the power to see the dramatic consequences of his act of self-denial. He observes that while having the power to make a (free) act of choice, man has no power to undo what he has once done or to undo the consequences of what he has once chosen, and hence he is not in the position to undo the consequences which affect himself. St. Paul's famous words refer precisely to this matter. It is from the depth of the split in the structure of his inner and rationally free self, which he has himself brought about, that he asks a most dramatic question: "What a wretched man I am!" ... doing what I do not approve of! "Who will rescue me from this body doomed to ... death?"

Similar words can be found in Euripides' *Hippolytus*: "We know and recognize what is good, but we do not follow it", or in Ovid: *Video meliora proboque deteriora sequor*. Cf. also on this problem: R. Buttiglione, *Etyka w kryzysie* (*Ethics in Crisis*), Lublin 1994; T. Styczeń, *Być sobą to przekraczać siebie. O antropologii Karola Wojtyły*. Posłowie do: Karol Wojtyła, *Osoba i czyn oraz inne studia antropologiczne* (*To Be Oneself is to Transcend Oneself. On Karol Wojtyła's Anthropology*. Afterward to: Karol Wojtyła, *The Acting Person and Other Anthropological Studies*), Lublin KUL 1994, pp. 493-526; and by the same author *Na początku była prawda. U genezy pojęcia osoby* (*In the Beginning Was the Truth. At the Origin of the Concept of Person*), "Ethos" Facing Postmodernism, 9 (1996) 1-2, pp. 15-30.

[16] "There is an even more profound aspect which needs to be emphasized: freedom negates and destroys itself, and becomes a factor leading to the destruction of others, when it no longer recognizes and respects its essential link with the truth". (EV, No 19, emphasis put by JPII).

"This ultimately means making freedom self-defining and a phenomenon creative of itself and its values. Indeed, when all is said and done man would not even have a nature; he would be his own personal life project. Man would be nothing more than his own freedom!" (VS no 46). The root of the "totalitarian distortion" of a democratic state lies precisely in such a vision of freedom.

Cf. H. Arendt, *Korzenie totalitaryzmu* (*The Origins of Totalitarianism*), Warsaw 1989, Niezależna Oficyna Wydawnicza, Chapter IV, *Sprawa Dreyfusa* (*The Dreyfus'Case*), pp. 75-96. Cf. also M. Schooyans, *La dérive totalitaire du liberalisme*, Editions Universitaires, Paris 1991; cf. also by this author: *L'avortement: enjeux politiques*, Québec 1990, in the Polish translation: *Aborcja a polityka* (*Abortion and Politics*), Lublin 1991. Cf. also K. Wojtyła's analysis of the "felicity bringing union between freedom and truth", made in paragraph 6 *Happiness and the Person's Transcendence in Action* of the work *The Acting Person*: Chapter IV: *Self-Determination and Fulfillment*, esp. the points: "Self-Fulfillment as a Synonym of Felicity", and "Truth and Freedom as Sources of Felicity".

Thirdly, we have to do here with an **act of self-deceit and self-enslavement of particular persons as human beings and citizens, and thus with an act of their moral suicide**.

Therefore, this diagnosis points *sui generis* to a triple death:
1) the death of the institution of the law,
2) the death of the institution of the state as the lawgiver
3) **the moral death of the citizens of the state – that is law-making subjects: voters and their representatives in lawmaking bodies – and ultimately their moral death as humans.**

This is why John Paul II – in the encyclical *Evangelium vitae* – calls this phenomenon the **"culture of death"**[17], noticing a real threat of the decline of culture in it.

The described state of affairs shows clearly that the role of the ethician is finally results in a demonstration of the above diagnosis, and – through it – in unmasking this law as an act bringing the **absurdity of the "culture of death"** to existence. His reason is to hinder the process of the **death of culture**. The moral imperative of the moment is to make people sensitive to the powers of the absurdity of the **"culture of death"**, which though sometimes invisible to their eyes, bring about the destruction of man's subjectivity. The thing at stake here is **to be or not to be of man's identity** at a turning point of history which is particularly dangerous to him.

3. BETWEEN VALIDITY AND ACCEPTANCE OF MORAL NORMS

It might seem that an ethician will reach his aim when he makes two steps, in an intersubjectively controllable way, namely:

---

[17] John Paul II writes in *Evangelium vitae*: "[...] *a new cultural climate is developing and taking hold, which gives crimes against life a new and – if possible – even new sinister character, giving rise to further grave concern: broad sectors of public opinion justify certain crimes against life in the name of the rights of individual freedom', and on this basis they claim not only exemption from punishment, but even authorization of the State, so that these things could be done with total freedom and indeed with the freed assistance of health-care systems*" (EV 4).

And further: [...] "This reality is characterized by the emergence of a culture which denies solidarity and in many cases takes the form of a veritable "culture of death" (emphasis: TS). [...] it is possible to speak [...] of a war of the powerful against the weak (emphasis: TS). In this way a kind of "conspiracy against life" is unleashed (emphasis: (TS, EV 12).

A detailed analysis of this leading subject is taken up between No. 68 and No. 70, where John Paul II continues and supplements the considerations included in *Centesimus annus* and *Veritatis splendor*.

The most significant texts where the term "culture of death" appears, can be found in Numbers: 12, 19, 21, 24, 26, 28, 50, 87. The term "conspiracy against life" appears in Numbers: 12 and 17.

1. when he proves the **universal validity** of the statement that all action that contributes to realizing an absurdity is absolutely inadmissible and morally destroying for man as a rationally free being – even if it be subjected to his freedom;

2. when he demonstrates the **objective validity** of the statement that this absurdity does take place whenever a person – as a citizen – participates in the "plot against life", either as a voter or as his representative in a lawmaking body.

In order to succeed in making the first step, it will suffice to ask – oneself and every other person[18] – a banal question, yet one revealing a lot, thanks to its obviousness:

Can I (you) deny the truth which I (you) have recognized, even if I am (you are) able[19] to do it?

Indeed. What is the reason why logicians demand that the proposition **(p∧~p)**, called **contradiction** in logic, should be preceded by the symbol of negation: , which is rendered in the common language as: **"it is false that"**, and so, we receive the proposition: **~(p∧~ p)**, whose essence absolutely excludes any possibility of its ever being rationally questioned by anyone?[20] I

---

[18] I am one who must not deny the truth which I have recognized; you are one who must not deny the truth that you have recognized; you are all together – and everyone individually – ones who ... etc. R. Spaemann aptly notes and interprets this fact: "Es gibt keine Ethik ohne Metaphysik. Yet he immediately adds: "[...] Ontologie und Ethik werden durch die Intuition des Seins als Selbstsein – das eigenen ebenso wie des anderen – uno actu konstitutiert". Cf. by this author, *Glück und Wohlwollen. Versuch über Ethik*. Stuttgart 1989, p. 11.

[19] The fact that "I can deny (the truth of) what I have myself recognized", identical with the fact that "I don't have to confirm with an act of my free choice (of truth) what I have recognized", bears inevitable consequences. Firstly: while denying with an act of free choice what I have recognized with my own cognitive act, I bring about radical decomposition of the identity of my own ego, which is the union of the cognitive subject and of the one of free choice. In a way I stop being myself. Moreover, I stop being free since I choose what I do not approve of myself. Hence I stop being self-dependent; I submit myself to some constraint, and it is no longer significant that I do it voluntarily. I agree to making myself dependent on a thing that is not myself. While distorting myself in this way, I enslave myself, I deny my freedom – even if I do so by the power of its dynamism. Is this not a sufficient – and at the same time necessary – basis of distinguishing the true freedom from the untrue one, the latter distorting itself and accepting this self distortion?

This is why, to save the truth, to save freedom, and to save oneself (one's moral identity) mean the same. Cf. T. Styczeń, *Wolność w prawdzie (Freedom in Truth)*, Roma 1987. It is in this spirit that John Paul II – in his address outside Brandenburger Gate – warned us against the mistake of identifying freedom with randomness, and – consequently – against identifying the right to freedom with the right to randomness.

[20] Deontic logic treats the aletheic copula "it is untrue that", or "it is not that"; as paralleling the deontic one, in a way rendering the logical law of contradiction by means of the formula: it is forbidden that (p∧~p).

think that an attempt to take such an absurd step was already considered by Duns Scotus, and he indirectly excluded it by formulating his famous theorem: $(p \wedge \sim p) \rightarrow q$. *Ex falso quodlibet*[21].

In his study, which in the Polish translation bears a significant title: "Can People Be Rational?", B. Blanshard, following M. E. McTaggart, warns everyone who would dare to make such a step: "No one has ever broken the laws of logic, yet logic has broken many who have tried to." Blanshard expressively makes his point by saying that "Originality at all cost would not be heroism in this case, but a suicide"[22]. This is how contemporary logicians teach us ... ethics[23].

The demonstration of the second step has already been attempted above, in the way that enables everyone to control it rationally against a mere insight into the essence of an act of legalizing abortion. What does a law making act ultimately express, if its essence lies in depriving the evidently innocent and the helpless from any protection, and if those who kill them are not applied any sanctions against, but even assisted by the power of the law? Does it not express another attempt at carrying out a logical contradiction?[24] Paradoxically (!), only after these two steps have been taken does it turn out possible to see successfully – from the point of view of the method that ethics adopts – the heart of the matter concerning efficient demonstration of truthfulness or falsehood of the propositions that ethics puts forward, including the ones concerning a "law against life".

Ethics is a domain where, unlike in mathematics, we continually note the painful fact of the hiatus between the **universally valid** statements and the **universally recognized** ones. Showing the universal validity of a statement in ethics does not necessarily mean convincing *eo ipso* everyone about it. Neither does it mean making everyone accept it, or observe the norm of action which such a statement expresses. What is necessary and sufficient in mathematics does not always suffice in ethics.

So, what is there to be done?

Here is where the *crux ethicorum* as well as the one of the method of ethics lie.

---

[21] Cf. in this matter: W. Marciszewski, *Sztuka dyskutowania (The Art of Leading a Discussion)*, Warszawa 1994, pp, 251-252.

[22] Cf. Brand Blanshard, *Czy ludzie mogą być rozumni? (Can People Be Rational?)* in: J. Krzywicki (ed.): *Filozofia amerykańska. Wybór rozpraw i szkiców historycznych (American Philosophy. A Selection of Works and Historical Sketches)*, Boston 1958, p. 120.

[23] It is probably worth paying attention to still another thing: wherever the logic of propositions says "it is untrue that: $p \wedge \sim p$", deontic logic simply says "it is forbidden that: $p \wedge \sim p$". Why is that so? What is the basis of such a smooth inference of "ought to, ought not to" from "is, is not", "it is true that, it is untrue that"? Have logicians forgotten about Hume's warning, or have they treated it as not *"ad rem"*?

What is an ethician supposed to do, having once recognized that the absolute prohibition of abortion, a **universally valid** thesis, which is *de iure* intersubjectively controllable, *de facto* is not only **unaccepted**, but directly rejected by many cultural circles all over the world?

4. BETWEEN THE DIAGNOSIS AND THE THERAPY

A drastic example of the attitude described above was the case of the "plot against life", made by the world's political and cultural circles when the UNO Conference in Cairo was approaching, right before the 50th anniversary of the foundation of the UNO. Is it possible to imagine a more expressive context of demonstrating the so-called option for **"safe abortion"**[25], that is of promoting a particularly brutal form of a "law against life", if we have in mind the **reason why the UNO was founded**?

Was it not born out of the calling of conscience of the whole world, out of the calling: **"Never more!"**, which was the reaction to the shock at the

---

[24] Therefore I consider a statement made by a well-known Polish member of Parliament as particularly peculiar, since he argued that: "Life is stronger than logic". According to the author of these words, the people's consent to acts of abortion is a sufficient condition to legalize it, even if such a legal act – logically speaking – bears an internal contradiction. Cf. T. Styczeń, *Nienarodzony miarą demokracji* (*The Unborn as the Measure of Democracy*), Lublin 1991, pp. 168-172. Cf. also V. Possenti, *Le società liberali al bivio. Lineamenti di filosofia della società*, Genova 1991, p. 335 and next, where the author of an interesting dissertation on the face of the contemporary democratic states presents H.Kelsen's commentary on Pilate's attitude. The prosecutor finds out that the Defendant is innocent, and then – as if unaware of what he has just recognized, and publicly announced – leaves the decision on the fate of the Accused to plebiscite, asking the people: Which of the two do you want me to release for you? "Agendo cosí – conclude Kelsen – Pilato si comporta da perfetto democrata: affida cioe' il problema di stabilire il vero e il giusto all "opinione della maggioranza". Cf. the text by Bishop Julian Herranz, *La struttura moralle della libertà*, already quoted in note no 3.

[25] "*Safe Motherhood for example, a typical case of the "politics of meaning" so abused in these UN sessions, and ostensibly a concept towards which all could agree to work, was demonstrated to be defined in other UN languages to include access to legal abortion. The bracketing of this term by Latin Americans, backed by the Holy See, caused tremendous anger in April of 1994 at Prepcom III*". – wrote one of the active Vatican delegates to the UNO Conference in Cairo. Cf. Christiane Vollmer, *Cairo: A Clash of Two Civilizations*, in: *Twenty Years of Family Sciences*, Warsaw 1995, Wydawnictwa Akademii Teologii Katolickiej, p. 287. "*These delegates [...] then preceded [...] to do battle with the greatest and richest powers on earth and to fight against the worst parts of the document, which stated that children all over the world were to have the right to abortion, sterilization and so on, without parental notification. Abortion was included in the document scores of times under a number of euphemistic phrases. Such terms as health, have official definitions clearly indicating their true meanings, at World Health Organization, for example, but these definitions were not easily available to the delegates*" (p. 289).

tragic consequences of the first – in the history of mankind – case of a "law against life"? The source and basis of this "law" was then the will to broaden the "living space" (*Lebensraum*) and the scope of freedom (*Freiheitsraum*) of the people of some special race (Blut und Ehre) at the cost of the people of some other race. The symbols of these costs – as well as of their consequences – became **Auschwitz** with its "*Homo homini* ... on the Block of Death", and **Nürnberg** with the judges' dilemma, unprecedented in the history of judicial procedures: did each of the accused of crime against mankind not prove that he had been acting in accordance with the state law, with the law of a state whose government had been chosen in the way of democratic elections?![26]

This is a peculiar memory, peculiar awareness of our identity, and a peculiar gift to world's culture and to the future history of mankind, on the occasion of the 50's anniversary of the foundation of the UNO; 50 years after Auschwiz and Nürnberg[27]. The ethician is the one who must not forget or fail to see – by means of contrast – the connection between these two events, in the situation when it is no longer recognized by the UNO[28]. What is the so-called right to safe abortion, justified by the so-called right to a choice (pro choice), which was postulated in the proposal of the closing document of the UNO Conference in Cairo? What is it, but another – if not identical – attempt at justifying the violence exerted by some over others? Hence it is only a slightly different mode of modern totalitarianism: the totalitarianism which tries to justify – under the guise of the law – some people's claim to the right to kill others whose existence is inconvenient to them. The only difference is that the criterion which is to justify this extreme violence done to the human being is not his belonging to a given race, as it was the case in the Nazi totalitarianism, but his age[29].

---

[26] Cf. Robert Spaemann, *Obrona człowieka przed nieograniczonymi żądaniami* (*The Defence of Man Against Unlimited Demands*), in: Wokół encykliki "Veritatis splendor" (*On the Encyclical "Veritatis splendor"*), "Biblioteka Niedzieli", Częstochowa 1994, pp. 113-121 (Jarosław Merecki, SDS, (ed), transl. from Italian: *Una difesa dell'uomo contro pretese illimitate, in: Lettera Enciclica Veritatis Splendor del Soemmo Pontefice Giovanni Paolo II. Testo e commenti*, Libreria Editrice Vaticana 1994, pp. 182-185).

[27] Cf. Yannis Thanassekos, *L'evento- Auschwitz nella coscienza della modernità*, in: Giuseppe Vico e Milena Santieri, *Educare dopo Auschwitz* (ed). Milano, Vita Pensiero. Piemme, Milano 1996, pp. 35-59, esp. pp. 50-51.

[28] The ethician asks here the question which is the "truth test" for the culture of the whole history of mankind, insofar as this history is to remain the history of culture: *Can history flow against the stream of conscience?* (Karol Wojtyła, *Myśląc Ojczyzna – Thinking Fatherland*).

[29] Cf. Michel Schooyans, *Aborcja a polityka* (*Abortion and Politics*), Lublin 1991 (*L'avortment: enjeux politiques*, Quebec 1990), and also by this author: *La dérive totalitaire du liberalisme*, Paris 1991.

So, how is the ethician then supposed to cope with the burden of this problem, without losing anything from the discovery, made by Socrates, that man is a being that feeds on truth, a capax veri? What is an ethician supposed to do bearing no illusions as to the fact of how few patients he – as if a doctor responsible for the spiritual delivery – has nowadays, if the patients are still at all interested in their need for the therapy?

Let us firstly consider the possible diagnoses of the case. There are *prima facie* three possibilities which involve three respectively differentiated ways of **therapy**. These diagnoses are as follows:

1) **they either have not accepted because they did not recognize** – which lets them live in "peace and quiet": nocentes sed innocentes quia insipientes, we shall repeat after Abelard: the dangerous ones yet innocent, because unintelligent;

2) **or they have recognized, but have not accepted** – avoiding the trouble to bear the burden of the truth about the greatness of man: bonum arduum, arduous good, "tough talk";

3) **or they do not want to recognize** – having in advance considered false the assumption that the truth about man is something to be discovered by means of a cognitive act[30], and to be accepted by a free act; and that it is not merely to be decided, and carried out, by a free act itself, drawing on the creative invention of reason[31].

---

[30] Conscience is the "creative reason" ("schöpferische Vernunft"), it is not the *lector* of the truth about man, but its creator! Gewissensurteil gives way to Gewissensentscheidung. The point here is the so-called Copernican turn in anthropology (anthroplogische Wende, svolta antropologica); as its result, the key anthropological and ethical terms, such as "freedom" and "truth", and in consequence also "conscience", have acquired a meaning that is radically contradictory to the one existing so far, due to the reversal of the relationship of dependence between freedom and truth. The terms, though, have remained unchanged, which brings about dangerous confusion. Cf. R. Buttiglione, *La crisi della morale*, Roma 1991; cf. also A. Szostek, *Nature-Vernunft-Freiheit. Philosophische Analyse der Konzeption "schöpferische Vernunft" in der zeitgenoessischen Moraltheologie*, Verlag Peter Lang Gmbh, Frankfurt am Main 1992; cf. also A. Laun, *Aktuelle Probleme der Moraltheologie*, Wien 1991, pp. 24-30; cf. also the special edition of the Quarterly published by John Paul II's Institute at the Catholic University of Lublin and the International Academy of Philosophy in the Principality of Liechtenstein, devoted entirely to the question of the ethos of freedom: "Ethos". Zum Ethos der Freiheit. Vierteljahrschrift des Johannes-Paul-II-Institut der Katolischen Universität in Lublin – Internationale Akademie für Philosophie im Fürstentum Liechtenstein. Sonderausgabe No. 1 (1993).

[31] Actually, John Paul II's entire encyclical *Veritatis splendor* is devoted to this particular question (No. 1 and No. 32). Cf. also T. Styczeń, SDS: *Wolność z prawdy żyje (Freedom Lives on Truth)*, in: Jan Paweł II, *Veritatis splendor*. Tekst i komentarze (John Paul II *Veritatis splendor*. The Text and Comments), A. Szostek (ed), Lublin 1995, pp. 127-168, (*La libertà vive della verità*. "Anthropotes" 2 (1996), pp. 235-255).

The therapy in the case of the first diagnosis is the one of **awakening** by means of education: by using the **informative** function of the language of ethics.

The second diagnosis requires the therapy of **mobilization**: taking advantage of the **parenetic** (performative) function of the language of ethics.[32]

The third diagnosis involves the simplest, yet the most difficult therapy, which consists in the proposal to **refer once again – humbly – to the sources of anthropology and ethics**, and to look again – in their light – at one's own vision of freedom; in readiness to accept all the consequences which logically follow from it, and among them ....

Thus, in the first case an ethician will suggest the question if they have considered all the possible addressees of the formula "safe abortion", and if they have ever taken the trouble to consider the question: "For whom is abortion «safe»?"[33] – and then he will patiently wait for the time of their awakening. He remembers: every man is a *capax v(V)eri*, bearing in himself the grounds for resistance to falsehood. Everyone is subjected to truth, be it at least "in embryo". Thus an ethician, a deliverer, does not give up. He awaits the moment of birth. He wants to help.

Wherever the second diagnosis is correct, the ethician following Socrates – makes use of the second dimension of the language of ethics and adds the performative moment to the information which he conveys, addressing those who have not accepted, though they have recognized. He insists. He is not ashamed to beg. And though he continually repeats the same, he puts new, mobilizing accents. He will remind *"Happier is the victim of murder than the murderer"*, but he will also add: *"The point is not only to live, but how to live good"*, and then he will reach for an admonition: *"Save the victim in order to save yourself!"*

Finally, the ethician will suggest that the representatives of the third group[34] should once again regard their freedom in the perspective of each

---

[32] St. Kamiński calls it stimulating function.

[33] A similar method of posing a test question could be used in the case of the authors of the verdict given by the Constitutional Tribunal in Karlsruhe: *rechtswidrig/straffrei*. Would the main addressee of this verdict, namely the child, express his gratitude for this concern about him, manifested by the Highest Instance of Justice, saying spontaneously: "Thank you!"? Cf. T. Styczeń, SDS, *Discurso del Dr. Tadeusz Styczeń. Discursos Pronunciandos en la investidura del grado de doctor "honoris causa", Universidad de Navarra*, Pamplona 1995, pp. 43-48: cf. also by this author: *For European Solidarity*. "Ethos", Quarterly of the John Paul II Institute at the Catholic University of Lublin – The International Academy of Philosophy in the Principality of Liechtenstein. Special Edition No.2, 1996. pp. 49-50.

[34] This vision of freedom is considered to be a product of the so-called modernism; yet according to the *Book of Genesis*, exactly the same vision of freedom as the power to decide about good and evil, was proposed to the first men by the "snake from the Garden of Eden".

cognitive act – **and fact** (!) of their own; and that they should confront their own vision of freedom with the one that reveals itself to them as the power to question what they have themselves stated. He will further suggest that they should draw the ultimate consequences from this confrontation. "Am I able to deny what I have myself recognized?" – "Yes, I am". "However, can I do it?" "Also when the result of the sum 2+2 is concerned?" "Why not?"[35] The ethician trusts that a *colloquium* will become an impulse for a salutary *soliloquium*[36]. He never loses the perspective of man as a being that is himself thanks to truth only.

Yet he will not hesitate to remind his interlocutors which vision of freedom laid the foundations of the law in the name of which people did what the notice: "*Homo homini ...*" warns us against. Was it not against such a vision of freedom that the calling of conscience decided about the foundation of our UNO fifty years ago? Can we thus repeat once again the same

---

[35] And here we enter the path of elementary anthropological and ethical insights, some of which we have already presented in the "socratic" note 15. And if we have agreed that an identical vision of freedom lies both at the basis of the "right to safe abortion" and of the "law" to which the accused at Nürnberg referred, should not those who today still want to accept it – for the sake of being consequent – apologize to Adolf Eichmann, and to all his companions, for the insults made and harms done to them in the meantime due to a lack of a mature knowledge of the essence of humanness? Cf. H. Arendt, *Eichmann in Jerusalem. A Report on the Banality of Evil*, London 1963; the Polish edition: *Eichmann w Jerozolimie. Rzecz o banalności zła*, Kraków 1987. Cf. also G. Herling-Grudziński: *Demon naszych czasów* (*The Demon of Our Times*), in: by the same author: *Godzina cieni. Eseje.* (*The Hour of Shadows. Essays.*), Kraków 1993, pp. 132-142. Reading the extracts selected by G. Herling-Grudziński from a book by H. Arendt (pp. 137-142!) is a deeply moving experience as it not only shows what could happen with people, but it also if not above all – shows what can happen to us.

Cf. an equally penetrating philosophical analysis of the genesis of totalitarianism and of its being rooted in Fichte's concept of freedom, made in the dissertation by W. Chudy: *Rozwój filozofowania a "pułapka refleksji". Filozofia refleksji i próby jej przezwyciężenia* (*The Development of Philosophizing and the "Trap of Reflection". The Philosophy of Reflection and the Attempts to Overcome It*), Lublin 1993, esp. pp. 89-135, 335-353.

[36] Let us remind: having once "discovered" man as capax v(V)eri – in the sense of one to whom t(T)ruth has been entrusted, the ethician is aware that he is confronting someone that he would betray if he did not give him a chance of self-discovery, and so a chance of a "second birth"; a chance of being himself as being free in truth. He knows that man finds himself and identifies himself – to use a metaphor – "in the embrace of truth and embracing truth". Hence Pascal's expressive statement: "You would not seek for me had you not found me" (*Pensées*). It does not suffice to grasp the truth about oneself in order to choose it, but one cannot choose it without having grasped it. *Nihil volitur nisi praecognitur*. This is why, St. Augustine inseparably connects his: Dilige et quod vis fac! with: Noverim me – noverim Te! Cf. also A. Szostek, *Wokół godności, prawdy i wolności* (*Around Dignity, Truth and Freedom*). Lublin 1995, pp. 160-178; and also T. Styczeń, *Wolność w prawdzie* (*Freedom in Truth*), Rome 1988.

experiment with freedom and ... law, the same mistake of history **in the UNO itself** (!), if the reason why we founded this organization was to overcome such mistakes and to eliminate them once and for all times from the history of the culture of man?[37]

However, what happens if an ethician, while merely wanting to help the patients from the mentioned groups, only irritates them?[38] If they do not want to tolerate him any longer, or even try to remove him – democratically – from their sight? Will it be not better for him rather to disappear: to escape? But does escape not mean taking the last chance of salvation away from them, and thus a betrayal?[39] And also a betrayal of oneself?

---

[37] Human weakness gives power to false ideas – or half-truths proclaimed by their makers as the truth. This is probably one of the main reasons why the idea of so-called "creative conscience" enjoys such enormous popularity in today's world, and unfortunately, also in the contemporary Catholic theology; being sometimes rendered by a suggestive pastoral slogan: Das Gewissen soll entscheiden! The concept of "creative conscience" – which is also a grave temptation – constitutes an alternative of the moral duty to carry the burden of the truth of man's essence (nature), which is rendered by ethics in the shape of moral norms which are absolutely binding human freedom. The vision of "creative conscience" aims at providing man himself with the power to determine the truth about himself. Hence all moral norms, with no exception, turn out to be always open to exceptions, bearing the nature of the so-called open truths. This is why the judgement of conscience (Gewissens-Urteil) disappears from the "new theology", replaced with the decision of conscience (Gewissens-Entscheidung). In this way the category of erroneous conscience practically disappears from the horizon of ethics and morality. From now on there are as "many truths" as there are "decisions of conscience" made by particular people. The concern that the Author of the encyclical *Veritatis splendor* shows centres around this issue above all. Cf. e.g. no. 46-48.

In this context, we must critically examine statements such as e.g. "There are as many kinds of 'nature' as there are 'theoreticians of nature'. Hence one may be afraid that there will be equally many natural laws'". Cf. J. Tischner, *Wolność w blasku prawdy* (*Freedom in the Splendour of Truth*) "Tygodnik Powszechny" 47 (1993) (48); cf. also T. Styczeń, SDS, *Wolność z prawdy żyje. Wokół encykliki "Veritatis splendor"* (*Freedom Lives on Truth. Around the encyclical "Veritatis splendor"*), in: Jan Paweł II, *Veritatis splendor. Tekst i komentarze* (John Paul II, *Veritatis splendor. The Text and Comments*), A. Szostek, MIC (ed), Lublin RW KUL 1995, pp. 127-168. Another text worth attention in this context is written by Jesuit theologian from Munich: Giovanni B. Sala, SJ, Die Königsteiner Erklärung *25 Jahre danach*, in: Forum Katolische Theologie 10 (1994) 97-123. Cf. also Estera Lobkowicz, *Ukradziony Sobór* (*The Stolen Council*) (pp. 8-26), in: Fronda, no. 7 (1996), (esp. pp. 24-25, devoted to the above mentioned publicist of "Tygodnik Powszechny".

[38] I. F. Stone (*The Trial of Socrates*, London 1988) proposes that a new trial against Socrates should be held nowadays, with the same verdict, on behalf of the contemporary "open society".

[39] Christ orders the man released from possession of demons to stay in Gheraza. Among his own people. Why must he do so? "To bear witness for them". From now on, the people of Gheraza must find their reflection in him, as if in a mirror. They must still recall anew that they had made the Man who miraculously healed their friend from the

5. THE ETHICIAN: A TEACHER OR A WITNESS?

At this point a Christian ethician sees – with the eyes of his imagination – God-Man – the Ethician par excellence – at the feet of man. During the Passover. At the beginning of the Passion.

But also an ethician who follows Socrates notices that he has not exhausted all the possibilities, having used all the options of the language of ethics. He has only exhausted the verbal possibilities. But there still remains **action** and the possibilities that it offers: namely **bearing witness,** which constitutes **an ethical argument** par excellence.

Therefore Karol Wojtyła, in his poem entitled *"Stanisław"*, speaks as an ethician and a poet, for the Bishop of Cracow, a witness of truth:
"The word did not help, blood will."

******

Socrates is a symbol of this argument.

He was given an opportunity to bear witness, by his fellow citizens, who democratically, according to majority rule, condemned him to death for undermining peace in their state with his moral doctrine[40]. But there is still a trial more difficult than death that awaits him in prison: the temptation to fall into doubt as to the sense of his mission. Is it not at the same time the greatest chance for a witness?

And then, in the middle of the night, his most ingenious disciple, Plato, appears in his cell offering him a chance to escape, to be free again[41].

"To be free"? So even Plato has not understood anything if he advises me to commit moral suicide. Maybe now there is a chance for me to help him see? And the Master says to his disciple: "You will go home alone. Without me."

Is Socrates not a bad loser, if he has failed to win with all, in the plebiscite which God-Man Himself seemed to have lost in Jerusalem on that Friday on which a skeptic was to utter unexpectedly the words **"Ecce Homo!"** – **"Here is the man!"**, almost simultaneously with his "ethical-cultural creed": **"Quid est veritas? – Don't you see that I can let you go free or put you to death on the cross?"** (Cf. J 19,5 – J 18, 38 – J 19, 10)?.

---

weakness of being possessed, leave their town. And they must recall why they had done it. What will be the result? It will also depend upon them. Christ does not intend to save them a chance of awakening and of the drama of making the choice which is their only chance. The choice will depend on them. Cf. also Fr. von Dürrenmatt: *Besuch der aelteren Dame* (film screenplay).

[40] Cf. Plato, *Defence of Socrates*.
[41] Cf. Plato, *Crition*.

Socrates did not have a chance to learn anything about his disciple's further life. Plato's way led him from the prison gate that he had vainly opened to his Master, to still another gate. Between these two gates – not without the help of his absent Deliverer, Plato gives birth to man in Plato[42]. He gives birth to something else: to his Academy, on whose gate he will put the notice which from now on will welcome his pupils with the sentence that constitutes the heart of Book VI of his *Politea*:
Diligere veritatem, omnem, et in omnibus.[43]
To love all truth and to love it in Everything.
And to be able to die for it if need be ...

***

"The word did not help. Bearing witness did".

***

A hundred years after his death ... Socrates awakens the Athenians: they erect his monument in order to get rid of the disgrace which had thrown a gloomy shadow on the prestige of democracy and of their state-polis: they had killed a Witness of humanity in man, in the name of the law and the democratic state.

Seventeen hundred years later Abelard will entitle his ethical treaty: *Scito te ipsum! – Know yourself!* And he will even suggest that the Litany to All Saints should be supplemented with the invocation: St. Socrates!

And here is my conclusion from the above analysis:

The hour of witnesses of truth has come: the hour of bearing witness to solidarity with man. Only witnesses – unyielding in resistance to lawlessness (which is deceitfully called the law), and uncompromising in front of the new totalitarianism appearing under the guise of a democratic state, will

---

[42] Cf. Plato, *Politea* (488 E). Cf. also Werner Jaeger, *Paidea*, Vol. II, Warsaw 1964, esp. the entire concluding chapter of the second volume of this monumental work: *Państwo jako "przestrzeń życiowa" dla filozofa* (*The State as the "Living Space" for the Philosopher*), pp. 306-326. Cf. also Card. J. Ratzinger, op. cit., pp. 208-209; cf. also Givanni Reale, *Saggezza antica. Terapia per i mali dell'uomo d'oggi*, Milano 1995, Epilogo, p. 233 and next.

[43] Cf. Josef Seifert, *Diligere veritatem omnem et in omnibus – Miłować prawdę wszelką i we wszystkim (wszystkich)*, "Ethos", Jana Pawła II wizja Europy (John Paul II's Vision of Europe), No. 28 (1994), and also by this author: *To Love all Truth and to Love it in Everything*, "Ethos" Quarterly of the John Paul II Institute at the Catholic University of Lublin – the International Academy of Philosophy in the Principality of Liechtenstein, Special Edition No. 2 1996, pp. 53-69. The author comments on Plato's statement from the perspective of the present Rector of the International Academy of Philosophy in the Principality of Liechtenstein, whose motto is the above statement made by the Founder of the Academy at Athens.

manage to save humanity at this turn of history. Everything that can be called the culture of man, the legal culture and the culture of the State, depends on bearing witness – on everyone of us[44]. The only chance of the survival of the culture of man, and the chance to save the institution of the State from its ultimate decomposition, lies in the solidarity with the most helpless of all, with ones excluded from legal protection and condemned to death before the majesty of the caricature of a democratic state. The reason is that the attitude towards the life of the **"Smallest"** is the measure of the rectitude and culture of man, as well it is the measure of the rectitude and culture of the law and State that he makes[45]. *Iustitia est quae **maxime** prodest ei qui **minime** potest* (Wincenty Kadłubek) – recalling the principle of the great jurist from Kraków which constitutes the basis of the geniune ethico-political interpretation of the principle of justice.

Hence we must not give up as long as even a single child – somewhere in the world – has to fear for his life, because of the law proclaimed by his elders in the state in which they themselves gave life to him (John Neuhaus).

* * *

Since I am speaking convinced that I am among Sisters and brothers in faith in God-Man: in Jesus Christ, I dare recall a significant element of the teaching of the Gospel here:

---

[44] In order to comprehend the depth of John Paul II's concern for this matter, it suffices to listen to the words that he said during the Angelus prayer – in the context of the approaching UN Conference in Cairo – in Rome, on the day of the Holy Trinity celebration, May 29th 1994, straight after his return from the Gemelli Polyclinic to Vatican. Cf. "L'Osservatore Romano", May 30th 1994, Il dono della sofferenza (the gift of suffering). Cf. also Christiane Vollmer, op. cit., pp. 292-293.

[45] H. Arendt concludes her work *The Origins of Totalitarianism* with a significant historiosophic reflection: "It remains true also that each ending in the history is simultaneously a new beginning; this beginning is a promise, the only "message" that an ending may ever produce. Before a beginning becomes a historical event, it is man's greatest skill; in the respect of politics it is identical with human freedom (emphasis: T. Styczeń). *Initium ut esset homo creatus est* – "man was created in order to be the beginning", said St. Augustine (*De Civitate Dei*, Book 12, chapter 20). This beginning is guaranteed by every new birth; every new man is this beginning" (emphasis: T. Styczeń). Cf. p. 365.

Another reflection comes up as a *post dictum* to this statement:

This is why no human freedom can kill any begetting human being, in any conditions; this is why absolutely no life can be destroyed. It would be not only the murder of a man who is being born, and hence the murder of the freedom that is being born together with him. It would also be the moral suicide of the one who kills him.

The language of experience continually confronts the language of the Revelation, if only freedom wants to allow itself to be spoken to by the truth of recognition ...

"So he called a little child to him whom he set among them". (Cf. Mt 18, 1-2).

What is more, He particularly identified himself with the weakest of Them All. Let us listen to His *ipsissima verba*:

"In so far as you did this to one of the least of these brothers of mine, you did it to me. In so far as you neglected to do this to one of the least of these, you neglected to do it to me" (Cf. Mt 25, 40; Mt 25, 45).

And finally: "Anyone who welcomes one little child like this in my name welcomes me" (Mt 18, 5).

He who does not accept this child ... ???

Let everyone give the ending himself.

* * *

We all know who Mother Theresa of Calcutta is to the world. We are happy to have her. While bending down over the weakest she awakens us. Her gesture is caught by the eye of the camera, and thanks to what she does the whole world can see her and rejoice to have her.

But we are made equally rejoiced also by other, sometimes completely unknown and anonymous heroes of the solidarity with the Weakest. Some of them find it sufficient to be known only to God Himself. Some do good to others during the night of "loneliness, away from God", which is not always due to their faulty disbelief in Him.

So, please, let me dedicate them – the Unknown Heroes of the Solidarity with the Weakest – the words written by a Polish poet, C.K. Norwid:

"I cherish the conviction that there is nothing more beautiful than
when one man challenges even the whole world to fight.
Maybe only people, maybe only they did something.
Old Socrates (...) Christopher Columbus (...)
Maybe only they did something, and they are men.
Maybe the whole mystery of Golgotha means only this.
Only man will win and triumph. (...)
It will often be after centuries have passed that he will win, but he will! (...)
It does not matter – it is an eternal Mass – each victory came in this way.
"(...) it was announced to us on Golgotha that truth had won
and that we are thus entering the succession of this fulfilled truth".

* * *

Hence the moment when God-Man says His victorious:
Consummatum est! It is fulfilled! (J 19, 30),
should not escape our attention. *A cruce regnat Deus*.

WŁADYSŁAW STRÓŻEWSKI
Jagiellonian University in Cracow
Poland

FREEDOM AND VALUE

The aim of this paper is to consider the relation between freedom and value in our basic axiological experience.

Let's begin with some preliminary remarks concerning freedom. Very often it is understood in opposition to determinism and necessity. Before we examine the correctness of this opposition, it will be useful to present some other oppositions, also taken into acount in analysing freedom; there are, among others: liberty – slavery; independence – dependency; indeterminism – determinism; freedom of choice – impossibility of choice etc.

Freedom, in each of its kinds, is treated generally as a positive value, its opposition – as a negative one. It is especially clear in considering the *freedom from*, in relation to *freedom to*, which is often treated as axiologically neutral. But when we pose the question concerning the relation between freedom and value, we think, first of all, about the *freedom to*, namely: the freedom towards value.

I shall focus my attention on three kinds of values: epistemological, moral and aesthetical. To make things more simple, I shall call them truth, good and beauty. I am, of course, aware that in each of these kinds (or groups) of values we have to distinguish many types of peculiar values, but I am also convinced that these peculiar values are subordinated to the most important and – so to say – highest among them, and that due to participation in it they receive an essential moment of their general validity. For example: certainty is valuable because of participation in truth, nobilility – due to participation in moral goodness, sublimity – due to participation in beauty (even if, according to some great aesthetitians, it constitutes an absolutely different aesthetic category). In the language of I. Kant we can say that truth, good and beauty are the *regulative ideas* of the distinguished groups of values. The highest values (or directive ideas) are very often given to us intuitively, without adequate definition of them, but by no means certainly and clearly. Lack of definition does not exclude knowledge: it is enough to remind G. E. Moore's analysis of good in order to make this statement evident.

The main thesis of my paper is that our freedom differs basically in our experiences of different kinds of values. In other words: there is another mode (kind) of freedom in experiencing truth, still another in experiencing good, another in the experience of beauty.

I. FREEDOM AND TRUTH

For we can do nothing against the truth, but for the truth.
(II Cor 13, 8)

We have to distinguish the ways of approaching truth and the truth itself.

The ways of conquering truth imply absolute freedom in choosing adequate scientific (or even unscientific) methods, in consequence – a possibility of failure, and a necessity of doubt.

The situation changes when the truth is received. The freedom of searching for truth is replaced by acceptance of the truth which manifests itself by itself. The acceptance of truth belongs to the essence of our experience of it and is absolutely necessary: therefore we can say that freedom is just surpassed (in Hegelian sens of the word) by necessity. But is this moment of necessity evident in each experience of truth and in relation to each definition of it?

As we know well, there are various definitions of truth, from the classical, "correspondence" definition, to the pragmatic one. St. Thomas Aquinas in the *Questiones disputatae de veritate* 1, 1 mentions 8 definitions of truth and divides them into three groups:

I. "Secundum id quod praecedit rationem veritatis, et in quo verum fundatur":

1. *Verum est id quod est*;
2. *Veritas cujuslibet rei est proprietas sui esse quod stabilitum est rei*;
3. *Verum est indivisio esse, et ejus quod est*;

II. "Secundum id quod formaliter rationem veri perficit":

1. *Veritas est adaequatio rei et intellectus*;
2. *Veritas est rectitudo sola mente perceptibilis*;

III. "Secundum effectum consequentem":

1. *Verum est manifestativum et declarativum esse*;

2. *Veritas est qua ostenditur id quod est*;
3. *Veritas est secundum quam de inferiioribus judicamus*[1].

It is interesting to note that some of these definitions are valid for today; e.g.: II 1 was reinterpreted by A. Tarski. III 1 and 2 are similar to some proposals made by phaenomenologists, I 1 could be interpreted as prior to Heidegger.

For our purpose the definitions of truth as "adaequatio" and "manifestatio" are the most important ones. The moment of necessity of truth is evident in both of them. When we reach the adequate fulfilment of our intentional act by the matter (content) of its transcendent object, we have no reason for any doubt. If being manifests itself in the sense of Heideggerian *aletheia*, there is no place for scepticism.

There are, of course, many kinds of truth, there are also same degrees of its importance. The judgements: "2+2=4", "$E=mc^2$", "Winston Churchill was the Prime Minister of Great Britain during the Second World War" belong to different kinds of sciences: mathematics, physics, historiography, but each of them is true, and they are of the same value for everybody who understands them.

The value (and at the same time the necessity) of being true is also independent of the importance of a true judgement. The judgement: "Peter Kowalski has been elected to the post of the president of the Society of Friends of Ants" is less important than the judgement: "Karol Wojtyła has been elected the Pope", but the truthfulness of both is the same, if only Peter Kowalski has in fact been elected to the mentioned post.

As we have mentioned above, the freedom for seeking truth is replaced by the necessity of acceptance of the truth received. In this case freedom and necessity do not constitute an opposition. On the contrary: necessity must be understood here as the fulfilment and perfection of freedom.

In the light of this conclusion we are able to understand better the words of Christ: "And ye shall know the truth, and the truth shall make you free" (John 8, 32). The freedom of truth depends not only on freedom from failure, uncertainty and doubt: it means also the freedom from the necessity of choice. The choice of truth can be one and only one. It is not determined by any accidental circumstances. It is guaranteed by the evidence of the deepest basis of truth: the being itself. *Verum est id quod est. Verum est manifestativum et declarativum esse.*

---

[1] Definitions I 1 and III 2, 3 are derived from St. Augustine (*Soliloquia 5; De vera religione 36 and 31*), I 2 and 3 from Avicenna (*In Metaph. XI, c. 2*), II 1 from Isaac, II 2 from St. Anselm (*De veritate c. 12*), III 1 from St. Hilarius.

II. FREEDOM AND GOOD

Why callest thou me good? there is none good but one, that is, God.
(Mk 10, 18)

The human approach to good implies, first of all, the freedom of choice.

There are different kinds of good governed by the axiological hierarchy, in various ways defined by philosophers. The common statement depends on the conviction that there are goods of higher and lower level and that we are obliged to make a correct choice among them. In making this choice we are relatively free. Our freedom, however, is not absolute: its limitation is caused by various factors that in many cases are independent of us. Enough to say that we "are not an island", that we live in a society, which makes definite laws that oblige us, that we are determind by certain biological, ethnical, cultural and many other factors.

On the other hand, there exists a particular "vocation for value" which induces us to accomplish this or that choice. But in a greater number of situations this choice is not determined by necessity. If we tried to perform this vocation in a kind of judgement, this judgement would assume the character of an implication: "if you want [...]" This situation implies a distiction between absolute and relative values: if you want to reach an absolute value A, you have to accomplish a value R, which is a necessary means to obtain A – and therefore is related to A. In other words: the value R is related to the value A as to its aim. Some examples: *Si vis pacem, para bellum*: war is, paradoxically, a value related to peace as its necessary condition; "[...] if thou wilt enter into life, keep the commandments" (Mt 19, 17); "If thou will be perfect, go and sell that thou hast [...] and come and follow me". (Mt 19, 21).

We are free not only in accepting the absolute value, but also in choosing the values that lead to it. The relation between A and R is not always unique: very often we can find various R leading to A. But if we really want to receive A, we must be aware that the ways to do this are not infinite. Great religions, as well as greatest thinkers, try to show the best possible ways leading to absolute values. They often appeal to the deepest desire of the human being: the desire of happiness, and they argue that only thanks to the highest values will we be able to achieve it. For example: If you want to be happy, "live according to nature" (the Stoics). Or: "It is not possible to live pleasantly without living prudently, and honourably, and justly [...]" (Epicurus)[2]. Or: If you want to be happy, dont't treat the earthly goods as the highest ones.

---

[2] Cfr. F. Copleston, *A History of Philosophy*, vol. I: *Greece and Rome,* Part II: Image Books, New York 1962, pp. 139 and 153.

It seems to me that even Kant's categorical imperative: "Act only on that maxim through which you can at the same time will that it should become a universal law"[3] is in fact hypothetical, as we may ask: "Why do I have to act this way?" The "universal law" must be rooted in something which justifies it, finally it may only be value (goodness) in itself, understood either as an universal happiness or universal peace etc. (By the way, it is not accidenal – I think – that one of the late Kantian treaties, which can be treated as a kind of supplement to the *Critique of Practical Reason*, is devoted to the analysis of the necessary conditions of eternal peace). What is, then, the ultimate aim of Kantian ethics? The answer is: virtue. Defining the "summum bonum" Kant wrote: [it] "means the whole, the perfect good, in which, however, virtue as the condition is always the supreme good, because it has no condition above it; whereas happiness, while it is certainly pleasant to him who possesses it, is not of itself absolutely and in every respect good, but always presupposes morally right behaviour as its condition"[4].

For our purposes the difference between modes of freedom linked with the supreme good and the ways that lead to it is highly important. It is to emphasize that – paradoxically – we are more free in accepting the supreme good than in accepting the means to receive it. In other words: the relative values that lead to the absolute value are necessary, while the acceptance of the absolute value depends on our freedom.

If our considerations are true, we have to accept the conclusion that in opposition to the identity of the truthfulness of true judgements, the moment of value, which constitutes various goods, is not unique.

But there is one thing which decides that in the situation of free choice between goods we also find a moment of higher necessity. This mysterious thing is love. The choice made by love excludes all possible values except this one which is just chosen. The choice of love may be rational but it may also be absolutely irrational; it may depend on reasonable arguments but it may also depend on pure intuition. In each case love overcomes any accidental choice: I choose it becouse I love it.

Love does not limit my freedom but fulfils it. I am not able to abandon my treasure, and "[...] where your treasure is, there your heart be also" (Mt 6, 21).

---

[3] Cfr. F. Copleston, *A History of Philosophy*, vol. 6: *Modern Philosophy*, Part II: *Kant*, Image Books, New York 1964, p. 116. Source of quotation: *Groundwork of the Metaphysics of Morals*, transl. T. K. Abbott, *Kant's Theory of Ethics*, London 1909, s. 421.

[4] Op. cit. p. 129. Quotation is from Cr. Pr. R., transl. by T. K. Abbott, London 1909, p. 199.

As an important consequence of this situation a new dimension of freedom appears, best expressed by St. Augustin in his famous sentence: *dilige et quod vis fac* ... Love does not close but opens new horizons of freedom, which is now subordinated only to the highest values. This way the peculiar axiological circle comes to its end: free choice of the supreme good is in fact caused by the love of it, and – at the same time – this love opens new ways of further choices, i.e. new modes of freedom subordinated only to the real values, participating in the highest good.

III. FREEDOM AND BEAUTY

Muß es sein? Es muß sein.
(Beethoven)

The last set of values I would like to consider in respect of our freedom belongs to aesthetics.

It is necessary to distinguish two fundamental aestetic experiences: passive and active. The former belongs primarily to the attitude of the artistic (aesthetic) receiver, the latter – to the process of artistic creation.

The passive attitude is often experienced as absolutely free. I can accept or reject aesthetic objects according to my taste, which can change arbitrarily, and make my aesthetic judgements independently of any norms or rules. *De gustibus non est disputandum.* In fact the situation is not so simple. My taste is determined by at least – as H. Taine remarked – *temps, milieu momenmt historique*, but also by education, influence of various authorities, customs, good and bad preferences. Going deeper and deeper I will find other determinations, which are probably connected with my biological, particularly physiological structure.

It is well known that the process of artistic creativity is not only active. In its framework we find also moments of acceptance of the traditional ideas and tools, of passive contemplation and affirmative judgements. More important, however, is the active aspect of this process. It seems – at the first glance – that the activity of an artist, particularly the possibility of choosing different means of artistic expression, is here unlimited. The history of art gives us numerous examples of changing artistic ideals, rules, norms, materials, tools, etc. The artist seems to be absolutely free.

In fact his situation is more complicated. He is limited not only by various historical circumstances but is also subordinated to a specific axiological vocation of the world of values. The greater the artist the deeper the sensitivity toward the vocation of value. We discover a particular *aesthetics a priori*, which in its highest form leads even to the supra-aesthetic values. Subordination to the domain of values does not mean any determinism. It is rather a way to axiological fulfilment of the work of art which is just created by the artist. This subordination is not experienced as determination that limits an artistic attitude but rather as liberation from accidental circumstances, and as necessity which is strictly connected with the essence of value itself.

It does not mean that an artist is able to reach this value immediately. Everything he can do is to prepare the necessary conditions or – in other words – the place for manifestation of value. He must feel the *a priori* vocation of it, he must do all the best for keeping it in his mind, but the final manifestation of beauty does not depend on him. On the other hand: if he does not try to reach it, it will never appear. The dialectic between the freedom of an artist and the liberty of manifestation of beauty is perhaps the greatest mystery of artistic creativity.

How could one find the necessary ways leading to the necessity of value? Some artists know them intuitively, some others search for them in deepest intellectual endeavours and emotional tension. Let Mozart be an example of the former, Beethoven of the latter. But when the correct way is discovered, the necessity of it becomes absolutely evident: *muß es sein? Es muß sein ...* The artistic freedom is finaly fulfiled by the highest necessity.

This moment of necessity reflects itself also in the final result of the perfect creative process – the masterwork. According to the classical definition of beauty, which we find also in L. B. Alberti's famous *De re aedificatoria*, "[...] beauty is the harmony of all parts in relation to one another, in which parts are in such agreement with and proportion to the work in which they inhere that nothing can be either added or taken away without ruining the whole. With certainty this is a great and divine thing; the attainment of perfection in this taxes talent and intellect to the limit, and rarely is it given to anyone, even to nature herself, to create a completely finished work that is perfect in everything"[5].

CONCLUDING REMARKS

The essence of freedom depends on the openness towards value.

The essence of value does not limit our freedom but fulfills it.

It is to distinguish axiological and deterministic (i.e. physical, biological, physiological, historical, etc.) necessity.

The higher position of value in axiological hierarchy, the stronger the character of its axiological necessity. *Navigare necesse est, vivere non est necesse*.

---

[5] Cfr. W. Tatarkiewicz, *History of Aesthetics*, vol. III: *Modern Aesthetics*, ed. D. Petsch, The Hague-Paris-Warszawa 1974, p. 93-94.

But: the higher the moral value, the greater freedom of its choice.

In the domain of truth we experience apodictical, in the domain of good – hypothetical necessity.

The acceptance of truth is apodictical, freedom belongs to the choice of means for seaking it. On the contrary: the acceptance of good is free ("if you want"), but the choice of means is ruled by necessity ("you have to" or even "you must").

The ultimate reason for choosing the real, particularly the supreme good, is love.

Unlimited freedom is characteristic of the domain of aesthetic taste, but there exists an aesthetic *a priori* which governs the very artistic endeavours towards beauty.

In everyday language we sometimes distinguish the category of "true values", e.g. "true good" or "true beauty". This way of speaking is deeply rooted in the heart of matter: the so called true values participate in the essential moments of truth, namely in its evidence and its apodicticity.

Therefore: truth is the highest value. The dignity of other values depends on their participation in truth (on their truthfulness).

VITTORIO POSSENTI
University of Venice
Italy

DIALECTIQUE DE LA LIBERTÉ
VERS UNE PHILOSOPHIE INTÉGRALE DE LA LIBERTÉ

1. En un premier temps j'avais proposé aux organisateurs de développer le sujet "La constitution politique de la liberté". Ensvite j'ai changé avec leur assentissement le titre, qui maintenant est le suivant: "Dialectique de la liberté. Vers une philosophie intégrale de la liberté". Le changement a été suggéré par une considération des images de la liberté circulant dans la culture et par l'idée qu'elles sont inadéquates. Alors que très fréquentes sont les références à la liberté politique, économique, juridique, religieuse, bien mince se présente aujourd'hui la réflexion sur la liberté comme telle et sur sa dialectique.

La position initiale de cette relation réside donc dans l'idée que la conception de la liberté, qui à présent se fait passer pour canonique, se borne très souvent à la liberté socio-politique et, dans les problèmes relatifs à la praxis humaine, à la liberté de choix (question du *liberum arbitrium*). De nombreuses questions qui se rapportent à l'écologie, à l'éthique, aux chances de vie de la personne, sont aujourd'hui traitées par la culture philosophique en demeurant à l'intérieur des susdites coordonnées.

Légitime semble donc la question de savoir si l'idée de liberté n'est pas sévèrement réduite et émiettée en plusieurs problématiques sectoriales. Une série de signes avertit cependant qu'un temps favorable à une conception substantive de la liberté, en connexion avec l'ontologie, l'anthropologie et l'éthique, peut se présenter à nouveau:
1) le déclin de la primauté de l'épistémologie et le retour de la question ontologique, et avec elle celle de la problématique des "modalités d'être", capable de répondre à la question: quelle modalité d'existence revient aux choses?

2) la crise de la soi disante "loi de Hume" sur l'infranchissable séparation entre être et devoir être. Cet événement ouvre à nouveau la route aux questions d'éthique substantive, donnant une place secondaire à celles métaéthiques, abstraites, procédurales. En stimulant de nouveaux problèmes sur l'homme, il favorise une reprise de l'éthique de la vertu et de la félicité;
3) l'homme est aujourd'hui plus conscient que jadis que le binôme science-technique dépose entre ses mains un immense pouvoir, et il est nécessaire d'en user avec le sens de la responsabilité. L'appel qui, de plusieurs côtés, s'adresse à une éthique de la responsabilité, entraîne une réflexion et une réformulation du thème de la liberté en rapport au problème écologique, et en général à une question sur son sens et finalisme dans la vie de la personne.

2. Le développement de ces problèmes requiert une réflexion renouvelée sur la liberté. A côté des facteurs favorables auxquels on a fait allusion, on doit reconnaître la présence de noeuds qui font obstacle, et qui se reportent à des dichotomies depuis longtemps cristallisées: la séparation entre métaphysique et morale; entre le bien et le juste, sous la présupposition que le premier concept vaudrait seulement pour le domaine privé et le deuxième seulement pour le domaine public; entre raison pratique et raison spéculative, dans la tentative encore et toujours abondamment suivie de dégager la première de la seconde. Cependant certains facteurs nouveaux, peut-être capables de dissoudre les cristallisations auxquelles on a fait allusion, s'annoncent: on peut ici rappeler par exemple l'étroit rapport posé par H. Jonas entre métaphysique et morale, à un point tel que l'axiologie est jugée comme un simple secteur de l'ontologie[1]. Dans la sphère de la pensée politique il semble qu'un obstacle soit créé par l'accent emphatiquement posé sur le libéralisme, dans lequel se cristallise une signification restreinte de la liberté, assez fréquemment identifiée à la seule liberté de choix. La théorie et la praxis de ce type de liberté ont été trop soulignées aux dépens d'autres formes de liberté, oubliées au moins partiellement.

En parallèle à l'idée que la liberté est une propriété très intime de l'esprit, dont elle révèle la noblesse spécifique, s'est imposé, comme expression d'un anthropocentrisme radical, le mythe de l'homme comme sujet pur, autonome et inconditionnellement libre, de l'homme conçu identique à une liberté pure. Cette conception a été fréquemment nourrie par le dualisme entre nature et liberté, dans lequel on adopte une idée empirique-phénoménique, non ontologique, de nature. Elle serait seulement une infinie multiplicité de phénomènes, dont s'occupent la physique et les autres sciences associées, tandis que le royaume de la liberté se placerait ailleurs, à une distance sidérale de la nature physiquement considérée. Opposition entre

---

[1] Cfr. *Il principio responsabilità*, Einaudi, Torino 1993, p. 101.

nature et liberté, rendue un lieu commun par Kant et par sa *Critique de la raison pratique*, et après devenue contrapposition sans médiation entre être et liberté chez Gentile et Sartre, mais qui doit être soumise à la réflexion. À une considération attentive deux propositions résultent comme bien fondées: la sphère de la liberté, présuppose et repose sur celle de l'être et de la nature selon la loi générale de l'insertion de l'ordre de l'action dans celui de l'être; les deux ordres restent distincts, en vertu de la différence générale des objets représentés par l'existence et par l'agir. Une liberté pure, une liberté nouménique sans sujet est impensable. Nous connaissons seulement la liberté de sujets personnels, qui sont plongés dans l'existence et le devenir. Ce n'est pas la liberté qui est à l'origine de la personne, mais celle-ci de la liberté, qui est bien sûr une propriété essentielle et imprescriptible de l'être-personne. Elle revient de droit à une nature spirituelle, à un sujet intellectuel.

Ces brèves remarques détournent l'idée que le sujet libre puisse être entendu comme un abîme de pure indétermination et séparé de toute nature. Comme faculté d'un sujet intellectuel la volonté possède une détermination nécessaire: le désir du bien comme tel et l'imuable attraction vers ce qui comble et rassasie, la félicité comme fin ultime. La liberté aussi a une nature, possède un objet immuablement déterminé, sans lequel elle n'existerait pas. Et c'est sur la nécessaire volition de la parfaite félicité que se fonde la liberté de choix vers tous les biens finis, qui en tant que tels ne peuvent pas combler la volonté.

3. Dans la philosophie de la liberté à laquelle nous nous addressons, la volonté est pensée comme un *appetitus*, une faculté d'appétance et de tendance, qui de par sa propre nature va avec tout son poids vers le bien. Selon une solution apparemment paradoxale, proposée par Thomas d'Aquin, la liberté de choix est possible car la volonté n'est pas libre devant le bien parfait et sans limites, devant la béatitude. Solution paradoxale car le Docteur commun fonde la liberté de choix sur la nécessaire orientation de la volonté vers la parfaite félicité[2]. Dans cette perspective l'homme, doué de liberté, est posé loin du déterminisme comme de l'indétermination: il est justement pensé comme sujet doué d'autodétermination, comme maître de ses propres actes selon trois formes: maître de procéder à choisir, de s'abstenir du choix, de choisir entre différents objets.

À cette position on peut adresser l'objection que, si tous les hommes désirent par nécessité de nature le bien et si celui-ci est conçu comme félici-

---

[2] Cfr. *S. Th.*, I II, q. 13, a. 6; I, q. 19, a. 10, où on distingue entre l'appétition nécessaire du bien parfait et l'élection libre des biens partiels. Selon saint Thomas la *necessitas coactionis* est contraire au libre arbitre, non la *necessitas naturalis*.

té, alors on n'y aurait pas de liberté, car la connaissance du bien la déterminerait nécessairement. On peut efficacement répondre que l'inclination naturelle nécessaire vers la félicité est hautement indéterminée en rapport à ce en quoi consiste l'authentique félicité pour l'homme et les moyens qui y conduisent. En outre l'intellect peut certainement proposer à la volonté diverses conceptions du bien (sans concept il n'y a pas de liberté), mais en dernière instance c'est la volonté avec son pouvoir illimité à orienter le jugement de l'intellect où elle veut. Une adéquate reflexion sur le péché de l'Ange serait ici nécessaire pour démentir toute forme d'intellectualisme éthique. L'Ange ne connaissait–il pas parfaitement la vérité sur Dieu? Et n'a-t-il pas opté contre cette vérité?

La situation de la liberté est dramatique car le sujet doit choisir non seulement les moyens pour la fin, mais aussi entre les diverses fins mêmes celle en laquelle consiste le bien parfait. La position ici soutenue est parfois taxée d'eudémonisme car, dit-on, elle serait dirigée par le désir de la félicité. Mais la philosophie déjà entrevoit, et la Révélation confirme en plénitude, que le désir naturel et humain de félicité se purifie et s'approfondit en devenant amour du bien comme tel et en dernière instance amour de Dieu, aimé *amore Dei*, non *amore mei*. Et c'est par amour de Dieu que le sujet veut, en la transfigurant, la félicité.

4. Ceci présupposé, et en nous faisant les élèves de la *Seinsphilosophie* (philosophie de l'être et non du paraître, disait Jean Paul II en 1979, en commémorant le premier centenaire de l'encyclique *Aeterni Patris*), notre but est d'explorer la dialectique de la liberté, à partir de son stade initial jusqu'à un possible point terminal d'aboutissement. Il est hors de notre propos de développer une entière philosophie de la liberté, quoique les parties traitées pourraient y être intégrées à bon droit. Dans la tradition de la philosophie de l'être la notion de liberté se présente comme plus ample et complexe que Le concept de *libre arbitre*. Celui-ci est pour l'homme non une conquête, mais un cadeau ou bien un équipement de nature, quelque chose que la personne se trouve à posséder par le fait même d'être personne. Propriété ontologique originaire, et donc *liberté initiale*, la liberté de choix du sujet connaît de nombreuses victoires et autant de défaites. Elle doit se développer dans la registre psychologique et moral, à travers une capacité toujours renouvelée de l'homme à faire bon usage de son *liberum arbitrium*. Elle est donc ordonnée à quelque chose de divers et de plus haut que le choix, à un aboutissement, que la sagesse de toutes les époques et latitudes (asiatique, grècque, chrétienne) a conçu essentiellement comme une *libération* des maux et limites de la condition humaine. La dialectique de la liberté, en impliquant la vie et les plus profondes aspirations de la personne, possède une forme *sociale* et une forme *spirituelle*.

Sur le premier plan la conquête de la liberté se déroule à partir de la condition d'un sujet qui, en se sachant soumis à une infinité de conditionnements, lutte pour s'en libérer et pour monter à un niveau d'existence plus élevé. Le mouvement essentiel de l'histoire humaine est animé par un effort, qui traverse toutes les époques, pour se libérer des grandes limites de la condition humaine: libération de la misère, de la maladie, de la tyrannie, de l'ignorance. Sur le plan spirituel, profondément enraciné dans le noyau le plus intime de la personne, est son nostalgique désir d'atteindre la condition d'une totalité concrète, capable d'un sommet de spontanéité et d'exultation, dans l'ouverture à soi-même, au grand Tout universel, à Dieu.

En se libérant des maux et limites sociaux propre à la condition humaine, et en se dirigeant vers sa fin ultime absolue, la personne atteint une vie plus haute, une plénitude relative de *liberté terminale*, qui dans sa forme pure se réalise seulement en Dieu comme liberté divine, dont l'homme jouit par participation, et qu'on peut appeler liberté d'autonomie, d'indépendance, de spontanéité et enfin d'exultation: d'autonomie et spontanéité, car le sujet accomplit avec un parfait naturel et sans aucune contrainte ce qui est demandé par la loi morale[3]; liberté d'indépendance, car il cherche à se dégager de conditionnements hétéronomes; liberté d'exultation, car dans son sommet une telle liberté donne une plénitude d'existence, de floraison et de fruit. C'est pour l'acquisition de cette liberté que nous sommes doués du libre arbitre: la liberté de choix n'est pas une fin en soi, ni une fin à soi-même. Elle est finalisée à l'acquisition de la liberté terminale: Autant la première est donnée à l'homme comme un cadeau de nature, autant la deuxième est une dure conquête, où les échecs sont plus fréquents que les succès.

Le sens où la finalisation de la liberté est orientée vers une plénitude d'être: est de monter à de plus hauts niveaux d'existence. Condition de la liberté est l'étendue transcendantale du désir dirigé à la totalité de l'être et attiré par l'amabilité du bien: c'est le désir qui explore la géographie du possible. En confondant liberté de choix et liberté d'autonomie, une partie de la culture contemporaine, sceptique en ce qui concerne les fins, place la liberté suprême seulement dans la première, et donc l'étendue intégrale de la liberté n'est pas comprise.

Pour rendre plus plastique la différence entre les deux formes de liberté, on dira que dans le concept de libre arbitre est inclue l'idée de *libertas a*

---

[3] Cette idée d'autonomie se révèle différente de celle kantienne, et à notre avis plus vraie et adéquate. Selon Kant il y a véritable liberté quand celle-ci procède en totale autonomie du seul sujet et sans aucune régulations du côté de l'objet. Dans la liberté d'autonomie dont nous traitons, la régulation de l'objet reste mais interiorisée et rendue spontanée.

necessitate (l'objet n'exerce pas une détermination nécessaire sur l'acte de la liberté), alors que l'autre concept de liberté renvoie à la *libertas a coactione*. Cette liberté de la co-action peut et doit être interprétée d'une façon non strictement physique, mais plus ample jusqu'à inclure la liberté vis-à-vis du péché, de la culpabilité, de la mort, de la loi qui écrase la volonté mauvaise. En ce sens la *libertas a coactione* signifie une autonomie morale et spirituelle intérieure qui constitue une montée et un perfectionnement.

5. Dès le nouveau départ cartésien, la question de la liberté a peut-être constitué *le* problème de la pensée moderne. Chez Descartes une place centrale est occupée par la liberté divine, pensée comme une efficacité infinie, déliée de toute nécessité à un tel point qu'elle aurait pu créer des cercles carrés et des montagnes sans vallées sur la seule base de son choix arbitraire. Dans une autre phase, après la conception de Leibniz qui conçut la nature de l'être comme unité originaire de *perceptio* et *d'appetitus*, la doctrine de l'idéalisme schellingien soutient que l'être originaire (*Urseyn*) est volonté. Dans la philosophie de Kant la liberté est une propriété nouménique du sujet. Enfin en Heidegger la liberté prend un poids tellement puissant que la vérité se rapporte à elle; l'essence de la vérité est la liberté, lit-on dans *Sur l'essence de la vérité* dans une formule douée d'un haut taux d'ambiguïté. En rapport à la dialectique de la liberté reste le problème, que nous ne voulons pas aborder ici, de savoir si les deux formes de liberté, dont on a traitées, ont reçu une considération adéquate chez les auteurs cités.

6. Nous ne croyons pas secondaire que dans la question de la liberté, la foi chrétienne confirme par voie indirecte ce que la philosophie découvre. Si la liberté était seulement celle de choix, le sujet serait "condamné" à toujours choisir. S'il ne choisissait pas, il ne serait plus personne, car il n'exercerait pas la liberté qui le constitue comme sujet. Cependant, alors que le libre arbitre restera finalement en repos – il ne s'exercera pas dans la vision béatifique – la liberté de floraison et d'exultation durera toujours. À son sommet, en elle, s'exprime la parfaite spontanéité d'une nature spirituelle unie à Dieu.

En philosophie se rencontrent des avantages, en posant en comparaison les questions sur l'homme et celles sur Dieu. Le thème de la liberté ne fait pas exception. Si la liberté divine se donne surtout comme une liberté de spontanéité et d'exultation, qui en Dieu, est aussi une parfaite nécessité selon la loi qu'on pourrait appeler de la *coincidentia oppositorum* où on rejoint le secret jaloux de la Transcendance, il est aisé de comprendre que le sommet de la liberté humaine ne se place pas dans celle de choix. En suggérant cette réflexion, la philosophie chrétienne se meut dans l'espace entre-ouvert par la révélation selon laquelle l'homme est *imago Dei*: en tant qu'image, il l'est aussi dans la sphère de la liberté.

7. Le dynamisme de la liberté possède une forme *sociale* et une forme *spirituelle*, nous l'avons dit. À son tour la première forme se dédouble en un niveau plus typiquement interpersonnel, auquel on fera seulement une brève allusion, et en un niveau plus typiquement social, qui dans notre contexte exige une attention plus poussée. Au niveau interpersonnel l'homme existe dans le rapport avec l'autre, et dans ce rapport la liberté du sujet rencontre une autre liberté: ici commence la dynamique de la mutuelle reconnaissance qui, quand elle se déroule en termes positifs, donne aux sujets certification d'eux-mêmes dans la conscience d'être une personne et de se sentir reconnue comme telle.

Dans la vie socio-politique est-ce que l'homme recherche d'abord des libertés particulières (liberté d'opinion, de pensée, de presse, etc)? Ou bien cherche-t-il à premier lieu à parvenir à la liberté d'autonomie et d'indépendance, en vertu de laquelle la personne procède à son aboutissement? La forme sociale de la liberté d'autonomie a pour fin d'une part de garantir un domaine d'indépendance par rapport à la volonté arbitraire d'autrui; et d'autre part de secourir la personne, de réparer les blessures infligées par la nature matérielle (maladie, misère, cataclysmes). On sait bien quelle immense partie de la vie sociale et du cycle économique et productif dépend de la nécessité de s'occuper du côté matériel de la vie.

Il n'est pas douteux que l'idée de liberté, plus que celles d'égalité et de fraternité, donne l'inspiration à de nombreuses philosophies politiques modernes. Or, en rapport à la liberté socio-politique on peut individuer trois conceptions dans l'époque moderne:
– la perspective individualiste-libérale, dans laquelle la vie sociale prend comme but de favoriser la plus ample extrinsécation de la liberté de choix des individus. Société et politique tournent autour de cette liberté, tandis que sur celle d'autonomie et de libération descend un voile. Elle est abandonnée au côté privé de l'existence, où se déploient les préférences des individus;
– la perspective totalitaire (au sens large), où avec le sacrifice de la liberté de choix, la vie sociale est adressée à la production de puissance et à un effort collectif, dans lequel l'individu peut se reconnaître et dans une certaine mesure se libérer. Ici se fait valoir l'idée que la liberté n'est pas seulement celle du choix (durement contrainte dans les sociétés totalitaires), alors que l'autre signification de liberté est au même temps reconnue, diminuée et finalisée vers une issue collective de puissance;
– une troisième perspective, à laquelle convient le nom de personnalisme communautaire, bien que reconnaissant l'importance de la liberté de choix,

entend la vie sociale polarisée par la recherche du bien commun d'un peuple uni. Dans son idée est inclus le but de favoriser l'entrée des citoyens à une adéquate jouissance de la liberté d'autonomie et à une libération des principaux maux de la condition humaine. Dans cette perspective de philosophie politique la conquête de la liberté terminale contemple la présence active de deux piliers de toute société passablement organisée: la justice et l'amitié civique.

Une question importante surgit à propos des sociétés libérale-démocratiques: il s'agit de comprendre leur rapport avec la conception de la liberté qui a été esquissée. Dans une section considérable de leur culture et praxis on estime nécessaire de pousser toujours plus loin la liberté de choix et l'éventail des options des individus, dans le présupposé que tel soit le but de la vie sociale. Mais si une vie sociale adéquate n'incorpore pas seulement la liberté, mais plutôt le bien commun et la félicité politique, le seul développement des options peut comporter anomie, destruction de relations et de liens, et enfin déclin du bien-être collectif. En rapport au constant élargissement des options, qui a constitué le cheval de bataille des politiques libérales et démocratiques pendant un siècle, il semble désormais nécessaire de consolider l'éventail des options, et d'opérer pour le rétablissement des liens.

Cet objectif est suggéré non seulement par la culture du personnalisme communautaire, mais aussi par les courants plus réfléchis du libéralisme. Selon R. Dahrendorf la théorie politique de la liberté s'est tellement concentrée sur les options, qu'elle a perdu de vue l'importance des liens et relations: "La tâche du libéral concerne le plus difficile des objectifs sociaux, la création de liens, l'encouragement à établir des relations, le renouveau du pacte social"[4].

8. Dans la conquête de la liberté un relief spécial revêtent l'art, la philosophie, la religion, capables de donner vie à des formes *spirituelles* de libération, où la liberté terminale de floraison atteint le noyau le plus intime de la vie personnelle. Aucune vie sociale ne peut garantir l'accès à la liberté spirituelle d'autonomie, qui dépend de L'épanouissement de la culture, de la transcendance et des biens de l'esprit, et auxquels la vie civile peut seulement préparer de loin.

Dans l'effectuation de la liberté terminale le niveau plus haut revient à la religion, où on atteint le sommet de la liberté d'exultation dans l'union par grâce entre personne divine et personne humaine. Ceci est le lieu de la sainteté, quand le sujet créé, dans la parfaite spontanéité d'une nature spirituelle, payée au prix d'un déchirement toujours surmonté, accomplit libre-

---

[4] R. Dahrendorf, *La libertà che cambia*, Laterza, Roma-Bari 1981, p. 52.

ment, par amour et sous la motion du Saint Esprit, ce que la loi exige, en entrant en dialogue avec l'Absolu. Dans la vie de l'esprit la liberté terminale de spontanéité et d'exultation constitue la forme accomplie de la liberté des enfants de Dieu. En dernier ressort le libre arbitre nous a été donné pour ce couronnement. Dans son sommet on rencontre ici le paradoxe étrange et à la fois lumineux que plus l'homme obéit à Dieu, plus il est intérieurement libre, car il a intériorisé la règle.

Dans une telle dynamique s'éclaircit ultérieurement ce que l'analyse philosophique déjà entrevoit, c'est-à-dire que la structure morale de la liberté ne consiste pas dans l'obéissance à soi-même, mais plutôt dans l'obéissance au juste et au bien. "Freedom is not simply the absence of tyranny or oppression. Nor is freedom a licence to do whatever we like. Freedom has an inner 'logic' which distinguishes it and ennobles it: freedom is ordered to the truth, and is fulfilled in man's quest for truth"[5]. Il ne semble donc pas sage que l'on donne une place toujours plus ample à la liberté de choix dans la societé sans favoriser au même temps une élévation de la maturité et responsabilité morale, où la volonté *libre* se transforme au prix d'une sévère lutte en volonté *bonne*.

9. À une philosophie adéquate reviendrait la tâche d'explorer l'immense gisement de la liberté: une responsabilité urgente à une époque où l'être-pour-la-mort, le nihilisme, l'angoisse ont marqué en profondeur la pensée en créant un milieu moins favorable au déploiement de la liberté de la personne et habité par une prédominance du négatif. À cette situation spirituelle ont réagi avec un succès variable d'autres expressions de la culture, parmi lesquelles le "principe responsabilité" de H. Jonas et le "principe espérance" de E. Bloch. Plutôt que de les opposer – le principe responsabilité incorporerait une plus grande sagesse et réalisme que l'autre, qui s'accorderait d'effrénées projections utopiques – il serait sage de les coordonner à la lumière de l'idée que l'esprit et la liberté ne sont pas un immobile miroir du monde[6]. Nous avons fait allusion ou fait que dans la dialectique de la liberté est esquissée une géographie du possible. Celui-ci, d'abord conçu à travers l'élan de la liberté qui se penche sur le futur, est appelé à l'existence par son acte même. Moyennant le passage du possible au réel, la liberté a une liaison intime avec l'espérance, qui se projette vers le "pas encore". Le

---

[5] Jean Paul II, „*From the Human Rights to the Rights of Nations*", Address to the General Asembly of the United Nations Organization, New York, October 5, 1995.

[6] En coordonnant "principe responsabilité" et "principe espérance", nous n'entendons pas réduire la force de la critique élevée par Hans Jonas au concept d'utopie de Ernst Bloch (cfr. *Il principio responsabilità*, pp. 227-291). À notre avis la position du premier en faveur de la responsabilité ne nie pas le rôle de l'espérance, au moins d'une espérance fondée et ouverte à la recherche du possible.

désespéré n'attend rien du futur, il estime que l'exercice de la liberté est une passion inutile. Il y a espérance s'il y a des possibilités ouvertes: la vérification de leur existence revient à une ontologie de l'être capable de faire place à la potentialité, le *dynamei on* d'Aristote. Un grandiose gisement du possible est représenté par l'âme, lieu du pas-encore-conscient, du pas-encore-explicité, source dont jaillissent des projections de libération. La dialectique de la liberté se développe au-delà de la conception close et statique de l'être.

GEORGES COTTIER O. P.
Teologo della Casa Pontificia
Vatican

LIBERTÉ CRÉE
LIBERTÉ ET OBÉISSANCE – RÉFLEXIONS PHILOSOPHIQUES

INTRODUCTION

1. Le philosophe qui conduit sa méditation en ayant pour horizon les lumières supraphilosophiques reçues de la Révélation, y puise la conviction, qu'il lui appartiendra ensuite de fonder en raison, de la transcendance de la personne humaine. Il sait d'emblée que la dimension déterminante de l'être humain n'est pas donnée dans son rapport de partie à tout, tel qu'il se vérifie au plan du cosmos ou de la société, mais dans son rapport constitutif à ce Tout transcendant qu'est Dieu. Au delà des médiations naturelles, la personne humaine est appelée à vivre une relation spirituelle directe avec Dieu. Dans cette relation, elle découvre la grandeur inouïe de sa liberté. Qu'il suffise d'évoquer ici, avec Kierkegaard, la figure d'Abraham, ou encore cette jeune fille d'Israël, Myriam, au consentement de laquelle Dieu a voulu, pour ainsi dire, suspendre la réalisation de l'Incarnation.

Le philosophe retiendra comme un fait majeur et décisif cet apport de l'héritage biblique et chrétien à la culture. Dorénavant l'humanité sait l'extraordinaire dignité de la personne et de sa liberté et sa dimension transtemporelle et transhistorique. Les négations acharnées, les déviations et les abus eux-mêmes ne se comprennent que dans la perspective d'une prise de conscience suscitée par la rencontre avec la Révélation. Cela l'humanité ne peut pas l'oublier. Elle est appelée à en dégager progressivement certes non sans aléas et possibles reculs, les implications.

Ainsi le sens de la liberté de la personne et de sa noblesse est, dans un premier temps, objet de conviction, conviction assez puissante pour porter le dynamisme de la vie sociale et l'affirmation des individus, mais aussi conviction fragile et menacée, pour autant précisément qu'elle demeure au stade de la conviction.

En un second temps, un effort d'élucidation est donc requis qui en établisse la nature, les fondements et les conséquences. Et de fait, le thème de la liberté tient une place centrale dans la pensée philosophique moderne. À ce niveau se rencontrent, comme l'on sait, des divergences et des contrastes. Développer une philosophie de la liberté, qui soit en consonance avec la Révélation, est sans doute une des tâches majeures qui attendent les penseurs chrétiens.

I

LIBERTÉ DE LA PERSONNE

2. Je vous propose ici quelques brèves réflexions qui doivent être considérées comme autant de jalons indispensables pour nous permettre d'aborder le problème de l'obéissance.

Une première considération doit porter sur le *sujet* de la liberté. Elle est nécessaire pour autant que parmi les théories modernes de la liberté, certaines font de celle-ci une hypostase ou un équivalent de l'Absolu, tandis que d'autres identifient purement et simplement personne et liberté. Or la liberté est une prérogative de la personne. De plus, notre propos porte sur la personne humaine et sur sa liberté. On rappellera l'adage: *actus sunt suppositorum*. Cet adage indique que pour comprendre les actes libres, il faut remonter à une métaphysique de ce sujet qu'est la personne, ainsi que de ses puissances ou facultés. Mais à l'inverse, il signifie aussi que c'est la personne qui se révèle et se manifeste à travers ses actes libres. Il n'est pas inutile de souligner ce point, car certaines conceptions de la liberté tiennent, à l'opposé, que la condition même de l'affirmation de la liberté, serait le désengagement du sujet à l'égard de ses actes, aussitôt que ceux-ci ont été posés. C'est comme si l'acte, par sa détermination concrète, signifiait une mort et une négation de la liberté, qui doit sans cesse se reprendre et revenir à son indétermination originelle. Il faut, au contraire, souligner que, à travers ses actes libres, actes *siens*, c'est-à-dire sur lesquels elle exerce son dominium et son pouvoir, la personne s'édifie elle-même. Elle est responsable de ses actes; c'est *en* eux que s'exerce sa responsabilité et non pas dans l'instant qui précède leur production. Les actes libres s'intègrent dans l'édification morale de la personnalité qui affirme ainsi son inscription dans la durée et son historicité.

Il faut aussitôt ajouter une précision essentielle. La personne comme la liberté sont des notions analogiques. Elles ne sont pas circonscrites dans la sphère humaine, elles sont attribuables *proprie* aux esprits purs et à Dieu lui-même. Elles ont, pour reprendre une expression de Maritain, une portée *transnaturelle*. Elle ne sont pas enfermées dans les limites spécifiques de notre nature particulière. C'est pourquoi, en vertu même de leur valence analogique, elles tendent à outrepasser ces limites. Autrement dit, leur pleine compréhension suppose la métaphysique de la participation, au sens où elle est présupposée par la *quarta via* de saint Thomas. Celui-ci n'a pas craint de dégager le dynamisme propre à ce qui dans l'être humain ressortit aux dimensions transnaturelles, comme dans sa doctrine du désir naturel de voir Dieu[1].

Mais n'est-ce pas aussi à ce caractère transnaturel, quand la nature des exigences dont il est porteur n'est plus perçu avec précision, qu'à leur manière rendent témoignage les déviations elles-mêmes que constituent les différentes formes d'autodéification de la liberté?

VOLONTÉ

3. Notre seconde considération a pour point de départ une double question que pose saint Thomas (*Sum. Theol.* I, q. 83, a. 3 et 4) le libre-arbitre est-il une puissance (*potentia*) de l'âme ressortissant à *l'appetitus?* Cette puissance est-elle identique à la volonté?

La distinction entre l'âme et ses facultés a son fondement dans la composition de tout être crée en acte et en puissance; elle est d'ordre métaphysique.

Le concept *d'appetitus*[2] est lui aussi un concept métaphysique. Il découle de la nature essentiellement dynamique de l'être. Sa portée est analogique. En effet, tous les êtres tendent vers leur bien propre, mais chacun le fait conformément à sa propre nature. Saint Thomas, citant Aristote, donne cette quasi définition du bien: *bonum est quod omnia appetunt*. Le mouvement de tout être, son désir (au sens métaphysique et non psychologique) le porte vers son bien et, celui-ci une fois atteint, à se reposer en lui. Ainsi la volonté est-elle définie comme un *appetitus rationalis*, c'est-à-dire *appetitus* enraciné dans l'intellect. Son objet est le bien désirable (*appertibile*), tel qu'il est saisi par l'intellect. Celui-ci saisit le bien en tant que bien, c'est-à-dire dans son constitutif intelligible (sa *ratio*).

La distinction entre connaître et vouloir, entre intellect et volonté a été éclipsée chez plus d'un penseur moderne. L'idéalisme n'est pas étranger à

---

[1] Je ne peux pas ici m'arrêter au sens exact de cette formule.
[2] Je renonce à traduire ce terme, auquel il faut conserver son sens technique, qu'appétit ne traduit pas adéquatement.

la confusion qui tend à s'établir ainsi. Le primat affirmé de la raison pratique, puis de la praxis, sont à cet égard symptomatiques.

Retenons qu'alors que, dans la connaissance, la chose connue existe dans l'intellect d'une existence intentionnelle, la volonté se porte vers la chose en tant qu'exerçant son existence propre.

L'appetitus des êtres inférieurs, qui fait un avec leur être, est une inclination inscrite en eux par le Créateur. Avec les animaux, capables de connaissance sensible, l'inclination porte sur un bien particulier, tel qu'il est présenté par le sens. L'*appetitus* intellectuel ou rationnel a pour objet le bien sous la raison de bien, saisi selon toute son amplitude, le *bonum secundum communem boni rationem*[3]. C'est vers ce *bonum in communi* et vers sa possession qui constitue la béatitude, que se porte spontanément la volonté. Cette donnée de base est présupposée à l'analyse du libre-arbitre, qui nous occupera bientôt.

4. Auparavant il nous faut dire un mot de la nécessité. N'avons-nous pas dit que c'est spontanément que la volonté tend à la béatitude? Et la liberté ne se définit-elle pas par opposition à la nécessité? L'élucidation de ce point est décisive pour la doctrine de la liberté.

Nécessité s'entend en plusieurs sens, en fonction des principes qui font qu'une chose ne peut pas ne pas être[4]. Il faut donc se reporter aux causes dont dépend la nécessité. Si le principe est intrinsèque, matière ou forme, nous avons affaire à la nécessité naturelle et absolue. Mais la nécessité peut provenir encore d'un principe extrinsèque, la fin ou l'agent. En ce qui concerne la fin, une chose peut être nécessaire en ce sens que sans elle la fin ne peut pas être atteinte ou ne peut pas être atteinte d'une manière satisfaisante. Tel est le domaine de l'utile.

En ce qui concerne l'agent, il y a nécessité quand celui-ci exerce une contrainte. À cela appartiennent les diverses forme de coaction. La nécessité de coaction est totalement opposée à la volonté. On parlera alors de violence. Est violent, en effet, ce qui agit contre l'inclination d'une chose. Or le mouvement même de la volonté est une inclination vers un bien. Et de même qu'on appelle naturel ce qui est selon l'inclination de la nature, on appellera volontaire ce qui est selon l'inclination de la volonté. Comme il est impossible qu'un acte soit à la fois violent et naturel, il est impossible qu'absolument parlant (*simpliciter*), un acte soit à la fois posé sous la contrainte et la violence et volontaire.

Il convient de relever ce parallèle entre le naturel et le volontaire, le premier terme permettant de pénétrer l'intelligence du second. La philoso-

---

[3] Cf. *Sum. Theol.*, I, q. 60, a. 4.
[4] Cf. *Sum. Theol.*, I, q. 82, a. 1.

phie moderne, depuis Descartes et surtout Kant, ne pose-t-elle pas une opposition entre nature et liberté? C'est que le concept de nature a subi, au cours de l'histoire de la philosophie, de profondes métamorphoses. Il est sans doute l'un des concepts qui reflètent le mieux les changements de points de vue qui commandent dans chaque cas l'ensemble d'une réflexion philosophique. Disons que le concept moderne est d'origine épistémologique en ce sens que les philosophes font leur le concept de nature qui est à la base des sciences nouvelles nées avec Galilée puis Descartes. La nature se présente avec le double caractère d'être mathématisable et objet d'observation empirique. Ce double caractère est patent chez Kant.

Il ne va nullement de soi que le nouveau concept de nature, concept mécaniciste, rende caduc le concept antérieur. Mais il est nécessaire de s'aviser qu'ici et là le même mot a cessé de recouvrir la même réalité.

Le concept thomasien de nature, élaboré à partir d'Aristote[5] est un concept ontologique. La nature est dans chaque être le principe interne de "mouvement", d'activité. Ce concept est analogique; il est applicable à Dieu et la théologie en a besoin pour exprimer les plus hauts mystères de la foi.

L'un des sens de naturel est la spontanéité. Dans cette perspective, le mouvement de la volonté tendant au bien, qui suppose que le sujet est un être spirituel, peut être considéré comme une réalisation éminente de cette spontanéité dont les êtres inférieurs, et notamment les animaux[6], présentent comme des ébauches imparfaites. Il n'y a pas lieu de poser une opposition, là où existe une hiérarchie des êtres, marquée certes par des seuils.

5. Pour qu'il y ait acte volontaire, il faut que le principe de l'acte soit intérieur et qu'il ait connaissance de la fin[7].

Et de ce qui précède nous pouvons conclure que la nécessité de la fin ne répugne pas à la volonté. C'est évident là où il n'est possible d'atteindre la fin que d'une seule manière. De même la nécessité naturelle ne répugne pas à la volonté. Il faut affirmer davantage: comme l'intellect adhère nécessairement aux premiers principes, de même la volonté tend nécessairement vers la fin, qui est la béatitude.

Aristote l'avait relevé: la fin est dans l'ordre opératif ce qu'est le principe dans l'ordre spéculatif. Ainsi toute l'activité volontaire est portée par le mouvement naturel qui porte la volonté vers la fin. Il y a là une nécessité naturelle qui, loin de supprimer la liberté de la volonté, la fonde. La motion

---

[5] Voir mon étude *Le concept de nature chez saint Thomas*, in *Physica, Cosmologia Naturphilosophie Nuovi Approcci*, Roma Herder – Università Lateranense, 1993, p. 37-64.

[6] Saint Thomas n'hésite pas à parler de *volontaire*, dans un sens diminué, pour les animaux, *Secundum rationem imperfectam*, cf. *Sum. Theol.*, I-II, q. 6, a. 2.

[7] Cf. *Ibid*.

de la cause ultime (au sens où la fin meut en étant désirée) est présupposée à la vie de la volonté, et elle n'appartient pas à ce dont nous avons le *dominimum*[8].

Ce dernier point ne doit pas prêter à malentendu. La volonté nécessaire de la fin ultime s'étend à tous les biens qui sont en connexion avec la béatitude[9]. Encore faut-il que cette connexion soit connue. Or en Dieu seul est la vraie béatitude. Cependant, avant que l'on ait l'évidence de cette connexion par la certitude de la vision divine, la volonté n'adhère pas à Dieu et aux choses divines nécessairement. La volonté de celui qui a la vision de Dieu adhère à Dieu nécessairement, comme, d'une manière analogue, ici-bas nous voulons nécessairement être heureux. Aussi bien la volonté ne veut-elle pas nécessairement tout ce qu'elle veut.

Ainsi quand la personne devra délibérer d'elle-même et de sa destinée, ses choix décisifs porteront sur la fin dernière elle-même, puisque nous n'avons pas l'évidence de l'identité de Dieu et de la béatitude. Notre connaissance de Dieu est médiate et imparfaite. Seule la vision de Dieu révèlera l'ordre des connexions nécessaires. Alors l'adhésion de la volonté sera parfaite et la liberté, loin d'être abolie, sera comblée. Mais pour comprendre ce point, il nous faut réfléchir à la liberté comme libre-arbitre. Retenons pour l'instant qu'avant d'être pouvoir de choix, la volonté est d'abord *appetitus*.

LIBRE-ARBITRE

6. La troisième considération découle immédiatement de ce qui précède. Elle porte sur la liberté comme libre-arbitre ou faculté de choix.

C'est la connaissance qui propose son objet, le bien (réel ou apparent), à *l'appetitus*. C'est pourquoi le constitutif (*ratio*) de la liberté dépend du mode, du type, de connaître.

Saint Thomas note que le jugement est au pouvoir de celui qui juge selon qu'il peut juger de son propre jugement. Or cela appartient à la seule raison, qui réfléchit sur son propre acte et qui connaît le rapport (*habitudo*) des objets dont elle juge et par lesquels elle juge. C'est dans la raison que se trouve la racine de toute liberté[10].

Ainsi par sa raison l'homme juge des actes à poser et il peut juger de son arbitre ou jugement en tant qu'il connaît la fin en tant que fin (sa *ratio*) et ce qui est ordonné à cette fin ainsi que le rapport et l'ordre de l'un à

---

[8] Cf. I, q. 82, a. 1 et ad 1, ad 2.
[9] Cf. I, q. 82, a. 2.
[10] Cf. *De Veritate*, q. 24, a. 2.

l'autre. C'est pourquoi l'homme n'est pas seulement cause de soi dans la motion, ce qu'on peut dire de l'animal; il est cause de soi dans le jugement. Dire qu'il possède le libre-arbitre revient à dire qu'il possède le libre jugement en ce qui concerne agir ou ne pas agir[11]. Et non seulement ceci, mais encore il n'est pas mû d'une manière nécessaire par les biens qui se présentent à lui ou par la pulsion de ses passions, qu'il peut accepter ou écarter.

Et s'il en est ainsi, c'est parce que, connaissant la raison universelle du bien, il peut à partir d'elle juger que telle ou telle chose est bonne, et sous quel rapport elle l'est ou cesse de l'être.

Or les actes que nous sommes amenés à poser sont contingents et devant ce qui est contingent, la raison demeure ouverte aux opposés, comme le montrent les syllogismes dialectiques et les artifices de la rhétorique.

Ainsi devant une action à faire, le jugement de la raison n'est pas déterminé, il peut pencher dans un sens ou dans l'autre.

Comme nous l'avons vu, la volonté, faculté du bien, veut nécessairement ce à quoi elle est naturellement inclinée. Elle veut nécessairement la béatitude. Elle ne peut pas ne pas vouloir le bien et tout ce qu'elle veut, elle le veut sous la raison du bien. Mais l'objet des actions que nous posons, est contingent, il n'épuise pas en soi l'universelle *ratio boni* et ne peut en conséquence nécessiter ni le jugement ni la volonté. Tel est le fondement du libre-arbitre.

L'acte propre du libre-arbitre est l'élection ou le choix. Celui-ci présuppose une délibération de la raison aboutissant au "conseil" qui le guide. Le choix est-il affaire de la raison ou de la puissance d'appétition? Sur ce point, Aristote avait hésité. Saint Thomas tranche: le choix est un acte de la puissance appétitive, il consiste à accepter le jugement du "conseil". Son objet est ce qui conduit à la fin, ce que Thomas appelle l'utile (dans un sens qui n'est pas celui de l'utilitarisme).

Ainsi le libre-arbitre est une puissance de l'âme. On peut aussi l'appeler la puissance de choix (*vix electiva*). Cette puissance est-elle distincte de la volonté? Puisque c'est dans la raison qu'est la racine du libre-arbitre, la réponse sera commandée par l'analyse des démarches de notre intellect. Celui-ci est, selon ses activités, *intellectus*, vue directe et simple, où s'origine et où aboutit la connaissance, et *ratio*, qui renvoie au mouvement par lequel on passe de la connaissance d'un premier objet à la connaissance d'un autre, ce qu'est précisément le raisonnement[12]. De même la volonté se porte spontanément et nécessairement vers le bien et elle opère des choix, choisir étant précisément désirer un objet en vue d'un autre qu'elle veut à titre de fin.

---

[11] Cf. *ibid.* q. 24, a. 1. En fait, la liberté porte sur l'exercice et sur la spécification.
[12] Cf. mon étude *Intellectus et ratio* in "Revue Thomiste", t. LXXXVIII, 1988/2, p. 215-228.

7. Nous devons apporter ici one précision, qui est essentielle. En insistant comme nous l'avons fait sur l'enracinement de la liberté dans la raison, nous avons mis l'accent sur un aspect des choses. La racine de la liberté, dit saint Thomas, est la volonté comme son sujet, mais, comme sa cause, c'est la raison. En effet, si la volonté peut se porter à divers biens, c'est parce que la raison peut avoir diverses conceptions du bien. D'où la définition du libre-arbitre que donnent les philosophes: un libre jugement procédant de (*de*) la raison, la raison étant ainsi la cause de la liberté[13]. *Diversae conceptiones boni*. Cajetan explique ainsi: parce que la volonté naît du bien connu, la volonté libre naît de biens opposés, sans détermination à l'un d'eux.

Mais il faut considérer encore un second aspect. Par leurs actes, intelligence et volonté s'enveloppent (*includunt*) l'une l'autre. L'intelligence connaît la volonté qui veut, la volonté veut que l'intelligence connaisse. Et le bien est un certain vrai, le vrai est un certain bien désiré[14]. Dans ce mutuel enveloppement, c'est tantôt l'intelligence tantôt la volonté qui, selon les points de vue, a la prééminence[15]. Ici se vérifie le principe de la réciprocité des causes selon divers ordres de cause.

Ce mutuel enveloppement et cette causalité réciproque éclairent l'analyse de la séquence des actes de la raison et de la volonté qui conduisent au choix[16]. Celui-ci dans son unicité, bien qu'il dépende de la mouvance de la loi universelle, est en lui-même contingent. Au niveau de practicité qui est le sien, sa vérité se mesure par sa conformité à *l'appetitus* droitement orienté et c'est la volonté qui fait sien le jugement pratico-pratique qui l'éclaire.

Si je rappelle cette doctrine, c'est pour souligner que la conception thomasienne de l'acte libre, tout en reconnaissant l'importance fondamentale de la raison, n'est pas une conception intellectualiste. Pour Thomas le problème de e'âne de Buridan est un faux problème.

LA VOLONTÉ ET LE BIEN

8. Ici vient se greffer une quatrième considération. Selon les connotations inspirées par certaines philosophies modernes, la volonté s'entend en un sens volontariste d'affirmation de soi, de pouvoir et de domination. Quant à la liberté, elle se présente, alle aussi, comme auto-affirmation de son autonomie, décision souveraine, et à la limite, autocréation.

---

[13] Cf. *Sum. Theol.*, I-II, q. 17, a. 1, ad 2.
[14] Cf. *ibid.*, I, q. 82, a. 4, ad 1.
[15] Cf. *ibid.*, q. 82, a. 3.
[16] Cf. Les analyses développées dans les questions 11 à 17 de la I-II de la *Sum. Theol.*

Il faut tenir, au contraire, que la volonté libre est faculté du bien, qui a raison de fin. Mais le bien ne pourrait exercer son attirance à laquelle est suspendu l'ensemble du processus libre, si le sujet qui tend vers lui n'avait une aptitude ou proportion à sa fin. Cette aptitude ou proportion de *l'appetitus* au bien est l'amour, qui n'est rien d'autre que la *complacentia boni*; le mouvement vers le bien est le désir; et le repos dans le bien atteint et possédé est la joie ou la délectation[17].

Aussi bien l'affirmation de la volonté comme faculté du bien, implique une métaphysique de l'amour. Dire que le dynamisme entier de la volonté et de son libre-arbitre procède du bien, c'est dire que la volonté avec son libre-arbitre trouve dans l'amour son accomplissement. Ce point demanderait à être développé. Notons ceci: l'amour n'est pas univoque, il varie selon les types de biens aimés. Son achèvement est dans la réciprocité de l'amitié. Et la Révélation de la divine charité nous a appris que c'est à l'amitié avec les divines Personnes qu'est appelée la personne humaine.

Ce point est en contraste avec les thèses du libéralisme philosophique. Celui-ci, par sa logique propre, pose une liberté par laquelle e'individu se complaît dans son autosuffisance et inévitablement dans l'égoïsme, à l'instar de la monade sans fenêtres dont parle Leibniz. Et s'il est encore question de l'amour, il s'agit d'une passion de l'âme qui n'atteint pas au niveau de souveraineté de la liberté. À moins qu'on le ramène aux besoins sexuels comme besoins de l'individu en tant que tel.

Si j'ai employé la formule: métaphysique de l'amour, c'est parce que l'exaltation individualiste de la liberté, ignore la générostié de l'être. Elle dessine devant l'esprit l'image d'un monde d'avarice et de lutte.

CAUSALITÉ

9. Notre considération, en cinquième lieu, doit porter sur la causalité ou, plus précisément, sur la liberté comme cause. Est libre celui qui est cause de soi, c'est-à-dire cause de son propre jugement; par là il dispose de soi, il décide de sa propre destinée, dans le temps et pour l'éternité, en dépit de tous les conditionnements qui pèsent sur l'être humain en vertu de sa corporéité et de ses dépendances sociales. Par sa liberté, la personne est en lien avec l'Absolu. Devant un tel pouvoir et la sorte d'infinitude qu'il comporte, d'aucuns sont pris de vertige et d'ivresse. Mais en faisant de soi son idole la liberté devient son propre tombeau.

Pour autant qu'elle détermine ce qu'est pour elle la fin dernière, le bien pleinement saturant, en quoi consiste la béatitude à laquelle elle tend néces-

---

[17] C'est à propos des passions que Thomas donne cette analyse, cf. *Sum. Theol.*, I-II, q. 25, a. 2. elle s'applique analogiquement aux actes de la volonté.

sairement, la volonté libre est souveraine. Cette souveraineté doit être bien entendue, elle n'est pas synonyme d'arbitraire, comme s'il appartenait à la volonté libre de décréter du bien et du mal. La vraie béatitude ne se trouve qu'en l'union avec Celui qui est le souverain Bien. Parler d'idolâtrie, c'est précisément désigner l'acte par lequel la personne engage sa destinée en faisant d'un bien qui n'est pas l'Absolu un substitut du souverain Bien subsistant.

Nous rencontrons ici une thèse essentielle de la dotrine thomiste. Dieu, cause première, créateur de tous les êtres, les élève également à la participation à la "dignité de cause", en proportion de leur degré de perfection ontologique. Par rapport à la causalité de la cause première, les créatures exercent les unes par rapport aux autres la causalité de causes secondes. Or cette causalité ne doit pas s'entendre comme une diminution apportée à la causalité de la cause première, ou un retrait de sa part. Un effet crée est tout entier effet de la cause première et tout entier effet des causes secondes plus ou moins immédiates dont il dépend. Concevoir ici un partage ou une concurrence, c'est s'interdire la compréhension de l'agir divin au coeur des activités créés. C'est en vertu même de sa suprême transcendance que la causalité divine est immanente à la causalité des causes secondes, les portant et les soutenant sans leur faire subir la moindre violence.

Or dans l'ordre des causes créées, de même que la personne est ce qui est le plus haut et le plus noble dans toute la création, la causalité la plus haute et la plus noble est celle de la liberté. De soi, la liberté représente ainsi le mode le plus élevé de participation à la causalité. En exerçant sa liberté souverainement la personne adhère avec pleine autonomie au souverain Bien. Et l'amour unitif à Celui qui est le souverain Bien est tout autant la pleine affirmation de soi.

Dans cette perspective s'éclaire une précision essentielle apportée par saint Thomas. Il n'appartient pas nécessairement à l'essence de la liberté que l'être libre soit la cause première de soi, tout comme le fait qu'un être soit la cause d'un autre ne requiert pas qu'il en soit la cause première.

Seul Dieu est la cause première qui meut et les causes naturelles et les causes volontaires. Quand il meut les causes naturelles, il ne prive pas leurs actes d'être naturels. De même quand il meut les causes volontaires, dont la causalité est le mode de participation le plus haut à la causalité première, il ne prive pas leurs actions de leur qualité de volontaires; c'est plutôt ce qu'il réalise en elles, car il opère en chaque être selon le mode qui lui est propre (*non aufert quin actiones earum sint voluntariae, sed potius hoc in eis facit; operatur enim in unoquoque secundum eius proprientatem*[18].

---

[18] Cf. *Sum. Theol.*, I, q. 83, a. 1, ad 3.

La réflexion sur la métaphysique de la volonté perçoit aisément ces points. Mais comment s'exerce la causalité de la cause première au coeur de cette causalité seconde qu'est la liberté de la volonté créée? Cela reste pour nous mystérieux. Et ceci parce que notre expérience immédiate porte sur les activités cosmiques et humaines, qui sont de l'ordre des causes secondes. Pour répondre pleinement à la question il faudrait avoir la vision directe de l'agir divin.

PECCABILITÉ

9. De plus qu'en est-il de l'exercice de la causalité divine quand la volonté libre de la créature est défaillante? Comment en d'autres termes comprendre la permission du mal de la part de Dieu? Je ne peux ici que mentionner ce problème crucial. Cependant, pour notre propos, il convient de proposer une double considération, qui porte d'abord sur la peccabilité de la liberté créée et, ensuite, sur le rapport de cette dernière au mal.

La peccabilité désigne la possibilité de faillir dans l'exercice de la volonté libre. La peccabilité n'est pas encore le péché ou la faute, même pas à titre de germe de faute. Elle dit une pure possibilité. Or il est impossible pour Dieu de faire une créature impeccable; cette impossibilité tient dans le rapprochement des deux termes; il s'agit d'une contradiction comme est contradictoire l'idée d'un cercle carré.

L'impeccabilité, en vertu de sa nature, n'appartient qu'à Dieu seul, parce que la bonté divine, fin dernière de toutes choses, est la nature même de Dieu. Il est acte pur, sans mélange de potentialité, et par là bonté pure et absolue.

À l'inverse toute créature, ange ou homme, parce qu'elle est mêlée de potentialité, peut faillir dans son activité volontaire. Sa nature, en effet, est un bien particulier, elle n'est pas la fin dernière. Il peut donc y avoir faute si sa volonté reste fixée dans son bien propre sans tendre, au-delà, vers le souverain Bien, qui est sa fin dernière.

C'est sa structure métaphysique qui explique l'impossibilité pour une créature d'être naturellement impeccable et confirmée dans le bien. Cette impossibilité traduit une contradiction. Elle a sa raison dans la composition d'acte et de puissance propre à tout être créé. Et s'il en est ainsi, c'est que la créature est tirée du néant[19].

10. Ajoutons ici une remarque qui concerne, non plus la peccabilité, mais l'acte peccamineux lui-même. À propos de tout bien particulier qui

---

[19] Saint Thomas est revenu à plusieurs reprises sur ce point, cf. Par exemple, *De Veritate*, q. 24, a. 7, *Comp. theol.*, I, c. 113.

sollicite la volonté, c'est parce que la raison connaît la loi morale qu'elle est capable de mesurer sa conformité ou sa non-conformité à la fin dernière. Par ses choix, la volonté à chaque fois se porte vers un bien particulier; c'est un jugement pratique particulier, qu'elle fait sien qui lui présente ce bien comme *hic et nunc* désirable. Un tel jugement ne peut pas être contraire à l'appétition[20].

Dans le cas d'un acte peccamineux, la volonté passe à l'acte en étant guidée par un tel jugement pratique particulier, sans considérer la règle générale de la raison qui lui aurait montré la non-compatibilité de l'objet de son désir avec la poursuite de la fin dernière. La non-considération de la loi en soi n'est pas le péché; elle devient constitutive du péché quand elle est voulue, c'est-à-dire quand la volonté passe à l'acte, en suivant le jugement particulier, tout en écartant délibérément cette considération qui assurerait la vérité pratique, la rectitude de son agir.

La conscience sait bien que le jugement particulier de désidérabilité n'est pas conforme à la loi morale. Mais dans le jugement invisceré dans le choix concret, cette considération est mise de côté et ce qui éclaire l'acte c'est un jugement particulier présentant le bien particulier désirable "absolument", c'est-à-dire soustrait à la normale mensuration de la loi morale.

Nous avons rencontré la formule remarquable: la raison, pour l'exercice du libre-arbitre, juge de son propre jugement. Cela signifie que la raison est capable de saisir la *ratio boni* et le bien dans toute son amplitude universelle, ainsi que le rapport d'un bien particulier au bien parfait qui a raison de fin dernière. Elle juge de la conformité ou de la non-conformité d'un jugement pratique particulier avec la loi morale universelle exprimant les exigences de la fin dernière. Agir en mettant volontairement de côté cette référence vitale, parce qu'elle contredirait dans le *hic et nunc* le jugement particulier au service d'une appétition désordonnée, tel est le propre de l'acte peccamineux.

La rupture entre liberté et vérité, dont parle *Veritatis Splendor* s'entend comme la rupture de la liberté avec la vérité du bien – la vérité du souverain Bien et de ses exigences.

11. Il nous faut dire un mot du rapport entre le libre-arbitre et le mal. Nous touchons là à une opinion extrêmement répandue: le libre-arbitre se définirait comme faculté de choix entre le bien et le mal.

La volonté, nous l'avons vu, est dite libre selon qu'elle ne veut pas nécessairement ce qu'elle veut. Cettre liberté doit être considérée à un triple point de vue: d'abord quant à l'acte, la volonté peut vouloir ou ne pas

---

[20] Cf. *De Veritate*, q. 24, a. 2: *Sed iudicium de hoc particulari operabili, ut nunc, nunquam potest esse contratium appetitui.*

vouloir; ensuite quant à l'objet, elle peut vouloir tel objet ou son opposé, ceci se vérifie non quant à la fin (béatitude, *bonum in communi*), mais pour tout ce qui est ordonné à la fin; enfin, elle peut vouloir le bien et le mal, ce qui couvre aussi le domaine de ce qui est ordonné à la fin. Ceci se vérifie dans l'état où la volonté peut défaillir. Les bienheureux sont délivrés de cette faillibilité. C'est que vouloir le mal, n'est pas la liberté, ni une partie constitutive de la liberté, bien qu'il y ait là un certain signe de la liberté, ou de la liberté créée. Que la volonté penche (*flexibile ad*) vers le mal, elle ne le tient pas selon qu'elle vient de Dieu, mais selon qu'elle est tirée du néant[21].

Une réflexion sur le nihilisme ne peut ignorer la relation au néant inscrite dans la peccabilité et le péché. Il ne s'agit évidemment pas de juger les personnes, mais de nous interroger sur l'essence du mal moral, comme néantement ou néantisation.

II

UNE DIMENSION D'INFINI

12. Par sa liberté, la personne est cause de soi, elle est maîtresse de ses choix et de ses motions. Par là elle détermine sa propre destinée, dans le temps et pour l'éternité; elle a donc une dimension d'infini, sa souveraineté la confronte directement à l'Absolu.

La liberté créée représente ainsi la forme la plus haute de participaton à la "dignité de cause". Saisir ce point, c'est tenir la clef des problèmes de la liberté et, par mode de conséquence, la signification pour la personne libre d'exercer l'obéissance.

La liberté créée constitue un paradoxe. D'une part, la participation dit limite; d'autre part, par son acquiescement au souverain Bien ou par son rejet, la créature libre touche à l'Absolu. Nous avons noté, à ce propos, qu'il faut écarter l'illusion de la symétrie, comme si "l'indifférence dominatrice" de la liberté présupposait une sorte d'équivalence entre le bien et le mal. L'élan vers l'union au souverain Bien appartient à l'essence de la volonté, la possibilité du choix mauvais est la rançon du statut de la créature en tant qu'elle est tirée du néant.

J'aimerais ici proposer quelques brèves remarques.

La première concerne le contexte actuel qui est celui d'une culture sécularisée, quand la sécularisation est délibérément voulue[22].

---

[21] Cf. *De Veritate*, q. 22, a. 6, et ad 3.
[22] On sait que pour certains la sécularisation, philosophiquement entendue, constituerait l'essence de la "modernité", en donnant à ce terme un sens normatif. Cette manière de voir est hautement contestable.

Quand la personne occulte ou mortifie sa connaturelle relation à l'Absolu transcendant, elle se condamne à déployer les requêtes de la liberté, qui sont marquées du sceau de l'infini, à l'intérieur du temps et des horizons terrestres. Elle entretient donc en elle-même une perpétuelle insatisfaction, elle est constamment inquiète, elle est sans cesse tentée par la transgression ou par la subversion.

La conscience de son infinité ne pouvant être totalement étouffée, la liberté s'affirmera contre le monde. Dès qu'elle aura satisfait son désir, prise par la crainte de se trouver engluée dans l'objet de son choix, son premier souci sera de s'en libérer. Tout se passe comme si la liberté, faculté de choix, se perdait en choisissant et se retrouvait en se désengageant. C'est qu'elle a fait d'elle-même son propre objet, suprême Vacuité se posant en s'opposant à l'univers des choses.

LA LOI MORALE

13. La seconde remarque porte sur la loi morale. Il importe de souligner que la loi est mesure et règle de l'agir parce qu'elle appartient à la raison: *lex est aliquid rationis*[23].

Le concept de loi est analogique. Les exigences morales ont leur fondement dans la loi éternelle, définie par saint Thomas comme "raison de la sagesse divine, selon qu'elle dirige la totalité des actes et des motions"[24], par lesquels Dieu gouverne l'univers et, d'une manière particulière, le monde des personnes libres. La loi naturelle est dans les êtres créés et selon la modalité propre de chacun, participation à la loi éternelle[25]. Et s'il en est ainsi c'est parce que la causalité créatrice est attribuée à la science de Dieu selon que la volonté lui est conjointe[26].

La causalité créatrice présuppose la sagesse et le vouloir. Certes Dieu est sa sagesse et Dieu est sa volonté, dans la simplicité transcendante de son être. Mais la volonté, selon l'ordre des raisons, présuppose la sagesse.

On sait que la conception sapientielle de la loi a été fortement contestée par les diverses écoles volontaristes. L'inspiration volontariste et nominaliste est évidente chez Descartes.

---

[23] Cf. *Sum. Theol.*, I-II, q. 90, a. 1.

[24] *Ratio divinae sapientiae, secundum quod est directiva omnium actuum et motionum*, ibid., q. 93, a. 1.

[25] *Ibid.*, ad 1.

[26] *Ibid.*, I, q. 14, a. 8: *secundum quod habet voluntatem conjunctam*. Cf. aussi q. 19, a. 4.

14. Pour Descartes, la volontgé toute-puissante de Dieu, elle-même déterminée par rien, a déterminé la vérité des choses. Si les trois angles d'un triangle sont égaux à deux droits, si les contradictoires ne peuvent être ensemble, c'est que Dieu a voulu qu'il en fût ainsi: "il est maintenant vrai que cela est ainsi, et il ne peut pas être autrement". Que tel acte soit moralement bon, cela dépend du fait que Dieu "a ainsi voulu faire"[27]. Et si notre entendement ne peut pas voir les choses autrement, cela tient à ce qu'il est ainsi constitué. Sartre pourra conclure que chez Descartes la liberté est le fondement du vrai.

"Il n'y a que la seule volonté, que j'expérimente en moi être si grande, que je ne conçois point l'idée d'aucune autre (puissance) plus grande et plus étendue: en sorte que c'est elle principalement qui me fait connaître que je porte l'image et la ressemblance de Dieu".

Certes, en raison de la connaissance et de la puissance, la volonté est incomparablement plus grande en Dieu qu'en moi. Cependant "si je la considère formellement et précisément elle-même", "elle ne me semble pas toutefois plus grande". C'est que l'indifférence qui la constitue est indivisible.

Cependant, il semblerait que Descartes opère un total renversement quand il s'agit d'expliquer la possibilité du péché. La volonté "étant beaucoup plus ample et plus étendue de l'entendement, je ne la contiens pas dans les mêmes limites, mais je l'étends aussi aux choses que je n'entends pas; auxquelles étant en soi indifférente, elle s'égare fort aisément, et choisit le mal pour le bien, ou le faux pour le vrai. Ce qui fait que je me trompe et je pèche".

La liberté illimitée en soi se trouverait ainsi, à ce qu'il semble, limitée dans son exercice par sa dépendance à l'égard de la connaissance. Tant que mon choix porte sur un objet dont j'ai une idée claire et distincte, je suis sûr de ne pas me tromper. Le "bon sens" est précisément la capacité de me guider dans la vie en fonction des idées claires et distinctes.

On pourrait être tenté de s'en tenir à ce point. On aurait ainsi affaire à une conception intellectualiste du libre-arbitre, le péché étant ramené à un manque de connaissance claire.

En réalité, un autre aspect doit être pris en considération. Il concerne le jugement. Celui-ci n'est pas l'acte de l'intelligence en qui s'accomplit la connaissance. Descartes l'attribue à la volonté. Il est consentement de la volonté à une idée conçue par l'intellect. Il est de l'ordre de la croyance.

---

[27] Descartes revient à plusieurs reprises sur ce thème de la liberté. Voir par exemple, la quatrième *Méditation métaphysique, Réponses aux sixièmes objections, 6. Lettre au P. Mesland du 2 mai 1644*. Sur Descartes, voir mon étude *Liberté et Vérité* in "Revue Thomiste", XCIV, 1994, p. 179-194.

La volonté n'est pas un *appetitus* tendant vers le bien. Elle consiste "seulement en ce que nous pouvons faire une même chose ou ne pas la faire". Le souverain Bien est défini subjectivement: il est dans la ferme volonté de bien faire.

L'entendement lui-même se trouve ainsi, par le jugement, subordonné à la volonté qui décide, c'est-à-dire qui affirme le bien avant de l'élire. Par le biais du jugement, Descartes pose le primat de la volonté, qui affirme ou qui nie, sur l'entendement qui, dans un premier temps, semblait, en vertu des idées claires et distinctes, restreindre le champ de la liberté.

D'ailleurs, le discours cartésien dans son entier n'est-il pas suspendu à un acte de la volonté, qui décide de douter, afin de fonder le savoir sur des certitudes que le sujet ne devra qu'à lui-même?

Il y a là une démarche paradigmatique de la pensée moderne. Le volontarisme, dont l'archétype est posé en Dieu, investit la raison dans sa version cartésienne.

15. La conception cartésienne n'est qu'une première manifestation du volontarisme que nous pouvons considérer comme un des traits caractéristiques de la philosophie moderne. Schelling attribuera ainsi à l'idéalisme d'avoir permis pour la première fois d'élaborer le concept de la liberté. On sait que Heidegger attachait aux *Recherches sur l'essence de la liberté humaine...* (1908) une importance majeure. Ce texte n'est pas d'interprétation facile, à cause notamment d'une sorte de va-et-vient entre la liberté de Dieu et la liberté humaine. Il semblerait aussi que le problème de la liberté soit comme absorbé par le problème de la nature du mal. La liberté, en effet, y est présentée comme pouvoir du bien et du mal, lequel est positif.

Relevons quelques aspects particulièrement significatifs pour notre propos.

Schelling fait sienne l'intention exprimée par Lessing d'élaborer les vérités révélées en vérités rationnelles nécessaires. En réalité, le philosophe, comme le fera de son côté Hegel, emprunte à la révélation et à la théologie chrétiennes un ensemble de concepts auxquels il confère un contenu nouveau. L'influence de Boehme et d'Oetinger est ici patente. La conséquence en est une philosophie qui tient de la gnose et de la théosophie.

En polémique contre le mécanicisme de Spinoza et de Leibniz, Schelling pose au centre de sa réflexion le concept de vie; mais ce concept n'est jamais pleinement dégagé du vitalisme, lequel sera transporté jusque dans l'Absolu. La production des êtres, la "création", est autorévélation de Dieu. De la nature le philosophe propose une image dynamique. La vie est activité; l'activité est liberté, au sens de spontanéité. Schelling dira ainsi qu'il n'y a pas d'autre être que le vouloir.

Schelling s'inspire du concept platonicien et néoplatonicien de matière pour élaborer le concept de fond (*Grund*). Ce fond est vivant dans la nature. Bien plus il est la condition de l'existence de Dieu. Pour que le mal ne soit pas, dit-il, il faudrait que Dieu lui-même ne fût pas. Le mal est nécessaire à la révélation. Pour qu'il y ait effectivité, l'opposition est nécessaire. Ainsi la souffrance et le devenir sont transportés jusque dans l'Absolu. Car là où il n'y a pas lutte, il n'y a pas vie. Ainsi Dieu possède en soi la condition qu'il surmonte (*Ueberwindung*) par l'amour. L'amour, par delà l'Esprit qui unifie, est ainsi unification de deux principes antagonistes. Il y a mal quand il y a scission et déchirement. La personnalité, déjà en Dieu, s'affirme par cette unification. Doit-on parler d'autogenèse? Schelling ajoute que les deux principes ne sont pas ce qu'il y a de plus originaire: au-delà, il y a l'*Urgrund* ou *Ungrund*, l'indifférence primordiale, le non-fond. C'est là, précise-t-il, le seul concept possible de l'Absolu.

L'intention du philosophe est certes de maintenir la distinction entre la liberté divine et la liberté humaine. Le repli sur soi, dans sa *Selbstheit*, de la liberté humaine, est maintien dans la scission et l'irrationnel. Il reste qu'on trouve dans les *Recherches*, par l'affirmation d'une dualité dialectique au niveau même de Dieu, le fondement d'un concept de la volonté comme force cosmique, irrationnelle, telle qu'il sera développé chez Schopenhauer et chez Nietzsche. Chez Schelling, la victoire de l'amour sur la dualité continue d'être lumière et raison, mais les principes sont posés d'une conception radicalement irrationnelle de la volonté. Cet aboutissement était contenu en germe dans le volontarisme. Là est sans doute la forme la plus radicale du divorce entre liberté et vérité.

III

PUISSANCE OBÉDIENTIELLE

16. La liberté créée peut donc être définie comme forme éminente de la causalité participée; dans cette formule est comprise la raison d'être de l'obéissance.

Son fondement métaphysique est dans le rapport de l'être créé au Créateur. Une créature peut être envisagée dans sa propre nature. Elle possède un certain nombre de puissances (*potentiae*), actives et passives, qui lui permettent d'acquérir ce qui concourt à sa perfection et d'atteindre sa fin propre. On parle pour désigner ces puissances de puissances naturelles. Mais on doit encore envisager, plus radicalement, la créature en tant même que créée. À ce titre elle est sous la dépendance du Créateur qui peut en disposer et la porter à des actes ou à un état, qui dépassent les propres capacités de sa nature, comme dans le cas du miracle ou de l'élévation à la vie de la grâce. On parle alors, et l'expression est significative, de puissance obédientielle. Il y a là une profonde intuition métaphysique. La toute-puissance de Dieu s'exerce sans arbitraire ni violence, précisément parce qu'elle rencontre dans la créature une disponibilité radicale, une ductibilité, en un mot une obéissance à se laisser conduire et élever par le Créateur. La nature des êtres qui donne à chacun d'être ce qu'il est et de pouvoir agir en conformité à ce qu'il est, n'est pas close sur elle-même.

L'être participant tend à la perfection du participé, en l'occurence à la perfection divine. En vertu des limites de sa propre nature, il ne peut satisfaire par lui-même à ce dynamisme et à cette aspiration. Mais, de par cette même aspiration, il est ouvert à l'action et au don du Principe. Il est en puissance obédientielle à son égard.

17. Si maintenant nous considérons le domaine de l'agir au sens le plus large, nous noterons que les activités les plus nobles, qui sont les activités immanentes de connaissance et d'amour, comportent réceptivité et accueil. L'acte de connaissance, par lequel le sujet connaissant devient intentionnellement le connu, reçoit, dans son acte même, le don de l'être. Il en va, d'une manière analogue et encore plus patente, pour l'amour d'autrui. La raison dernière de cette réceptivité est qu'aucune créature n'est acte pur. Et Dieu, acte pur, est suprême générosité.

On se gardera, certes, de confondre la connaissance et l'amour avec l'obéissance. Mais la question est de savoir pourquoi, dans le contexte culturel moderne, il est si difficile de percevoir le bien-fondé de l'obéissance. Cette difficulté est un héritage de l'idéalisme. Dans la perspective de ce dernier, l'activité spirituelle se présente essentiellement comme auto-position, la raison est conçue avant tout comme raison pratique, "créatrice" de l'objet et, à la limite, par sa médiation, de soi-même, l'amour se trouve relégué au plan inférieur du sentiment, et, en ce qui touche la structure du sujet, la distinction entre puissance et acte est ignorée et l'acte (*Handlung, Tat*) est opposé à l'être. Il est significatif que G. Gentile, pour décrire précisément l'auto-position du sujet, utilise l'expression *actus purus*.

DEUX SENS D'OBÉISSANCE

18. C'est avec l'ordre éthique que nous rencontrons l'obéissance au sens propre du terme. Mais il n'était pas inutile de jeter auparavant un regard sur les fondements métaphysiques et anthropologiques de cette vertu.

Une première distinction se présente à nous, qui est intérieure au domaine de l'éthique et de la spécification des vertus.

Dans un premier sens, général, l'obéissance désigne l'inclination de la volonté à remplir, conformément à sa nature, les commandements divins. Le volonté créée n'étant pas à elle-même sa propre loi, est guidée par la loi, morale vers les biens qui lui conviennent. Elle est spontanément encline à obéir à cette loi morale. Cette obéissance est incluse dans toute vertu, parce que la totalité des actes des vertus tombent sous les préceptes de la loi divine. L'obéissance nous apparaît ainsi comme attitude fondamentale du sujet éthique. Elle est la marque, dans l'agir moral de la personne, de la conscience de sa condition créaturale, elle est, à la racine de tout agir moral, la reconnaissance vécue, existentielle, de son identité de personne et de liberté créée, de sa vérité.

On saisit ici l'importance décisive d'une conception exacte de la nature de la loi morale comme reflet de la sagesse divine. Obéir à la loi morale, c'est s'insérer, par l'exercice autonome d'une volonté polarisée par le bien, dans la vérité de son être et participer à l'ordre de la sagesse divine.

Dans un second sens, l'obéissance désigne une vertu spéciale, la vertu d'obéissance. Celle-ci est une inclination de la volonté à obéir aux préceptes, aux ordres du supérieur[28]. Elle rend au supérieur ce qui lui est dû. C'est pourquoi l'obéissance se rattache à la justice. Cela suppose que le supérieur soit légitime et que soit délimité le champ de ce qui est dû. Celui-ci est déterminé par les exigences du bien commun. Car s'il y a nécessité de la vertu d'obéissance et d'abord nécessité de gouvernement c'est parce que la personne, dans son individualité, est membre d'une société, s'insère dans un ordre. Pour chacun cette appartenance est multiple, il est membre de la famille, de la société politique, etc. Chacune de ces sociétés a pour raison d'être la réalisation d'un bien commun qui lui est propre; le mode et le style du gouvernement et de l'obéissance, à chaque fois, en découlent.

C'est pourquoil il importe d'avoir une idée claire de la *ratio superioritatis*, c'est-à-dire de la nature du gouvernement et de l'obéissance qui lui est due en proportion des exigences du bien commun spécifique qu'il doit servir. L'oeuvre législative a pour but d'exprimer ces exigences et leurs limites.

C'est à partir de la suprême supériorité, celle de Dieu, que se prend la mesure de cette délimitation. Car l'homme est soumis à Dieu, absolument, en toutes choses, intérieures et extérieures, il doit donc lui obéir en tout. L'affirmation de Pierre devant le Sanhédrin a valeur de principe: "il faut obéir à Dieu plutôt qu'aux hommes" (Act, 5, 29)[29]. Ainsi reconnaître que

---

[28] Saint Thomas propose cette distinction, entre autres, à propos de l'expression paulienne d'obéissance de la foi (cf. Rm, 1, 5). Il remarque que, prise dans le premier sens, l'obéissance est requise par la foi; dans le second, elle en est une conséquence, cf. *Sum. Theol.*, q. 4, a. 7, ad 3.

[29] Cf. *Sum. Theol.*, II-II, q. 104, a. 5.

l'homme doit obéir en toutes choses aux préceptes divins, c'est du même coup poser les limites de toute autorité humaine.

On n'a pas à obéir à l'ordre d'une autorité subordonnée qui s'opposerait à l'ordre d'une autorité supérieure. Pour ce qui est de l'autorité politique, on est tenu de lui obéir "en tant que l'ordre de la justice le requiert", aussi n'est-on pas obligé d'obéir à un usurpateur ou à une autorité qui donnerait des ordres ou directives contraires à la justice[30].

L'homme n'est pas tenu d'obéir à l'autorité humaine en ce qui touche l'intériorité, qui est du domaine de Dieu seul. À l'autorité humaine, il doit la prestation des actes extérieurs, étant entendu qu'il ait l'intention droite du respect dû à l'autorité là où elle s'exerce légitimement.

C'est par notre corps que s'exercent les activités extérieures, mais cela ne signifie pas que l'autorité politique ait droit d'intervenir en tout ce qui concerne le corps. En effet, pour ce qui touche à sa nature, l'homme n'est pas tenu d'obéir à une autorité humaine, mais seulement à Dieu, parce que tous les hommes, pour ce qui est de la nature humaine, sont égaux; c'est le cas pour la nourriture et l'entretien du corps ou la génération. Ainsi l'homme est libre quand il s'agit de contracter mariage ou se décider pour le célibat consacré. Ces exigences qui découlent de la nature humaine sont, pour la plupart, reconnues par les Déclarations des droits de l'homme. Mais il n'est pas impossible que dans les années qui viennent se lèvent de nouvelles menaces contre la personne humaine et ses droits.

Ainsi, c'est toujours dans un champ limité que s'exerce l'autorité humaine. Elle n'a aucun droit sur le fors interne. En dehors du cercle de sa compétence, l'homme est soumis immédiatement à Dieu, qui l'instruit par la loi naturelle ou par la loi révélée.

Ajoutons que, la société humaine étant une société de personnes, son bien commun, que les personnes comme membres de la société doivent servir, doit à son tour être au service des valeurs transcendantes et des personnes. Car la personne libre n'a pas son horizon ultime dans la société, elle est appelée à entrer en relation immédiate avec le Dieu transcendant, bien commun séparé, et, à ce titre, le bien commun politique lui-même est subordonné au bien des personnes.

19. Les conceptions volontaristes de la loi qui ne reconnaissent en celle-ci d'abord que l'affirmation de la volonté du souverain ou, au-delà, de la toute-puissance divine, en ignorant toute référence à la sagesse, ne permet-

---

[30] *Ibid.* Ad 3. Saint Thomas ajoute: si ce n'est peut-être *par accidens* afin d'éviter un scandale ou un danger. Quand le précepte est directement opposé à la loi naturelle, l'objection de conscience devient légitime et s'impose. Cette doctrine récemment proposée par le Magistère connaîtra sans doute encore d'importants développements.

tent pas de rendre justice aux distinctions libératrices que je viens d'esquisser. Ainsi la distinction entre les deux sens de l'obéissance que nous avons rappelée tend à perdre sa pertinence; il en va de même de l'instance médiatrice du bien commun et de la justice. Le volontarisme conduit également à concevoir le rapport entre le supérieur et le sujet d'une manière conflictuelle. Quand, avec Luther, le liberté créée se présentera avant tout comme volonté pécheresse, le rapport à l'autorité, divine ou politique, deviendra un rapport d'opposition. Ce rapport se maintiendra au coeur des philosophies de l'immanence dont la responsabilité est grande dans la genèse du léviathan totalitaire en notre siècle.

Ces brèves notations exigeraient des développements. Elles suffisent ici pour indiquer que la crise de l'obéissance ne peut être totalement dissociée de conceptions erronées du pouvoir et de l'autorité et des abus qui s'en sont suivis.

PERSPECTIVES ECCLÉSIALES

20. Quelques mots encore en guise de conclusion. Je m'en suis tenu à une considération philosophique des problèmes de la liberté et de l'obéissance.

Mais il va de soi que le philosophe chrétien développe sa méditation sur l'horizon des données de la Révélation, dont l'incidence sur la culture est incontestable.

Dans cette perspective proprement surnaturelle, la liberté découvre de plus grandes profondeurs et l'obéissance une richesse nouvelle.

La méditation théologique s'arrêtera d'abord à l'obéissance du Christ sur la Croix, comme suprême expression de son amour du Père et du don de la rédemption. Par là est révélé le drame du péché, comme désobéissance à Dieu, selon qu'elle s'oppose à l'obéissance au premier des sens que nous avons discerné.

En second lieu, la méditation portera sur la grâce de filiation nous introduisant dans la vie d'amour des trois Personnes divines elles-mêmes. La charité est ainsi une amitié; or le propre de l'amitié est de faire que les amis communient dans le vouloir: *idem velle et nolle*. C'est pourquoi il ne peut pas y avoir charité sans obéissance[31]. La conscience chrétienne ne peut pas ne pas aimer la vertu d'obéissance.

Enfin, la méditation se fixera sur le mystère de l'Église et sur la signification proprement ecclésiale de l'obéissance. S'il y a crise de l'obéissance dans l'Église, c'est sans doute parce que nous subissons le contre-coup de la crise

---
[31] Cf. *Sum. Theol.*, II-II, q. 104, a. 3.

culturelle. Mais c'est surtout parce que le sens de l'Église comme mystère de foi a décliné dans bien des coeurs.

Avec ces quelques indications, j'entre dans un nouveau champ de réflexions, qui n'est plus strictement celui que je m'étais assigné. Il m'a semblé que nous ne pouvions pas isoler les problèmes actuels de l'obéissance dans l'Église en faisant abstraction de la crise culturelle. Ces problèmes en sont souvent le contre-coup. Ils pénètrent dans la conscience des chrétiens, dès que le sens théologal vient à fléchir, mais cela mériterait un nouveau discours.

GEORGE F. McLEAN
Secretary of the World Union of Catholic Philosophical Societies
United States

FREEDOM AS THE BASIS OF CIVIL SOCIETY:
THE TRANSFORMATION OF CHRISTIAN PHILOSOPHY AT THE DAWN OF THE NEW MILLENNIUM

In present efforts to develop democratic societies one major contemporary issue for Christian philosophy must be to renew its understanding of human freedom. The present deep cultural transformations are a creation of this freedom. Hence we cannot safely proceed without a better understanding of its nature. As the prior totalitarian structures slip away and new human sensibilities and aspirations emerge our questions deepen to a second order, namely, to the very nature and status of Christian philosophy itself. This proposes not only a specific new task, but basic new capabilities and horizons which can enable a far richer sense of philosophy than hitherto realized and engaged.

It is difficult if not impossible to catalogue or even survey the broad spectrum of a fundamental cultural change. What is feasible is to select an example and to unfold its meaning. In this sense we note the profound change in the work of the United Nations. For almost fifty years this body was dominated by the debates of two powerful political blocks in the Security Council divided according to economic ideology. Now, however, the Security Council is seldom heard from. Instead one hears of great conferences in Rio, Cairo and Beijing, which names, indeed, have come to stand for environment, family and women.

People's concerns have shifted from the competition of political powers over economic goals, that is, from quantitative concerns, to qualitative ones regarding the dignity of human life. As a result, the present comes to be characterized by people freely taking up responsibility for the quality not only of their personal life, but of their community and world. This constitutes an operational definition of civil society.

Let us then consider, first, what is the nature and content of civil society understood as a people's responsible exercise of freedom; second, why does this need to be rediscovered and especially in what terms can it be re-elaborated in our days; and third, what is needed in order for Christian philosophy to be able to respond to this need? This should enable us to identify the needs for an appropriate development of Christian philosophy at this turn of the millennia.

I. THE NATURE AND CONTENT OF CIVIL SOCIETY

As a notion civil society is in full transition. This should not be surprising for it concerns the basic realization of human community at a point of epochal, indeed millennial, change. If it could be clearly defined the issue would be closed, forward progress would be stopped and we would live once again in the closed horizons of a battle of ideologies.

It may be helpful to look first not at what civil society is or can become, but at the sources of the elaboration of the notion, if not of the reality, in Greek philosophy. For this Aristotle would point our attention not to the theoretical sciences which concern what is, but to the practical sciences which regard what we do or make. Note that whereas the principle for the former are to be found in the object, the principles for the latter are to be found in the subject who makes or does this. Consequently, a search for the nature of civil society must be directed toward the human persons as they implement the governance of, in and by their community. This he terms *koinōnia politika*. Let us look at each of these words separately.

The root of governance is to be found in the term *arché*. There are two ways of misunderstanding this, each of which can help to highlight its essence. The first misunderstanding is characteristic of the modern effort to think all in terms of power and control. In such terms *arché* is taken to mean an autocratic affirmation of will which suppresses the freedom of the people. In fact, *arché* expresses a beginning or source. As to freedom as self-determination, this means that the will is not determined by anything other than itself. As such, it is essentially, responsible for the act and for its sequelae. Hence, *arché* as the root of governance is essentially a matter of the exercise of responsible freedom.

A second misinterpretation of the notion was by Aristotle himself. He seems first to have understood governance in terms of the search for private interests. As a result this would best be exercised by those sufficiently wealthy not to have pressing personal needs. These, however, being few in number this would imply government by the few, an oligarchy, which nevertheless would be preferable to a democratic government in which the many but more needy citizens are responsible. In another sketch on governance, however, Aristotle enters what could be taken as a corrective of the above. If participation in governance is to be expanded, as is the broad desire of humankind in our days, then it would appear that governance must be exercised on a different basis – not for the private benefit of those who rule, but but for the common good of all[1]. On this new qualitative basis it becomes possible to undertake the democratic effort to engage the broad populace in the work of governance.

Christian philosophy adds substantively to this democratic sense of governance by tracing all to an absolute source, God. As this cause is all wise, the created nature which derives therefrom is not a Stoic fatalistic order to which all must surrender blindly, but a wise pattern for human welfare and in which our conscious life enables us to engage. Further, as the source is all-loving the goal of creation is the good of people as rational, free and possessed of an inalienable dignity. Finally, as the source is one and indeed unique all are united therein and hence one with all others. They live this by acting according to natural law for the common good.

The second term: community or *koinōnia* entails two notions: solidarity and subsidiarity. Solidarity adds the element of multiplicity to the sense of the one source. This implies that the unity of society will be one of order. Consequently, the exercise of responsible freedom with and for others will be through an interactive community which is united in one source and one goal[2].

The other notion is that of subsidiarity. This adds a structural principle for ordering social units with increasingly broader responsibilities. In view of what has been said above the task of the broader unit is not to withhold the exercise of freedom from the more immediate communities, but to promote the exercise of responsibility by those solidarities in their concrete engagements in education and labor, health and environment, and religion and the quality of public life. Their goal is the exercise of responsible freedom by those most engaged in these affairs and hence knowledgeable and naturally interrelated in these regards.

In this sense civil society is the responsible exercise of freedom for the common good by the multiple solidarities according to structures of subsidiarity.

---

[1] *Politics*, III, 7-8.
[2] *Nichomachean Ethics*, IX, 6, 1167 b 13; and *Politics*, I, 2, 1253 a 20-37.

II. THE PRESENT TRANSITION IN HUMAN AWARENESS

In these days we find a renewed interest in civil society and a sense that there is urgent need that it be rebuilt. In order to respond, however, this need must be understood. How is it that the earlier sense of the social exercise of responsible freedom was forgotten or limited as with the Scots as to seem, even to such of its proponents as Hegel and Marx, to be in need of being superseded. To understand this one should return to the grounds of the Enlightenment and the sweeping cultural violence of its groundclearing operation. For Bacon all "idols" of market place, theater, etc. were to be swept away; for Locke the mind was to be voided of all content till it resembled a blank tablet; for Descartes all was to be bracketed by a systematic doubt except the sole idea which proved indubitable. All was removed, leaving the mind as an aseptic laboratory into which in a strictly controlled manner were to be introduced ideas derived exclusively from either the senses or the intellect. On the former basis the Anglo-Saxon tradition developed the materialistic empirical and analytic visions restricted to single material entities and reflected in individualistic capitalist ideology. On the latter basis the continental traditions developed the idealistic visions (and their materialistic inversions) focused upon unity even to the extent of depersonalizing community. The ultimate denouement of this bifurcated product of the rationalist laboratory were the hot and cold wars of a uniquely vicious 20th century.

What had been lost, and what do people now seek to restore? Shortly after Descartes Jean Baptiste Vico noted that this dual reductionism left no place for person, for probabilities or possibilities, for sensibility or feeling, for imagination or creativity, in a word, for all the elements involved in the development of a culture. What would result, he foretold with great insight, would be a brute – and what is worse, an intellectual brute[3]. What then is to be restored, rebuilt or developed anew can be expressed in a word: culture. It is no accident then that in the collapse of the cold war and the end of the battle of ideologies a whole new agenda emerges for philosophy. No longer is attention directed to Marx's abstract category of species with total loss of attention to the person, or to the single individual as viciously self-concerned according to Hobbes. Rather attention is directed to the person as truly unique in his or her subjectivity and freedom, but now as prime image of God and hence responsible regent of society, world and cosmos.

---

[3] Giambattista Vico, *The New Science*, transl. T. Bergin and M. Fisch, Ithica: Cornell University Press 1988. See also Lu Xiaohe, *G.B. Vico and the Contemporary Civil World*, in *Civil Society in A Chinese Context*, Washington, D.C.: The Council For Research in Values and Philosophy, 1996.

This includes not only rationality as an instrumental technology of quantitative ideas, but also the reasonableness of truth regarding the quality of life; it includes knowledge, but also love; it includes the recognition of given objective realities, but also creativity by way of the imagination and regarding new possibilities. Together these generate cultures as the creation of peoples; indeed, this creation of culture now comes to be seen as pertaining to the very essence of the human character of persons, communities and peoples. In retrospect the power achieved by the enlightenment comes now to be seen as having been purchased at enormous costs paid in human suffering and life. The present effort to transcend this without losing the achievements of rationalism constitutes the philosophical challenge of our day. How can it be met?

This is a question of the greatest import because it concerns not only the addition of one or another particular insight which previously had been elaborated, but for some reason not yet fully explored. On the contrary, it concerns the essence of the person, which is the core insight of Christian philosophy as a *philosophia perennis*. Something dramatic must be happening not only to the content of philosophy, but to the very character of philosophizing itself. For if one fails to develop philosophy in proportion to the new sensibilities to person, the vision available to us in the next millenium will not exceed that of the past. Inevitably, the history of the coming century will be repeat the violence of the past, now in higher octaves of power and violence. On the contrary, if truly new sensibilities were to be available and philosophy developed accordingly then there would be reason to hope that a new age can be dawning and that the richness of human life can be expanded.

To focus attention to these challenges and possibilities I would like to take up briefly three points: the development of aesthetic awareness in philosophy and its implications for the religious character of philosophy, and the place of Christ in a Christian philosophy.

III. PHILOSOPHY IN AESTHETIC TERMS

Looking back at the history of philosophy in the last two millennia, it can be seen that during those periods philosophy developed insight in terms of two of the transcendental properties of being. During the first millenium of the Christian era there emerged an awareness of being as *esse*. The history of this emergence has been written especially by Cornelio Fabro in his studies on participation[4]. He shows that the Christian sense of the creation

---

[4] Cornelio Fabro, *La nozione metafisica de partecipazione secondo S. Tommaso d'Aquina*, Torino: Societá ed. Internazionale 1950, pp. 75-122.

of being, as well as the deepened sense of freedom as the response of Christ's redemptive invitation to new life, carried the human mind beyond the Greek understanding of being in terms of form to a new appreciation of the existential character of being. As a result the unity or identity of each being stood forth from the generic or specific with unique force and the person was able to be appreciated in his or her uniqueness.

The second millenium focused especially upon the truth of being and the power of human reason. This was related to the reintroduction of Aristotle to the West in the early part of this period and its magnificent elaboration in the high Middle Ages. The structure of the *Organon* and its implications for scientific knowledge were decisive. The period of the Fathers was replaced by that of the theologians whose concern was to develop knowledge, even of the Christian myseries, in scientific terms. This did not omit the mystical dimension, but neither did it give great attention thereto; today this is considered a basic difference of the Roman from the Orthodox traditions of Christian thought.

As noted above this focus upon truth was radicalized with the Enlightenment and its exclusion from the realm of philosophy of all but ideas and of these only those which are clear and distinct. Pascal and Kierkegaard might object that there are other "reasons", but their thought would be definitely marginal.

Neo-Scholasticism was born in the full tide of 19th century rationalism. Hence, it focused upon truth, particularly objective truth. Until the mid 1950s its key figures were at best reticent and more commonly hostile to attention to subjectivity. It could be said without exaggeration that Vatican II was called to explore whether, to what degree and how Christian thought could integrate the awareness of subjectivity which, with the emergence of phenomenology, could no longer be pushed aside.

While Vatican II clearly affirmed the appropriateness, indeed the essential richness, of the new sensibilities to human subjectivity in reading Scripture, participation in Church structures and liturgical and pastoral practice, it was not in position to evolve a philosophy to undergird these developments. This task was rightly left to Christian philosophers. Delays in effectively implementing this task have resulted in no small tension within the Roman Catholic community and between it and its confreres within and beyond Christianity as the new aspirations of freedom and creativity continue to be recognized to in terms of objective truth at the expense of creative engagement with the ongoing progress in human awareness[5].

---

[5] G. F. McLean, ed., *Ethics at the Crossroad*, vol. I: *Normative Ethics and Objective Reason*, vol II: *Personalist Ethics and Human Subjectivity*, Washington, D.C.: The Council for Research in Values and Philosophy in Bucharest, Romania: Paideia Publisher 1996.

There are resources in the classical tradition of Christian philosophy for responding to these challenges. Thomas' extensive *Disputed Questions on Truth (De Veritate)* is a most extended and detailed study on the tanscendental properties of being: unity, truth and goodness. Each of these is convertible with being and hence partakes of the dynamic nature of being according not only to its essence, but especially to its existence. Each unfolds or "explicates" being; each so includes and expresses the inner life of being that it is distinct from being only by the minimal minor distinction of reason between what is actually present but not explicitated (being), on the one hand, and what is explicitated (unity), on the other. Unity is being itself in its very identity; truth is this same identity as essentially related to the intellect or "intelligible"; and the good is this identity as not only intelligible, but further as desirable to the will. Hindu philosophy expresses this particularly well when it states the character of the divine not in abstract, but in concrete and living terms: Brahma is not just one and true and good, but existence (*sat*), living truth or consciousness (*cit*), and experienced goodness or bliss (*ananda*).

Thomas points out further that these transcendentals are not simply parallel or indifferently related; they are sequenced so that being is included in the formal definition of one or unity, which in turn is formally included in the definition of truth, and truth in the formal definition of goodness. This means, of course, that the good cannot be chosen without the true (or justice), according to the dictum that nothing can be willed unless it is first known. Thus, concern over the direction of freedom has centered upon objective and universal laws of nature – whether the physical laws of the material world or the natural law of universal human nature.

This corresponds well with the emphasis upon reason characteristic of the second millenium, but is it sufficient to respond to the new sensibilities of this point of transition to the third millenium? In the sequence of the transcendentals, this is to proceed to the exercise of freedom according to the meaning of being only as true, that is, as what can be known to be or to have been, rather than as good, namely, that which is desirable as end or goal. Since truth precedes the good and does not explicate that which is unfolded by the good, this is not to take full account of the good. It considers only whether something makes sense and is according to law, rather than responding to its attractiveness as goal which draws us forward. This is analogous to driving a car while looking only in the rear mirror.

To live freedom a new stance becomes necessary. One must bring forward not only being, unity and truth, but also the good, and assemble all these before one's vision or consciousness in order to be able to respond creatively to the attraction of being. Only then can one respond to the challenges of life, search out its possibilities and create life that is new and harmonious. This is precisely the nature of the fourth transcendental, beauty. As "that which pleases when seen" it integrates the previous three transcendentals in a manner which maximizes and transcends the meaning of any one taken simply or even of all three taken serially.

But if we are truly to philosophize in terms of the beauty of beings then we must be sure that we do not return to a rationalism centered upon truth and relatively insensitive to the good or to beauty. On the contrary, we must look into human subjectivity as it responds freely to the good and works creatively to unfold its possibilities. These can then be reassembled actively, imaginatively and creatively in terms of beauty with an art focused upon realizing a social life marked by harmony and dignity. This calls for a philosophy in which the aesthetics plays a key coordinating role.

This can be seen in Kant's evolution of a third critique. In initiating the decade in which he wrote his three critiques Kant did not have the third critique in view. He wrote the first critique in order to provide methodologically for the universality and necessity of the categories found in scientific knowledge. He developed the second critique to provide for the reality of human freedom. It was only when both of these had been written that he could see that in order to protect and promote freedom in the material world there was need for a third set of categories, namely, those of aesthetic judgement integrating the realms of matter and spirit. Their harmony can be appreciated in terms neither of a science of nature as in the first critique nor of society as can be worked out from the second, but of human creativity working with the many elements of human life to create meaning which can be lived as an expanding and enriching reality.

This can be seen through a comparison of the work of the imagination in the first and the third critiques. Kant is facing squarely a most urgent question for modern times, namely: how can the newly uncovered freedom of the second critique survive when confronted with the necessity and universality of the realm of science as understood in the *Critique of Pure Reason*?

– Will the scientific interpretation of nature restrict freedom to the inner realm of each person's heart, where it is reduced at best to good intentions or to feelings towards others?

– When we attempt to act in this world or to reach out to others, must all our categories be universal and hence insensitive to that which marks others as unique and personal?

– Must they be necessary, and, hence, leave no room for creative freedom, which would be entrapped and then entombed in the human mind? If so, then public life can be only impersonal, necessitated, repetitive and stagnant.

– Must the human spirit be reduced to the sterile content of empirical facts or to the necessitated modes of scientific laws? If so, then philosophers cannot escape forcing upon wisdom a suicidal choice between either being traffic directors in the jungle of unfettered competition or being tragically complicit in setting a predetermined order for the human spirit.

Freedom then would, indeed, have been killed; it would pulse no more as the heart of mankind.

Before these alternatives, Kant's answer is a resounding No! Taking as his basis the reality of freedom – so passionately and often tragically affirmed in our times by Gandhi and Martin Luther King – Kant proceeded to develop his third *Critique of the Faculty of Judgment* as a context within which freedom and scientific necessity could coexist, indeed, in which necessity would be the support and instrument of freedom. Recently, this has become more manifest as human sensibilities have opened to awareness that being itself is emergent in time through the human spirit and hence to the significance of culture.

To provide for this context, Kant found it necessary to distinguish two issues, reflected in the two parts of his third *Critique*. In the *Critique of Teleological Judgment*[6], he acknowledges that nature and all reality must be teleological. This was a basic component of the classical view which enabled all to be integrated within the context of a society of free men working according to a developed order of reason. For Kant, if there is to be room for human freedom in a cosmos in which man can make use of necessary laws, if science is to contribute to the exercise of human freedom, then nature too must be directed toward a transcendent goal and manifested throughout a teleology within which free human purpose can be integrated. In these terms, nature, even in its necessary and universal laws, is no longer alien to freedom, but expresses divine freedom and is conciliable with human freedom. The same might be said of the economic order and its "hidden hand". The structure of his *Critiques* will not allow Kant to affirm this teleological character as an absolute and self-sufficient metaphysical reality, but he recognizes that we must proceed "as if" all reality is teleological precisely because of the undeniable reality of human freedom in an ordered universe.

If, however, teleology, in principle, provides the needed space, there remains a second issue of how freedom is exercised, namely, what mediates it to the necessary and universal laws of science? This is the task of his *Critique of the Aesthetic Judgment*[7], and it is here that the imagination reemerges to play its key integrating role in human life. From the point of view of the human person, the task is to explain how one can live in free-

---

[6] Immanuel Kant, *Critique of Judgment*, transl. H. H. Bernard, New York: Hafner, 1968, pp. 205-339.

[7] *Ibid.*, pp. 37-200.

dom with nature for which the first critique had discovered only laws of universality and necessity, and especially how the free person can live in the structures of society in a way that is neither necessitated nor necessitating?

There is something similar here to the *Critique of Pure Reason*. In both, the work of the imagination in assembling the phenomena is not simply to register, but to produce an objective order. As in the first *Critique*, the approach is not from a set of *a priori* principles which are clear all by themselves and used in order to bind the multiple phenomena into a unity. On the contrary, under the rule of unity, the imagination orders and reorders the multiple phenomena until they are ready to be informed by a unifying principle whose appropriateness emerges from the reordering carried out by the productive imagination.

However, in the first *Critique* this reproductive work took place in relation to the abstract and universal categories of the intellect and was carried out under a law of unity which dictated that such phenomena as a house or a receding boat must form a unity – which they could do only if the multiple phenomena are assembled in a certain order. Hence, although it was a human product, the objective order was universal and necessary and the related sciences were valid both for all things and for all people[8].

Here in *The Critique of the Aesthetic Judgment*, the imagination has a similar task of constructing the object, but not in manner necessitated by universal categories or concepts. In contrast, here the imagination, in working toward an integrating unity, is not confined by the necessitating structures of categories and concepts, but ranges freely over the full sweep of reality in all its dimensions. Its search is to see whether and wherein relatedness and purposiveness or teleology can emerge and the world and our personal and social life can achieve its meaning and value. Hence, in standing before a work of nature or of art, the imagination might focus upon light or form, sound or word, economic or interpersonal relations – or, indeed, upon any combination of these in a natural environment or a society, whether encountered concretely or expressed in symbols.

Throughout all of this, the ordering and reordering by the imagination can bring about numberless unities. Unrestricted by any *a prori* categories, it can nevertheless integrate necessary dialectical patterns within its own free and, therefore, creative production and scientific universals within its unique concrete harmonies. This is properly creative work. More than merely evaluating all according to a set pattern in one's culture, it chooses the values and orders reality accordingly.

---

[8] Immanuel Kant, *Critique of Pure Reason*, transl. N. K. Smith, London: Macmillan 1929, A112, 121, 192-193; Donald J. Crawford, *Kant's Aesthetic Theory*, Madison: University of Wisconsin 1974, pp. 83-84, 87-90.

This is the very constitution of a culture itself, which is the productive rather than merely reproductive work of the human person as living in his or her physical world. Here, I use the possessive form advisedly. Without this capacity humans would exist in the physical universe as other objects, not only subject to its laws but restricted and possessed by them. They would be not free citizens of the material world, but mere functions or servants. In his third *Critique* Kant unfolds how one can truly be master of his or her life in this world, not in an arbitrary and destructive manner, but precisely as creative artists bring being to new realization in ways which make possible new growth in freedom.

In the third Critique, the productive imagination constructs a true unity by bringing the elements into an authentic harmony. This cannot be identified through reference to a category, because freedom then would be restricted within the laws of necessity of the first *Critique*, but must be recognizable by something free. In order for the realm of human freedom to be extended to the whole of reality, this harmony must be able to be appreciated, not purely intellectually in relation to a concept (for then we would be reduced to the universal and nesessary as in the first *Critique*), but aesthetically, by the pleasure or displeasure, the attraction or repulsion of the free response it generates. It is our contemplation or reflection upon this which shows whether proper and authentic ordering has or has not been achieved. This is not a concept[9], but the pleasure or displeasure, the elation at the beautiful and sublime or the disgust at the ugly and revolting, which flows from our contemplation or reflection.

Maritain takes this further in terms of a realist metaphysics pointing out in his *Creative Intuition in Art and Poetry*[10] how the aesthetic integrates the material and the spiritual, the universal and the concrete, the intellect as ground of truth and the will as ground of the good. Moreover he suggests that this unity of beauty corresponds properly not to any particular human faculty such as intellect and will, but more deeply to the very center of one's personhood. This explains then how the uniqueness of one's personality is reflected not by any single possession or act, but by all the actions and dispositions of one's life as these form a distinctive unity and harmony. It is in terms of beauty that the person, long neglected and repressed in a rationalistic universe, seeks now to flourish and be expressed.

---

[9] See Kant's development and solution to the problem of the autonomy of taste, *Critique of Judgment*, nn. 57-58, pp. 182-192, where he treats the need for a concept; Crawford, pp. 63-66.

[10] J. Maritain, *Creative Intuition in Art and Poetry*, New York: Pantheon 1953.

One finds this prefigured as well in the classical studies of Thomas' position on freedom. Though the realistic character of his position often is most strongly noted, upon close analysis it becomes manifest that the act of freedom consists centrally not in the choice of a thing or an action, but in a practical judgment as is noted elsewhere in this volume in the chapters of Professors Krąpiec and Cottier. Such judgments are not given, but are created by the person; it is here – and particularly with a consciousness appropriate for the aesthetic order – that we must look if we are to respond to the creative needs and possibilities of the millenium now upon us.

Concretely, this is necessary if we are to integrate into our philosophical vision that most distinctive of human creations, namely, the cultures of peoples. In the past philosophy largely has ignored culture and sought only what is necessary and universal. Indeed, as with Kant's categorical imperative, it has taken formal universality to be precisely its philosophical warranty. In contrast, what was proper to a people and expressive of its unique life in time and space was depreciated as of no philosophical significance. The result could only be a philosphy in which the significance of human life – the heroic daily striving and ingenious creativity in the protection and promotion of families, peoples and universe – was lost to philosophical appreciation, which in turn was left immune to any enrichment of its content and meaning. It is no wonder then that this last century has been marked by so great a depreciation of, and the violent attack upon, human life in all its dimensions from beginning to end.

In contrast, integration of aethetic modes of awareness into human life now makes possible attention to culture. It makes it possible to take account of the concrete prioritizing of multiple goods which constitute the values of a people and their pattern. It makes it possible to take account as well of the properly human capabilities, strengths or virtues which a people develops in the exercise of these values or priorities. And it becomes possible finally to take into account the way in which this pattern of values and virtues as the cumulative exercise of responsible freedom through time comes to constitute a tradition. Culture indeed is the union of all three: values, virtues and tradition. In order for a philosophy to be able to recognize and give due importance to the human reality with its properly temporal mode, that is, to the existential reality of the lives of persons and peoples, the aesthetic dimension of human awareness now becomes essential to the philosophical project.

IV. A RELIGIOUS PHILOSOPHY

A second challenge to a Christian philosophy in our days is to integrate the properly religious character of human life, and indeed of all reality. We know not only by faith, but by reason that God created all things. This is the essential content of Thomas' five ways. In theology these appear at the very beginning, i.e., in the second question of the first part of his *Summa Theologica*[11]. However, in philosophy after the Aristotelian manner, reasoning to the divine comes only at the end (Book XII of Aristotle's *Metaphysics*). Hence, we proceed through the entire extent of philosophy as if we are making sense of reality without taking account of God. When, however, we do carry out the reflection at the end of the Metaphysics we find that indeed no reality makes sense except in relation to the divine as absolute being. In contrast the Hindu *Vedanta Sutras* states this up front, in the very second sutra, namely that "Brahma is that from which, in which and into which all is". Parmenides at the very aub of Western metaphysics, immediately upon establishing the principle of contradiction separating being from non being, proceeded to demonstrate that being as such must be one, eternal and unchanging. This is not the last, but the first of philosophical truths. If reasoning to the divine life is taken up at the end of metaphysics in order that being, causality and reasoning be well in hand, it is nonetheless crucial to appreciate the meaning of their conclusion, namely, that God is the first being and that in him alone do all things have their being and meaning.

What is more, the act of creation as conservation is continuous in its effect. Hence, God works continuingly and creatively in all cultures; it is only in and by him that peoples face the challenges of their life and cooperate in the creation of new human meaning. The most proper task of philosophy then is to engage in the development of a culture, to enable this to be conscious of its divine source, and beyond an instrumentalization of human life to keep this open to the full dignity of the human quest in its origin from God, in imaging Him in time and in striving toward religious realization.

Here Christian philosophy has a truly missionary character. It must be concerned to go to all cultures for all are reflections of divine creation. It must engage these cultures in philosophical interchange and in this it must assist in a number of ways. In this it must be recognized at the outset that in many if not most cultures awareness of the divine source, meaning and goal will be more intense than in Christian philosophy as developed in the Western tradition. Indeed, it is the promise of our times that Christian

---

[11] *Summa Theologica*, I, q. 2, a. 3.

philosophy done on the basis, for instance, of the Indian philosophical tradition will vastly enrich the heritage of Christian philosophy thusfar attained. In this light the coming century and millenium bear the promise that Christian philosophy will be vastly more deep and the life of humankind immeasurably enriched.

But here the task is not only one of harvesting insights; it has elements of Lawrence Scupoli's *Spiritual Combat*[12] as well. The history of philosophy is rife with reductionisms as philosophers become fascinated by their own insight and proceed to attempt to reduce all philosophy and human life thereto. "Let's suppose that all is matter", says the materialist, or "Let's suppose that all is spirit", says the idealist. As a purely speculative enterprise this can be helpful, but philosophy has a way of being transformed into practical life. As a result such exercises become vicious projects of human reduction either by the coercive power of the state and its means of visiting even death upon those who oppose it or by the new powers of the media to dominate the human spirit and instrumentalize it as a consumer in the economic process. These elements of modernity constitute major assaults on all peoples of our times; but they are transferred especially from the West to many cultures not previously exposed to such menaces and which are poorly equipped philosophically to cope. It must be a task of the Christian philosopher in the West to help others to respond the these missive secularizing assaults upon the religious roots of their cultures.

Hence, both in the positive sense of expanding horizons and in the defensive work of protecting them, Christian philosophy has a crucial missionary task to perform in our day. It is not that of proselytizing; rather it is the effort to uncover, defend and promote the work of the spirit in the lives and cultures of all peoples.

V. CHRIST IN CHRISTIAN PHILOSOPHY

In this does the Christian philosopher work in the image of Christ or, as is often the case, of Aristotle; in other words how Christian can Christian philosophy be while still remaining philosophy? Escpecially working in terms of aesthetics, recent work in hermeneutics can be helpful in integrating the normative, inspirational and mobilizing reality of Christ and thereby helping to constitute a more properly Christian "Christian philosophy". H.G. Gadamer sees tradition as a double source. As extending through time it makes possible a process of learning by trial and error: we are able

---

[12] Lawrenzo Scupoli, *Spiritual Combat*, London: Burns, Oates and Washbourne, 1935.

to see what does not work and adjust until we find what does. But beyond this utilitarian level cultures possess classical examples which by their balanced and integrated perfection express in a unique way the perfection of a culture. Due to the fact that humans are oriented to the good or perfection, the very existence of such classic examples exercises an attractive and orienting force which shapes our life. Examples of this might be the Parthenon in classical architecture and the Lord Buddha in the lives of many peoples. What is to be said of Christ in relation to a Christian philosophy which is sensitive to the aesthetic and hence to the beauty of the singular and concrete existent?

Certainly, Christ can be taken account of as a classical instance of humanity, exemplifying in himself ideals of physical, emotional and spiritual life. A Christian philosophy can reflect also the riches of a Christian culture in which the gospel ideals have been preached and lived. Indeed, here the distinction of nature and supernature begins to dim as examples of devotion and self-sacrifice in one's family or towards the common good of one's community or nation open new horizons of love and social responsibility. These are carried out by grace, but they convey an outlook, attitude and way of acting externally visible to all. The nature of one's inspiration and goal may be able to be appreciated fully only by grace, but a special quality of one's actions, their beauty and attractiveness, are open to all.

But can one go further; can one say that the person of Christ as divine also can be appreciated and enter into philosophical reflection? As was said above, aesthetic awareness brings forward the unity, truth and goodness of being so that its beauty stands before our eyes and imagination in the form of a compelling masterpiece inspiring and guiding our action. Can this be said of the figure of Christ appreciated as a divine person living according to human nature?

It may be too soon to draw up a response to this question, but a number of clues begin to accumulate and invite exploration:

1. that the characteristic of aesthetic knowledge is to be able to take account of the unique and to integrate matter and spirit;

2. that metaphysics has God not among its object, but as the cause of its object; and hence that awareness of the divine pertains integrally to metaphysics even when taken in the strict sense of an Aristotelian science;

3. that Thomas' five ways bring us by reason to a knowledge of God and His characteristics (as treated in the divine names);

4. that the fourth way presents us with almost immediate knowledge of the divine truth, goodness, nobility, etc. when these pure perfections are encountered in varying degrees among the beings of our daily life;

5. that the openness of spirit and hence of the human intellect and will is limitless;

6. that knowledge by connaturality makes possible a deep and immediate response by the holy person to the divine;

7. that a beautiful masterpiece or classic instance of perfection is so compelling that it is not to be changed in itself, but inspires limitless other instances of beauty; and

8. that divine perfection, its love and wisdom, exercises decisive attraction upon the human heart and mind; thus, it was noted that great crowds were drawn to Christ and that the hearts of the apostles were burning in his presence on the way to Emaus.

These clues might suggest that it is possible to integrate into Christian philosophy gospel teachings and the example of Christ not regarding such properly revealed matter such as the Trinity of divine persons and the economy of redemption, but the inner dynamism of being found in the Trinitarian relations of knowledge and love, and its implications for the deeper meaning of human life and the cosmos.

Then the philosophical history of this crucial transition to the new millenium is written this may well be described as the time when philosophy turned decidedly and creatively toward the creation of the future as a work of human freedom shared in creatively by all philosophies and cultures. In this Christian philosophy will find an urgent and exciting mission in this world and may learn even how to integrate the power and beauty of the God-made-man. If so in this Third millenium Christian philosophy finally will have come home.

LOTHAR KRAFT
Director of the Konrad Adenauer Stiftung
Germany

"TO ENJOY FREEDOM WE MUST BEAR RESPONSIBILITY". FREEDOM AS SEEN BY THE CHRISTIAN DEMOCRATIC UNION OF GERMANY

I. POLITICS AND RELIGION

In the course of its 50-year history, the German CDU has examined the notion of freedom again and again. Sources available for reconstructing these past debates include a multitude of preserved speech manuscripts as well as, and most importantly, the programmes of the party. In my contribution, I intend to describe the notion of freedom as it is interpreted by a political party, the Christian Democratic Union of Germany. In consequence of the unusual situation prevailing after the overthrow of the dictatorship in 1945, the party's founders chose to call it "Christian Democratic", the term "Union" being added to signify cooperation between Catholic and Protestant Christians in politics. In a speech given on August 28, 1948, Konrad Adenauer said, "It is our intention to re-shape the political life of Germany on the basis of intellectual foundations that have been created by Western Christianity in the course of many centuries...". To this extent, "the party is firmly rooted in Christian philosophy".

"Personal freedom is and will always remain man's most precious property". This "fundamental political postulate" sets us apart from the enemies of freedom and from dictatorships where might goes before right, where governmental power is everything, and the individual is nothing. In its 1994 party programme, the CDU once again affirmed its commitment to "a Christian interpretation of man and his world", engaging at the same time "to preserve the values of Christianity in our democracy".

In our time with its plurality of world views, its well-developed secularisation, and its segregation of church and state, as the church retreats to focus on its proper mission, notions like "Christian politics" or "Christian democracy" are very much in dispute. Thus, the concretisation of Christianity in this world reveals one of the fundamental strains of Christian existence. We need to distinguish clearly between the church as a community of believers sharing a common religious creed, and politics as an area where politicians, acting responsibly, may instil Christian values in political ethics.

II. FREEDOM AND PERSONAL DIGNITY

Speaking in March 1946, when he was chairman of the CDU in the British Occupied Zone, Konrad Adenauer expressed the party's fundamental position with regard to the notion of freedom as follows: The CDU follows Christian ethics in its core concept – the value of each individual is inestimable, and each individual has his own unique personal dignity. From this, governmental, economic, and cultural constitutions necessarily evolve. The power of government is held in check by the dignity and the freedom of the individual. A state is a community of responsible individuals, a community based on legality and freedom. "Personal freedom is not to be equated with licentiousness and arbitrariness; rather, its beneficiaries are under a constant obligation not to neglect the responsibility they bear for their neighbours as well as for the entire nation."

III. THE VISION OF FREEDOM

Together with the age of enlightenment, a great vision was born at the end of the 18th and the start of the 19th century – that a society based on civic freedom had become attainable (thus Biedenkopf). This concept of freedom derives from the dignity of the individual and from his identity, his uniqueness as a person. Personal freedom implies providing protection for privacy and private property, just as it implies personal responsibility towards others. Together with the idea of personal dignity, the idea of freedom forms the ethical hub of politics.

Recognition of the dignity and freedom of man forms "the basis of the CDU's cooperative effort"; furthermore, "implementing the freedom of the individual remains ethically impossible without responsibility being assumed by the individual both for himself and for his community." (1994 CDU Party Programme).

Our own freedom is limited by the freedom of others. Our relations with others are a mixture of freedom and dependence. We are free, and then again we are not. "Let us measure our freedom by the relationships in which we live, and by the decision-making options we enjoy in our various roles" (Amelung). A permanent dialectical relationship exists between freedom and government, the power that strives to hold its own. Whenever it encounters unjust government and opression, freedom may imply resistance and rebellion. It is part and parcel of personal freedom that the individual should be prepared "to fight for it and repel any totalitarian encroachment" (CDU Party Programme).

IV. THE EROSION OF FREEDOM

Freedom may vanish in a moral vacuum. Freedom may erode; civil courage and personal responsibility may be lost; and freedom may be threatened by internal or external developments, by gradual humiliation and disfranchisement. Without order, freedom dissolves. As Ludwig Erhard said, freedom may lose itself in wantonness and even brutality, evading any humane and ethical restrictions.

Then again, there are a growing number of people who express their understanding of freedom by saying, "I reject all taboos; I consider myself emancipated from everything; I will not accept orders from anyone; I can do as I please". These are random wanderings without orientation, "an anarchic absence of all criteria" (Alexander Schwan).

V. FREEDOM AND THE LAW

This is the reason why freedom always appears paired with other terms: Freedom and authority; freedom and order; freedom and solidarity; freedom and justice; freedom and responsibility; and, most important of all – freedom and the law. Commenting on this, E. W. Böckenförde said that freedom cannot exist without the law, as it is both the goal and the purpose of legality. It is the law that imbues freedom with security and order. In fact, freedom under the law is an option. Freedom in reality, freedom in practice, empirical law, and positive legal orders often fail to come up to the ideal, and are often abused; in other words, discrepancies arise between the idea and reality, a frequently painful experience in our everyday existence. Freedom and the law are anything but heavenly gifts; they are not spontaneous births but cultural achievements, the product of human action.

VI. FREEDOM AND GOVERNMENT

The grandest concept in politics is to protect the citizen's freedom through the rule of law. A democratic and social state under the rule of law is seen as the creation of free, mutually responsible citizens.

"The authority of the state draws its legitimation from its allegiance to fundamental civil rights and human dignity. Such a state obeys a code of values, aims to achieve the 'bonum commune', and is committed to justice" (Forster).

This term, "bonum commune", may define the ultimate purpose of the state. A democratic state seeks to further the interests and benefits of its citizens in pursuit of the "bonum commune" principle. Its goal should be to safeguard peace at home and abroad, and to protect freedom and justice as the supreme objectives of the law. Virtues and rules enable people to live together, and "bonum commune" must rely on the insights and virtues of the citizen. In all this, political action must be firmly based on moral and legal norms which, in the ongoing struggle for scarce goods and objects of desire, are our only protection against the emergence of a "status naturalis" with its attendant risks of egotism, the brutal pursuit of individual advantage, a war where every man's hand is turned against his neighbour, with the tough fighting the pliant, the strong fighting the weak.

It is, therefore, necessary to prevent any instance of "torture, coercion, humiliation, or exploitation of humans", as Franz Böhm said.

Consequently, we should follow Richard Löwenthal in remembering "that a state of tension exists between the freedom of the individual and the capacity of a society and community to survive".

VII. THE SOCIO-ECONOMIC FOUNDATIONS OF FREEDOM

Freedom is impossible to implement at a level of social and economic existence that is so low as to be offensive and injurious to the dignity of man. There is a very distinct relationship between freedom and water, electric lighting, education, health care, life expectancy, shelter, income distribution, property, and security. Freedom-oriented policy requires social receptiveness, so that social policy becomes an important field in liberal politics.

Analogously, the same might be said about the economy. No society can be free in a command or planned economy without private ownership, free markets, free competition, and freedom for producers and consumers to decide what to do.

VIII. FREEDOM IN EVERYDAY LIFE

Freedom is not merely an ethical and religious idea, it has social and political connotations as well. It is being debated by philosophers, and it is an issue of importance for all of us. Those who enjoy freedom believe this state to be perfectly natural. However, if one takes a closer look at our world, at our factories and institutions, and at the past 100 years of our history, one will see immediately that freedom is exposed to an unceasing succession of hazards and requires constant defence.

Freedom in everyday life is an issue of importance to all who "are about to lose their life, health, and happiness, and are fighting for their liberation" (Roman Herzog). This manifestation of freedom concerns all those "who show consideration, who help those who are no longer able to help themselves, who respect the honour of others, who do their work well, who do not cheat, and who assist the young and the old".

Regarded in this light, freedom may well turn into an exacting obligation, freedom and responsibility being interdependent. The measure of the worth of constitutions, laws, and governments as well as party programmes is "their value in everyday life", as Roman Herzog said.

IX. WESTERN VALUES?

If we blend man's freedom and dignity with the fact that he is answerable to his own conscience, we begin to approach the transcendental justification of human freedom – religion and theology. Religions leave their stamp on cultures. What is so frequently described as "Western culture and Western values" these days is formed by a cultural heritage consisting of christian tradition, a Christian background, and a philosophical anthropology all claiming universal truth and universal validity. These, then, are the points currently being debated: The universality of human rights; Western versus Asian values; universalism versus particularism; mutual relations between cultures and religions; relations between these two on the one hand and politics and political ethics on the other; belief, fundamentalism, enlightenment, and secularisation.

X. TO SUPPORT AND SHAPE FREEDOM AND THE LAW

Let me conclude with some thoughts by Alexander Schwan, a professor of political theory who died in 1989, with whom the author fully agrees. Political ethics is predicated on a variety of philosophical anthropology that reflects the normative foundations of liberal policy, i.e. a balanced, personalist anthropology of individuality and sociality which relates the rights and obligations of the individual to the interdependence of freedom and responsibility. Thus, the dignity of mankind becomes the measure and principle of the design of communal existence. "This being so, personalism should be seen as a kind of liberal solidarism, a philosophical approach which may serve as a basis for the implementation in theory and practice of pluralist, active, and social democracy under the rule of law, the objective being to achieve a maximum of freedom and equality for the people living in our historic era."

"That every person is imbued with dignity entitles him or her to a life under the established rule of law and under a constitution of freedom. Once this has been irrevocably achieved, any person, any individual, and any citizen will be correspondingly obliged to support both this rule of law and this liberal constitution, and share in its development and maintenance."

XI. CONCLUSION

At the 1956 general meeting of Catholics in Cologne, the then Federal Chancellor Konrad Adenauer addressed the following message to those among the audience who had come from the Soviet Occupied Zone of Germany: "Your day of freedom will come! On that day, we shall all be united in peace and freedom in our country of Germany." His address was entitled "Freedom – a Sturdy Foundation".

ANTON RAUSCHER
Universität Augsburg
Deutschland

DAS RECHT AUF RELIGIONSFREIHEIT IN EINER SÄKULAREN GESELLSCHAFT

Für das Verhältnis von Glaube und Welt, von Kirche und Gesellschaft ist die Religionsfreiheit im modernen weltanschaulich neutralen Staat konstitutiv. Auch wenn die geschichtliche Entwicklung der christlichen Kultur in Europa von einem engen Miteinander von Kirche und Staat, von Thron und Altar, von geistlicher und weltlicher Macht bestimmt wurde, so blieb doch immer die Forderung Jesu lebendig: „Gebt dem Kaiser, was dem Kaiser gehört, und Gott, was Gott gehört" (Mk 12,17). Das Christentum steht im strikten Gegensatz zu jedwedem innerweltlich-politischen Totalanspruch, wie er im Kaiserkult des Römischen Reiches kulminierte und deshalb zur Unterdrückung und Verfolgung der neuen Religion führte, wie er gleichfalls in den totalitären Machtsystemen des Nationalsozialismus und des Kommunismus zur Herrschaft gelangte. Auf der anderen Seite ist auch eine Theokratie mit der Forderung Jesu unvereinbar. Die Kirche soll das Evangelium der Erlösung und des Heils allen Menschen verkünden, aber nicht „im Namen Gottes" diese Welt regieren und eine Oberhoheit über den Staat beanspruchen. Die Zwei-Reiche-Lehre beziehungsweise die Lehre über Staat und Kirche als „societates perfectae", die unabhängig voneinander sind, gehört wesentlich zur christlichen Sichtweise des Verhältnisses von Staat und Kirche.

I. ZUR ENTWICKLUNG DES RECHTS AUF RELIGIONSFREIHEIT

So bedeutsam freilich dieser Grundsatz für die Gestaltung der gesellschaftlich-kulturellen und der politischen Verhältnisse in Europa auch war, so kam es weder im frühen Christentum, noch im Mittelalter, auch nicht in den religiösen Stürmen der Reformation in Deutschland zur Ausbildung der Idee und eines Rechtes auf Religionsfreiheit. Nicht der einzelne hatte ein Recht, sich zu seiner religiösen Überzeugung zu bekennen und sie zu leben, vielmehr bestimmte die weltliche Obrigkeit, welche Konfession auf ihrem Territorium legitimiert war, auch wenn im Zuge der weiteren Entwicklung „Ausnahmen" unter bestimmten Bedingungen zugelassen wurden. Wie der evangelische Theologe Martin Heckel zutreffend feststellt, entwickelte sich die Religionsfreiheit einerseits aus dem Reichsverfassungsrecht des konfessionellen Zeitalters, das für ganz Europa galt, andererseits aus den Vorstellungen der Aufklärung des 18. Jahrhunderts über die „natürliche Religion" und Moral[1]. Den Hintergrund, auf dem die Religionsfreiheit wie auch alle anderen Freiheitsrechte allmählich Konturen annahmen, bildete das Hervortreten der „Gesellschaft" mit ihren vielfältigen Strukturen zwischen den einzelnen, die in der Großfamilie beheimatet waren, und dem modernen Staat. Diejenigen Stimmen, die heute dem Christentum und der Kirche Vorhaltungen machen, warum sie nicht von Anfang an für die Religionsfreiheit eingetreten seien, machen sich zu wenig Gedanken über die geschichtlichen Voraussetzungen der Freiheitsrechte. Diese sind als Abwehrrechte gegenüber dem absolutistischen Staat entstanden, aber sie konnten nur entstehen, weil sich die Gesellschaft an der Schwelle zur Moderne als ein eigenes soziales Gravitationsfeld zwischen der Familie und dem Staat entwickelte. Dies darf freilich nicht zu dem Fehlschluß verleiten, früher habe es keine gesellschaftlichen Freiheitsräume gegeben. In besonderem Maße gilt dies für den Glauben und die Taufe. Die Kirche hat immer daran festgehalten, daß diese nicht erzwungen werden können und dürfen, daß sie vielmehr allein in der freien Entscheidung eines Menschen liegen.

Erst auf dem Boden der modernen Gesellschaft gedeiht die Religionsfreiheit. Es ist das Verdienst Joseph Listls, den Entwicklungslinien des Grundrechts der Religionsfreiheit nachgegangen zu sein. Er verweist auf den Jahrhunderte dauernden geistesgeschichtlichen Prozeß, in dessen Verlauf der Mensch sich in zunehmendem Maße seines Rechtes bewußt wurde, auf dem Gebiet des Glaubens und der Religion unabhängig vom Einfluß des Staates seine Entscheidungen zu treffen[2]. Nicht nur der katholischen Kirche fiel es schwer, auf dem II. Vatikanischen Konzil ihre traditionelle Position, wonach nur die Wahrheit und die wahre Religion ein Existenzrecht haben

---

[1] Martin Heckel, *Religionsfreiheit: I. Geschichte und Grundsatzfragen*, in: *Staatslexikon*, 7. Aufl., Bd. 4 (1987), Sp. 822.
[2] Joseph Listl, *Die Religionsfreiheit als Individual- und Verbandsgrundrecht in der neueren deutschen Rechtsentwicklung und im Grundgesetz*, in: *Essener Gespräche zum Thema Staat und Kirche*, hrsg. von Joseph Krautscheidt und Heiner Marré, H. 3, Münster 1969.

und Anspruch auf staatlichen Schutz erheben können, aufzugeben und eine Neuorientierung ihrer Lehre über das Grundrecht der Religionsfreiheit und über die Verpflichtung des Staates zur Gewährleistung staatsbürgerlicher religiöser Freiheitsrechte vorzunehmen. Erinnert sei an das Engagement des heutigen Papstes Johannes Paul II., damals noch Erzbischof von Krakau, für die Religionsfreiheit.

Das Konzil geht von der Würde der menschlichen Person aus, die das Recht auf Religionsfreiheit hat. „Die Freiheit besteht darin, daß alle Menschen frei sein müssen von jedem Zwang sowohl von seiten einzelner wie von gesellschaftlichen Gruppen wie von jeglicher menschlicher Gewalt, so daß in religiösen Dingen niemand gezwungen wird, gegen sein Gewissen zu handeln, noch daran gehindert wird, privat und öffentlich, als einzelner oder in Verbindung mit anderen – innerhalb der gebührenden Grenzen – nach seinem Gewissen zu handeln"[3].

Auch der Staat gelangte erst nach vielen Um- und Irrwegen und über verschiedene Vorstufen dazu, allen Machtansprüchen des früheren Staatskirchentums zu entsagen und die Religionsfreiheit für alle Bürger und Religionsgemeinschaften zu gewährleisten[4].

Im 19. Jahrhundert schälte sich zuerst die Religionsfreiheit als Grundrechts des Glaubens, Gewissens und Bekenntnisses und der freien Religionsausübung für jedermann heraus. Allerdings wurde die Religionsfreiheit zunächst vornehmlich von Freigeistern und Dissidenten in Anspruch genommen, wohingegen die große Mehrheit der Bevölkerung in der Volkskirche des immer noch christlichen Staates beheimatet war. Auch wer nicht glaubte und bekannte oder anderer Überzeugung als die Mehrheit war, konnte sich auf die Religionsfreiheit berufen und sicher vor staatlichen Sanktionen sein. Im Zuge der Französischen Revolution und der gesellschaftlichen Umbrüche trat dieses eher antireligiöse Moment der Religionsfreiheit hervor. Reli-

---

[3] Zweites Vatikanisches Konzil, *Erklärung über die Religionsfreiheit* (1965), Nr 2. Diese Freiheit darf nicht losgelöst werden von der Verpflichtung aller Menschen, „die Wahrheit, besonders in dem, was Gott und seine Kirche angeht, zu suchen und die erkannte Wahrheit aufzunehmen und zu bewahren" (ebd., Nr. 1). Das Bekenntnis des Konzils zur Religionsfreiheit darf deshalb nicht in der Weise interpretiert werden, als ob die Kirche von der Verpflichtung des Menschen zur Gottesverehrung und zur Suche nach der Wahrheit irgendwie abgerückt wäre. – Einer der Wegbereiter der Erklärung über die Religonsfreiheit war der nordamerikanische Theologe John Courtney Murray. Vgl. zu Person und Werk die Studie (mit umfassender Bibliographie): Reinhold Sebott, *Religionsfreiheit und Verhältnis von Kirche und Staat* („Analecta Gregoriana" Bd. 206), Roma 1977.

[4] Vgl. Martin Heckel, *Zur Entwicklung des deutschen Staatskirchenrechts von der Reformation bis zur Schwelle der Weimarer Verfassung*, in: „Zeitschrift für evangelisches Kirchenrecht", Bd. 12 (1966/67), S. 34 f.

gionsfreiheit erschien damals als Kampfbegriff, als Abwehrfreiheit für einzelne und Minderheiten gegen die noch bestehenden Verhältnisse von Staat und Kirche. Erst mit der Säkularisierung der Gesellschaft und der Trennung des Staates von der Kirche gewinnt die Religionsfreiheit in Deutschland schon während der Kulturkampfzeit und verstärkt im 20. Jahrhundert für die Mehrheit der Gläubigen und der kirchenzugehörigen Bevölkerung reales Gewicht und rechtliche Relevanz, und zwar als „positive Religionsfreiheit": als Freiheit des Bekennens, des Gottes- und Nächstendienstes in der Welt, mithin auch des Geltendmachens der eigenen religiösen und sittlichen Überzeugung bei der Gestaltung der gesellschaftlichen und politischen Verhältnisse[5].

II. DIE SOZIALE DIMENSION

Von der individuellen Religionsfreiheit muß die soziale Dimension der Religionsfreiheit unterschieden werden. Sie betrifft die Freiheit der Kirche beziehungsweise das Verbandsgrundrecht. Erst im 20. Jahrhundert setzte sie sich mit dem Abbau der staatlichen Kirchenhoheit und des landesherrlichen Kirchenregiments durch[6].

Um das, was mit „sozialer Dimension der Religionsfreiheit" gemeint ist, verstehen zu können, muß man die geistesgeschichtlichen Zusammenhänge befragen. Die Freiheitsrechte und die Idee der Menschenrechte wurden unter dem Einfluß der liberalen Bewegung als Grundrechte des Individuums gesehen, die gegen den überkommenen absolutistischen Staat und gegen die traditionelle Verbundenheit von Thron und Altar erkämpft werden mußten. Unter diesen Prfämissen war die Religionsfreiheit als Grundrecht des Individuums denkbar, aber nicht in ihrer sozialen Dimension als Kirchenfreiheit. Die liberale Losung der Trennung des Staates von der Kirche und der Kirche von der Schule, die dann auch von der sozialistischen Bewegung übernommen wurde, war die Kampfparole, die sich gegen die „alten Mächte" richtete.

Noch gravierender jedoch war das liberale Credo, das die gesellschaftlichen Wirklichkeiten in ihrer öffentlichen Dimension nicht anerkennen wollte, sondern sie in den Privatbereich verbannte. Dies galt für die Organisierung der industriellen Wirtschaftsverhältnisse ebenso wie für die kulturellen und religiösen Bereiche. Die liberalen Parteien taten sich schwer, Gewerkschaften und Arbeitgeberverbände als Ordnungsträger der wirtschaftlichen

---

[5] Martin Heckel, *Religionsfreiheit*, a. a. O., Sp. 824.
[6] Vgl. Gerhard Anschütz, *Die Verfassungs-Urkunde für den Preußischen Staat vom 31. Januar 1850*, Berlin 1912, S. 184 f.

und sozialen Verhältnisse anzuerkennen, weil sie darin Störfaktoren für den Markt erblickten, was sich nur nachteilig auf die Wohlfahrt auswirken konnte. Aus denselben Denkansätzen heraus trat man zwar für die Assoziationsfreiheit der Individuen in allen gesellschaftlichen Bereichen ein, aber die Assoziationen sollten im privaten Bereich verbleiben und keine das Individuelle übergreifende soziale Struktur werden. Die Gesellschaft wurde nicht in ihrer eigenen Qualität erkannt, sondern nur als Summe von Individuen, die bei Bedarf „Verträge" mit anderen schließen (Ehevertrag, Arbeitsvertrag, Gesellschaftsvertrag). Die individualistische Sicht der Gesellschaft ist die eigentliche Wurzel für die Auffassung, wonach Religion und auch Kirche Privatsache seien, die als solche selbstverständlich den staatlichen Gesetzen, die für alle galten, unterworfen wären und ihre Angelegenheiten nur so weit „selbständig" regeln können, wie sie sich in das staatliche Reglement einfügen.

Anders verlief die Entwicklung in Nordamerika. Hier fehlte der Kampf gegen die „etablierten Mächte", der sich allenfalls gegen die politische Abhängigkeit von Großbritannien richtete. Der weltanschaulich neutrale Staat wiederum trug den religiösen Überzeugungen bei den verschiedenen Einwanderergruppen Rechnung und verhinderte, daß der Gedanke einer Staatskirche überhaupt an Boden gewinnen konnte. Es kam aber nicht zu der antikirchlichen und auch antireligiösen Stoßrichtung, wie sie in Europa die Entwicklung belastete. Während die Französische Revolution und die liberale Bewegung von einer rein innerweltlich begründeten Idee der Menschenrechte ausgehen, heißt es in der amerikanischen Unabhängigkeitserklärung von 1776: „Folgende Wahrheiten halten wir für selbstverständlich: daß alle Menschen gleich geschaffen sind; daß ihr Schöpfer ihnen gewisse unveräußerliche Rechte verliehen hat; daß dazu Leben, Freiheit und das Streben nach Glück gehören". Die Überzeugung, daß der Mensch aus der Schöpferhand Gottes hervorgegangen und mit unveräußerlichen Rechten von Gott ausgestattet ist[7], die Überzeugung also von der Existenz Gottes und einer universalen sittlichen Ordnung ist die Grundlage des sozialen Lebens – nicht eine „neutrale" Indifferenz und schon gar nicht eine kämpferische Antihaltung.

Von diesen Grundlagen her besitzt die Religionfreiheit auch eine soziale Dimension, so daß sich die Religionsgemeinschaften und auch die Kirchen in Freiheit und Unabhängigkeit entwickeln konnten. Glaube und Religion waren und sind in Nordamerika gesellschaftliche Wirkkräfte – nicht Privatsache, so wie auch die weltanschauliche Neutralität des Staates nicht als

---

[7] Albrecht Langner, *Die politische Gemeinschaft*, Köln 1968, S. 26-29. – Auch der Einwand, daß bei den Vätern der amerikanischen Verfassung deistische Vorstellungen mit am Werk waren, ändert an dem Sachverhalt nichts.

Wertneutralität verstanden wurde, wie es das Bekenntnis zum Schöpfer--Gott in der Verfassung zeigt.

Nach dem Ende der Gewaltherrschaft des Nationalsozialismus und nach den Verheerungen des Zweiten Weltkrieges kam es in Europa zur geistig--kulturellen Erneuerung. Die Menschenrechtserklärung der Vereinten Nationen (1948) folgte der nordamerikanischen Tradition, ebenso die Europäische Menschenrechtskonvention des Europa-Rates (1950). Damit war der Weg frei für eine unbefangene Sicht des Glaubens und der Religion, der Kirchen und der Religionsgemeinschaften, auch wenn die bisherigen Verkrustungen in einzelnen Ländern noch lange nachwirken sollten. In Deutschland, wo die religiösen und sittlichen Zerstörungen besonders tief gegangen waren, waren die Erneuerung und die Besinnung auf das kulturelle Erbe das Gebot der Stunde. Viele Christen engagierten sich in allen Bereichen des öffentlichen Lebens. Das Grundgesetz bekennt sich zur Verantwortung des deutschen Volkes vor Gott, zur unantastbaren Würde jedes Menschen und zu seinen Grundrechten, die auch demokratische Mehrheiten in ihrer Substanz nicht ändern können. Die Religionsfreiheit in Art. 4 des Grundgesetzes wird nicht nur als individuelles Grundrecht anerkannt, sondern auch in ihrer sozialen Dimension. Die Rechtssprechung des Bundesverfassungsgerichts hat seither die Freiheit der Kirchen, ihre Angelegenheiten in eigener Zuständigkeit und Verantwortung zu regeln, weiterentwickelt[8].

Auch das Konzil hat die Freiheit der Religionsgemeinschaften betont und sie in einem ursprünglichen Zusammenhang mit dem persönlichen Recht auf Religionsfreiheit gesehen: Die Freiheit als Freisein vom Zwang in religiösen Dingen muß den einzelnen auch zuerkannt werden, wenn sie in Gemeinschaft handeln. „Denn die Sozialnatur des Menschen wie auch der Religion selbst verlangt religiöse Gemeinschaften"[9]. Sie haben die Freiheit, daß sie sich gemäß ihren eigenen Normen leiten. Sie dürfen nicht durch Mittel der Gesetzgebung oder durch verwaltungsrechtliche Maßnahmen der staatlichen Gewalt daran gehindert werden, ihre eigenen Amtsträger auszuwählen, zu erziehen, zu ernennen und zu versetzen. Sie dürfen keine Behinderung bei der öffentlichen Lehre und Bezeugung ihres Glaubens in Wort und Schrift erfahren, auch nicht, was die besondere Fähigkeit ihrer Lehre zur Ordnung der Gesellschaft und zur Beseelung des ganzen menschlichen Tuns betrifft. Das Konzil argumentiert nicht mehr entlang der früher vertretenen Linie, sondern sieht die Freiheit der Kirche im Recht auf

---

[8] Hier sei nochmals auf die schon genannten Arbeiten Joseph Listls verwiesen, die neuerdings gesammelt vorliegen: *Kirche im freiheitlichen Staat. Schriften zum Staatskirchenrecht und Kirchenrecht*. Hrsg. von Josef Isensee und Wolfgang Rüfner in Verbindung mit Wilhelm Rees, Halbbd. 1 und 2, Berlin 1996.

[9] Zweites Vatikanisches Konzil, *Erklärung über die Religionsfreiheit*, Nr. 4.

Religionsfreiheit begründet, „wonach Menschen aus ihrem eigenen religiösen Sinn sich frei versammeln oder Vereinigungen für Erziehung, Kultur, Caritas und soziales Leben schaffen können"[10].

III. LAIZISTISCHE TENDENZEN

Allerdings gibt es heute in nicht wenigen Ländern in Europa, auch in den USA, gegenläufige Tendenzen, die sich, wenn sie sich durchsetzen könnten, sehr einschränkend auf die Religionsfreiheit auswirken würden. Im Zuge der neuen „Aufklärung" und Säkularisierung und der 68er Revolutionen kam es auch in Deutschland zu einem Wiederaufleben liberaler Positionen aus dem 19. Jahrhundert. Die so wohlklingende Maxime „Freie Kirche im freien Staat" sollte dazu herhalten, erneut Glaube und Religion zur Privatsache zu erklären und die Kirchen und Religionsgemeinschaften aus dem öffentlichen Leben zurückzudrängen. Die neuralgischen Bereiche sind nicht nur die Politik, wo die sozialliberalen Kräfte die Stellungnahmen der katholischen Kirche zur Abtreibung, zu Ehe und Familie, zu grundsätzlichen Wertorientierungen als eine nicht legitime Einmischung zurückgewiesen haben. Es gibt Tendenzen, die viel weiter reichen, die, wie dies im Jahre 1995 besonders deutlich wurde, das Kreuz, überhaupt religiöse Symbole und Zeichen nicht nur aus staatlichen Einrichtungen, sondern aus den gesellschaftlichen Lebensräumen verbannen möchten[11]. Hier werden laizistische Strömungen virulent, die versuchen, über die Massenmedien und in zunehmendem Maße über die Gerichte an Einfluß zu gewinnen und ihre kulturkämpferischen Ziele der anders gesinnten Mehrheit des Volkes aufzuzwingen. Auch in den USA haben die laizistischen Gruppierungen, die über viel Geld verfügen und vernehmlich in den Ballungszentren der Ostküste wirken, über die Medien einen großen Einflußbereich. Besonders schlimm wirkt sich aus, daß das höchste Gericht, der Supreme Court, seit den sechziger Jahren unter dem Deckmantel der weltanschaulichen Neutralität des Staates immer heftiger für eine sittliche Wertneutralität des öffentlichen Lebens eingetreten ist. Eine Reihe von Urteilen steht im offenen Gegensatz zu den Grundlagen der Amerikanischen Verfassung und den Überzeugungen der großen Mehrheit des Volkes.

In diesen Auseinandersetzungen spitzt sich die Frage darauf zu, ob der positiven oder der negativen Religionsfreiheit der Vorrang gebühre. Unter der negativen Religionsfreiheit versteht man das Recht des Menschen, seine

---

[10] Ebd.
[11] Vgl. *Schule ohne Kreuz?* Mit Beiträgen von Peter Lerche, Hans Maier, Anton Rauscher, Walter Ziegler, in: „Kirche und Gesellschaft", Sonderheft, Köln 1995.

religiöse Überzeugung nicht offenbaren zu müssen. Die Problematik beginnt dort, wo daraus gefolgert wird, daß dieses Recht so weitreichend sei, daß es auch die Ausübung der positiven Religionsfreiheit blockiere, wenn die negative Religionsfreiheit in anderer Weise nicht gesichert werden kann. Wenn ein Schüler, weil seine Eltern eine atheistische Erziehung praktizieren, nicht am Schulgebet in der Klasse teilnehmen will, oder wenn er durch den Anblick des Kreuzes im Klassenzimmer sich in seiner „Religionfreiheit" beeinträchtigt fühlt, dann sei ihm das nicht zuzumuten. Deshalb habe das Schulgebet zu unterbleiben und müsse das Kreuz aus dem Klassenzimmer verschwinden.

Die Privilegierung der negativen Religionsfreiheit würde nicht nur religiös-sittliche Wertorientierungen in Grundsatzfragen der staatlichen Ordnung treffen, sondern überhaupt Glaube und Religion aus der Gesellschaft verdrängen. Auch die Kirchen und Religionsgemeinschaften würden nicht mehr als für die Gesamtgesellschaft wesentliche und unverzichtbare Kräfte gelten, vielmehr würden sie über kurz oder lang tatsächlich nur noch zur „Privatsache" werden. Glaube und Kirche wären nicht mehr gesellschaftliche Dimensionen der menschlichen Existenz, sondern würden in den Bereich subjektiver Beliebigkeit fallen. Dies würde auch darauf hinauslaufen, den universalen Verkündigungsauftrag der Kirchen einzuschränken und zu reglementieren[12].

Welches Gewicht Religion und Glaube bei den Bürgern hat, und welche Zuordnung von Staat und Kirche sein soll, ob eine feindselige Trennung, ein mehr oder weniger Nebeneinanderher oder eine offene und von beiden Seiten interessierte Zuordnung gelten soll, dies hängt in der pluralistischen Gesellschaft und im konfessionell und weltanschaulich neutralen Staat nicht von der Gunst der Regierenden, nicht von rechtlich eingeräumten oder geschichtlich zugewachsenen Privilegien ab. Der weltanschaulich neutrale Staat hat keine Zuständigkeit für religiöse Wahrheiten. Aber das bedeutet nicht, daß der Staat der Religion gegenüber „neutral" oder gleichgültig sein könnte. Dies ergibt sich aus seiner Gemeinwohlaufgabe, wozu, und zwar an oberster Stelle, der Schutz für die Grundwerte und Grundrechte gehört. Der Staat kann sie nur schützen und sichern, wenn und insofern sie nicht nur für die Staatsbürger und für die Gesellschaft, sondern auch für den Staat selbst von grundlegender Bedeutung sind. Zu diesen Grundwerten und -rechten gehört die Religionsfreiheit, die auch die Freiheit der Kirchen und der Religionsgemeinschaften einschließt. In diesem Sinne betont das

---

[12] Vgl. die Aussage der Pastoralkonstitution *Gaudium et spes* des II. Vatikanischen Konzils, Nr. 76: Die Kirche kann durchaus auf Privilegien und legitim erworbene Rechte verzichten, aber nicht auf das Recht, in wahrer Freiheit den Glauben zu verkünden und ihre Soziallehre kundzumachen.

Konzil: „Der Schutz und die Förderung der unverletzlichen Menschenrechte gehört wesenhaft zu den Pflichten einer jeden staatlichen Gewalt"[13]. Der Staat ist gehalten, durch gerechte Gesetze und andere geeignete Mittel den Schutz der Religionsfreiheit aller Bürger wirksam zu gewährleisten und für die Förderung des religiösen Lebens günstige Bedingungen zu schaffen, damit die Bürger ihre religiösen Rechte auch wirklich ausüben und ihre religiösen Pflichten erfüllen können.

Die Religionsfreiheit ist auch bedeutsam für die Wahrung des sittlichen Kerns der übrigen Grundwerte und damit der Verantwortlichkeit der Staatsbürger für diese Grundwerte. Wenn es für den Staat und seine Aufgaben gleichgültig wäre, ob sich die Bürger, ob eine Mehrheit von Staatsbürgern sich zu ihrer Verantwortung vor Gott bekennt, ob sie desgleichen die Grundwerte und Grundrechte als vorgegebene Grundwerte und Grundrechte achten und bejahen, dann würde sich die Wertgebundenheit des Staates reduzieren auf innerweltlich erkannte Notwendigkeiten für das Zusammenleben. Wenn aber, wie das Zeitalter der Ideologien und des Totalitarismus, auch des Aufeinandereinschlagens der Völker gelehrt hat, die Besinnung auf Gott die Entartung des Menschen, der Gesellschaft und des Staates verhindert, dann wird sich der Staat seiner Wertgebundenheit bewußt sein müssen, nämlich jener sittlichen Werte, um an einen Gedanken Ernst-Wolfgang Böckenfördes zu erinnern, die er zwar nicht selbst hervorbringen kann, auf denen er jedoch aufruht.

Der Laizismus ist wie der Atheismus bisher den Beweis schuldig geblieben, daß er auf die Dauer in der Lage ist, das Humanum zu sichern und nicht in die Inhumanität abzugleiten. Wie Hans Maier betont, war und ist Deutschland kein „Etat laíc". „Staat und Kirche stehen – wie auch Richter des obersten Gerichts jahrzehntelang betont haben – in einem auf «Wertoffenheit» und wechselseitigem Verständnis begründeten Verhältnis der «Koordination» und «Kooperation». Gewiß, es gibt keine Staatskirche. Der Staat bekennt sich nicht zu einem Glauben. Aber er schützt die christlichen Bekenntnisse und arbeitet mit ihnen zusammen, er sieht in ihnen wichtige Faktoren des öffentlichen Lebens – wohl wissend, daß er die geistig-weltanschaulichen Voraussetzungen, auf denen seine eigene Wertordnung beruht, nicht selbst geschaffen hat und schaffen kann"[14]. Der religiös-sittliche Be-

---

[13] Zweites Vatikanisches Konzil, a. a. O., Nr. 6. – Hier sei darauf hingewiesen, daß zur Schutzaufgabe des Staates auch gehört, gegen Mißbräuche, die unter dem Vorwand der Religionsfreiheit vorkommen können, vorzugehen. Die Anhänger von Teufelskulten beispielsweise können sich nicht auf die Religionsfreiheit berufen; ihnen muß im Interesse der öffentlichen Sittlichkeit Einhalt geboten werden (vgl. ebd., Nr. 7).

[14] Hans Maier, *Geschichtsblind und schulfremd. Zur kulturpolitischen Bedeutung der 'Kreuz-Entscheidung'*, in: Schule ohne Kreuz, a. a. O., S. 9 f.

reich darf nicht, wie Klaus Stern hervorhebt, aus der staatlichen Existenz ausgeklammert werden und in einen Laizismus mutieren, der alle religiösen Elemente aus dem öffentlichen Leben verbannt und zur offiziellen Etablierung einer säkularen Weltanschauung ohne Gott führt[15].

Ob in einem Staat und in einer Gesellschaft und im öffentlichen Bewußtsein die Religionsfreiheit, und zwar die positive Religionsfreiheit lebendig ist, dadurch ist auch der Bestand der anderen Freiheits- und Menschenrechte bedingt. Richtig verstanden kann man sagen: Die Religionsfreiheit ist die Garantie der Grundfreiheit und der Fähigkeit einer Gesellschaft, Übergriffen gegen die Würde und die Grundrechte eines jeden Menschen entgegenzutreten und die Freiheitsfeindlichkeit totalitärer Machttendenzen zu entlarven.

---

[15] Klaus Stern, *Die Fehler der Richter*, in: „Die politische Meinung", 40. Jg. (November 1995), Nr 312, S. 8.

FRANCESCA RIVETTI BARBÒ
Università degli Studi di Roma
Italy

LIBERTÉ ET VÉRITÉ.
DU SAVOIR COMMUN À LA PHILOSOPHIE

I. CRISES DE NOS SOCIÉTÉS – MULTIPLES CONCEPTIONS DE LA LIBERTÉ

Aujourd'hui il y a bien des conceptions de la liberté, tout-à-fait différentes les unes des autres. C'est un signe du fait que, actuellement, nos sociétés occidentales sont décidément multiculturelles. L'idée que l'on se fait de la liberté dépend en effet, précisément, de notre culture: que chacun partage, normalement, avec un groupe de personnes ou un autre.

La multiplicité des conceptions de la liberté, qui caractérise nos sociétés occidentales, est un symptôme des crises culturelles parmi lesquelles nous vivons. Elle en est aussi une des causes: peut être, sa cause principale.

Quantà vous, mes amis polonais, vous avez bien su lutter pour défendre votre culture contre ces cultures totalitaires, que l'on a cherché à vous imposer par la violence. C'est de toutes vos forces, et à tout prix, que vous les avez combattues! Ainsi, vous avez su préserver votre culture, en même temps que votre vraie liberté; vous l'avez même rendue plus forte.

Ces crises culturelles – qui se représentent souvent, de nos temps, quoique de façons différentes – peut-on les surmonter? Certes oui! Pourvu que nous combattions pour un renouveau de nos cultures fondé sur la vérité.

1. *Que faire? Former une nouvelle «culture de la vérité»!* Que faire donc, pour sortir des crises culturelles de nos sociétés? Il nous faut lutter, même à contre courant, pour une nouvelle «culture de la vérité» (c'est ainsi que je voudrais l'appeler), enracinée dans la sagesse chrétienne de nos peuples.

Justement cette «culture de la vérité» est en état de de fonder une «civilité de l'amour»!

Ce lien (entre cette culture et la civilité de l'amour) est dû, avant tout, au fait que notre vraie liberté est strictement attachée aux vérités que nous réussissons à reconnaître: ceci ressort clairement dès que l'on parvient à une conception correcte de la liberté (ainsi qu'on va le voir, par la suite). Il s'agit en premier lieu de notre vraie liberté intérieure: la plus importante puisque, sans elle, il n'y aurait aucune vraie liberté extérieure.

Cette «culture de la vérité» est donc condition indispensable de notre vraie liberté et de son épanouissement. Par conséquent il est extrêmement important qu'elle prenne pied et se répande, grâce, si possible, aux efforts de tout le monde.

Parmis les vérités les plus importantes voici, successivement, tout ce qui concerne notre liberté intérieure: c'est à dire ces vérités qui nous font comprendre ce qu'est la vraie liberté humaine intérieure. Il s'agit surtout de certaines vérités qui ressortent mieux (ainsi qu'on va le voir) si on les compare aux difficultés que l'on rencontre à ce propos. En tant que «philosophe», c'est à nous qu'il revient de l'expliquer: voilà justement mon sujet[1].

Je vais commencer par une description d'un de nos actes libres, qui donne un aperçu des richesses de ses composantes [*n. 2*]. Ainsi je pourrai dessiner, en ébauche, soit une conception correcte de notre liberté [*n. 2.10*], soit quelques-unes des principales façons (tout à fait différentes les unes des autres [*n. 2.11*]) dont les gens usent de leur liberté.

Sur cette base, nous chercherons à comprendre quelles sont les raisons de principe des difficultés que l'on rencontre à ce propos. Il s'agit des raisons mêmes, qui sont aussi à l'origine des dites différences entre conceptions de la liberté[2], aujourd'hui si remarquables et si répandues.

De ces difficultées, on peut donner des explications différentes, situées à deux niveaux: d'une part des explications plus simples [*n. 3*], d'autre part des raisons plus profondes [*n. 4*].

Ces dernières sont les plus importantes: quoiqu' il arrive que l'on ne les remarque pas!

Ainsi l'on parviendra au noeud du problème [*n. 5*], on trouvera de quoi franchir tout obstacle [*nn. 6 et 7*] et de quoi mettre en évidence soit les

---

[1] Je devrai me limiter à des esquisses très rapides. C'est pourquoi je vais ajouter ici des notes, où j'indiquerai quelques-uns de mes écrits précédents, ainsi que quelques textes classiques.

Deux descriptions et analyses de la liberté se trouvent en F. Rivetti Barbò', *Lineamenti di antropologia filosofica*, Jaca Book, Milano 1994, pp. 254: chap. 6, «La liberté», pp. 161-192; et dans mon *Essere nel tempo. Introduzione alla filosofia dell'essere, fondamento di libertà*, Jaca Book, Milano 1990, pp. 247: chap. 15, pp. 215-232.

[2] Pour une justification de la thèse, d'après laquelle la multiplicité des conceptions contemporaines de la liberté dépend des difficultés que l'on rencontre à s'en faire une conception correcte, cf. F. Rivetti Barbò', *La fondazione della libertà umana: Dio-Amore*, dans A. Piolanti (curatore) «Atti del IX Congresso Tomistico Internazionale, San Tommaso d'Aquino, Doctor Humanitatis», 24-29 sett. 1990, vol. I, L.E.V., Roma 1991, pp. 224-236: nn. 1-6, pp. 224-232.

fondements de notre liberté [*nn. 8.1 et 8.2*], soit la raison principale de son ampleur [*n. 8.3*].

Que faire donc pour affirmer notre vraie liberté, grâce à une «culture de la vérité»? Il faut en parler à tout le monde, surtout aux plus jeunes: de façon compréhensible, pour eux. Mais... «on ne se comprend plus!». Ceci, est une expression tout à fait juste aujourd'hui, puisque même le langage est changé! Pour faire comprendre une terminologie, il faut donc la réintroduire à nouveau [*n. 2*]; pour ceci, rien de mieux que des exemples.

II. DESCRIPTION DE LA LIBERTÉ, À L'AIDE D'UN EXEMPLE

Je commencerai par une de nos expériences, des plus communes. Cela devrait être un discours qui s'adresse à tout le monde!

Qu se passe-t-il, quand nous prenons une décision libre?

Avant tout chaque décision libre est un acte vital[3], effectué par un être réel: substance vivante[4], homme-ou-femme, qui connaît et qui a des tendance. «Je décide, librement, d'escalader cette montagne, avec ces amis et ce guide». Pourquoi? Car ça m'attire!

1. [*Les objets de mes souhaits.*] Voici en effet ce que je me souhaite: la vue de là haut, si belle! Une journée avec ces amis: si bonne! Un bon guide...! J'organise ce projet en vue d'un repos avantageux pour l'ensemble de ma vie, considérée dans son unité: de façon que tout cela puisse aussi s'harmoniser, dans une unité ultérieure ... Ce guide, ces amis, ce repos ..., ils sont tous véritablement bons! En outre, tout ce qui a été énuméré jusqu'ici, c'est quelque chose (= est un «être»).

2. [*Les objets de mes choix: complexes, changeants, unis par des liens qui en forment des «réseaux».*] Voyons, de plus près, comment tout ceci se présente; ce que je choisis (c'est à dire ces êtres, si beaux et si bons), c'est bien complexe, et ça change. Par dessus le marché, tout ces êtres sont liés les uns

---

[3] Toutefois, pour en parler, il nous est indispensable d'utiliser des concepts, que l'on peut prendre de façon abstraite: donc même indépendemment de la vitalité de ces réalités dont on est en train de parler.

Ceci on doit le souligner, du fait que bien des discours philosophiques sont considérés, parfois à tort, comme «abstraits» et «statiques». D'autant plus que cette opinion peut dépendre du manque d'une conception correcte de notre façon de penser et de parler. Dans ce dernier cas, cela dépend donc d'un préjudice. A ce propos, cf. F. Rivetti Barbò', *Dubbi, discorsi*, verità, en *Lineamenti di filosofia della conoscenza*, Jaca Book, Milano 1985[1], pp. 206, 1991[2], pp. 216: surtout les chap. 6, 7 et 8, pp. 59-118.

[4] Pour une explication de la notion de substance individuelle et vivante, cf. mon *Lineamenti di antropologia*... cit., chap. 2, «Nous mêmes et les autres, substances vivantes», pp. 35-65.

aux autres (et avec d'autres choses encore), de façon à former des «réseaux»[5] (qui sont eux aussi extrêmement complexes, et en mouvement).

3. [*Mes projets: qui visent au réel et regardent des possibilités.*] Je choisis ou tel ou tel projet, en prévoyant qu'il se réalise! Entre-temps, c'est seulement une possibilité, quelque chose de possible.

4. [*Ma fin dernière.*] Mes décisions libres, je ne peux jamais les isoler du reste de ma vie: c'est donc toujours en vue d'un certain but global, que je me décide.

5. [*Des difficultés.*] Malheureusement, quelque mauvais accident peut toujours arriver!

6. [*Mes expériences intérieures.*] Mes «habitus» (vertus, vices, habitude à la maîtrise de soi ou bien facilité à perdre le contrôle...) ont une influence remarquable sur mes décisions libres. En mon for intérieur: voici la «voix de ma conscience» qui se fait entendre.

7. [*Ce que je pense, à ce propos.*] Tout ceci je le sais (plus ou moins clairement). Je me dis en effet: «c'est vrai: ce guide est vraiment bon!» Ou bien: «c'est vrai: cette promenade est vraiment reposante!» Etc.

8. [*Ce que je veux.*] Tout ceci je le veux, par des actes de volonté.

9. [*Je m'abstiens de décider.*] Parfois je décide de ne prendre aucune décision, par rapport à quelque chose.

10. [*Synthèse.*] La liberté humaine est donc constituée par des séquences d'actes (agir ou ne pas agir) qui sont, *a*) effectués par un homme-ou-femme; *b*) composés par des actes de connaître, et de tendre-à, quelque chose, y compris, en tout cas, à des actes de penser et de vouloir, *c*) conditionnés par ce qui est en rapport avec celui qui agit; en outre, *d*) chacun de ces actes a son influence sur les actes libres, successifs, de la même personne; tout ceci contribue donc à la formation de sa personnalité.

Ces composantes et ces caractéristiques se trouvent en tout acte libre, humain.

11. [*Quatre constatations sur l'immensité de notre liberté: soit, 1) à notre détriment, soit, 2) à notre avantage; ou avec, 3) des élans vers un idéal, ou bien avec, 4) des «rêveries» illimitées.*] Quant à liberté humaine en ce monde, on pourrait ajouter bien d'autres constatations. Je m'arrête à quatre, des plus importantes.

Chacun est tout à fait libre, tout le long de sa vie en ce monde. A tel point que, d'une part, 1) l'on peut se ruiner, il suffit de s'adonner à la drogue..., mais ça, c'est une contrefaçon de la liberté! D'autre part, 2) chacun

---

[5] «Tout se tient»: c'est le fameux mot de Ferdinand De Saussure, à propos du langage, que l'on doit appliquer à notre monde de l'expérience.

peut prendre de bonnes décisions et développer ainsi sa personnalité, voilà la vraie liberté[6].

Par dessus le marché, voici des désirs qui portent à l'infini[7]. Ainsi, 3) quelqu'un s'élance vers un idéal. Ou bien, 4) l'on se laisse prendre par «des rêveries», quelqu'un s'imagine aussi un «paradis terrestre»[8].

Il y a donc des façons bien différentes, de vivre la liberté. Par conséquent, il y a aussi des différences radicales entre les idées que l'on se fait, à ce propos. De quoi celà dépend-il?

III. VIS À VIS DES PROBLÈMES CONCERNANT LA LIBERTÉ PREMIÈRE SORTE D'EXPLICATIONS

Les raisons essentielles des différences entre les diverses façons de prendre des décisions libres se trouvent certes dans les composantes, si nombreuses, qui y contribuent (celles qui ont été partiellement indiquées au nn. 2.1 - 2.9). Ceci conditionne aussi nos différentes conceptions de la liberté.

Je vais mettre ceci en évidence très rapidement, et seulement à propos de quelques points. Après quoi je passerai [*au n.4*] aux raisons plus profondes, et peut-être les plus intéressantes.

1. [*Sur les «vérités sémantiques» face à la «vérité ontologique».*] En premier lieu, voici le plus important: les convictions[9] de chacun [*voir le n. 2.7*]. Il s'agit de ces «vérités» que chacun de nous reconnaît, en son for intérieur, par rapport aux composantes de nos décisions libres.

A ce propos, il nous faut nous souvenir du fait suivant; une proposition est «vraie» en tant qu'elle «dit» ce qui «est», en son objet[10]. Une propositon vraie s'accorde donc à la «vérité de cette chose» (sous tel ou tel aspect): sa

---

[6] Pour la différence entre «liberté vraie» et «contrefaçons de la liberté» (c'est à dire «pseudo-liberté»), cf. mon *Essere nel tempo...*, cit., chap. 15, nn. 15.3, 15.4, 15.5 et 15.6, pp. 220-232, et mon *Lineamenti di antropologia...* cit., chap. 6, nn. 6.2 et 6.3, pp. 163-171; cf. aussi mon *La fondazione della libertà umana...*, cit. nn. 3, 4, 5 et 6, pp. 226-232 et n. 8, p. 234.

[7] A ce propos, cf. mon *Essere nel tempo...*, cit., chap. 14, n. 14.2, pp. 190-193, et chap. 15, n. 15.6, pp. 231-232, et mon *Lineamenti di antropologia...* cit., chap. 4. nn. 4.6.5 pp. 122-123, et chap. 6, n. 6.6.2.2 et 6.6.3, pp. 190-191.

[8] Ceci est décrit très brièvement dans mon *Essere nel tempo...*, cit., chap. 14, n. 14.4.6, p. 202.

[9] La dernière décision de tout acte libre dépend d'un de nos actes de volonté [*cf. n. 2.8*]. C'est pourquoi nos actes de volonté sont importants, eux aussi, mais puisqu'ils sont guidés par nos convictions, ces dernières sont (à mon avis) encore plus importantes.

[10] Les propositions (qui sont le signifié de nos énoncés) sont en effet des expressions de notre pensée, que nous reconnaissons êtres vraies ou fausses; cf. mon *Dubbi, discorsi, verità*, cit., chap. 8 et 9, pp. 99-137.

«vérité ontologique»[11]. La «vérité des propositions» je l'appelle «vérité sémantique»[12], justement pour la distinguer de la susdite «vérité ontologique».

2. [*Vérités sémantiques concernant la liberté.*] Les vérités sémantiques qui entrent en jeu dans nos décisions libres regardent, en premier lieu, ce que l'on considère bon[13] (plaisant, utile, avantageux, honnête...); elles concernent surtout ce qui est plus ou moins bon. En l'occurence, l'on juge aussi de ce qui est plus ou moins beau[14].

En tout cas, on le pense ceci toujours en vue d'un certain but qui unifie la vie, peut-être par rapport à un certain idéal[15].

A propos des choix que l'on peut faire (qui devraient regarder ce qui est un «bien») l'important est de comprendre «ce que les choses sont», en réalité. Quant aux décisions qui concernent des évènements de nos vies, il s'agit d'être informé par raport à «ce qui se passe», réellement. Tandis qu'il n'est pas du tout important, de savoir ce que tel ou tel personnage a dit[16]...

---

[11] Quand on dit que ceci ou cela a «un sens», l'on rend explicite une première ébauche de notre connaissance de la «vérité ontologique» ou «vérité de l'être», que l'on appelle aussi «vérité transcendentale», puisque c'est un des «transcendentaux» (voir le n. 4).

[12] J'use «sémantique» pour indiquer ce qui regarde les signifiés de notre langage. Remarquons que tout signifié d'un énoncé, vrai ou faux, est une proposition, vraie ou fausse, exprimée par quelqu'un d'entre nous. En tant qu'il s'agit d'un signifié, la proposition relève donc de la «sémantique». Pour ce dernier concept, cf. F. Rivetti Barbò', *Semantica bidimensionale. Fondazione filosofica, con un progetto di teoria del significato*, ed. Elia, Roma 1974, pp. 476: pp. 13-26.

[13] Cf. St. Thomas, *In I Eth.*, l. 1, ed. Spiazzi, nn. 9-11, et S. Th., I, q.6, a. 2, ad 2um.
Pour la façon dont chacun de nous se forme le concept de «valeur vraie», et donc du «bon» (à partir de nos connaissances immédiates de certaines valeurs), cf. mon *Essere nel tempo*..., chap. 14, nn. 14.4, 14.5, 14.6, pp. 196-213.

[14] Cf. St. Thomas, S. Th., I. q. 5, a. 4, ad 1um; et ibid., q. 39, a. 8, c. Je ne peux pas m'arrêter sur ce point. Quand-même, voici un exemple: quelqu'un apprécie une «belle chanson», un autre aime un «beau rock and roll»...

[15] Pour une brève description, cf. mon *Essere nel tempo*..., cit., chap. 14, nn. 14.2 et 14.3.

[16] Cf. St. Thomas, *De Coelo et Mundo*, lb.1, lec. 22, nr. 9 «Studuim philosophiae non est ad hoc quod sciatur quid homines senserint, sed qualiter se habeat veritas rerum». C'est justement cela, qui devrait guider nos choix!
A propos de l'enseignement des «maîtres à penser», cf. St. Augustin, De Magistro, 13,45 (14) «...quis tam stulte curiosus est, qui filium mittat in scholam, ut quid magister cogitet discat?» Une idée semblable est écrite par A. Rosmini: «c'est rendre un service extrêmement précieux, que de soumettre à une juste critique certains enseignements des personnes les plus admirées: puisque ainsi l'on aide le public à séparer ce qu'il y a de faux dans leur célébrité, et à se rendre compte de ce qu'il y a de vraiment grand» (*Apologetica*, Milano 1840, «Prefazione», cit. en «Charitas», année LXX, mai 1996, pp. 150-151; traduit de l'italien).
A propos de notre connaissance de la «vérité des choses», voir aussi J. Baudrillard, *Le crime parfait*, ed. Galilée, Paris 1995; le titre de la traduction en italien (par G. Piana, ed. Raffaello Cortina, Milano 1996) est complété par *«La télévision, a-t-elle tué ce qui est réel?»*.

Par dessus le marché, toute «vérité sémantique» concernant ce que l'on décide pour l'avenir (qui est donc, pour l'instant, seulement quelque chose de possible [*cf. n. 2.3*]) ne peut pas être définitivement vraie; c'est une vérité «pratique».

Il n'est donc pas du tout si facile, de connaître tout ce qui est important en vue de la réalisation de notre vraie liberté! D'autant plus, que toute chose doit être considérée soit dans sa complexité, soit en tant que placée dans certains «réseaux», soit en tant que changement [*cf. n. 2.2*].

On pourrait s'arrêter aussi sur d'autres facteurs qui influencent notre liberté, mais je les laisse de côté.

3. [*Sur l'infini, que nous aimons désirer.*] J'ajoute un seul mot, sur nos désirs toujours inassouvis[17] qui s'expriment soit sous la forme d'aspiration à un idéal, soit quand on poursuit un «rêve», parfois même irréalisable [*cf. n. 2.11, sous 3) et 4)*]. Voici ce qui est fondamental, pour en donner une première explication; nous pensons en exprimant des concepts universels, et aussi, surtout, moyennant des concepts analogues. Ceci concerne, en particulier, le concept de «bon» (qui est en effet analogique[18]). C'est pourquoi notre volonté, qui suit notre pensée, est portée à désirer, constamment, quelque chose de plus et de mieux.

Ceci s'avère exact, surtout par rapport à tout l'ensemble de la vie de chacun. C'est bien à cause de cela, que l'un s'élance vers un idéal alors que l'autre est porté à «rêver» un «bonheur infini (= non-fini)», qui toutefois se réalise «en ce monde fini». Peut-être, arrive-t-il à le choisir, mais cela, c'est vouloir «l'impossible»! (Si ces termes sont pris ou sens «strict»).

4. [*A la recherche de raisons plus profondes.*] La façon dont on se sert des composantes de nos actes libres conditionne donc tout libre choix, ainsi que la conception de la liberté que l'on se fait. Ici se trouve une première explication de nos multiples façons d'envisager la liberté. Pouvons nous peut-être (à côté des explications du genre de celles données jusqu'ici) trouver des raisons plus profondes, pour expliquer ce qui concerne notre liberté?

A mon avis, oui!

C'est un fait que, de nos jours, l'on met en doute la possibilité même de connaître le réel, d'affirmer des vérités. Le «crime» dont parle Baudrillard semble donc être «parfait»! (Du moins en tant qu'il s'agit d'un doute).

Quand même, il y a toujours quelqu'un qui réussit à s'opposer à ce «crime», et avec succès. Pour une défense de cette thèse, cf. F. Rivetti Barbò', *Al di là della crisi delle verità*, en «La cultura europea del XX secolo. Le sue crisi e oltre», Atti del Seminario di Cadenabbia, 18-20 aprile 1986; ed. Konrad Adenauer Stiftung, Urbino, 1987, pp. 153-156.

[17] Cf. mon *Essere nel tempo...*, cit., chap. 14, n. 14.2, pp. 190-193, et chap. 15, n. 15.6, pp. 231-232, et mon *Lineamenti di antropologia...* cit., chap. 4. nn. 4.6.5 pp. 122-123, et chap. 6, n. 6.6.2.2 et 6.6.3, pp. 190-191.

[18] Cf. mon *Essere nel tempo...*, cit., chap. 14, nn. 14.5. 1, -2, -3, pp. 205-208.

IV. LE MANQUE D'ÉVIDENCE IMMÉDIATE DES TRANSCENDENTAUX: RAISON PROFONDE DES OBSCURITÉS CONCERNANT LA LIBERTÉ

La «vérité des choses» (ou «vérité de l'être» ou «vérité ontologique») a été mentionnée tout à l'heure, ainsi que le «bien», le «beau», l'«un», et aussi (dès les premières descriptions) l'«être». Qui a une certaine culture philosophique y reconnait cinq transcendentaux[19] (dans le sens que ce mot a, d'après la terminologie de la tradition qui remonte à Aristote): c'est à dire l'«être» et quatre de ses propriétés.

Néanmoins, ceci n'est pas immédiatement évident à tout le monde! Ces termes sont en effet connus, par la majorité des gens, de façon tout à fait superficielle. Il est même assez facile de les estropier, quant à leur signification: il en est ainsi, dès que l'on laisse de côté toute explication philosophique.

Pour le rendre tangible, voyons ce qui se passe à propos des termes qui sont les plus importants, pour comprendre notre liberté.

1. [*Par rapport au «bien».*] Il s'agit avant tout du «bien». Chacun de nous en a une connaissance initiale, en tant qu'il considère que ceci ou cela est, pour lui-là même, soit une valeur à réaliser, soit quelque chose qui est utile ou qui plait... C'est à dire, en tant que ceci ou cela est bon, pour celui même qui le prend en considération. C'est donc par rapport à soi que l'on comprend, en premier lieu, ce qu'est un «bien», cependant, il s'agit d'un point de vue extrêmement unilatéral! Par conséquent, notre façon d'envisager le «bien» est fortement conditionnée par nos habitudes, nos convictions morales, et aussi par les influences culturelles que l'on subit. C'est quand même à partir de cela, que chacun se forme une première idée du «bien». (Des considérations semblables sont valables aussi par rapport au «beau».)

Par dessus le marché, tout «bien» dont nous avons l'expérience, en ce monde, est complexe, se trouve placé en des «réseaux» d'êtres, et change continuellement (ainsi que nous l'avons dit plus haut *[n.2.2]*).

2. [*Par rapport au «vrai».*] Quant à ce qui est «véritablement bon», en principe, il s'agit du «bien», en tant que fondé sur la «vérité de l'être» ou «vérité transcendentale».

Nous voici donc face à la «vérité transcendentale» et à nos «vérités sémantiques», qui devraient s'y rapporter, car c'est suivant les «vérités sémantiques», que l'on peut connaître ce qui est «vraiment bon» ou «vraiment beau», etc. C'est à dire, exactement, c'est ainsi que l'on peut connaître ce

---

[19] Cf. St. Thomas, *De Ver.*, q. 1, a. 1, c. Ce terme à été introduit par la scholastique postérieure.

qui est tel en sa «vérité ontologique», puisque tout «être» est connaissable grâce à sa «vérité ontologique».

La «vérité ontologique» est donc la «splendeur» qui rend connaissable tout «être», et chacun de ses aspects, y compris sa «bonté», sa «beauté», son «unité»...

Toutefois, en ce monde, notre connaissance de la «vérité ontologique» de chaque être est, elle aussi, extrêmement superficielle, il suffit de penser à l'énorme limitation de toute connaissance en biologie, en physique, etc., et à la difficulté d'acquérir des connaissances philosophiques mieux fondées et plus profondes...

3. [*Synthèse, par rapport à tous les transcendentaux.*] Des considérations semblables pourraient aussi bien être faites pour chacun des autres transcendentaux.

Voici donc, en cette superficialité de notre connaissance des transcendentaux, une raison plus profonde expliquant les difficultés - que chacun de nous rencontre – à prendre des décisions qui soient véritablement libres, car ce sont bien les transcendentaux, qui se trouvent à la base de toute décision libre. (Pour s'en assurer, il suffit de voir la description donnée plus haut [*précisément au n. 2.1*]).

Cette superficialité est aussi une cause de l'ampleur de notre liberté, celle, en vertu de laquelle l'on peut même se droguer..., et s'acheminer ainsi vers une pseudo-liberté. Cette superficialité dépend à son tour d'une raison que l'on peut indiquer [*voir le n. 8.3*], pourvu que l'on pousse plus loin notre recherche.

4. [*Par rapport à tout «être» créé, en tant que tel: notre pensée vise surtout son «essence», notre vouloir vise surtout son «existence».*] On peut trouver une raison encore plus profonde éclaircissant certains aspects de notre liberté, si l'on considère le fait que tout «être» créé est réellement composé de son «essence» et de son «existence», et si l'on remarque[20] que ce qui est envisagé de préférence: a) par notre pensée, c'est son «essence»[21], b) par notre volonté, c'est son «existence»[22]. (Il s'agit seulement d'une «préférence», par rapport à l'«essence» et à l'«existence». Il ne s'agit pas du tout d'une exclusion de l'un ou de l'autre «côté» des «êtres» créés, d'autant plus qu'il ne peut y avoir «essence» sans «existence», et réciproquement.) Chaque acte libre est le résultat des deux, pensée et volonté. Justement à ce propos l'on peut trouver (ainsi que je vais le dire, très brièvement) une raison ultérieure à bien des difficultés de nos vies.

---

[20] Cf. mon *La fondazione della libertà umana...*, cit., n. 7.1, pp. 233-234.
[21] Cf. St. Thomas, *De Ver.*, q. 21, a. 1, c., vers la fin.
[22] Cf. ibid., et *C. Gent.*, I, chap. 37.

D'une part, 1) ce que nous désirons, surtout par des actes de volonté, devrait devenir réel (avoir, tôt ou tard, une existence réelle). D'autre part, 2) ce que l'on pense (de nos objets de désirs) devrait être infini: car il nous est facile de le penser ainsi. Pour mettre en évidence ce deuxième point, il nous faut nous souvenir du fait que (comme je l'ai dit plus haut) c'est suivant des concepts universaux et parfois aussi analogiques que notre pensée envisage tout, de sorte que ces concepts expriment aussi (en tant qu'il sont universaux et analogiques) des possibilités ultérieures, à l'infini! Mais en ce monde, tout être réel est fini, pas du tout infini.

Voici donc une raison encore plus profonde expliquant bien des chagrins, dus au déchirement entre notre soif d'infini et notre désir de réaliser nos espoirs, alors que ce qui nous manque, en ce monde, ce sont des réalisations effectivement infinies[23].

V. UNE CONCEPTION GLOBALE DU «TOUT»: INDISPENSABLE POUR BIEN COMPRENDRE NOTRE LIBERTÉ

Pour avoir des idées bien claires, quant à qu'est notre liberté, il nous faut avoir recours à une conception globale du «tout». Ceci on peut l'entrevoir, à partir des remarques faites jusqu'ici; toutefois on pourra le comprendre clairement, seulement sur la base de ce que nous allons dire d'ici peu.

Grâce à cette conception globale nous arrivons à comprendre quels sont les fondements de notre liberté [*cf. nn. 8.1 et 8.2*] et l'on peut remonter à la raison fondamentale de l'ampleur de son étendue [*cf. n. 8.3*].

VI. RÉVÉLATION DANS LE CHRIST ET APPROCHE PHILOSOPHIQUE DE LA VÉRITÉ GLOBALE

Cette vérité globale, c'est Jésus Christ qui nous l'a révélée. En Lui nous trouvons aussi la solution du problème du mal [*cf. n 2.5*]. Lui, qui nous offre l'aide – immense – de la grâce.

Nous pouvons quand même obtenir aussi une vue globale et vraie sur le «tout» par des raisonnements philosophiques. Ces raisonnements nous permettent en effet de remonter à la raison première de notre liberté, Dieu-Transcendant et Créateur, et puis de redescendre vers nous. Ceci nous per-

---

[23] Pour une explication de ce point, cf. mon *Lineamenti di antropologia...* cit., chap. 6, n. 6.6.2, pp. 189-190 Par dessus le marché, ce qui ne se réalise pas est source de désillusion, car plus l'espoir est intense, plus forte est la désillusion.

met de résoudre (du moins sous leurs aspects théoriques) bien des difficultés concernant notre liberté.

VII. DIEU, PROUVÉ SUR LA BASE DE NOTRE LIBERTÉ

Notre liberté nous offre un point de départ, pour un des «chemins» qui remonte à Dieu-Créateur. C'est un raisonnement «par l'absurde».

Si nous n'étions pas créés par Dieu-Transcendant, alors nous, et le monde entier, nous serions là: 1) par hasard; ou bien, 2) en tant que dérivations nécessaires d'un Absolu immanent, soit, a) comme une émanation nécessaire de l'Absolu, soit, b) comme un des moments d'une dialectique de type hégelien). Dans ces deux cas, nous ne pourrions pas agir librement.

En effet: 1) si tout est «par hasard», alors il n'y aurait rien de «bon» ou de «valable», et nous n'aurions aucune raison, de choisir quoique-ce-soit: puisque toute raison de choisir est une certaine valeur[24].

D'autre part, 2) si tout est une dérivation nécessaire de l'Absolu, alors rien ne peut être libre: pas même les individus humains.

Par conséquent: puisque – dans certains de nos actes – nous sommes libres, il s'en suit que, 3) nous sommes créés par Dieu-Transcendant.

En outre l'on peut prouver, en philosophie, que, 4) Dieu, Créateur du monde entier, est Amour-donneur[25].

VIII. NOTRE LIBERTÉ, FACE À DIEU AMOUR-DONNEUR

Ces vérités [3) et 4)] nous donnent une vue globale sur le «tout» qui nous assure, avant tout, que notre liberté nous est donnée par Dieu afin que la personnalité de chaque homme-ou-femme s'épanouisse pleinement.

Par dessus le marché, ces vérités nous permettent de comprendre, soit, 1) quels sont les fondements de notre liberté [*cf. nn. 8.1 et 8.2*], soit, 2) quelle est l'origine de son étendue [*cf. n. 8.3*]: qui, en ce monde, est illimitée.

---

[24] Pour une preuve de cette thèse, cf. F. Rivetti Barbò', *Speranza e verità, tra filosofia classica ed escatologia*, dans «Rivista di Filosofia neo-scolastica», LXXXVI, 1994, pp. 749-760.

[25] Cf., pour Dieu-Amour, St. Thomas, S. Th., I, q. 19, a. 1 et q. 20, a. 1.
Une nouvelle preuve de Dieu-Amour-donneur est en F. Rivetti Barbò, *Dall'essere-pregnante all'Assoluto-che-dona*, II. *L'ascesa*, dans «Riv. di Filosofia Neoscolastica», LXXI, 1979: fasc. 2°, pp. 245-289: P. III, pp. 280-289; cette preuve est reformulée dans mon *L'Assoluto è Amore-Vivente*, «Aquinas», 1988, n. 1, pp. 137-145.

1. *Le fondement premier de notre liberté*; Dieu. Voici le résultat des argumentations[26] qui mettent en évidence le premier de ces deux points.

Dieu a créé tout «ce qui est»; c'est pourquoi tout «être» est nécessairement pourvu de certaines propriétés. En effet, quant à tout ce qui est créé, 1) en tant qu'il est pensé par Dieu, le Souverain-Vrai, c'est un «être» qui a sa propre «vérité», sa «vérité ontologique»: que nous pouvons donc penser; 2) en tant qu'il est voulu par Dieu, le Souverain-Bien, c'est un «être» qui est «bon»: que nous pouvons donc aimer (en ce qu'il a de bon); 3) en tant que (en sa «vérité ontologique» et en sa «bonté») il reçoit de Dieu, Souveraine-Beauté, une certaine capacité d'éblouir, c'est un «être» qui est «beau»: que nous pouvons donc admirer (en ce qu'il a de beau).

Voici donc les transcendentaux dont dépend notre liberté; nous comprenons que leur présence en toute créature est nécessaire, en tant qu'elle est due à l'acte créateur de Dieu, Celui-qui-Est, souverainement Vrai, Bon, Beau.

C'est donc la présence, en tout, de ces transcendentaux, qui est assurée par la création de tout, de la part de Dieu; et c'est par rapport aux transcendentaux, que notre liberté peut exister [*cf. n. 4 et n. 2.1*].

Par conséquent Dieu, Amour-donneur, est le fondement premier[27] de la liberté humaine.

2. *Le fondement proche de notre liberté, l'«être», en tant que «vrai», «bon» et «beau»*. Le «vrai ontologique», le «bien» et le «beau» sont donc des propriétés de l'«être», de tout «être», soit de Dieu, soit de toute créature. (On l'a mis en évidence, tout à l'heure).

Puisque notre liberté est telle, par rapport au «bien», au «beau», et à la «vérité ontologique», puisque ceux ci, sont des propriétés de l'«être» en tant que tel, il s'ensuit que ce qui rend possible notre liberté c'est l'«être».

C'est donc l'«être», qui fonde notre liberté; c'est son fondement proche.

Toutefois il nous a fallu faire un détour, pour arriver à le comprendre. en fait, les résultats énumérés plus haut [*au n. 8.1*] ne sont pas du tout immédiatement évidents! Pourquoi nous trouvons nous en cette situation? Voici la raison.

---

[26] Ici je donnerai seulement un abrégé de quelques résultats de raisonnements d'une théologie philosophique, aux – quels l'on devrait ajouter ce qui concernee l'«unité» de l'«être».

[27] Cf. mon *La fondazione della libertà umana: Dio-Amore*, cit., n. 9, pp. 234-236 et mon *Libertà e fondazioni della bioetica: di fronte al morire*, dans S. Biolo (curatore) «Nascita e morte dell'uomo. Problemi filosofici e scientifici della bioetica», Atti del 46° Convegno docenti universitari, Centro studi filosofici di Gallarate, 4-6 aprile 1991, Marietti, Genova 1993, pp. 231-237.

3. *Dieu caché: cause de l'ampleur de notre liberté, en ce monde.* Nous n'avons aucune vue immédiate de l'Acte créateur de Dieu. C'est pourquoi nous n'avons pas non plus aucune évidence immédiate des raisons de l'appartenance des transcendentaux à tout être de ce monde. Par conséquent, il ne nous est pas facile de comprendre ces mêmes appartenances; nous arrivons seulement à les entrevoir.

C'est à cause de cela que, pendant notre vie en ce monde, l'amplitude de notre liberté arrive à son maximum: à tel point, que chacun peut choisir aussi ce qui est une contrefaçon de la liberté (voir celle de se droguer...).

Pour nous assurer la surabondance de notre liberté, Dieu, en ce monde, se «cache» bien. Ainsi, chacun peut même prendre un chemin qui le conduit loin de Dieu; toutefois, cela aussi est un don de Dieu! Lui, qui renonce à se faire tout de suite aimer par ses créatures intelligentes, pour nous donner une liberté plus large.

4. *Un point de vue hyper-optimiste sur notre surabondante liberté.* Chacun de nous a donc, en cette vie, une liberté surabondante: de telle façon, que c'est par des actes d'amour tout à fait libres, que chacun de nous est appelé à s'élancer vers Dieu.

Quand même, puisque Dieu est Amour-donneur, c'est en Lui que chacun peut trouver son assurance, pour affronter toute décision, en toute liberté. Voici donc une clarté nouvelle, qui illumine notre liberté d'un optimisme magnifique.

JEAN LADRIÈRE
Université Catholique de Louvain-la-Neuve
Belgium

LIBERTÉ ET ÉVÉNEMENT

La liberté peut être considérée en ce qu'elle est en elle-même, dans son essence. Elle se révèle alors comme une propriété de la volonté, qui est elle-même comprise comme puissance d'opération appartenant, en tant qu'accident d'ordre essentiel, à la substance que constitue l'étant humain. En tant qu'elle est une telle propriété, elle ne peut être atteinte ni par intuition ni par déduction, mais seulement par une analyse régressive, de caractère spéculatif, remontant de ce que la volonté manifeste d'elle-même jusqu'à son essence et à ses propriétés caractérisantes. Comme toutes les puissances d'opération, la volonté libre ne peut être connue qu'à travers les actes qu'elle produit, en tant qu'ils peuvent eux-mêmes être rejoints à travers les effets qu'ils engendrent. Ce en quoi la volonté libre se rend manifeste, et donc accessible à l'analyse, c'est son effectivité. L'étude de la volonté en elle-même procède de l'effectivité de la volonté à son essence. Mais une fois que l'on a formé le concept de la volonté libre, on est amené à retourner vers son effectivité, qui pose un problème spécifique, distinct de celui de l'essence: comment la volonté libre, qui est une puissance de l'esprit, peut-elle avoir une effectivité, c'est-à-dire s'insérer dans le cours du monde? Comment peut s'effectuer le passage d'une intériorité à l'extériorité? Ou bien la liberté n'est réelle que comme pouvoir purement intérieur, et elle n'est alors effective que des attitudes spirituelles de consentement ou de refus qu'elle peut commander, mais elle n'influe en rien sur les situations mondaines. Ou bien elle a une effectivité extérieure, mais alors il faut pouvoir comprendre comment cette conversion en extériorité est possible.

Cette question a été posée de façon assez radicale par Kant, dans un contexte culturel qui était marqué par une vision déterministe de la nature.

Il l'expose dans la troisième antinomie de la raison pure, qui concerne la causalité: "On ne peut concevoir que deux espèces de causalité par rapport à ce qui arrive, la causalité selon la nature et la causalité par liberté. La première est, dans le monde sensible, la liaison d'un état avec l'état précédent auguel il succède suivant une règle". Quant à la liberté, au sens cosmologique que Kant lui donne dans le contexte des antinomies, il la définit comme "la faculté de commencer de soi-même un état dont la causalité n'est pas subordonnée à son tour, suivant la loi de la nature, à une autre cause qui la détermine quant au temps". On retrouve dans la formule "de soi-même" l'idée classique de l'auto-déterminarion et dans la condition négative de non-subordination à une causalité naturelle l'idée classique de l'indépendance à l'égard de toute contrainte extérieure. Ce qui donne à la formulation kantienne son accent spécifique, c'est la référence à l'idée de "loi de la nature" et par là à une conception générale de la nature inspirée par la mécanique newtonienne.

La solution de l'antinomie est donnée par Kant sur la base de la distinction entre l'ordre nouménal et l'ordre phénoménal, correspondant à la distinction entre les deux espèces de causalité. Établir cette distinction revient à affirmer l'irréductibilité de la causalité libre à toute forme de causalité naturelle. Dans le vocabulaire de Kant, la liberté en tant que telle n'est pas un phénomène. La distinction étant posée, elle explique la compatibilité entre les deux formes de causalité, mais elle ne prouve pas encore la réalité de la causalité nouménale. Kant entreprend de l'établir dans son étude de la "raison pratique", en remontant de l'analyse de l'agir moral à ses conditions de possibilité. Cette démarche régressive est spéculative, non scientifique.

Mais une fois établies l'irréductibilité et la réalité de la liberté, il reste à aborder de façon positive le problème du rapport entre les deux formes de causalité. Montrer leur compatibilité n'est qu'une démarche préalable, mais elle ne suffit pas. Deux processus peuvent être compatibles tout en restant totalement extérieurs l'un à l'autre. Or s'il y a une effectivité de la liberté, c'est en tant qu'elle inscrit réellement sa marque dans l'ordre phénoménal. Si on peut parler d'une "causalité" de la liberté, c'est précisément parce qu'elle change quelque chose dans le monde. Dans l'acte libre s'effectue un passage entre un processus intérieur et un processus extérieur. Ce passage est un processus de métamorphose, de structure d'ailleurs fort complexe. Il y a d'abord la préparation de l'acte, au cours de laquelle le sujet agissant reconnaît le contexte dans lequel son action est appelée à s'inscrire, envisage les différents cours d'action possible, les évalue en fonction de ce qu'il sait des circonstances, des raisons qui peuvent recommander ou au contraire disqualifier chacun d'eux, des valeurs qui sont en jeu, de ce que prescrit, par rapport à la situation où il se trouve, la loi morale, et finalement forme le projet de l'action à entreprendre. Il y a ensuite le moment de la décision, où la volonté libre se résout effectivement à agir; c'est en ce moment que se concentre pour ainsi dire l'intervention de la liberté. Et enfin il y a la motion volontaire, qui prolonge la décision en exécutant, ou à tout le moins en tentant d'exécuter le projet qui a été élaboré. C'est dans ce troisième moment que s'effectue la rencontre entre une initiative intérieure, qui se donne son contenu dans le projet, et le cours du monde, en lequel ce contenu doit se projeter. L'acte libre s'engrène alors dans le flux de la réalité historique et cosmique. D'une part cette réalité impose à l'action des conditions, qui sont pour elle des contraintes, dont le projet doit tenir compte. Et d'autre part elle ouvre pour l'action un champ de possiblilités. Pour être raisonnable, l'agent doit inscrire son action dans ce qui lui est ainsi présenté comme possible, ou en tout cas dans ce qui lui apparaît possible, du point de vue où il se trouve.

Or cette insertion pose un double problème. D'une part, si la réalité phénoménale est absolument rigide, il n'est pas possible d'y introduire des déterminations qui ne seraient pas précontenues dans les lois qui régissent son évolution. Il n'est même plus pertinent de parler du possible dans ces conditions, car tout est nécessaire. D'autre part, l'inscription de la volonté libre dans l'univers n'est réelle que dans la mesure où elle s'y manifeste de façon visible, directement ou indirectement. C'est cette condition que Kant a en vue lorsqu'il parle de "la faculté de commencer de soi-même un état" non subordonné à une autre cause "suivant la loi de la nature". Ce qui est présupposé dans cette formulation c'est l'idée de série phénoménale: les phénomènes s'enchaînent dans le temps suivant une loi dynamique. La loi gouverne le passage de chaque état à l'état suivant, mais pour que la série soit entièrement déterminée il faut que soient fixées les conditions initiales. Ce que Kant suggère c'est que la liberté agit non pas sur la loi, mais sur les conditions initiales: elle est la capacité de poser d'elle-même le premier terme d'une série. Son intervention est effective dans la mesure où l'état qu'elle fait exister n'aurait pu être produit sans son intervention, par le cours normal de la nature. Une condition initiale posée par la liberté est une réalité empirique, phénoménale selon la terminologie kantienne. Mais elle entre dans l'existence en vertu d'une causalité qui n'est pas celle dont dépend l'enchaînement des phénomènes, qui est capable de susciter *par elle-même* son effet, autrement dit qui a le caractère d'une initiative. Ce qui pose problème c'est que c'est la même condition qui est le contenu de l'initiative et l'état empirique qui est au premier moment d'une nouvelle série phénoménale dans le monde. Comment s'effectue la transmutation de l'initiative, qui est de la nature d'un acte, dans un terme empirique comparable comme tel à tout autre? C'est très exactement en ce point que se situe le problème de l'articulation entre la liberté et le cours des choses.

Dans la troisième *Critique*, Kant invoque la finalité, qu'il met en contraste avec les aspects de la nature régis par le mécanisme. Les "lois de la nature" rendent compte de ce qui relève du mécanisme, mais elles ne déterminent que très partiellement la nature. La pensée "réfléchissante" doit introduire l'idée de finalité pour rendre compte de ce qui demeure irréductible au mécanisme, c'est-à-dire à ce qui est déterminable par les lois. Cet irréductible c'est tout le règne de l'organique, c'est-à-dire ce qu'on pourrait appeler les architectures de la nature. Cette distinction du mécanique et de l'organique donne une indication suggestive en ce qui concerne le premier problème, puisqu'elle permet de comprendre que la nature est loin d'être rigide. Quant au deuxième problème, la troisième *Critique* suggère l'idée d'une sorte de convergence entre la finalité naturelle, qui régit l'ordre des phénomènes, et la finalité nouménale, qui est la finalité morale poursuivie par la volonté libre. Mais ce que pourrait rendre possible une telle convergence ce serait l'assomption dans la finalité de la liberté des finalités de la nature. Il y aurait ainsi un emboîtement de l'ordre phénoménal dans l'ordre nouménal. Mais ce qu'il faut expliquer, pour rendre compte de l'effectivité de la liberté, c'est que le *même* terme est *à la fois* produit de l'initiative de la liberté et élément d'une série phénoménale.

Ces suggestions ayant été ainsi évoquées il faut reprendre à nouveaux frais l'examen des deux problèmes de la malléabilité de la nature et de l'initiative.

* * *

Examinons d'abord le problème de la malléabilité de la nature. Il est clair que si la nature est gouvernée par un déterminisme absolu, la liberté ne peut agir, au mieux, que sur des états purement intérieurs. La question est de savoir si, de fait, il y a un déterminisme absolu. Il convient tout d'abord, par rapport à la question qui nous occupe, d'écarter le recours à l'indéterminisme quantique. D'abord la question du statut de cet indéterminisme reste largement ouverte. Il se pourrait fort bien qu'il ne soit qu'une conséquence de l'incomplétude de la théorie quantique; il serait alors de nature épistémologique plutôt que de nature ontologique. Autre chose est la description qu'il est effectivement posible de donner de la nature, autre chose cette nature elle-même. De plus, même s'il y a un indéterminisme objectif, de nature ontologique, autrement dit s'il y a des lacunes de causalité, on ne peut assimiler un acte libre à un saut quantique. S'il y a effectivement de l'aléatoire pur dans la nature, le fait que telle possibilité se réalise plutôt que telle autre est sans raison. Or la liberté, dans son exercice, n'est pas sans raison; l'analyse de l'acte libre montre précisément qu'il n'est pas une sorte de "fiat", relevant d'une factualité pure, mais un acte raisonnable, c'est-à-dire fondé sur des raisons et capable de se justifier par les raisons qui l'inspirent.

L'indéterminisme quantique étant ainsi mis hors de cause, on peut dire qu'il y a déterminisme là où les conséquents sont déterminés univoquement par les antécédents selon des lois dynamiques. On pourra faire remarquer entre parenthèses que, de ce point de vue, la mécanique quantique doit être considérée comme déterministe, puisque les états d'un système quantique sont liés entre eux de façon univoque par une loi d'évolution. S'il y incomplétude, elle se situe dans la description de l'état, non dans la loi dynamique. Mais le point essentiel, dans l'examen de la question posée, c'est que tout ne s'explique pas par les lois dynamiques. C'est précisément ce que suggérait l'argument kantien de la troisième *Critique*. D'abord, comme on l'a déjà rappelé, même en ce qui concerne les processus évolutifs pour lesquels les lois dynamiques sont pertinentes, la détermination des états dépend non seulement des lois mais aussi des conditions initiales. Et celles-ci renvoient, de proche en proche, à des conditions de nature cosmologique, qui sont peut-être de l'ordre d'une factualité pure, et sont alors contingents de la contingence du factuel pur, ou qui pourraient éventuellement dépendre de certaines contraintes de caractère global, tout à fait distinctes des lois dynamiques, et qui alors seraient contingentes de la contingence de ces contraintes. Mais il n'y a pas dans la nature que l'aspect dynamique; il y a aussi ce qu'on pourrait appeler l'aspect structural, que visait le rôle attribué par Kant au „jugement réfléchissant". La nature se présente sous forme de systèmes plus ou moins complexes, susceptibles de se décomposer en sous-systèmes ou de s'intégrer dans des systèmes plus complexes. La structure de ces systèmes et les possibilités de construction ou de déconstruction qui leur appartiennent sont gouvernées par des contraintes, qui s'expriment sous forme de principes d'organisation. Le "principe de Pauli" (interdisant l'occupation du même état quantique par deux électrons) et le principe d'énergie minimale (prescrivant qu'un électron doit se placer dans un état d'énergie minimale disponible), en mécanique quantique, qui régissent les constructions atomiques, en sont un exemple. Ces contraintes sont de même nature épistémologique que les contraintes cosmologiques dont il vient d'être question: le cosmos comme tel peut en effet être traité comme un système global, contenant tous les autres et leur imposant par lui-même du reste des contraintes spécifiques. Or les effets de ces contraintes structurales, qui rendent intelligibles les architectures de la nature, dépendent des "conditions-frontières", qui expriment l'incidence du milieu extérieur sur le système, et peuvent donc être modifiés par modification de ces conditions. Ainsi un changement de température peut entraîner la dissociation des composants d'une molécule, dont la structuration est pourtant commandée en définitive par des règles quantiques. Rien ne s'oppose donc dans l'organisation de la nature à des interventions extérieures susceptibles de produire des effets artificiels de destructuration ou de restructuration, éventuellement selon des principes d'organisation inédits, pourvu que les contraintes naturelles soient respectées. On peut comprendre ainsi qu'il soit possible de construire un objet complexe, qui n'existe pas dans la nature, comme par exemple une machine à calculer. On peut remarquer du reste que les contraintes organisationnelles comportent un aspect de finalité, qui les rend analogues aux principes qui commandent la construction d'un objet artificiel. Dans le cas d'une architecture naturelle, la contrainte impose aux éléments mis en oeuvre d'interagir entre eux de telle manière que telle condition globale soit remplie. On le voit particulièrement bien dans le cas où la contrainte s'exprime sous la forme d'une loi d'extremum. De telles lois ont un caractère finaliste évident. Dans le cas d'un objet artificiel, la contrainte globale est l'effet à réaliser, par exemple la capacité de l'objet à réaliser un certain type de performance. Elle est donc bien de caractère finaliste. De part et d'autre, le mode d'action de la contrainte globale est d'intégrer l'action des lois dynamiques et celle des contraintes partielles qui s'imposent aux composants et à leurs interactions, sous l'égide d'une condition englobante, exprimant la finalité imposée au système global. C'est l'idée que Kant avait introduite dans la troisième *Critique*, en parlant de l'intégration du mécanisme dans le finalisme.

Mais il faut examiner de plus près comment, concrètement, se présente ce qu'on pourrait appeler le champ d'intervention de la liberté. Il convient pour cela de distinguer trois domaines d'intervention possible: celui de la nature extérieure, celui de la société et de l'histoire, et celui du soi de l'agent.

I. L'ACTION SUR LA NATURE

Pour que la volonté libre puisse avoir une effectivité dans le domaine de la nature extérieure il faut non seulement que celle-ci la laisse intervenir, passivement, mais aussi qu'elle lui offre un appui, qui doit rendre possible l'inscription effective du vouloir dans le cours du monde. La contribution demandée à la nature c'est une potentialité positive. Celle-ci doit être complémentaire d'une contribution venant de l'agent. Or cette contribution est essentiellement l'introduction locale, dans le fonctionnement normal de la nature, d'un concept organisateur, s'exprimant sous la forme d'un plan d'action et axé sur la production d'un système complexe de nature artificielle, répondant à certaines contraintes de caractère finaliste. Pour que le plan puisse se réaliser, l'agent doit pouvoir disposer de matériaux appropriés. La potentialité sur laquelle il espère pouvoir prendre appui c'est donc la disponibilité d'un segment de la réalité naturelle à l'égard d'une idée organisatrice. L'action effective est l'appropriation de ce segment naturel, constitué de me on le voit clairement déjà dans le deuxième livre de la *Physique* d'Aristote, il y a une analogie entre l'action organisatrice et le processus naturel de formation d'un nouvel organisme. De part et d'autre une finalité est à l'oeuvre, venue de l'extérieur dans un cas, immanente au processus lui-même dans l'autre.

On peut se représenter schématiquement une intervention dans l'univers naturel comme un processus de transition entre deux états, un état initial constitué d'un ensemble de composants, fournis par la nature, directement ou indirectement, à travers des interventions antérieures, et un état final constitué d'un système dans lequel ces composants sont intégrés en un tout organisé. En reprenant une expression utilisée par Whitehead on pourrait dire que la transition s'effectue entre un ensemble d'éléments donnés "disjonctivement" et ce même ensemble d'éléments donnés "conjonctivement". Le surplus de détermination qui s'ajoute à l'ordre disjonctif pour produire l'ordre conjonctif est de nature informationnelle. Cette détermination, à la différence des composants, ne vient pas de la nature mais d'une démarche d'invention, dont le résultat s'objectifie sous la forme d'une certaine représentation, dans laquelle l'agent se donne une anticipation de ce qui est à réaliser. La capacité de produire la représentation d'un état encore inexistant est une forme de spontanéité qui correspond dans l'ordre de la représentation à celle qui est caractéristique de la volonté libre dans l'ordre de l'action. Dans le schéma de l'intervention l'état initial ne peut évoluer de lui-même vers l'état final. Mais les éléments dont il est constitué ont des propriétés telles qu'ils sont réceptifs à l'égard de l'information, fournie dans la représentation, qui apporte le plan d'organisation selon lequel est engendré le produit de l'intervention. L'état initial est ainsi la contribution de la nature à la réalisation du projet.

Mais pour que la représentation soit effectivement projetée dans le réel il faut l'action et donc la mobilisation de la volonté libre, qui en est le principe. Or on peut légitimement se demander si elle est vraiment libre et donc si l'initiative de l'intervention est vraiment une initiative. En partant de l'hypothèse spéculative selon laquelle tout est absolument déterminé, on pourrait tenter d'interpréter l'action volontaire de façon déterministe. Ainsi on imaginera que les processus cérébraux, fonctionnant de façon entièrement déterministe selon des lois dynamiques compliquées, peuvent transformer des informations venant du dehors en représentations de nouveaux schémas d'opération et ensuite déclencher les gestes concrets qui doivent contribuer à la réalisation de ce qui est ainsi représenté. Et on invoquera éventuellement l'analogie d'une machine capable de créer des représentations inédites grâce à des processus purement opératoires. On obtient ainsi un modèle de l'action dans lequel le premier moment n'est pas une initiative mais une information venue d'autres systèmes, tout s'enchaînant à partir de là selon des lois dynamiques de même nature que celles qui régissent le jeu des forces cosmiques. Cette façon de voir met en jeu une certaine conception des rapports entre le mental et le somatique, ou, selon une terminologie plus métaphysique, entre l'âme et le corps, selon laquelle les états mentaux ne sont que des configurations d'états cérébraux. Une telle conception ramène la sucession d'états mentaux conduisant d'une représentation à une effectuation par l'intermédiaire d'une décision à un enchaînement d'états cérébraux liés déterministiquement. Elle aboutit donc à naturaliser l'esprit, et en particulier la volonté libre.

Une telle conception est-elle tenable? Pour en décider, il n'y a pas d'autres arguments que ceux que peut fournir une analyse de l'acte, considéré en tant que producteur de nouveauté, qu'il s'agisse de l'acte d'invention, ou de la décision, ou de la motion volontaire. L'acte peut être objectivé, mais la forme d'objectivation de l'acte n'est plus acte. Ainsi la pensée qui engendre une représentation nouvelle est un acte, mais la représentation objectivée qu'elle produit n'est plus elle-même acte. Et d'autre part l'acte peut avoir des conditions de possibilité de nature somatique. Ainsi il est très vraissemblable qu'un acte de telle ou telle espèce ne puisse être posé que moyennant l'occurrence préalable ou simultanée de certains états cérébraux. De tels états ont une objectivité qui les rend en principe accessibles à l'analyse scientifique. Mais l'acte comme tel n'est pas un état. Et il ne peut être conçu comme projection d'un état. Car ou bien la projection est elle-même un état, et alors si l'acte n'est pas un état il ne peut pas non plus être la projection d'un état. Ou bien ce qu'on entend par projection, c'est la relation de possibilisation qui relie un état à l'acte que cet état conditionne. Mais la possibilisation n'est pas une production, et une condition nécessaire n'est pas une condition suffisante. On ne voit pas comment un état peut se transformer de lui-même en un acte, même s'il en est une condition nécessaire, selon le rapport constitutif qui relie, dans le statut de l'être humain, la dimension de corporéité à celle qui est classiquement désignée par le terme "esprit". L'acte introduit une réalité qui est d'une autre nature que les états. Il est productivité pure, non prédéterminée, initiative, position absolue de lui-même, survenance, création d'inédit, introduisant dans le cours des choses une nouveauté irréductible, et suscitant par conséquent un effet de coupure dans le flux des phénomènes. En un mot, l'acte est de caractère événementiel.

II. L'ACTION SUR LA SOCIÉTÉ ET L'HISTOIRE

Il y a dans l'histoire et de façon générale dans tout phénomène social un aspect d'objectivité qui a suggéré l'idée que la société est une seconde nature. Si elle est "nature", en tout cas, c'est selon une signification très particulière, qui ne permet nullement de la réduire à un fragment de la nature cosmique. Il faut donc considérer à part l'action historique et de façon générale toutes ces formes d'action qui contribuent à tisser et à modifier la trame des relations interhumaines. Que l'on porte l'attention sur de grandes péripéties historiques ou sur des interactions de caractère très local, on peut concevoir schématiquement l'intervention, dans le domaine des relations sociales, comme dans le cas des interventions sur la nature extérieure, sous la forme d'un processus de transition entre états. Mais, bien entendu, il ne s'agit plus ici d'états de type cosmologique mais de réseaux de relations relativement isolables et relativement unifiés par certaines conditions-frontières. Le passage d'un état à un autre s'effectue en fonction de certaines représentations, appuyées sur des motivations de différents ordres, de ce qui est considéré comme objectif à réaliser.

On pourrait, comme dans le cas précédent, envisager une interprétation entièrement déterministe de l'action sociale. En partant de l'idée qu'un réseau social est une réalité objective et que son évolution est soumise, comme celle de tout système, à des lois dynamiques contraignantes, on pourrait tenter de ramener ce qui est en apparence une initiative au statut d'un simple chaînon dans une dynamique déterministe et d'en expliquer ainsi l'occurrence comme suite inévitable d'états antérieurs, éventuellement en intercalant dans le schéma purement sociologique de l'explication des hypothèses relatives au rôle des états cérébraux dans la genèse des représentations et des actions qu'elles inspirent. Ce serait là en somme une interprétation systémique tout à fait radicale de la société et de l'action sociale.

Mais il faut examiner de plus près en quoi consiste un réseau de relations de nature sociale. Comme l'a montré Max Weber, les rôles sociaux, qui sont en quelque sorte les noeuds du réseau, sont constitués par des systèmes d'attentes, relatifs aux comportements d'autrui et relativement stabilisés par le système culturel. Or les attentes elles-mêmes sont basées sur les significations que les acteurs sociaux reconnaissent aux comportements d'autrui et aux règles, implicites ou institutionnellement fixées, qui déterminent les formes d'ajustement des rôles. Et la signification qui s'attache, pour un acteur social, à une situation est le mode selon lequel elle est interprétée par lui. Les significations renvoient donc à un processus d'interprétation et un tel processus renvoie à son tour à un schème général de compréhension, qui définit la perspective selon laquelle l'acteur voit le monde social et sa propre position dans ce monde. On ne peut traiter un schème de compréhension comme un système dynamique rigide. La façon dont un acteur social perçoit les situations peut certes se transformer, en fonction des informations qu'il reçoit et en fonction de changements d'ordre psychologique ou moral, mais la transformation d'un schème de compréhension n'est pas du tout de même nature que la transformation d'un état physique en un autre "suivant des règles", car un tel schème n'est nullement réductible à un état physique.

Une interprétation a toujours un caractère hypothétique et est toujours, de soi, ouverte à des remaniements, éventuellement à des modifications radicales. Les significations qu'une interprétation attache aux êtres, aux choses et aux situations sont donc de nature fluide et doivent être traitées comme des potentiels de nouveauté. On retrouve ici, formellement, la condition de potentialité positive dont il avait été question à propos de la nature extérieure. Mais il faut préciser que la potentialité d'une signification est d'une autre espèce que la potentialité d'un état physique. Ce qui fait la potentialité d'un état physique c'est qu'il se situe dans un espace d'états possible, et que dans un tel espace il est relié par des chemins praticables (en vertu des lois de la nature ou moyennant une intervention extérieure) à un certain nombre d'autres états. Ce qui fait la potentialité d'une signification c'est qu'elle se profile sur l'horizon général du sens et que son rapport à cet horizon est constitué par un système d'anticipations qui ouvrent des chemins possibles vers d'autres significations, susceptibles de fournir de meilleures approximations de ce qui est à comprendre.

Comme dans le cas de l'action sur la nature, cependant, la transformation d'une configuration sociale en une autre suppose l'intervention d'un élément nouveau qui est d'ordre informationnel. Le processus de transition lui-même est, comme on vient de le voir, une réinterprétation. Mais celle-ci comporte un aspect créatif, qui est de l'ordre de l'invention. L'initiative transformatrice se projette en une représentation, qui propose une configuration à réaliser, autrement dit un projet. Et c'est ensuite l'action qui relaye la représentation en assumant ce projet dans une intervention effective, qui est le fait de la volonté libre. On pourrait évoquer ici la même idée d'une reconstitution entièrement déterministe de l'action volontaire qu'à propos de l'action sur la nature cosmique. Mais elle appellerait la même remarque concernant d'une part la différence radicale entre l'acte et sa représentation objectivée, et d'autre part la nature de la relation qui relie l'acte à ses conditions somatiques.

III. L'ACTION SUR SOI DE L'AGENT

Il y a des formes d'action qui concernent non la nature ou le monde socio-historique, mais le soi de l'agent lui-même. Il peut s'agir d'un acte simple, d'ordre intérieur, comme l'acceptation ou le rejet, en pensée, d'une situation, ou un jugement intérieur porté sur autrui. Et il peut s'agir aussi d'une suite d'actes délibérément orientés dans une certaine direction et contribuant à créer un nouvel état du soi, comme dans le cas de la formation d'un "habitus". Ici aussi on peut recourir au schéma de la transformation d'un état dans un autre. Mais il faut sans doute distinguer l'action sur soi qui consiste à modifier un certain état somatique et l'action sur soi qui vise l'être moral du soi comme tel.

Dans le premier cas on a affaire à la transformation d'un état somatique en un autre. Comme il est toujours possible de traiter un état somatique dans une perspective purement objectiviste, comme le fait l'approche scientifique, on pourrait considérer qu'une telle transformation est exactement du même type que la transition d'un état pyhsique à un autre. Mais une telle façon de voir est purement abstraite. Dans sa réalité concrète un état somatique est toujours un moment dans le déroulement d'une existence. Autrement dit, il est un état du soi. Et ce qui le constitue comme tel c'est sa signification existentielle, c'est-à-dire la manière dont il s'inscrit dans le cours d'une vie. L'absorption d'un médicament dangereux est un acte qui, sans doute, transforme de façon constatable l'état somatique du soi. Mais un tel acte a d'emblée une signification existentielle, en ce que, par lui, le soi risque de porter atteinte à l'intégrité de son être. La modification d'un état somatique est donc en fait une transformation d'une signification en une autre. On doit donc utiliser ici le même type d'analyse que pour l'action qui porte sur des configurations sociales. Et comme dans ce cas ce qui fait la potentialité de la situation de départ c'est la plasticité des significations, dont le rapport à l'horizon du sens est essentielement mouvant, une signification n'étant jamais qu'un moment dans un processus incessant de réinterprétation qui accompagne le mouvement de l'existence.

Dans le cas où l'action porte sur un état moral, la transformation qu'elle induit est une transition de cet état moral donné à un autre. De nouveau ce qui rend la transformation possible ici c'est qu'un état moral ne consiste pas en une détermination rigide mais n'est jamais qu'un moment dans un processus qui n'est pas un enchaînement de phénomènes mais l'existence même du soi, le devenir-soi du soi. La transformation dont il s'agit pourrait à juste titre être qualifiée de "transformation de nature spirituelle". Dans une telle transformation il y a toujours un aspect d'innovation, l'intervention d'un moment inventif, en lequel se concrétise, par rapport à des situations données, l'effort du soi pour assumer son être, la mise en jeu de sa responsabilité à l'égard de lui-même.

Il faut aborder maintenant le second problème, qui concerne l'articulation entre la liberté et le cours du monde. Dans la mise en oeuvre de la volonté libre il y d'abord une initiative. Mais cette initative comporte en elle-même l'exigence de son effectivité. Et ce qui lui donne son effectivité c'est l'inscription de l'initiative dans le cours ds choses. La volonté pose un état original. Une fois cet état posé, il évolue suivant les lois de la nature et les contraintes des circonstances (dont un traitement dynamique tient compte sous forme de "conditions aux frontières"). L'initiative qui, comme telle, est de la nature de l'acte et est une réalité purement intérieure, doit pouvoir se transformer en une réalité extérieure, qui engendrera des conséquences dans le milieu de l'extériorité. (Dans le cas de l'action qui porte sur le soi de l'agent, on retrouve ce moment d'extériorisation, de façon évidente lorsque l'action porte sur un état somatique, et de façon indirecte quand il s'agit de l'état moral de l'agent, un tel état étant toujours susceptible de se traduire en comportements). Comment cela est-il possible?

Pour qu'une telle transformation soit possible il faut que l'action puisse se produire en un lieu qui appartienne d'une certaine manière à la fois au milieu de l'intériorité et au milieu de l'extériorité. Or il y a effectivement, dans la structure ontologique de l'être humain, une instance qui constitue précisément un tel lieu: c'est le corps, lieu ontologique dans lequel ne cesse de s'opérer le passage de l'intérieur dans l'extérieur et réciproquement. Envisagée dans sa réalité concrète, en son effectuation, l'action passe toujours par une mise en jeu téléologiquement organisée du corps, sous forme de gestes et de paroles. L'action sur les états naturels s'effectue en définitive par des gestes, même s'ils sont très élémentaires, comme dans le cas où l'action se sert de dispositifs informatiques. L'action sur les configurations sociales s'effectue par la parole, même si celle-ci se projette et s'objectifie dans des règles, des rôles sociaux, des institutions, des formes culturelles durables. Et l'action sur soi est soit mise en jeu du corps par rapport à lui-même, comme dans l'exemple de la prise de médicament, soi modification d'intentions, d'attitudes, "d'habitus", bref de propriétés dispositionnelles, qui prennent leur sens de ce à quoi elles disposent, à savoir des comportements, donc des actions extériorisées qui mettent en jeu le corps comme puissance d'action précisément.

Dans le processus de l'extériorisation de l'acte libre il y a une superposition entre le contenu de l'acte, déterminé par le projet qui le sous-tend, et l'état nouveau introduit dans la réalité, cosmique, sociale ou existentielle. Le moment crucial dans l'effectuation de cette superposition c'est la motion volontaire, cette intervention de la volonté qui met en branle le corps et oriente ses moyens propres d'intervention – le geste et la parole – pour les faire concourir à l'objectif qu'elle poursuit elle-même en tant que volonté. Le processus somatique par lequel l'action devient effective est en quelque sorte la face objective de l'acte posé par la volonté. Mais il demeure adhérent à cet acte pendant son effectuation. Ce qui suppose que s'exercent en lui simultanément deux fonctions, l'une par laquelle il répond à la motion volontaire et qui correspond à l'aspect d'adhérence, l'autre par laquelle il se manifeste dans l'extériorité, et qui correspond à l'aspect d'effectivité. On reconnaît dans cette double fonction le statut ontologique très singulier du corps qui est à la fois un organisme naturel et une source de signifiance, à la fois être cosmique et être de sens. La parole que prononce un sujet est d'une part la forme objectivée d'un processus intentionnel, dont elle est l'aboutissement, et d'autre part, simultanément, l'effectivité d'un phénomène acoustique par lequel elle peut se faire entendre.

Mais pour qu'un processus somatique puisse ainsi recueillir et exprimer concrètement ce qui est visé dans un acte de volonté, il faut que cet acte comporte en lui-même déjà la dualité que comporte de son côté sa réalisation somatique. D'une part, en tant qu'il se pose sans prédétermination, à partir de lui-même, il est un processus purement intérieur. Mais d'autre part, en tant qu'il met effectivement en mouvement de façon appropriée les puissances corporelles, il se donne une forme qui est capable de se prêter à un processus de transcription dans l'ordre somatique. Comme visiblement un comportement somatique téléologiquement orienté est commandé par une certaine organisation neuronale, qui en est comme l'esquisse préalable, on peut dire que cette forme transcriptible de l'acte est la matrice d'une organisation neuronale qui elle-même est le schème effectif du processus somatique correspondant. Si tout n'est pas neuronal, s'il y a une priorité de l'acte sur les processus de nature physique, il faut bien qu'il y ait entre l'acte et le comportement ce processus de transposition qui à la fois objectifie l'acte et prépare le comportement. Le fondement de la possibilité d'une telle transposition se trouve dans le statut énigmatique de la corporéité, dans ce qu'avec Gabriel Marcel nous pouvons appeler le mystère de l'être incarné.

Mais s'il y a bien, dans l'exercice effectif de la liberté, priorité de l'acte, il faut que l'acte possède en lui-même la capacité d'introduire dans la réalité une détermination qui n'adviendrait pas sans lui. Cette capacité s'exerce doublement: dans le moment de la décision, où la volonté se détermine par rapport à la représentation de ce qui est à réaliser, et dans le moment de la motion volontaire, qui effectue la conversion de la représentation en processus somatique. Par le moyen de cette conversion l'acte s'insère dans le flux cosmique ou dans le flux historique et y fait apparaître effectivement quelque chose de nouveau, des situations inédites. Ce qui survient ainsi n'est pas attribuable au jeu des lois ou aux contraintes naturelles. C'est une détermination qui vient d'ailleurs. Sa survenance est à proprement parler événement.

Mais l'effectivité de l'acte, ce par quoi il devient visible en ce qu'il produit, renvoie à la source d'où provient la nouveauté, à savoir l'initiative, qui est au coeur de l'acte. À vrai dire l'initiative n'est pas une sorte de "fiat" absolument simple. Elle est un processus qui s'articule en plusieurs phases, étroitement solidaires les unes des autres. Dans ce processus il y a la formation de la représentation-projet, l'élaboration d'un schéma d'action, la délibération et puis la décision qui la conclut. Mais comme la décision est définie en son contenu par le projet en fonction duquel elle s'effectue, et comme le projet a été élaboré dans le moment de la représention, la décision réassume en elle tout le processus. Elle est le moment véritablement central de l'initiative. Et c'est elle qui est au sens fort événement, ce qui arrive dans le monde n'étant par rapport à elle événement qu'en un sens dérivé.

Mais il faut préciser en quoi consiste au juste cet événement. On ne peut le concevoir comme l'apparition d'une nouvelle réalité substantielle. S'il y un aspect créatif dans l'acte de la volonté, ce n'est pas au sens fort de la position d'un être nouveau mais au sens faible de la position d'un état nouveau. L'acte libre peut introduire localement dans la nature des arrangements inédits, il peut introduire dans la réalité socio-historique des figures nouvelles d'interaction, il peut introduire dans l'agent lui-même de nouvelles dispositions ou un nouvel état moral, mais ces déterminations nouvelles ne font qu'affecter une réalité substantielle préexistante. Ces déterminations sont des configurations, des types d'ordre, des systèmes de relations, et leur événementialité est précisément celle de l'émergence d'un nouveau type d'ordre. Si, à la manière de Wittgenstein, on définit le monde comme l'ensemble des états de choses, donc des arrangements possibles entre les composants fondamentaux de la réalité, on pourra dire que la nouveauté est la survenance d'un autre monde. Si on définit le monde comme le support substantiel des arrangements possible, on devra dire que la nouveauté est l'apparition d'un nouvel arrangement.

L'événement lui-même est la transition entre deux ordres, mais une transition qui n'est pas réductible à une succession d'états suivant une loi, qui est inattendu, imprévisible, singulier, pure discontinuité. Reliant des ordres, l'événement est lui-même de la nature d'une relation. Mais en tant que survenance, il est le pur passage, l'entre-deux, l'intervalle qui sépare l'ordre initial de l'ordre final. S'il est relation, il faut le concevoir comme relation pure, considérée abstraction faite des termes qu'il relie. La liberté est puissance d'événement. Si elle est auto-déterminante, c'est qu'elle tire d'elle--même la nouveauté qu'elle introduit. En la posant elle franchit d'elle-même la distance qui sépare l'ordre donné de celui qu'elle instaure. En son acte, elle pose donc une relation, et c'est en posant cette relation qu'elle fait apparaître le nouvel ordre. Dans l'effectivité de la liberté, c'est bien la relation qui est première. Et c'est dans la relation que gît l'événementialité de la liberté.

Si l'événement est vraiment ainsi pure transition, non nomologiquement déterminée, si c'est la liberté qui fait passer la réalité d'une configuration à une autre, il faut penser que l'intervalle est purement et simplement coupure, sans détermination propre. Il y a dès lors en lui quelque chose d'abyssal. Et la vertu de la liberté c'est d'être capable de franchir l'abîme. Qu'elle soit auto-détermination cela veut donc dire qu'elle a ce pouvoir extraordinaire de se lancer pour ainsi dire, par ses seules forces et sous sa propre responsabilité, au-dessus de l'abîme, vers un terme qui n'existe pas, qui n'existera que de cet élan lui-même. La liberté se confie au vide de l'intervalle et se recueille de son acte même, de l'initiative qu'elle est. Elle est donc risque. Non pas insensé cependant, car elle agit sur base de raisons. Mais ces raisons valent par rapport à un futur qui n'est encore présent que de façon anticipative, dans la représentation. En assumant ce risque, la liberté fait exister le contenu de la représentation, elle lui donne réalité, elle lui confère ainsi un poids ontologique que la représentation n'a pas par elle-même, elle l'inscrit dans l'être comme qualité nouvelle, sous la forme d'un ordre irréductible aux dynamiques nomologiques. Elle a donc par elle-même une force ontologique, qui est son être même. Elle est donc créatrice à sa manière, selon son statut de liberté finie, au sens précisément de la capacité de poser la relation. Par là elle contribue à ce qu'il y a d'événementiel dans la réalité créée, et singulièrement à cette forme de l'événementialité qui est de l'ordre de l'esprit.

JOSE A. IBAÑEZ-MARTIN
University Complutense of Madrid
Spain

ABOUT THE EUROPEAN CULTURAL CONSCIENCE: HUMAN CONDITION AND THE DIVINE PERSON

I. INTRODUCTION

The point I want to tackle is this: Is the European Union an artifice put together in response to defensive interests – whether economic or military – or is it the political expression of a common culture? Obviously I know that if we turn to the recent origins of the European Union, we seem to find a political structure built to protect economic and military defensive strong interests. Nevertheless, every union is really very weak if it depends only on economic basis, as we see in the recent rebirth of nationalism. My thesis is that the European Union is not a simple agreement among merchants or capitalists. Rather, it is based on a cultural reality that, as historians say, has been three thousand years in the making. The fact that the union has been strengthened over the last half century by means of economic instruments is because of a determinate appraisal of the social circumstances of the times, but with the wish of moving toward a political configuration more in accord with Europe's cultural community. Although it is not easy to know whether that appraisal was correct, we certainly can say that one of the key proponents behind the European Economic Community, Jean Monnet, stated near the end of his life that if it were possible to go back and start the process of a European union again, it would have to begin with culture. Moreover, the place selected for this International Congress express indirectly the idea that it was untrue that the borders of Europe were the borders of the EEC. This shrinking of Europe's limits was years ago frantically defended whenever anyone recalled that what lay behind the Iron Curtain was also Europe. As Seton-Watson pointed out in 1984, some people even thought that remembering Europe's true size was akin to predicting nuclear war. Seton-Watson, an important historian of Russia, insisted that "nowhere in the world is there so widespread a belief in the reality, and importance, of an European cultural community, as in the countries lying between EEC territory and the Soviet Union"[1]. He continued by warning of the need to stop regarding the Soviet colonial empire as something permanent, stating "there is just one statement that historians can safely make about history: that in history nothing is permanent. How change will come, historians are poorly qualified to predict"[2]. Seton-Watson, like most everyone, could not imagine that change happening in less than five years, and without following a nuclear war.

The communism has been defeated, but the problems have not disappeared. Nowadays we are in a situation in which it is a taboo to speak clearly about the main elements of this European cultural community, and perhaps for the fear for recognizing the central place of Christian religion in our common heritage. This problem is not new. Let's begin making a brief historical notice about the discussion of what are the essential elements that characterize a common European culture.

II. EUROPE: A CONTINENT WITH CONTENT

The title of this section is taken from Ortega's brilliant words expressing his position on the existence of a "European cultural conscience"[3]. Of course, it is one thing to defend this common content, whose weakening, as Ortega warned in 1937, had brought Europe to "a state of war substantially more radical than ever before in its history"[4]. But it is another matter entirely to clarify the essential characteristics of whatever unites us in this continent. Indeed, the three main papers by Ortega published in the aforementioned book on Europe were left unfinished, probably because they could not end without first entering into this matter, and analyzing it meant taking a stance on highly controversial questions.

In other words, I consider Ortega's writings to fall short in regards to this matter, though they do not elude it completely. In fact, a close reading of the book brings us to the conclusion that European culture has one fundamental characteristic, from which we can derive an important conse-

---

[1] H. Seton-Watson, (1995) *What is Europe, Where is Europe?*, "Encounter"? v. 64-65, July, p. 14. The same idea is defended by L. Kołakowski, (1990) *Education to Hatred, Education to Dignity*, in: *Modernity on endless trial* (University of Chicago Press), p. 255.

[2] Id.

[3] J. Ortega y Gasset, (1985)? *Hay hoy una conciencia cultural europea?*, in: *Europa y la idea de nación*, p. 21 (Madrid, Revista de Occidente en Alianza Editorial).

[4] Id. *De Europa meditatio quaedam*, in o. c., p. 109.

quence that may be interpreted in very different ways. To Ortega's mind, the cultural customs of the European nation have nothing at all to do with simple "folk tradition", which is "the prototype of everything homey"[5]. Instead, "added to the own life of the traditional customs in which man lives by inertia were ways of living that, though well articulated with traditional ones, attempt to represent a 'way of being man' in the highest sense; an aspiration to be precisely the most perfect way to be man, and thus, well-founded and projected on the future"[6]. Beyond a doubt, these words are quite significant, and so should be analyzed and contrasted with care.

Ortega does not mean to discard traditional customs, which must be articulated into any solid future project; he does, however, point out their limitations and the orientation needed to transcend them. If we turn to a historical allegory, we could say that this feature of a European culture became manifest at the commotion with which Europeans received the news of the burning of the ancient library at Alexandria, and the burning in our times of the one in Sarajevo. Europe has always cherished its books, fretted over its past, and watched over the research of those who went before us. The European, as has often been said, from John of Salisbury to Newton, has felt "like a dwarf raised up onto the shoulders of a giant". This, too, should be the object of reflection.

In truth, what is meant by that "giant?" In some way, this picture expresses not only a few interpretations or behavior patterns consolidated by untold repetition (inertia), but also someone with his own outstanding strength and vigor. Our past must be known, not out of an inclination for mere erudition but out of a love for ethnography. The basic idea of this search is to reach "the most perfect way of being man". Socrates stated that only the life examined is worth living, and Aristotle indirectly pointed out that such examination is not a simple exercise in introspection, but a necessary means for solving the central problem of our existence, which is finding out how to attain a worthwhile life, a good life. Indeed, life is not good for however sluggardly we choose to live it with greater or lesser independence from the pressures of the dominant mentality. There are choices which lead us to thrive, and choices which dehumanize. We can discover which goals make us more authentic, and distinguish them from those which alienate us. This is no easy feat, and thus the European tries to learn what the important people preceding us in time have said (the giant), to try to ponder it (find out its pondus, or weightiness) and either take it in or reject it, seeking new horizons without feeling obliged to repeat unthinkingly what he has received. If a European feels as if raised on the shoulders of a giant, it is

---

[5] Id. *De nación a provincia de Europa*, in o. c., p. 18.
[6] Id. o. c., p. 16.

because he/she thinks the giant has found valuable things, but also that he/she himself/herself can reach further than his/her predecessors could.

All this leads us to identify a central element of European culture, repeated from Plato to Husserl and Allan Bloom. The myth of the cavern allegorically shows us that "folk tradition" (as Ortega would say) is a cave unbefitting our being, though custom has made us forget our chains and we feel at home inside. The human person is meant to leave hand-me-down ideas behind in search of the truth. The philosopher is the one who should jab at the comfort of his/her fellow men/women so that they may abandon their niche, and help them confront the reality of things as they really are, not just the shadows they cast in the sunlight. If we address the essential meaning of these ideas, we come to the conclusion that European culture is first and foremost characterized by the central role given in human existence to reason, able to attain the truth and impel human persons to follow it however difficult hat may be[7].

This basic surety is best represented by one of the most specifically European institutions: the University, a gathering of masters and scholars with the will and understanding to learn "the knowable" (as Alfonso X the Wise said). It is an institution that at one and the same time is a place of searching for and communicating knowledge, as well as a revolutionary "center for social advancement based on success in examinations rather than on birthright"[8], in an undeniable tribute to intelligence, so that the force of the desire to have does not suffocate the natural inclination to know.

Needless to say, any surety can be poorly administered. This was the tack taken by Cartesius. Rationalism and enlightenment by the "lights of reason" have led to an imperialism of reason wholly willing to give explanations *more geometrico*, to the alienating use of science denounced by Husserl as seeking to dominate man/women instead of freeing them from need, to a technical reason concerned only with means, whose perverse consequences have been brilliantly analyzed by Adorno and Horkheimer, to the Hegelian belief in a necessary unfolding of reason in the history of Europe, the center of the universe, in which all other peoples should look, etc. These phenomena lie at the base of the current distrust of reason. What once proved so much has today turned out for many to prove nothing at all. It would seem urgent to forget about "great stories" and dedicate life to the "small story" of our own traditions, which has led Bloom to conclude that the modern mind has suffered a process of shrinking, of closing off, which

---

[7] An analysis of the consequences of the collapse of this Platonic myth could be seen in my article: Ibañez-Martin, J. A. (1994) *Formación humanística y filosofía*, „Revista Española de Pedagogía" 52:198, mayo-agosto, pp. 231-246.

[8] J. Le Goff, (1994) *La vieille Europe et la nôtre* (Paris, Ed. du Seuil), p. 32.

makes us "feel too dependent on history and culture"[9]. Furthermore, even attempting to speak of a common goal is, for many, the worst social threat imaginable, since they consider that "if truth and ethos leave the private domain and aspire to a public value, they leave the bounds of the permissible and loom as a totalitarian attempt to subjugate man to the yoke"[10], forgetting that the truth is not aggressive; it is offered meekly to intelligence, and those who do not open up to it (the only road to reaching self-fulfilment) end up subjugating themselves to the whims of fickle majorities.

At the beginning of this section, I said that, according to Ortega, European culture has a fundamental feature (which we have analyzed) that leads to a consequence susceptible to a variety of interpretations. This consequence is that Europe is prone to "suffering periodic crises. This means it is not a closed culture like others, crystallized forever. For this reason, it would be a mistake to try to define European culture by specific contents. Its glory and strength lie in that it is always willing to go beyond what it was, beyond itself. European culture is perpetual creation. It is not an inn, but a road to be taken. Cervantes, who had lived a long life, said in his old age that the road is better than the inn"[11].

These words by Ortega are a brilliant sum of hits and misses, and make up a position that has especially today been gaining popularity. It is true that Europe suffers periodic crises because it is willing to go one step further, which recalls Emperor Charles V's motto *plus ultra*, literally "more far". It is no surprise that the first coin minted in the European Union bears the effigy of Charles V. But these words forget that real progress is made when "a crisis comes to a good close", e.g., when whatever mistakes found are modified, and a further step is taken. Ortega's theses are repeated today by Edgar Morin, who insists that what European culture can call its own is that the habitual cultural dialogne is not limited in Europe's case by dogmas or prohibitions, but is open to discussion "in which none of the constituent parties vanquishes or exterminates the others, nor does it even produce a lasting hold on its hegemony"[12]. Of course, this position fails to explain how it can be integrated with the wish to find "the most perfect way to be man", since at the extreme, every interpretation of doing so would have the same validity. This position also forces us to accept that promoting human dignity is just as specifically European as trading in slaves, often sold by the chieftains of enemy tribes.

---

[9] A. Bloom, (1989) *El cierre de la mente moderna* (Barcelona, Gedisa), p. 393.

[10] J. Ratzinger, (1993) *Una mirada a Europa* (Madrid, Rialp), p. 20.

[11] J. Ortega y Gasset, (1985)? *Hay hoy una conciencia cultural europea?*, in o. c., p. 28. It is meaningful that the manuscript of this lecture is unfinished, ending with this paragraph.

[12] E. Morin, (1987) *Penser L'Europe* (Paris, Gallimard), p. 128.

Europe's lengthy path through history has been covered with steps of uneven correctness and always open for discussion. But such discussion has led to some conclusions that have molded the European spirit, even if they vary in strength and ordinarily lack any pretense of annihilating those who hold the opposite view. Europe is aware of its errors, as when it turned to preying on its weaker peoples, to arrogance, to imposing rules that were clearly harmful to the legitimate interests of other countries. However, being aware of an error is not just acknowledging certain behavior, but recognizing it as mistaken. And what we recognize in ourselves is our concrete culture.

It is, then, time to make a positive, and perhaps risky, proposal about the main lines of the European culture.

III. CENTRAL ELEMENTS OF THE EUROPEAN CULTURE: A PROPOSAL

It is well known that the term "culture" contains a great many meanings; we cannot hope to analyze them all here even in passing. In general terms, we could say that culture can be given an objective meaning generally without valuative connotations, and a subjective meaning generally with a value judgement. In the first sense, culture is the whole of the interpretations of reality and the behavioral patterns in effect in any given society. They set the pace for personal growth, taking into account the lack of effective instincts that characterizes the human species. Just as our parents gave us a walker to help us learn to walk, society forms us initially by means of its particular culture to give us our orientation as individuals and as members of a society. In the second sense, we subjectively speak of a cultured person when referring to the exercise and cultivation that our higher faculties have been subject to in order to put them in shape to yield the best fruit possible. If we stay with the objective sense, cultures are usually distinguished mainly by the way they characterize man and the slack there is in it between what he receives from society and the personal future he projects, by the way of understanding the relationships among people, and by the type of presence/absence of divinity in personal and social life.

I have already pointed out that journeying into these questions is stepping into a land full of complexities. But I believe that the construction of a democratic Europe obliges all of us to make the cultural proposals we find most fruitful. We will, then, move on now to an interpretation of the position of European culture on each one of these aspects.

1. THE HUMAN CONDITION: HISTORY AND PROJECTION

The question of human condition is the most ancient and the most current. Man is a mystery to man, since we know ourselves to be open to the whole, we are aware that our private assumptions shape our very face, yet our intuition surely informs us that not all behavior is equally human nor humane. Ortega correctly said that, while tigers cannot de-tigerize themselves, humans can certainly dehumanize themselves, which, *a sensu contrario* indicates that among all the possible choices, only certain ones lead to fulfilment, to becoming more humane. Europe is primarily Greek. European culture has accepted the Aristotelian definition and sees human beings as rational animals who live, as Aquinas later said *arte et ratione*[13], thanks to reason and ingenuity, and to work. Living thanks to reason means distancing oneself from Gobineau-type biologists views and from any kind of cultural relativism. San Martin correctly points out that one very European feature is discovering a truth without making ethnic references[14]. This has a two-sided consequence: on one hand, the truth can be shared with those of other blood, of other origins. On the other hand, truths from outside cannot be discriminated against on the basis of race, sex, or social class. Nobody in Europe is troubled over the color of Saint Augustine's skin; they are only concerned with analyzing his books, studying his contributions to better understand the complexities of the human heart.

The human person is *logos*, but he/she is also liberty. Sartre criticized those who felt proud that the Emperor and the slave could argue together, and that the slave, *dans les fers*, could feel freer than his master. Sartre was right, since freedom requires being also present in society and politics. Still, *a rebours*, he pointed out the importance that inner freedom, the source of all liberty, has always had in European culture from the times of Epictetus to Bernanos, who declared that "Europe has always bet on mankind. And the sure-fire proof is that Europe falls when liberty falls. He who saves freedom saves Europe. He who loses freedom loses Europe"[15].

The study of human reason and free will shows man's infinite openness and the consequent impossibility of living off strictly corporeal matters, which are by definition limited. We thus find that we have spiritual faculties which require an equally spiritual principle, which we call "soul". European culture, from Aristotle to Denis de Rougemont, has always believed firmly in the human soul. de Rougemont even organized the European Culture

---

[13] Aquinas, *Comm. in Analyt. Post.*, n° 1.

[14] Cfr. J. San Martin, (1993) *El sentido de Eurpa*, in: Garcia Marza, V. D. and Martinez Guzman, V., *Teoría de Europa* (Valencia, NauLlibres), p. 46.

[15] G. Bernanos, (1989) *El espíritu europeo y el mundo de las máquinas*, in: *La libertad, para que?* (Madrid, Encuentro Ediciones), p. 164.

Foundation to stress what he called – paraphrasing a principle of trial security – *habeas animam*, every person's right to a soul, whose development must be nurtured and whose existence cannot be ignored. To the Greeks, the "most perfect way to be man" implied *kalokagathía*, beauty of the body and mind, as a goal of education. Such beauty, though, is clearly the one of the mind, the one which is achieved with *areté*, through the virtuous exercise of freedom.

Among the many properties of the human soul, one has been the object of constant debate: immortality. It has been rejected by some, like D'Holbach. Others have put forth lengthy arguments to demonstrate it, as did Plato, Aquinas, and Cartesius. Still others, such as Cicero[16] and Kant, consider it unwaveringly even though they do not support their belief with rational arguments (Kant, in fact, held it as a postulate of practical reason). The European Christian heritage believes not only in the immortality of the soul, but in the resurrection of the dead, which has had numerous cultural consequences.

Along with these characteristics outlining the way Europeans have interpreted the human condition, some observation must be made as to how they have interpreted strictly human activity, and how such actions are telling of man's origins and his ability to project. Europeans soon overcame the spreading temptation of fatalism. Of course, the past is cumbersome; it is also the foundation of life, even when it remains unseen, as happens with the roots of a tree. Nevertheless, man/woman is not a tree; he/she is beckoned to overcome the circumstances of his/her birth, to tame the forces of nature, to modify the context in which he/she saw the light. The human person is master of his/her own life and can come to tame the earth, thanks to science and his/her own enterprising spirit. As Díez del Corral states, "Europeans spread their rule through Asia not because they were richer in consumer goods [...] but because they had a slight margin of superiority in their spirit of adventure, in their ability at military and commercial organization, and in the will to dominate"[17].

The European's life is an adventure. The adventure of Marco Polo, of Christopher Columbus, of Livingstone, and of Gagarin. The adventure of Shakespeare and Dalí. The adventure of Cyril and Methodius and Theresa of Jesus. The adventure of the Beatles and of Victoria de los Angeles. The adventure of Galileus and of Madame Curie. It is the adventure of the many who do not consider that *les jeux sont faits* from circumstances of their birth; instead, they tried, serenely, sure of the bases of reality, to step beyond the barriers of the given.

---

[16] Vid. what is called "the Dream of Scipionis" in his work *Lelius or about friendship*, IV, 13 and 14.

[17] L. Diez del Corral, (1974) *Prólogo a la edición de "El Rapto de Europa" por Alianza Editorial*, in: *El rapto de Europa* (Madrid, Alianza Editorial), p. 67.

2. THE HUMAN PERSON AS A SOCIAL AND POLITICAL ANIMAL

"No man is an island, entire of itself; every man is a piece of the continent"[18]. This famous verse by Donne, newly brought to the minds of the Spanish people through Hemingway's novel, expresses the European's attitude toward other people. We are social by nature. Friendship, said Aristotle, is the most precious gift human beings can receive, since happiness lies not in the things outside, but in the unity of hearts among beings who stand out because of their dignity. Needless to say, Europeans have also concocted legal falsehoods to abuse others, even to the point of intentional extermination: they were barbarians, they did not have Roman citizenship, they worshipped the wrong gods, they belonged to a "cursed" race, and so forth. But it was a falsehood for silencing the conscience that held that all men have a common dignity, and that nobody can be treated as merchandise, as an instrument, as an inferior being bound to the arbitrariness of the powerful. This is the conscience that moved the King of Spain to dictate the Laws of the Indians, the conscience seen in *Fuenteovejuna*, the conscience that leads Kant to state that man has dignity but not price.

Because of this, Europe is the birthplace of democracy, of dialog and conversation based on reasons, of the rule of law and due process showing equal respect to all citizens, of social justice, of tolerance, of monogamy, of care for the weak. Because of this, Europe has played a decisive role in the Universal Declaration of Human Rights, and the Council of Europe has opened its doors – often with considerable discussion, such as in the case of Russia – in recent years to many countries that are not part of the European Union but are nevertheless willing to commit themselves to obeying the European Convention on the Rights of Man.

3. THE HUMAN PERSON AND THE DIVINE PERSON. GOD, SO CLOSE AND YET SO FAR

One element present in all cultures is the concrete way in which the relation to divinity is perceived. This relation could simply be said to develop in Europe along the lines of Christianity. Seton-Watson points out that "the interweaving of the notions of Europe and of Christendom is a fact of history which even the most brilliant sophistry cannot undo"[19]. Even so,

---

[18] J. Donne (1573-1631). The famous novel of Hemingway about the Spanish Civil War took its title of one of these lines: *For whom the bell tolls*.

[19] H. Seton-Watson, o. c., p. 16. About this problem, in the most recent bibliography, it could be consulted G. Davie, (1994) *The Religious Factor in the Emergence of Europe as a Global Region*, "Social Compass", 41:1, pp. 95-112 and G. Mucci, (1995) *La presenza della cultura cristiana in Europa*, "La Civiltà Cattolica", 18.3.1995, quaderno 3474, pp. 553-566.

there are many movements today that deny or play down this fact. The first are especially represented by those who call themselves the "new right" in France, led by Benoist[20] and the most fervent laymen. Notable among the second are the less combative lay movements and most of the official documents of the European Union, which tend to avoid any religious reference at all.

It is hard to call denying Europe's Christian roots as anything but blatant manipulation. It is of course true that those roots have sprouted into a variety of shapes and sizes, and that not all of their developments have been equally positive. For that reason, it may be that some deny it not so much out of an *odium religionis* as out of the fear of a resurgence of past displays that only irrelevant fringe groups would wish to restore. No one can even consider making Christianity a prerequisite to being European, especially after Vatican II. It is clear that only by an act of free choice do we sincerely join a religious faith, and yet we can all be Europeans by birth. Moreover, from the point of view of social organization, it is clear today that no kind of society will satiate the scatological perfection to which mankind aspires. The articulation of political coexistence has its own autonomy, just as religious life is not in the hands of the political powers. After many ups and downs, European culture rejects the principle from the Peace of Augsburg (1555) *cuius regio eius religio*; it rejects theocracy as a system which hands over the management of temporal affairs to the religious authorities; it rejects "Caesar-as-Popeism" as pretext for political power to rule over the Church and to demand religious obedience from its citizens, having been given, primarily by the Roman Catholic Church, a deeper meaning of religious freedom.

From this stance, God is far from ordinary life. From another point of view, however, God is nearby, being not only the keystone of European culture, but also open to keeping a relationship of intimacy with the human person[21]. Indeed, it is worth bearing in mind that if Europeans are characterized by a spirit of adventure, many non-Europeans feel strongly attracted to the European civilization after coming into contact with it. This spontaneous attraction may have some basis in the Hegelian considerations on the universality of European culture, able to move those who, according to Hegel, live in singularity themselves. Specifically, one of the most remarkable motives for attraction is Europe as the birthplace of science and modern technology. Naturally, the question to be asked, as Díez del Corral did, is

---

[20] Vid. about this subject the article of P. A. Taghuieff, (1993-1994) *From Race to Culture: the new right's view of European identity*, "Telos", winter-spring, vol. 98 and 99, pp. 99-125.

[21] Cfr. R. Brague, (1992) *Europe, la voie romaine* (Paris, Criterion), p. 168.

the following: "Why did modern science start in Europe instead of in China?"[22]. To this he replied elliptically, drawing on a quote from Needham in which he says that both the absence in China of the idea of a creator-deity, and thus of a supreme lawmaker, as well as the organicist view from Taoism, gave little room for the laws of nature. This idea is further developed in the work of the renown American cosmologist Stanley Jaki, who argues that modern science was born in a cultural matrix that made it possible. This matrix has three primary characteristics: the trust in the existence of a rationally ordered universe outside us, the certainty that our mind is able to investigate that order, and finally, the sense of responsibility at knowing we are the only ones in the world who can[23]. To Jaki, any real history of science must individuate that cultural humus given by the Christian faith in which science finds its possible conditions. These conditions are often forgotten when attention is focussed on trivialities and legends. We can thus say that Christianity is the cornerstone on which the effort of Western reason was built, and point out its decisive importance when putting unconditional limits on the exercise of liberty. Seneca said that "man is a holy thing to man"[24], and Kołakowski stresses that, when a culture loses its sacred dimension, it also loses its sense. The thrill of unlimited possible changes and the disappearance of moral reins on desire lead man to a vacuum, and society to the empire of the violent, to the downfall of the operative validity of human rights, to the degradation of the earth, and to the destruction of culture[25].

God, then, is quite close to European man/woman. Of course, political power has no authority to demand that closeness of anyone. But that does not mean we have to forget our roots and assure ourselves that all our law depends on majority decisions, specially since the acceptance of the criteria of the majority is based on the Christian idea of a dignity common to all. If to God there is neither Jew nor Gentile, neither are there the powerful nor the weak. As nowadays Communitarians rightly remark, society is not a group of heterogenous individuals, who arranges its legal structure according to the desires of the moment. Every sane society has a common ground

---

[22] o. c., p. 31.

[23] Cfr. S. L. Jaki, (1978) *The Road of Science and the Way to God* (The University of Chicago Press), pp. 326-327. Jaki has been working for years on this subject and for his results received, in 1987, the known Templeton Prize.

[24] Seneca, *Epist. ad Lucilium*, 95, 33.

[25] Cfr. L. Kołakowski, (1990) *The Revenge of the Sacred in Secular Culture*, in: *Modernity on endless trial*, o. c., pp. 69-74. Vid. et. J. Le Goff, o. c., p. 64. In his recent book *La libre afirmación de nuestro ser. Una fundamentación de la ética realista*, A. Millan Puelles (1994) shows brilliantly how the last foundation of the moral imperative is in the Absolute Person (Madrid, Rialp), pp. 396-421.

of values, a prior basic agreement about how living together, in which positive law acquires its full sense.

Consequently, neither the Christian faith nor Christian moral criteria need be reduced to the scope of private conscience, since in that case, Europe would be lacking the "forces which can shape a community and keep it together"[26].

IV. CONCLUSIONS

We have made a proposal to identify the fundamental elements of the glue that joins Eurpeans together. Those elements must be the object of special attention by any minimally lucid education and cultural policy. Europe has always fallen into decadence whenever it did not know how to be creatively true to its historical vocation[27].

Many have pointed out the serious cultural crisis we find ourselves in at the verge of the third millennium. Giving an imaginative and profound answer to the challenges of our times is not an easy task. Perhaps, then, it would be best to conclude by pointing out the most notable challenges we must find an answer to if we are not to disappear as a culture.

First, Europe must take efforts to redefine the meaning of reason and its place in human existence, its possibilities and its limits. To Husserl, "the crisis of European existence has only two ways out: either the decadence of Europe in a distancing from its deep rational sense of life and the sinking of the spirit into hostility or barbarism, or the rebirth of Europe through the spirit of philosophy by means of a heroism of reason that triumphs definitively over naturalism"[28]. Of course, that heroism of reason has nothing to do with a rationalist imperialism.

Second, Europe needs to give up narrow nationalisms, which does not mean wiping legitimate national identities from the slate, but does require taking into account the horizon of a united Europe and rejecting any form of ethnic sacralization, which would end up in thinking with bloodlines, as the Nazis advocated.

Third, it is necessary to overcome economicism and the thirst for private gain, without becoming carried away by the pressures of those who reduce everything to material welfare, from which many are generally excluded. As Le Goff says, "Europe should set the example to the world of putting the economy and economists in their place"[29].

---

[26] J. Ratzinger, o. c., p. 24.
[27] Cfr. G. Bernanos, o. c., p. 169.
[28] E. Husserl, (1969) *La Filosofía en la crisis de la humanidad europea*, in: *La Filosofía como ciencia estricta* (Buenos Aires, Nova, 2ª ed.), p. 172.
[29] J. Le Goff, o. c., p. 65.

Fourth, Europe must to recover ethical and religious conversation in the public forum, openly and freely, and without political pressures, aware that moral demands outweigh any other considerations based on expediency[30].

Fifth, it is necessary to promote a new cultural synthesis for the times. Curzio Malaparte told of the Nazi colonel who, leading the troops he belonged to in the Second World War, decided to execute the Russian prisoners who could read and write. When asked by Malaparte what would happen to the German prisoners if the Russian soldiers followed the same criterion, he replied that it was not the same thing, since Germany was a people of a great *Kultur*. A great tragedy of our times is cultural fragmentation[31], the inability to act unitedly in the various ranges of existence. It is a unity of action that will have to be recovered if we do not wish to disappear as a result of dispersion and contradictoriness.

---

[30] Isaiah Berlin in the last pages of his work *El supuesto relativismo del pensamiento europeo del s. XVIII*, gives a clear view of how the degradations we have seen in these years remark more and more the universality and objectivity of certain moral calls, in: *El fuste torcido de la humanidad* (Barcelona, Península), pp. 185-194.

[31] Vid. about this subject the very interesting book of J. L. Del Barco, (1995) *La civilización fragmentaria* (Madrid, Rialp).

Conceptions of Freedom

EDUALDO FORMENT
Universidad de Barcelona
Spain

QUE ES SER HOMBRE?

I. LA VULGARIDAD IMPUESTA

Con mi comunicación, desearía ayudar a la reflexión sobre algunas cuestiones, que me parecen de gran importancia, en estos momentos de inseguridad generalizada, tanto en el orden intelectual como en el de los órdenes más prácticos. Como mi vida gira en torno a la Universidad, comenzaré con unas advertencias de un gran universitario, José Ortega y Gasset. Afirmaba el eminente catedrático de metafísica que el „mal radical" de las muchas cosas, que ocurren en nuestra época, puede situarse en diferentes causas, pero: „Si se busca el ápice de esa raíz, aquello de que todo lo demás brota y emerge, nos encontramos con algo que tolera sólo un nombre adecuado: la *chabacanería*. De lo alto a lo ínfimo penetra toda nuestra existencia nacional, la anega, la dirige y la inspira".

Precisaba que: „El abandonarse, el 'de cualquier manera', el 'lo mismo da', el 'poco más o menos', el 'iqué importai', eso es la chabacanería"[1]. Esta insubstancialidad y banalidad, en que consiste lo que denominaba „chabacanería", es también una „falta de decoro mínimo, de respeto a sí mismo, de decencia"[2].

Lo que es más grave es su dificultad para superarla, porque la ordinariez: „Se acostumbra a sí misma, se encuentra cómoda a sí misma y tiende a *generalizarse* y *eternizarse*"[3]. Además: "El alma vulgar, sabiéndose vulgar, tie-

---

[1] J. Ortega y Gasset, *Misión de la Universidad,* Madrid, Revista de Occidente, 1936, pp. 21-22.
[2] Ibid., p. 20.
[3] Ibid., p. 21.

ne el denuedo de afirmar el *derecho* de la vulgaridad y lo *impone* dondequiera".

Los hombres chabacanos constituyen lo que llama la „masa". Según Ortega lo es: „Todo aquel que no se valora a sí mismo -en bien o en mal- por razones especiales, sino que se siente 'como todo el mundo' y, sin embargo, no se angustia, se siente a sabor al sentirse *idéntico* a los demás"[4]. Para el hombre vulgar o masificado: „ser diferente es indecente"[5]. Explica que, por ello: „Masa puede definirse, como *hecho psicológico*, sin necesidad de esperar a que aparezcan los individuos en aglomeración".

En consecuencia, añade: „La división de la sociedad en masas y minorías excelentes no es, por lo tanto, una división en clases sociales, sino en *clases de hombres*, y no puede coincidir con la jerarquización en clases superiores e inferiores"[6]. Los hombres que, en cambio, *se conducen* a sí mismos y *se esmeran* en perfeccionarse, aunque no les sea posible conseguirlo, por motivos individuales propios o por otros extrínsecos y circunstanciales, no pertenecen al género de la masa. Explica Ortega: „Imagínese un hombre humilde que al intentar valorarse por razones especiales -al preguntarse si tiene talento para esto o lo otro, si sobresale en algún orden-, advierte que no posee ninguna cualidad excelente. Este hombre se sentirá mediocre y vulgar, mal dotado; pero no se sentirá «masa»".

El hombre, que no es masa, o „El hombre selecto no es el petulante que se cree superior a los demás, sino el que *se exige* más que los demás, aunque no logre cumplir en su persona esas exigencias superiores (...) Lo decisivo es si ponemos nuestra vida a uno u a otro vehículo, a un máximo de *exigencias* o a un mínimo". De ahí que: „La división más radical que cabe hacer de la humanidad es ésta, en dos clases de criaturas: las que se exigen mucho y acumulan sobre sí mismas dificultades y deberes, y las que no se exigen nada especial, sino que para ellas vivir es ser en cada instante lo que ya son, sin *esfuerzo* de perfección sobre sí mismas, boyas que van a la deriva"[7].

II. LA VULGARIDAD VOLUNTARIA

La vulgaridad que, según Ortega, es „el mal radical de lo español"[8], puede identificarse con la *medianía*, de la que habla Caturelli. El eminente pro-

---

[4] Idem, *La rebelión de las masas*, Madrid, Revista de Occidente, 1937, p. 40.
[5] Ibid., p. 42.
[6] Ibid., pp. 40-41.
[7] Ibid., p. 40.
[8] Idem, *La misión de la Universidad*, op. cit., p. 22.

fesor universitario la describe del siguiente modo: „Hay un estado común, o mejor aún, propio del hombre medio, de la medianía o mediocridad (...) Esta medianía implica un encadenamiento, un estar esclavizado (sin saberlo) a la inmediatez de los entes"[9].

Los hombres mediocres son los que: „Están situados en la servidumbre de la inmediatez, como los hombres del mito platónico de la caverna, están 'atados por las piernas y el cuello' y deben mirar siempre adelante 'pues las ligaduras les impiden volver la cabeza'. Esto es un no poder ver sino las 'sombras' de sí mismo y de las cosas proyectadas por la luz del fuego sobre la pared, que está frente a los hombres; por eso, para este hombre de la medianía lo real es, precisamente, lo no real, la sombra; la verdad, la no verdad; el ser, el no-ser"[10].

La medianía, que, como también afirma Caturelli: „es el máximo peligro para la vida del espíritu"[11], es un vicio del que debe liberarse todo hombre, pero también debe ayudar a la posible liberación de todos los demás, al igual que el hombre del mito de la caverna de Platón. Ortega creía que ello podría hacerse con la *cultura*. Sería posible liberar al hombre de la mediocridad, con la: „Enseñanza de la cultura o transmisión a la nueva generación del sistema de ideas sobre el mundo y el hombre que llegó a madurez en la anterior"[12].

El filósofo tomista R. Garrigou-Lagrange distingue entre una mediocridad ética y otra intelectual. „La mediocridad *moral* no es (...) más que un medio entre el bien o el justo medio verdadero y las formas opuestas del mal"[13]. En cambio, la autentica vida moral o vida según la virtud no lo es, en este sentido, porque toda virtud es un extremo respecto a los vicios opuestos por exceso y por defecto, y es sólo un medio entre el exceso y el defecto de las pasiones[14].

En el orden *intelectual*: „la mediocridad consiste (...) en tomar como reglas las opiniones existentes verdaderas o falsas, en aceptar cualquier cosa por medio de un eclecticismo arbitrario y en hacer una elección o compromiso oportuno entre todas. La esencia del oportunismo. Pero hay muchas maneras de ser mediocre. Se puede ser de una manera *vulgar*; es también a veces una actitud maduramente reflexionada, estudiada, que supone un ta-

---

[9] A. Caturelli, *La Universidad. Su esencia, su vida, su ambiente*, Córdoba, Argentina, Universidad Nacional de Córdoba, 1963, pp. 17-18.
[10] Ibid., p. 18.
[11] Ibid., p. 56.
[12] J. Ortega y Gasset, *La misión de la Universidad*, op. cit., p. 42.
[13] R. Garrigou-Lagrange, *Dieu, son existence et sa nature*, Paris, Beauchesne, 1933, 6Æ ed., p. 731.
[14] Cf. Santo Tomas, *Summa Theologiae*, I-II, q. 64, a. 1, ad 1.

lento real, y bajo esta segunda forma, la mediocridad puede llegar a ser un aspecto engañador del mal más sutil y más profundo"[15]. Hay una *vulgaridad vulgar*, no querida directamente, y otra *vulgaridad querida*, porque se busca el ser vulgar para conseguir unos fines útiles.

III. NECESIDAD DEL HUMANISMO

El celebre escritor francés Georges Bernanos, que en sus novelas y ensayos combatió siempre la mediocridad, escribió en 1947, un año antes de morir que: „La civilización moderna se ha basado en una definición *materialista* del hombre que lo representa como un animal perfeccionado".

Con la cierta rudeza e ironía que le caracteriza, añade: „Los imbéciles se han imaginado siempre que un individuo que no cree en Dios, y considera a sus semejantes y a él mismo como monos, sólo podía ser un hombre despreocupado, de faz rubicunda, que come y bebe bien, que es mujeriego, pero por lo demás, como dice Rabelais, el mejor hijo del mundo"[16]. Lo que es patente que no es así.

Esta deformación en la concepción del hombre tiene también una importancia extraordinaria. De tal manera que: „El problema que se plantea hoy en día, porque el destino de la humanidad depende de su solución, no es un problema de régimen práctico o económico -democracia o dictadura, capitalismo o comunismo- es un problema de *civilización*". En la actualidad: „de buena gana se califica a esa civilización de inhumana ¿Qué puede ser eso, una civilización inhumana? Es evidentemente una civilización basada sobre una definición del hombre *falsa o incompleta*"[17].

Desde sus inicios, la civilización o cultura occidental ha sido *humanística*, porque puede considerarse la realización del humanismo, que no es más que el „desarrollo del hombre en orden a su perfección humana"[18], o del „acrecentamiento del hombre hacia su plenitud"[19]. De ahí que el humanismo, así como la misma cultura o civilización que lo lleva a cabo: „Se estructura como un recorrido entre dos términos: entre el hombre tal cual es, y el hombre tal cual debe ser, o más brevemente, entre el ser y el deber-ser del hombre"[20].

---

[15] R. Garrigou-Langrange, *Dieu, son existence et sa nature*, op. cit., p. 732.
[16] Georges Bernanos, *La libertad ¿para qué?*, trad. de O. Boutard, Buenos Aires, Librería Hachette, 1955, pp. 83-84.
[17] Ibid., p. 75.
[18] O. N. Derisi, *Naturaleza y vida de la Universidad*, Buenos Aires, Editorial Universitaria de Buenos Aires, 1969, p. 73.
[19] Ibid., p. 77.
[20] Ibid., p. 73.

Por esta falsa o incompleta antropología, la civilización ha perdido su finalidad esencial. En sentido propio: „No (es) una civilización, sino una *contra-civilización,* una civilización hecha no para el hombre, sino que pretende *esclavizar* al hombre, hacer al hombre para ella, a su imagen y semejanza, usurpar de este modo el poder de Dios"[21].

IV. EL PROBLEMA DE LA ECONOMÍA

Uno de lo principales medios que utiliza la civilización para „esclavizar" al hombre es la *técnica.* La importancia hegemónica de la técnica lleva a que se pueda preguntar: „Si la técnica dispondrá en cuerpo y alma de los hombres por venir, si decidirá no sólo de su vida y su muerte, por ejemplo, sino también de las circunstancias de su vida, como el técnico del *criadero de conejos* dispone de los conejos de su conejera"[22]. El dominio de la técnica en la civilización: „Sólo es la consecuencia de esa especie de *'despersonalización',* síntoma análogo y de significado idéntico a cualquier otra victoria de la colectividad sobre el individuo"[23].

La técnica en sí misma no es mala. Por ello, dirá Bernanos: „No se trata de destruir las máquinas, se trata de levantar al hombre, es decir devolverle, con la *conciencia de su dignidad,* la fe en la *libertad de su espíritu*"[24]. La técnica es un instrumento y como tal debe ser utilizada por el hombre. La técnica debe estar al servicio del humanismo, pero no dirigirlo o hasta sustituírlo. No debe reemplazarse la civilización humanística por otra *civilización tecnológica.* La no sumisión de la técnica al hombre hace que se convierta en un peligro para él mismo[25].

La libertad humana se ve amenazada no sólo por la civilización técnica, sino también por el *Estado moderno.* La célebre frase de Lenin „la libertad, ¿para qué?", según Bernanos: „Expresa con brillo y lucidez terribles esa especie de desapego cínico hacia la libertad que ya ha corrompido a tantas

---

[21] G. Bernanos, *La libertad, ¿Para qué?,* op. cit., p. 87.
[22] Ibid., p. 76.
[23] Ibid., pp- 77-78.
[24] Ibid., p. 87. „La técnica es la actividad del hombre por la que fabrica artefactos útiles y en los cuales se proyecta y participa" (A. Caturelli, *La Universidad. Su esencia, su vida, su ambiente,* op. cit., p. 127).
[25] "Todo aquello que siendo relativo se absolutiza, tiende a su propia aniquilación y en nada es más evidente que en la técnica" (A. Caturelli, *La Universasidad. Su esencia, su vida, su ambiente,* op. cit., p. 132). Véase: M. Heidegger, *La pregunta por la técnica,* trad. A.P. Carpio, , en „Epoca de Filosofía" (Barcelona), I/1 (1958), pp. 7-29.

conciencias (...) La frase de Lenin se ha convertido en el 'slogan' del Estado moderno, se pretenda éste demócrata o no"[26].

Advierte seguidamente que considera que: „La democracia significa mucho menos libertad que igualdad, la democracia es infinitamente más *igualitaria* que *libertaria*. Cada victoria de la igualdad parecía al hombre de 1900 una victoria de la libertad. No se daba cuenta de que era primero y ante todo una victoria para el Estado. De cada victoria de la igualdad, cada ciudadano podía sacar algunas ventajas y una satisfacción de amor propio, pero el beneficio real era sólo para el Estado. Reducir todo a un *denominador común* facilita enormemente el problema de las dictaduras. Los regímenes totalitarios son los más igualitarios de todos. La igualdad completa es la esclavitud completa"[27].

Además, sostiene que en la democracia se ha dado un *reduccionismo económico*. Se pregunta, por este motivo: „En la mayoría de los países, ¿acaso la democracia no es en primer lugar y ante todo una *dictadura económica*? Este es un hecho importantísimo y que basta para demostrar la degradación profunda de la sociedad moderna"[28]. Por ella, el hombre, dice más adelante: „ya no existe frente a la economía, su autonomía está desapareciendo, se encuentra envuelto en cuerpo y alma en la economía, representa la verdadera aparición de una nueva clase de hombre, el hombre económico, el hombre que no tiene prójimo sino cosas"[29].

El problema no es meramente económico, sino humano, porque:"Quien dispone de los bienes siempre termina por disponer un día de las personas. Quien se acostumbra a robar corre el riesgo de volverse asesino"[30]. El hombre ha quedado convertido en „material humano", puesto que: „La civilización de las máquinas no puede concebirse sin un material humano siempre disponible". De ahí que al Estado moderno le interese tanto la cuestión de la *justicia social*. „Un material humano ha de ser tan debidamente cuidado como cualquier otro material, pero la libertad, lejos de favorecer su rendimiento, no haría sino disminuírlo en cantidad y calidad"[31].

---

[26] G. Bernanos, *La libertad, ¿Para qué?*, pp. 65-66.
[27] Ibid., pp. 67-68.
[28] Ibid., p. 66.
[29] Ibid., p. 74.
[30] Ibid., p. 81.
[31] Ibid., p. 96. Según Heidegger, por la técnica las cosas: „no se presentan al hombre ni siquiera como objeto, sino exclusivamente como reserva-disponiobe („Bestand"). El hombre en el seno de estos no-objetos, no es más que el que hace la reserva disponible. Entonces el hombre camina junto al borde del precipicio, esto es, va hacia allí donde él mismo va a ser considerado como reserva-disponible" (M. Heidegger, *La pregunta por la técnica*, op. cit., pp. 26-27).

A esta denuncia airada, añade otra más concreta al escribir:. „El mundo moderno no conoce otra regla que la eficiencia. Por eso las democracias mismas han aprisionado su material humano en las redes de una *fiscalización despiadada*. En nombre de tal fiscalización las vemos reforzar hipócritamente cada día el poderío del Estado"[32].

V. EL PROBLEMA DE LA LIBERTAD

Por este creciente poderío: „Esta pregunta 'la libertad, ¿para qué?' el Estado moderno la formula a sus ciudadanos, quiero decir a sus *contribuyentes*, pues en casi todas partes el contribuyente ha reemplazado al ciudadano: 'la libertad, ¿para qué?' ¿Para qué, imbéciles? Concédanme un poco más de tiempo, trabajen de firme y pronto yo los tomaré totalmente a mi cargo, los aseguraré contra todos los riesgos (menos contra la pérdida de la libertad, claro está), los casaré, educaré a sus hijos; ¿qué más podrían pedir? La libertad, ¿para qué? Puesto que yo hasta me tomaré el trabajo de *pensar por ustedes,* también podré ser libre yo en vez de ustedes"[33].

Para Bernanos, por consiguiente: „el mundo moderno es esencialmente un mundo sin libertad"[34]. Además, no solamente se ha dado una apropiación de la *libertad human*a, sino que también los hombres: „Han perdido su libertad más preciada o al menos sólo conservan de ella una parte cada día más pequeña. Su *pensamiento* ya no es libre. Día y noche, casi sin darse (...) cuenta, la propaganda bajo todas sus formas los trata como un modelador trata al *bloque de cera* que amasa entre sus dedos"[35]. A los hombres actuales: „El Estado los alivia algo más cada día de la preocupación de disponer de su propia vida, mientras espera el día cercano -llegado ya para millones de hombres, sí, para millones de hombres en este mismo momento- en que los eximirá de *pensar*"[36].

La pérdida de la capacidad de pensar por propia cuenta, de juzgar o valorar, es una pérdida de salud espiritual. Esta *enfermedad del espíritu* es como una anemia profunda. Sostiene Bernanos que: „El síntoma más general de esa *anemia espiritual*, contestaré con seguridad: *la indiferencia* ante la

---

[32] G. Bernanos, *La libertad , ¿Para qué?*, op. cit., pp. 95-96.
[33] Ibid., p. 71. Escribe más adelante: „La libertad, ¿para qué? ¿De qué puede servir en el mundo de las máquinas? Más aún, sólo puede tornarse cada vez más peligrosa" (Ibid., p. 96).
[34] Ibid., p. 95.
[35] Ibid., p. 97.
[36] Ibid., p. 71. "El estado moderno sólo tiene derechos, ya no se reconoce deberes" (Ibid., p. 81).

verdad y la mentira. Hoy en día, la propaganda prueba lo que quiere y se acepta más o menos pasivamente lo que propone". Añade, Bernanos, con el mismo tono profético, que *ha encantado a unos e irritado* a otros, que: „Esa indiferencia oculta más bien un cansancio, una especie de *asco* de la facultad de juzgar. Pero la facultad de juzgar no puede ejercitarse sin cierto compromiso interior. Quien juzga se compromete. El hombre moderno ya no se *compromete* porque ya no tiene nada que comprometer"[37].

Si „la pasión por la verdad va unida a la pasión por la libertad"[38], al desinterés por la primera le sigue el desinterés por la segunda. Parece que al hombre actual no le importa perder al libertad, usurpada por el estado moderno con la técnica. Lo que es más grave que el mismo hurto, porque: „La peor amenaza para la libertad no es que nos la dejemos tomar – pues el que se la ha dejado robar siempre puede reconquistarla – sino que se desaprenda a amarla o que ya no se la comprenda"[39].

Las conclusiónes de Bernanos -que, como la mayoría de sus afirmaciones y tesis, es considerada por algunos como *descentrada* o como expresión de una *censura exagerada,* aunque no indican las que serían las ponderadas-, son que: „La humanidad entera está *enferma*"; y que, „se debe curar a la humanidad".

Para ello, añade a continuación que: „Ante todo y en primer lugar se debe *'reespiritualizar'* al hombre"[40]. Ante esta „des-espiritualización" o „atrofia de la vida interior"[41]. En segundo y último lugar, propone en este escrito: „Una movilización general y universal de todas las fuerzas del espíritu, con el objeto de devolver al hombre la *conciencia de su dignidad*"[42].

VI. LA PREGUNTA POR EL HOMBRE

Para que pueda redescubrirse esta dignidad del ser humano, de cuyo olvido se lamenta Bernanos, puede ser muy útil volver a reflexionar lo que es el hombre. Se debe intentando contestar a la pregunta kantiana, siempre actual: „¿Qué es el hombre?"[43]

---

[37] Ibid., p. 97. Véase: Charles Moeller, *Literatura del siglo XX y cristianismo*, Madrid, Editorial Gredos, 1961, vol. I, *El silencio de Dios,* pp. 455 y ss.

[38] Ibid., p. 98.

[39] Ibid., p. 65.

[40] Ibid. p. 100. „La humanidad entera está enferma. Se debe ante todo y en primer lugar reespiritualizar al hombre" (Ibid., p. 87).

[41] Ibid., p. 84.

[42] Ibid., p. 99.

[43] Kant, *Logik*, A, 25.

Una de las respuestas más completas y acordes con la realidad se encuentra en el pensamiento griego. En el mundo helénico: „El hombre fue concebido como *confín* de dos mundos, como *horizonte*. Por encima de su cabeza se alza todo el mundo infinito de los espíritus, de las inteligencias, de las substancias separadas. Por debajo todo el universo en cuya composición entra la corporéidad y tiene el peso de la materia. El hombre es ese punto de inserción de dos grandes *pirámides invertidas*"[44].

Explica Santo Tomás -que asumió integramente esta imagen del hombre, aunque al profundizarla, la completó-, que en el panorama metafísico griego, o más concretamente en el neoplatónico, el universo se concibe jerarquizado en una *escala de seres* superiores e inferiores, que, a pesar de su discontinuidad, por sus diferentes grados de ser, guardan una continuidad de *orden*.

Tal graduación sigue la siguiente ley: „Siempre está unido lo ínfimo del género supremo con lo supremo del género inferior, como algunas especies inferiores del género animal exceden en muy poco la vida de las plantas, por ejemplo, las *ostras*, que son inmoviles y sólo tienen tacto y a modo de plantas se agarran a la tierra".

Añade el Aquinate que la aplicación de este principio al hombre, lleva: „A considerar lo *supremo* del género corpóreo, es decir, el cuerpo humano, armónicamente complexionado, el cual llega hasta lo *ínfimo* del género superior, o sea, el alma humana, que ocupa el último grado del género de las substancias intelectuales, como se ve por su manera de entender"[45].

Revela que el alma humana es la última de las subtancias espirituales, la naturaleza de sus facultades superiores. El *entendimiento humano*, por ejemplo, es puramente potencial. No sólo en cuanto que posee una capacidad receptiva de lo inteligible, al igual que las substancias intelectuales inmediatamente superiores, sino también en cuanto que, por carecer del modo de conocimiento por inteligibles innatos, únicamente puede recibirlos, a través de los sentidos sensibles, de las cosas materiales. Por eso Aristóteles equiparaba al entendimiento humano con: „una tabla en la que nada hay escrito en acto"[46].

Por el contrario, el *cuerpo humano* es superior al de los demás animales, tal como muestra su conocimiento sensible. Algunos animales le superan en los sentidos externos, pero no, en los internos – la imaginación, la memoria, etc. – De ahí que: „El hombre posea la complexión *más equilibrada* entre todos los animales"[47].

---

[44] Ibid., pp. 86-87.
[45] Santo Tomas, *Summa Contra Gentiles*, II, c. 68.
[46] Aristoteles, *De anima*, III, c. 4, 429b31.
[47] Santo Tomas, *Summa Theologiae*, I, q. 91, a. 3, ad 1.

La superioridad corpórea del hombre sobre los animales se manifiesta por su *posición erecta*. Argumenta Santo Tomás que: „El tener la estatura recta le fue conveniente al hombre (...) porque los sentidos le fueron dados no sólo para proveerse de lo necesario para vivir, como sucede en los animales, sino para *conocer*. De ahí que, mientras los demás no se deleitan en las cosas sensibles más que en orden al *alimento* y a la *procreación*, sólo el hombre se deleita en la *belleza* del orden sensible por la belleza misma. Por eso, dado que los sentidos están situados la mayor parte en el rostro, los demás animales lo tienen inclinado hacia la tierra, como para buscar el alimento y proveer a su nutrición, mientras que el hombre tiene el rostro erguido, para que por medio de los sentidos, sobre todo por medio de la vista, que es el más sutil y percibe muchas diferencias de las cosas, pueda conocer libremente todas las cosas sensibles, tanto en la tierra como en el firmamento, en orden a descubrir la *verdad*"[48].

La superioridad del cuerpo humano e inferioridad del espíritu humano, con respecto a otro espíritus, que justifica la caracterización del hombre „como *horizonte* y *confín* de lo corpóreo e incorpóreo", queda perfectamente explicada con la doctrina metafísica del hombre de Santo Tomás.

VII. EL CUERPO Y EL ALMA

En su antropología metafísica se demuestra que su alma es „*sustancia* incorpórea, *forma*, sin embargo, del cuerpo"[49]. El alma es substancia inmaterial, porque realiza operaciones, como el entender y el querer, en que no interviene intrínsecamente lo corpóreo. La materia en los actos de entender y de querer es sólo su *condición*, porque concurre en ellos de una manera *extrínseca* e *indirecta*. Por lo mismo que es substancia inmaterial, el alma es también forma del cuerpo, porque *necesita* de sus sentidos para pensar y amar.

En el hombre, sin embargo, *no hay una dualidad profunda*. Es una única substancia, aunque compuesta de la substancia alma -que necesita unirse esencial y, necesariamente al cuerpo- y este último.. „Los dos componentes son *coprincipios* respectivamente. El alma es alma de un cuerpo, el cuerpo es relativo al alma. Uno sin el otro no constituyen al hombre"[50].

---

[48] Ibid., I, q. 91, a. 3, ad 3. Cf. A. Lobato, *El cuerpo humano*, e en Idem (Ed.), *El pensamiento de Santo Tomás de Aquino para el hombre de hoy*, vol. I, A. Lobato, A. Segura, E. Forment, *El hombre en cuerpo y alma*, México-Bogotá-Valencia, Edicep, 1994, pp. 101-275

[49] Idem, *Summa Contra Gentiles*, II, c. 68.

[50] A. Lobato, *Il rapporto medico-malato: la dimensione etica secondo San Tommaso*, en Idem (ED.) *Etica dellátto medico*, Bologna, Edizioni Studio Domenicano, 1991, pp. 11-41.

Según esta concepción del ser humano, denominada hilemórfica, porque alma y cuerpo son forma y materia, según la filosofía de Aristóteles, hay que afirmar que: „Consta de cuerpo y alma, íntimamamente enlazados. *El uno es para el otro. El uno no actúa sino a través del otro*"[51] De ahí que todo lo que llega al alma es a través del cuerpo, y todo lo que brota del alma lo hace con algún concurso del cuerpo.

A la unión del cuerpo y el alma, Santo Tomás la denomina „*conexión admirable*"[52]. Como explica el profesor Lobato: „En la unión de los dos órdenes de la realidad no hay mera yuxtaposición, no hay absorción de un elemento en otro, hay una auténtica unidad de las dos esferas del ser, y por ello se produce un cierto milagro natural, una sorpresa. Por medio del hombre surge en el universo escalonado un *anillo* que abraza al mismo tiempo al espíritu y a la materia, en una conexión estupenda: *mirabilis connexio*".

Añade, a continuación: „La sorpresa sube de punto cuando se piensa que los dos órdenes del ser, unidos y no confundidos en el hombre, tampoco están en igual peso y proporción, porque en la *balanza* tiene mayor peso el espíritu. Es el alma la que confiere la especie, la que informa la materia y la constituye en el orden del ser, es el espíritu el que le da al hombre su dignidad y su distinción"[53].

La corporéidad, a pesar de su valor, es al mismo tiempo una *limitación*. El cuerpo es también una barrera para el hombre. „La materia es límite estructural a las posibilidades del hombre, porque no se adecúa totalmente al alma, porque reduce las posibilidades del espíritu, que de suyo es abierto a la totalidad. La disposición de la materia ya influye en el ser del alma y del individuo con mayor o menor perfección, y por lo mismo condiciona el obrar. Por la corporéidad acontece la fatiga, el dolor, la incapacidad de realizar muchas cosas. En la adquisición de las virtudes, tanto en la vida intelectual, cuanto en la perfección moral la corporéidad puede ser obstáculo"[54].

No obstante, estas limitaciones quedan *compensadas* por el espíritu, porque: „El alma como forma del cuerpo y substancia espiritual al mismo tiempo *penetra* todo lo humano. Porque afecta al ser del hombre nada se escapa

---

[51] Idem, *Primacía de lo intelectual en la comunicación interpersonal*, en „Revista De Filosofía" (Madrid), XXI/80-81 (1962), pp. 89-94, p. 92.

[52] Santo Tomas, *Summa Contra Gentes*, II, 68.

[53] A. Lobato, *La antropología de Santo Tomás y las antropologías de nuestro tiempo*, en Idem (Ed.), *El pensamiento de Santo Tomás de Aquino para el hombre de hoy*, vol. I, op. cit., pp. 25-98, p. 44.

[54] A. Lobato, *La humanidad del hombre en Santo Tomás de Aquino*, en *San Tommaso d'Aquino Doctor Humanitatis*, Atti del IX Congresso Tomistico Internazionle, Pontificia Accademia di S. Tommaso e di Religione Cattolica, Libreria Editrice Vaticana, 1991, vol. I, pp. 44-82, p. 65.

a esta presencia y a esta dignificación que viene del espíritu (...) La condición del alma horizonte está cualificando toda la realidad humana"[55].

En definitiva, por su naturaleza espiritual, el alma humana es *distinta* de la de los animales, pero también lo es de los otros espíritus, que no informan a ningún cuerpo. Sin embargo: „Porque el alma humana es espiritual, pero no es un espíritu separado de la materia, no es adecuado al pensamiento tomista hablar de ella como si fuera *espíritu en el mundo* o *espíritu encarnado*. Hay en todo un resto de platonismo, y la expresión no refleja la realidad de ser alma forma del cuerpo"[56]. El hombre es cuerpo y espíritu, constituyendo ambos una única substancia.

VIII. EL ALMA ESPIRITUAL

El hombre, sin embargo, es superior a los otros seres del cosmos por su *alma*, que revaloriza a su cuerpo, haciéndole participar de su dignidad. La presencia dignificadora del alma espiritual se manifiesta en todo el obrar humano. Incluso en las mismas *actividades económicas*. Como ha señalado Millán-Puelles: „Solamente en virtud de que en el hombre hay espíritu, puede darse en el ser humano una cierta necesidad de cosas artificiales, o sea, de cosas que no llegan a existir, ni pueden tampoco ser usadas, sin que funcione el poder de nuestra razón"[57].

La grandeza del alma espiritual se patentiza en que, como afirmó Aristóteles, es „en cierto modo *todas las cosas*"[58]. Comentando este importantísimo texto, explica Santo Tomás que: „El alma fue dada al hombre en lugar de todas las formas para que el hombre sea en cierto modo todas las cosas, ya que su alma es receptiva de todas las formas"[59].

Lobato ha advertido asimismo que: „La frase aristotélica, el hombre es en cierto modo todas las cosas, *quodammodo omnia*, tenía un sentido preciso. Se trataba de poner de relieve la capacidad típica del hombre, por la cual emerge entre todos los animales: hacia adentro la *mente*, y hacia afuera la *mano*. Por la mente y la mano el hombre va más allá de los propios

---

[55] Idem, *Anima quasi horizon et confinium*, en Idem (Ed.), *L'anima nell'antropologia di S. Tommaso D'Aquino*, Atti del Congresso della Società Internazionale S. Tommmaso d'Aquino (SITA), Milano. Massimo, 1987, pp. 53-80, p. 69.
[56] Idem, *La humanidad del hombre en Santo Tomás de Aquino*, op. cit., pp. 73-74.
[57] A. Milan-Puelles, *Léxico Filosófico*, Madrid, Rialp, 1984, p. 531.
[58] Atistoteles, *De Anima*, III, 431b 21.
[59] Santo Tomas, *In De Anima*, III, Letc. 13, n. 790.
[60] A. Lobato, *La antropología de Santo Tomás de Aquino y las antropologías de nuestro tiempo*, op. cit., pp. 79-80.

confines y puede llegar a superar cualquier límite en el pensar y en el hacer"[60].

También comenta Lobato, sobre la afirmación de Aristóteles: „La mano es el instrumento de los instrumentos"[61], que: „Se le han dado las manos al hombre, como parte integrante de su ser. Por las manos entra en contacto con el contorno. Aristóteles veía en las manos el órgano por excelencia, el medio de la acción productiva, el instrumento humano de mayor alcance. Tomás de Aquino apunta la razón de esta singular eficacia de las manos del hombre. Guíadas por la inteligencia pueden adquirir una dimensión ilimitada. Originan nuevos auxiliares de su acción, una cadena sin fin de instrumentos, que tiene en la mano su primer anillo, y pueden servir para producir un número incontable de efectos"[62]. Por consiguiente, como indica en otro lugar: „La mano humana no es comparable con ninguna mano animal, es un *instrumento de espíritu*"[63].

IX. EL ECLIPSE DEL HOMBRE

Tal es la dignidad humana , que todo lo demás esta a su servicio Como ya decía Santo Tomás de Aquino, al inicio de una de sus obras: „Todas las ciencias y las artes se ordenan a una sola cosa, a la *perfección del hombre, que es su felicidad*"[64]. Unicamente a los seres humanos, a cada una de ellos en su concreción y singularidad, se subordinan todas las ciencias, teóricas y prácticas, las técnicas, las bellas artes, toda la cultura y todas sus realizaciones. Siempre y todas están al servicio del hombre. A la felicidad de los hombres, a su plenitud de bien, es aquello a lo que deben estar dirigidos todos los conocimientos científicos, sean del orden que sean, e igualmente la misma tecnología, y todo lo que hace el hombre.

Puede aceptarse teóricamente la suprema dignidad humana y que todas las cosas son siempre relativas al hombre, que no hay nada, en este mundo, que sea un absoluto, porque todo está siempre referido a la felicidad de los seres humanos, y, sin embargo, no descubrir y reconocer en algunos hombres al ser humano con toda su dignidad. Parece que en ciertas situaciones se *eclipsa* la dignidad humana

El profesor Gonzalo Herranz, en un interesante trabajo, cuenta que en sus cursos realiza una prueba, que efectuó Paul E. Ruskin. Consiste en que

---

[61] Aristoteles, *De Anima*, III, 8, 432a 1.
[62] A. Lobato, *El problema del hacer humano*, en „Salmanticensis" (Salamanca), 13/2, pp. 283-325, p. 284.
[63] Idem, *La humanidad del hombre en santo Tomás de Aquino*, op. cit., p. 67.
[64] Iidem, *In Metaphysicam Aristotelis Commentaria,* Proem.

los alumnos de enfermería y de medicina describan su actitud y estado de ánimo, si tuvieran que asistir a un caso como el que se les presenta: „Se trata de una paciente, que aparenta su edad cronológica. No se comunica verbalmente, ni comprende la palabra hablada. Balbucea de modo incoherente durante horas, parece desorientada en cuanto a su persona, al espacio y al tiempo, aunque da la impresión que reconoce su propio nombre. No se interesa ni coopera en su propio aseo. Hay que darle de comer comidas blandas, pues no tiene piezas dentarias. Presenta incontinencia de heces y orina, por lo que hay que cambiarla y bañarla a menudo. Babea continuamente y su ropa está siempre manchada. No es capaz de caminar. Su patrón de sueño es errático, se despierta frecuentemente por la noche y con sus gritos despierta a los demás. Aunque la mayor parte del tiempo parece tranquila y amable, se pone muy agitada y presenta crisis de llanto inmotivado".

Explica el Dr. Herranz que la respuesta más mayoritaria de los alumnos es del tipo siguiente: „Cuidar a un paciente así sería devastador, un modo de dilapidar el tiempo de médicos y enfermeras". Otra más minoritaría es ésta: „Un caso así es una prueba muy dura para la paciencia y la vocación del médico o de la enfermera. Desde luego, si todos los enfermos fueran cono el caso descrito, la especialidad geriátrica sería para médicos y enfermos santos, pero no para médicos y enfermeras comunes". Se replica señalando que tales posiciones son discriminatorias e incompatibles con la ética, pero no acostumbran a convencerse. Este rechazo desaparece, porque: „La prueba de Ruskin termina haciendo circular entre los estudiantes la fotografía de la paciente referida: una preciosa criatura de seis meses de edad"[65].

Esta prueba es muy útil para advertir lo difícil que es ver siempre en el hombre -sobre todo al débil o al necesitado y al incapacitado- su carácter humano, y también que cualesquiera diferencias de peso, de edad, de expectativa de vida, merecen los mismos cuidados y atenciónes. En definitiva, sirve para comprender el principio ético del respeto a la debilidad en general. Los débiles o los debilitados por la edad, por la enfermedad, por el dolor, y por la soledad, deben ser aceptados y protegidos.

Este principio es, sin duda, uno de los elementos de progreso de las ciencias de la salud como de la misma sociedad. Gracias a la tradición deontológica cristiana, se ha avanzado éticamente, al comprenderse que los débiles no son despreciables y que la sociedad debe ayudarles, e incluso ponerse a su servicio Podría decirse que con esta idea nació la civilización, así como las mismas profesiones sanitarias, las propias de la enfermería, de la medicina, de la farmacia, etc.

---

[65] Gonzali Herranz, „El paciente terminal y la ética de la medicina paliativa", en *Cuadernos de Bioética* (Santiago de Compostela), 16 (1993), pp. 5-19, pp. 14-15.

Es innegable, que todavía, después de dos siglos, este pilar básico sigue encontrando *resistencia* en la sociedad y también en cada uno de nosotros. Probablemente esta oposición se explica porque en los momentos actuales de nuestra cultura se *rechaza* la debilidad. La misma *economía de producción-consumo* y la vida profesional actual, que conlleva la lucha por el *poder*, comportan el desdén por lo improductivo y por el fracaso, y con ello el desprecio por lo débil. Incluso la misma debilidad, la pobreza en todos los ordenes se *oculta*. No se tolera la debilidad. Además, el *hedonismo*, que acompaña al afán de dinero, de poder y de éxito, no reconoce ningún tipo de sufrimiento, por considerarlo indigno.

Se ha dicho incluso que: „Estamos a poca distancia ya de hacer oficial la ética nietzscheana: el cuiadado y la compasión por el débil y por quien es poca cosa son propios de una moral de esclavos, de una humanidad decadente y empobrecida en sus instintos. Se impone la ética de la voluntad, de la fuerza, del poder"[66]. Para *Nietzsche* el espíritu de abnegación y de sacrificio, el espíritu de humanidad, las entrañas de misericordia, el amor al prójimo, la compasión, y la misericordia, son vistas como debilidad, como propios de una „*moral de esclavos*". El auténtico hombre es duro, sin piedad para los débiles. Por su voluntad de poder, que constituye su vida humana en cuanto tal, no atiende al dolor ajeno ni a su propia conciencia.

Desde esta ética de la voluntad de poder, todas las profesiones que tienen por objeto directo al hombre, pueden ser vistas como el de los talleres de reparación de automoviles, cuya función sería arreglar los desperfectos del cuerpo, de un mero conjunto de moléculas o de órganos, para que continúen actuando en un mundo en el que sobreviven los mejores dotados biológicamente.

X. EL ELEMENTO INTERPERSONAL

Ante estas degradaciones, cerradas al mundo de los valores, al mundo propiamente humano, y que representan su empobrecimiento y hasta su brutalización, es preciso no sólo procurar *no colaborar* con esta lucha injusta y aberrante de los fuertes contra los débiles, sino también tratar de que ni social ni individualmente se discriminen a estos auténticos hombres débiles o pobres „pobres". Para ello, es preciso que se *reintroduzcan* los valores humanísticos en las relaciones entre los hombres

Es preciso asumir la afirmación de Séneca, el filósofo español del siglo I: „*Homo res sacra homini*"[67], pero sin excluir al necesitado. También él es

---

[66] Ibid., p. 14.
[67] Seneca, *Epistolae*, 95, 33.

algo sagrado: „*Homo debilis res sacra homini*", el hombre débil es algo sagrado para el hombre. Todo niño, enfermo, anciano, en su condición de necesitado se impone como lo más digno, lo más sagrado. Ante él, hay que ver no lo externo o superficial sino la persona.

Por otra parte, y consecuentemente, hay que procurar que toda relación con la persona, aunque sea débil o necesitada, sea personal. Luchar contra el egoísmo, el amor desordenado de sí mismo, que hace cerrarse dentro de sí y que es el principio y fundamento de todos los males éticos.

En un reciente libro de una octogenaria, se lee: „Hace algún tiempo, un anciano se quejaba de soledad. Vivía en una residencia en la que nada le faltaba. Pero se sentía solo. Le faltaban -según él- tres palabras que empiezan por la letra C. Y son éstas: *Cariño; Comprensión; Compañía*. (Pensamos que hay otra -también con C- de la que pueden arrancar las otras tres...¿No será Corazón?)"[68]. Todos los problemas actuales no son meramente económicos, ni técnicos, sino humanos, de *corazón*.

Vivir como hombre es *amar*. El sentido de la vida del hombre es amar. Esta amor, exclusivo de los hombres, es donación. El amor humano es la benevolencia hacia otra ser humano, el querer el bien no para sí, sino para el otro. Consecuentemente, engendra la *reciprocidad* y, con ella, la unión afectuosa y el deseo de comunicación. El amor es una aspiración a ser comprendido, apreciado, acogido, es decir, a ser amado, pero también implica necesariamente la difusión, el derramarse, el darse. Tan necesario es recibir el amor, como comunicarlo. Lo natural en el hombre es la bondad de corazón y, cuando no la apaga y lo endurece, recibe el amor de los demás, porque el bien que se hace, al igual que el mal, siempre *vuelven* a su autor.

La bondad de corazón se manifiesta en el trato delicado, en la sonrisa dulce, en las palabras nunca hirientes ni mortificantes, ni tampoco bruscas ni imperiosas, en la alabanza sin adulación, en el cuidado en no lastimar, en el ser complaciente e indulgente, en el desinterés y la generosidad, en el no regatear el tiempo para los demás, en la conversación agradable para con todo el mundo, en el saber escuchar e interesarse por los otros, en el ser profundamente agradecido, en definitiva, en *hacer siempre el bien.*

Quiero terminar con este mensaje realista y universal del amor humano, lo más gratificante de todo, que no sólo debe practicarse en las relaciones que también debe ser enseñado a los mismos niños, enfermos y ancianos y a todos los hombres en general. Uno de estos últimos decía hace poco en una entrevista: „Cuando se ha recorrido la mayor parte de la existencia personal, cabe tomar tres rutas diferentes. Por la primera, el hombre, la mujer, se va haciendo más difícil de tratar, está cada día más irritable, impertinente y

---

[68] Aamalia de Miguel, *La oración de la tercera edad,* Madrid, BAC, 1994, p. 110.

protestón; es el camino del *cascarrabias*. La segunda lleva a la desconfianza, al desánimo y al decaimiento; es el camino del viejo quejica o *encogido*. Por la tercera, la persona se va haciendo más atenta, más amable, más indulgente; es el camino del anciano *comprensivo*. Mostrar la imagen de serenidad ante los acontecimientos y de comprensión hacia las personas es justamente el gran servicio que los mayores pueden prestar a la sociedad"[69].

Lo humano no es únicamente la juventud, la belleza o el placer, sino el amor. El amor de donación es lo más propiamente humano. El amor vale para todos y para todas las etapas y situaciones de la vida, porque el amor nunca cambia y en cualquier circunstancia siempre se puede y debe amar. El amor permanece siempre. Además, si somos cristianos sabemos que al final de nuestra vida terrena se nos juzgará por el amor.

---

[69] Victor Garcia Hoz, „Habla un eminente octogenario", en *Palabra* (Madrid), 362 (1995), p. 71.

ABELARDO LOBATO OP
Pontificia Universita S. Tommaso
Italy

LA LIBERTAD Y EL FUTURO DEL HOMBRE
LA PERSPECTIVA TOMISTICA

La conciencia del hombre actual es muy sensible al hecho y a las exigencias de la libertad, que ocupa uno de los puestos más altos en la escala de los valores. Nos encontramos todavía en el horizonte de la modernidad que se caracteriza por su preferencia por la libertad y trata de ponerla como fundamento. Se diría que el hombre de nuestro tiempo tiene más hambre y sed de libertad que de verdad, que cual otro Esaú, vende gustoso sus posesiones por gozar de libertad. Se trata una libertad más bien anhelada que poseída, como la libertad soñada por el prisionero en la cárcel que proyecta su vida para cuando se le abran las rejas. Sea como fuere, esta conciencia colectiva de la humanidad es un hecho, y es un testimonio muy poderoso del proceso ascendente hacia la conquista de la plena humanidad. Comprendemos el lento proceso hacia conquista de la plenitud de lo humano por lo que experimentamos en el individuo que somos cada uno de nosotros. Es lenta la maduración del ser personal, pero es constante y por sus grados. De hecho se realiza en el tiempo un descubrimiento progresivo del ser del hombre, del misterio de su humanidad.

El hombre es siempre más de lo que entiende de sí mismo. Incitado por su proprio misterio vuelve sobre sí y topa consigo en los fenómenos que más le sorprenden. La modernidad se ha sorprendido ante la libertad, y hoy nos interrogamos con cierto estupor por este hecho, por el ser libre, en busca de su verdad y su sentido.

El hombre de nuestro tiempo tiene la certeza de que en la libertad se concentra la esencia de lo humano, de que en ella se juega su dignidad y su destino. Esta poderosa vivencia de la libertad interroga de modo especial al pensamiento cristiano, llamado a conjugar la libertad y la verdad, conforme al célebre pasaje del evangelio de Juan: *Conocereis la verdad y la verdad os hará libres* (Jn, 8,32), precioso *apax legomenon* del evangelio que ha tenido en nuestros días un espléndido comentario en la encíclica „*Veritatis splendor*" de Juan Pablo II[1]. La certeza de que todo hombre, solo por el hecho de ser hombre, es libre ha entrado en el mundo por el anuncio del evangelio. Hegel esto proclama: „Esta idea ha venido al mundo por obra del cristianismo, para quien el individuo como tal tiene valor infinito, y siendo objeto del amor de Dios está destinado a tener una relación con Dios como espíritu, y a conseguir que este espíritu more en él: es decir el hombre está destinado a la suma libertad"[2]. El hombre era libre desde el principio, pero no siempre ha sido consciente de ello, no ha podido gozar de su libertad. Gusdorf ha podido hablar de la „humanidad sin libertad durante milenios"[3]. La idea del hombre en plenitud y su realización se ha verificado en el primer hombre y la hemos conocido en Jesucristo[4].

Los pensadores cristianos han glosado este don de Dios al hombre, en el cual reside su dignidad. El hombre cristiano es libre y ha sido liberado por Cristo. Descartes expresaba con una frase feliz el puesto que ocupa el don de la libertad en el pensamiento cristiano, al contarlo como una de las tres maravillas de la omnipotencia divina: Dios ha hecho el mundo de la nada, la libertad en el hombre, la encarnación en la historia[5]. El pensador cristiano se sitúa ante el hecho de la libertad con el estupor que siente ante las grandes obras de Dios. La historia de la salvación se efectúa por la intervención directa de Dios que realiza lo que ha sido designado como *magnalia Dei*[6]. Tres hechos admirables se imponen entre todos: el primero es el mundo, el segundo el hombre como ser libre, el tercero dios con nosotros, hombre entre los hombres. La analogía entre estos tres „milagros", bien merece una glosa[7]. En los tres se verifica un salto hacia el infinito que solo Dios puede realizar.

La libertad del hombre es un don de Dios, en la misma línea de la creación desde la nada, de la redención que se efectua solo por amor, como un cierto vínculo entre ambas. En el principio está la libertad creadora, de

---

[1] Juan Pablo II, Enc. „*Veritatis splendor*", 6 agosto, 1993. Cfr. „*Veritatis splendor, Testo integrale e commento filosofico teológico*", a cura di R. Lucas, San Paolo, Roma 1994.

[2] G. W. F. Hegel, *Encyclop*, § *482*. Ed. Laterza, Bari 1951, p. 443.

[3] G. Gusdorf, *La signification humaine de la liberté*, Paris 1962, p. 15 ss.

[4] Cfr. Ef. 4, 13, Col. 1,28, etc.

[5] R. Descartes, „*Tria mirabilia fecit Dominus: res ex nihilo, liberum arbitrium et hominem deum*", en *Cogitationes privatae*, Opera edi. Adam-Tann, X, 228.

[6] Cfr. Ex. 14,13; Sal. 70,19; Hech. 2,11, etc.

[7] La hemos desarrollado en otro estudio. Cfr. A. Lobaćto, *Experiencia radical de la libertad*, en „Asprenas" 24 (1977) 401-420.

la cual todo procede. El pensamiento cristiano está llamado a mantener viva esta conciencia de la libertad que va a la par con la dignidad del hombre, a desarrollarla aún más y a orientarla hacia su destino, que tiene que ser conforme a su origen. La filosofía cristiana de nuestros días se siente interpelada por la libertad, y es justo que de ella se espere una nueva luz.

Tomás de Aquino se encontró en su tiempo ante este problema de la libertad y del libre albedrío y lo tratò a fondo[8]. Su profunda comprensión de la humanidad del hombre y la inserción en ella de la libertad, nos ayuda en esta tarea de intérpretes de la libertad actual del ser humano. Tres problemas nos piden espiecial atención: comprensión de la *situación*, retorno al *fundamento*, y *paideia* cultural adecuada para la orientación de la humanidad del hombre en el tercer milenio. El futuro del hombre depende del ejercicio de su libertad.

El hombre es libre, y su libertad tiene un sentido bien preciso. Procede del ser espiritual y se ordena a su expresión y a su complemento. La libertad por un lado es inherente a la dignidad humana, es integrante de la estructura del hombre, por otro es su riesgo, su peso y su tarea. Compete al pensador cristiano redescubrir este don, desvelar su fundamento, orientar su proceso para que sea factor de desarrollo de la plena humanidad del *homo viator*.

I. SITUACIÓN

Para una adecuada comprensión de la libertad es preciso partir de la vivencia de la misma. La libertad es existencial, concreta, se comprueba en el mundo de los fenómenos vividos por el hombre. Es un hecho. El filósofo Bergson, apasionado por la libertad del espíritu, pero reacio a cualificar como libre cualquier acto humano, afirmaba: „La libertad es un hecho, y entre los hechos que observamos, no hay otro más claro"[9]. Los hechos se constatan, pero de suyo no se dejan apresar de modo definitivo. Requieren una categoría, un horizonte de universalidad en el cual se mueve nuestro entendimiento. Por ello nos resulta difícil dar razón de la situación de libertad vivida. Tenemos que aplicar el método agustiniano, de acceso al interior y de subida a una altura de transcendencia: *intra in te ipsum, transcende teipsum*[10].

---

[8] Santo Tomas, QQ. DD. *De Malo*, q. VI: De electione humana. Cfr. A. Lobato, *El principio libertad, El dinamismo originario de la voluntad en la q. VI De Malo de Santo Tomás de Aquino*, en „Doctor Communis", 30 (1977) 33-81.
[9] H. Bergson, *Essai sur les donnés de la conscience*, Paris 1889, p. 169.
[10] S. Agustin, *Conf. 7, 10*.

Si entramos en lo profundo de los hombres de nuestro tiempo, en especial en los conformados por la llamada cultura occidental, todavía la única que tiene irradiación universal, y de modo particular en las nuevas generaciones que son índice de la marcha de la historia, constatamos una situación dramática, que puede ser descrita como el epílogo de la marcha de la libertad en la hora moderna. La experiencia de la libertad es real, pero resulta fatal. El hombre libre de nuestro tiempo es el nuevo Prometeo, capaz de escalar el Olimpo, víctima de su latrocinio, atado a la roca del Cáucaso, mientras los buitres le picotean las entrañas. La libertad de hoy es como la verdad de antaño, se esconde en un pozo profundo y, como decía Demócrito, cuando sale fuera todos corren tras ella pero pocos la alcanzan. El drama singular de nuestra civilización es un drama de libertad, es de tipo espiritual.

La agresividad de los hombres y los pueblos jóvenes, es índice de un anhelo no saciado, y de la frustración consiguiente. La libertad vivida no se identifica con la liberación anhelada. Las nuevas generaciones buscan ante todo la libertad que rehuye toda coacción, por incompatible con ella. La coacción procede desde fuera, es un obstáculo que se interpone en el camino. La experiencia de la libertad está en la superación de los obstáculos.

El proceso es gradual. Se comienza por saltar las barreras interiores, las que impone la moral con los imperativos del *tú debes*, luego las que dicta la religión con la presencia del absoluto que implica dependencia y destino. La huida de toda coacción se extiende más tarde a las que se estiman barreras exteriores, y se encuentran en las estructuras usuales de la vida humana: la familia con sus lazos de sangre, la sociedad civil con sus leyes y normas de comportamiento. Este proceso no tiene límites hasta eliminar todo aquello que pueda ser obstáculo a la libertad. La vivencia moderna de la libertad consiste en admitir como libre solo lo que tenga el carácter de espontáneo, que brote del interior como el agua de la fuente. La libertad humana lleva siempre un sello del espíritu: tiene exigencias de absoluto, lo mismo cuando camina hacia su destino que cuando vaga extraviada.

Esta vivencia de la libertad resulta dramática. Al contrario de lo que se podía esperar, el ejercicio de la pura espontaneidad produce monstruos, engendra esclavos. Los resultados están a la vista. Las nuevas generaciones respiran el aire de la libertad sin trabas y gozan de ella en la casa, en la escuela, en la vida social. A. Mitscherlich describe este predominio de la libertad como espontaneidad en la sociedad sin padres y sin maestros[11]. La rebelión de la juventud en 1968 era su primer producto. La sequela ha sido muy numerosa y los resultados del mismo signo negativo en todas las expe-

---

[11] Cfr. H. Seidl, *Teologia del padre e società senza padri*, en el vol. „La nuova evangelizzazione e il personalismo cristiano", a cura di A. Lobato, Bologna ESD, 1994, pp. 151-167.

riencias. Ese ejercicio de la libertad como pura espontaneidad es apto para derribar barreras y saltar las vallas de todas las Bastillas, pero nada más. En realidad con ella se han fabricado los nuevos paraísos artificiales, de la droga, del sexo, de la *new Age*. Y con ello tenemos el drama y la tragedia, los nuevos esclavos, a veces desde muy temprana edad, los infiernos de nuestro tiempo a la puerta de los cuales también tienen que dejar toda esperanza de vuelta a la humanidad los que van entrando.

Una libertad que sea solo un rechazo de toda coacción de dentro o de fuera no es todavía humana. Es solo un primer paso. Al hombre no le basta no ser oprimido o coaccionado por agentes internos o externos, necesita ser dueño de su ser personal y dirigirlo hacia su adecuado destino. La libertad dramática de nuestro tiempo se pierde en su propio laberinto y muere en la misma fosa que ella está excavando. Trata de ser pura espontaneidad y por ese camino pierde el sello de lo humano, la racionalidad, la disciplina, la virtud.

Podemos intentar otro modo de comprensión del fenómeno, desde una perspectiva más amplia. La situación requiere un horizonte de totalidad para ser valorada. Nos ofrece una primera pista su dimensión hisórica. La libertad es existencial, concreta. Se vive en el tiempo y en el espacio. El momento trágico actual de la libertad en nuestra situación cultural tiene sus antecedentes. Nada ocurre sin su razón suficiente. El pasado deja su huella y a veces revive de nuevo. Nuestra sitación viene descrita como „postmoderna". En efecto estamos en un horizonte cultural que sigue al de la modernidad: aquellos polvos trajeron estos lodos. La libertad humana en el pasado ha recorrido tres etapas fundamentales. Este momento tiene algo de las tres, en una nueva amalgama.

La primera experiencia de la libertad humana, con su teoría y su praxis social, fue la griega. Era una libertad cívica, social, política. El pueblo griego se había liberado de los „bárbaros" y conquistó a gran precio su libertad. Atenas es la primera ciudad libre del mundo antiguo. Esa experiencia de libertad fue el germen de la especulación y de la comprensión más profunda de la libertad, pero tenía sus límites bien precisos. Apenas penetró en lo profundo del hombre, porque no logró la superación del horizonte del cosmos, y la entendió como espacio cerrado dentro del horizonte de la necesidad. Para el hombre griego la fatalidad domina siempre y cada ser humano, como en las tragedias, es víctima de su destino. La libertad actual hereda de esa concepción el acento político, y el recurso al horóscopo. En cierto sentido seguimos siendo griegos. Cada vez que el hombre occidental se extravía en su camino, retorna como Anteo, a sus raices cósmicas. La libertad actual trata de ser liberación frente al mundo. Es una libertad que se contenta con lo periférico, con el trascender sin trascendencia[12].

---

[12] Cfr. M. Pohlenz, *La libertà greca*, Paideia, Brescia 1963; V. Guazzoni Foa', *La libertà nel mondo greco*, Genova 1974.

Mayor es la huella no borrada de la libertad cristiana. Es esta la que ha modelado a occidente, la que ha revelado que la libertad externa cuenta poco frente a la interna, la que ora por la liberación del mal, la que comprende el evangelio como anuncio de liberación y a Cristo como liberador, que „nos ha liberado para la libertad"[13]. Con el anuncio cristiano de la liberación, el hombre se comprendió a sí mismo en su verdad, porque logró situarse a solas frente a Dios. El hombre descubrió su verdadero rostro, su dignidad de *imago Dei*, su vocación singular de ser colaborador en la obra de Dios en su triple dimensión, de creación, de redención y de santificación, su terrible poder de decir sí y no a Dios, su responsabilidad ante el bien y el mal, su destino consiguiente. El hombre cristiano ha reconocido su dignidad, su pertenencia al mundo espiritual, su situación en la escala de los seres. Esta herencia cristiana y esta comprensión de la libertad, para el bien y para el mal, es la piedra angular de la cultura de occidente[14]. Esta huella profunda de su origen cristiano persiste en la cultura actual. A partir de Nietzsche este hombre libre necesita gritar en la plaza *Gott ist tot*, proclamar que no hay más dios que el hombre: *homo homini deus*!. Ese anhelo de infinito y esa sed de absoluto, es de origen cristiano, una de las ideas cristianas, que al decir de Chesterton, se han vuelto locas al dejar la casa paterna.

En la genealogía y el atavismo de la libertad hay que contar también entre sus progenitores a los filósofos del iluminismo. Son ellos los que han proclamado la „salida del hombre de la minoría de edad", los que han puesto la piedra angular de la libertad como la gran respuesta a la pregunta kantiana *Was ist der Mensch?*. Fichte es el discípulo de Kant que identifica el ser con la libertad, que va más allá de Nicolás de Cusa, que daba a la libertad el privilegio de elevar al hombre a un *secundus deus*, para hacerlo un absoluto. El nuevo Prometeo sube al Olimpo y se sitúa a sí mismo en el puesto de los dioses. „El hombre, condenado a ser libre, porta el peso del mundo entero sobre sus espaldas: es el responsable del mundo y de sí mismo en cuanto modo de ser", dirà con su habitual osadía Sartre[15]. La libertad actual es el hijo pródigo que salió de esa casa del padre y se encuentra ahora, al final de su proceso descendente, con algunos harapos del antiguo vestido.

El proceso de la modernidad, que exaltaba al hombre y sus dotes, que negaba toda transcendencia y se proclamaba ateo, ha concluído su periplo. No restan sino los efectos de esa huída del ser y de Dios, el nihilismo, ya

---

[13] Gal. 5,1. Cfr. J. Moltmann, *El cristianismo como religión de libertad* en „Convivium", 26 (1968) 39-70.

[14] Cfr. A. Lobato, *La filosofia cristiana de la libertad*, Primer Congreso Mundial de Filosofia cristiana, Córdoba, Argentina, 1982, vol. II, pp. 357-370.

[15] J. P. Sartre, *L'être et le néant*, Nagel, Paris 1965, p. 665.

profetizado por Sartre y justificado por Heidegger[16]. La tragedia histórica de este proceso de la libertad está en que anhela el absoluto y concluye en el nihilismo.

Desde las dos lecturas de la situación de la libertad actual, la de la vivencia, y la de la genealogía, podemos obtener una cierta comprensión del fenómeno. Para la conciencia cristiana esta lectura dramática y nihilista de la libertad es toda una sacudida cultural, ante la cual no se puede dar un rodeo y pasar como si nada ocurriera. Es un síntoma de extrema gravedad. La suerte del hombre está en juego y nada humano nos puede ser ajeno.

Cómo ha sido posible este proceso? Qué hacer para remediarlo? Una de las causas de este desvío cultural de la libertad y origen de la situación en que se encuentra puede detectarse en la ruptura que se ha producido entre naturaleza y cultura, entre la dimensión natural y la cultural del hombre. El hombre es a un tiempo una conjunción de ambas. La libertad es el puente que une las dos orillas. En nuestros días el puente no es apto para transitar por él. La cultura ha tratado de imponerse a la naturaleza en ver de ser una expansión de la misma.

De hecho el hombre es un ser cultural, y todo hombre es sujeto y objeto de la cultura. La cultura del hombre es el envolvente de las situaciones históricas, la esfera humana que se prolonga más allá de la naturaleza. Este horizonte es necesario, pero si se enfrenta a la naturaleza, resulta nefasto. La naturaleza es el fondo persistente y consistente. La cultura es siempre frágil, quebradiza. El hombre culto fácilmente deja paso al bárbaro que llevamos dentro y parece siempre pronto a despertar a través de los instintos. La cultura moderna ha ignorado la condición real del hombre en su estado de naturaleza caída, en su condición de ser menesteroso, frágil, quebradizo. Ha mitificado la libertad, la ha hecho una diosa. En nombre de la libertad a lo largo y ancho del siglo XX se han hecho los crímenes más horrendos de la historia. El ídolo fabricado con manos humanas, ha saltado por los aires, hecho pedazos.

La filosofía cristiana, en esta hora de nihilismo cultural, está llamada a volver por los fueros de la libertad, porque pertenece a la esencia del hombre y rescatarla de las ruinas que la han sepultado. La libertad del hombre actual se encuentra herida. El hombre de hoy es el que describe la parábola del buen samaritano, es el hombre a la vera del camino, expoliado, herido, desangrado, semimuerto que pide ayuda a los que pasan a su lado[17]. Hay en el hombre una herida original, que tiene parte en esta situación histórica.

---

[16] Cfr. A. Lobato, *Gli ostacoli all'incontro con Dio nella cultura odierna*, en el vol. „L'incontro con Dio", ESD, Bologna 1993, pp. 11-35.

[17] Lc. 10, 30-37.

Tomás de Aquino nos da la clave para penetrar en nuestra condición de expoliados al borde del camino. En verdad la naturaleza humana, después de la caída originaria, conserva los elementos esenciales que la constituyen, y las propiedas que brotan della, como las potencias, el entendimiento y la voluntad, la sensibilidad y las pasiones, porque „el bien de la naturaleza ni se quita ni se disminuye por el pecado"; ha perdido el don de la justicia original del que gozó el primer hombre; y si no ha perdido la inclinación natural a la virtud, sí ha disminuído esa inclinación, al crecer la contraria que le incita al pecado: „porque el pecado es contrario a la virtud, y por lo mismo que el hombre peca, se disminuye el bien de la naturaleza que es la inclinación a la virtud"[18].

La situación actual de la libertad humana es muy ambigua. Es un „signo de los tiempos" el hambre y sed de libertad que siente el hombre de hoy, tanto a nivel singular como a nivel de pueblos. No es posible concebir la vida humana sin la promoción de las libertades fundamentales y de los derechos del hombre como ser personal y ser cultural[19]. Esa ansia de libertad en índice de la profunda realidad humana, cuya estructura implica la libertad. Pero por otro lado, el abuso de la libertad, la carencia de fundamento, el total olvido de sus raices cristianas, y la obstinación en ignorar la naturaleza del hombre, han dado origen al nihilismo y a los infiernos modernos. La filosofía cristiana está interpelada por estos signos y por esta situación y obligada a dar una respuesta a este problema. Nada humano nos es ajeno, y en cada hombre se juega la suerte de la humanidad[20]. La superación de esta triste situación requiere descubrir la verdad integral de la libertad. Esta es un poder, es esponteneidad, tiende al absoluto, es el signo de la dignidad del hombre, pero es también responsable, necesita de la luz y la claridad de la inteligencia, debe someterse a la disciplina y ser ayuda en la conquista del bien y camino que lleva a Dios. Para el pensamiento cristiano el hombre libre de nuestros tiempos está descrito en las primeras secuencias de la parábola del hijo pródigo: reclama su parte de herencia, deja la casa parterna, se aleja a una región lejana, es víctima de sus pasiones y se encuentra sirviendo a otro señor, añorando la libertad perdida. Con ella pierde a girones su humanidad. Con el alba del tercer milenio se propicia la segunda parte: la entrada en sí mismo, la carrera hacia el padre, la fusión de ambos en un abrazo de encuentro, el vestido nuevo y la libertad en casa y en fiesta[21].

---

[18] S. Tomas, *Sum. Theol.* I. II, q. 85, 1.

[19] Cfr. A. Lobato, *Nuevos horizontes de los derechos humanos. La Iglesia y los derechos de los pueblos*, en „Angelicum", 73 (1996) pp. 185-216.

[20] Cfr. A. Lobato, *Coscienza morale e storicità dell'uomo*, in „Crisi e risveglio della coscienza morale nel nostro tempo", Bologna, ESD, 1989, pp. 9-46.

[21] Cfr. Lc. 15, 11-32.

Este Congreso de Filosofía cristiana está llamado a ser el primer paso del largo camino de vuelta a la verdadera libertad del hombre.

II. FUNDAMENTO

Frente a la situación dramática y nihilista de la libertad en la cultura actual la filosofía cristiana está invitada a dar su respuesta. La tarea fundamental que se espera de ella es la que la que corresponde a la filosofía, una palabra clarificadora. La filosofía tiene el cometido de buscar, encontrar y comunicar la verdad, responder a la pregunta sobre el ser de la libertad en el hombre. Esta gran vocación del filósofo como buscador de la verdad, le impone la tarea correlativa de combatir el error contrario. El filósofo cristiano tiene que asumir esta doble función y ordenarla al servicio de la verdad que propone la fe. Tomás de Aquino, *Studiorum Dux*, fiel a su vocación de filósofo y teólogo cristiano, se trazó para sí mismo este ideal desde el principio de su obra[22]. Nuestra situación cultural tiene una cierta vivencia de la libertad, pero tiene una profunda necesidad de conocer la verdad de la libertad, sin la cual no puede decirse dueño de sí mismo y verdaderamente libre. La respuesta al nihilismo contemporaneo, ya anticipado por Lenin y practicado por todos los regímenes totalitarios, – *La libertad, para qué?...* – solo es válida cuando se conoce bien qué es y qué no es la libertad del hombre. Podemos glosar a S. León Magno que invitaba a conocer la dignidad del hombre y en ella incluía la libertad: *Agnosce, oh chritiane, libertatem tuam!*[23].

La verdad accesible al hombre se apoya en el ser, pero se verifica en el juicio, en el cual se da la adecuación del entendimiento a la cosa y de la cual se sigue el conocimiento de la realidad[24]. La libertad humana no es fácil de apresar en ese orden. El entender humano no va directamente ni a los singulares, ni al horizonte apetitivo. La libertad le presenta las dos dificultades: se realiza en el orden existencial y pertenece de modo especial a la voluntad. Pero como todo lo que tiene acto de ser, es inteligible, el entender humano, aunque sea dando los rodeos de la *conversio ad phantasmata*, y de la analogía, llega a percibir de algún modo el llamado „milagro de la libertad humana".

---

[22] S. Tomas, *Cont. Gent. I, 1-2.* Cfr. A. Lobato, *Filosofia y teología. El uso y el abuso de la filosofia en la teología enlas primeras obras de Santo Tomás*, en AA. VV. „San Tommaso Teologo" a cura di A. Piolanti, Lib. Editrice Vaticana 1995, pp. 59-84.

[23] San Leon Magno, *Sermo I de Natívitate Domini*, PL, 54, 192: *Agnosce, oh christiane dignitatem tuam!*

[24] Cfr. A. Contat, *La relation de vérité selon Saint Thomas d'Aquin*, [Studi tomistici, 62] Libr. Editrice Vaticana, 1996.

La indagación sobre el ser de la libertad se reduce a las dos grandes cuestiones que el hombre se plantea: la de su existencia, y la de su modo de ser o esencia. La existencia es el punto de partida. Es preciso topar con ella. No se deduce de ningún principio. Es preciso comprobarla en el orden de lo real. En la cultura actual la existencia de la libertad no es un problema especial, una cuestión disputada, como lo ha sido en otros momentos. Su existencia tiene un consenso universal, que guizá nunca ha tenido tan amplia aceptación como en nuestro tiempo. En una situación análoga, Tomás de Aquino para demostrar la imposibilidad de un entendimiento único y separado, contra Averroes y los discípulos que él por vez primera designó como „averrfoistas", recurrió a la experiencia de cada hombre – *hic homo singularis intelligit!*[25]. Este mismo recurso lo emplea en nuestro tiempo Sartre y trata de darle valor para negar la existencia de Dios. Si yo actúo con libertad, no hay espacio para Dios: *Il n'y avait que moi: j'ai décidé seul.. moi l'home. Si Dieu existe, l'hommne est néant; si l'homme existe...*"[26]. La existencia de la libertad parte de la experiencia interna, en el cual el sujeto está presente a sí mismo, con la capacidad de transcender la corriente de los actos y penetrar en la estructura de los mismos. Para Tomás de Aquino la existencia de la libertad viene vorroborada desde tres posiciones complementarias, la fe, la experiencia y la razón, en las cuales el hombre obtiene la solución fuera de toda duda. En efecto la fe cristiana implica la libertad del ser personal, la fenomenologia de la libertad lo hace presente en el acto de elegir, la razón lo prueba en el análisis del acto libre del cual es causa solo el hombre[27]. Esas pistas de aproximación a la existencia del acto libre siguen conservando todo su valor en nuestro tiempo. Cada hombre es capaz de topar con la libertad en sí mismo. El cristiano corrobora su certeza desde las exigencias de respuesta personal que implica la llamada de parte de Dios a la vida nueva.

La cuestión disputada en nuestro tiempo no es la de la existencia, sino la de la esencia, la del origen del acto libre, por el cual el hombre se convierte en *causa sui*, conforme a la feliz expresión que Aristóteles aplicaba a la metafísica y Tomás de Aquino adaptó a la libertad humana[28]. Es claro que la verdad sobre la libertad del hombre, presupone la verdad sobre el hombre mismo. Y es aquí donde ha centrado su reflexión el hombre de la

---

[25] S. Tomas, *De unitate intellectus contra averroistas*, nº 62.

[26] J. P. Sartre, *Le diable et le bon Dieu*, Gallimard 1951, p. 267.

[27] S. Tomas, *QD, De veritate*, 24, 1: „Absque omni dubitatione hominem arbitriuo liberum ponere oportet. Ad hoc enim *fides* astringit, cum sine libero arbitrio non possit esse meritum vel demeritum, iusta poena vel proemium. Ad hoc enim *manifesta indicia* inducunt, quibus apparet hominem libere unum eligere et aliud refutare. Ad hoc etiam *evidens ratio* cogit".

[28] Aristoteles, *Met. I, 2, 982 b 26-27*. S. Tomas, *In I Met. Lect. III*, nº 58-59.

modernidad, La antropología es la gran cuestión. La seducción del pensamiento kantiano ha sido decisiva: *Was ist der Mensch*? En la práctica esta cuestión ha sustituido la pregunta que para Aristóteles retorna siempre a la mente humana: τό τί ὄν;. Este intento kantiano ha provocado no solo la revolución copernicana, el giro antropológico, sino también el olvido del ser, y la negación de Dios. Hasta Heidegger se interroga sobre la validez de esta propuesta arrogante de reducción de todo el saber, el deber y el esperar al hombre. En verdad las espaldas de este Atlante moderno no son capaces de soportar el peso del ser[29].

En realidad el concepto de natroplogía ha cambiado de signo. Ya no se trata de prolongar los antiguos tratados *De Homine*, sino de penetrar en un sujeto cuyo horizonte tiende siempre al absoluto. A partir de Kant se puede decir que ha nacido un „neoaverroismo", con la aparición del „ego trascendental", que domina todo el desarrollo del pensar postkantiano. Se hecha en olvido la realidad del hombre en cuerpo y alma, del hombre de carne y hueso que proclamaba con razón el pensador español Miguel de Unamuno. No es necesario seguir aquí el hilo de esta vuelta y las consecuencias que implica para la filosofía. Pero sí tenemos que denunciar el desvío y exigir un retorno a la comprensión del hombre en sus justos límites, de ser finito, a un tiempo corporal y espiritual, con una estructura de cuerpo y alma, con una dignidad personal, abierto al ser *y capax Dei*. El retorno a una antropología sensata y real es una condición previa para la comprensión adecuada del hombre como ser libre.

La humanidad del hombre tiene también su gran maestro en Tomás de Aquino, cuyo pensamiento está abierto a todas las aportaciones valiosas de la modernidad[30]. El pensamiento cristiano tiene su mejor expresión acerca del hombre en la *imago Dei*. Tal es el espejo en que se debe mirar y desde el que se debe juzgar toda antropología. El ser del hombre precede al ser libre de cada hombre. La libertad se sitúa en la esfera del dinamismo, de la acción que sigue al ser.

Los desvíos nunca son puro error. El pensamiento moderno, centrado en el horizonte de lo humano, a partir de Kant, ha estimulado la búsqueda del ser libre del hombre, porque pone la libertad como fundamento de su nuevo sistema. Se trata de un fundamento que sostiene todo el edificio, pero escapa de algún modo a nuestra comprensión. Kant no tenía escrúpu-

---

[29] Cfr. M. Heidegger, *Kant et le probléme de la metaphysique*, Gallimard, 1953, $ 38, pag. 270 y ss.

[30] Cfr. A. Lobato, *La humanidad del hombre en Tomás de Aquino*, en el vol. „San Tommaso d'Aquino Doctor humanitatis", Atti del IX Congresso Tomistico Internazionale, Libr. Vaticana, 1991, pp. 51-82: ID. „*Antropologia y metantropologia. Los caminos actuales de acceso al hombre*", en „Aquinas", 30 (1987) pp. 5-41. ID. *El hombre en cuerpo y alma*, Valencia, EDICEP, 1994.

los en afirmar: „la libertad es un problema ante el cual son vanos los esfuerzos de los hombres"[31]. Quizá por esta incitación a la búsqueda de ese tesoro oculto de cada hombre los discípulos y herederos del pensamiento kantiano se apasionaron hasta el extremo por el tema de la libertad. Basta enumerar los tres grandes del idealismo: Fichte, Schelling, Hegel. Su aportación al problema, aún dentro del extravío inicial en torno a la antropología, deslumbrados por esa ilusión del absoluto, ha producido abundantes efectos. Uno de los más acertados y vistosos es la superación de las categorías del cosmos para describir lo humano. La nueva filosofía, amasada con „sangre de teólogos", al decir de Nietzsche, prefería un lenguaje y unas categorías cristianas, para expresar sus contenidos. Pierden importancia tanto el alma, como el cuerpo, para describir lo humano, pero entra bajo arcos de triunfo el espíritu.

En esta nueva orientación la libertad se entiende no solo como espontaneidad, sino como causalidad originaria. De ella depende la posición del ser, el ser mismo en su novedad irrepetible. La realidad es proceso y el ser se entiende como dinamismo espiritual que todo lo pervade. Hegel puede afirmar: „La libertad expresa a la vez la esencia y el vértice del hombre como espíritu, es decir como elevación de la voluntad a la realidad absoluta de la idea"[32]. Cada ser humano está llamado a tener una relación de Dios como espíritu. Esta relación es directa, un salto al encuentro con el absoluto. Kierkegaard, desde su posición aún los antípodas de Hegel, sitúa el individuo ante Dios y recurre también a la omnipotencia divina para la fundación de la libertad[33].

Hay que agradecer al pensamiento moderno esta insistencia en la categoría del espíritu y esta pasión la novedad del ser, como fruto de la libertad. Pero al tratar de la libertad humana hay que volver a la realidad concreta que es el hombre, cuyo dinamismo procede del ser y de sus estructuras de ente finito.

Tomás de Aquino ha sido presentado como „maestro de libertad", y en realidad lo es[34]. El punto de partida es la inserción de la libertad humana en el ser del hombre. Una vez dado a conocer el ser humano, cuyo origen es porvía de creación, y tiene su mejor comprensión cristiana como *imago Dei*, Tomás estudia „el fenómeno" y el ser humano, desde la dimensión espiritual del alma, por ser ella la forma única del cuerpo, cuya esencia, potencias y operaciones abren el horizonte de la libertad. El dinamismo del

---

[31] E. Kant, *Kritik der praktischen Vernunft*, B, 116.
[32] F. W. Hegel, *Enz.* § 482.
[33] S. Kierkegaard, *Diario*, 7a 181.
[34] Cfr. C. Fabro, *San Tommaso, maestro di libertà*, en „Studium" 70 (1974) pp. 155-168.

hombre pertenece al orden existencial, y tiene su origen en el supuesto que es la persona. La libertad del hombre va con el ser mismo por su condición espiritual, pero no se confunde con el ser, porque en la creaturas ser y obrar nunca coinciden. San Pablo había afirmado que la libertad se da donde hay espíritu, y que la libertad cristiana está donde está el Espíritu del Señor que libera al hombre: *Ubi Spiritus ibi libertas*[35]. El espíritu se encuentra en el creador y en las creaturas espirituales. Tomás analiza cómo se encuentra la libertad de modo diferente en cada una de estas categorís de los seres espirituales: en Dios, en las sustancias espirituales, en el hombre. El espíritu en el hombre está constituído por el alma. El alma del hombre no es material, es de naturaleza espiritual. Hay que recurrir a ella para encontrar el fundamento de la libertad. El alma humana es espiritual, creada directamente por Dios, forma sustancial del cuerpo.

A diferencia de Avicena, que se figuraba el alma humana, ya creada por Dios en el acto de venir como en vuelo a su corporeidad, y le atribuía actos de pensar y de querer, el *cogito y el volo*[36], Tomás excluye la posibilidad de cualquier acto del alma antes de ser infundida en el cuerpo y animar el corazón, *primum vivens et ultimum moriens*. El hombre es un *sinolon*, un todo, compuesto de cuerpo y alma, y las operaciones son del todo, del cuerpo animado por una sustancia espiritual. El alma humana, por su condición espiritual, y por su destino de ser forma sustancial del cuerpo, se sitúa en el horizonte de los dos mundos, el del espíritu y el de la materia, y tiene relaciones con ambos[37]. Por su condición de espíritu le competen operaciones que trascienden la materia para las cuales está dotada de principios o potencias que brotan de la misma esencia del alma. En vez de las tres potencias del alma que proponía la tradición augustiniana, Tomás, dejando a parte la memoria, solo admite entendimiento y voluntad, si bien el entendimiento, conforme al pensamiento de Aristóteles, es doble, agente y posible, el que forma los intelegibles y el que entiende.

Hay una primacía del entendimiento sobre las demás potencias, en el origen, en el objeto, en la orientación de todo el proceso del desarrollo del ser personal. De suyo el entendimiento no es libre. La fuerza de las cosas se le impone, y el entendimiento se mueve desde la evidencia de la realidad que es su medida. Pero el alma no es puro entendimiento, no es solo cognoscente, es también volente. Hay en ella una potencia espiritual, que se designa como apetito, o voluntad, por la cual se dirige hacia las cosas cono-

---

[35] II ad Cor, 3, 17.

[36] Cfr. A. Lobato, *Avicena y Santo Tomás en la teoria del conocimiento*, Granada 1956, pp. 35-50.

[37] Cfr. A. Lobato, *Anima, quasi horizon et confinium*, en AA. VV. „L'anima nell'antropologia di San Tommaso", Roma, PUST, 1987, pp. 52-80.

cidas en su realidad existente. Estas dos potencias del alma son el puente de encuentro entre el hombre y la realidad. Por el conocer el alma tiene en sí de modo intencional todo lo que ella es y lo que hay fuera de ella. El conocer es un proceso intencional *a rebus in animam*. Por el apetito racional, la voluntad, el hombre puede ir a las cosas que conoce dentro y fuera. Es un proceso hacia afuera *ab anima ad res*. Esta circularidad comienza en el alma: inteligencia y voluntad radican en la misma alma, proceden de ella, se destinan a su perfección, por ella todo lo conocido puede ser querido, y todo lo querido puede ser conocido. El alma humana está presente a sí misma, se posee. Esta presencia y dominio se ejerce mediante los actos del conocer y del querer. Las potencias espirituales tienen esta capacidad de vuelta sobre sí, de reflección, de compenetración. Hay en ellas un proceso que brota del alma y una primacía alternativa, en los dos órdenes, el del conocer y el de mover. Nada es apetecido si no es previamente conocido, nada pasa al acto si la voluntad no lo mueve[38]. La voluntad humana tiende al bien por su misma inclinación natural y lo apetece necesariamente si se le presente como puro bien. En los casos en que solo se presenta un bien concreto, que es apetecible como bien, pero no sacia la sed de infinito de la voluntad, esta queda libre, y está invitada a ejercer su determinación. Así nace el àmbito de la libre elección, de la opción por el fin y los bienes concretos. La voluntad se mueve a sí misma y mueve las demás potencias en el ejercicio, con dominio de su acto y elección de su objeto. Es aquí donde radica todo el poder de la voluntad libre, que es el horizonte de la *voluntas ut voluntas*[39].

La libertad tiene aquí su raíz, en la espiritualidad del alma y en la capacidad de esta de conocer y de apetecer. El centro radical es el ser personal, constitutivo, en el cual encuentran unidad todos los elementos y estratos que pertenecen al hombre. El ser personal es concreto, un todo bien compacto, inalienable, incomunicable, con esa alta dignidad que da el ser espiritual. Tiene el más alto grado de ser, que es el supuesto, y el más alto grado de modo de ser que el espiritual. Tomás ha puesto de relieve esta centralidad de la persona, de la cual brota la interioridad, la presencia de sì a sí, la dignidad del ser humano, y al mismo tiempo la capacidad de apertura y de

---

[38] S. Tomas, *QD De Veritate*, 22, 12: „Potentiis autem animae superioribus, ex hoc quod inmateriales sunt, competit quod reflectantur super seipsas; unde tamvoluntas quam intellectus refelctuntur super ser et unum super alterum, et super essentiam animae et super omnes eius vires. Intellectus enim intelligit se, et voluntatem et essentiam animae et omnes animae vires, et similiter voluntas vult se velle, et intellectum intelligere, et vult essentiam animae et sic de aliis".

[39] S. Tomas, *QD, De Malo*, q. VI. „De electione humana: voluntas movet seipsam et omnes alias potentias. Intelligo enim quia volo, et similiter utor aliis potentiis et habitibus".

relaciones en el orden intencional. En la persona se concentra el ser, por su condición espiritual el ser personal se distiende y se hace como advertìa Aristoteles, *quodammodo omnia*[40]. Esta capacidad intencional del sujeto humano es su riqueza. Tomás no solo acogió la feliz fòrmula de Aristóteles sino que la desarrolló en todos los campos de lo humano[41]. Por la condición espiritual del alma humana es posible la correspondencia del hombre con el ser y con todas sus propiedades. El ser, además de uno, es verdadero, bueno y bello. Las facultades del alma hacen posible el desarrollo del hombre como apertura hacia la toalidad, y hasta su capacidad de encuentro con el Absoluto. Esta apertura alcanza su grado más alto en la expresión que define al hombre como *capax Dei*[42].

Tal es el proceso tomista para la fundación de la libertad humana. Queda bien fundada al describir el ser el hombre como imagen de Dios, y participar de su espiritualidad, de estar destinado a convivir con él. El alma y sus potencias de entender y querer son fundamento del ser libre del hombre. A partir de ahí se busca el fundamento inmediato tanto en el entedimiento cuanto en la voluntad. Ambas potencias del alma resultan implicadas. Los antiguos han preferido hablar de libre albedrío, o libre juicio, para indicar la pertenencia de las dos facultades al acto libre. El ser funda la actividad. Esta se ejerce solo en el orden existencial. Por ello hay que llegar a un acto de la libertad, y este se encuentra en la elección. Tomás ha comenzado su itinerario del hombre hacia Dios, poniendo como punto de partida la libertad humana, la capacidad de dominio sobre los actos humanos, citando unas palabras de Juan Damasceno, que Tomás ha hecho célebres. Hay una conección entre el hombre imagen de Dios, y el ser libre, que es principio de sus actos, capaz de dominio sobre ellos[43].

En un intento de diálogo con el pensamiento moderno, en la misma línea en que Tomás se movió, como pensador esencial y dialogante, entre los tomistas actuales se discute apasionadamente si no ha llegado el momento de superar la visión de la libertad tomista, anclada en la distinción de la voluntad, *ut natura et ut voluntas*. En la concepción tomista se da razón del acto libre, pero no se advierte fácilmente el tremendo poder de ese acto

---

[40] Aristoteles, *De anima*, III, 8, 43 1 b 21.

[41] Cfr. J. Girau, *Homo quodammodo omnia según Santo Tomás de Aquino*, Toledo, 1995.

[42] S. Tomas, *Sum. Theol.* III, 9, 2.

[43] S. Tomas, *Sum. Theol.* I. II. Prol. „Quia sicut Damascenus dicit (De Fide Orthodoxa, II, 12, PG, 94, 920) homo factus ad imaginem Dei dicitur secundum quod per imaginem significatur intellectuale et arbitrio liberum, et per se potestativum, postquam praedictum est de exemplari, scilicet de Deo... restat ut consideremus de eius imagine, id est de homine, secundum et ipse est suorum operum principium, quasi liberum arbitrium habens et suorum operum potestatem".

personal, cuando se sitúa frente a Dios, ni resalta la novedad en el ser que implica, para bien o para mal, el acto de la libertad radical. La posición cristiana de Sören Kierkegaard parece haber llegado más a fondo en la comprensión de la relación de la libertad y el ser del hombre. El diálogo con Kierkegaard ha sido una de las cuestiones que el P. Fabro ha planteado a los tomistas actuales. Con anterioridad Fabro había encontrado en Tomás la solución al problema y la acusa lanzada por Heidegger contra la filosofía occidental, el del olvido del ser. De modo análogo creyó poder encontrar también en Tomás, de quien se profesó siempre discípulo fiel, la radicación de la libertad en el ser y la primacía de la voluntad en el hombre. Fabro dedicó gran atención a este problema y realizó una lectura nueva de los textos tomistas, tratando de superar toda huella de la primacìa del entendimiento, como herencia aristotélica que debía ser superada. En vez de afirmar con Tomás la radicalidad del entendimiento que hace posible la libre elección y se expresa en la fórmula: *radix totius libertatis est in ratione constituta*[44], Fabro prefiere el recurso al fundamento, al ser espiritual imagen de Dios, familiar a Dios, y por ello capaz de participar en la emergencia de la realidad mediante el poder de la libertad. El hombre por la libertad alcanza a gozar de una creatividad participada, al modo como lo proponía y resolvía S. Kierkegaard[45].

El debate sigue abierto. Mientras los discípulos de Fabro estiman que es compatible dar razón de la libertad humana en la línea tomista, tanto de la novedad radical que implica el acto libre como de una creatividad participada, la mayoría no admite esa lectura de Tomás. Ello implicaría la primacía de la voluntad sobre el entendimiento, y un poder que es exclusivo de Dios.

La cuestión debe seguir abierta, porque el diálogo con el pensamiento moderno, pude ser provechoso para un ulterior desarrollo de la libertad humana. La coincidencia de Tomás y los modernos está en la afirmación de la libertad y en el rol que tiene en la vida personal. Las discrepancias se sitúan en la diferencia entre el ser y la libertad, en el rol del entendimiento en el acto libre del hombre. Entre los discípulos de Tomás se discute cómo dar un sentido a las expresiones del maestro. Es cierto que el hombre participa de la dignidad del ser espiritual, por su alma. Pero la participación del hombre en la escala del ser no quita la distancia infinita que lo separa de Dios. La creatividad participada puede entenderse al estilo del *secundus deus* de Nicolás de Cusa. El hombre, por su dignidad espiritual es un colaborador en las obras de Dios, y es responsable, a diferencia de los demás seres, porque es libre.

Las obras de Dios son la creación, la redención, la santificación. Se trata de obras exclusivas de Dios, en las cuales ni los ángeles tienen poder

---

[44] S. Tomas, *DQ De veritate, q. 24, 2.*
[45] C. Fabro, *Riflessioni sulla libertà*, Maggioli Editore, Rimini, 1983.

para intervenir. Nuestro lenguaje puede ser más elástico, pero manteniendo esa distancia. Hablamos de creaciones humanas, de colaboración en la redención y en la santificación. Dios ha creado todas las cosas por sì mismo, pero quiere cooperación en la ejecución del plan de su providencia. El salto de la nada al ser en el acto libre, que no existiría si yo no lo hago, para el bien y para el mal, para salvación o condenar, es análogo a la novedad que desde Aristóteles se pone en el proceso de las creaturas cuando algo pasa de la potencia al acto. Hay verdadero cambio sustancial, novedad. Pero la creación implica el poder de emanación de todo el ser y por ello dominio de la totalidad del ser que no compete al hombre. El hombre es libre por el dominio de sus actos, y por ello de sí mismo y de su destino, cosa que lo eleva de rango por encima de los otros seres del cosmos. En este sentido cabe aplicarle las palabras elogiosas del salmo, *"ego dixi: dii estis"*[46]. La libertad humana no tiene que ser exaltada hasta hacerla infinita, porque no tolera la rivalidad de Dios. Más bien el proceso es el contrario, hay que fundarla en Dios. Solo Dios crea al hombre libre y le ofrece la garantía de respeto y de absoluto que necesita para su ejercicio. Si no hay Dios tampoco es posible ningún hombre libre. En esa relación de obediencia y de entrega a Dios, se manifestó Jesús como hombre libre y dió la medida máxima de la libertad humana[47].

La libertad humana tiene por tanto un fundamento en el ser personal del hombre, en su naturaleza espiritual, en la mutua compenetración del entendimiento y la voluntad y por ello es capaz de elección de medios y de fines concretos, mediante los cuales desarrolla sus posibilidades de ser hombre en plenitud o de no serlo. Tal es el dilema humano al que le lleva el privilegio y el peso de su condición de ser libre! Esta alta dignidad merece respeto y cuidado, por ello debe ser promovida. Se nace libre y se llega a vivir en libertad.

III. LA PAIDEIA DE LA LIBERTAD

El *homo viator* es y deviene, su ser personal es el mismo desde el principio, pero su personalidad sigue el ritmo de la temporalidad y de la historia, tiene sus fases de crecimiento y de erosión, de esplendor y de miseria, es fruto de sus decisiones y de los agentes que la van modelando. El hombre cuando inicia su itinerario es un cúmulo de posibilidades. Este número se va limitando en la medida en que toma decisiones en un sentido o en otro. La elección es al mismo tiempo ejercicio y negación de la libertad. Al optar

---

[46] Salmo, 81, 6.
[47] Cfr. C. Ducocq, *Jesús hombre libre*, Salamanca, 1975.

por un modo concreto de vida, se niegan otros infinitos posibles. El hombre se hace y se deshace mientras camina, gracias a su libertad, por la cual, mientras se realiza en el tiempo, entra también en la historia.

La libertad enfrenta al hombre en cada momento con el futuro. El futuro de la mera temporalidad adviene inexorablemente en el paso lento e implacable de los instantes y de las horas hasta que se corta con la muerte. El futuro del hombre, cuyo espíritu trasciende el tiempo, se crea en la distensión del alma en el proyecto. Es un futuro que se va crando en la medida que el proyecto se encarna. En el tiempo humano los instantes no tienen la misma duración e intensidad. Los hay anodinos y los hay decisivos, como si concentraran toda la existencia y dispusieran de ella para darle sentido.

La conciencia de ambas dimensiones de la libertad, la temporal y la humana, se acentúan en algunos momentos. Así parece acontecer en los fines de siglo y más en los cambios de milenio. Como si se tratara de una escalada alpina, al llegar a la cumbre, instintivamente el hombre siente una invitación a la contemplación: mira hacia atrás y recorre en un instante lo que ha sido su camino. Es normal que se encuentre insatisfecho. No ha vivido conforme al ideal de hombre que lleva dentro. Mira hacia adelante y se siente llamado a comenzar de nuevo. La hora del milenio es aún más incitante, porque no solo invita a pensar en la propia trayectoria, sino en la de la humanidad. Este es el drama del final del siglo XX y del alba del tercer milenio. Es el drama cristiano de la realización del evangelio en la historia. En el fondo es el drama de la libertad del hombre y del cristiano. El proyecto paral resto del camino debe ser más exigente. La humanidad tiene que ir hacia adelante y hacia arriba, recorriendo el círculo completo de la existencia. La libertad es la palanca de este proyecto[48].

Ya hemos visto que en el hombre no hay plena coincidencia entre ser y libertad, pero sí hay una estrecha relación. La libertad del hombre se inscribe en el plano del obrar, y solo mediante la acción incide de nuevo en el ser del cual procede. Esto se puede entender con la imagen del cìrculo: es como el agua que el calor del sol evapora en el mar, forma las nubes, cae sobre la tierra, brota en las fuentes, forma los rios y vuelve al mar, su punto de partida. Del acto primero de ser, brotan los actos segundos del obrar, entre ellos el acto libre. Todo ser es para la acción y tal es el ser, tal es el obrar.

Tomás de Aquino llega más adentro y entiende que cuanto más alto es modo de ser más íntimo es lo que brota de él[49]. De esos dos principios

---

[48] Cfr. A. Lobato, *Itinerarium evangelizationis ieri e oggi*, en el vol. „La nuova evangelizzazione e il personalismo cristiano", Bologna, ESD, 1994, pp. 11-44.

[49] S. Tomas, *Cont. Gent.* IV, 11: „Secundum diversitatem naturarum diversus modus invenitur in rebus; et quanto aliqua natura est altior, tanto id quod ex ea emanat est magis ei est intimum".

Tomás presenta un panorama de la totalidad de los procesos desde lo más ínfimo que es el mundo inanimado, hasta lo más alto que es la vida íntima de Dios, en la cual se produce la generación del Verbo. En la escala de este proceso, que pasa por los diversos grados de los vivientes, se encuentra el grado supremo de la vida que es la espiritual, que tiene su expresión en el entender y el querer del hombre. Ya aquí aparece la intimidad, en la conciencia y en la posesión, pero todavía se precisa algo extrínseco porque toda actividad cognoscitiva está suscitada desde fuera, y no hay conocer sin fantasma, y el conocer suscita la tendencia hacia el bien propuesto y termina fuera.

Se comprende que la naturaleza es el principio de la operación y tal es el ser, tal es su obrar. El ente es lo que es por su acto de ser. De ese acto fontal primero brota todo el dinamismo. Los actos llamados segundos, suponen el acto primero, en el cual está la participación del ser. Pero a su vez se ordenan a la mayor plenitud del ser. De este modo hay una ontología del obrar que se verifica en un cierto círculo. Si los actos son expresión y como una salida del ente más allá de sì mismo, el proceso revierte en el ser porque los actos contribuyen al devenir del ser. Si el ser es para la acción, los actos son para realizar el devenir y con ello la perfección del mismo. El paso de la posibilidad a la realidad, de la potencia al acto, del poder ser al ser se verifica en el dinamismo de la acción. Este proceso, aplicado a los actos libres, indica cómo el hombre deviene mediante el ejercicio de la libertad.

El horizonte de la libertad no abarca todo el dinamismo de lo humano, sino solo el de los llamados *actos humanos*, que son aquellos de los cuales el hombre es dueño[50]. Este dominio implica conocimiento y poder de elección. La esfera de lo humano es la que sigue a la dimensión espiritual del alma, que se desarrolla en tres grandes horizontes, el del conocer, el de obrar y el del hacer. El hombre expande su vida en la teoría, la praxis y la poiesis. En todos esos campos que son los de sus potencias se realiza la vida humana y el hombre adquiere el desarrollo de su personalidad. Al mismo tiempo el hombre crea la cultura y es recreado por ella. Hay que advertir que la incidencia en el ser del hombre no es la misma cuando se trata del conocer y del hacer que cuando se trata de la actividad del obrar. Aquellas dos actividades pueden ser perfeccionadas por los hábitos dianoéticos y factivos, y mediante ellos el hombre promueve el saber, da origen a productos de la mente y de la mano, forma el mundo y lo domina.

No ocurre lo mismo cuando se trata del obrar humano. Los actos tienen una incidencia directa en el ser del hombre, por ser buenos o malos, hacen bueno o malo al hombre. En el orden del saber la inteligencia no es libre. Debe dejarse vencer por la fuerza de las cosas. La verdad está en el juicio

---

[50] Cfr. S. Tomas, *Sum. Theol. I. II, 1.1*.

en la medida en que éste se adecua a ellas. La obra de arte tiene sus exigencias y el artista, llevado de su inspiración, tiene que seguirla. Pero en el obrar humano el hombre es libre, dueño de su acto para ponerlo o evitarlo, para optar por uno u otro de los posibles a su alcance. Por esto es responsable. Porque, siendo libre, el hombre es reponsable y está llamado a conformar su espontaneidad con la doble norma que brota en su mismo interior y le da la regla para su acción, la objetiva del entendimiento práctico y la subjetiva de la conciencia. El hombre libre está llamado a seguir el deber de hacer el bien y a no ponerse nunca a su propia conciencia. Solo así es fiel a sì mismo, y el ejercicio de su libertad es el camino de la promoción del hombre[51].

Por esta incidencia en el devenir humano, del individuo y de la humanidad la libertad necesita ser cuidada, promovida, desarrollada. El hombre libre tiene que conquistar su plena libertad en la liberación. Es aquí donde entra la fuerza de la paideia, del hombre y del cristiano. Podrìa parecer una paradoja la exigencia de la paideia de la libertad. Nuestra cultura de la libertad como espontaneidad lo entiende asì y prefiere dejar la libertad a sus anchas. Pero la realidad es la contraria. La naturaleza libre tiene que adquirir la virtud del ejercicio sano de la libertad. Hay una ley que se verifica en los procesos naturales, en la adquisición de las ciencias, y en la conquista de la plenitud de lo humano. No es posible el desarrollo teniendo en cuenta solo los factores externos, los agentes; tampoco se logra atendiendo solo a la misma naturaleza en su espontaneidad. Esto acontece en la escuela y en la vida política. Es necesaria la via media. El factor principal es siempre el interno, donde radican las posibilidades, sobre todo cuando se trata de las personas. Toda violencia es contraproducente. Pero tampoco basta la espontaneidad, porque hay fuerza e instintos contrarios al proceso normal. Así acontece en la salud, en la formación escolar, en la misma naturaleza. Tomás de Aquino advertía la analogía que existe en tres clases de procesos: los de la naturaleza que pasa de la potencia al acto, los del saber que hacen posible la adquisición de las ciencias desde la fuerza de los principios que ya tiene la mente humana, y los de la virtud que requieren la adquisición de hábitos teniendo en cuenta la fuerza de las grandes inclinaciones de la naturaleza humana[52].

El problema de nuestro tiempo es cómo llevar a cabo la paideia de la libertad. Las escuelas de todo tipo han seguido la pueril indicación de Hu-

---

[51] Cfr. A. Lobato, *Coscienza morale e strocità dell'uomo in San Tommaso d'Aquino*, en el vol. „Crisi e risveglio della coscienza morale nel nostro tempo", Bologna, ESD, 1989, pp. 9-46. ID. *El „sentido moral" en situación de peligro en la cultura contemporánea*", en „Angelicum", 72 (1995) pp. 41-62.

[52] S. Tomas, *QD, De Veritate, XI, De magistro, art. 1*.

me, de que la moral describe, pero no prescribe y han dejado todo intento de educación y forja de la libertad que era el principal intento de la escuela clásica. Rousseau propuso al „buen salvaje" como modelo ideal y la vuelta al idilio de la naturaleza. El „pensiero debole" de nuestro tiempo más que doctrina es justificación de la vida sin trascendencia. Son grandes claudicaciones de la cultura occidental, cuyas consecuencias se pagan tarde o temprano. La verdad está en los antípodas: La libertad requiere paideia. El no ejercerla, sobre todo en los períodos decisivos de la vida, la niñez y la juventud es condenarse al imperio de los instintos ciegos que brotan del inconscio del hombre y lo arrastran. La libertad sin educación en la virtud cae muy pronto en los determinismos inconsciente.

El futuro de la humanidad, en la parte que está en manos del hombre, como agente de la historia, depende de la paideia de la libertad. También la pedagogía de la libertad tiene un especial significado en la vida del cristiano. Pablo lo ha recordado en su epìstola a los Gálatas. El hombre con la nueva ley pasa de niño a adulto, de escalvo a libre. Cristo es nuestro pedagogo, quien nos ha liberado de la ley antigua que era externa y nos ha hecho pasar a la nueva, que es más bien ley infundida, interna, espiritual. Así la libertad queda liberada. „Cristo nos ha liberado para que seamos en verdad libres"[53]. Tomás de Aquino ha clarificado de modo magistral la conexión entre la naturaleza y la gracia. El hombre precede al cristiano. La libertad humana moderada por la paideia es camino de preparación para el evangelio: „La gracia no destruye sino que perfecciona la naturaleza"[54]. La libertad cristiana es la libertad que brota del conocimiento de la verdad, cuya paidea está confiada a la obra del Espíritu. Por su fuerza estamos llamado a la *sequela Christi*, el hombre libre en plenitud.

* * *

El futuro del hombre depende, en buena medida de la libertad, por esa conexión que la libertad tiene con el ser y el hacerse del hombre concreto. Reside en ella un poder, al mismo tiempo sagrado y satánico, por el cual el hombre se realiza o se pierde. Tomás de Aquino reconoció a la libertad esta fuerza de causalidad, porque orienta al hombre hacia el fin. Es una causalidad que racae sobre sí mismo, sin contradecir el principio de que nada es causa de sí mismo. El hombre recibe el ser, es causado, pero lo recibe de tal nobleza que se le confía su desarrollo, el hacerse hasta lograr la plenitud hacia la cual tiende por naturaleza. La libertad de que goza todo hombre es este poder de hacerse a sí mismo en cierta medida. En la volun-

---

[53] Ad Gal. 5, 13.
[54] S. Tomas, *Sum. Theol.* I, 8 ad 2.

tad libre reside el secreto para realizarse y ser *causa sui*. En esta prerrogativa excelsa consiste la dignidad del hombre. Tomás escribe: „La voluntad humana tiene una cierta superioridad porque impera sobre todas las potencias del alma, en cuanto su objeto es el fin; por lo cual muy propiamente se encuentra en ella la cúspide de la libertad: se dice libre es que es causa de sì mismo"[55]. Al entrar en el tercer milenio, con el temor y temblor que nos produce la situación actual, abrigamos la esperanza cristiana que empuja hacia el futuro y confía en el poder de la libertad, guiada por la paidea del Espíritu. Así es posible realizar el imperativo que ya expresaba Marco Aurelio: ελευθερος εσσω![56].

---

[55] S. Tomas, *In II Sent*. D. 25. Q. 1. a. 2. ad 4: „Tamen voluntad quodammodo superior est, secundum quod imperium habet super omnes animae vires, propter hoc quod obiectum eius est finis; unde convenientissime in ipsa summum libertatis invenitur, liber enin dicitur qui causa sui est, in in II Met c. 2 dicitur". *I. Cont. Gent*. III, 112: „Quod dominium sui actus habet liberum est in agendo, liber enim dicitur qui sui causa est".

[56] Marco Aurelio, *Mem*. IV, 3, 9.

ANNA-TERESA TYMIENIECKA
World Phenomenology Institute
USA

FREEDOM
IN HUMAN CREATIVE CONDITION

"What is freedom?" The way in which we usually employ this term conceiving of it spontaneously is that which we can express only poetically as the "breath of life" – only poetically, because what we mean by "freedom" does not fall under any ontological category. Fredom is neither an object, a thing, a living being, (individual), an idea, a class, a quality, a process, an event, a force, a function... not even a relation. And yet freedom is undeniably, nay, primogenitally a modality of life.

That freedom is a constant matter of concern in human life is an obvious and striking fact. Humanity at large is locked in an unrelenting struggle for the freedom of nations, social groups, institutions, and human beings. What this really amounts to is that it is the freedom of the human person, as it is nowadays formulated, that is at stake. However, when we consider the freedom of the human being, the human person, the fact should impress itself on us that freedom is most intimately involved with life and consequently has to be considered with respect to all living beings-for higher living beings of the higher species of animals are also persons.

With this preamble, it is clear why in order to approach the question of freedom in a foundational fashion we have to situate it first within its proper context. Only situating it within the network of the generative life functions spurring freedom's emergence can we do justice to the role of freedom-a germ of which at least is essential to this emergence itself. It is by following that development that we may then grasp freedom's significance for human life. I propose that the appropriate context in which to treat and discover plausibly the conditions and parameters, the virutalities and functions proper to its emergence and its assumption of a specific role within the world of life, the world of living beings, is the philosophy/phenomenology of life, a philosophy of life that is integral and scientific. Freedom concerns life in a unique fashion. That is to say, within its context we have to seek to differentiate the modalities of life which acquire the expression 'freedom' conveying it to living-beings-in-action in order that they may "act freely".

I submit that it is my phenomenology/philosophy of life, integral and scientific that may serve in a unique way as the context of freedom, as well as the groundwork from which to extract the roots out of which freedom grows. (See my *Logos and Life*, Book 1: *Creatiave Experience and the Critique of Reason*, Analecta Husserliana, XXIV; Book 2: *The Three Movements of the Soul*, Analecta Husserliana, XXV; Book 3: *The Passions of the Soul and the Elements in the Ontopoiesis of Culture. The Life Significance of Literature Logos and Life* (Dordrecht: Kluwer Academic Publishers, 1988, 1988, 1990).

I. FREEDOM AS THE PRIMOGENITAL MANIFESTATION OF LIFE

What is more obvious, and yet it usually eludes our attention, than the fact that the bursting out of life as such is an emergence of a novel, original phenomenon, novel with respect to its premises, original with respect to its source? It is an emergence into the "open" while its premises remain in the self-enclosed area; emergence into "light" while its premises remain in the "dark", exhaling a breath out of an inert area. There is ignited a spark for a fire that spreads, a manifestation of a life-engine that may pull inert energies into the process of becoming. Becoming is a factor at the presiding and carrying out of the constructivism of life and its spread into existential modalities unprecedented in matter. In brief, to breathe, to move, to feel, to think, to desire and the struggle for existence is an exercise of freedom. How wonderfully free are we living beings in breathing the air, in thinking and feeling and desiring and moving and expanding ourselves this way, in projecting tentacles of our very own outside selves. Indeed, we are free to project them *from within and without*.

In this respect each manifestation of life as this expanding from within is a manifestation of freedom; we human beings share it with everything-there-is-alive: plant, animal. And yet there are-as hinted at above-marked differences in this *primogenital freedom*, differences in *extension*, in *modalities*, in *inner control*.

Indeed in line with great thinkers such as Aristotle, Leibniz, Thomas Aquinas, Hegel, Kant and others after them, we discover ever anew that life as an eventful emergence as well as a process-like development which proceeds all from within and is worked out by living individual's functioning, unfolded within the enactment of each and every move.

And yet, as has been pointed out often, there is, first, a great differentiation of types of living beings with respect to the variety of their inner systems of functioning and corresponding to that differentiation integration within the circumambient sphere of life. It is precisely in the spread of the active tentacles that the living being throws around itself that, its range of possibilities as well as its power to control the inward/outward directed progress from within that life's unfolding expands.

Having recognized as freedom the promogenital expansion from within one's own virtualities and powers, we will recognize the growth in complexity in the ecolutive differentiation of life as growth in *degress of freedom*. In fact, with the advance of the complexity of types there goes a larger range of possibilities of the living individual to match his innermost existential needs with the available means in order to satisfy them. From the rootedness of plants and trees to the simplest animal is a radical and most significant jump in mobility, be it the least mobility, yet it allows for a novel line of freedom to "seek" and to "choose".

Indeed, while with the lowest species, those simplest in functioning, vital needs are satisfied simply by a "fitness" with the materials available in the circumambient environment (I have established the term 'fitness' in this sense in my monograph "Moral Sense in the Foundations of the Social World", Analecta Husserliana, Vol. ...), whereas with the higher sensitivity of more complex functionig, this satisfaction of needs is guaranteed by the *sentient features of the inward propensities*, so that at the level of acquired motility, the mobility of a living being goes together with its further developed "discernment", with its sentient recognition of the nature of needed as well as available resources, recognition that paves the way to its exercising an 'inclination' toward such or other choice. However, it is obvious that there is a close and stable correspondence, matching the vital needs and the range of their possible satisfaction and the available resources of the environment. The crucial point is that both of these express the laws of life itself. That is to say, it is an inner code of the individual's functioning that carries with itself the traditional indications for this correspondence between the indivudual unfolding life and the environmental conditions indispensable for it.

The laws of life are represented by the inner code-which I have termed the 'enterlechial nucleus' of a living being-by which the rules of life's unfolding strictly implement the laws of life itself. Thus, the primogenital freedom in its range of choice, selection, and deliberation is strictly circumscribed by these laws.

The emergence of the Human Condition within the evolutive advance of the forms of life is a radical novum-even with respect to the types of higher animals, which, the ape for example, have a seemingly vast referential system by which to satisfy their needs. It is the surging forth from nature of elements that are heterogeneous vis-à-vis that system that brings about a transformation of the entire vital functioning by expanding it into the human mind. As a result the living being loosens its bondage to Nature-Life, opening upon a uniquely different sphere of existence.

This transformation occurs precisely around the human mind, the axis of a novel kind of freedom, a freedom that on the wings of *imaginatio creatix* proposing ever new possibilities, informing with ever new tendencies, and prompting the faculties of the mind, soars far beyond the circumference of the avital laws, often defying them. *Imaginatio creatix* proceeds by always seeking its satisfaction within the specifically human significance of life that the creativity of the mind brings about. Thus is the sphere of the human spirit coaxed forth.

The main question that I want to treat now is this: In virtue of which factors of the creative virtualities does specifically human freedom emerge and unfold?

But we have first to bring forth the innermost manifestation of this specifically human freedom beyond the existential web of life as embodied through the human person.

II. CREATIVITY AND THE DRAMA OF HUMAN EXISTENCE

Let us repeat that the Human Creative Condition involves a radically novel modality of freedom in which desire, selection, and choice are not circumscribed by the strict laws of the entelechial nucleus in its attunements to circumambient conditions, but, to the contrary, go far beyond those conditions with the entrance upon the scene of *imaginatio creatix* and the new factor of invention, which proposes new avenues of life.

This new creatively expanded and projected network of specifically human life opens a new, most complex type of freedom, one which-not being strictly circumscribed by life's laws-becomes as it were the engine of a *drama* that inwardly and outwardly tears the human person apart, pulls in various directions, brings in new existential categories of defeat, disaster, and misery as well as of victory, accomplishment, and happiness, etc., that are absent from animal existence.

The point is that, as present day social life most acutely demonstrates, the possibilities for realizing one's own dreams, intentions, pursuits depends upon the situation within the societal world. There is a limited societal space for realizing each individual's pursuits. As in the animal kingdom, so in the human societal world the existence of one individual means co-existence with others. This means a tightly spun network of interaction, interrelation in which (unless societal circumstances are favorable to a certain type of life accomodating numerous individuals) each individual is allotted within the common net its space of action in which to push his own intentions while renouncing others so that the social law's protection of one's 'rights' infringes upon the rights of a fellow man. One's self-instigated exercise of free selection, invention, promotion may, and often does, infringe in some way upon the rights of others. While we individually and as a race tend toward "absolute" freedom, should not that goal be seen as a utopia in fact?

The drama of the human aspirations that raise the human being high above his frame and of the defeats that plunge him into despair, the drama of legitimate aspirations, heroic efforts to fulfill them and of the indomitable forces of life that cut their wings and annihilate them, this drama of existence is rooted in the scarcity of goods in the natural and social worlds, in the limited possibilities offered for the exercise of our imagination, and in the inner and outer struggle we engage in as we strive at some or all cost to express the force of the spirit as prompted by a yearning to accomplish, win, gain, reach something particularly significant in our existence.

Success and satisfaction, disappointement and distress, these are the extremes between which the pendulum of human freedom swings. Moving from the vital level of freedom as the primogenital engine of life to that of human freedom, we discover in the latter the engine of the human drama.

The transformation of the modality of freedom from the vital to the specifically human significance of life is such that we have to raise *the question of what is the specific coincidence of elements in the human condition, of what is the original virtuality* that moves the creative orchestration of the human mind toward that configuration of factors that makes specifically human freedom surge-a freedom that is on the one side unbound imaginative/inventive promptings and on the other conditioned by the entanglements of the natural/social world of life. What are the reasons for which humanity denounces and struggles against the direction exercised by governments, cultural expectations and social groupings? If left without direction society degrades into a spectacle of mutual abuse among its members. The law and the systems of ethics meant to protect in an even-handed way the rights of all individuals fall short in their implementation, and this reveals that they lack sufficient power of appeal to us as human beings to begin with. What would be objectively applied in a particular instance somehow misses the internal 'measuring stick' within the person, if there be one. The indispensable resonance that would make the prescription work in each case does come about. Law and ethics lack the power to convince that would awaken a desire and willingness to implement the ruling of ethics or law even when recognized as fitting if that ruling hinders or goes against our interests. We are tempted to go around the rules avoiding the proper resolution of conflicts and finding beside the point, meritless excuses for doing so. We will just lull ourselves into thinking that right.

Having thrown out our question, we will now go deep into the roots of the free human person as it crystallizes itself from the virtualities of the human condition and so trace to its origins this conditional freedom in order to answer our question.

III. THE PROMOGENITAL MOVE OF THE MORAL SENSE AS THE IGNITING OF THE SPECIFIC FREEDOM OF THE HUMAN SPIRIT

I have previously proposed the moral sense-as the 'benevolent'/'malevolent' sentiment-as the factor of humanness that emerges from the creative virtualities of the human condition. I see in it the primogenital experience that first 'humanizes' the living individual; second, it simultaneously throws a hook towards human companions as partners in the game of life.

Indeed, as I have described before, there takes place-in the first stages of the human being's evolution from the sharing-in-life of gregorious herd existence-an encounter of the living individual with another. (See my "Moral Sense in the Foundation of the Social World", Analecta Husserliana, Vol. XXII, 98). This is an encounter in which simple animal herd feeling do not prevail, being a 'con-frontation', a kind of measuring up of the other in which, first of all, the possible intentions of affect-distrust, fear, indifference-are superceded by the benevolent sentiment that the creative virtualities of the moral sense release from the Human Condition in this confrontation. It is like a synergy, a prompting force that carries the factors of significance in it. With the release of the 'benevolent'/'malevolent' sentiment (it can be a negative event), there follow the *three founding moments* establishing the humanity of the person, the humanity that, although it means a transformation of the very innermost core of the individual in his inwardness, bonds or refers the individual to another, prompting the throwing out of links that create a new kind of 'togetherness' in life.

In the first moment of this transformatory experience that the benevolent/malevolent sentiment releases, there is a recognition of the being confronted as having a likeness to oneself, that he is "like myself", or to put it more strongly is "an *other* self"*. The second moment follows, which consists in the attribution to the "other myself" an equivalence with myself in the vital significance of life and beyond. These two moments give rise to a

---

* Paul Ricoeur's concept of 'Un autre moi-meme' was put before the public ten years after my widely-discussed monograph "Moral Sense in the Foundations of the Social World", Analecta Husserliana, Vol. XXII, 1987, vol. XXXL, 1990.

third, namely, they prompt the *gesture*. The gesture, an exchange of a gift, lifts itself to a higher level of significance; it acquires the significance of an action that transcends itself, of a *trans-action*. This act transcends its vital setting, transcends the pragmatic giving and receiving of goods by raising all to a specifically novel sense in which the exchange of goods bestows upon the occasion 'moral sense'. The gesture means the freeing of the moral sense lying there in wait as a factor of sense among the avirtualities of the Human Condition now playing an active role in the advance of life.

The emergence of the moral sense bestowing a specifically human significance upon life is borne upon the three-moment primogenital establishment of the basis for the human equitable experience-of-oneself-and the-other, the self-awareness of our sharing-in-life and of the equality of rights among human beings and of a measure for apportioning rights to living beings other than man. It finds a measuring stick in the ontopoietic design of life's individualization within the networks of interactive relationship in the unity-of-everything-there-is-alive, the basis of the differentiation between good and bad. (See my "Measure and the Ontopoietic Self-Individualization of Life", *Phenomenological Inquiry* 19(1995), pp. 26-51).

Lastly, but foremost, the release of the moral sense accounts for the capacity to decide about oneself, which is the full-fledged meaning of decision.

With these three moments of the new meaningfulness of the reality of life the moral life is established. The benevolent/malevolent sentiment, its carrier, is a prompting force of a nature entirely different from those of vital energies. It is not only that vital spontaneities and synergies carry only the *vitally* significant rationalities for the meaning bestowing that is dedicated to the promotion of natural life, but, as said before, their meaningfulness follows strictly the schema of life. The synergy of the moral sense brings in rationalities which transcend the circumference of the vital significance of life; they even contradict the vital self-interest by such moments as generosity, denial of self for others..., which means putting the interest of the other before one's own and the renunciation of my own interest for the benefit of the other. Here the sharing-in-life common to all higher animals is taking a new turn. It is grounded in the specifically human rationalities that the creative orchestration of the faculties captures from the entire spectrum of the emerging new meaning bestowing virtualities. Under the aegis of the ever actiave Imaginatio Creatrix, human beings can in self-awareness of their interests project at the novel level of imaginative planning, using their intellectual knowledge on the platform of life-interrelations.

Now due to the synergies of the moral sense, this new platform sinks roots in the inter-action among human individuals, which means a sharing-in-life on a higher level than that of the gregariousness of higher animals.

This inter-action is moderated by reference to individual rights in sharing, by applying the highest principles of Good and Evil, and any of the variety of systems of human values that the intellect constructs upon the instigation of the moral sense.

The understanding, the acceptance, the application of the moral precepts of ethics and law and recognition of the validity of moral values depends not only upon intellectual analysis of the situation-its understanding in terms of *moral valuation* established by the exercise of the moral sense in human transactions, but first of all upon the *force of the moral synergy of the benevolent/malevolent sentiment* of human persons.

Here we are reaching the focal statement that emerges from the foregoing inquiry. With the emergence of the synergetic moral sentiment there came forth a specifically human freedom, springing from within the unfathomable depth of the human soul that nurtures all the human functions of the creative orchestration, a freedom to invent, to plan, to evaluate, and to decide upon the sharing-in-existence with others of a common life in life's fullness.

Human life is engendered in the freedom of this self-awareness with others. Hence, the unquenchable thirst for freedom. As I mentioned above, the freedom to act of one person may, and often does, encroach upon that of another. The game of freedom between myself and my fellow man carries, however, all the prerequisites for harmonious attunement in the proper understanding and exercise of the moral sense. The very root significance of *my* freedom lies in my recognition of the equivalence of the rights of other fellow men.

The last but not the least result of our inquiry, which did not come to my attention in my previous study of the moral sense, concerns the extra-vital origin of the moral sense that ignites the specifically human freedom. I attempted above to emphasize that this freedom appears as a unique emergence within the avital life-system of a trans-vital moment, on the one hand, and transcends all vital necessities and determinations, on the other hand. Thus is brought in the inward freedom of the human being, who emerges self-conscious and self-deliberating and deciding not only about himself with respect to others, but with respect to himself. Personal self-evaluation leads to the questioning of human destiny and opens the gate for the transnatural longings, premonitions, forebodings of the supernatural, etc. In other terms we may see in this transnatural ingression of the moral sense into nature and ingression of the supernatural, which leads to the relgous intuition of sense into nature and ingression of the supernatural, which leads to the religious intuition of the Creator. Finally, this opening toward the trans-natural on reaching the founts of the human soul, allows it to draw upon its own resources for its transnatural destiny. (See my *Logos and Life*, Book 2: *The Three Movements of the Soul*, Analecta Husserliana, XXV [Dordrecht: Kluwer Academic Publishers, 1988]).

Summarizing, it comes clearly to light that specifically human conditioned freedom emerges in the wake of the moral sentiment that prompts it and which distributes the moral principles, emotional qualities, evaluative standards and leads toward the intellectualization of this entire network of moral values. Hence, it is also clear that this modality of freedom is simultaneously the promotor of the individual modalities of expansion within the world of life, the unity of natural and societal coexistence, inasmuch as it is essentially mindful of the possibilities of the expansion of the other fellow human being.

The intellectualization of this system tends to take over. While the intellectual calculus of values that we tend to make in applying strictly rational means of evaluating our part in a transaction and making decisions then is easily twisted by our egotism and self-interest and we may evade the distribution of justice by false calculations of merits and dues, it is reference to the moral sentiment that is the source from which the distribution of the equal rights and responsibilities of the human person flows and to it human persons as humans should naturally have recourse.

In conclusion: no sterile debate about the respective validity of socially competing ethical theories will help solve the social disarray and perplexity of our present age. It is the revival in human persons and social groups of the primogenital moral sentiment alone that will give us true direction.

JAN VAN DER VEKEN
Katholieke Universiteit Leuven
Belgium

CAN THERE BE FREEDOM IN A DETERMINIST WORLD?

I. Determinism is the view that, given the state of the world in the past, everything that happens now *has* to happen. It could not have turned out differently.

Many proponents of the scientific outlook at reality feel that all that happens now is to be seen as the consequence of previous conditions and laws: it could not have happened otherwise. Science – at least natural science – has been remarkably successful at finding theories and laws that enable us *to predict* what will happen in the future on the basis of what has occured in the past. The capacity to predict and the worldview of scientific determinism are strongly connected.

Admittedly, the so-called human sciences have not been so successful in predicting what a human being is going to do. This, however, according to an increasing group of people, is due to the fact that the initial conditions are far more complex, and that we just cannot tell what the determining factors of our behaviour are. The contemporary influences of an evolutionary worldview and of sociobiology make it even more convincing that all what we are and do has arisen in a long evolutionary process. There seems to be no reason to claim that human freedom would be an exception to an overall deterministic worldview.

Determinism and necessitarism go together. Determinism and freedom seem to be mutually exclusive.

II. Many authors in the past have tried to counter that challenge. Most of all Kant should be mentioned. He accepts – according to the worldview of his time – that determinism reigns supreme on the level of the phenomenal world. On the level of the noumenal world, determinism does not apply.

Freedom, the existence of God and immortality are postulates of practical reason.

Today, we would not make such a clearcut distinction between the phenomenal world and the noumenal world. Why should we? But what Kant really intended to say is still valid for us: it is another thing to *predict* on the level of the events that can be studied by science, and to *assume responsibility* for one's actions.

A problem hardly addressed by Kant is the very possibility of the emergence of those two very different realms of reality in the evolutionary process. The later Merleau-Ponty has also seen that the phenomenological distinction between subject and object – even when they are conceived as truly interrelated – somehow begs the question. How is it possible that consciousness can arise at all, if it is not present right from the beginning? For that reason, Merleau-Ponty was looking for an interplay between subjectivity and objectivity "at all the levels of the world". Either subjectivity – in the broad sense of "putting itself together" – is present right from the beginning, or it will never appear.

When we apply these insights to the problem of freedom and determinism, it might well be the case that freedom also is a universal, which applies in some broad and restricted sense to all there is. We do realize that this argument should be handled with care. An uncritical appeal to indeterminism on the level of quantum physics is not enough. In this sense we fully agree with Karl Popper's position in *Indeterminism is not enough*.

III. In the third and concluding part of my talk I will present the position of Whitehead - Hartshorne as somehow in line with the Kantian approach. It combines determinism and freedom in the very structure of every actual entity. This view throws some unexpected light upon the interpretation of scientific determinism itself.

Thesis 1-8
Let me now state in a succinct way – under the form of theses, which should be developed at length – the main thrust of my argument.

Thesis 1. *If* we have to choose between "incompatibilism" and "compatibilism", between determinism and freedom, compatibilism is by far the better choice. If the argument runs as follows:
M. Determinism and freedom are mutually exclusive
m. Determinism is true.
C. Hence, freedom is at best a subjective feeling, and at worst an illusion; *then,* of course, that conclusion is for most of us unacceptable. We want, somehow, to "save" human freedom. The easiest way is to reject the incompatibility-thesis. It *must* be the case, in order to avoid the unhappy

conclusion which would deny what is dearest to us, that the incompatibility thesis is false. Put in this way, the rejection of the incompatibility thesis is rather a question of presuppositions than a reasoning based on argument. In any case, except for those accepting a truly materialistic outlook on reality, compatibilism has to be the winner.

Compatibilism somehow edulcorates the tension between determinism and freedom. Hence, a distinction between hard and soft determinism has been introduced in the literature. B. F. Skinner as a scientist, and Baron d' Holbach as a philosopher, can be considered to be hard determinists. Philosophers who accept basically that all that happens, happens necessarily, but who do not want to deny human freedom for that matter, can be called "soft determinists" or compatibilists. They accept the basic assumptions of a deterministic or a scientific worldview and redefine freedom in such a way that determinism and (a redefined form of) freedom are mutually compatible. Most of us are – or have been – "compatibilists". However, with W. James, who rejected both hard and soft determinism, we should ask the question whether soft determinism does not land us in a "quagmire of evasion". Whereas James has a kind of respect for hard determinism -the kind of respect one has for an honest, straightforward adversary – for soft determinism, on the other hand, he has nothing but contempt. Although soft determinism is even today extremely "fashionable", there is a good deal of truth in James' claim that soft determinism is an evasion. Hence our second thesis:

Thesis 2. Compatibilism is not enough.

Compatibilism can be grounded in the possibility of coexistence of two different worlds, or of two different language-games. When we accept a clearcut distinction between the level of the appearances and the level of the noumenal, then, following Kant, we can leave the whole sphere of events that happen in this world to the rule of iron law. This realm is the realm of necessity: things happen the way they should happen. It makes no sense to oppose the reign of necessity and forseeability: necessity and forseeability are the very tools of understanding. This is the way our mind works. On the other hand, and equally certain, there is within us the level of moral responsibility, which would lose any meaning without positing the realm of freedom as an implication of the very sense of obligation: "You are capabl of being morally obliged: so you are free". Kant is clearly the most prominent advocate of the *coexistence* of the two spheres: the sphere of the phenomenal and the sphere of the noumenal, the sphere of iron necessity and the sphere of human action and responsibility.

Contemporary ways to solve the question of freedom and necessity, by pointing towards our different attitudes towards the world, or towards two different language-games are not structurally different from the Kantian position.

Somehow, it must be possible to behave as free and responsible persons in a world which is to a large extent governed by the laws of nature. For that reason, for most scientists who are also interested in human affairs, compatiblism is an acceptable position. They feel that they can, at the same time, "believe" in science, and still make sense of their lives and their responsibilities. Compatibilism is still a respectable position, which we would not like to give up, but we must be philosophically more demanding than just *stating* the coexistence of two wholly different spheres of existence.

Hence, according to our thesis 2, compatibilism is not enough. Kant himself surmised that he could not really *explain* how the two orders of reality could coexist. He was impressed as well by the starry heavens as by the moral law inside his heart. He could not possibly know how the two could be part of the same universe. The very idea of the emergence of human subjectivity in a world governed by iron law was, for Kant, unconceivable.

Thesis 3. Indeterminism is not enough.

Much has been said and written about the developments of modern science. Some authors, pointing to quantum mechanics and the indeterminacy principle of W. Heisenberg feel that, at last, the problem of determinism and freedom can be put in new terms. Because there seems to be some indeterminacy on the subatomic level, it makes sense to them to surmise that after all the so-called iron laws of nature are only stochastic processes, to be expressed in the language of probabilities rather than of certainties. If the outcome of no physical process is one hundred procent certain, there is, indeed, "room for freedom"[1].

Karl Popper has devoted many pages to defending a non-determinist worldview. It is all the more saying that he thinks that indeterminism – the kind of it that he accepts – is, as such, not enough to defend human freedom. Hence, I can side with Karl Popper in stating: indeterminism is not enough. "Not enough" means that, even if indeterminism is to be accepted as the worldview which best accounts for all observable phenomena, it is still wanting as a sufficient ground for freedom. I could state his (and my) position as follows: indeterminism is a necessary but not a sufficient condition for freedom[2].

---

[1] Gerard Bodifée, *Ruimte voor vrijheid. De onvoltooide natuur en het menselijk initiatief*, Kapellen, DNB/Uitgeverij Pelckmans, 1988.

[2] Karl R. Popper, *The Open Universe. An Argument for Indeterminism*, Towata, New Jersey, Rowman and Littlefield, 1982. See more especially: Addendum 1: Indeterminism is not enough: an afterword. p. 113-130.

Thesis 4. Determinism is an *idealized* case, characterizing a huge amount of processes, which cannot strictly be described within a hard determinist framework.

Determinism, which has been widely accepted by what nowadays is called "classical science", is only a rough approximation of a far more intricate relationship between cause and effect, or between the past and the actual occurences. If determinism was *absolutely* true, then nothing could really happen. Then, according to Laplace's famous hypothesis of a Spirit larger than ourselves, knowing the actual state of the world and the laws of nature, everything that could ever occur, would be strictly forseeable. It is fashionable, also in scientific circles, to stick to Laplace's hypothesis, and to state that it is just a matter of practical impossibility to determine the exact initial conditions. This, however, seems to be an untenable position. It is, according to my understanding, *in principle* impossible to determine fully the initial conditions of a very complex system, without interacting with that system. On the macroscopic level, this interaction is negligible. When we *look at* the sun, that hardly affects the solar energy. But there is some interaction, just as if we climb the tower of Pisa, we affect the rotation speed of the earth. For all practical purposes such an influence of the observer is negligible. On the microscopic level, however, it seems to be the case that it is impossible in principle to describe the system without interacting with it. Hence a description from the outside, which would leave everything as it is, is *in principle* impossible. The famous hypothesis of Laplace describes a universe without an observer. *To know is to interact.* Laplace demon, knowing the initial conditions of the system, *has already interfered*.

On the basis of such arguments, however, we should not reject scientific determinism in favour of overall indeterminism. To a very large extent the determinist laws of mechanics do apply. For that reason we can foresee with any amount of relevant precision, the future trajectories of the heavenly bodies, the time of eclipses, etc. Even in a new field such as the so-called determinist chaos, where a different relationship between cause and effect applies – where minute causes may have large effects (the so-called butterfly syndrom) – determinism is still a tool which allows for calculation. It is, however, important that we are here always working with an understanding of natural law which has to take into account that the studied relationships between cause and effect are an idealization of a far more complex relationship.

Thesis 5. Classical determinism does not explain the emergence of real newness.

The emergence of real newness, and of a being capable of asking questions about its very being in the universe, cannot be explained within a purely deterministic framework. It is absurd, taking into account what we know today about the emergence of reflective subjectivity in this universe, that the coming into being of subjects, capable of reflective thought, had to occur exactly in the way it has occured. To explain the emergence of subjectivity into an overall deterministic world, the proponents of determinism have no choice: they can appeal only to chance (or to a divine creator bringing about something completely new). I think that mere chance is not enough for an explanation. The appeal to a divine intervention is too much a "deus ex machina" to be a workable hypothesis.

Thesis 6. "Subjectivity" can have a far broader meaning than just *human* subjectivity. It allows for degrees.

If subjectivity is defined as "the inner side" of an event or an entity, then subjectivity allows for minimal and maximal degrees. As far as the animal kingdom is concerned, it seems obvious that some feelings, some meaningful reactions should be attributed to man's best friend. But also plants are somehow putting themselves together. Great authors of the past like Aristotle and Aquinas have seen enough reasons to talk about an animal and a vegetative soul. If any event or entity has an inner and an outer side, then it makes sense to say that the outer side is what an event or an entity is for the other, whereas the inner or subjective side is the way an entity or an event puts itself together.

Thesis 7. Determinism can be accepted as an overall framework to describe processes where the level of subjectivity is minimal. In that case, strict determinism may be accepted as an idealized case to express the relationship between cause and effect.

Stones and planets have no subjectivity (Fechner not withstanding). A lot of nonsense has been said to the defense of a panpsychic outlook on reality. Clouds do not think, have no intentions, no psychè. But it might be the case that the very constituents of every reality whatsoever have an inner and an outer side. Think about Leibniz's monads. They all have at least a minimal degree of mentality. Of course, microscopic events do not think, and in this sense, they do not have "feelings". If "feeling" however receives a broader connotation, namely to react in a meaningful way to meaningful information, then any occurrence can be said to take into account the given world, and to react meaningfully to it. On the physical level, the amount of newness is negligible. Hence, most processes on the macro-scopic level can be described as fully determined: i.e., here an absolute reciprocity between cause and effect seems to apply. This, however, is an idealized case, which in fact never expresses fully what really happens.

Thesis 8. The emergence of subjectivity can be accounted for only if subjectivity is present "at all levels of existence". The later Merleau-Ponty has seen that the relationship between "to see" and "to be seen", "to feel" and "to be felt" is absolutely universal. What happens concretely in our bodies (the reversal between the "to see" and the "to be seen", "to feel" and the "to be felt") must belong to the very stuff of the world. Hence his somewhat puzzling expression about "the flesh of the world". The level of perception, of language and of thought cannot be juxtaposed. They presuppose one another, by a movement of mutual implication. Merleau-Ponty refers to the Husserlian notion of *Fundierung*, to clarify the relationship between perception and thought, between the pre-reflexive and the reflexive, between perception and language, or between perception and thought. This *Fundierung* is a relationship which applies in both directions. Language and thought do presuppose perception, but on the other hand, perception is only fully human, when permeated by language and thought.

Human freedom is neither absolute, nor is it an illusion. It is somehow imbedded in our bodily existences. Sartre, in fact, is an advocate of absolute freedom. Sartre is in fact a dualist: he accepts pure consciousness, which is nothing else than the opposite of the *en-soi*. Merleau-Ponty in his later writings, before all, objects to that type of Sartrean dualism. It cannot possibly be the case that freedom and our bodily existences belong to an entirely different world. Already in the Phenomenology of Perception, Merleau-Ponty states : "There must be a «slope» of the spirit" ("*Il faut qu'il y ait une pente de l'esprit*"). Not everything is equally probable. Freedom and some necessity presuppose each other.

Thesis 9. The account of A.N. Whitehead is fully consonant with the views presented in this paper[3]. For Whitehead, *any* actual entity has a physical and a mental pole. In physical occurrences, the physical pole is almost allpervasive. The mental pole is merely the handing over of the same form to each new occasion. A molecule of iron enacts itself *almost* endlessly, transmitting the same form to each new occurrence. For that reason, a molecule of iron will have the same qualities "for ages". It will behave in a stable way. On the level of life, there is clearly far more room for newness. Here we can talk about "creativity" (in the broad sense of the word). The emergence of life is a most creative happening, and it cannot be accounted for in terms of strict determinism. Not everything has been programmed right from the beginning. Many things "could have happened otherwise".

---

[3] See a.o. George R. Lucas, Jr., *Two Views of Freedom in Process Thought. A Study of Hegel and Whitehead*, AAR Dissertation Series 28, 1979.

The emergence of always more intricate forms of life makes good sense within a Whiteheadian framework. The more complex instances help us to understand the less complex ones, and not the other way around. Within a Whiteheadian framework, the laws of nature are not "iron": they describe in an approximate way the more stable features of the universe we live in. But stability is never absolute: it is only an aspect of a phenomenon which is creative through and through. For that reason, a philosophy of freedom is not an exception. It rather characterizes an overall feature of creative becoming. To be sure, it may not be appropriate to talk about "freedom" (with all its human connotations) on the subhuman, and even on the animal level. On the other hand, it is equally impossible to make a clearcut distinction between the natural realm and the human realm. A system as Whitehead's can account at the same time for the observed regularities *and* for the evident experience of value in a universe which is far more to be conceived as organic than as a clockwork in which in a miraculous way someone to look at the clock has been brought into existence.

In a time of increasing influence of a naturalistic outlook on reality, it is all important to develop a richer view of nature, so that it would not be necessary to "double" a naturalistic account of nature, of which we are part, with an unintelligible emergence out of the blue of a subjectivity which has no real place in the world. In such a world, man would still be an alien, and he would not *really* be free.

STANISŁAW JUDYCKI
Catholic University of Lublin
Poland

FREEDOM AND DETERMINATION

I. CATEGORIAL FREEDOM

When speaking about freedom, we often mean „independence of external influences". In this sense any system which is made up of components organized in some way, and which is partly isolated from other systems can be said to be „free". Such a system may consist of physio-chemical or biological elements, or it may represent a society or a social group. Such a system may also represent some individuals as (to some extent) isolated units within larger systems. In turn, each of these individuals is also composed of some subsystems, which are free, that is, at least to some extent, independent of other systems comprising that individual.

Within such a context the following questions may arise: first, does the thing we call the Universe comprise only one system of organized elements or, in other words, are all the components of that system exclusively subject to physical causality? Are there any relatively isolated systems within that system of a higher order, that is within the Universe? Are there any totally isolated systems within it, in the sense that they are subject to an entirely different sort of determination than the physical causal one? In this last case a system would be free in the sense of having at its disposal a different sort of organizing principle than physical causality to arrange its components. However, such a system would not be totally isolated in that its peculiar sort of organizing principle would have to fit in with the determining principle operative in other systems.

One might go on asking questions. Is it not the case that some kind of isolation – in the sense of having at its disposal a mode of determining other than physical conditioning – is not illusory, e.g. teleological determination might in reality be no more than a causal determination of a very complex sort? Is it not the case that the particular mode of determining the characteristic of human persons which we call free-will is only an introspective epiphenomenon that is something derivative from the (underlying) physical causal determination? And possibly any relative isolation is merely an appearance, for if anything only partially depends on something else, then, in effect, it is totally dependent, unless it possesses its own peculiar mode of determining, which only fits in with the principle of determination operating in the rest of that very same system. And finally; what does coordination and fitting of various modes of determination mean?

Naturalism, which nowadays is a prevailing mode of thinking among philosophers, is the thesis that all facts within the Universe are natural facts.[1] This means that they can be properly recognized and explained by the natural sciences. The naturalist reduction of logic and mathematics, and the naturalist interpretation of the essence of mind do not pose such disturbing problems as those posed by the naturalist interpretation of human freedom. If being free means no more than being a system of physical causal connections which is capable of consciously experiencing acts of volition (this is how modern compatibilists interpret freedom)[2], then clearly a suspicion arises that nobody can be held morally responsible for anything he does. Thus the problem of freedom appears to be the greatest obstacle to naturalism. The explanatory and prognostic success of the modern natural sciences made the monistic naturalism look a much more serious alternative than was the case in the times of Aristotle or Thomas Aquinas. A formerly widely upheld view that there exists a plurality of modes of conditioning (determining) things and events has nowadays been replaced by the notion of one and only one mode of conditioning, that is the physical causal one.

The main difficulty in understanding the nature of human freedom consists in the problem of the correct interpretation of the relationship of human freedom to physical causality. One can define determinism in many ways: it can mean, for instance, the thesis that every event has its cause, which in turn means that every event is predictable given the preceding conditions and natural laws. Determinism then, would be the thesis that whatever exists is subject to physical determination. One should notice, though, that such a determination itself is independent of any external influences and in that sense it is free. In our world this sort of determining happens to be coordinated with the teleological and logical-mathematical conditioning.

---

[1] On this topic cf. S.J. Warner/R. Warner, *Introduction*, in: *Naturalism. A Critical Appraisal*, ed. S. J. Wagner/R. Warner, Notre Dame 1993, pp. 1-21.

[2] Compatibilism is the thesis that freedom of will can be reconciled with determinism. Th. Hobbes and D. Hume are regarded as the first to embrace that position.

Of course we may object that it is only coordinated with these modes of determining provided they are really distinct from physical conditioning. I am not going to discuss this problem now, assumimg for the time being that there exists as rich a repertory of various modes of determining as possible. The teleological and logical-mathematical modes of determining are also free in the above sense, for taken in themselves both of them are independent of external influences. Teleological and physical determining share the same objects which they condition, namely the concrete physical and organic objects. This is not true of the logical-mathematical conditioning, for its objects are of a different sort than physical and organic. However, taking into account nature's capacity for being treated mathematically, one has to indirectly accept that also logical-mathematical determination ought to be compatible with the physical and teleological one. These connections are contingent ones, which is proved by the possibility of envisaging a nature that would lack teleological conditioning, as well as a nature that would not allow mathematical treatment. One may therefore speak of a categorial freedom, that is of an independence of one mode of conditioning from other such modes, with each categorial realm possessing an appropriate mode of conditioning. Hence the problem of human freedom can be formulated as the question of whether there exists any mode of determination different from physical, teleological and logical-mathematical conditioning, that is proper to human persons. Before discussing the problem of the existence of such a mode of determination, I will present the main components of the notion of determination in general.

II. THE NOTION OF DETERMINATION

The notion of determination can be reckoned as one of the most general metaphysical (ontological) concepts.[3] The most widely accepted kind of determining is physical causal determining. I will take this as an example to illustrate the main components of the general notion of determination.

Determining of any sort is determining of some elements by another set of elements. In the case of physical causality such determination has all the characteristics of a dynamic chain. In a chain of this kind a feature passes from element to element in accordance with the direction of the time sequence. The essence of physical determining cannot be grasped if we only take into account time sequence alone, or the diversity of particular phases

---

[3] On this cf. N. Hartmann, *Der Aufbau der realen Welt. Grundriss der allgemeinen Kategorienlehre*, Berlin 1940, pp. 309-318 and by the same author, *Ethik*, Berlin 1949, pp. 621-685.

of a physical process. Nor can it be done from the point of view of the substance enduring throughout the process.

In determining of any sort one can distinguish at least three structural elements. These are, for one thing, objects (things or substances) that undergo determining. Then there are observable connections between the elements which undergo determining; in „our world" these are regular in character, which makes it possible for us to formulate physical laws. Finally there is the simple „how" of determining, that is that „force" which makes one object change another object (or make it change itself). The mystery of that „how" consists in the fact that the force engendering changes can be deduced neither *a priori*, that is by analysing the nature of the objects which are physically determined, nor *a posteriori*, that is through analysing the regularities themselves (Hume). These same distinctions (albeit with certain important modifications) apply to other than physical modes of determining, that is to the teleological and logical and mathematical mode.

Now free will can be considered as a mode of determining that is characteristic of the human person, a different mode from physical, teleological or logical-mathematical conditioning. In the case of the human being, then, freedom does not above all mean *libertas indifferentiae*[4], but it consists in there being in a human person a positive power capable of determining objects of various kinds. It is, therefore, not only independence of other modes of conditioning that human freedom has in common with other kinds of categorial freedom, but also being some sort of positive force. However, free will also contains components which make it an entirely unique mode of determining. It is spontaneous (in the sense that is yet to be determined), it is connected with self-consciousness, with reason, with „I", and it is in an essential way sensitive to values. Despite these differences, however, the essential community with the other modes of determining can be seen in the fact that in the case of free will too, the three element structure present in other modes of conditioning can be discovered. Here too we have the objects which are determined by free will. These objects may be physical, as in the case of free actions mediated by the body, or purely mental, as in the case of free actions aiming at changing one's attitude, temperament, convictions etc. Also in the case of free will there are noticeable regularities, e.g. people in some circumstances will typically behave in a certain way. Still, the difference from the other modes of determining is enormous: given the tem-

---

[4] Freedom as *libertas indifferentiae* is to be opposed to freedom understood as *libertas spontaneitas*; see on this W. Vossenkuhl, *Analytische und transzendentale Argumente für eine kausale Handlungstheorie* in H. M. Baumgartner (ed.), *Prinzip der Freiheit. Eine Auseinandersetzung um Chancen und Grenzen transzendentalphilosophischen Denkens*, Freiburg/München 1979, pp. 97-100.

perament of a man and the circumstances, one cannot predict what the man will do (or think) in a given situation. That particular mode of determining that is free will, does not allow strict (logical) generalizations, nor does it allow an inductive generalization with the degree of precision we have in the physical world. That sort of generalization that is compatible with the determination by free will can be falsified in each particular case. The third structural element (which free will has in common with other modes of determining) is the existence of the force which determines those objects of various kinds. It is something different from those objects and it cannot be reduced to the regularities through which it makes its appearance.

III. NECESSITY AND CHANCE

So far all of our reflections have assumed that there is such a thing as that peculiar mode of determining that is human free will. The arguments for its existence are a separate question. At the moment we are only concerned with the idea of freedom and not with proving its existence or answering the question whether it can be reduced to other modes of determining or whether it is compatible with physical determination. Now I would like to discuss the problem of how free will (as a mode of determining that is specifically human) is related to modal concepts such as necessity, possibility and chance.

Freedom is most often opposed to necessity.[5] Frequently the problem of freedom is put in such a way, that human freedom is seen as a certain introspective illusion opposed to the „actual reality" constituted by the all-embracing physical determination. It was at this sort of opposition that the inescapable paradox characteristic of the notion of freedom would emerge. If determinism is true (by determinism, I mean the necessity produced by physical determination), then nobody can really decide on what he or she does. If, however, determinism is false, our acts of choice are entirely accidental. Nobody can have choice concerning an event which is the result of an accident. In such a case nobody is able to choose freely. Yet a statement

---

[5] Therefore one may entertain the supposition that freedom is another modal category, along with such modal categories as possibility, chance and necessity. If we oppose freedom to necessity, we are then obliged to say that a certain event can be necessary, possible, contingent, or „free".

That would mean that it was not determined by the preceding conditions. Would, then, free events be chance events? In what way would they be different from possible events? It is hard to say to what extent one can operate with a concept of freedom as a modal category. Is the modal logic of freedom possible?

like this sounds paradoxical for it is contrary to our deeply rooted intuition that there are situations in which we can blame (or praise) people for what they have done[6].

In view of the above reasoning one may, however, ask whether the opposition between the categories of necessity and chance is correct. On the one hand we would have physical determination and the necessity it produces, on the other hand, however, we would not simply have a lack or absence of physical determination, but another positive mode of determining. The notion of chance, if it has any meaning at all, is only valid within a definite mode of determination, and even here one can only attribute it an epistemological and not a metaphysical sense. In the physical world only those events appear to be accidental whose causal path is not entirely apparent to us. If we knew all the factors which were operative in the production of the event A we would not think of A as accidental. Thus in the physical world we are only concerned with empirical necessities.[7] The mode of existence of empirical possibilities constitutes a separate problem here. If there were such things as chance events in the physical world, that would mean there existed events without causes. Such events may exist, but they cannot be thought to be without contradiction.

Besides this epistemological sense of the notion of chance one can point to one more way of construing it. The „how" of each sort of determining is hidden from our cognition. In view of that, even empirical necessity taken in the sense of there being all the factors necessary to produce an event has to be regarded as an entirely chance necessity. One can speak of a „necessity" in any situation involving a set of conditions from the point of view of which a certain event can be considered necessary. However, if we look on physical determing taking into account the „how" of that determination, rather than any conditions preceding the caused event, every physical event can be regarded as a chance event. We do not know the principle of physical condi-

---

[6] "Random choice, as a blind and arbitrary throw of a dice or the spin of a wheel of fortune, does not seem to be any more desirable than determined choice. Indeed many have thought that it was *less* desirable, and have gone on to propose alternative reconciliations of free will with determinism (different varieties of *reconciliationism* or, as it is more frequently called, *compatibilism*)" (D. C. Dennett, *Elbow Room. The Varieties of Free Will Worth Wanting*, Oxford (Clarendon, Press) 1984, p. 2).

[7] This position only implies necessitarianism with regard to the physical world. It assumes that empirical possibilities (as distinct from ideal possibilities) exist merely in „our minds" and as such result from our incomplete knowledge of a given causal path. Whether empirical possibilities also exist as Platonic ideas (like ideal possibilities and necessities) is another problem. Physical necessitarianism does not have to be universal necessitarianism, as (according to the view just presented) free will is one of the factors which can be coordinated with various causal paths in the physical world.

tioning just as we do not know the principle according to which free will determines specifically human events. Even Laplace's daemon i.e. a being knowing all the conditions necessary for an event to happen would be quite helpless here. All he would be able to do was precisely to foresee the occurrence of an event, and this only assuming that the force linking the causal chains extended in time would go on generating those events as it had been doing hitherto.

Consequently we do not have to choose between determinism and indeterminism when trying to solve the problem of free will. The existence of free will means that there exists a mode of determining that is specific to the human person; the mode that concerns mental events of various kinds as well as (through the mediation of the body) physical events. The existence of such a mode of determining is about as puzzling as the existence of other modes of conditioning. The effects generated by free will are just as mysterious as the effects resulting from the constant functioning of physical causality. This is how things are if we look on them from the point of view of the very „how" of a mode of conditioning rather than from the point of view of the conditions preceding any event.

Such an analysis, I think, makes it possible for us to eliminate, at least in part, the chance versus determinism riddle from the problem of free will. It also makes it possible to deal with another difficulty often raised in this context. In our twentieth century G. Ryle made out a case for there being a problem of infinite regression implicit in the concept of free will[8]. The presence of acts of volition makes us call some actions free. A question might be asked, though, if acts of volition are themselves free acts of the mind. If acts of volition are not themselves free, any action resulting from them is not free either. If they are free, they must result from previous acts and so *ad infinitum*.

One can make the following reply to this argument: if we think of determining (physical or otherwise) as something extended in time, the problem of an infinite regression (formulated in Ryle's spirit) arises for any mode of determining. We will have to deal with it also in relation to physical causal determination. Does it follow from the fact that here too we can formulate the problem of infinite regression that there is no such thing as physical causality as a mode of determining extended in time? If we were to take Ryle's paradox seriously we would have to stop believing in the existence of physical causality. This paradox will no longer arise if we observe that at the root of any mode of conditioning extended in time we have to accept the existence of a „force" which joins together the separate objects subject to

---

[8] Cf. G. Ryle, *The Concept of Mind*, London 1949, p. 67.

that determination. It no longer makes sense to ask about the conditions preceding that force: one has to accept that it is a self-driven „mechanism".[9]. Both the notion of „force" and the notion of „mechanism" are to be regarded as mere metaphors here. Thus we reach the limits of the intelligibility of either the phenomenon of free will or the phenomenon of physical causality.

IV. DETERMINATION AND TIME

The analyses presented so far might suggest that free will is a sort of „blind force" manifesting itself in the human person. In this respect it would not be any different from the „blind force" which manifests itself in the physical universe and binds together concrete physical objects existing therein. However, when thinking about free will we mean by the notion something which enables us to shape our own selves rather than something that only makes itself apparent in our persons as something indepedent from ourselves. It is ourselves who are masters of our free will or, in other words, it is ourselves who possess free will which we may use in accordance with reasons which we consider to be right. Thus there immediately arises another paradox: if free will is wholly determined by rational motives or by the features which comprise what we call our self-conscious „I", it is no longer free. Again, if free will is not wholly determined by our self-conscious „I" nor by rational motives it is totally arbitrary, that is chance-driven. Its effects are events without causes. And so we come to the moment where it is necessary to define the relationship obtaining between the concept of free will so far outlined and such „objects": as: „I", „reason", and „self-consciousness".

Free will, then, is a „force" (or that mode of conditioning) which manifests itself along with other characteristics. These characteristics show the distinct identity of free will as compared with other modes of determining.

(1) Free will is the sort of „force" that can function within the area delimited by consciousness and self consciousness. Not all conscious beings possess free will (e.g. higher animals and children up to a certain point in

---

[9] There is a limit to the intelligibility of the way in which any mechanism functions. Knowing the conditions necessary for „installing" various components of a given mechanism, as well as knowing their possible relationships with respect to the effect we want to obtain by constructing that mechanism is not the same as knowing „how" that mechamism functions. This „how" is always hidden, as we do not know the force (or forces) which makes the relations between the components of that mechanism function as they do.

[10] McGinn says that rationality presupposes intentionality, but he also affirms that the opposite claim is less obvious. He also adds that it is not clear to what degree rationality and

their development), but it seems to be impossible for any being to possess free will without being conscious.[10]

(2) The connection between free will and self-consciousness is a distinguishing mark of free will as a mode of determining. Free will, unlike other modes of conditioning, is spontaneous. The quality opposed to spontaneity is passivity. In the case of physical determination this means that certain physical state t is the effect of all the preceding physical states which are (directly or indirectly) connected with it. The co-occurence of free will and consciousness makes it possible for a subject to adopt an attitude of distance to the events preceding a given decision. Thus spontaneity means that there is a distance with regard to the past and also openness to the future and an identification with the future. This identification often takes the form of an active, anticipating resolution to remain faithful to the decision now being made. Nothing like this can be found in physical determining. The passivity of that determination consists in total dependence (lack of distance) of each stage of a causal chain on the preceding stages. There is no such thing as a conscious anticipation in the case of physical conditioning.

(3) Free will is operative not only in the area of self-consciousness but also in the area of reasoned motives as well as in the area of values. However, it is not identical with these realms. It is free from teleological determination which the apprehended values exert on it; it can never be entirely determined by rational motives. If the former were the case we would be no more than axiological automata, i.e. the sort of beings that always automatically choose what is of highest value. In the latter case we would be rationalistic mechanisms, i.e. beings who are always motivated by the reasons regarded at a given time as the more compelling.

(4) Free will – as a different mode of determining from physical and teleological determining – is to some extent able to resist causal determination. The „how" of that possibility of resisting causality is not available to us, nor do we know how far we can resist bodily impulses in every case. Yet we are always aware of there being such a possibility.

---

consciousness presuppose each other, or, in other words, if rationality can exist without consciousness. (C. McGinn, *Consciousness and Content*, in: R. J. Bogdan (ed.), *Mind and Common Sense. Philosophical Essays on Commonsense Psychology*, Cambridge 1981, p.89). Rationality without consciousness can be thought of as a possibility of an unconscious robot which behaves in an appropriate way in his surrounding world. Such a robot would not transform information received from his surroundings into experiences possessing phenomenal qualities. It seems, though, that one cannot think without contradiction of a creature which would be able to make free decisions while being only capable of processing information in an unconscious way.

To summarize all these characteristics of free will, one may say that free will is the mode of determining which is spontaneous, which operates within the field of self-consciousness, within the field of the rational and within the realm of values. Free will too, is capable of distancing itself from physical determination. In giving these characteristics, however, we have not yet given even a clue to the solution to the problem that Kant treated as one of the so-called antinomies of pure reason, namely how it is possible for free will to be different from teleological determination, from rational motivation and physical determination without thereby becoming something totally transintelligible[11]. It seems to me that one might suggest the following direction of reasoning to weaken the paradoxical character of the problem.

The problem of the incompatibility of causality with free will arises only when we regard physical causality as a series of events extended in time. Yet according to our previous discussion of the problem, what manifests itself in time is a mere sequence of events, and the very force which makes some objects regularly cause changes in other objects does not reveal itself. The same is true of free will as a mode of determining. So if we say that free decisions are casual as being independent of reason, valuations and physical causes, we only mean that it is not possible to relate them to any events preceding them in time. However, from the mere fact that it is not possible to establish a connection between free decisions and preceding events it does not follow that free will is not conjoined with rational motives, valuations and physical causality. The „how" of those connections is not something that can be characterized as a series of events extended in time, so in effect there does not arise any problem of absolute chance-character (casualness) of free will. This problem only arises when we treat both physical and other sorts of determination as phenomena occurring in time. One may, however, suppose that it is only the effects of the functioning of various sorts of determination that possess extension in time and not these modes of determining themselves. The very mode of conditioning that is free will and the way it conjoins with other modes of determining are not available to our cognition. What is cognitively available to us are their manifestations in time. Hence free decision is not an event without a cause in the sense that it is ultimately based on a timeless way in which various modes of determining tie up with each other. However, from a temporal point of view we have to

---

[11] Cf. I. Kant, *Critique of Pure Reason*, A448/B476. Without going into the details of the solution Kant propounded for his third antinomy of pure reason, one may point to the fact that the proposed solution referred essentially to the empirical world, that is, to one „immersed" in time, on the one hand, and on the other hand to „the world of things in themselves" which are not subject to conditioning by time.

interpret each free decision as an event without causes, for not only is it the case that all modes of determining become apparent to us in time, but also our thinking about these modes is essentially temporal in its character.[12] Hence arises the paradox of events without any causes.

V. IS THERE SUCH THING AS SELF-DETERMINATION?

Is it at all possible to entertain doubts that human beings have at their disposal a mode of determining other than physical and teleological determination? Usually the doubts with regard to this problem result from an impossibility of achieving a reconciliation between freedom and determinism, or else from difficulties of understanding what free will is. To try to avoid these difficulties one may try and adopt the position (the prevalent one among philosophers today) that is termed referred to as compatibilism. The point of view I defend here is compatibilist in so far as it affirms a fundamental possibility of diverse modes of determining in the world coexisting. However, this point of view is not full compatibilism, for I do not accept that free will is to be construed exclusively as a freedom of acting as one wishes[13]. Free will cannot be reconciled with determinism for it is a mode of determining entirely different from physical or teleological determimation. The doubts resulting from the problematic character of the very concept of free will, that is the doubts concerning the chance character of free will and the infinite regression of acts of volition appear to have been removed (at least in part) by the above discussion of them. However, is it really the case that there exists free will as a separate, specifically human mode of determining?

A suggestion for an answer to that question may be seen to be included in another question: are there any reasons to suppose that physical determination is something merely „superficial", that is, the entire structure of the physical causal connection is in reality constituted by a completely different mode of determining and by completely different sorts of objects being

---

[12] This thesis is not contradicted by the fact that logical determination is not characterizible as a dynamic series of phases extended in time as even in this case we have to think of determination passing from conditions to their consequences. Therefore the necessity we notice in this way is also a necessity relative to the „preceding" conditions. The paradox of freedom as an event without a cause looms so large for it is only in this that we have to deal with „empty" consciousness of pure activity. Free will is the only mode of determining given to us „from inside", whereas all other modes are given to us „from outside" as well as being always mediated by conditions extended in time.

[13] On the falsity of compatibilism and determinism see P. van Inwagen, *An Essay on Free Will*, (Clarendon Press), Oxford 1985.

bound together. It seems we do not have any such reasons. This in turn means that we have to accept that physical determination is not only a superficial but rather an ultimate, irreducible factor to any further mode of determining. This does not seem to hold true of teleological determining. With regard to this mode of conditioning it is widely believed, as a result of the development of biochemistry and physics as well as reductionist tendencies becoming more and more widespread, that such a mode can be eliminated and replaced by physical determination. Even though there is some case for such a reduction, I do not think one will ever succeed in an attempt to eliminate (either empirically or conceptually) the belief that certain events are determined by their purpose.

The impossibility of a reduction of any modes of conditioning to other modes is even more clearly seen in the case of the attempts to reduce logical and mathematical determination to physical causality. Perhaps, therefore, one should affirm that all the fundamental categorial objects, events and processes are just what they are and nothing above and beyond that. One also ought to remember that all the successful reductions of one theory to another which the physical reductionists adduce have taken place within categorially homogeneous realms[14].

Now if we take into account any description of the characteristic features of free will as a mode of determining it should be clear, at least from the phenomenological point of view, that free will is a radically different mode from other modes of conditioning. Spontaneity of free will stands in opposition to the passivity of physical determination, transcendence with respect to time, that is distance from the past and identifying openness to the future, set free will apart from both physical and teleological determining. A holistic tie up with rational motives makes for the contrast between free will and the linear functioning of causal determination. The essential tie up of free will with self-consciousness differentiates it from „blind" causal and teleological determination. One may add here, as is usually done, the phenomena of feeling guilty or feeling morally blameless, which would be something totally incomprehensible if man (as a product of cosmic determination) was completely conditioned by physical and axiological reality. True enough, the existence of all these descriptive features, as well as the existence of the

---

[14] The so-called successful intertheoretical reductions, e.g. a reduction of thermodynamics to statistical mechanics, have always taken place within a qualitatively homogeneous area. In the reductions of that sort there was no necessity of a switch to a qualitatively radically different sphere. Such a radical difference obtains e.g. between the sphere of conscious experience and the sphere of processes in the brain. A similar qualitative gulf also characterizes the relationship between physical causality and the phenomenal features of free will as a mode of determining.

phenomena of feelings of guilt and moral blamelessness does not, of itself, invalidate the supposition that the free will we experience is only a surface phenomenon underlain by causal determination. Here, as in all problems involving scepticism, the burden of proof lies with the one who doubts the actual existence of apparent features of a given phenomenon. The sceptic doubter has to point out the reasons which would compel us to suppose that freedom is just an illusion. The sceptic would also have to demonstrate the way other modes of determining are transformed so as to create the illusion of freedom. So far no such reasons have been produced, and reasoning in accordance with the principle of the best explanation would rather make us assume that the singular ontological position of man consists in man having at his disposal a unique mode of determining, which combines with reason and the ability to appreciate values.

RYSZARD LEGUTKO
Jagiellonian University in Cracow
Poland

FREEDOM OF THOUGHT
AND INVIOLABILITY OF CONSCIENCE

This paper describes an evolution what the two major concepts -liberty of thought and inviolability of conscience – underwent in the course of the development of a modern idea of freedom. It is to identify the development of a modern idea of freedom. The aim of the paper is to identify the difference that separates a modern liberal attitude from that which appeared at the beginning of modernity. The two concepts in question – distinct, but often confused – emerged in the great debate about religous toleration which began in the wake of Reformation and lasted until the era of the Enlightenment.

Both concepts marked two principle positions in the debate: one held by advocates of religious liberty and the other – by political authoritarians defending a strong state as the best means to secure public peace. It was then the former who, rather expectedly, claimed a protected status of human conscience while it was the latter who – somewhat paradoxically – ascribed to it a status of natural inner freedom. Referring to those two positions, I will speak of the authoritarians' and libertarians' arguments, respectively.

Let us start with the authoritarians' argument. Historically speaking, it grew out of two sources: Reformation and Neo-Stoicism. The reformation, it will be recalled, claimed to have shifted the centre of religious life from the outward to the inward; what mattered in religion was thus an internal process, and consequently – though some would object to the logical grounds of such a consequence – what happened externally did not belong to religion and, therefore, did not have the protection that was naturally granted to religion. To this was added a Neo-Stoical proposition that a human identity was developing internally, not externally, that is, through penetrating into a deeper layers of our consciousness: if we are threatened by the outside world, we can always recede more deeply into ourselves to find a safer and more basic foundation of our identity. The argument about liberty of conscience had thus a following structure:

(i) The human mind is autonomous, independent of external factors: coercion can prevent a man from expressing his thoughts, but it cannot prevent him from thinking;

(ii) intellectual independence can therefore coexist with political dependence as the latter does not deprive a man from control over his own mind;

(iii) whoever desires to preserve a freedom of thinking must develop a certain typer of intellectual and moral virtue that would enable him to withstand external pressure and, in the face of political and social destinies, to secure integrity of his own mind.

The argument could be and, in fact, was sometimes used to justify an unlimited power of government. It provided an excuse to employ political coercion almost indiscriminately since every coercive measure could be minimized as not being directed against religion; a liberty of conscience was located so deeply that it had a scarce mitigating effect on the sovereign who wanted to exert his political power on the subjects. If used in this sense, the argument did not have much value, but was merely a propaganda ploy to be conveniently applied by the powers that were. But there was a deeper, more rational core in it which rehabilitated this argument and which is still worth reflecting on.

It cannot be denied, however, that when assessed from a modern perspective the argument seems somewhat anachronistic. It belongs, one would think, to the now closed period of a widespread belief in enlightened political absolutism with its claim *cuius regio eius religio* – one state, one religion. Nowadays there are surely no thinkers or ideologies in the Western world who would contend that religion is a basic cohesive political force and that therefore all citizens should observe its outward forms as their political duty while being free to believe privately in whatever they like. There are however contentions – at least such an argument sometimes comes to the fore in polemics – that some form of secular ideology has replaced religion as the political unifying force, with religion being moved into a private sphere. In short, some contend that we today observe a reversal of the authoritarians' old argument. I do not think that there is an exact symmetry between these two ideological patterns, and will not analyse the problem in this paper. I will concentrate instead on two other aspects in which the authoritarians' argument appears vulnerable today. First, unlike the authoritarians we no longer distinguish politically between a freedom of thinking and a freedom of expressing one's thoughts; second, unlike the authoritarians we have rejected an interpretation of reality, social, political and economic, in terms of destiny to which we ought to conform.

Let me tackle the first of these. There is a lot to be said in support of today's reluctance to distinguish between an internal freedom of thought and a political freedom of speech: since thinking cannot develop without a dialogue, an exchange of arguments, a freedom to articulate our thoughts in public seems to be a prerequisite of all other freedoms and all political and social procedures. It would be, indeed, unwise of me to waste time trying to cast some doubt on this assumption. I think that today the problem lies elsewhere, which explains why we find it so hard to understand the rational core of the authoritarians' argument. The problem lies not in diminishing the value of expression, to which a possible authoritarian of today would be tempted – such a temptation is not worth giving in – but in diminishing the value of an inward act of thinking, and it is to this that we seem to be at present inclined. There is not much importance – we believe – in free thinking if it is not accompanied by free expression. And it is precisely this thesis which I find somewhat presumptuous. Once we accept it, we tend to see freedom almost solely in political terms, also politicising those domains which should not be politicised. It is no incident that the idea of disinterested contemplation as a way of life has been on the wane for some time: it contains precisely what the modern notion of freedom cannot easily espouse – withdrawing from the necessaries of life, from political commitments and from the logic of utility. As Aristotele put it in Book X of the *Nicomachean Ethics*: "The just man needs people towards whom and with whom he shall act justly, and the temperate man, the brave man, and each of the others is in the same case, but the philospopher, even when by himself can contemplate truth, and the better the wiser he is; he can perhaps do so better if he has fellow workers, but still he is the most self-sufficient. And this activity alone would seem to be loved for its own sake; for nothing arises from it apart from the contemplating, while from practical activities we gain more or less apart from the action".

The authoritarians' argument was of course not about philosophy but about religion; still I think by a similar type of dualism – that of body and soul – which had underlain Aristotle's argument for the superiority of contemplative life, was also at the root of what the authoritarians said about inner freedom; they were clearly influenced by the Cartesian dichotomy of *res cogitans* and *res extensa*. We can invest so much faith and hope in the life of the mind or the life of the soul if we treat this mind or this soul as an equally viable alternative to body and action. I do not think it particularly controversial to claim that in the modern world the life of the mind or of the soul is no longer considered an equally viable alternative to an active life in a community. As a consequence, intellectualism as previously understood lost its appeal. That does not mean of course that people lost interest in acquiring knowledge through thinking; far from it. It means that acquiring knowledge, though widespread on an unprecedented scale, is not any more accompanied with the moral and spiritual expectations it once was. It is certainly not considered to be a vehicle for spiritual self-improvement; in other words, it no longer serves as a means to cultivate one's soul.

The second aspect in which we differ from the authoritarians is a question of destinies. The concept of destiny has become suspect since it came to be seen as an ideological smokescreen for domination: it is assumed that people will not rise to change their inferior status as long as they believe it belongs to the sphere of destiny. For reasons too complex to expound here the concept of politics that we have today has gradually eliminated any idea of destiny: no political goal seems to lie outside political ideologies, if not outside political programs; no political structure is immune against human intervention. But rejection of destiny is not limited to politics; it has also occurred in the social and moral sphere: no social and communal bonds are aviewed as permanent as free exit is considered to be the primary condition of social interaction of individuals; no commitments are unbreakable if one can prove they are against basic entitlements of an individual (marriage may be a case in point). Probably the only area where we had, until recently, an element of destiny was economy, at least in some free market theories. Capitalism, as has been often pointed out, preserved some form of belief in destiny, or providence; the verdicts of the market are what they are, neither just or unjust as Hayek said, but to be accepted as a necessary outcome of the processes which we cannot control, or rather, which we would be better off not controlling. This tenet of capitalist philosophies is hard to reconcile with the idea of the individual emancipation and the power of individual initiative which these very same philosophies proclaim, which has led to a permanent internal tension within the capitalist doctrine. Anyway, the post-Hayekian thinkers appear less prone to give their theories a fatalistic tinge, and thus are less exposed to the charge raised against older market theorists that they had made some form of submission a morally honourable attitude. Putting economy aside, we are probably left with only one sphere of life – that of biological existence – where we still feel a sense of destiny; so far death, to my knowledge, has not been abolished.

This depreciation of the idea of destiny has an important consequence. Our moral horizon no longer encompasses certain type of virtues, those that develop as our moral response to the processes and events that affect us but are beyond our control. During the toleration debate the Neo-Stoics restored the old stoic category of *ataraxia* which denotes precisely this: an ability not to be moved by the arbitrary changes of destiny. Others used a Latin term '*constantia* in more or less the same meaning. These virtues expressed two seemingly contradictory notions: on the one hand, a sense of aloofness or superiority or even condescension towards power, that stemmed from the inner freedom of a learned and cultivated mind; on the other, an acceptance of and submission to this power as a huma fate. The fact that this combination of attitudes seems foreign to modern taste signifies, probably, a considerable shift in the way we see the world. *Ataraxia* and *constantia* conveyed a sense of the tragic, and it is here that the early modern and the present sensibilities diverge. I am not saying that we are no more capable of experiencing the tragic. I am saying that we are no longer responsive to the tragic or rather no longer able to see the tragic in the areas in which the existence of the tragic was once obvious, politics being the obvious case. We do not see destiny in political power, which of course does not mean that we control this power; realistically speaking, for many of us it still remains a sort of destiny but we simply refuse to see it as such.

Let us now turn to the libertarians' argument. At its historical root we also find an idea of the internalisation of religion that the Reformation gave prominence to. Another possible inspiration, yet having roughly the same consequences, came from the more and more deeply felt gap between science and faith; the growth of scientific knowledge pushed religion more and more into the sphere of the subjective, and bring more vividly into light the qualitative difference between the experience of knowledge and the experience of faith.

The libertarians' argument had the following structure:
(i) religious experience derives its strength from a believer's sense of certainty; this type of certainty is strictly individual and cannot be objectively verified;
(ii) an experience of faith in a true religion is therefore indistinguishable from an experience of faith in a false religion;
(iii) both these experiences are thus entitled to the same rights; hence conscience understood as an idividual conviction of the truth of one's own religious faith is inviolable.

The libertarians' argument sounds more in accord with modern liberal sensibilities but it, too, has undergone substantial modification. Let us note that the force of this argument stemmed from a certain interpretation of religious experience as something above the objective knowledge of science; its subjectivity could therefore not be identified with the subjectivity impression or opinions, i.e., with the subjectivity of what is below the objective knowledge of science. Religious experience was thus regarded not as pre-scientific but rather as post-scientific; it was an attempt to go beyond science towards the ultimate, but such a venture, it was claimed, could only lead to an individual certainty, untranslateable into the experiences of other people and therefore entitled to the same treatment as those other experiences. The argument had – at least in some verisions, notably in Pierre Bayle's – a clear trace of scepticism: objective rational knowledge cannot give us the ultimate truth, leading us often to antinomies and doubt; the only way to overcome those antinomies and doubts is religion, but the price we pay for transcending the sphere of science is subjectivity and unverifiability.

The libertarians' argument in the above formularion had two definitely non-libertarian, or to be precise, authoritarian elements. The first is a consequence of the fact that, as it has been pointed out, originally conscience was restricted to religious experience; it did not include moral convictions. In fact one of the reasons why philosophers argued for toleration was an assumption that freedom of religion could be separated from a question of moral conduct; in the latter there was no freedom, that is, the state took over the function of a moral guardian; even liberal philosophers, such as Locke, thought it necessary that the legal system defended moral virtues and punished moral vices. In short, morality was not a matter of conscience but largely a matter of law or, at least, of the sovereign's concern. This view, as it is easy to see, sharply deviates from the modern liberal idiom where there is no asymmetry between religious and moral toleration, and where the notion of inviolability of conscience is usually interpreted as inviolability of strongly subjective moral. I would wish to say – religious about something, they deserve to have their conscience inviolable. This is the grounds on which one can defend promiscuity, considerable liberalisation of sexual ethics, euthanasia, abortion, etc. Inviolability of moral conscience with respect to those questions is seen to be almost identical as inviolability of aesthetic tastes: all of these belong to a private sphere of rights and individual choices, and are thus structurally and psychologically indistinguishable from religious sensibilities which are also protected as belonging to the sphere of individual rights and choices.

The other authoritarian element which was present in the libertarians' argument and which is absent today is the restriction of its applicability to Christian religion. The argument, if made use of consistently, did not of course limit itself to Christianity, but implied religious egalitarianism: all religions, real and potential, great and small, adhered to by great civilisations and by minute sects, must be seen as equally true, equally false, or equally arbitrary. But it is precisely this consequence which people like Bayle did not want to espouse. They made a reservation – somewhat ad hoc, one might say – that the argument as an argument for toleration should apply solely to Christian religion; they thus assumed that all Christian religions are equally legitimate, i.e., equally Christian in their search for God as long as they are animated by a sincere and profound faith. (Toleration of non-Christian religious groups was grounded differently: on a utilitarian argument of reciprocity). This had important political consequences. It allowed philosophers to talk of a Christian society, that is, of a society where one could legitimately speak of crucial common values having a common source; Christianity as a social fact was a common concern because it represented an essential part of spiritual and moral identity of this society, and was therefore granted, as a religion, a privileged position within a political community. Of course, the fact that toleration became a hotly debated issue proved that there was a lot of confusion about this spiritual and moral identity, that it was more an ideal than a fact, that division and conflicts more often came to the fore than a bond of Christian brotherhood; yet it must be noted that the aim of the debate over toleration was not to marginalize Christianity but to secure for it a central role in a modern society.

Today this limitation of the argument no longer holds in liberal political theory, and religious egalitarianism seems to prevail. Religion, Christian or non-Christian, is not included either in the description of a modern society or in the initial set of values (state of nature, original position, etc.) in the light of which the basic rules of co-operation are said to be established. Religion, if it exists as a social fact, is considered to be more a conflict-generating problem that needs to be solved by a lawmaker or a theorist of justice than a possible source of a rule-making process; in short, it no longer belongs to a sphere of authority.

The conclusion of the above remarks is somewhat banal. The original concepts of freedom of thought and inviolability of conscince had more authoritarian presuppositions than a modern liberal use of these concepts would allow. Whether this is a change for the better or for the worse, may be for some people an open question, although a liberal would certainly have an unequivocal stand on this issue. My own position is more ambiguous. I would say that a balanced assessment of gains and losses would not be possible unless and until we have analysed the nature of the new authoritarianism which replaced the old one. That such authoritarianism exists I do not doubt since each conception of freedom establishes its own rules of discipline.

ANDRIUS VALEVIČIUS
Université de Sherbrooke
Canada

FREEDOM AND PERSONAL AUTONOMY

This paper is a reflection upon one the outflows of our contemporary culture of freedom, the concept of autonomy. Autonomy, whether individual or collective, has become a new universal maxim, a categorical imperative placed upon all facets of life in Western society, and maybe even elsewhere now. First of all, I can only speak for my own North American culture, but I suspect that the same trends are well entrenched in Western Europe and it is probably only a question of time before they reach Central and Eastern Europe if they have not already done so.

In Canada, when children begin school at the age of five, or even pre-kindergarten at the age of 4, one of the subjects on their report card and for which they receive a mark (satisfactory, highly satisfactory, etc.) is „autonomous behaviour." I have never really been able to figure out what exactly autonomous behaviour refers to at this early stage of the game. Does it mean that the child is able to tie his or her own shoelaces, get dressed alone, not have to be told to pick up his or her crayons and so forth? Generally speaking, does it refer to independent behaviour? And this behaviour, from the first days of school onwards, where the child will remain for the next twelve or thirteen years, is highly valorized. There is nothing that the teachers praise more. Therefore, we should feel free to assume that this form of behaviour is good and healthy. Or, can autonomous behaviour also be taken to mean individualistic behaviour? The ideologues of autonomy will not doubt deny this. However, now that autonomy has become nothing less than a virtue[1], what happens to the child who is less autonomous, who

---

[1] Robert Paul Wolff speaks of the "the virtue of autonomy" in his *In Defense of Anarchism*, 1970, pp. 12-19. Reprinted in Arthur J. Minton and Thomas A. Shipka, *Philosophy. Paradox and Discovery*, New York: McGraw Hill Publishing Co., 1990, pp. 462-467.

needs help at tying his or her shoelaces, buttoning up his or her coat or in deciding what to do? Are the autonomous children taught that it is equally important for them to help less autonomous ones even though the latter do not have a place on the report card?

Similarly, adolescents and young people are to be autonomous. For young people, leaving the parental home and living on their own, having a part-time job, having money in the bank and owning a car, in other words, working evenings and weekends at MacDonald's or elsewhere in order to support this independence (along with the pressure to separate oneself from the crowd forced upon them by the teen-age fashion industry), is somehow the more progressive style of life than just simply staying at home with your parents, being content with few personal material goods and spending evenings reading or studying instead of working.

As young adults, the pursuit of a career is everything. This is something that nothing is allowed to compromise, not even marriage. Even here, in Holy Matrimony, the same ideal of autonomy is carried over. Both husband and wife must respect each other's autonomy, each other's freedom. Both have the same equal right to a career and to the development of their interests which help to realize and fulfil the Self. Both should have their own source of income and each have his or her "own money". Further, today it is considered foolish not to have a marriage contract. Children should not be an obstacle to personal self-fulfilment either. Personal parental attention can easily be replaced by the day-care system where children can be raised institutionally and learn to be autonomous even while still in diapers.

Finally, the ideal of autonomy has also been imposed upon a part of society that probably heard very little of the word when they were young, that is to say, our senior citizens. The ideal of autonomy has been pushed upon them, at an age when human beings naturally become less and less autonomous, by a much younger = class of bureaucratically-minded, career orientated, individualistic, freedom and fun-loving middle age or baby-boomer generations. These technocrats and bureaucrats, or just sons and daughters, expect all pensioners to be financially independent and autonomous in terms of health as well. If they require any kind of daily care, then it is better that they be autonomous in a senior citizen's home rather than a burden on their offspring who have no time to care for them, otherwise they might loose some of their own autonomy. It does not matter whether you are old and sick and dying of cancer, you must be autonomous. If you feel that you can't be autonomous any longer because your isolation and pain is too great or because it costs so much that it is diminishing the amount of your children's inheritance, it is now becoming possible in some Western countries to autonomously choose the moment of death.

Furthermore, the pressure to be autonomous has received the support of "the great global capitalistic financial enterprise", because autonomy multiplies needs. Thus, it greatly boosts consumer spending and this, in turn, is considered to be good for the economy. How often autonomy is equated with credit. Being autonomous means being able to obtain credit. There are numerous books on the subject, published both privately and by government agencies[2]. In other words, being able to get oneself into debt is understood to be something positive because it is a demonstration of financial autonomy.

Last but not least, autonomy has even received the prestigious support of organized religion. How many courses in ethics and theology, the latter often being now nothing more than a pious form of pop-psychology, exalt the virtues of autonomy. If an unwanted pregnancy is a threat to the autonomous self, serious questions must be asked in order to decide upon the options, as if there were any options in a Christian context. If your marriage is an obstacle to your self-realization and self-fulfilment as a human being, maybe it is time to see whether you were really married in full sense of the sacrament? If not, then there was no real marriage in the first place and you are free to regain your autonomy.

Saint Augustine in the *City of God* talks about the two cities, the City of God and the earthly city as *perplexae et permixtae*, tightly intertwined with one another. In Augustine's perspective, it would be inconceivable to separate them before the fullness of time at which point the latter will be blended into the former. Yet, even Vatican II did not miss the opportunity to exalt the notion of autonomy. Paragraph 36 of *Gaudium et spes*, subtitled "Rightful autonomy of earthly affairs", reads as follows: "If by autonomy of earthly affairs is meant the gradual discovery, exploitation, and ordering of the laws and values of matter and society, then the demand for autonomy is perfectly in order: it is at once the claim of modern man and the desire of the creator. By the very nature of creation, material being is endowed with its own stability, truth and excellence, its own order and laws. These man must respect as he recognizes the methods proper to every science and technique."[3]

---

[2] For a few titles, cf.: Nicole Chardin, *Le contrat de consommation de crédit et l'autonomie de la volonté*, Paris: Librairie Générale de Droit et de Jurisprudence, 1988; Monique Frappier, *L'autonomie financière de nos ainés et les enjeux pour la société québecoise*, Québec: Insitut Québecois de recherche sur la culture, 1991; *Les femmes et le crédit: accéder l'autonomie financière*, Québec: Ministre du conseil executif, Secrétariat de la condition feminine, 1988.

[3] *Vatican II. The Conciliar and Post Conciliar Documents*, editied by Austin Flannery, Northport: Costello Publ. Co., 1975, p. 935.

Personal autonomy, as we know it today, is a relatively modern phenomenon. It can be traced back to Descartes, Kant and the German idealists Fichte and Schelling. Then there is the sudden burst into contemporary culture where it occupies an enormous place now in educational, psychological, ethical and feminist literature. It is basically taken to mean "being in charge of your own life". It is a combination of two Greek words, "autos" and "nomos" which mean self-rule, i.e., the condition of living according to the laws that one gives oneself, not being under the control of another. However, the Greeks knew nothing of personal autonomy as we understand it, the term autonomy was applied to city-states. The autonomy of Athens consisted in its not being ruled by another city. Instead of speaking about personal autonomy, the Greeks had other concepts to emphasize personal freedom. In Plato's *Republic*, one such concept was the virtue of courage; the ability to do what one believes to be right despite the swaying of emotion and passion. Then, wisdom, temperance and justice were the other basic constituents of the free man, or of the autonomous person as we would call him today.

Aristotle, in his *Politics* and *Ethics* uses the term "autarchy" which means self-sufficiency. It is a concept which can be applied to both the city-state and to the individual. It is the ability to provide for one's own needs so that one may be free to seek happiness while living the virtuous life. Thus, for Plato and Aristotle, autonomy, if the term could be applied to the individual, would have meant trying to be as human as possible; fitting into the definition of what it is to be a human being to the best of one's ability. This kind of autonomy had a very definite finality to it, the individual knew exactly what he had to become, a rational animal.

In today's world it is not enough to desire to be a human being, to be rational or to be virtuous. If anything, calling someone virtuous is far from being a compliment. It is much more an embarrassment, especially for teenagers. Autonomy today is a form of hyper-individuality. Lawrence Haworth calls it "making a demonstration of my uniqueness..." The autonomous person is "one who has individuated himself vividly"[4]. The autonomous person is thus one who is capable of being an agent of action although this does not answer the question of the why or whereafter of the action, other than just wanting to be different. Again, this fits well with our "performance" geared society and economy. It is accepted as self-evident that performance must always improve in order to maximize efficiency and productivity, and this is the best indication of progress. "[...] Material being is endowed with its own

---

[4] Lawrence Haworth, *Autonomy. An Essay in Philosophical Psychology and Ethics*, New Haven: Yale University Press, 1986, p.13.

stability, truth and excellence, its own order and laws" and performance and individuality seem to be two of them.

Autonomy can also be understood as a striving for competence, or the ability to do things for oneself. It is an assertion of one's independence and basically a rejection of parentalism, as psychology informs us. But, this form of discourse ignores man's fundamental desire for dependence, for belonging, for living in community with others. Man's willingness to accept the situation of being a hostage, in the words of Levinas. One of the principles of the proponents of autonomy is not to do harm to others, but the Gospels teach us not only to abstain from doing harm, but to love others, even to the point of self-sacrifice. The entire notion of self-sacrifice, the kenotic attitude, is completely foreign to the concept of autonomy. Here, it would be called self-determination, one chooses to give of oneself, as if such occasions are planned and rationally meditated upon, as if they came from the mind instead of from the heart.

The autonomy and performance orientated education which we give our young people teaches them to be assertive, demanding and aggressive, whereas the Gospels tell us that "I must become smaller so that He be greater". The age-old wisdom of humility, meekness, tenderness, find no place in today's jungle ideology where sometimes being just plain animal may get you further than being a rational animal.

Saint Augustine in the *Confessions* said, "too weak to find the truth by ourselves, we need the authority of divine books". Today's culture of autonomy automatically nurtures a rejection of authority: parental authority, institutional authority, moral authority and from there the next step is the rejection of any Divine authority. Everyone is "autonomos". The decalogue is irrelevant. I recently put together a bibliography on the Decalogue using a computer data base. To my amazement, over the past twenty-five years almost nothing has been written on the Decalogue in Catholic circles, more has been done in Protestant circles, but the only centres of study which continue to write serious commentary and do research on the Decalogue are the rabbinical schools. The Decalogue, in essence, is also about freedom, but a freedom founded upon a pre-described law. Ten basic principles according to which men and women must live. Its "minimal" character in terms of paragraphs, along with its elasticity of application, allowed for a relatively free lifestyle, nonetheless, in societies which upheld these principles as law. However, once the existence of every principle has vanished, the necessity of legalism takes over. Since there are no longer any external principles in Western society which would be binding to all, for autonomy requires that we be the creators of our own laws, it is necessary to multiply laws everywhere and codify life to the point where, even though we may believe ourselves to be autonomous, we are in reality less and less free and more and more dominated by the state. It cannot be otherwise. With individuality as strong as it is nowadays, there must a great multiplication of laws, otherwise society would not be governable.

The tradition of early Christian writings has always upheld freedom as the greatest of man's qualities. To describe freedom, Gregory of Nyssa uses words such as *ἀδέσποτος* (freedom from every form of dominion) and *ἄδουλατος* (the absence of any form of slavery). He describes the free person as *Αυτεξούσιός*, the one who "is of himself." The free person becomes Godlike according to Gregory, *ισοθεον γάρ έστι το αύτεξούσιον*. However, despite this immense freedom, the ontological truth of man is beyond all philosophy, beyond the realm of Platonic ideas, beyond the theory of emanations of the Gnostics, beyond the soul, beyond matter, beyond personality. Man's ontological truth lies in his being created in the image of the invisible God. In this perspective, autonomy as such cannot even exist because, even if autonomy theoretically allows for the existence of God, God can never be an exterior principle upon which man is dependent since He is man's ontological origin. God is the very centre of human existence and man must live centred upon God. So too man's activity, his laws, his choices in life. Anything short of this is atheism.

For Gregory of Nyssa, every human being, even though he be extremely free, is, in so far as he is a created being, in a state of dependence (*δουλεία*). Dependence is a constituent part of a creature (for he is dependent upon his creator for his existence) and it is only by way of this dependence that the human being can find his natural nobility. Moses, for Gregory, symbolizes true freedom because he is a true servant of God: "Moses is worthy of being called the sublime servant of God, which is equal to saying that he was superior to all"[5].

Autonomy is when the parental lineage to God is cut and as such, it is a form of pseudo-freedom. As Vatican II informs us, science, matter, world order, are good in themselves, but if they are separated from their ontological source, the Godhead, if they become completely autonomous, they risk running a very dangerous course. Then scientific discovery, instead of being used to improve life, as an autonomous and exchangeable entity, can become an instrument of war. We have seen enough of this and the thought requires no clarification. The same for many of the human sciences: psychology, once it becomes an autonomous science and a marketable entity, instead of healing the soul, it can be used to manipulate people's emotions, desires and convictions. Economics, instead of working for a equal distribution of wealth in the world, as God would have wanted it, as an autonomous

---

[5] In J.-P. Migne, *Patrologia graeca cursus completus* (PG), 1857-1868, vol. 44, col. 428B.

science it can end up serving the interests of some to the impoverishment of others.

Thus, what is the future of a society which continues to encourage autonomy? Can it be governed freely without resorting to totalitarianism? Can it ever be strong enough to overcome a major crisis? Will it be able to mobilize its population for the attainment of a common good? To witness the devastation that theories of autonomy have brought to the family and to family values, how can any positive results be expected on the large-scale family, the nation? Most of all, can it cure the deep depression of Western man? Depression which has been brought on by fragmentation and isolation. Finally, which one of the three persons of the Trinity is autonomous with respect to the others?

ALESSANDRO GHISALBERTI
Università Cattolica del Sacro Cuore
Italy

LE RAPPORT ENTRE LIBERTÉ ET FÉLICITÉ DANS LA PHILOSOPHIE MÉDIÉVALE: RELECTURES CONTEMPORAINES

Cette intervention se propose de faire émerger les points les plus significatifs de la discussion concernant le rapport entre la volonté libre de l'homme et la félicité sur le plan de l'éthique, dans la seconde moitié du XIIIe siècle et la première du XIVe.

En affrontant l'exégèse de l'*Ethique à Nicomaque* d'Aristote, les penseurs latins (nous examinerons la position de Thomas d'Aquin) trouvèrent d'abord une solution qui sauvegardait le primat de la morale théologique. Celle-ci, selon la tradition principalement inspirée de Saint Augustin, défendait l'accomplissement supraterrestre de la fin dernière de l'homme, dans la vision *post mortem* béatifiée.

Au cours du dernier quart du XIIIe siècle, cependant, l'idée d'une félicité naturelle acquiert une crédibilité toujours plus grande. Cette félicité naturelle serait toute entière mondaine, et l'homme la poursuivrait avec ses facultés proprement humaines, en particulier par l'exercice de la contemplation intellective. Cette idée culmine dans la discussion, développée par Jean Buridan, concernant l'autonomie possible de l'éthique philosophique par rapport à l'éthique révélée.

I. FÉLICITÉ ET FIN DERNIÈRE: LA FONDATION DE L'ÉTHIQUE CHEZ THOMAS D'AQUIN

Le donné commun à toutes les actions, qui réside dans l'être des "mouvements", non pas au sens de mutations, mais au contraire au sens d'acquisition d'un donné supplémentaire, exprimable par la formule classique du passage de la puissance à l'acte, n'échappe pas à l'appartenance à l'ordre de la fin ou des fins: la fin est ce en vue de quoi chaque agent agit, et la cause finale coïncide avec l'objectif qui pousse la cause efficiente à "mouvoir", c'est-à-dire à opérer le passage de la puissance à l'acte. Mais il semble que cela ne s'applique pas toujours, ni à toutes les actions de l'homme, parce que s'il est vrai que l'homme agit en vue d'une fin lorsqu'il décide délibérément de poursuivre un certain résultat, il y a d'autres situations où il agit sans délibération et sans penser à ce qu'il fait: gesticuler avec les mains ou les pieds, se lisser la barbe, etc.

Il convient ici d'établir une distinction préalable entre les actions proprement humaines, que l'homme accomplit en tant qu'homme, c'est-à-dire dans la totale maîtrise de ses propres actes, à travers la raison et la volonté, et les actions que l'homme accomplit non par une délibération consciente de sa volonté, mais d'une manière inconsciente ou irréfléchie, à partir de stimulations ou de conditionnements divers de son organisme. Thomas, comme on le sait, parle d'*actiones humanae* dans le premier cas, et d'*actiones hominis* dans le second[1]; et il est clair, suivant cette distinction, que le domaine des actions proprement humaines comprend tout le vaste champ de la praxis assujetti à l'éthique, qui exige, pour que l'on puisse parler d'éthique, une mise en jeu de la responsabilité du sujet agissant, tant dans la capacité de viser par l'intention que dans celle de choisir ou de vouloir librement.

Toutes les actions qui procèdent d'une puissance sont causées par elle relativement à l'objet propre à cette puissance: dans le cas de la volonté, l'objet propre qui la détermine à agir est la fin, qui s'identifie concrètement avec un bien à poursuivre et à atteindre grâce à l'action mise en acte. Thomas conclut pour cela que "quod omnes actiones humanae propter finem sint". Naturellement, à chaque acte en général, à chaque action, quel que soit l'être capable d'être actif qui l'ait produite, il appartient d'avoir une fin: les agents naturels, privés de raison, ne connaissent pas cette fin, ils ne se la représentent pas, et pour cela, ils ne la poursuivent pas à partir de la tendance introduite par un autre agent (comme dans le cas de la flèche mue par l'archer qui atteint la fin (la cible) ou par déterminisme naturel, c'est-à-dire par la constitution biologique des organismes (le poirier qui produit les poires).

---

[1] "Actionum quae ab homine aguntur, illae solae proprie dicuntur humanae, quae sunt propriae hominis inquantum est homo, differt autem homo ab irrationabilibus creaturis in hoc, quod est suorum actuum dominus; est autem homo dominus suorum actuum per rationem et voluntatem; unde et liberum arbitrium esse dicitur facultas voluntatis et rationis; illae ergo actiones proprie humanae dicuntur, quae ex voluntate deliberata procedunt: si quae autem aliae actiones homini conveniant, possunt dici quidem hominis actiones, sed non proprie humanae, cum non sint hominis inquantum est homo" (*Summa theol.* I-II^{ae}, q. 1, art. 1, resp.).

Par rapport à ces derniers exemples, la nature rationnelle de l'homme se distingue par un *proprium*, "ut tendat in fine quasi se agens, vel ducens ad finem"[2]. La volonté agit seulement si elle choisit un objet comme fin de l'acte du vouloir, et la première caractéristique de l'objet de la volonté est celle de se présenter comme un bien, un *bonum in universali*, c'est-à-dire comme une chose désirable parce que positivement constituée et dont la possession est susceptible de produire un plaisir.

Thomas se place dans un contexte historico-doctrinal qui connaissait des réponses précises au thème volonté-bien, élaborées en profondeur par la tradition grecque, platonique et aristotélicienne, et par la tradition chrétienne, en particulier augustinienne, qui avait exclu toute valence métaphysique du mal: le non-bien comme tel n'existe pas, et ne peut exister, dans la mesure où il coïncide avec le non-positif, avec le non-être. Par conséquent, ce que l'on veut, l'objet-fin de la volonté, ne peut qu'être un bien en général: "obiectum voluntatis est finis, et bonum in universalis"[3].

Le bien en universel constitue l'objet en général de la volonté, au sens où, en définissant la volonté de l'homme comme une puissance rationnelle tendue vers l'action, c'est-à-dire vers la poursuite (*appetere*) de quelque chose qui la détermine positivement, on doit dire que sa tendance (*appetitus*) est vers quelque chose de bon, vers n'importe quel objet qui entre dans la notion de bien en général; il reviendra à la délibération individuelle de discerner un objet concrètement désirable, un *bonum* particulier, que le mouvement de la volonté transforme en bien possédé en acte, tandis qu'auparavant, il n'était possédé qu'en puissance, dans la mesure où il était inclus dans la notion de bien en universel.

Le bilan de ces premières analyses concerne surtout l'acquisition de la transcendantalité du rapport action-fin (il n'y a pas d'action sans fin) et en second lieu le lien de coextensivité entre la fin et le bien, dans lequel le bien a comme caractéristique de satisfaire une tendance, de contenter un appétit, de susciter un félicité proportionnelle à l'acte de possession de ce bien-fin.

Nous touchons ainsi à un autre problème: entre les différentes fins de l'action humaine, existe-t-il un ordre, ou connaissent-elles une distribution de fait, privée de stratégies ponctuelles et d'objectifs ultimes? Avec le langage de Thomas, ont pourrait dire: existe-t-il une fin dernière de la vie humaine, ou bien procède-t-on à l'infini dans la série des fins?

Il convient de rechercher une indication de fond dans l'équivalence déjà établie entre bien et fin: si la fin est un bien, projeter les biens dans le règne de l'incomplétude, dans une "succession à l'infini", équivaut, du point de

---

[2] Ibid., art. 2, resp.
[3] Ibid., art. 2, ad 3.

vue spéculatif, à les situer dans un horizon privé de tout sens achevé (infini veut dire ici incomplet). Et pour cette raison, cela revient à destituer le bien de sa raison même de bien: la *ratio boni* réside en effet, comme nous le savons, dans l'être désirable de ce que la chose est en soi et pour soi, pour sa constitution définie.

Mais il y a une instance plus forte pour décider de l'impossibilité d'une progression à l'infini dans l'ordre des fins; cette instance vient d'Aristote, qui a établi, dans ses oeuvres décisives du point de vue théorique (*Métaphysique, Physique, Ethique à Nicomaque*), que la progression à l'infini d'une série d'êtres ne permet pas de définir le principe qui institue ce rapport initial, et que, dans la mesure où le critère qui institue la série manque, la raison d'être des êtres qui entrent en relation à travers une référence commune à ce premier critère tend à s'estomper. On peut trouver l'application la plus connue de l'impossibilité de procéder à l'infini dans les textes d'Aristote où celui-ci soutient l'impossibilité de procéder à l'infini dans les causes du mouvement, quand bien même elles fûssent causées: avec la régression à l'infini disparaîtrait la possibilité d'établir l'existence d'un premier moteur, dont le mouvement procèderait et qui expliquerait la transmission du mouvement effectuée par les causes motrices-mues. Thomas reprend intégralement l'argumentation concernant la régression infinie dans l'ordre des fins, que ce soit dans l'ordre des fins-intentions (*ordo intentionis*) ou dans celui des fins-exécutions (*ordo executionis*). Ce qui est premier dans l'ordre de l'intention équivaut au principe qui pousse la volonté à délibérer; comme procéder à l'infini reviendrait à ne pas poser ce principe qui "meut" la volonté, s'il n'y avait cette fin première qui "intentionne" (*in-tendit*) la volonté, celle-ci ne se meuvrait pas, puisque rien ne l' "intentionnerait".

C'est la même notion de fin dernière qui inclut cette exigence d'exclusivité: la fin dernière est l'objet capable de satisfaire totalement le désir de l'homme, c'est-à-dire capable de remplir chaque mouvement d'appétition, de sorte que chaque aspiration de la volonté soit satisfaite entièrement et définitivement. Une fin dernière ainsi définie correspond à la notion de souverain bien, de bien dans sa plénitude et dans sa perfection: et comme il ne peut y avoir deux biens, de la même façon il ne peut y avoir deux fins ultimes, c'est-à-dire susceptibles de contenter totalement et définitivement ce désir de bien qui définit structurellement la volonté humaine.

Ces acquis spéculatifs deviennent les prémisses d'un nouvel ordre de conclusions: en particulier, ce qui constitue la fin dernière est ce que l'homme poursuit à travers chacune de ses actions volontaires. L'acte humain se définit en effet comme volontaire, c'est-à-dire résultant d'une délibération de la volonté qui est mue par l'intention de poursuivre un bien particulier. Chaque bien particulier réalise la notion de bien en tant qu'il est possession partielle du bien entier, du bien plein et suprême: chaque désir d'un bien particulier s'inscrit comme partie constitutive du désir du bien total, et pour cela l'articulation du souverain bien ou de la fin dernière à l'acte de désir est incluse dans chaque acte humain de désir ou de volonté. Cela reste vrai si l'individu singulier n'en a pas une conscience claire: "sed virtus primae intentionis [la force de ce qui est principe de chaque in-tention], quae est respectu ultimi finis, manet in quolibet appetitu cuiuscumque rei, etiamsi de ultimo fine actu non cogitetur: sicut non oportet quod qui vadit per viam, in quolibet passu cogitet de fine"[4].

Même le bien "ludique", ce bien que l'on recherche dans le divertissement, le jeu ou le repos, n'est pas un bien isolé, soustrait à la fin globale, mais il entre lui aussi dans l'horizon du bien qui réalise le désir du sujet et il s'inscrit par conséquent, comme un fragment de félicité, dans l'ordre de la félicité totale. Nous pourrions paraphraser la doctrine de St. Thomas en ces termes: tout bien particulier, poursuivi par une activité quelconque, fût-elle répétitive, ne se laisse ni isoler ni dissiper par manque d'inhérence au bien qui satisfait le désir de félicité; nous sommes en présence de fragments de bien, qui entrent de droit dans le giron du souverain bien, comme son "inchoatio", forme germinale qui ne peut être ni supprimée ni exclue, parce qu'elle a la force du positif et parce que, comme telle, elle échappe par soi-même au négatif. Tout ce qui peut être poursuivi comme fin, dans sa forme spécifique, ne peut l'être que dans la mesure où cette fin participe de la *ratio boni*; nous savons que c'est l'intention de l'agent qui décide de la nature morale du résultat, de sa configuration comme moralement bon ou moralement mauvais. Le mal ne croît pas comme tel, s'il n'y a pas une volonté qui le vise et qui articule quelque chose de positif à une fin disproportionnée ou abusive pour une nature dotée de raison et de volonté. Dans l'articulation des fins à la fin dernière, Thomas réserve aussi une place au *bonum* de la philosophie: même le bien que l'on poursuit en spéculant, celui qui contente le désir de connaissance par lequel se manifeste le désir de félicité du philosophe, est inscrit dans l'ordre du souverain bien, et, pour cela, de la fin dernière[5].

Tous les hommes partagent le fait de tendre vers la fin dernière, dans la mesure où ils désirent tous leur propre félicité et leur propre perfection: dans ces notions de félicité et de perfection est incluse de droit la notion de fin dernière comme celle du bien plein, capable de conférer la félicité ou la perfection. Si ce dernier n'existait pas, la notion même de félicité ou de perfection perdrait de sa réalité pour n'exister qu'à des degrés partiels.

---

[4] Ibid., art. 6, ad 3.

[5] "Et similiter dicendum ad secundum de scientia speculativa, quae appetitur ut bonum quoddam speculantis, quod comprehenditur sub bono completo et perfecto, quod est ultimus finis" (*Ibidem*, ad 2).

Mais tous les hommes n'ont cependant pas une conception adéquate, c'est-à-dire une représentation identique, de ce que pourrait être concrètement la chose absolument satisfaisante qui réalise la notion de fin dernière: certains considèrent que la plus haute félicité est produite par la richesse, d'autres la mettent dans les plaisirs, d'aucuns dans la renommée, la gloire, la science, la théologie. Le donné de l'expérience n'annule pas les conclusions que nous avons atteintes plus haut, puisqu'il est difficile de construire une évaluation de ces hétérogénéités dans les fins ultimes de fait, à la lumière du concept rigoureux de fin dernière de droit. Les différences anthropologiques attestent des comportements factuels qui n'effacent pas le donné univoque et permanent, qui est invoqué par la caractéristique commune à tous les hommes, c'est-à-dire par le fait qu'ils soient dotés de raison et de désir.

II. FÉLICITÉ MONDAINE ET BÉATITUDE ÉTERNELLE: L'ACHÈVEMENT HUMAIN SELON SAINT THOMAS

La caractéristique générale de la félicité est liée au fait que le désir se satisfait en atteignant le bien désiré, et que, dans cette satisfaction, le sujet éprouve contentement, plaisir, *delectatio*. Cette expérience du plaisir est maximale lorsqu'il s'agit de l'accès à la fin dernière, au souverain bien, capable de rassasier totalement et définitivement le désir. A partir de là se profilent donc deux types de félicité: la félicité mondaine, consécutive à l'accès à des biens finis, et la félicité éternelle, qui dérive du souverain bien. Thomas parle d'une "beatitudo imperfecta, quae habetur in hac vita", et de "beatitudo perfecta, quae in visione Dei consistit"[6]; l'éthique philosophique s'occupe de la première, dans le sillage des doctrines éthiques d'Aristote, et la théologie s'occupe de la seconde. Le corps participe lui aussi de la félicité mondaine, mais Thomas considère qu'il faut fixer pour cette *beatitudo* le même caractère formel que celui de la *beatitudo* ultime de l'homme, c'est-à-dire son caractère d'accompagnement d'une activité humaine qui veut connaître, contempler, "comprehendere" le bien. La félicité de l'homme, celle qui est mondaine et imparfaite, entre donc dans l'espèce de félicité propre à l'homme, à sa capacité de comprendre et de vouloir, qui le porte à se réaliser précisément dans ces attitudes formelles. Aristote avait déjà vu dans l'aspiration de l'esprit humain à la connaissance totale et parfaite des réalités simples le trait caractéristique de la recherche humaine de la félicité. Thomas le répète en s'appuyant sur la dialectique intellect-volonté: l'intellect se réalise dans la *visio* du bien et la volonté dans la *delectatio*, qui accompagne la vision de l'intellect. A ce stade de l'analyse, nous savons donc que le

---

[6] *Summa Theol.*, I-II{ae}, q. 4, art. 5, resp.

corps participe de la félicité imparfaite, mais dans la mesure où, dans cette vie, la connaissance intellective de l'homme se développe avec l'aide des organes corporels de la connaissance, qui prédisposent le matériau nécessaire (le *phantasma*) à la connaissance abstraite des universaux. Cette exigence est moindre dans le cas de la béatitude éternelle, parce que l'objet de la connaissance ou vision, est constitué par l'essence du souverain bien, c'est-à-dire par l'essence divine. Et pour cette vision, aucun fantasme n'est requis, et il serait absolument impossible que l'essence divine fasse l'objet d'une connaissance développée selon les modalités de la connaissance sensible.

L'inclusion du corps est par ailleurs acquise dès que l'on parle de la félicité mondaine de l'homme, qui exige la "bona dispositio corporis" en vue de consentir à l'homme de déployer son activité propre au plus haut degré de sa puissance. N'importe quelle forme de maladie ou d'infirmité corporelle a une incidence sur la capacité de l'homme à traduire dans des actions parfaitement réalisées ses propres facultés rationnelles, l'intellect et la volonté; ainsi, l'élévation de l'esprit à la contemplation de Dieu n'exige pas en soi la participation des organes corporels, et cependant une lésion de ces organes corporels peut empêcher la contemplation des essences abstraites et spirituelles. D'une façon analogue, Thomas établit que certains biens matériels contribuent à la félicité mondaine: nous savons déjà que la nature de cette félicité imparfaite est homogène à celle de la félicité ultime, c'est-à-dire qu'elle réside dans l'activité des facultés rationnelles de l'homme, dans les vertus et les habitudes virtuoses que l'homme acquiert pour faciliter son activité proprement humaine, qui est l'exercice de la *dianoia*, de la contemplation pure et désintéressée. Il faut considérer le besoin de biens matériels comme auxiliaire et instrumental là où l'homme montre qu'il en a besoin pour se conserver en vie, pour avoir les énergies nécessaires à l'activité de son organisme, pour exprimer des activités artisanales et exercer des vertus actives. Dans la mesure où ces choses et ces activités sont des biens, et où, en tant que biens, elles sont capables de contribuer à la félicité mondaine de l'homme, elles conservent une instance de définitivité, c'est-à-dire qu'elles seront d'une certaine manière accueillies dans la totalité du bien: "Bona ista deservientia animali vitae non competunt vitae spirituali, in qua beatitudo perfecta consistit: et tamen erit in illa beatitudine omnium bonorum congregatio: qui quidquid bonum invenitur in eis, totum habebitur in summo fonte bonorum"[7].

L'affirmation selon laquelle la félicité théorisée par la philosophie, et caractérisée par la contemplation des êtres abstraits, ne doit pas être considérée comme totalement distincte de la béatitude éternelle, constitue un

---

[7] Ibid., art. 7, ad 2.

acquis dans les oeuvres de la maturité de Thomas d'Aquin, et en particulier dans la *Summa theologiae*. On peut trouver dans ses affirmations une subtile continuité entre les biens qui produisent la félicité mondaine et le souverain bien qui donne la béatitude éternelle. C'est l'identité de l'objet, c'est-à-dire du bien, qui maintient ces deux félicités solidaires: dans la vie actuelle, l'intellect voit et contemple le bien sous une forme abstraite et sujette à la fragmentation en de multiples biens particuliers; dans la vie éternelle, le bien est vu intuitivement et dans sa totalité pleine.[8]

Toutefois, comme le souligne à juste titre A. J. Celano, la position de Thomas est précisée par la double acception de la notion de fin qu'il développe dans la *Summa theologiae*, I-II[ae], q. 1, art. 8: il convient de distinguer entre *finis cuius* et *finis quo*. *Finis cuius* est ce qui inclut en soi la même *ratio boni*, c'est-à-dire l'objet que les actions entendent poursuivre; *finis quo* est en revanche l'usage ou la poursuite de l'objet désiré. Thomas précise que l'objet final de l'homme (*finis cuius*) est Dieu, dans sa pleine bonté formelle; atteindre cet objet est la fin de l'activité, c'est-à-dire de la praxis éthique.[9]

Pour Thomas d'Aquin, l'éthique, y comprise celle d'Aristote, ne s'occupe que du *finis quo*, sans étendre sa propre enquête au *finis cuius*, c'est-à-dire à Dieu lui-même, bien qu'il constitue l'objet ultime de la contemplation.[10] En suivant l'orientation dominante des théologiens de l'époque, Thomas offre une lecture de l'*Ethique à Nicomaque* qui en fait une oeuvre s'étendant au seul domaine de la praxis, comme un discours sectoriel qui a besoin de la métaphysique pour s'élever à la pleine détermination du souverain bien, et de la révélation chrétienne pour fixer les modalités de jouissance du même souverain bien, dans la béatitude éternelle.

Il n'en ira pas ainsi pour les commentateurs d'Aristote postérieurs à Thomas; nous voudrions maintenant nous arrêter sur le commentateur le plus important de l'*Ethique à Nicomaque* de la première moitié du XIVème

---

[8] Cf. A. J. Celano, *Act of the intellect or act of the will: the critical reception of Aristotle's ideal of human perfection in the 13th and early 14th centuries.* in Ahdlma, 57 (1990), [92-119], pp. 98-100.

[9] "Dicendum quod, sicut Philosophus dicit in 5. Metaphysic., finis dupliciter dicitur, scilicet *cuius*, et *quo*; idest ipsa res, in qua ratio boni invenitur, et usus, sive adeptio illius rei [...] Si ergo loquamur de ultimo fine hominis quantum ad ipsam rem, quae est finis, sic in ultimo fine hominis omnia alia conveniunt, quia Deus est ultimus fini hominis, et omnium aliarum rerum" (*Summa Theol.*, I-II[ae], q. 1, art. 8, resp).

[10] "Thomas realizes well that the focus of the *Eth. Nic.* is the human activities of contemplative and moral virtue, and not the object which is contemplated. Thomas' successors did not limit their discussion of Aristotle's *Ethics* so strictly, as they considered the *finis cuius* as well as the *finis quo* to be legitimate concerns of moral sicence", A. J. Celano, *The "finis hominis" in the Thirteenth Century Commentaries on Aristotle's Nicomachean Ethics*, in Ahdlma, 53 (1986), [23-53], p. 37.

siècle, Jean Buridan, qui revendique pour la philosophie un espace de discours autonome, c'est-à-dire capable de déterminer la félicité mondaine de l'homme, en lui permettant de poursuivre sa propre fin dernière naturelle, saisie à travers le parcours de l'intelligence et de la volonté, en laissant de côté la caractérisation de la béatitude offerte par la révélation.

3. JEAN BURIDAN: LES "APPÉTITS" DE L'HOMME ET LE FINALISME

Dans le commentaire par questions du premier livre de l'*Ethique à Nicomaque*, Buridan demande si le bien constitue l'objet de chaque appétit. Il semblerait que la question, ainsi formulée, ne puisse recevoir de réponse affirmative, parce que la notion de bien varie selon les natures, et il convient de la rapporter à celle de perfection; pour cela, un être imparfait, lorsqu'il désire le bien, désire être préservé dans sa nature imparfaite, tandis que pour l'être absolument parfait, désirer le bien équivaut à désirer sa propre perfection.

La difficulté qu'il y a à délimiter une notion univoque du bien est résolue en faisant appel à l'unicité du souverain bien, du meilleur bien, qui coïncide avec Dieu, dans lequel il n'y a aucune séparation entre connaissant et connu, aimant et aimé: toutes les choses sont bonnes dans la mesure où elles entretiennent un certain rapport de similitude avec leur cause. Il se produit donc avec la perfection de la bonté ce qui se produit avec la perfection de l'être: de même qu'il y a un être en soi, parfaitement existant, il y a aussi un bien en soi parfaitement réalisé; et ce n'est qu'en rapport à ce meilleur bien que tous les autres êtres peuvent être dits bons, par bonté dérivée (*secundum quid*).

La bonté des êtres se présente ainsi, en premier lieu, comme la ressemblance qu'ils ont avec leur cause; en second lieu, lié à cette ressemblance, il y a l'appétit ou l'inclination des êtres vers le bien, comme le montre la tendance des corps naturels (eau, terre, air, feu) à revenir à leur lieux naturels (le haut ou le bas). Cette inclination serait complètement inutile si elle n'était pas poursuivie à travers une tendance (*motus*) actuelle vers le bien propre, ou si toutes les choses n'avaient pas les inclinations ou les facultés de mettre en oeuvre cette tendance vers le bien par leurs propres opérations.

Dans l'univers, tous les êtres tendent (*appetunt*) au même bien, mais avec des modalités différentes: les êtres les plus parfaits, qui disposent d'un degré élevé de perfection, sont plus proches de l'être simple et absolument parfait et en jouissent immédiatement: les êtres dont la perfection est moindre tendent à un bien proportionnel à leur nature, et c'est à travers ce bien qu'ils se rapportent au souverain bien. La tendance universelle vers le souverain bien se manifeste donc de diverses façons, parce qu'elle peut être immédiate, ou médiatisée par la ressemblance du bien propre à des natures particulières avec l'être premier, source de tout bien. En suivant Aristote, Buridan précise que même les nature qui ne sont pas dotées de capacités cognitives tendent vers le bien, et que leur tendance est le résultat de l'action directrice d'une nature connaissante, c'est-à-dire des natures intelligentes hérarchiquement supérieures.

Buridan distingue ensuite l'appétit naturel, l'appétit sensible et l'appétit intellectif; il définit l'appétit naturel comme inclination de n'importe quelle puissance naturelle, active ou passive, vers un acte qui lui est propre et qui lui convient, sans connaissance préalable. De cette façon, "l'intellect est naturellement incliné à connaître avant même qu'il ne connaisse, et la volonté à vouloir avant même qu'elle ne veuille"[11].

L'appétit sensible est l'inclination vers une chose connue de façon sensible, à travers le jugement des sens portant sur la bonté ou la malice caractéristique de cette chose.

L'appétit intellectif coïncide totalement avec la volition, ou avec la volonté si celle-ci est comprise comme l'acte de vouloir, qui est décrit comme "l'inclination vers la chose connue à travers le jugement de l'intellect portant sur la bonté ou la malice caractéristique de cette chose. Pour cette raison, je ne concède pas que tout appétit de la volonté soit un vouloir; le vouloir est en effet libre, tandis que l'appétit précédent est naturel"[12].

Cette partition de l'appétit sert à déterminer l'horizon précis de la problématique concernant la tendance universelle des êtres vers le bien: c'est ici qu'apparaît notement le problème de savoir comment il faut comprendre la tendance vers le bien chez les êtres incapables de connaissance, qui ne disposent que de l'appétit naturel ou sensible, par rapport aux êtres, qui disposent aussi de tendance ou d'appétit intellectif.

On se demandera aussi si la tendance de toutes les choses au bien comme à leur propre fin naturelle peut être interprétée comme la mise en acte ou la réalisation de leur puissance naturelle, et pour cette raison comme la tendance de toutes les choses à la félicité, qui réside dans la fin dernière propre à chaque nature.

En répondant à ces interrogations, Buridan se détache de la lecture orthodoxe de nombreux aristotéliciens, et il déclare que la tendance vers la fin, comme conscience d'une fin dernière à atteindre à travers des fins intermédiaires, est une prérogative de l'homme. Un passage très clair de son

---

[11] J.Buridan, *In I Ethic.*, q. 4, f. 5 r b; nous citons la réimpression anastatique (Francfort, 1968) des *Quaestiones super decem libros Ethicorum*, Paris 1513.

[12] Ibid.

commentaire de la *Physique* précise la différence entre l'agir des vivants selon la vie végétative et sensible, et celui des vivants selon la vie rationelle:

> Parmi les agents naturels, je pense que l'hirondelle, lorsqu'elle s'accouple et lorsqu'elle fait son nid et pond ses oeufs, ne connaît pas les poussins qu'elle doit produire plus que l'arbre ne connaît le fruit qu'il doit produire lorsqu'il porte des feuilles et des fleurs. Je ne pense pas non plus que l'accouplement, la nidification, ou la ponte des oeufs de l'hirondelle dépendent dans leur être et dans leur forme des poussins, mais que le contraire est vrai; je ne pense pas non plus que ce soient les poussins qui déterminent l'hirondelle à agir de cette façon, mais au contraire que c'est la forme et la nature de l'hirondelle, les corps célestes, à des moments donnés, et le Dieu suprême, à travers son infinie sagesse, qui déterminent l'hirondelle à s'accoupler, ce dont la fécondation et les oeufs sont le résultat[13].

Le moment discriminant, pour Buridan, est marqué par la capacité de l'agent rationnel à se représenter la fin, à connaître les directions (intentions) et les appétits qui le conduisent à l'action, capacité dont ne disposent pas les animaux irrationnels. A ce stade, Buridan reprend la double acception de la notion de fin, et il l'insère dans le contexte de son discours: il s'agit de la distinction entre fin d'intention première et fin d'intention seconde, distinction proche de celle de Thomas d'Aquin que nous avons abordée plus haut. La fin d'intention première (ou *finis gratia cuius*, fin en vertu de laquelle l'agent se réalise dans l'action) est la fin au sens premier, en vertu de laquelle l'agent développe sa propre capacité d'agir de façon intrinsèque; la fin d'intention seconde (ou *finis quo*, la façon de procéder qui permet d'atteindre la fin) coïncide avec le résultat extrinsèque de l'opération. Dans l'exemple d'un homme qui construit une maison, le *finis quo* est la maison, fin d'intention seconde, tandis que le *finis gratia cuius* est l'homme lui-même, la réalisation de son projet d'artisan, fin d'intention première[14]. Buridan précise aussi dans quelle acception du terme fin on doit entendre l'affirmation, que nous avons examinée auparavant, selon laquelle toutes les choses tendent vers le bien: toutes les choses sont bonnes en rapport avec leur fin au sens premier, c'est-à-dire en rapport au souverain bien qui est la fin universelle *gratia cuius*; le *finis quo* dépend étroitement du *finis gratia*

---

[13] "Sed de naturalibus ego credo quod hyrundo coiens, nidificans et ovificans nichil plus cognoscit pullos generandos quam arbor frondes et flores congnoscit fructum generandum, aut hyrundinis coitus nidificatio et ovificatio dependent in esse et ordine eorum ab illis pullis, sed econtra; nec illi pulli determinant hyrundinem ad sic operandum, sed forma et natura hyrundinis et corpora caelestia, determinatis temporibus, et deus summus per suam sapientiam infinitam determinant hyrundinem ad coitum, ex quo consequenter sequitur generatio ovorum" (J. Buridan, *In II Physic.*, q. 13; éd. Venise, 1509, f. 40 r b).

[14] Cf. J. Buridan, *In II Physic.*, q. 7, f. 35 r b.

cuius: en d'autres termes, la bonté des fins secondaires est décidée par la bonté des fins premières[15].

Revenons à ce qui nous occupe: en quel sens dit-on que l'homme tend vers la fin dernière, vers le bien parfait en rapport à sa nature, et qu'il trouve la félicité en ce bien?

En reprenant la conclusion à laquelle nous sommes parvenus plus haut, à savoir que toutes les opération humaines tendent vers une fin, parce que l'on ne peut désirer que le bien, et que le bien désiré participe à la notion de fin, on répondra en soulignant comment, dans la caractérisation de la fin que donne Aristote, est incluse l'affirmation selon laquelle on ne peut procéder à l'infini dans l'ordre des causes finales: en effet, avec la disparition de la fin première (ou dernière) disparaîtrait aussi la possibilité de constituer des fins intermédiaires, et l'appétit qui incline l'homme au bien resterait frustré.

On pourrait objecter que l'homme n'atteint parfois la fin-bien que s'il se la propose préalablement, et que pour cela il peut arriver que son désir reste frustré, en particulier s'il s'agit de désirs "irrationnels", qui n'impliquent pas foncièrement l'ordre rationnel de l'homme. Buridan répond que, même dans le domaine des appétits irrationnels, la notion d'appétit postule un objet appréhendé et, d'une certaine façon, visé dans l'intention, lequel développe pour cela la raison de fin; en général, on doit donc dire que chaque action humaine tend non seulement vers une fin, mais vers la fin dernière: cette tendance n'est pas la même pour tous les hommes, ni selon l'espèce, ni dans les modalités de sa manifestation. Buridan est un observateur attentif du comportement humain, et il rejoint Ockham pour reconnaître que l'expérience ne montre aucune homogénéité dans la tendance des hommes vers une fin dernière qui serait identique pour tous, ni que les hommes admettent de tendre vers la félicité lorsqu'ils s'orientent vers la fin dernière. L'identité de la fin dernière qu'impliquent toutes les actions humaines doit être accordée avec la pluralité des "opinions", c'est-à-dire des façons d'entendre la fin dernière elle-même:

> Chacun poursuit en effet comme fin dernière ce qui lui semble être la meilleure fin, comme dans le cas de celui qui se suicide par désespoir; il lui semble en effet en retirer la meilleure chose possible lorsqu'il est libéré de l'angoisse qui l'étreint; pour cette raison, en vue de cela (*gratia huius*), il se suicide[16].

Buridan prend ici parti d'une façon extrêmement nette: son approche de l'éthique entend rester sur le plan des analyses rationnelles, empiriquement

---

[15] Cf. J. Buridan, *In I Ethic.*, q. 12; f. 12 r b.
[16] J. Buridan, *In I Ethic.*, q. 5; f. 5 v b.

contrôlables, avancées dans le texte aristotélicien que le maître parisien est en train de commenter. La fin dernière, qui est discutée du point de vue éthique, est celle qui est affirmée en vertu de l'impossibilité de procéder à l'infini dans l'ordre des fins, sans que disparaisse pour autant la notion de fin; mais chaque homme suit une approche personnalisée de la fin dernière: l'expérience nous apprend que tous les hommes ne partagent pas une "opinion" unique au sujet de l'objectif prioritaire qu'ils entendent poursuivre *hic* et *nunc*. Cette observation empirique ne s'oppose pas à l'affirmation rationnelle selon laquelle la fin dernière coïncide avec le souverain bien en abolu; bien des hommes ne sont pas à même de se représenter correctement le souverain bien en absolu, et "sont de l'avis" que le souverain bien consiste en un bien qui, à bien y regarder, n'est ni le souverain bien ni le bien auquel on s'est résolu, mais qu'il y renvoie. C'est avec une vigilance phénoménologique que la philosophe découvre que:

> [...] en chacune de ses actions, l'homme ne poursuit pas formellement le bien final de l'homme, qui est la félicité humaine; en chacun de ses actes, l'homme tend plutôt vers un bien partiel, qui détient une certaine similitude avec cette félicité, et qui se rapporte à travers cette similitude à la félicité elle-même. En effet, aucune action n'est à ce point mauvaise qu'elle ne vise pas à poursuivre quelque chose d'utile, ou de beau, ou d'agréable, de façon directe ou indirecte. Ceci manifeste déjà une similitude avec la félicité elle-même, qui est le meilleur, le plus beau, le plus agréable et le suffisant en soi-même[17].

Cette fondation du finalisme ne se caractérise pas seulement pas sa nature éminemment phénoménologique; sur le fond, elle reprend aussi la lecture avancée par les aristotéliciens latins, postérieurs à Albertus Magnus et à Thomas d'Aquin, connus aussi sous le nom d' "averroïstes latins": il n'est donné qu'à quelques hommes, aux contemplatifs, aux philosophes qui parviennent au sommet de la spéculation théorique, d'atteindre réellement la fin dernière, cette félicité de l'esprit qui s'obtient par la plus grande activation de l'intellect. La plupart des hommes poursuivent des objectifs plus limités, parce qu'ils sont dominés par les passions et les jugements sensibles, ce qui les empêche d'exprimer toutes les potentialités de leur nature rationnelle. Cette situation ne préjuge en rien de la validité de la thèse philosophique concernant la visée d'une fin dernière qui coïncide avec ce qu'il y a de meilleur pour l'humanité, parce que, même si la majorité des hommes ne l'atteint pas, il reste indiscutablement vrai que tous possèdent une nature qui a la faculté de l'atteindre et de connaître la félicité la plus élevée.

---

[17] Ibid.

IV. LE RAPPORT FÉLICITÉ – LIBERTÉ DANS QUELQUES RELECTURES CONTEMPORAINES

Avec Buridan, nous sommes parvenus à la conclusion qu'il n'y a de la félicité que là où il y a de l'intellect et de la volonté, c'est-à-dire là où il se trouve une liberté capable d'adhérer au bien qui contente son désir. Pour déterminer cela, on reconnaît à l'éthique la tâche d'examiner non seulement le *finis quo* aristotéliquement défini comme "l'animae operatio secundum virtutem perfectissimam", mais aussi le *finis gratia cuius*, l'objet-même qui produit la félicité. En décrivant celle-ci, Buridan observe que, selon le même Aristote, "optimum igitur et pulcherrimum delectabilissimum felicitas; tale autem non est nisi unum; quia quod per superabundantiam dicitur, uni soli convenit"[18].

Selon A.J. Celano, le premier auteur qui ait appliqué la double acception de la notion de fin mentionnée plus haut au concept aristotélicien de *souverain bien* a été Boèce de Dacie: en examinant le *summum bonum hominis*, Boèce observe que l'on ne peut exclure la considération de la fin dernière, comprise comme Dieu, de la considération de la fin dernière de l'homme. Dieu étant l'objet le plus haut de l'aspiration humaine à la connaissance, la connaissance de Dieu dont l'homme est capable appartient aussi à la considération de la fin dernière, relativement à l'objet des activités intellectuelles humaines[19].

Pour Boèce de Dacie, l'extension de l'enquête éthique réalisée par la seule raison philosophique est claire:

> Et quia summum bonum quod est hominis possibile est eius beatitudo, sequitur quod cognitio veri et operatio boni et delectatio in utroque sit beatitudo humana[20].

Chez Boèce donc, comme du reste chez Buridan, l'enquête éthique inclut le *finis cuius*, Dieu, comme objet de la contemplation de l'intellect humain et achèvement de son désir, c'est-à-dire comme le lieu de la félicité qui n'est plus appelée imparfaite. D'autres auteurs ont marqué le passage historique de Thomas à Buridan, outre Boèce de Dacie: en restant dans le domaine de l'aristotélisme de la fin du XIIIème siècle et des premières décennies du XIVème, nous pouvons ajouter les noms de Siger de Brabant, Giacomo da Pistoia, Dante Alighieri et Jean de Jandun, qui partagent tous la valorisation de la "béatification à travers l'intellect".

---

[18] J. Buridan, *In X Ethic.*, q. 4, f. 209 r b.
[19] Cf. A. J. Celano, *The finis hominis...*, cit., p. 32.
[20] Boèce de Dacie, *De summo bono*, ed. N. G. Green Pedersen (Corpus philosophorum danicorum medii aevi, VI, 2), Copenhague 1976, p. 371.

F.-X. Putallaz, en développant une lecture brillante de R.-A. Gauthier, caractérise ainsi la nouveauté du passage à une perspective éthique autosuffisante:

> L'homme trouvera en lui-même la force et le secret de son bonheur; libre et maître de ses actes, il sera l'artisan de sa destinée; c'est parce qu'il est libre qu'il peut se libérer. L'homme trouvera ainsi son bonheur dans une activité qui vient de lui-même et qu'il exerce par elle-même: seule la vie d'étude l'accomplit, la vie philosophique, car l'activité de l'intellect est la plus noble et la meilleure part de nous-mêmes. Voilà le lien de l'autonomie et de la liberté; l'homme existe de son propre fait et non du fait d'un autre [...]. Par l'étude et l'application, par la philosophie, l'homme conquiert par lui-même son bonheur et sa liberté; d'où la défiance d'Aristote pour tout ce qui ne vient pas de l'homme: le bonheur n'est pas un don des dieux; il n'est pas aléatoire. C'est par ce côté que se dévoile le sens de l'humanisme aristotélicien: il est "un humanisme de cette terre. Le seul bonheur qui soit permis à l'homme d'espérer, c'est le bonheur de cette vie" [R.A. Gauthier] L'homme y sera heureux, comme un homme[21].

Le point le plus significatif du passage de Thomas à Buridan, pour ce qui concerne l'éthique, est la reconnaissance du fait que la félicité dont parle la philosophie ne coïncide pas avec la félicité imparfaite dont parle Thomas, parce que cette dernière n'est pas une vraie félicité pour l'homme, étant donné que le qualificatif même d'"imparfaite" renvoie à la vraie félicité, pleine et supraterrestre.

La lecture d'Aristote qui était celle des théologiens du XIIIe siècle jusqu'à Thomas avait déjà été mise à mal par certains passages d'Albert le Grand, comme l'ont souligné les études d'Alain de Libera: Albert avait reconnu que le discours sur les vertus infuses et sur la béatitude poursuivie *post mortem*, c'est-à-dire le discours de la tradition théologique d'Augustin à Thomas, n'a aucun rapport avec la félicité dont parle Aristote, liée à l'activité de l'intellect, qui est l'artisan autonome de la félicité humaine: le véritable homme (heureux) est le philosophe qui active pleinement son intellect[22].

La discussion suivante voit s'insérer les condamnations du *Sillabo* parisien, oeuvre d'Etienne Tempier, qui considérait que l'intellectualisme éthique défendu par les philosophes était dangereux; et l'on ne doit pas oublier le problème que l'éthique philosophique laissait en suspens: si l'état naturel de

---

[21] F.-X. Putallaz, *Insolente liberté. Controverses et condamnations au XIIIe siècle*, Editions Universitaires Fribourg Suisse, Editions du Cerf, Paris, 1995, pp. 294-295.

[22] Cf. A. de Libera, *Albert le Grand et la philosophie*, Paris 1990, pp. 268-291; Idem, *Averroïsme éthique et philosophie mystique. De la félicité intellectuelle à la vie bienheureuse*, in Coll., *Filosofia e teologia nel Trecento. Studi in ricordo di Eugenio Randi*, Louvain-la-Neuve 1994, pp. 33-56.

l'homme qui active pleinement sa nature intellective et accède ainsi à la félicité, est celui du philosophe, qu'en est-il alors des autres hommes, de tous ceux qui ne pratiquent pas la contemplation intellectuelle? De quelle marge de liberté et de félicité peuvent-ils bénéficier? Une réponse intéressante se trouve dans les *Quaestiones in Metaphysicam* de Jean de Jandun, qui dit que l'aspiration humaine à la félicité n'implique pas nécessairement que tous les hommes y accèdent. Pour que la désir naturel ne soit pas vain, il est suffisant que quelques hommes seulement le portent à sa réalisation, que quelques uns atteignent "per adeptionem" la fin bienheureuse, c'est-à-dire qu'ils atteignent la connaissance simple et intuitive, avec laquelle l'intellect actif, la dernière des intelligences séparées, connaît les autres substances spirituelles, par la convenance naturelle qu'il entretient avec elles[23].

La réponse de Buridan au même problème se révèle encore plus intéressante, dans la mesure où elle est formulée au terme d'un parcours rigoureux, à travers lequel le maître parisien a reconstruit un parcours autonome de l'éthique philosophique, sans toutefois nier le fait que l'objet final de l'éthique philosophique coïncide avec celui de la morale théologique. L'homme poursuit la félicité proprement humaine à travers ses actions, avec les moyens dont la nature l'a doté, qui doient être soumis à une activité subjective rigoureuse; si cette activité s'affaiblit, il en résulte une carence correspondante d'accès à la félicité:

> Secundo dicendo quod felicitas provenit hominibus ab humana causa, quod patet ex eius diffinitione. Est enim operatio secundum virtutem ipsius perfectissimam, propter quod non est dubium si virtutes hominis insint a causa humana quin felicitas sit a causa humana. Virtutes autem tam morales quam intellectuales ab humana causa proveniunt, quia ex huminis operationibus acquiruntur: hae quidem per disciplinam et studium, aliae per assuefactionem et exercitium[24].

En arrivant à une distinction proposée par certains théologiens, Buridan parle d'une "felicitas praemiatoria" et d'une "felicitas meritoria": de la félicité récompensante est exclus tout mal, qu'il soit "malum culpae", volontairement contracté, ou "malum poenae", contracté involontairement, dérivant des conséquences pour l'humanité de la chute originelle. Tandis que seule la félicité récompensante inclue tous les biens dont l'homme est digne, la félicité méritoire inclue aussi les biens dont l'homme est digne, mais pas tous. C'est de la félicité méritoire que s'est occupé Aristote, comme d'une opération absolument parfaite, conforme aux vertus,

---

[23] Cf. Jean de Jandun, *Quaestiones in Metaphysicam*, II, q. 4; éd. Venise 1560, cc. 121-127.

[24] Buridan, *In I Ethic.*, q. 17, f. 17 r a.

[...] quia est dei sollicita et continua contemplatio secundum quod est possibile in hac vita[25].

Le chemin vertueux mis en oeuvre par le philosophe qui recherche la félicité mentale, en même temps que l'effort pour se maintenir dans cette vie au plus haut niveau de contemplation méritoire de Dieu, amène Buridan à conclure que la félicité méritoire ne peut rester extérieure ou exclue de la félicité récompensante; il est en effet tout à fait cohérent que la philosophe s'attende à une récompense après la mort, pour l'activité et l'effort qu'il a déployés pour vivre selon la tempérance et la continence:

> Ergo si philosophus de suo labore nullam expectaret remunerationem post mortem, valde esset inconveniens ponere felicitatem humanam in opere philosophiae, et non in divitiis[26].

De l'attente et de la cohérence, on ne passe à l'affirmation réelle qu'à travers la révélation, dans l'éthique théologique; pour cela, la philosophie continue de parler de félicité humaine, poursuivie en activant la nature, même si cette félicité qui se tient en deçà des limites de la condition de l'homme historique est une félicité au conditionnel, non absolue.

Nous partageons par conséquent l'avis de ces spécialistes, comme J. B. Korolec et J. J. Walsh, qui voient dans l'effort de Buridan la présence d'un téléologisme éthique équilibré, qui se construit positivement sur l'admission d'une fin dernière de l'action humaine et sur la revendication de la liberté de l'homme dans le domaine éthique; nous prendrons en revanche de la distance par rapport à ces interprètes qui, comme E. J. Monahan et O. Pluta, lisant dans le texte de Buridan un scepticisme de fond par rapport aux doctrines théologiques ou l'orientation vers une éthique matérialiste[27].

---

[25] Ibid., f. 17 v a.

[26] Ibid., f. 17 v b.

[27] Pour les auteurs cités ici, nous renvoyons aux essais suivants: J. B. Korolec, *L'Ethique à Nicomaque et le problème du libre arbitre à la lumière des Commentaires parisiens du XIIIe siècle et la philosophie de la liberté de Jean Buridan*, in "Miscellanea Mediaevalia", 10. *Die Auseinardersetzungen an der Pariser Unversität im XIII. Jahrhundert*, Berlin–New York 1976, pp. 331-348; J. J. Walsh, *Teleology in the Ethics of Buridan*, in "Journal of History of Philosophy", 18 (1980), pp. 265-286; E. J. Monahan, *Human liberty and Free Will according to John Buridan*, in "Medieval Studies", 16 (1954), pp. 72-86; O. Pluta, *Ewigkeit der Welt, Sterblichkeit der Seele, Diesseitigkeit des Glücks - Elemente einer materialistischer Philosophie bei Johannes Buridan*, in B. Mojsisch – O. Pluta, hrsg, *Historia philosophiae Medii Aevi*, Amsterdam–Philadelphie 1991, pp. 847-872. Sur le thème de la liberté, cf. A. Ghisalberti, *Giovanni Buridano dalla metafisica alla fisica*, Milan 1975; sur les problèmes d'ensemble de l'éthique, cf. G. Krieger, *Der Begriff der praktischen Vernunft nach Johannes Buridanus*, Aschendorff, Münster 1986.

PHILIPPE CAPPELLE
Institut Catholique de Paris
France

LIBERTÉ PHILOSOPHIQUE ET ONTOLOGIE THÉOLOGALE[1]

Je voudrais faire écho aux thèses de Dominique Dubarle[2] sur la notion de Liberté philosophique. Initialement formé à la logique mathématique et à l'épistémologie des sciences, suivant la voie tracée par Aristote et Saint Thomas d'Aquin sur le front de l'ontologie, le Père Dubarle a noué un incessant dialogue avec la pensée hégélienne. Réfléchissant sur les enjeux de la "modernité", il a, au cours d'une période à la fois trouble et foisonnante, cherché à repenser les liens entre métaphysique et liberté, sciences et philosophie, vérité et acte philosophique. Il laisse une oeuvre considérable de plus de six cents titres dont une petite partie est connue du catholique de Paris, "*Philosophie & théologie*", a symboliquement programmé pour son premier numéro, la publication du cours parmi les plus significatifs de son projet intellectuel d'une "ontologie théologale": *L'Ontologie de Thomas d'Aquin*[3].

La mention de cet ouvrage me permet de désigner d'emblée la perspective ontologique dans laquelle Dominique Dubarle a organisé ses réflexions sur la liberté philosophique: "Je n'ai cessé, écrit-il dans son cours de Métaphysique donné pendant l'année universitaire 1974-75, de rêver d'un progrès de la réflexion logicienne qui permettrait, et ceci au niveau des convictions

---

[1] Conférence donnée le 23 août 1996 à l'Université de Lublin (Pologne), à l'occasion du Congrès mondial de philosophie chrétienne.

[2] Professeur à la Faculté de philosophie de l'Institut catholique de Paris de 1944 à 1980, doyen de cette même Faculté de 1967 à 1973.

[3] D. Dubarle, *L'ontologie de Thomas d'Aquin*, Collection "Philosophie & Théologie", Paris, Ed. du Cerf, 1996. Cf également *Dieu avec l'être. Essai d'ontologie théologale*, Collection Philosophie, Paris, Beauchesne, 1986.

les plus radicales de l'esprit, l'instauration d'une meilleure 'politique' de la liberté au sein de la conversation humaine travaillant à se faire raisonnable. Or, il me semble – à tort, qui sait? – que c'est à même la pensée de "l'être" et nulle part ailleurs que se forme la puissance de la logique qui permet aux hommes la conversation *communicante*"[4]. Ce propos à la fois testamentaire et programmatique s'entend à partir de ce qui, selon notre auteur, constituait la nouvelle "donne" des relations entre la philosophie et la foi religieuse.

I. PHILOSOPHIE ET FOI RELIGIEUSE. LA "TROISIÈME POSITION"

L'un des axes fondamentaux de la recherche du Père Dubarle a consisté à relire l'histoire des rapports entre les deux traditions philosophique et théologique et à tenter un diagnostic sur leur situation contemporaine.

La première "position" de la philosophie par rapport à la foi religieuse dont Dubarle opère la reconstruction et qu'il nomme "la position antique", porte sur la période qui va de la naissance de la philosophie en Grèce jusqu'au début du XVIème siècle. À partir de ce que fut l'exercice de la philosophie naissante – à savoir un rapport de distance, de critique et de transposition de la religion – et avec l'entrée en scène de la foi chrétienne, Dubarle relève ce qu'il estime être l'organisation et le prolongement d'un oubli majeur. Cet oubli, c'est l'appartenance de la philosophie et de la foi chrétienne à un fond religieux humain. Ainsi la philosophie, instaurée à l'origine comme autorité de l'esprit jusqu'à l'égard des faits religieux, se trouve-t-elle à l'ère chrétienne en position inverse de sujétion vis à vis de l'autorité religieuse[5].

D'où la remontée de l'énergie philosophique qui détermine à l'époque moderne, la "seconde position". Outre les facteurs socio-culturels et institutionnels que Dubarle ne minimise pas, une double expérience, explique-t-il, préside à la rupture avec la position antique; d'une part, ce qu'il appelle "l'expérience de l'expérience" et qui constitue le principe d'*autorité de science*; d'autre part, l'expérience de l'énergie originaire du "vouloir libre"[6]. Cette double expérience reçoit sa traduction philosophique, quelque soient les vections propres de Descartes, de Kant, de Spinoza et de Hegel, dans la légitimation théorique de l'absorption philosophique de la religion.

---

[4] "Pourquoi j'ai pris le parti d'un essai de remise en chantier de l'ontologie", *Cours de Métaphysique*, 1973-1974, Archives de l'Institut catholique de Paris, p. 144; publié dans la *Revue de l'Institut Catholique de Paris* (désormais RICP), 26 (avril-juin 1988), p. 135.

[5] *Cours de Métaphysique* 1973-1974, Archives de l'Institut catholique de Paris, Texte ronéoté, p. 11.

[6] Ibid., p. 13.

La "troisième position" n'indique certes pas un moment synthétique, une sorte d'*Aufhebung* récapitulatrice, mais énonce une prise de parti au sein de l'époque présente: "celle d'une philosophie consciente de se trouver en présence d'une énergie de la foi elle-même consciente de soi et se tenant, elle aussi, de façon consciente, en présence de l'énergie de la philosophie"[7]. Qu'est-ce à dire? Qu'il faut se résoudre à une *double irréductibilité* et la penser comme telle: 1) irréductibilité de l'énergie de la philosophie qui est attention et considération vis à vis de ce qui est donné, y compris le religieux; 2) irréductibilité de l'énergie de la foi, d'une expérience théologale forgée dans une connexion de sens qui "fait le poids" devant la totalité des énergies intellectuelles, philosophiques et scientifiques.

L'on pourra certes, en dépit des nuances apportées par Dubarle lui-même et dont on n'a pu faire ici état, faire valoir une complexité plus grande de l'histoire effective des rapports entre la philosophie et la foi religieuse, en monde grec et en monde chrétien; elle ne saurait cependant atténuer la force de cette position fondamentale: "La vie de l'esprit peut être le lieu, jusqu'à l'intérieur de l'individu humain, d'une pluralité – existence plurielle et pluralisme théorisable de façon cohérente – des consciences noéticoépistémologiques"[8]. Autrement formulé: l'énergie de la foi religieuse peut se tenir au coeur même de la puissance de raison, sans mettre en cause l'irréductibilité de cette puissance propre; inversement, l'oeuvre de raison peut pénétrer l'intelligence croyante sans corrompre l'originarité spécifique de celle-ci.

Cela indiqué, nous sommes maintenant en mesure d'explorer, comme annoncé, les thèses de Dubarle sur les conditions[9] ontologiques de la liberté philosophique dans l'état contemporain de la culture[10].

---

[7] Ibid., p. 21.

[8] Ibid., p. 27.

[9] Le thème de la "condition" traverse, à partir de l'année universitaire 1974-1975, l'essentiel des écrits du Père Dubarle; il y désigne la posture proprement "moderne" de la pensée, c'est-à-dire l'attention inédite portée à la phénoménalité "brute" introduite par l'évolution des sciences et des disciplines pratiques; Dubarle ressaisit ce thème en posant la question du statut d'une ontique dans l'ontologie. Voir à ce sujet l'étude de H. Faes "La philosophie de la condition du Père Dominique Dubarle", *Revue des Sciences philosophiques et théologiques*, 77(1993), pp. 373-398.

[10] Ces thèses sont formulées au moment de la douzième leçon du *Cours de Métaphysique* donné pendant l'année universitaire 1973-1974, dans un long développement intitulé "*De la condition et de la conduite de la raison dans l'espace de la liberté philosophique*" (p. 103-111). Afin d'éclairer certaines des procédures par lesquelles ces thèses sont posées, je me référerai à deux autres textes tirés du Cours de Métaphysique donné pendant l'année universitaire 1976-1977 et intitulés: "*Sur les rapports entre ontologie, vécu religieux et théologie*" (Archives de l'Institut catholique de Paris p. 389-395; *RICP*, p. 107-114), "*Philosophie de la conscience, ontologie de la subjectivité et conditions contemporaines de la philosophie*" (id. p. 461-473; *RICP*, p. 119-136).

II. RAISON ET LIBERTÉ. LA LOGIQUE DE LA PHILOSOPHIE

Thèse 1: *"Au nom de ce que nous pouvons appeler authentiquement raison, il n'y a pas de produit de l'intelligence philosophique qui soit universellement normatif pour toutes les intelligences accédant à la raison philosophique"*[11].

Cette première thèse combat deux préjugés majeurs qui ont présidé, selon Dubarle, à l'auto-compréhension de maints discours philosophiques. Ce qui est visé avec le premier, qualifié de préjugé "objectif", c'est l'équivalence entre le rationnel et le nécessaire, l'idée tenace que "par-dessous la variété buissonnière des formes prises par la pensée philosophique, il subsiste en principe une constitution fondamentale de l'habitude intellectuelle, assise première de toute conceptualité"[12]. Est stigmatisée ici non pas seulement une certaine conception chrétienne de l'à *priori* de toute rationalité mais aussi bien, le type de savoir achevé par Hegel qui, en dépit du renversement qu'il opère vis à la vis de la scolastique, ne parvient pas à se départir d'un "en soi" de la raison philosohique.

Le second préjugé, subjectif, s'exprime assez bien avec l'expression française: "avoir raison" qui résume la volonté de faire venir à sa pensée et à sa position, les pensées et les raisonnements de tout autre sujet humain. Il n'a ni plus ni moins que le poids d'une réplique donnée par le personnage de Sganarelle dans le pièce de Molière *Le médecin malgré lui*: "Quand j'ai bien bu et bien mangé, je veux que tout le monde soit soûl dans ma maison"[13]. Par-delà cette référence amusée, la question grave que pose ici Dubarle est celle des fondements de la "catholicité" de la pensée. Cette question pèse avec d'autant plus de force que la détermination subjective de l'"avoir-raison" devient celle non pas ceulement d'un individu, mais d'une collectivité organisée, d'une institution. C'est toute la prétention d'une catholicité du savoir et de la raison qui est ici visée jusque dans son report sur les aires conquérantes de la *philosophie des Lumières*. Ce type de catholicité, fausse catholicité du savoir que Dubarle appelle "la catholicité doctrinaire de la raison philosophique"[14], ne résiste pas aux implications de sa propre inscription dans le champ de la *communication* et de la *raison communicante*.

Telle est la sanction d'un "second deuil": après le moment d'éclatement des discours philosophiques et le renoncement obligé à un discours philoso-

---

[11] *Cours de Métaphysique*, 1973-1974, p. 104.
[12] *Cours de Métaphysique*, 1976-1977, p. 389.
[13] Molière, *Le médecin malgré lui*, acte 1, scène 1; cité in *Cours de Métaphysique*, 1973-1974, p. 104.
[14] *Cours de Métaphysique*, 1973-1974, id.

phique unitaire – moment qui, avec Engels et *L'essence du christianisme* notamment, marquait la fin de l'idéalisme classique – est venu le temps de la blessure de la "subjectivité", de la mise en question de sa constitution[15]. Non seulement la raison philosophique relève toujours de l'*épistémê* d'une époque, voire s'abîme dans les fixations d'école, mais plus profondément, ne peut éluder le caractère de liberté de l'intelligence elle-même; en deçà des choix qu'elle systématise et débordant toute détermination strictement subjective, la liberté philosophique appartient à une "logique" que Dubarle cherche à caractériser. D'où la seconde thèse.

Thèse 2. *"La philosophie, d'une part se meut elle-même au dedans d'elle-même, dans un mouvement qualitatif de l'intelligence qui est progression historique de la compréhension, et d'autre part ne cesse d'aller se nourrissant de son propre passé, dans la rumination intellectuelle de la connaissance historique de ce passé"*[16].

Le passage de la catégorie "nécessaire" à la catégorie "liberté" qu'organise cette seconde thèse, ne recouvre en aucun cas l'alternative entre la disposition à l'*universel doctrinaire* et l'option pour le *relativisme infini*. Car ce qui serait irrémédiablement perdu là et que Dubarle entend justement préserver, c'est l'espace d'une pratique féconde de communication entre philosophes *comme tels*. Or, le relativisme ne sait pas plus honorer les requêtes ultimes de la communication que la raison doctrinaire ne sait inscrire l'universel auprès de l'irréductibilité de la liberté de l'intelligence. C'est à partir de cette préoccupation maintenue que doit donc être comprise la thèse de Dubarle sur la "logique de la philosophie".

Suivant Eric Weil et son célèbre ouvrage, Dubarle admet dans la constitution de tout discours philosophique, un jeu entre une logique d'irréfutabilité et la réorganisation conciliante des discours antérieurs. Mais de manière originale, il fait d'abord ressortir la "logique de la philosophie" sur la base de deux déterminations complémentaires et articulées: 1) comme jeu *essentiellement temporel* d'épreuve et de maturation; 2) comme faits de *décision libre* sur les contenus d'intelligibilité eux-mêmes, c'est-à-dire tout à la fois "césure qualitative" et émergence d'une *originalité indépendante* de tout point de vue immédiatement conciliateur. L'engagement à penser jusqu'au bout le statut de cette décision libre implique aussi bien le renoncement à l'idée d'une décision philosophique unique, universellement valide et obligée, voire ambitieusement englobante, que "l'abandon passif aux fatalités

---

[15] "Philosophie de la conscience, ontologie de la subjectivité et conditions contemporaines de la philosophie", op. cit., p. 461-462.

[16] Ibid., p. 105.

du devenir et des interactions des doctrines (...) supposées devoir produire à la longue le réel progrès de l'esprit"[17]. Cet engagement trouve une assise fondamentale dans l'attitude qui fut celle-là même de Saint Thomas d'Aquin et que le Père Stanislas Breton vient de réévoquer avec passion[18]: *respondeo dicendum*, (*Je réponds qu'il faut dire*). Il s'agit là de l'initiative propre, libre de l'intelligence, jaillie dans un esprit de responsabilité, au sens il est dit en français: "j'en réponds".

Poussant son analyse, Dominique Dubarle distingue dans le libre parti irréductible de l'intelligence philosophique, quatre déterminants de nature fort différente est lui-même porté par: 1) la référence à tout un arrière plan d'intelligibilité, indicateur de vécus particuliers, 2) l'horizon indéfini de l'intelligibilité comme telle 3) le langage d'un système fortement codifié et socialisé, sorte de "dotation naturelle" faite à l'intelligence et 4) l'usage spécifique de la faculté générale de communiquer[19]. Ces quatre déterminants ne suffisent cependant pas encore à définir l'espace propre de l'élaboration philosophique. Dans un exercice de comparaison avec l'état actuel de la recherche mathématique – comparaison dont il sait mieux que quiconque les limites – le Père Dubarle fait remarquer comment celle-ci a fait oeuvre de libération "en renonçant à une épistémologie dogmatiste des axiomes et en découvrant à chaque fois leur caractère d'hypothèses rationnelles s'offrant à la liberté de l'intelligence. (...) Comme l'a dit Cantor – le fondateur de la théorie moderne des ensembles – c'est la liberté qui donne son essence vraie à l'être mathématique"[20]. Le rapport entre les théories axiomatiques et l'espace de liberté de la logique mathématicienne, devient alors pour Dubarle, l'indicateur, par analogie, d'un rapport entre la philosophie en ses discours particuliers et l'ontologie. D'où une troisième thèse qui honore le plan ontologique de la question d'ensemble.

Thèse 3. *La raison philosophique "se trouve devenir elle-même en faisant une sorte d'arbitrage touchant à ce qu'il faut penser (du) vécu extrême de la durée qu'il est donné au sujet pensant de vivre au moment de la liberté"*[21].

La spécification de la liberté philosophique ne tient pas seulement en effet à la prise en compte des points de trajets, des "carrefours de la liberté" où diverses voies semblent ouvertes et entre lesquelles il faut choisir; elle se

---

[17] Ibid., p. 99.
[18] Stanislas Breton, "Sur la difficulté d'être thomiste aujourd'hui" in *Le statut contemporain de la philosophie première*, Ph Capelle (Ed.), Paris, Beauchesne, 1996, p. 338.
[19] Ibid., p. 106-107.
[20] Ibid., p. 108-109.
[21] Ibid., p. 110.

dit au plus profond dans la situation d'*appel* qui est celle de la raison vis à vis de ce que Dubarle nomme "les deux faces de sa durée vécue": le temps et l'éternité: 1) celle qui mène de l'action à l'être, c'est-à-dire de la durée de l'énergie mentale à ce qui s'annonce comme la limite de cette durée; en ce premier sens, l'arbitrage est "l'acte de disponibilité existentielle ouvert à autre chose encore, *si* autre chose il y a". Une telle disponibilité peut être à bon droit portée par quelque conviction venue d'ailleurs; 2) celle qui, ressaisissant les deux faces de la durée vécue, le temps et l'éternité, fait coïncider cette fois le terme de la montée de l'esprit en sa plus haute libération et son moment d'éternité; d'où la dénégation de tout autre monde que ce monde-ci, qui caractérise l'essentiel de la pensée philosophique "moderne".

Telles sont les deux formes de l'auto-détermination, de la détermination *libre* de la philosophie: *disponibilité*, inscrite dans l'économie de la pensée, à un autre monde et *coïncidence* finale entre le monde pensé et la pensée de son éternité. Faut-il dès lors en rester, avec ces deux formes d'auto-détermination, à une sorte d'indécidable entre deux décisions irréductibles? Il est possible d'aller plus profond. Car deux gestes de "reconnaissance" sont appelés par une telle situation: 1) *auto*-reconnaissance du "libre parti", engagée par la raison philosophique; 2) reconnaissance *réciproque* de ces „libre parti" comme tels.

Une autre époque vient ainsi – et telle était la conviction profonde de Dubarle – où peut s'articuler dans un acte de liberté souveraine, la conversation véritablement *communicante* entre ces deux formes de la liberté philosophique: "Dans cette reconnaissance réciproque des formes libres de l'auto-constitution philosophique, par-delà la controverse des thèses divergentes ou le combat des contenus, peut alors prendre place l'*entretien*, libre lui aussi, sur les arrière-plans du vécu et des intelligibilité profondes, domaine de la communication à l'intérieur duquel il se peut que chacun des membrements libres de la liberté philosophique ait encore beaucoup à apprendre de l'autre, sans pour autant devoir se départir de la façon dont (...) il s'est philosophiquement déterminé"[22]. La position de Dubarle organise ainsi audacieusement un double plan de liberté philosophique: – liberté des discours philosophiques portée par les déterminants exposés ci-dessus – et liberté au second degré en quelque sorte, espace ontologique qui permet certes la position d'écoute et de discours modeste, mais qui offre bien davantage: l'éventualité, voire la chance de presser le rendez-vous attendu et de percer, dans l'entretien, l'énigme d'une éternité insoupçonnée.

---

[22] Ibid., p. 111.

III. LA RAISON PHILOSOPHIQUE EN UNIVERSITÉ CATHOLIQUE

Ces thèses fondamentales ne sont pas sans incidences sur le statut de la raison philosophique en monde catholique. Nous relèverons ainsi brièvement et en manière de conclusion, deux genres de réflexions programmatiques du Père Dubarle, restées pour partie confidentielles, qui concernent la spécificité de l'exercice philosophique au sein du dispositif universitaire catholique et plus largement au sein de l'intelligence croyante.

1. "(La philosophie) dans un système universitaire catholique, ne peut être une discipline close, étant au contraire son domaine de frontière sur l'ensemble du système universitaire humain. Elle ne peut être la discipline se faisant simplement l'auxiliaire humaine de la foi et des pensées théologiques, la ménagère des sciences sacrées. Elle a sa liberté intellectuelle en et pour soi dans toute la mesure où elle est intellectuellement située. Elle ne peut servir vraiment la théologie au sein de la culture moderne qu'en se tenant résolument au sein de cette liberté constitutrice"[23]. Plusieurs affirmations se conjuguent ici qui, enregistrant l'absence d'un substrat philosophique universel, font valoir aussi bien l'*irréductibilité* de l'épreuve philosophique que le principe de *conversation* de la philosophie. La philosophie est ainsi chez elle tant dans l'université profane que dans l'université confessionnelle et religieuse: "D'une manière ou d'une autre, elle a toujours la moitié de sa 'Faculté' hors d'elle et c'est très précisément cette condition [...] qui met la philosophie en position médiatrice"[24]. Fidèle à la mémoire évangélique, la Faculté catholique de philosophie[25] se doit d'être un organe de recherche libre et d'invention pensante; c'est sous ce rapport qu'elle se rend en mesure de faire jaillir l'unité entre l'université profane et l'université confessionnelle; et c'est comme telle qu'elle peut fournir à la théologie les ressources de la pensée en "raison".

2. Si, dans le libre parti de son intelligence et dans les conditions de liberté telles qu'elles ont été rapportées ci-dessus, la philosophie d'inspiration chrétienne n'est/ne saurait être ni une "philosophie entamée" ni une

---

[23] D. Dubarle, Mémoire adressé au début de 1968 à la "Congrégation romaine des Séminaires et des Etudes" en vue de la révision de la Constitution *Deus Scientiarum Dominus*, Archives de l'Institut Catholique de Paris, (texte ronéoté) p. 5.

[24] Ibid., p. 6.

[25] Nous nous permettons de renvoyer au texte de notre conférence "Tâches et mission d'une Faculté catholique de philosophie" donnée à l'UNESCO le mardi 10 octobre 1995, lors du colloque du centenaire de la Faculté de philosophie de l'Institut catholique de Paris, et publiée in *Le statut contemporain de la philosophie première*, op.cit. po. 343-354.

"théologie déguisée", reste néanmoins posée la question de son rapport à la *fides quaerens intellectum*. Cette célèbre formule anselmienne désigne certes le travail de l'*intellectus fidei*, mais elle indique aussi, selon Dubarle, un espace original qui est celui de la *fides quaerens rationem*, mieux, de la *fidelis intellectus rationis*. Cette affirmation décisive n'est en réalité rien que conséquente avec l'irréductibilité de l'intelligence philosophique au sein de la recherche intelligente de la foi; elle tient sa légitimité de la nécessité ultime, tant pour la philosophie que pour la théologie, de maintenir "à vif" en quelque sorte, l'économie d'une vérité première, celle de *la liberté native de l'esprit*[26]. La formule canonique *fides quaerens intellectum* comporte donc une double détermination: celle du théologien engagé dans l'intelligence de la foi comme foi – et celle du philosophe, lorsqu'il est croyant et viscéralement tenu à l'inspiration chrétienne, engagé dans la fidélité à l'intelligence en raison.

De ces deux réflexions résulte une série de conséquences qui définissent une Faculté catholique de philosophie à l'écart de toute représentation "à étages" des rapports philosophie-théologie, comme autre chose qu'un faire-valoir culturel au service de la théologie, mais plus profondément, comme un organe spécifique qui manifeste au sein d'une Université catholique, l'acte vivant de l'esprit duquel jaillit une production de sens.

Cet acte vivant, "à vif", de l'esprit en sa liberté ontologique, peut être aussi bien compris comme celui de la pensée religieuse: "L'ontologie qui est un produit de la pensée réfléchissante supposant une demande de la pensée vivante et vivant immédiatement un certain déploiement substantiel d'elle-même [...] ne peut que se conjuguer à la pensée religieuse vive [...] pour autant que cette pensée religeuse est ainsi en acte vif"[27]. Se présente alors un champ encore inexploré que le Père Dubarle a voulu appeler non pas, justement, une ontologie théologique, mais une "ontologie théologale", une ontologie qui revendique pleinement le titre d'ontologie philosophique.

---

[26] D. Dubarle, "*Fides quaerens rationem*. La philosophie dans un Institut catholique", in: *Humanisme et foi chrétienne. Mélanges scientifiques du centenaire de l'Institut catholique de Paris*, Y. Marchasson et Ch. Kannengiesser (Ed), Beauchesne, 1976.

[27] "Sur les rapports entre ontologie, vécu religieux et théologie", op.cit., p. 392.

ANDRZEJ WALICKI
University of Notre Dame
USA

MARXIST COMMUNISM AS A CONCEPTION OF FREEDOM

Marx's philosophy of freedom should not be reduced to its critical part, i.e. to Marx's well-known critique of the "bourgeois liberty". Neither should it be identified with the problem of determinism versus freedom in historical materialism. Its most important (although, paradoxically, more esoteric and much less known) part was the theory of communism. It is an integral, holistic theory but for heuristic purposes it can be discussed under two headings: as a proposal to define freedom in a way diametrically opposite to the liberal conception, and as a vision of the final outcome of a dialectical process of self-realization of human species essence. It is important to stress that the theory of this process, conceived as a process of self-enriching alientation, is larger in scope than historical materialism: the latter deals only with the "kingdom of necessity", i.e. with history within the structure of alienation, whereas the vision of communism describes the final phase of human development: the positive abolition of self-alienation in the future "Kingdom of Freedom"[1].

---

[1] For a detailed reconstruction of Marx's philosophy of freedom, as well as a study of its historical fates, see my book *Marxism and the Leap to the Kingdom of Freedom. The Rise and Fall of the Communist Utopia*, Stanford Univ. Press, Stanford 1995. (Polish translation: *Marksizm i skok do królestwa wolności. Dzieje komunistycznej utopii*, PWN, Warsaw 1996). Among the relatively new books, dealing with the problem of freedom in Marx's thought, the best ones are, in my view, Allen Buchanan, *Marx and Justice: The Radical Critique of Liberalism*. London, 1982 and G. Brenkert, *Marx's Ethics of Freedom*. London, 1983. James J. O'Rourke's, *The Problem of Freedom in Marxist Thought* (Dordrecht–Boston, 1974) deals mostly with the problem of determinism vs. freedom in historical materialism. In the Polish literature on the subject the two books by S. Rainko contain many valuable insights. See Rainko, *Świadomość i historia* (Warsaw 1978) and *Świadomość i determinizm* (Warsaw 1981).

The classical-liberal conception defined freedom "negatively" -as "independence of the arbitrary will of another"[2]. The subject of such freedom was obviously the concrete individual, living here and now. A necessary condition of the liberal freedom was the existence of a pluralistic civil society, enabling everybody to pursue his own individual aims, and a monetary-exchange economy, guaranteeing maximization of choices in the sphere of consumption. Dependence on the impersonal, reified forces of the market was seen as a necessary price for personal freedom. The idea of reducing the uncertainties of life through collective self-mastery, i.e. through rational collective control of economic and social forces, was perceived as incompatible with individual choice and free pursuit of happiness. Freedom, as Friedrich Hayek put it, "means that in some measure we entrust our fate to forces which we do not control"[3].

In all these respects the Marxist theory of freedom was paradigmatically different from the liberal conception. It defined freedom not as an absence of external coercion or constraint, but as the ability to live in accordance with man's essential nature, that is, as the opposite of dehumanization. The subject of such freedom was not the human individual but the human species or, more precisely, the human species of the communist future-since only under communism the human essence would be reconciled with the human existence. A necessary condition of the communist freedom was seen in a radical overcoming of the divisive, egoistic pluralism of civil society and in putting an end to man's dependence on the blind forces of the market; spontaneous social forces, as Engels put it, had to be transformed from "master demons" into "willing servants"[4]. It was not denied that liberation from the impersonal rule of the market would increase the scope of dependence on public authorities. Marx (in *Gruindrisse*) said explicitly that dependence on the market ("objective dependence") is inversely proportional to personal dependence; that the liberation from the reified power of money must entail the proportional increase of the power of community which binds the individuals together[5]. But this was not perceived as a threat to freedom for at least two reasons. First, the founders of Marxism saw "objective dependence" – the dependence on things-as much worse, much more dehumanizing than personal dependence. Second, they assumed that in the

---

[2] See F. A. Hayek, *The Constitution of Liberty*, The Univ. of Chicago Press, Chicago 1960, pp. 11.

[3] F. A. Hayek, *Law, Legislation, and Liberty*, Routledge and Kegan Paul, London 1982 (three volumes in one-volume paperback), vol. 2, p. 30.

[4] F. Engels, *Anti-Dühring: Herr Eugen Dühring's Revolution in Science*, Moscow 1978 (1947), p. 339.

[5] K. Marx, *Grundrisse: Foundations of the Critique of Policial Economy*, Penguin, Harmondsworth 1973, pp. 157-158.

communist society of the future individuals would become fully socialized, identifying their true selves with man's species essence and, therefore, perceiving the power of community as realization of their own freedom.

Thus, in contrast to liberalism, Marx defined freedom not as individualistic freedom from control but as conscious collective control over conditions of life, as proud mastery over collective fate, liberating people from the domination of things and from the dehumanized forms of social life. The specifically Marxist element of this ideal of collectivist prometheanism was the emphasis on the crucial role of humankind's capacity to control the conditions of its own self-objectification, that is, of the entire sphere of production and exchange.

The identification of freedom with communism meant in practice that the full liberation of humanity could be expected only at the end of a long and convoluted process of the self-actualization of the human essence in history. Marx defined this process as the history of self-enriching alienation, that is, a development through alienation, as a necessary phase of exteriorizing and reifying the species forces, towards the full unfolding of human species nature, revealing all its inherent capacities and its potential richness. In this perspective history of freedom had two aspects: "man versus nature", that is ability to exercise conscious, rational control over nature, and "man versus society", that is ability to consciously shape the social conditions of human existence, thereby eliminating the impersonal power of alienated, reified social forces (read: market-bound forces of the civil society). These two aspects of freedom corresponded to two successive phases in the process of human liberation: maximizing the productive powers of the species at the cost of alienation (capitalism) and the disalienation of these powers by rational planning (communism). Following Hegel's *Phenomenology of Spirit* Marx saw the capitalist epoch as the most alienated and most progressive so far, since in the past progress had to be paid for by alienation. From the point of view of man's power over nature, capitalism was the greatest triumph of freedom, but with respect of the power of humankind over its own social relations it represented at the same time the greatest denial of freedom, the most complete domination by alienated and reified forces[6]. Marx did not hesitate to draw from this the conclusion that capitalism, contrary to the liberals, brought about not an increase of freedom but a drastic diminution of its scope. What the bourgeoisie called personal freedom (we read in *The German Ideology*) amounted, in the end, to leaving the fate of

---

[6] Thus, the relation between the two aspects of freedom was, historically, inversely proportional: "In the same measure in which mankind achieves power over nature, man seems to fall under the power of his own baseness". (K. Marx, F. Engels, *Collected Works*, New York 1975, vol. 14, p. 655).

individuals to the play of chance, which was simply the other aspect of the blind necessity that governed social relations as a whole[7].

Marx's vision of communism as the "true realm of freedom" presupposed gaining total conscious control over economy, that is, total abolition of commodity production and market exchange, including the abolition of money. Contrary to the social democratic interpretation of Marxism this great change was not to be implemented in a gradual way, through a piecemeal social engineering; it was tgo be a radical break with the past, involving *from the very beginning* the abolition of the market and the replacement of money with labor certificates which would enable the extension the principle of collective planning to the sphere of individual consumption. True, in his *Critique of the Gotha Program* Marx divided communism into two phases: the lower one (Lenin called it "socialism"), applying the principle "to each according to his work" and preserving thereby a "right of inequality", and the higher one, in which, owing to the unprecedented increase of social wealth, "the narrow horizon of bourgeois right" would be crossed in its entirety and society would implement the principle "from each according to his ability, to each according to his needs". But this distinction, important as it was, had nothing in common with the idea of a transitional period combining markets with planning, money economy with communal ownership of the means of production. The capitalist rules of the game were to be abolished at once. Lenin's policy before the NEP-the policy of a direct transition" to communism-was fully concordant with this vision.

The social-democratic interpretation of Marxism, characteristic of the Second International, drew support from the anti-voluntaristic spirit of historical materialism. In reality, however, the only logical connection between historical materialism and the communist soteriology was Marx's conception of a necessary breakdown of capitalism. What was to happen after this catastrophe was beyond the grasp of historical materialism almost by definition. After all, historical materialism, as a science of objective law of socioeconomic development, dealt by definition with the "Kingdom of necessity", and not the "Kingdom of freedom". This is what Lukács had in mind when he described it as "the self-knowledge of capitalist society" – that is, as the theoretical explanation of man's enslavement by things, and not as a theory of communist freedom[8]. (A similar point has been made by Father Jean-Yves Calvez)[9]. Indeed, a sharper contrast could hardly be imagined.

---

[7] Ibid., vol. 5, kpp. 78-79, 80-81.

[8] G. Lukács, *History and Class Consciousness*, Trans. R. Livingstone, The MIT Press, Cambridge, Mass. 1971, p. 229.

[9] Jean Yves Calvez, *La pensée de Karl Marx*, Editions du Seuil, Paris 1961, pp. 533-534.

The communist utopia presupposed total, collective control of historical processes whereas historical materialism explained why historical events always escaped such control. In other words, historical materialism was a theory of the unintended results of human actions, that is, of creating history within the structure of alienation, without the possibility of controlling its course and giving it a conscious direction. In contrast with this, Marx's theory of communism (including its "lower phase") presupposed the conscious steering of historical process, that is, the creation of history in accordance with the consciously chosen aims, expressing the innermost essence of our common human nature. Hence, it could not be derived from the so-called objective laws of economic development, discovered by historical materialism; the very essence of the communist ideal of freedom was the promise that such laws would cease to exist in the future.

Nevertheless, there is a viewpoint from which historical materialism ("Kingdom of necessity") and the communist utopia ("Kingdom of freedom") are meaningfully related to each other. As mentioned previously, this is the mythical story of self-enriching alienation. Historical materialism deals only with the second act of this drama-with the story of man's development *in* alienation and *through* alienation. In contrast with this, Marx's vision of communism concerns the second and final act: the story of humanity's de-alienation and reintegration. These two stories are structurally interrelated as parts of the great underlying myth, but not as parts of a single scientific theory.

The libertarian intentions of Marx's communist ideal should not obscure the fact that it was definitely and consistently anti-liberal, anticipating some features of the militantly communist regimes of the twentieth century. Freedom conceived as full, conscious control of people's collective fate presupposed the existence of a public *capable* of exercising effective control over all spheres of social life, and this, arguably, would entail the liquidation of the uncontrollable individual freedom. The replacement of self-regulating impersonal mechanisms by conscious decisions would severely restrict personal freedom, since all individual life-plans would be controled by the public authorities. The substitution of egoistic individual freedom by a harmonious unanimity, or species freedom, is obviously incompatible with pluralistic civil society, enabling the individuals to pursue their own interests and to be different from others. Universal participatory democracy, in which Marx sought a remedy against authoritarianism, may be good for small communities but not for large, complex, industrialized societies. Experience has shown, in particular, its complete incompatibility with the principle of collective planning; if Marx had thought that under communism different individuals could accept the same criteria of rationality, fully agree as to the common good and, consequently, harmoniously cooperate with one another in pursuing the same aims, it only shows that he saw them not as *individualized* human beings but as undifferentiated "species beings", reduced to their essential identity as specimen of the same species[10]. Finally-last but not least-Marx's view that the subject of true freedom is the entire species, and that the realization of freedom is possible only under communism, justified a principled rejection of ethical individualism, readiness to treat concrete individuals, as well as entire classes and nations, as mere instruments of historical progress, whose sufferings and destruction could be fully legitimized as paving the way for the universal human liberation in the future. In this way the communist ideal of the final liberation peformed the same function as the concept of "necessary laws of development" in historical materialism: both justified the cruelties of history, the lack of moral scruples in realizing the Great goal, and the utterly contemptuous attitude towards the "sentimental" concerns about the price of progress[11].

Yet, Marx's conception of the communist freedom was not a blueprint for communist totalitarianism. Despite his enormous intellectual arrogance, he did not claim the monopoly on truth and did not elaborate an all-embracing "scientific view of the world", pretending to contain ready-made solutions to all possible problems. He did not envisage the creation of an infallible vanguard party, indignantly rejected the view that "the working class of itself is incapable of its own emancipation" and, in the communist Manifesto, solemnly proclaimed that "the Communists do not form a separate party opposed to other working-class parties"[12]. His model for the dictatorship of the proletariat was the Paris Commune, despite the fact that it was

---

[10] In his *Main Currents of Marxism* (Oxford, Univ. Press. Oxford, 1981, vol. 1, pp. 161-62) Leszek Kolakowski strongly disagreed with this view (Cf. my critique of his position in *Marxism and the Leap*, pp. 59-61). In his later work, however, he discovered in Marx the ancient "dream of a perfectly unified community" and pointed out that "there is no reason to expect that this dream can ever become true except in the cruel form of despotism". (L. Kolakowski, "The Myth of Human Self-Identity", in L. Kolakowski and Stuart Hampshire, eds., *The Socialist Idea: A. Reappraisal*, London 1974, p. 35).

[11] This aspect of Marxism has been stressed by Nikolai Berdyaev in his famous essay "Socialism as Religion" (1906). He wrote about it thus: "The person is never a goal and always a means. The person himself possesses no worth and is valued only according to his usefulness in winning the proletarian-socialist paradise. [...]. The evil principle of Marxism is nowhere so manifest as in this atheistic and inhuman attitude toward the human face, toward individualism, and in this respect Marx himself sinned more than anyone". (Quoted from B. Glatzer Rosenthal and M. Bohachevsky-Chomiak, eds., *A Revolution of the Spirit: Crisis of Value in Rusai 1890-1924*, Fordham Univ. Press, New York 1990, p. 112).

[12] See K. Marx, F. Engels, *Selected Works*, 3 vols., Moscow 1969, vol. 2, p. 81 vol. 3, pp. 94 and 147, and vol. 1, p. 119 ("Manifesto of the Communist Party").

firmly controlled by his ideological rivals: a Blanquist majority and a Proudhonist minority. This shows beyond doubt that his concept of the proletarian dictatorship should not be confused with the monopolistic rule of one "truly Marxist" party[13].

Nonetheless, it is a fact that Marxism, ultimately, proved to be very well suited to the legitimization of the Soviet totalitarian regime, that the crimes of this regime were meant to serve the cause of the Marxist utopia, and that almost all Marxists in the world supported this regime without questioning its ideological legitimacy. To explain this fact we must devote some attention to the works of Marx's life-long friend and collaborator, Frederick Engels. It is good to remember that for three or four generations of Marxists Engels was, in practice, a more important and influential Marxist theorist than Marx himself[14]. It is especially true in the domain of philosophy. After all, Engels's philosophical works, such as Anti-Dühring, Socialism: Utopian and Scientific, and Ludwig Feuerbach at the End of Classical German Philosophy, inspired powerful revolutionary movements, while the works of young Marx, whose philosophical weight was much greater, remained unknown and could not lay claim to a comparable world historical significance.

From the point of view of the problem of freedom Engels' contribution to Marxism can be summarized in two points.

First, Engels wanted to present Marxism as a rigidly "scientific" form of socialist thought and did so at the expense of deemphasizing the libertarian aspects of Marx's communist utopia. Accordingly, he defined freedom not as the unfettered, many-sided development of man's species essence, but as the "understanding of necessity" and obtaining thereby "the control of ourselves and over external nature"[15]. In this way collective control over conditions of life, exercised through a comprehensive collective planning, came to be seen by him not as a precondition of freedom (or "freedom in the realm of necessity", as Marx put it)[16], but as freedom itself. A further consequence of this was his commitment to the saintsimonian principle of a cen-

---

[13] This was stressed by R. Hunt in *The Political Ideas of Marx and Engels*, vol. 2-*Classical Marxism*, Univ. of Pittsburgh Press, Pittsburgh, Pa, 1984, pp. 182-211.

[14] See G. Lichtheim, *Marxism: An Historical and Critical Study*, F. A. Praeger, New York 1962, p. 241, and L. Kolakowski, *Main Currents*, vol. 1, p. 261.

[15] F. Engels, *Anti-Dühring*, pp. 140-141.

[16] In the famous fragment of the unfinished third volume of *Capital* Marx said that "in fact the realm of freedom actually begins only where labor which is determined by necessity and mundane considerations ceases [...] The shortening of the working day is its basic prerequisite". (K. Marx, *Capital*, 3 vols., New York 1967, vol. 3, p. 820). From this point of view rational, conscious regulation of production was only freedom within the realm of necessity-a necessary *basis* of true freedom, that is of unfettered development of human capacities as an end in itself.

tralized and authoritarian organization. Following Marx's Capital[17], Engels made a sharp distinction between "division of labor in society" (implying free competition and, therefore, the anarchy of the market") and "division of labor in factory" (implying "production upon a definite plan"). Needless to say, he condemned the first, as bringing about the rule of "blind forces", and extolled the second, as representing the victory of consciousness and reason. He had no doubt that "factory despotism" was vastly superior to "freedom of the market". The increasing concentration and planned regulation of production under corporate capitalism was for him a progressive tendency, anticipating to a certain extent "the invading socialist society"[18]. The victory of socialism, seen from this perspective, was to be the culminating point in the process of replacing the spontanerous division of labor (and the market economy, bound up with it) by an organized division of labor and the conscious, planned allocation of products. Socialism was to transform society into a single organization, "one immense factory".

Thus, Lenin was a faithful disciple of Engels when he pictured the socialist society of his dreams as a single factory run from a single office[19]. And he did not forget Engels's warning that the regime of factory work presupposes severe discipline and an unquestioning subordination to public authorities, no matter how delegated[20].

Second, Engels transformed Marxism into an all-embracing pseudo-scientific philosophy of "dialectical materialism" (with historical materialism as its part). The liberating function of this philosophy was to provide a "correct", scientific understanding of the laws of necessity and, thereby, to make it possible to replace the domination of blind, irrational forces by an all-embracing rational control of social life, based upon comprehensive economic planning. In Engels's view this was the deepest meaning of the "leap from the kingdom of necessity to the Kingdom of freedom"[21]. But this emphasis on the salvationist role of "true knowledge" was in fact extremely dangerous to freedom. Claims to posses "correct", scientific knowledge of the general direction of future history undermined the democratic principle of power legitimation and justified instead a particularly self-confident, hence particularly repressive, authoritarian leadership. The conviction that an understanding of the "laws of development" supplies unambiguous

---

[17] See Marx, chapter 14 of the first volume of Capital ("Division of Labor in Society, and Division of Labor in Manufacture").

[18] F. Engels, Socialism: Utopian and Scientific, In K. Marx, F. Engels, Selected Works, vol. 3, pp. 136, 144.

[19] See Lenin's The State and Revolution, Chap. V, 4 (V. I. Lenin, Selected Works, 3 vols., Moscow 1977, vol. 2, p. 312).

[20] Engels, "On Authority", 1874 (K. Marx, F. Engels, Collected Worsk, vol. 3).

[21] F. Engels, Anti-Dühring, pp. 343-344.

directives as to the only correct action promoted a constructivist attitude to social change, disregarding the empirical realities of life, as well as the simple common sense, in the name of theoretical dogma. Finally, the conception of freedom as dependent on a comprehensive understanding of the "objective laws" of nature and history justified attempts at an ideocratic rule, based upon the total indoctrination of society. In this respect Engels's unintended contribution to Stalinist totalitarianism seems to be especially important: the systematic enslavement of minds could present itself as an attempt at bringing people to "true understanding", or "adequate consciousness", thus creating conditions for their liberaton.

As is known, Engels himself did not move in this direction; on the contrary-in his last years he tended to endorse the social-democratic interpretation of Marxism. A consistently totalitarian interpretation of Marxism was elaborated by Lenin. It appeared for the first time in Lenin's What is to be Done? (1902), as the theory of a centralizd vanguard party, embodying the "most advanced theory" and, at the same time, the "true class consciousness" of the workers; it culminated in Lenin's theory of the dictatorship of the proletariat-a dictatorship "untrammeled by any laws, absolutely unrestricted by any rules whatever, and based directly on force"[22].

The relationship between Leninism and Marxism has been a subject of many heated discussions and I do not pretend to say the final word in this matter. In particular, I do not intend to claim that Leninism, both as an ideology and as a movement, was a necessary, unavoidable consequence of Marxism. But, on the other hand, I cannot agree with the view that Lenin did not belong to the genuinely Marxist tradition and should be seen rather as a product of some specific features of Russian history. Even at its worst, Leninism was profoundly indebted to Marxism and, arguably, impossible without Marxism, Lenin's obsession with control was obviously derived from Marxism. His idea of the party's control over spontaneous workers' movement was a legitimate extension of the conception of freedom as conscious control; after all, modern trade unions belonged to the "blind forces of the market" – hence establishing a firm control over them by a "conscious", revolutionary minority was just a part of the communist program of liberating society from the rule of reified economic powers. Not only in Lenin, but also in Marx the word "spontaneity" (stikhiinost', Urwüchsigkeit) was associated with the dependence on blind, natural (or quasinatural) forces, and by no means with "true freedom". Despite its unprecedented brutality, Linin's definition of the proletarian dictatorship was deeply connected with the populist vulgarizations of Marxism, denouncing "bourgeois liberty" as

---

[22] V. I. Lenin, *Collected Works*, Moscow 1960-70, vol. 10, p.246, and vol. 31, p. 353.

"merely formal", fraudulent, and useful only for the rich. Even Lenin's rejection of "all rules" could not be separated from the Marxist vision of communism as an end-connected (teleocratic) order, consciously opposed to the aim-independent, rule-connected (nomocratic) civil society[23].

Does it mean that the experience of the Society totalitarianism has fully discredited the Marxian view of freedom, sending it to the proverbial "rubbish bin of history"? Yes, and no. Yes, because the communist utopia has indeed become fully discredited and is no longer revelant for informed discussions about humanity's future. No, because the core idea of Marx's conception of freedom-the idea of consious, rational control of human collective fate-is still fully relevant for defining the scope of our responsibilities. The ideal of freedom as total control has indeed compromised itself, and not only as a complete denial of individual freedom; it proved to be self-contradictory and untenable, producing unintended, uncontrollable consequences and therefore failing to realize its own objectives. It does not follow, however, that the only alternative to the visible hand of the communist party is the invisible hand of the market. Reliance on this invisible hand cannot absolve us from responsibility for the great and urgent problems of the world. Hence the classical-liberal "freedom from control" must be supplemented somehow by "freedom as responsible control" as envisaged, for instance, by the Catholic teaching on "subsidiarity". A wholesale denial of this practical compromise is possible only from positions of a right-wing libertarianism, which does not seem to be an acceptable option.

It seems, therefore, that the Marxist philosophy of freedom, despite all its inherent dangers, contains an element of truth which should not be suppressed by the trendy anticommunist triumphalism. But, on the other hand, a close study of its multiple and grave errors can show better than anthing else the truth and continued relevance of the essential liberal values.

---

[23] This useful typological distinction has been elaborated by F. Hayek. See Hayek, *Law, Legislation, and Liberty*, vol. 2, pp. 38-9. A similar distinction is to be found Karl Popper's *The Open Society and Its Enemies*.

RACHEL GAZOLLA DE ANDRADE
Pontificia Universidade Católica São Paulo
Brazil

RÉFLEXIONS ETHICO-POLITIQUES SUR LES RACINES DE LA NOTION DE LIBERTÉ DANS LA PHILOSOPHIE GRECQUE ANCIENNE

I. Pour commencer, je voudrais mettre au clair le Fait que, en parlant de la notion de liberté dans la philosophie ancienne, je serai naturellement menée à parler en même temps de sa signification moderne, dans un rapprochement qui souligne les ressemblances aussi bien que les différences présentes dans son développement historique. Le mot liberté est rarement laissé de côté dans les discours des hommes politiques, et nous l'entendons tous comme une valeur positive, sans être toujours d'accord sur son sens ou sa signification. On sait que la liberté dans la culture grecque ancienne n'a pas la même importance que nous lui accordons en tant qu'héritiers du libéralisme du XVIIe siècle et du rousseauisme du XVIIIe. Locke et Rousseau sont ceux qui nous donnent les bases de la notion de l'individualité, absente à l'époque ancienne. Être libre est pour un grec ancien ne pas être esclave. Mais cela ne nous dit pas grand-chose. Dans l'interstices des textes disponibles pour les recherches, on trouve cette affirmation extrêmement objective. Du point de vue des règles de comportement, c'est à dire du *ethos* en vigueur, 'être libre' s'appliquait à celui qui d'une manière ou d'une autre était considéré (et se sentait ainsi) supérieur à un autre, ou à un groupe. La liberté était présentée comme valeur extérieure en fonction de quelques spécificités, reconnues de la même manière par tous ceux qui les découvrent chez quelqu'un ou chez un groupe de personnes. Si nous cherchons les racines du mot *eleutheria* (liberté) ces spécificités deviennent plus claires.

Pour Émile Benveniste (in "Le vocabulaire des institutions indo-européennes") le mot *elutheria* a un radical indo-européen – *leuth* – avec l'idée de croissance, de développement liée à l'idée d'appartenance à un groupe, de partager les mêmes racines éthniques ou le même *génos*. Robert Muller, dans un article publié dans la revue 'Dialogue' (XXV, 1996, pag. 421) note que cette signification indique une qualité et non une comparaison, c'est à dire que quand on parle d'un homme libre ou d'un esclave, on ne compare pas la manière d'être antagonique entre l'un et l'autre mais on expose une qualité présente chez l'un deux. Bien qu'elle soit absente chez l'autre, dire qu'un homme est libre ne dépend pas de la négation chez l'autre de cette qualité pour qu'elle se vérifie chez lui.

Si nous acceptons l'explication de Benveniste, la liberté n'explicite pas le pouvoir d'aller et venir, ni n'émerge nécessairement de la relation 'seigneur-esclave', mais c'est une qualité de l'être supérieur du fait d'avoir des racines, d'avoir une identité à partir d'un *génos* ou d'une *Politiéia*. Être libre signifie s'appartenir, croître ou grandir, se développer et avoir une identité à partir d'un groupe qui est une extension de soi, c'est pouvoir reconnaître dans le groupe et à travers lui, pouvoir acquérir et montrer son identité personnelle. Il n'est pas difficile de trouver une telle signification dans les textes archaïques et principalement chez Homère. Que l'on se rappelle les noms de chaque famille liés au lieu d'origine, au *génos*. C'est la règle qui est aujourd'hui préservée dans nos noms de famille sans que nous fassions attention à leur origine. La soumission à des règles de groupes est prévisible car ce sont elles qui créent l'essence propre des hommes qui forment et maintiennent un groupe. Le sentiment de contrainte, de menace ou de violence est absent dans ce mouvement à deux sens, entre le groupe et l'individu. En effet, cet enracinement est ce qui qualifie l'homme dans sa *eleutheria* à laquelle vient s'attacher étroitement une autre notion, celle de *philia*, d'amitié, car avoir une terre, un nom, un *oikós* présuppose un don et le sentiment profond d'appartenance mutuelle et unificatrice.

Il fallait la naissance de la philosophie comme un nouveau savoir qu'émerge au VI-e siècle pour que s'élargisse cette première signification, et parce qu'elle est première, elle est, à mon avis, indélébile. Il fallait que les philosophies de Platon et d'Aristote fondent l'Éthique et la Politique comme de nouveaux domaines du savoir pour que la notion de liberté y lance les bases de son tissu historique.

II. La philosophie grecque ne sépare pas les savoirs nommés Éthique et Politique qui malheureusement ne maintiennent plus aujourd'hui les liens que les unissaient auparavant, liens que les études universitaires n'ont pas préservés non plus. Cet unique savoir cherche à comprendre le 'faire' humain, le *prattein*, se référant à l'action d'un seul homme (Éthique), aussi bien que l'action collective dans la cité (Politique). Le champ du *prattein* est déjà établi dans l'oeuvre de Platon comme divers du 'faire' technique – le *poiein*. *Prattein* est lié au pouvoir théorique ou noétique propre à l'âme humaine, c'est à dire, au domaine du *theorein* (contempler). Si nous examinons la notion de liberté chez Platon, nous verrons qu'elle s'y montre beaucoup plus en creux que par ses attributs positifs.

En privilégiant un dialogue, la *'Republique'*, Platon parle, dans le livre IX, de l'esclavage du tyran, un esclavage que émerge des désirs illimités, laissés dans leur démesure, rompant l'harmonie avec les deux autres *dynameis* de l'âme: la timocratique (*timoeidés*) et la logistique (*logistikón*). Par conséquent, la prédominance de la partie épitimétique ou des désirs sur les deux autres signifie l'éloignement du paradigme de la cité juste et de l'homme juste parce que le tyran touche l'animalité, soit dans l'insociabilité, soit par le désordre qu'il crée dans son âme et dans la cité tyrannique, en comparaison à la *physis* ordonnée. Platon voit la non-liberté dans le total esclavage aux désirs, ce qui signale une autre configuration mentale: être esclave c'est méconnaître le bon usage des trois puissances de l'âme, en se soumettant à la violence de l'une d'elles et spécifiquement à la tyrannie, de la partie épitimétique. Dans cette nouvelle structure de pensée le philosophe considère le pouvoir de savoir de faire et de désirer, sur un terrain commun dérivé de sa conception de l'âme, qui est pour lui fondamentalement la même dans l'univers, dans l'homme et dans la cité. La partie logistique de l'âme humaine (*logistikón*) étant hégémonique et décisive, parce qu'elle a le *lógos* et le *nous* (Inteligência), réunit la théorie et la pratique dans la recherche de la sagesse et de la vertu. On peut déjà deviner le sens de 'liberté': elle s'exprime dans le bon usage du *lógos*, dans le fait d'écarter les entraves qui menacent la reflexion qui est la seule voie conduisant à l'harmonie entre l'homme, l'univers et la *politéia*. Dans cette perspective, la sagesse et la vertu sont inséparables de *l'euletheria*.

Platon fait oeuvre d'innovateur en inaugurant la réflexion sur les origines d'une intériorité quand, suivant en partie la pensée de ses prédécesseurs, il crée une théorie de l'âme. On peut alors parler de la liberté comme d'un 'état intérieur' de non-menace, de non-contrainte. C'est ainsi encore qu'apparaît le sens le plus archaïque de la notion-contrainte. C'est ainsi encore que le sens le plus archaïque de la notion de liberté comme appartenance à un groupe se préserve. C'est ce qui fait ressortir les traits du tyran, un homme dont la marque est s'éloigner du groupe, se rendant esclave de ses propres désirs et qui finit par se détruire dans la solitude du pouvoir.

Ce n'est pas sans raison qu'Aristote, élève exemplaire de l'Académie pendant vingt ans, pourra dire dans sa *Politéia* qu'il y a des esclaves par nature ou par convention, quoique la première catégorie, celle des esclaves par nature, soit pour nous à l'époque moderne, un scandale. Aristote affirme seulement que la nature a fait les homme différents, et il est difficile de le nier: parmi les hommes il y a ceux qui peuvent commander parce qu'ils ont une vision d'ensemble, c'est à dire, qu'ils savent articuler, établir des relations, mesurer, calculer comme s'ils avaient reçu une portion du grand regard de Zeus. Ceux-là, puisqu'ils ne sont pas esclaves, ils ont le savoir qui les rend capables de créer et de dicter les règles pour ceux qui ne peuvent pas avoir la même vision de l'ensemble: les esclaves ne peuvent pas établir la plus petite articulation entre les causes et les effets et ne feront donc qu'obéir (in 'Politique', I et 'Métaphysique', A,1).

La logique de son argument est indiscutable. Comme chez Platon, Aristote affirme le pouvoir de savoir articulé au 'faire'. Dans l'esclavage par nature apparaît comme dans un miroir la liberté qu'Aristote étudiera dans l'Éthique à Nicomaque (livre III), ce qui signifie pouvoir utiliser la capacité noétique de l'âme pour la connaissance des dispositions. Quand il fait un 'choix', dit le philosophe, l'homme le fait de sa propre initiative – *hekousia* –, sans être contraint par des circonstances extérieures-*akoúsia*. L'action de délibérer (*voúlesis*) et l'action de choisir (*proaíresis*) de sa propre initiative (*hekousia*, parfois mal traduit par volontaire) forment le noyau de l'Éthique comme *phronésis*, l'action réfléchie. Aristote rend évident l'*autorchéia*, ce que veut dire les premiers principes du 'penser humain' relatifs à la vie pratique, pour que chaque homme, dans l'emploi de ses principes, puisse agir d'une manière éthique, c'est à dire 'librement', sans que son action découle des contraintes extérieures. Il ne s'agit pas de celui qui est seigneur par nature et peut commander comme dans la 'Politique', mais du début d'une nouvelle signification pour *eleutheria* venue d'*autarchéia* et que le philosophe relie à la réflexion politique.

Dans cet étroit chemin, Aristote, allant plus loin que Platon, établit les racines de la notion de liberté intérieure qui quelques siècles plus tard sera indispensable aux textes fondateurs de l'État Moderne. Il est évident que dans nos textes modernes un élément est absent des textes d'Aristote: celui de l'individu pensé comme atome social, dont je ne traiterai pas ici. L'idée qu'un philosophe grec puisse voir la *pólis* comme non pertinente à l'essence de l'homme est inacceptable. À mon avis, la notion de l'individualité a ses premières racines dans le sol hellénique, notamment chez les stoïciens, mais on ne peut pas lui attacher le sens que le libéralisme lui a donnné plus tard, puisque c'est la notion de nature qui est modifiée à la naissance d'une structure économique post-médiévale.

Un philosophe grec aura beau élaborer des théories sur l'intériorité et se référer à une individualité latente chez l'homme, mais il n'affirmera en aucun moment qu'un individu est responsable de tous ses actes, abstraitement seigneur de lui même, vue que c'est le cosmos et la cité qui établissent les fondements de son identité. Il n'y a dans la pensée grecque ni un Dieu créateur et sa créature, ni l'éloignement homme-nature que nous lisons dans la société moderne.

III. La réflexion grecque sur l'*eleutheria* maintient la liaison entre la vérité et la vertu, une paire que ne subsiste plus. Cette liaison a été relevée par les stoïciens à l'époque alexandrine et ce sont eux qui définitivement nous en parlent de plus près. Le souci-de-soi, très cher à M. Foucault (in 'Histoire de la sexualité') était déjà cher aux stoïciens. Prendre soin de soi-même signifie pour l'ancienne Stoa chercher son sol protecteur hors des institutions. C'est ainsi que, à une époque de désintégration des *póleis* et de désarticulation de l'empire alexandrin, cette philosophie pensera l'homme attaché à l'univers, son véritable et divin terrain protecteur, créateur de son être, tandis que les institutions historiques indiquent le règne de l'esclavage. Selon les fragments qui restent de la 'Politéia' de Zenon de Cícion, fondateur de la Stoa, on peut dire que l'histoire n'a jamais été ressentie aussi menaçante pour l'homme qu'elle ne l'a été pour lui. Pour Zenon, l'homme porte la cité dans son coeur et où qu'il aille, l'univers est avec lui, et les liens universeaux de la *philia* peuvent être mis en oeuvre et reconnus dans n'importe quel autre homme.

Le fait de reconnaître que tous les hommes sont égaux par nature revient à affirmer la notion d'appartenance cosmique selon le mode rationnel et divin de l'être humain et replace la liberté dans son premier sens d'appartenance, comme on l'a déjà vu, mais dans un autre cadre, le cadre philosophique: être libre c'est appartenir à l'univers et agir selon les règles qui sont inscrites dans chaque homme comme si sa nature était un *génons* amplifié, une fraternité universelle. C'est bien l'*autonomía* plus que l'*autharchèia*. Le Stoïcisme dans le sillage de l'Académie et du Lycée réaffirme la liberté intérieure mais à condition qu'elle se conforme à une nouvelle *physis* normative et divine, c'est à dire le pouvoir d'exercer le choix à travers la connaissance du tout. C'est dans cet espace possible de l'arbitre que s'installe, comme chez Aristote, le champ de l'Éthique.

Une maxime stoïcienne dit qu'il y a des choses qui dépendent de moi et il y en a qui ne dépendent pas de moi, et ce qui peut faire l'objet de l'exercice éthique se trouve dans la première affirmation. Être vertueux signifie exercer le *lógos*, se guider par les lois naturelles qui sont les lois rationnelles. C'est l'autonomie stoïcienne. Une telle lecture de la *physis* donne à la liberté une signification originale: être libre c'est suivre le *lógos*, et le suivre c'est vivre en accord avec lui. La soumission à la *physis* est pourtant une marque de la liberté. Apparemment paradoxale, cette réflexion laisse entendre que suivre le *lógos*, divin et ordonné, n'est pas une contrainte, bien au contraire, et sans doute cela a servi aux idées démocratiques fondées dans la représentativité. L'État Moderne, en soumettant, ne se soumet pas mais représente. Rousseau a été un bon lecteur des stoïciens.

Une fois de plus, on trouve dans les passions l'autre face de l'esclavage. Ce sont elles qui font irruption dans un va et vient incontrôlable, et comme

Platon, les stoïciens considèrent ce mouvement sans contrôle comme la négation d'être libre. Ce sont les passions sans contrôle qui desharmonisent l'homme dans le mouvement de l'ensemble en dérangeant le *lógos*. Une fois de plus ce sont elles qui peuvent menacer l'homme avec leur éventuelle démesure. Si la véritable identité humaine est une donation cosmique, les passions ont leur terrain préférentiel dans l'histoire, c'est à dire dans la variabilité inconrtournable des événements. Et pourtant commettre des erreurs de conformité avec le *lógos*, se laisser mener par les passions, c'est cela qui structure l'historicité; et les stoïciens le savent. L'histoire s'oppose à la nature car elle est le domaine des incorporels (comme on sait, le vide, le lieu, le temps et le *lékton*). Ce sont des presque-êtres qui se détachent de la réalité des corps, noyau original de la réflexion du Portique. Si les passions et la vie historique contraignent, et si la liberté se trouve en conformité avec l'univers, hors de l'histoire, alors c'est dans l'intériorité de chacun que se trouve le discernement des jugements, c'est dans le tremblement ou mouvement de l'âme de chaque individu, un tremblement non perçu de l'extérieur, que la liberté ou l'esclavage s'installent. Il n'y a pas de doute que la Stoa tient un langage très proche de la réflexion médiévale et moderne.

IV. En reprenant mes considérations, je dirais qu'il y a trois voies possibles pour traiter la question de l'*eleuthería*: a) la voie de la liberté comme appartenance éthnique; b) la voie de la liberté comme appartenance éthique; b) la voie de la connaissance de soi-même, dans la perspective de l'autarchéia, c'est à dire dans l'exposition de l'emploi du noyau dianoétique de l'âme; c) la voie de l'autonomie comme exposition d'une essence humaine qui provient d'une dogmatisation stoïcienne de la nature. Ces deux dernières voies ne sont pas totalement opposées à la première. Si les anciens grecs ont pris en considération dans leurs actions le poids inexorable du destin (*moira*), si le pouvoir contraignant des circonstances quotidiennes n'a pas été oublié, ni les déterminations organiques inconnues, comme le dit Aristote (in 'Éthique a Nicomaque', III), il reste un petit espace pour la liberté comme exercice de savoir-faire ouvert par la philosophie. Quelque éloignés que nous soyons apparemment de cette soigneuse et profonde réflexion, il ne me semble pas raisonnable d'employer le mot 'liberté' sans tenir compte de ses racines et ses significations possibles, toujours liées à ce que nous considérons comme menaçant, contraignant ou violent. Ce ne serait qu'un mot vide, répété comme une valeur indiscutable parce que personne n'oserait la nier sous peine de perdre l'identité avec son époque.

Finalement, que signifie être libre? Est-ce que c'est pouvoir aller et venir? Est-ce que c'est laisser fluer la force du désir, aujourd'hui canalisée vers les marchandises? Peut-être suivre ses propres principes de volonté rationnelle comme l'a voulu Kant en rappelant l'autonomie stoïcienne? Est-ce que c'est maintenir sa propre identité? Mais quelle serait cette identité? Identité personnelle, ou celle du groupe, de la famille de la nation? Peut-être que nous comprenons la liberté comme nous lisons le monde des végétaux, des animaux, considérés 'libres dans leur croissance', sans intervention humaine. Ou comme S. Freud, lecteur de Nietzsche, nous soutenons que la civilisation est une répression nécessaire, d'où cet incontournable malaise des civilisés? Une telle pensée n'est pas loin de la vieille matrice antagonique 'nature-culture'. Quelle que soit la réponse à toutes ces questions, la réflexion grecque reste pour nous un champ semé.

Il me semble que les philosophes grecs nous enseignent qu'il n'y a pas de liberté sans que son contraire soit signalé. Tantôtce sont les dieux, tantôt la vie imparfaite des hommes dans la domination sublunaire, tantôt les règles civilisatrices nécessaires, ou encore nos déterminations inconscientes. Tout ceci constitue le non-être de la liberté. Cette facette ne se détruit pas, on vit avec elle. Les philosophes grecs, amoureux de la mesure, diraient que l'*autarchéia* et l'autonomie sont des pouvoirs humains, indicateurs de la liberté de l'âme, indicateurs pourant être utilisés dans la recherche du bonheur. Et tout ceci dans la mesure du possible car comme il s'agit des êtres humains, il n'y a rien d'absolu. Sans l'optimisme dialectique de Hegel, les grecs ont signalé le poids du *theorein* dans le *prattein*. On ne serais pas en mauvaise posture en adoptant une telle indication.

Quelque soit le contenu qui change ou anime la notion de liberté que nous avons, il ne pourra pas être compris et effectué si nous savons théoriquement peu sur son contraire. Il faudra donc élaborer des théories, dans le sens grec du mot, ce qui n'implique pas s'éloigner de la *práxis*, bien au contraire, mais la rendre meilleure, face aux contraintes et aux empêchements. Enfin, la liberté est l'une de ces notions que le penser humain voudrait élire comme nucléaire, mais ne semble réussir à s'en approcher que par les bords.

PAUL RICHARD BLUM
Freie Universität Berlin
Germany

DER ORT DER FREIHEIT – ARGUMENTE AUS DER RENAISSANCE-PHILOSOPHIE

I. VORÜBERLEGUNGEN

Die Gedanken sind frei. Das ist ein großer Satz, den man gerne ausspricht. Er wendet sich gegen die Not der Unterdrückung der Gedanken und der Freiheit, zu handeln. Insofern ist es ein Satz, der immer zum Zweck der Negation einer Unfreiheit gesagt wird. Negativität ist der Kontext der Gedankenfreiheit. Sie negiert, sie protestiert gegen die Unterdrückung der generellen Freiheit. Die Gedankenfreiheit ist zumindest ein letztes Asyl der anderweitig bedrohten oder beschnittenen Freiheit. „Wir haben jetzt vollkommene Freiheit." Diese Aussage, gesprochen von einem tschechischen Philosophen Ende 1989, enthält daher folgende philosophischen Elemente:
 1. Es gibt vollkommene Freiheit.
 2. Freiheit kann eingeschränkt werden.
 3. Freiheit ist in der Zeit, jetzt, also etwa Ende 1989, realisierbar.
 4. Freiheit ist der Besitz eines Wir, Freiheit hat ein Subjekt, denn sie kann sogar von einem kollektiven Ich ausgesagt werden.

Freiheit ist nach diesen Vorüberlegungen ein Existenzial, eine Grundbestimmung eines Ich-sagenden Subjektes. Zugleich: als etwas, das man haben oder verlieren kann, und vor allem als etwas, das vollkommen sein kann, ist Freiheit ein Transzendentale. Denn zwischen «Freiheit haben» und «frei sein» kann man nicht unterscheiden, sofern Freiheit im «Frei-sein» liegt. Wie jedes Existenzial und jedes Transzendentale kann auch Freiheit in Defizienzmodi auftreten. Diese sind sogar der empirische Normalfall, denn sonst wären Metaphysik und Existenz ein Wissen und kein Forschungsthema. «Freiheit» ist folglich ein existenzphilosophisches und ein metaphysisches Thema. Das gilt auch für die Renaissance, die vielleicht eine Art Existenzphilosophie war, indem sie viele ethische und ontologische Themen aus der Referenz zum Menschen diskutiert hat, weshalb sie in vielen Aspekten auch als Humanismus bezeichnet wurde. Humanismus und Renaissance haben die Welt und den Menschen wiederentdeckt – diese Formel Jakob Burckhardts hat noch immer Sinn, denn das ist für Jean-Paul Sartre die Wahrheit des Humanismus: „der Mensch ist das Wesen, dessen Auftreten bewirkt, daß eine Welt existiert"[1]. Haben die Humanisten deshalb auch die Freiheit entdeckt? Von der Antike her wurde Freiheit immer als Handlungsfreiheit gedacht, diese wiederum als Willensfreiheit zwischen Alternativen, die grundsätzlich auf die ethischen Gegensätze «gut» und «böse» reduziert wurden. Dieses Gegensatzpaar wurde immer im Horizont des Transzendenten gedacht. Deshalb stand Wahlfreiheit als Handlungsfreiheit im Christentum – auch unter dem Einfluß Platons – im Angesicht der göttlichen Vorsehung: Gott kann die Freiheit aufheben oder bestätigen. Freiheit konnte daher auch heißen: Öffnung für die göttliche Offenbarung.

II. HINWENDUNGSFREIHEIT UND SPONTANFREIHEIT

Freiheit hat in der Tradition zwei Orte: den Menschen und Gott. Insofern der Mensch das Subjekt von Freiheit ist, bezeichnet sie seine existentielle Fähigkeit, aus sich heraus sich etwas zuzuwenden. Dies trägt den Namen «Willen». Die Willensfreiheit ist die typisch menschliche Freiheit. Es ist eine Hinwendungsfreiheit. Ihre Qualität richtet sich zunächst nach dem Ziel der Hinwendung und nach den Umständen. Die Einschränkung dieser Freiheit kommt von außen: es ist die äußere Einschränkung, gegen die die Gedankenfreiheit protestiert. Gebrauch, Mißbrauch oder Nichtgebrauch der Willensfreiheit mißt sich nach den Intentionen, d.h. nach den Absichten, nach den Objekten. Trotzdem denken wir den Willen als etwas dem Ichsagenden Subjekt Inneres. Dann aber sprechen wir von der Freiheit, deren eigentümlicher Ort Gott ist. Denn das wird an Ficino vor allem zu zeigen sein: Die Freiheit, die aus dem Wesen des freien Subjekts zu verstehen ist, hat die Struktur des Göttlichen:

> Jeder, der handelt, wird durch etwas anderes zum Tätigsein geführt, aber sie alle sind auf ein erstes Handelndes zurückzuführen, das in der Weise handelt, daß es sich selbst zum Handeln bringt, dermaßen, daß es sich selbst in seine Handlung verwandelt, und so, daß es erkennt und will, daß es tätig ist oder

---

[1] Jean-Paul Sartre: *Die cartesianische Freiheit*, in: Ders.: *Gesammelte Werke, Philosophische Schriften* I, 4, Reinbeck 1994, S. 99-116, hier: S. 116. Vgl. ebd. S. 117-155: *Der Existenzialismus ist ein Humanismus*. Auch wenn Sartre im Ansatz und Ergebnis atheistisch argumentiert, zeigt er doch, daß er die theologischen Implikationen der Freiheit genau kennt.

auch nicht, und dies wiederum so oder anders[2]. Was aber in dieser Weise aus Gott hervorgeht, geht bekanntlich aus freier Entscheidung hervor. Jeder Weise weiß allerdings, daß sich das Entscheiden bei Gott nicht vom Wesen unterscheidet[3].

Die göttliche Freiheit ist zwar auch eine Fähigkeit der Zuwendung oder Hinwendung, jedoch steht der Akzent nicht auf der Intentionalität oder gar der Richtung der Intention, sondern auf der Spontaneität. Das Aus-sich-heraus-frei-sein ist eine Form von Autonomie oder gar die Autonomie selbst[4]. Freiheit der Autonomie ist daher eine Spontanfreiheit im Unterschied zur Hinwendungsfreiheit. Ficino verwendet daher *voluntarium* und *spontaneum* als Hendiadyoin[5], weil willentliches Handeln immer aus einer Spontaneität hervorgeht. Angesichts der Kapazität, spontan zu sein, sind die Ziele indifferent, so wie die Geschöpfe in Relation zum Schöpfer als Schöpfer indifferent sind, sie haben grundsätzlich den gleichen Rang der Geschöpflichkeit und unterscheiden sich insofern gar nicht voneinander, obwohl sie gerade untereinander sehr wohl differenziert und wohl auch verschiedenrangig sind. Die Hinwendung des autonom freien Subjekts determiniert sich zunächst nicht aus dem Objekt, sondern aus der Spontaneität.

III. FREIHEIT, WOLLEN, WISSEN

Göttliche Freiheit interessiert den Menschen allerdings um des Menschen willen, so auch unter den Humanisten. Denn das ist Lorenzo Vallas Argument, mit dem er meint, Boethius zu schlagen: Boethius hatte in seiner *Consolatio Philosophiae* behauptet, Gottes Freiheit habe ihren Sinn in der göttlichen Allwissenheit, die überzeitlich sei und daher die Geschehnisse aller Zeiten zur Gegenwart habe[6]. Das ist nach Vallas Meinung ein abschlie-

---

[2] Soweit die allgemeine Struktur des Handelns!

[3] Marsilio Ficino, *Platonica Theologia de immortalitate animorum*, ed. Raymond Marcel, 3 Bde., Paris 1964-1970, zitiert nach Buch (römische Ziffern) und Kapitel (arabische Ziffern) sowie Band und Seite; hier: II 12, I S. 117: „agentia omnia quaecumque per aliud agunt ducunturque ad operandum, reducenda sunt ad agens primum, quod ita per se agat, ut seipsum ad agendum ducat, ergo ut in actionem suam penitus se convertat, ergo ut intelligat velitque operari aut non operari, rursusque ita vel aliter operari. Quae autem hoc modo proficiscuntur a Deo, nullus ignorat electione libera proficisci. Nullus tamen sapiens nescit electionem in Deo ab essentia non differe". – Alle Übersetzungen stammen, falls nicht anders vermerkt, von mir.

[4] „Autonomie" hat keine reflexive Konnotation, sondern meint die Ursprünglichkeit der Bestimmung der Akte im Handelnden. Vgl. R. Pohlmann, *Autonomie*, in: *Historisches Wörterbuch der Philosophie*, hg. v. Joachim Ritter u.a., Bd. 1, Basel 1971, Sp. 701-719.

[5] Ficino, *Platonica Theologia* II 12, I S. 114: maxime omnium voluntarium spontaneumque.

ßendes, philosophisch korrektes Urteil, das allerdings das Freiheitsproblem nicht löst, denn: „Wie kann ich hoffen, zur Erkenntnis der Einsicht und Ewigkeit zu kommen, der ich [als Mensch] vernunftbegabt bin und nichts außerhalb der Zeit kenne?"[7] Was nützt dem Menschen die Freiheit Gottes? Im Horizont des zeitlich und abhängig bestimmten Menschen entsteht immer dann Angst, die Freiheit des Menschen argumentativ zu verlieren, wenn die Konditionen der göttlichen Freiheit analysiert werden, weil der Mensch ihr unterstellt ist[8]. Die göttliche Spontanfreiheit, der gegenüber der menschliche Horizont beschränkt und abhängig erscheint, wird auch für Erasmus von Rotterdam zum Ernstfall der Freiheit des Menschen, nun allerdings der Freiheit überhaupt. In seiner Polemik gegen die Negation der Freiheit bei Luther und Karlstadt zeigt er, daß eine Bestreitung der Freiheit eines Christenmenschen die Freiheit überhaupt zerstören würde, auch die Denkbarkeit der Freiheit Gottes.

Die Gnadendiskussion[9] seit dem späten Mittelalter, derzufolge höchst komplexe Konstruktionen gemacht werden müssen, um im Rahmen der Vorsehung Gottes noch Freiraum für menschliches Handeln zu finden, führt entweder zum schlecht kaschierten Determinismus oder zur Rechtfertigung der göttlichen Freiheit aus der Freiheit des Menschen, spontan zu handeln. Lorenzo Valla hat die Antinomie dadurch verschärft, daß er hypothetisch einem Gott Apollo das Vorherwissen, das den Menschen zu determinieren scheint, und einem Gott Jupiter das Wollen, in dem Gottes Freiheit besteht, zuschrieb[10]. Auch Erasmus zeigt das Dilemma mittels der Verdoppelung der «Funktionen» Gottes: er zitiert die Unterscheidung Tertullians zwischen dem Gott des Alten Testaments, der für Gerechtigkeit (und Wollen) steht, und dem des Neuen Testaments, der für Gnade (weil vorher-

---

[6] Anicius Manlius Severinus Boethius: *Philosophiae consolationis* libri V, lib. 5, pr. 3: „Neque einim necesse esse contingere, quae povidentur, sed necesse esse, quae futura sunt, provideri, [...] necessarium esse eventum praescitarum rerum, etiam si praescientia futuris rebus eveniendi necessitatem non videatur inferre".

[7] Lorenzo Valla, *Über den freien Willen, De libero arbitrio*, lateinisch-deutsche Ausgabe, hg. und übers. von Eckhard Keßler, München 1987, mit der Seitenzählung der Ausgabe von Maria Anfossi, Florenz 1934, und der Paragraphenzählung der Ausgabe von Jacques Chomarat, Paris 1983; hier: S. 15, § 30 (Keßlers Übersetzung syntaktisch umgestellt).

[8] Erasmus von Rotterdam, *De libero arbitrio diatribe sive collatio*, in: Ders.: *Ausgewählte Schriften*, hg. v. Werner Welzig, Bd. 4, Darmstadt 1969, § I b 5, S. 28 f. polemisiert aus diesem und keinem anderen Grund gegen die zu enge Schriftauslegung: At ego iam homines confero cum hominibus, non homines cum deo. Vgl. §§ I b 7 und III a 17.

[9] Vgl. z.B. K. Reinhardt: *Gnadenstreit*, in: *Historisches Wörterbuch der Philosophie*, hg. v. Joachim Ritter u.a., Bd. 3, Basel 1974, Sp. 713 f.

[10] Lorenzo Valla, *De libero arbitrio*, S. 31 ff., §§ 67 ff. Vgl. Keßler in der Einleitung S. 48 f.

wissend) steht[11]. Aus der Spaltung der Subjekte geht scheinbar hervor, daß dem Menschen keinerlei Freiheit übrig bleibt. Allerdings gibt Valla schließlich zu, daß in Wirklichkeit (jedenfalls im Christentum) beide Potenzen in einem Gott vereinigt sind – und Erasmus nennt die Trennung von Gnade und Gerechtigkeit unfromm. Dann allerdings ist die Freiheit des Menschen zwar nicht beweisbar, aber immerhin möglich.

Wenn Gott alles restlos vorher weiß, stimmt er auch allem vorher zu: Gott kann nicht etwas nicht-wollen, von dessen Existenz er weiß, denn Gott weiß alles. Also will er auch alles. Falls es Böses gibt, will Gott auch Böses, oder andernfalls gibt es kein Böses. In jedem Falle kann folglich der Mensch entweder nichts Böses wollen oder aber dafür nicht verantwortlich sein: beides macht seine Freiheit zu einem leeren Wort. Wenn der Mensch nichts Böses wollen bzw. nicht schuldig sein kann, ist es belanglos, indifferent, ob er Gutes tun oder intendieren kann[12]. Deshalb nennt Erasmus die Spekulation um das göttliche Vorherwissen abseitig und überflüssig[13].

Die Frage bleibt dann nur noch, ob der Mensch überhaupt etwas aus sich heraus intendieren kann. Das läßt sich an Gott sozusagen beobachten. Denn alle Konstruktionen, die die Freiheit retten wollen, und sei es auch nur um des Beweises der Sündhaftigkeit des Menschen willen, operieren damit, daß sie das Wissen und Wollen Gottes differenzieren. Das Wollen geht dem zustimmenden Wissen voraus, während zugleich das wissende Urteil über eine Handlung vorübergehend die Augen verschließt, um Gelegenheit zur Sünde oder zur Heilstat zu geben, die – im Rahmen der Heilsordnung – als Handlung[14] für seiend, wirklich und gut gilt, gleichwertig ob sie moralisch und für das frei handelnde Subjekt gut oder böse ist. Die zeitlichen Kategorien in dieser Beschreibung sind vollkommen unangemessen, sofern sie sich auf Gott beziehen. Sie beschreiben aber exakt die Perspektive des Menschen. Deshalb betont Erasmus, daß in der Heilgeschichte der sündhafte Wille des Menschen vorausgeht, wenn Gott ihn seiner verwerflichen Gesinnung überläßt. „Wo aber reine und ewige Notwendigkeit ist, da kann weder Verdienst noch Schuld sein."[15] Gott ist der Ernstfall. Wenn Wollen und Wissen in Gott zu Antinomien führen, dann beschreiben sie um so exakter die Struktur des menschlichen Handelns. Gott müßte das Wissen abschalten, wenn er Böses zulassen würde. Die Eklipse der Vernunft gebiert die Dämonen. Richtiges willentliches Handeln wendet sich demnach dem

---

[11] Erasmus, *De libero arbitrio*, § IV 7, S. 168.
[12] Erasmus, *De libero arbitrio*, § IV 4, S. 164.
[13] Erasmus, *De libero arbitrio*, § I a 8, S. 12.
[14] Erasmus, *De libero arbitrio*, § III a 10.
[15] Erasmus, *De libero arbitrio*, § III a 10. (Übersetzung: Erasmus von Rotterdam, *Vom freien Willen*, übers. v. Otto Schumacher, Göttingen 1956, S. 52.)

richtig vorgestellten Objekt zu. Folglich handelt der Mensch – sofern er überhaupt frei handelt – durch Wissen seines Zieles. Andererseits sind Wollen und Wissen in Gott konvergent: Vallas Experiment mit den zwei Göttern hat bewiesen, daß dann nur Freiheit zum Bösen übrig bleibt. Freiheit beruht also umgekehrt auf dem Zusammenspiel von Willen und Weisheit.

Dem allgegenwärtigen Wissen Gottes entspricht in der zeitlichen Erstreckung der humanen Perspektive der beständige Drang zur Suche nach Wissen. Dieser Drang kann aber nicht mehr selbst durch Wissen, durch Objekte oder Ziele gesteuert sein. Die Indifferenz der Objekte gegenüber dem existentiellen Wollenkönnen des Menschen beschreibt die autonome Spontaneität des Wollens. Wenn (zwecks Theodizee) der göttliche Wille von seinem Vorherwissen absehen soll, heißt das nichts anderes, als Gott ein spontanes und nicht vom Objekt gelocktes Wollen zuschreiben. Da dies um der Theodizee willen, der Rechtfertigung der Freiheit des Menschen zum Bösen, geschieht, können wir das leicht in die Spontanfreiheit des autonomen Menschen übersetzen. Wenn der Mensch nicht autonom frei wäre, wäre Gott an sein Vorherwissen gebunden – und folglich selbst unfrei – nichts würde geschehen, was in Gott nicht schon vorherbestimmt ist. Gott selbst hätte keine Alternativen. Die von Gott gewollte und gewußte Freiheit des Menschen eröffnet paradoxerweise Lücken in der scheinbaren Prädetermination Gottes, die Gott sozusagen Gelegenheit geben, frei zu handeln, nämlich – und darin sind sich alle Freiheitstheologen der Reformationszeit einig – durch Gnade.

Das Existenzial Freiheit hat einen Aspekt der Hinwendung und einen Aspekt des autonomen Hervorgangs. Es hat sein Ideal in einer göttlichen Freiheit, deren Defizienzmodus die menschliche Freiheit ist. Die göttliche Freiheit erweist zudem aber Freiheit als ein Transzendentale, das ohne Schwierigkeiten mit dem Guten, Wahren, Einen und Seienden konvergiert, soweit das menschlich möglich ist: *Libertas est appetiblilis tanquam bonum*[16]. Insofern «gut», «wahr», «eins» und «seiend» verschiedenen transzendenten Akten zuzuordnen sind, die in Gott materialiter ununterschieden sind, gehört «frei» unvermittelt dazu. Denn nach Ficino fehlt Freiheit genau da, wo *esse, intelligere* und *velle* der Sache nach auseinander gehen. In Gott konvergieren sie mit Gottes Freiheit[17].

---

[16] Ficino, *Platonica Theologia* II 12, I S. 113.

[17] Ficino, *Platonica Theologia* II 12, I S. 114: „In quibus tria haec, scilicet esse, interelligere, velle, re ipsa inter se discrebant, in iis non est absoluta libertas. Vgl. II 11, I S. 106: Quidquid libertatis bonique esse potest usquam, id totum per summi principis bonique potentiam esse potest. Ebd. p. 110: quis divinum intellectum negabit praesens bonum suum, quod est omne bonum, per voulntatem libenter amplecti? [...] in sua bonitate vult bona omnia, quae et ipsius propagatione nascuntur [...]".

IV. AUS SICH HERAUSGEHEN

Die Vorfrage nach der Freiheit des Menschen ist die, wie es dem Menschen möglich ist, aus sich herauszugehen. Dies wird in der Regel als Lebensvollzug, als spezifisch menschliches Sein verstanden. Marsilio Ficino favorisiert hierfür die Metapher der Liebe[18]. Die zwischenmenschliche Liebe besteht im Austausch der Seelen der Liebenden, die sich selbst jeweils im anderen finden. Liebe ist für Ficino ein durch den anderen geläuterter Selbstbezug. Das Selbst konstituiert sich im Vollzug des Geliebtwerdens vom anderen her. Die Liebenden schaffen in der Wechselseitigkeit des Aus-sich-heraus-Tretens und des Sich-Findens eine Identität des Transzendierens. Diese Identität, also das ontologische Sich-beziehen-Können, das beiden gemeinsam ist, ist beiden auch transzendent. Der Selbstbezug der Liebe zum anderen ist in einer höheren Einheit aufgehoben, im wahren Sein des Menschen.

Insofern ist Ficinos Liebesphilosophie eine Lebensphilosophie: Menschliches Leben als ein menschliches existiert im transzendierenden Bezug. Kaum nötig zu sagen, daß dieser Lebensvollzug in der Liebe zu Gott und von Gott zum Menschen seine Vollendung findet. Nur im Transzendieren des Solipsismus lebt also der Mensch (als Mensch, muß man immer hinzufügen, damit die animalische Seinsweise ebenso ausgeschlossen ist, wie die engelhafte der erlösten Seele).

Um nun den ontologischen Status der Freiheit zu verstehen, ist es notwendig zu sehen, daß der *actus essendi* des Seienden als Seienden, wie er in der aristotelischen Philosophie gedacht wird, mit den Augen eines Renaissancephilosophen nach Analogie der humanen Seinsweise gedacht zu sein scheint. Der *actus* jedes Seienden ist ein Akt nach Analogie des menschlichen Lebens und Handelns. Existieren bedeutet für nichtbewußte Dinge die Zeitlichkeit des Seins. Diese Zeitlichkeit kann bei nichtbewußten Dingen nur von außen «gesehen» werden, nämlich von einem beobachtenden, zeitbewußten und urteilenden Bewußtsein. Der Seinsvollzug eines Dinges ist nur dann als Vollzug zu denken, wenn ein «vorher» oder «nachher» anzunehmen ist. Solange es solch eine zeitliche Begrenzung nicht gibt, gibt es auch keinen Bedarf an zeitlicher Bestimmung. Dann ist das Ding zeitlos. Es existiert nicht temporal, sondern ist in der Seinsweise des zeitlosen und fraglosen Seins. Es existiert ohne einen Vektor, ohne Herkunft, ohne Ziel – es sei denn, eine Beziehung würde von einem urteilenden Verstand oder auch

---

[18] Marsilio Ficino, *Über die Liebe oder Platons Gastmahl*, lat.-dt., übers. v. Karl Paul Hasse, hg. v. Paul Richard Blum, Hamburg 1994. Hierzu: Paul Richard Blum, *Selbstbezug und Transzendenz in der Renaissancephilosophie*, in: *Rationalität und Innerlichkeit*, hg. v. Peter Schulz und Horst Seidl (im Druck).

von einem emotionalen Empfinden hergestellt, etwa von der Art: «Dies dient zu jenem», oder: «Das ist hier, weil jenes da ist, oder ein anderes fehlt.» Dann kann das Vorhandensein zeitlich und vollziehend verstanden werden. Aber eine kritische Analyse wird dann immer die Zeitlichkeit des Seienden als Produkt oder Funktion des diskursiven Verstandes entlarven.

Die Zeitlichkeit wird allerdings auch unter gewissen Bedingungen den Dingen selbst zugestanden, etwa das Stürzen einer Lawine, weil das Wissen sich aus Gründen der immanenten Folgerichtigkeit gegen den kritischen Einwand wehrt, die Prozessualität[19] allein im Denken begründet oder gar verursacht zu denken.

An dieser Stelle melden sich die Lebewesen zu Wort: die selbstbewegte Natur des Aristoteles. Sie ist Vollzug an sich. Zwar geht das, was ist, definitorisch nicht aus sich heraus, und doch ist das lebendige Naturding gerade durch die Extreme bedingt, nämlich das «noch nicht» und das «woraufhin» des natürlichen Ablaufes; dieser ist sowohl natürlich – d.h. hier ontologisch und nicht gnoseologisch bestimmt – als auch prozessual und insofern indeterminiert zeitlich.

Angenommen, die so skizzierte Ontologie des Lebendigen ist zutreffend (d.h. sie wird vorkritisch verstanden und soll philosophisch Geltung behalten), dann verweist das lebendige Seiende schon selbst aus sich heraus auf das, was es selbst nicht ist. Und das, obwohl es (unter den geltenden Annahmen) weder ein Selbst eines potentiellen Selbstbezugs ist noch eine deiktische Funktion hat.

Wenn also schon der peripatetische Begriff des Seins ein Moment der Zeitlichkeit in den Seinsakt verlegt, so sieht man am aristotelischen Original des Seinsbegriffs als Vollzug des Lebendigen, daß eine Verweisung vom Seienden aus dem Seienden heraus eine ontologische Grundbestimmung ist. Die kritische Analyse wird sofort konstatieren, daß dies die Leistung eines ordnenden und urteilenden Bewußtseins ist. Aber selbst in strenger Ontologie wird ein Moment des Aus-sich-heraus gedacht. Um wieviel mehr ist es dann eine wesentliche Eigenschaft des Bewußtseins. Der kritische Einwand gegen eine teleologische Ontologie des Seienden als in Bewegung Seienden macht den Geist zum Ort des Strebens und folglich der Freiheit.

V. IMMANENZ DER ALTERNATIVEN

Geistiges Streben hat im Unterschied zu natürlichen Prozessen besondere Qualitäten, damit es den Charakter der Spontaneität hat. Dazu gehören

---

[19] «Prozessualität» wird hier im Sinne von Hans Wagner verwendet, der damit «kinesis» bei Aristoteles übersetzt: Aristoteles, *Physikvorlesung*, übers. von Hans Wagner, Berlin 1967.

die Alternativen der Ziele oder Objekte. Prozessual gedachtes Seiendes kann trotz des Bewegungsmomentes nicht wirklich auch etwas ganz anderes sein als es ist. Die Kontingenz liegt im Täter oder Schöpfer, nicht in der Tat oder im Geschaffenen, wenn es erst einmal «da» ist. Der Freiheit eignet die Alternative essentiell, nicht als verwirklichte, sondern als immanente Option[20]. *Post festum* läßt sich diese Alternative z.B. als Reue konstatieren. Tiere haben keine Reue, stellt Ficino fest. Das animalische Leben besteht zwar in einem immanenten Prinzip der Aktivität, aber ein konkurrierendes Prinzip ist nicht eingebaut, so daß es für den Lebensakt des Tieres nur ein einziges Ziel gibt. Nachträgliches Bedenken (*retractare*) ist ausgeschlossen[21]. Das bloß ungehinderte Ausführen des animalischen Aktes (*libertas a coactione*, wie Roberto Bellarmino es nennt) ist noch keine Freiheit[22]. Reue, nachträgliches Bedenken, darf natürlich nicht als bloßes Ressentiment verachtet werden. Wenn sie geeignet sein soll, über vergangene Taten zu urteilen, muß sie die Taten derart betrachten, daß sie auch wirklich hätten anders geschehen können. Dies geht so weit, daß im christlichem Bußsakrament die Reue dazu beiträgt, eine Tat moralisch sozusagen „ungeschehen" zu machen. Wäre jedes Ereignis im Nachhinein durch die faktischen Ursachen definitiv determiniert, hätten Reue und Bedenken nur emotionalen Sinn. Wenn aber Reue als humanes Denken möglich ist, markiert sie nachträglich den Ort der Freiheit im Akt des Entscheidens für eine bestimmte von wenigstens zwei Möglichkeiten – selbst wenn diese erst nachträglich als solche erkannt werden. Gerade die moralischen Bedenken umschreiben also noch einmal die offene Struktur freien Handelns, sie öffnen geschehene Taten, als wären sie nicht abgeschlossen, sondern eben frei. Das Freiheitsmoment an einer Handlung wird durch Retraktation als essentiell unzeitlich erwiesen, die Handlung selbst dagegen als Prozeß, der aus dem offenen Anfang heraus in die Geschichte geht.

Die Aktivität der animalischen Bewegung bleibt in einem gewissen Sinne immanent, weil sie auf das Ganze des Lebensvollzugs gesehen nicht wirklich «aus sich heraus» geht. Falls man überhaupt von einem Innen und Außen

---

[20] Karol Wojtyla: *The Acting Person*. Dordrecht 1979, S. 100: „Between the «I may» on the one hand, on the other, the «I need not» the human «I want» is formed, and it constitutes the dynamism proper to will". – Der Autor war bei Erscheinen des Buches inzwischen Papst Johannes Paul II.

[21] Ficino, *Platonica Theologia* IX 4, II S. 22.

[22] *Disputationes Roberti Bellarmini de controversiis christianae fidei*, 3 Bde., Bd. 3: Ingolstadt (Sartorius) 1596, controv. 3 generalis, controv. 1 principalis: *De gratia et libero arbitrio*, lib. 3, cap. 5, p. 656 C: „si ad liberum arbitrium constituendum sufficeret libertas a coactione, sequeretur etiam in pecoribus esse liberum arbitrium. Nam et illa sine coactione ulla sponte sua feruntur ad pabulum".

bei animalischen Aktivitäten sprechen darf, dann nach einem Reiz-Reaktions-Mechanismus, dessen Bewegungsprinzip im Körper liegt und von außen, etwa vom Futter-Reiz, angelassen wird. Eine Bewegung «aus sich heraus» im strengen Sinne gibt es nach Ficino bei Tieren nicht[23].

Umgekehrt ist für die freie Bewegung konstitutiv, daß sie aus dem Ursprungsort «heraus» geht, und das bedeutet, daß ihr die Alternative, das Sich-auch-anders-verhalten-Können immanent sein muß. Eine Mehrzahl von Alternativen erzeugt erst dann Freiheit, wenn sie nicht bloß untereinander gleichwertig sind, sondern für den, der wählt. Deshalb müssen die Alternativen im Wählenden selbst wirklich sein. Lorenzo Valla sagt daher, daß im göttlichen Vorherwissen nicht nur die tatsächlich eingetretenen Ereignisse enthalten sind, sondern auch die unterbliebenen. In der Freiheit sind nämlich alle Möglichkeiten wirkliche Möglichkeiten, obwohl sie *post festum* in bloße Optionen und Fakten unterschieden werden. Im göttlichen Vorherwissen ist die Freiheit in der Form gewahrt, daß alle Alternativen ontologisch gleichermaßen wahr sind[24].

Die Gleichheit der Alternativen ist immanent gesehen eine absolute Gleichheit; von außen gesehen, d.h. mit dem Bewußtsein der Prozessualität der Durchführung, handelt es sich um eine Gleichheit der Indifferenz. Denn vor dem Forum des intellektuellen Urteils sind die Alternativen zwar verschieden, die Urteilskraft ebenso wie die Prozessualität der Durchführung aber sind identisch indifferent jeweils eine[25]. Die Freiheit des Menschen äußert sich nicht zuerst im Handeln, sondern im Entschluß dazu; die Vielfalt der Handlungsweisen manifestiert die Nichtvorherbestimmtheit des prinzipiellen Handelnkönnens[26]. Derlei Indifferenz der Möglichkeiten untereinander wird dadurch aufgehoben, daß der Intellekt sie unter dem Gesichtspunkt der Realisation betrachtet.

Die Betrachtung der Realisation ist aber vor allem eine praktische Überlegung, und in diesem Sinne hat Ernst Tugendhat richtig beobachtet, daß alternative Möglichkeiten des Handelns im Überlegen verfügbar sein müssen und vom schlichten Überlegenwollen abhängen. Andererseits erschöpfen sich die Alternativen, die man meint, wenn jemand hätte anders handeln können, als er in Wirklichkeit tat, nicht in psychologischen, praktischen und

---

[23] Ficino, *Platonica Theologia* IX 4, II S. 21.
[24] Valla, *De libero arbitrio*, S. 28, § 61: „Nam quid obstat, haec simul vera esse? num quia potest aliter evenire continuo eveniat? [...]" S. 29, § 62: „Quare rata est praescientia, remanente arbitrii libertate".
[25] Ficino, *Platonica Theologia*, IX 4, II S. 19: „Itaque iudicium de rebus agendis non est natura sua ad aliquid unum determinatum. Est igitur liberum".
[26] Ficino, *Platonica Theologia*, IX 4, II S. 25: „Electiones autem hominis diversis viis tendunt ad finem tam in moribus quam in artificiis".

technischen Gegebenheiten. Freiheit besteht nicht darin, daß ein Geiger nur „frei" ist zu geigen, wenn er zunächst ein Instrument besitzt und geübt hat und schließlich auch noch will (so das Beispiel bei Tugendhat). Die Alternativen verbleiben sonst in der Betrachtung und Beurteilung von außen und *post festum* (aber ohne daß Reue mitspielte), ohne daß die handelnde Person selbst einbezogen wäre, denn nach Tugendhat werden Handlungen als Ereignisse ausschließlich von je anderen Ereignissen verursacht, nicht aber von einer Person, zumal es „nicht hinter dem natürlichen Geschehen eine solche Entität, genannt «die Person selbst», gibt"[27].

Die Natur des Menschen besteht auch in der Variabilität der Handlungen, die ihrerseits aus der Interaktion mit den Mitteln und Zielen und aus seiner Lernfähigkeit resultiert. Der Mensch geht mit sich zu Rate, bevor er agiert[28]. Dann ordnen sich die Alternativen, und es vergeht Zeit. Darin sieht Ficino den prinzipiellen Unterschied zwischen animalischem Handeln und freiem menschlichem Handeln, es vollzieht sich mit zeitlich gestreckter Überlegung[29]. Das menschliche Bewegungsprinzip hat ganz andere Qualität als die Tierseele, es ist die spezifisch menschliche Lebensform, die allen menschlichen Aktivitäten vorausliegt und ihnen gemeinsam ist. Die spezifisch menschliche Freiheit des Handelns besteht in der Indifferenz der Spontaneität gegenüber den Zielen. „Wir sind nicht auf eine einzige Aktionsweise beschränkt, sondern frei durchlaufen wir sie alle"[30]. Gegensätzliche Handlungen haben ihren Grund nicht exklusiv in abweichenden Umständen oder Zielen, sondern in der Freiheit der Spontaneität. Das geht nach Ficino so weit, daß wir beim Überlegen der Handlungsalternativen nicht uns (unsere Seele) den Umständen, sondern diese uns unterstellen[31].

Das distanzierende, in seinem Vermögen indifferente Urteil beweist die gleiche Distanz zur Vielfalt möglicher Handlungsalternativen wie die Spontaneität[32]. Trotzdem – wie an dem Vergleich mit den Tieren abzulesen – hat

---

[27] Ernst Tugendhat: *Der Begriff der Willensfreiheit*, in: *Theorie der Subjektivität*, hg. v. Konrad Kramer u.a., Frankfurt 1987, S. 373-393; hier zitiert nach: Ernst Tugendhat: *Philosophische Aufsätze*, Frankfurt 1992, S. 334-351, Zitat S. 342.

[28] Ficino, *Platonica Theologia*, IX 4, II S. 19: „Homines autem discunt, et opera sua variant semper: unam tamen et ab initio naturam habent".

[29] Ficino, *Platonica Theologia*, IX 4, II S. 22: „expergefacta et intenta ratione, consultamus in rebus agendis diu [...]".

[30] Ficino, *Platonica Theologia*, IX 4, II S. 23: „Ideo non uni agendi modo adstringimur, sed per omnes libere pervagamur".

[31] Ficino, *Platonica Theologia*, IX 4, II S. 23: „etiam dum corporalia manent similia, variae contrariaeque quodammodo fiunt electiones. Consultatione namque fit, ut non animam rebus, sed res animae nostrae subiiciamus".

[32] Ficino, *Platonica Theologia*, IX 4, II S. 19: „Itaque iudicium de rebus agendis non est natura sua ad aliquid unum determinatum. Est igitur liberum. [...] Cum igitur homo iudicium de rebus agendis non habeat a natura ad unum detrminatum, est necessario liber".

Freiheit nicht allein oder spezifisch den Intellekt oder das Urteilsvermögen zum Aktionsfeld, sondern die Potenz, aus sich heraus zu etwas zu streben, das gegenüber der Potenz gleichberechtigt möglich ist. Die Fähigkeit zu irren beweist, daß Freiheit nicht vom Intellekt abhängt, sonst wäre ja jede irrige Handlung *per se* unfrei. Vielmehr liegt die Freiheit dem Denken ontologisch voraus[33].

VI. MACHT ÜBER SICH HINAUS

Die Kategorie des «Aus-sich-heraus» muß betont und analysiert werden, weil sie jenseits der Diskussion um Wissen und Wollen, um Determinismus und Autonomie, vor allem auch jenseits des Gegensatzpaares von Freiheit und Gehorsam, die elementare Spannung im Freiheitsbegriff ausdrückt: das Potential, aus dem eigenen Selbst heraus nach außen zu wirken. Das manifestiert sich in Handlungen, die – sofern sie das Attribut «frei» verdienen sollen – aus nichts als dem inneren Selbst des Freien begründet sein sollen, was immer auch sonst noch an mitwirkenden Quellen und Umständen gegeben sein mag. Freie Handlungen sind nicht selbst Freiheit, sondern deren vollziehender Ausdruck. Freiheit liegt nach Karol Wojtyla den genuin menschlichen Akten voraus, und zwar genau insofern, als sie den Akten der menschlichen Person „efficacy" (Wirkmacht) gibt. Die Freiheit trennt die Tat vom Erlebnis, sie macht das Subjekt, das sich zu seinen Erlebnissen, Meinungen und Erfahrungen positiv (zustimmend) oder negativ verhalten kann, zu einer Person[34]. Sartre sagt: „Wirklichkeit ist nur im Handeln; (...) der Mensch ist nichts anderes als sein Entwurf, er existiert nur in dem Maße, in dem er sich verwirklicht"; dermaßen, daß „eine freie Tat eine absolut neue Schöpfung ist, (...) und daß Freiheit und Schöpfung eins sind"[35]. Damit radikalisiert er eine christliche Theorie der Spontanfreiheit mittels vorsätzlicher Eliminierung eines transenzenten Schöpfungsbegriffs. Beide Autoren wenden sich mit ihrer Philosophie gegen einen sozusagen quietistischen Begriff von Freiheit. Die spontane Richtung des freien Aktes, das „besondere Wort des Willens im engeren Sinne ist: «Du sollst existieren und wirst durch mich existieren»"[36].

---

[33] Ficino, *Platonica Theologia*, IX 4, II S. 19: „Homo vero a suo [intellectu], qui errare potest, ducitur [...]". Quod autem iudicet libere, ex eo coniicimus quod seipsum ducit ad iudicandum.

[34] Karol Wojtyla, *The Acting Person*, Dordrecht 1979, S. 100.

[35] Jean-Paul Sartre, *Der Existentialismus ist ein Humanismus* (wie Anm. 1), S. 130; und Ders.: Die cartesianische Freiheit, (wie Anm. 1), S. 114 f.

[36] Dietrich von Hildebrand, *Moralia*, Regensburg 1980 (*Gesammelte Werke* 9), S. 73.

Das «Aus-sich-heraus» der Freiheit bezeichnet die Macht, essentiell über sich selbst hinaus zu streben und seinen Bereich ontologischer Kompetenz zu erweitern. Freiheit ist eine Macht des Ich über sich hinaus. In dem traditionellen Gegensatz von «Freiheit von» und «Freiheit für» wird die Beeinflussung von außen abgewehrt und die Kompetenzerweiterung auf etwas außerhalb liegendes zugleich beansprucht.

Die stoische Freiheitsphilosophie dagegen reduziert Freiheit auf die Beurteilung des spezifisch menschlichen Bereichs dessen, «was in unserer Macht liegt», und bestätigt den Sinn des «Aus-sich-heraus» negativ. Wir sollen uns nach Meinung Epiktets von all dem frei machen, das von außen auf uns einwirken könnte. Zugleich sollen wir den Machtbereich so abstecken, daß jedes Handeln dadurch zum Ziel kommt, daß das Ziel in Reichweite des Selbst definiert bleibt. Da in dieser Vision das Wirken aus sich heraus nur noch in der Schwundform des Verzichtes vorkommt[37], richtet sich der elementare Freiheitsakt nur auf (oder sogar gegen) den Freien selbst: jeder soll sich selbst so belauern, als sei er sein hinterlistiger Feind[38]. Der stoische Weise ist in der Art frei, daß er auf sich selbst wie auf einen anderen wirkt.

Auch die lutherische Freiheit eines Christenmenschen kann wie eine Ableitung der Spontanfreiheit gelesen werden. Luther unterscheidet zwischen dem „inwendigen geistlichen Menschen" und dem „äußerlichen" bzw. „leiblichen" Menschen[39]. Indem er behauptet, der geistliche Mensch, die Seele, sei „über allen Dingen und niemandem untertan"[40], der äußerliche Mensch dagegen „ein dienstbarer Knecht aller Dinge und jedermann untertan", steckt er den Machtbereich menschlicher Aktivität ab: die weltlichen Dinge liegen nicht in seiner Macht, und sein Freiheitsstreben sollte nicht versuchen, sich auf sie auszudehnen. Im irdischen Bereich – das ist Luthers wortreiche Antwort auf Erasmus – ist alle Freiheit dadurch, daß Gott „omnia incommutabili et aeterna infallibilique voluntate et praesidet et proponit et facit", wie mit einem Blitz erschlagen[41].

Statt auf das Tun soll der Mensch seine Kompetenz auf den geistlichen Bereich ausdehnen. Dadurch werden alle dem Menschen zur Verfügung ste-

---

[37] Epiktet, *Diatriben* IV, 1: Freiheit „durch Abschaffung des Begehrens" (Epiktet, *Was von ihm erhalten ist*, übers. von J. G. Schulthess, bearb. von R. Mücke, Heidelberg o.J. (1926), S. 284.)

[38] Epiktet, *Enchiridion*, Kap. 48.

[39] Martin Luther, *Von der Freyheyt eynisz Christen menschen*, in: Martin Luther: *Werke* (Weimarer Lutherausgabe) Bd. 7, S. 20-38; hier zitiert nach: Martin Luther, *Von der Freyheyt eyniß Christen menschen*, Wittenberg 1520, Reprint München o.J., §§ 2 und 3. (Orthographie von mir modernisiert.)

[40] Luther, *Freiheit* § 1.

[41] Martin Luther, *De servo arbitrio*, in: Ders.: *Werke* (Weimarer Ausgabe), Bd. 18, Weimar 1908, S. 600-787, hier: S. 615.

henden weltlichen Mittel gegenüber der inneren Freiheit indifferent. Seine Freiheit besteht also nicht nur in der Neutralität der Aktionen gegenüber dem Handlungsimpuls, vielmehr degradiert sie alle Aktionen. Als Spontanimpuls christlicher Freiheit identifiziert Luther den Glauben. Alle menschlichen Werke werden durch ihn indifferent, und irdische Beschränkungen der Freiheit verlieren an Verbindlichkeit. Wer das beobachtet und mit dem stoischen Verzicht auf Wirkung nach außen verbindet, ist der späthumanistische Enzyklopädiker Laurentius Beyerlinck[42]. Der Christ wendet seinen Impuls, seine Kompetenz über sich selbst hinaus auf Christus[43]. Durch stoischen Verzicht auf materielle Macht wird „ein Christenmensch durch den Glauben so hoch erhaben über allen Dingen, daß er geistlich ein Herr aller Dinge wird, denn kein Ding kann ihm zur Seligkeit schaden"[44]. Sodann erkennt er, „warum Christus gekommen ist, wie man ihn brauchen und nutzen soll, was er mir gebracht und gegeben hat, nämlich – richtig ausgelegt – die christliche Freiheit, die wir von ihm haben, und wie wir Könige und Priester sind, aller Dinge mächtig"[45].

Da in der lutherischen Variante die Außenwelt nach dualistischem Muster negativ belegt wird, erscheint das Agierenwollen dort ebenfalls negativ. Freiheit darf sich folglich nicht als Herrschenwollen in dieser Welt manifestieren: das würde nämlich als Zugeständnis gegenüber dem Naturgesetz ausgelegt. Die Ausrichtung des Freiheitsimpulses auf Christus dagegen garantiert Herrschaft über die Dinge in Form von Weltverachtung und zugleich Einstimmung auf das Gesetz Christi: König und Priester zu sein mit Christus. An diesem Punkte macht sich der Christ zum Subjekt der Freiheit Christi, deshalb ist im lutherischen Sinne die Freiheit des Christenmenschen von der Gnade Gottes in der Sache nicht zu unterscheiden.

Die katholische polemische Theologie hat aus der protestantischen Abwertung äußerer Werke und der deklarierten Unverbindlichkeit von Gesetzgebung jeder Art vor dem inneren Menschen die Entstehung des Libertinismus abgeleitet[46]. Die Libertiner lehnten schließlich auch das Offenbarungs-

---

[42] Laurentius Beyerlinck, *Theatrum vitae humanae* [...], Lyon 1665/66, 8 Bde.; hier Bd. 4, littera L, S. 151 G: „Haereticorum recentiorum [Luther und Calvin] sententia est, Libertatem Christianam [...] in eo constitui, quod homo iustus immunis sit a debito legis divinae implendae coram Deo, si ut omnia opera illius sint indifferentia neque praecepta, neque vetita. [...] Denique in eo, ut rerum externarum usus habeatur pro indifferenti, easque omittere possit".

[43] Luther, *Freiheit* § 12.

[44] Luther, *Freiheit* § 15.

[45] Luther, *Freiheit* § 18.

[46] So schon Tommaso Campanella, *Atheismus triumphatus*, Rom 1631, Paris 1636; seine Definition der „machiavellisti, liberini e calvinisti" zitiert bei Giorgio Spini: *Ricerca dei libertini*, 2. Aufl. Florenz 1983, S. 84, mit der Vermischung von Religionskritik (nullam credunt esse religionem, Deum non esse), Selbstermächtigung (unumquemque debere seipsum

gesetz ab und wollten, daß der Mensch von jedem Gesetz frei sei und nur noch vom eigenen inneren Geiste geleitet werde, so jedenfalls der zitierte Beyerlinck[47]. Daran ist philosophisch richtig, daß das innere Diktat der Ort der Freiheit ist; der systematische Fehler liegt darin, daß die gegenüber der Freiheit geltende Indifferenz der Objekte und Umstände für deren Ungültigkeit und Unverbindlichkeit gehalten wird.

Die Einwirkung des Anderen oder Äußeren auf das Selbst oder zumindest dessen Widerständlichkeit wird als Notwendigkeit gedacht. Deshalb ist Freiheit als «Freiheit von» zunächst nur die Negation des äußeren Zwangs, und in diesem Sinne sind die Gedanken des Stoikers frei. Die meisten Bestimmungen der Freiheit als *sui ipsius imperare*[48], als Selbstbeherrschung unter Verachtung äußerer Zwänge, sind daher eine Rückwendung der ursprünglichen Außenkompetenz nach innen. So heißt es bei Horaz vom Sklaven:

> Fortis, et in se ipse totus teres atque rotundus,
> Externi ne quid valeat per laeve morari [...][49].

Die in sich ruhende Freiheit des Weisen ist doch nur die Freiheit des Sklaven[50], dem Horaz ironisch zuruft:

> ... Eripe turpi
> Colla iugo. Liber, liber sum, dic, age. Non quis [...][51].

Wer das Haupt aus dem Sklavenjoch erhebt und ruft: „Ich bin frei!" kann noch lange nicht frei handeln. Das hatte auch der anfangs zitierte tschechische Professor erfahren.

VII. AN DER SPITZE DER NOTWENDIGKEITEN

Positiv dagegen ist Freiheit so zu beschreiben, daß der Freie selbst Prinzip einer Notwendigkeit ist, die grundsätzlich sich nach außen richtet. Zwar

---

exaltare quot potest), Negation der Sünde unter der Voraussetzung der Existenz eines wirkenden Gottes, und Hedonimus (omnibus mundi perfrui voluptatibus).

[47] Laurentius Beyerlinck, *Theatrum vitae humanae*, Bd. 4, littera L, S. 152 D: „Libertini [...] solo [...] spiritu interno dictante, nos regi volunt: hominemque liberum a lege, sic ut nulla illius transgressione peccare possit, statuunt, omnesque humanas leges abolent, tanquam non obligatorias, et inanes".

[48] Pythagoras lt. Beyerlinck, *Theatrum*, Bd. 4, littera L, S. 132 H. Ficino, *Platonica Theologia* II 12, I S. 114: „Si quanto magis aliqua Deo propinquant, tanto minus servilia sunt magisque sui iuris evadunt, Deus sui iuris est maxime [...]".

[49] Horatius, *Satyrae* II 7.

[50] So der ganze Kontext von Epiktets *Diatribe* IV 1.

[51] Horatius, *Satyrae* II 7.

kann Freiheit sich auch in der Zustimmung zu Sachverhalten und Zuständen manifestieren, ihre eigentliche Funktion ist aber, „Tätigkeiten zu kommandieren, eine neue Kausalkette ins Leben zu rufen"[52]. Da die Notwendigkeiten notwendig Folgen zeitigen, ist unbezweifelbar und uneingeschränkt frei, wer Prinzip einer Notwendigkeitskette ist: *aut nusquam motus liber est, aut liber est ubi primus*[53]. Nach Ficino trifft das auf Gott zu. Als der Schöpfer ist Gott die Notwendigkeit selbst, durch die alles übrige Notwendige notwendig ist. Genau deshalb, weil in Gott die Notwendigkeit liegt, der keine weitere Notwendigkeit vorgeordnet ist, ist in Gott auch die höchste Freiheit[54]. Unter diesen Prämissen versteht es sich von selbst, daß in Gott, dem *summum bonum*, auch Notwendigkeit und Freiheit koinzidieren[55]. Anders als in Vallas Darstellung des Problems bilden Notwendigkeit und Freiheit in Gott keine Extreme, sondern sie resultieren bei Ficino auseinander. Die Macht der Freiheit äußert sich in Ficinos Analyse des Gottesbegriffes darin, daß Gott aus der Freiheit seines Willens sich in der Schöpfung nach außen zeigt[56]. Gott schafft anders als alle bekannten Naturprozesse, die unter gleichen Bedingungen gleiche Wirkungen erbringen, er schafft nämlich aus seiner eigenen Kraft die verschiedenen Dinge mitsamt der Verschiedenheit der Qualitäten und Stufungen[57]. Das folgt aus der in Gott anzunehmenden Einheit von Natur, Geist und Willen. Jede Art Naturprozeß spannt sich zwischen die Polarität von aktivem und passivem Element, und jeder intellektuelle Diskurs objektiviert diese Pole in sich. Deshalb vollzieht sich in Gott das Schöpfungsgeschehen sowohl «nach außen», nämlich vom Schöpfer hin zum Geschaffenen, als auch immanent als das Ganze der Schöpfung, mit der Gott auf theologisch komplexe Weise (quasi-pantheistisch) eins ist[58]. Hier liegt eine Antinomie vor, die bei platonisierenden Philosophen bekanntlich nicht mit Hilfe der Univozität oder der Analogizität des Seinsbegriffs aufgelöst wird. Die Immanenz der geschaffenen Formen kann bei Fici-

---

[52] Dietrich von Hildebrand: *Moralia*. Regensburg 1980 (*Gesammelte Werke* 9), S. 73 (Hildebrand spricht hier von „zwei Vollkommenheiten des Willens".)

[53] Ficino, *Platonica Theologia* IX 4, II S. 29.

[54] Ficino, *Platonica Theologia* II 12, I S. 113: „Necessitas autem ipse est Deus, per quem et caetera necessaria sunt quaecumque sunt necessaria".

[55] Ficino, *Platonica Theologia* II 12, I 114: „Si incitamentum boni in singulis maxime omnium necessarium est et maxime omnium voluntarium spontaneumque, certe in ipso bono summa naturae necessitas una cum summa voluntatis libertate concurrit [...]".

[56] Ficino, *Platonica Theologia*, II 11, I S. 105, Überschrift: „Deus voluntatem habet, perque illam extra se efficit omnia".

[57] Ficino, *Platonica Theologia* II 11, I. S. 107.

[58] Ficino, *Platonica Theologia* II 11, I. S. 108: „Operatio [enim] naturalis ab agente quidem incipit, sed desinit in id quod patitur [...]. Intellectualis autem utrumque terminum retinet in agente. Per hanc enim Deus dum se speculando versatur secum, undique versat externa [...]".

no nicht mit Hilfe des Seinsbegriffs vom Schöpfer distanziert werden, da der platonische Begriff des Seins immer dann mit Gott konvergiert, wenn er in seiner Fülle gesehen wird[59]. An Stelle dessen tritt hier der Begriff des Willens, der das veräußernde Moment der Schöpfung gegenüber dem ontologischen Immanentismus der Intelligibilität stark macht:

> Jeder Geist schafft eher wollend als sehend. Im Sehen reflektiert er nämlich die Formen nach innen, im Wollen entfaltet er sie nach außen; im Sehen betrachtet er das Wahre, dem Reinheit eigen ist, im Wollen erlangt er das Gute, dem Verbreitung eigen ist[60].

Die Antinomie der Richtung der Freiheit nach außen und der Immanenz ihres Wirkens im absoluten Prinzip findet ihre Parallele in der menschlichen Freiheit. Denn das Wirkenwollen «aus sich heraus» sucht um der wirklichen Freiheit willen danach, sich an die Spitze der Ursachenkette zu setzen. Bei Luther geschieht das in der Einheit von Glauben und Gnade. Im platonischen Hierarchiemodell, das weitgehend von der Stufung der Seelen in Platons *Nomoi X* beeinflußt ist[61], wird dies durch Partizipation an der göttlichen Schöpferkraft erklärt[62].

Nicht bloß durch göttliche Steuerung ist der menschliche Geist göttlich, sondern auch dadurch, daß er sich zum Höheren zurückwenden und davon „pro natura sua" Gebrauch machen kann. Ebenso kann der menschliche Geist auf niedere Stufen herabsteigen. Gerade durch Öffnung zur Inspiration wird der Geist frei in dem Sinne, daß er selbst Prinzip seiner Aktionen wird. Und insofern ist er göttlich[63]. Wenn man die theologische Dimension abschneidet, hat die menschliche Freiheit allerdings nicht mehr nur Ähn-

---

[59] Ficino weiß das genau, dafür spricht seine Anspielung in *Platnica Theologia* II 1, I S. 110: Ergo cum Deus sit, ut peripatetico more loquar, ens primum, [...]. Giovanni Pico della Mirandola versucht übrigens in *De ente et uno*, die platonische Eminenz des Seienden mit der Analogie-Differenz zu kombinieren".

[60] Ficino, *Platonica Theologia* II 11, I S. 110 f.: „Mens autem quaelibet volendo facit opera potius quam videndo. Videndo einm replicat formas intus, volendo eas explicat extra; videndo respicit verum, cui propria puritas est, volendo attingit bonum, cui propria est diffusio".

[61] Ficino, *Platonica Theologia* XIV 10, II S. 294 f.

[62] Eine systematische Entfaltung der Modelle von Partizipation, Analogie, Schöpfung und Dialog im Verhältnis der göttlichen zur menschlichen Freiheit bietet Julio Terán Dutari SJ: *Analogia de la libertad, Un Tributo al Pensamiento de Erich Przywara*, Quito 1989, S. 135-146.

[63] Ficino, *Platonica Theologia* IX 4, II S. 27 f.: „Sic enim divinae erunt hominum mentes, si moventur proxime a divinis. [...] Munus huiusmodi non prohibet animum nostrum ad lumen illud suo modo converti, pro natura sua uti, ac per illud libere ratiocinari atque eligere, praesertim quia noster animus interdum ad deteriorem partem in consiliis se confert. Instinctus autem mentium divinarum traheret semper ad optimum. Quapropter humanus ani

lichkeit mit der Schöpferfreiheit Gottes, sondern tritt an deren Stelle. Moralisches Ziel der Angleichung an Gott in der platonischen und stoischen Tradition war zum Teil nur die Verachtung der irdischen Welt, metaphysische Voraussetzung aber auch die Idee, daß der ein Gott ist, der selbst alles unter Kontrolle hat, was um ihn geschieht.

Mit der Macht, eigenes Prinzip der Notwendigkeit zu sein, geht einher, daß der menschliche Geist sein Wollen auf sich selbst richten und sich dadurch von allem frei machen kann. Wenn die Außenrichtung des freien Willens zirkulär wird, dann verzichtet er nicht einfach auf das Außen, sondern er macht das Wählenkönnen zwischen Alternativen zum Gegenstand des Wollens. Wollen und Nichtwollen sind dann selbst gleichwertige Objekte des Wollens. Das Ergebnis kann die Befreiung von allen Wünschen sein. Dann allerdings wird die Freiheit selbst zum Objekt des freien Strebens.

Das «Aus sich heraus» ist der Ursprung des Handelns überhaupt, hierauf lassen sich alle Motivationsketten logisch zurückführen. Ficino identifiziert das Freisein im Sinne von Selbst-frei-sein-Wollen mit Platons Selbstbewegung. Diese kommt der menschlichen Seele zu, bekanntlich noch mehr aber Gott. Deshalb tendiert der Mensch dazu, letztlich sein Sich-selbst-wollen auf das Prinzip zurückzuführen, bei dem Sich-Wollen und Etwas-Wollen dasselbe sind.

Aus dieser Perspektive kehrt sich die vermeintliche Mitwirkung Gottes an den Taten – wodurch allein die Frage der Mitverantwortung Gottes und der Theodizee aufkommt – um in die Aufgabe der Mitwirkung des Menschen am Heilsplan. Unter gewöhnlichen Umständen ist der Mensch zwar mit kontingenten Angelegenheiten befaßt, und gerade deshalb gehört die Differenz zwischen Freisein und Handelnkönnen zur *conditio humana*. Es kommt aber in der Geschichte vor, daß außergewöhnliche, heilige Menschen «ihre Seele mit Gott verbinden» – wie Ficino sagt – so daß Gottes- und Menschenwerk eins werden und beide «konkurrieren». Dann allerdings sind Wollen und Gebet, Werk und Wunder, Freiheit und Gehorsam nicht mehr zu unterscheiden. Oder Freiheit ist «aufgegeben».

---

mus inspirationem numinum in naturam suam trahit. Illinc quipe descendit stabilis. [...] itaque nihil obstat quo minus libera sit animi actio, cum nulli proprio movendi subiiciatur". (Nach der Ausgabe Ficino, *Opera*, Basel 1561, S. 210, muß es richtig heißen: moventi.) – Der Kontext ist die Kritik an der astrologischen Lehre, die höheren Geister könnten den Menschen beeinflußen und ihm die Freiheit rauben. Ficino kehrt die These um: der Mensch kann die Geister nutzen.

[64] Ficino, *Platonica Theologia* XIII 5, II S. 244: „Atque ita rebus contingentibus occupati, raro ut cupimus, assequimur, quia raro et sorte quadam com supernorum voluntate concurrimus. [...] Probant enim vota viri sanctissimi, praesertim si cum illo populi quoque vota concurrant, animos mirabiliter ita coniungere Deo, ut una quodammodo Dei animique operatio fiat, sed Dei quidem veluti artificis, animi autem tamquam instrumenti divini".

ANNA MAŁECKA
Academy of Mining and Metalurgy in Cracow
Poland

FREEDOM AND MORAL ACT IN THOMAS CARLYLE'S PHILOSOPHICAL THOUGHT

The essence of Thomas Carlyle's concept of freedom can be summed up in the following thesis:
– first, free is he who fulfils God-given duty;
– second, human duty consists in the performance of work understood as purely moral act.

The sources of this interpretation of the problem of freedom in the context of duty and moral activity can be traced back to the Calvinist tradition and to German idealism. Thomas Carlyle, the British writer and thinker living on the borderline of Romantic and Victorian epochs, belonged, since his childhood, to the Burgher Seceder Church, whose the creed was an offshoot of Calvinism; later, in his youth, he remained under the great influence of German idealist and Romantic philosophers and writers (especially Kant, Fichte, Schelling, Goethe), absorbing certain elements – after considerable transformations – to his own eclectic system.

The aforementioned three fundamental notions of Carlyle's ethics: duty, work and freedom, as well as relationships between them, should be analysed now.

I. DUTY

In his best known book, the masterpiece *Sartor Resartus*, compared in its surprising form to the contemporary *nouveau roman*, Carlyle calls duty "the divine Messenger and Guide"[1]. He even regards the symbolic presentation

---
[1] T. Carlyle, *Sartor Resartus*, London 1888, p. 112.

of the moral law, the law of human duty, as the essence of Christianity. Thus duty postulated by the moral law possesses a religious meaning: it is the revelation of God's will to man. In the spatio-temporal world of appearances, in the situation of man's apparent confinement, it confronts him with the godlike and the infinite (in this sense Carlyle speaks of the "infinite nature of duty"), and governs all his moral activity. The law of duty appears to be most deeply engraved in the human heart, found intuitively even at the moments of doubt and disbelief. Therefore Professor Teufelsdroeckh, the hero of *Sartor,* speaking of his crisis of faith can confess:

> was the infinite nature of Duty still dimly present to me: living without God in the world, of God's light I was not utterly bereft; if my as yet sealed eyes with their unspeakable longing could nowhere see Him, nevertheless in my heart He was present, and His heaven-written Law still stood legible and sacred there[2].

Carlyle, adopting terms from his German masters, describes duty as possessing the "transcendental nature". The moral law, the law of human duty, can be discovered only by the supra-individual consciousness, the "higher celestial ME" (akin to Fichte's absolute *Ich)* opposed to the "lower, happiness hungry self" (the individual empirical ego). The first preliminary moral act is identified with "Annihilation of self" (that's how Carlyle translated Novalis' term *Selbsttoedtung* into English). This ideal of self-resignation assumed the form of Puritan appeal to abandon all natural impulses and desires having their centre in the empirical ego, first of all the hedonist search after happiness. "Deny thyself"; he writes in his *Notebooks,* "whatsoever is thyself, consider it as nothing"[3]. Permanent and total negation of the lower, individual aspects of consciousness, determined by the emprical – illusory layer of the world, liberation from them, render possible the emergence of the so far hidden "higher celestial ME" in us, for which the world of appearances becomes, in Fichtean sense, "an object and material of our duty".

The recognition of the law of duty by this universal consciousness, the acceptance of its divine validity in the state of "Everlasting YEA" (the state achieved by the hero of *Sartor* in his mystical experience) is the first step on the path of freedom; the next one consists in the active and unceasing fulfilment of that law.

---

[2] Ibidem, p. 113.
[3] *Two Notebooks of Tomas Carlyle, from 23rd March, 1822 to 17th May, 1832,* wyd. C. E. Norton, New York 1898, p. 265.

2. WORK

Our whole duty, says Carlyle repeatedly in his writings, is to work in the right direction. The duty recognized by the higher celestial ME constitutes an impulse and guide for moral action, which Carlyle identifies with work. Such is the God-given task: to perform the work whose character is defined by the moral consciousness. Work means constant effort and externalization of one's inner potential. Carlyle again provides a religious justification for his thesis:

> He [man] is born to expend every particle of strength that God Almighty has given him, in doing the work he finds he is fit for; to stand up to it to the last breath of life, and do his best[4].

As in the Calvinist tradition, it is ordinary, everyday work that is exalted here, becoming, even in its seemingly most trifling forms, an occasion for the worship of God. *Laborare est orare* was one of Carlyle's favourite sayings.

Goethean appeal: *Do the Duty which lies nearest thee* becomes another of Carlyle's mottos, for which he seeks justification in the Bible. He paraphrases two passages in this context – the first one from Ecclesiastes 9,10: *"Whatsoever thy hand findeth to do, do it with thy whole might"*, and the second from John 9, 4: *"Work while it is called Today; for the Night cometh, wherein no man can work"* [5]. Let us remember remind that the fragment from the Gospel according to St. John is the one following the description of the healing of a blind man by Christ; so also human work may be compared to the light brought to the world by Jesus, the act of overcoming the dark forces of evil and falsity. We find here also a foreshadowing of Christ's death and a reminder of the duty to work before the end of the time we have been assigned.

Human work has a truly metaphysical and religious significance which consists in co-operating with what Carlyle calls "the real Tendency of the World", in actualizing God's plan, in revealing God-outlined ideal, and changing accordingly oneself and the whole world. *"Giant Labour is the truest emblem of God the World-Worker"*[6]. In his work man in the closest possible way approaches God, having the symbolic participation in His creative acts.

---

[4] Qoted after: N. Young, *Carlyle: His Rise and Fall,* Duchworth 1927, p. 299.

[5] T. Carlyle, *Sartor Resartus,* op. cit., p. 136.

[6] Cf. N. Young, op. cit., p. 203.

3. GOSPEL OF FREEDOM

Freedom can flourish only on the ground of ever-performed God-inspired work. As the real effects of work are spiritual, Carlyle means here, in accordance with Calvinist doctrine, the internal freedom. Following Kant and especially Fichte, he intends to show that this freedom of moral agent is possible in the world of necessity and, what is more, the world of necessity with all its obstacles and resistance, in which our "nearest duty lies", constitutes a constant challenge for our moral efforts, development and liberation:

> Our Life is compassed round with Necessity; yet is the meaning of Life itself no other that Freedom, than Voluntary Force: thus have we a warfare; in the beginning, especially, a hard-fought battle. For the God-given mandate, Work thou in Welldoing, lies mysteriously written, in Promethean Prophetic Characters, in our hearts; and leaves us no rest, night or day, till it be deciphered and obeyed; till it burn forth, in our conduct, a visible, acted Gospel of Freedom[7].

The concept of freedom seems to constitute Carlyle's last, concluding words in the field of his religion-oriented ethics; yet this issue has not been analysed in any detailed way in his own philosophy, inspiring further questions and discussion rather than giving ready answers.

The first of these questions may concern a solution of the duty/freedom paradox in this rigorous system. Freedom means for Carlyle a subordination to the law of duty, a consciously chosen constraint. So as in Kant's moral philosophy, the free agent is distinguished here not by the lack of constraint but by the peculiar nature of the constraint that governs him[8]. But Carlyle seems also to go further in his paradoxical understanding of freedom than Kant: this constraint is not only a postulate of our universal autonomous moral consciousness, this "higher celestial ME" but by means of its symbolizing power it turns to be a postulate of God himself, of God revealed in our ME as both immanent and transcendent. The true autonomy of the moral agent is founded upon the Highest Being. *"Whoso cannot obey cannot be free [...]"* we read in *Sartor*. *"Only in reverently bowing down before the Higher does he [man] feel himself exalted"* [9]. In Carlyle's ethics the free agent justifies the absolute moral authority of the law of duty over all human actions by appealing to God as its author. The subordination means here again the symbolical participation in God's glory and thus is the factor dignifying him and liberating from what is beneath him and, at the same time, freeing him for what is above.

---

[7] T. Carlyle, *Sartor Resartus*, op. cit., pp. 126-127.
[8] Cf. R. Scruton, *A Short History of Modern Philosophy*, London 1984, p. 155.
[9] T. Carlyle, *Sartor Resartus*, op. cit., p. 173.

Man, called the "Messiah of Nature", is to preach a "Gospel of Freedom" by act and word [10]. He has got the soteriological task of liberating all around him, of spiritualizing, in Fichtean sense, the world by his moral activity. Such is especially the role of the hero, Carlylean model man, the best symbol of God in the world, a person who mystically knows the truth and acts accordingly. He is destined to be a spiritual leader of masses; he deserves worship and almost limitless obedience. In his later works Carlyle seems to speak more of subordination to this representative of God than of subordination to God himself; as if the act of subjection to the God-given abstract moral law in the case of "ordinary people" were too difficult a task and required an intermediary and hermeneut.

Carlyle's hero-worship theory has evoked well known controversies and charges of inspiring several modern aberrations of political leadership and tyranny, which have brought an obvious threat to personal external freedom, freedom in its socio-political dimension. However, we should be more careful in acusing Carlyle for what others have done with his thoughts interpreted out of their original, however sometimes utopistic context. For Carlyle ethical principles are primary factors and constitute a warranty against political abuses. As he writes in his *Notebooks*: *"Politics are not our Life (which is the practice and contemplation of Goodness), but only the* house *wherin that Life is led"*[12].

CONCLUSION

In conclusion I should like to emphasise the meaning that Carlyle's concept presents for contemporary culture.

Firstly, it stresses the religious foundations of freedom. As if against, or maybe only in a supplement to strong "humanistic" trends of the modern civilisation, it defines freedom as overcoming the lower confinements of man not only in terms of one's own personal development; but, first of all, as steps towards subordination to the highest will, towards participation in it. As Carlyle says: *"in the Godlike only has he [man] strength and Freedom"*[12].

Secondly, freedom in this activistic philosophy is not only a prerequisite of moral acts, but a constant actualization of this potential in everyday efforts.

Thirdly, freedom has its "Messianic" dimension; it implies liberating influence upon the world around the moral agent.

---

[10] Ibidem, p. 152.
[11] *Two Notebooks*, op. cit., p. 141.
[12] T. Carlyle, *Sartor Resartus*, op. cit., pp. 132-133.

IGNACE VERHACK
Katholieke Universiteit Leuven
Belgium

THE TEMPORALITY OF FREEDOM

I. SOME BRIEF REMARKS ABOUT SELF-BEING AND THE TEMPORAL STRUCTURE AND MEANING OF FREEDOM

In the same way as there is no freedom without the constitutive character of our being as "being-possible" (*Möglichsein*[1]), there is also no "being-possible" without the capacity to relate ourselves effectively to this possibility, as to something that can be projected and appropriated by us. This appropriation occurs in the projection of our creative possibilities in the world through action. Man's being is a "being-possible" that is characteristic for an entity capable of creative action in an already existing world. Man has possibilities as his own. But not only does he have possibilities; his very being is a creative "being-possible". Man is not pre-determined to execute any particular or recurring patterns of action in the world; he is set free to be a "self", to give a personal figure to himself, and this by making choices and decisions. His being, therefore, is a "being possible", although not out of nothing. Nor is his being absolutely unqualified and void of all intrinsic meaning. I do not conceive this "being-possible" as the having-to-be of a sheer "da" without properties as Heidegger does suggest in *Being and Time*, §9. This being-possible, together with our capacity for the creative appropriation of it, we will call: "our freedom". As free beings, we are set free to be a "self", to become ourselves. This freedom or self-being realizes itself through choices and deliberate actions. But this freedom to do or not to do certain things in the world, is itself embedded in our inner relatedness to our *ownmost* possibility: it is embedded in our desire for the appropriation

---

[1] M. Heidegger, *Sein und Zeit*, p. 143 (§31).

of the most intimate sense of our being as being-possible. That to which we are related in that way is itself, however, nothing specific or determined in the order of things and possibilities in the world. But this absence of ontical determination in the ultimate meaning of our being-possible doesn"t leave it ontologically unqualified as if our being-possible would by itself remain indifferent to the many ontical determinations and qualifications which we attempt to give to it; as if it would deem them to be irremediably arbitrary and subjective with respect to the repulsive indetermination of our "being as such".

Being-possible is to be set free for the personal and creative appropriation of the meaning of our being through action. Such appropriation presupposes an understanding of being (Seinsverständnis[2]): an understanding of it as a possibility for us, but also a pre-understanding of its "sense" and qualitative meaning. The presence of such meaning shows itself in the fact that the full actualisation, i.e., appropriation, of our being is spontaneously felt and lived by us as the end-term of an all-encompassing desire *to be*, wherein being itself is naturally felt as a *good*. As object of desire, being is understood and lived as that which we passionately strive to fully assimilate and actualize in ourselves as actors. But the fullness of being is itself not like an "object" which we can "possess" in a thing-like way. It is something which we personally have to *be*, residing in our highest possible activity and creativity. Therefore, the full assimilation of the goodness of being is rather to be understood in such a way, that our ownmost activity may have reached a stage in which it may become identical, as it were, with the self-proliferation of the goodness of being in us, in the service of the whole of beings. It is that act of being in which there would be no longer any real distance between our own creativity and the self-dispersion of the goodness of being in us, so that this goodness may itself flow out from our most spontaneous creativity, and this to such a point that the originarity of self-dispersing being (encompassing in itself the totality of beings) and the originarity of our highest creativity in the *service* of beings as a whole, would have become one and the same: creativity having become the flourishing of being in us, and self-giving being passing immediately and without reserve in our ownmost creativity in the midst of beings. That state of "ontological" creativity would be the most divine-like in man.

But let us for the moment turn back to our freedom to be a self through action, to self-being as being-possible in a world. Some more reflection about this theme teaches us that freedom, thus conceived, has a *temporal* structure and meaning: self-being is only possible in terms of an orientation

---

[2] *Being and Time*, §4.

towards a *not-yet* from out of an *already-having-been*, and this, through active interaction in the *now* with that which surrounds us. Every singular free act is structured in this way. Still further reflection shows us that all free action can be seen as a kind of *recalling* of the past, and this in a twofold way. The having-been (past reality) is recalled in so far as free activity is an attempt to overcome the binding power that the past exerts on us, or that we ourselves sometimes give to it. Seen from this angle, freedom entails a moment of refusal, negation and deconstruction of the past. This is, however, only meaningful to the extent that the free act is able to recall this past in a new configuration that we ourselves have projected and willed. Every recollection of the past is, in this way, at the same time both a dissolution (destruction) and a calling-back of the past; a deconstruction of what has already been and at the same time a reconstruction of it into something new. Novelty or renewal, therefore, is the hall-mark of all true action in the world.

An action which would not be future-oriented would be nothing more than an imitative (or even ritually fixed) repetition of the past. But an action which cannot embody or embed itself in a past would also be no more than an empty formalism without any concretion in the world. This does not alter the fact, however, that future-orientedness is the very condition of possibility of all innovative acting. In this sense, the calling back of the past is only imaginable when we can call it back from out of our proper orientation towards an ideally conceived end which makes *novelty* and the *renewal* of reality possible. We can think here of our capacity to imagine the world and to assign its ideal possibilities to our actions as the goals to be reached by them. Yet, through action, we do not only try to realize external possibilities, i.e. new states of affairs in the world (as a synthesis of matter and form); in doing so, we also pursue some value or achieve a finality for ourselves. In acting, we undertake something for the sake of ourselves, in the name of our being-possible. We perform a synthesis of the ideal and the real with relation to ourselves. At this point, the ideal principle of our own novelty necessarily coincides with the constitutive ideal principle of the Synthesis that is *ours* and to which ideal project we are first and foremost directed from within ourselves. The fulfilment of our being comports a having-to-do, although not being identical with it. As a consequence, the ontological understanding of our ownmost Possibility (the "not yet" that we are after for ourselves in all action) can, in fact, not be separated from our reflective understanding of the ideal-*practical* meaning that our being-possible possesses for *us*. This is the ideal of practical possibility which is never completely fulfilled by any past realisation whatsoever and in the name of which this past can, therefore, be recalled again and again in and through innovative acting.

In this way, the practical understanding of our Possibility coincides in fact with the *projecting-in-advance* of our practical ideal in and over the social world of action. This practical understanding belongs to the understanding of the ultimate existential meaning of our own being-possible as it is *given to us*. This is a meaning of which we are not the creators, but which is given *to-be-understood* to us by Being itself as the giving ground of Possibility *in us*. This "self-opening" in us of the Possibility towards which we are internally moved (this first of all in a passible way), and consequently also the event of "giving itself for understanding" of the ideal meaning by which, in this very movement, we are also internally guided, here represents the a-temporal and non-projectable *beginning*, from which the temporal structure and dynamic of our freedom springs and in which it finds its source. It is also the source of freedom, once freedom is seen as a recollecting of the past out of our orientation towards the Possibility which flows from that beginning. For it is the source from which our own Possibility comes towards us in the midst of reality which surrounds us here and now.

II. THE BLIND ALLEY OF HEIDEGGER'S EXPOSITIONS ON WILL AND MOTION IN BEING AND TIME

The existential and ontological "grammar" of freedom which we briefly developed in the foregoing remarks, has to a great extent been inspired by our reading of M. Heidegger's *Being and Time*. Several of the utterances we made, could indeed be paralleled with some of the major statements of *Being and Time* with respect to the temporal meaning of the being of Dasein. But although the grammar of our exposition is Heideggerian, its deeper inspiration is far from being Heideggerian at all. The following comments on Heidegger's early masterpiece are meant to clarify the difference.

It is well known that Heidegger undertook his analysis of the being of Dasein in function of his renewal of the question of the meaning of Being. As the asker of the question, Dasein is the priviliged being to be interrogated in order to uncover the meaning of Being as temporality (§5). Less known, however, is that Heidegger also explicitly states that his existential analysis of Dasein is meant to free the living Dasein for its most extreme possibility of existence (§61, p. 303). The analysis should lead to the acquisition of a radically new insight into existential truth: this is an insight of which it is presumed that it possesses the liberating force of freeing Dasein to itself, by delivering it from the self-estrangement which is said to be proper of the daily routine in the world. Still less known is the implicit conviction which becomes, nevertheless, apparent towards the end of *Being and Time*, that this new account of the temporal meaning of the being of Dasein must also be seen as a new way of clarification of that which, by Heidegger, is not only called the riddle of Being but also "as has now been made plain, [...] that of *motion*" (§75, p. 392). Towards the end of *Being and Time*, it is plainly said that it belongs to the purpose of the final paragraphs "to face [...] the ontological enigma of the movement of historicizing ("das Geschehen") in general" (p. 389).

Unfortunately, this threefold purpose of *Being and Time* turned out to be a threefold failure as well. It was not entirely made clear, after all, how the analysis of the being of Dasein could lead us further with respect to the renewal of the question of being in general. But also the projected liberation of Dasein for its ownmost possibility leads us, as we will show, into a blind alley. It runs aground because of the fact that the existential analysis does not formulate a convincing answer to the not-so marginal question as to "by what" the will might be moved to really choose and will its withdrawal from the rapturous and quitening sphere of fallen routine, under the lead of the "They" (das Man). Let it be that Heidegger assumes the old adage of the gospel of John that truth makes us free[3]. Thus, it is only in the light of truth that we can discover our most proper possibilities. Unfortunately, however, the existential truth which is revealed in *Being and Time* is not meant as the intelligible presentation of any good or telos which moves us closer to ourselves, but as the unveiling of something which, if it does not repel us once and for all, at least will never omit to frighten us very profoundly. There is a good reason, therefore, to say like on p. 193 that daily failures are a way for Dasein to comport itself *unwillingly* to its possibilities. On which grounds, then, can it be said of this repelling and anxiety-giving truth that it has the force of moving the will to withdraw from the certainties and the apparent quietude of daily routine, in order to prefer instead that rather deterring truth of authenticity?

The consequences of this absence of a truely moving and motivating principle for Dasein in *Being and Time* will appear most clearly in what I would call the "cul-de-sac" of Heidegger's explanation of the *motion* of Dasein under the heading of "historicity". Heidegger ends up with an ontological reduction of the movement of Dasein to the voluntary suppression of all "real" future-directedness in the world, and in this sense also of the kind of hope and expectation which belongs to it. In fact, the true meaning of movement is ultimately thought in terms of "resoluteness" ("Entschlossenheit") (§74), that is, as the inner withdrawal ("Zurücknahme", p. 308) of Dasein from its immediate and everyday-attachment to its factical possibilities in the world, in order to free itself for the anticipation of death (p. 308-

---

[3] John, 8, 32.

309). This is not meant by Heidegger as a call for the suppression of all action as such, but rather as a radical acceptance of the ultimate nothingness of our being-in-the-world. Dasein is not a being that has to "realize" itself in the world as if it were itself a substance bound to the fulfillment of its own nature. The being of Dasein is the being of the ground of a nothingness (§58). In this way, the resolute acceptance of the hopelessness of existence is constitutive for the authenticity of Dasein. Not action, but "Entschlossenheit" (resoluteness) as the inner withdrawal of Dasein is, therefore, the "true" way of projection of Dasein"s being. Our critical question is the following. How can a philosophy of perspectivelessness bring us closer to a better understanding of the *movement* of Dasein? How can Dasein continue to be in motion under the explicit absence of any form of authentic and non-illusionary telos in and for its being? How can motion remain possible at all when the very possibility of Dasein *is* itself the withdrawal as such, that means, when there is nothing to be striven for, nor something to be hoped for by Dasein, except its own liberation to its freedom for death? Let us, therefore, look a bit closer at Heidegger's explanation of motion in *Being and Time*.

The way of being of Dasein is characterized first and foremost by its future-directedness (327). Dasein is "ahead of itself" (§41) in its projection of its own possibilities *to* be. This is the very definition of its freedom as being free *for* its own possibility (Seinkönnen). It is in the analysis of "Sorge" (care) (§41) that this being-ahead of oneself is uncovered as the finding-place of the temporal structure of Dasein, and hence of its freedom as "being-possible". This direction towards the future, however, may not be understood as a teleological movement towards a finalizing good, that means, as a striving for the good. To the contrary, it is constitutive of the existential thought of *Being and Time* to suspend (in an epochal sense) all ontical explanations of the movement of Dasein, in order to lead us to a more profound ontological understanding of that same movement in terms of a future-oriented repetition or recapitulation ("Wiederholung", re-delivery) of the historical past. The ontological reinterpretation of movement in terms of the temporal structure of Dasein becomes obvious here. In this way, the character of movement proper to Dasein is reduced to that which, at the end of the book, will be called the *historicity* of Dasein.

Historicity itself is to be understood from the fact that, for Heidegger at least, Dasein"s orientation towards the future is nothing else than its resolute anticipation of death. This death, however, cannot give or show us any factical possibilities to be projected (p. 383). Death does not motivate to anything at all; for sure, it is not something to be realised at all (p. 261). All that death can bring about is to throw us back (p. 384-385) upon our factical possibilities in the world. These are possibilities belonging to the social lifeworld, as possibilities which we inherit together with others from the past. The force of death, then, is to throw us back upon ourselves in the world, so that we may assume these possiblities as "ours" in the Situation, that is, in that free and always individual space of possibility which is opened up and determined by what is called "resoluteness" ("Entschlossenheit"; see especially §62). The personal *appropriation* of these factical possibilities is called by Heidegger "repetition" ("Wiederholung"). In this way, repetition is explained as the personal appropriation of something into which we are thrown. Expressed in terms of existential temporality, this means that repetition or recapitulation is to be understood as a future-orientedness which does not lead to a *forgetting* of the past. Such a denial of the past is proper to that kind of *creativity* with things (339[4]), or *modernity* (391) and *progress* (386), which consists, Heidegger says, in a clearing out of the past through a craving for novelty he calls it an ecstatical forgetting of the past (thrownness) as having-been (339). Repetition, therefore, is not a withdrawal from the past, but from the unreflected and immediate everyday-adherence to our factical possibilities in the world. This immediacy is characterized as a form of rigidity which can only be overcome through the resolute anticipation of death as Dasein's ultimate possibility (p.307). Repetition (redelivery) is the mark of Dasein's transcendance giving way to a recapitulation of the past by the inner withdrawal from all rigid self-attachment to the possibilities of the present (cfr. p.307). Hence, to repeat the past is to reintroduce an authentic futural character into that past which thus becomes our "having-been".

The profound paradox of this explanation of the meaning of existence can now be made plain. The primordial and essential future-directedness of Dasein, so much emphasized in §§65 and 74, must in no way be seen as a coming *close* to any fulfillment or attainment of the good, but as a withdrawal of such a kind of expectation. The meaning of being-towards the future is not one of expectation, but of anticipation: anticipation of death as the projection of Dasein's ultimate *impossibility*, in the name of which Dasein must withdraw itself from any form of "rigidity" in its situation. This cannot but mean that there is no moving-power operating at the heart of Dasein's direction towards the future. Such a future is not the arrival of something new, but only the source of a recapitulating endorsement of that element of factical non-transparancy which is inherent to being-thrown. This leads to a characteristic view on being authentic within one's own historical circumstances. These are first and foremost the circumstances in which Dasein's ordinary tendency of falling prevails (also called the improper future-directedness of Dasein; cfr. supra on creativity and modernity). However,

---

[4] "geschöpfte Möglichkeiten".

they are not contingent determinations from out of which I must try to "develop" my personality in a creative way. These are rather seen as an obtrusive and tempting multitude of factical possibilities (cfr. 384) from which I should withdraw, in order for me to choose for that in the situation, which really matters to me in the light of my finitude. What matters to me, is that what I am capable of (336), my being free for death (384), i.e. resoluteness and resignation. Only freedom for death can give to Dasein its "goal outright" ("das Ziel schlechthin"). This freedom is the appropriate criterium for choosing my historical possibility in the situation. What I have to choose, is my personal possibility or way to be free for death. This possibility is called by Heidegger one"s individual fate ("Schicksal", p. 384[5]). Understood in the usual way, fate is that which assigns to an individual what possibilities can befall him factually, that is, what experiences he can have. In Heidegger's use of the term, however, it is Dasein itself who, by its own choice, is responsible for the existential determination of its proper fate[6]. Fate, therefore, is the possibility to choose for and give a personal determination to one's own situation. In this way, the historical possibility for which I am choosing is handed down to me and personally chosen at one and the same time. It is the only authority to which I can be faithful (cfr. p. 391), because I am the one who is choosing *for* its being handed down to me as *my having been* (cfr. 339). Authentic historicity, therefore, consists in choosing one's heroes (371, 385) of resoluteness and resignation out of the historical heritage[7] of the past. These are the heroes from whose example Dasein can get its inspiration when facing *in its situation* the nothingness of its own "da" in an open and unconcealed way; that means, when the appeal of conscience is heard to open itself resolutely for the fortuities which are peculiar to its individual situation. We mildly pass over the fact that, in Heidegger's

---

[5] It must somehow be my own factical way of concentrating upon the finitude of my being, although this is not much clarified in the corresponding passage of *Being and Time*. Anyway, "repetition" is the recalling of the past *as* my ownmost factical possibility or "Schicksal" in the world.

[6] This leads to the most "unbelievable" thesis of *Being and Time*, according to which, in the name of authenticity, a total *existential* recuperation of our thrown being in its facticity be possible: a total recuperation, i.e., without remainder of passivity or rest of irrecuperable facticity, and this in a movement of *repetition* in which Dasein chooses and, by choosing, also autonomously posits its own "Schicksal". The "self" erects and constitutes itself as a self by overturning its throwness in a freely chosen factical possibility to be free for its own death. Such "autonomy", as a choosing for one"s own throwness and finitude (cfr. *amor fati* in Nietzsche), can only be thought on the basis of a total "possibilizing" of Dasein's being, where even the factical beginning and end of Dasein can become a possibility that can be projected by Dasein itself, although it finds itself first and for all as thrown in them.

[7] In fact a *cultural* heritage, although Heidegger himself avoids the use of this term.

view, every individual "fate" ("Schicksal") is guided and united in advance by the destiny ("Geschick") of one's people (p. 384).

That entity that, at the outset, seemed to be able to let come towards itself its own future in a very personal way, now appears to be reduced in its abilities to the "superior force" of choosing for its own choice, in order to deliver itself (on that very basis) to the "powerlessness" which consists in being affected and determined by the opaque accidentalities and by the uncontrollable particularities of one's own situation in the social life-world (p. 384). At the end of a long discourse, future-directedness seems to be reducable to a going back to the past (385; "die Rückgang in Möglichkeiten des dagewesenen Daseins") and this without the intervention of any principle of Novelty in the name of which the past would be called back and could be reconstrued.

This climbing down from future-directedness (or being ahead of oneself) to an authentic endorsement of the fortuities of a thrown past, cannot but make manifest the "cul-de-sac" of a philosophy of existence in which this being-ahead of oneself is by no means generated by an inner directedness towards a teleological principle by which Dasein would be moved and finalized from within. For Heidegger, Being-ahead of oneself has nothing to do with aiming at any final good attracting our will, nor is it a sign of being impregnated with the moving power of a transcendency from out of which we are given to ourselves and which affirms itself at the root of all desire. Being-ahead of oneself derives instead from being thrown in the anticipation of one's own possibility of ending, by the force of which we are thrown back in an inexorable manner on the facticities of our past as the only basis of historical concreteness available to Dasein. One could, of course, reply to our remarks that there is no serious reason for speaking of a "cul-de-sac" in a philosophy which claims of itself to be an ontology of the radical temporality and finitude of the being of Dasein. That I concede. My criticism, however, is addressed to the idea defended in §61 (p. 303), that that existential interpretation should also be able to *free* a living Dasein for its most extreme possibility of existence. To exist, however, is more than understanding, uncovering and conceiving. On top of all this, we should say that, even for Heidegger, to exist, is also a *willing*. Authentic existence consists in the preparedness of the will to appropriate as one's ownmost possibility that which has been uncovered to oneself in a "transparent" (§31) understanding of the totality of one's own being. (Existence is "die ausdrückliche Zueignung des Erschlossenen" 307; cfr. 222.) Existential analysis can bring us, as also anxiety can, to the threshold of our existential possibilities; it can, however, not enforce upon us any form of appropriation of them. Although existential understanding, as uncovering, does not connote in "*Being and Time*" something abstract and purely theoretical which would have no direct bearings on our existence, it does not follow from this that that which is projected in our understanding becomes also automatically willed by us. On p. 194, e. gr., Heidegger says that "In willing, an entity which is understood that is, one which has been projected upon its possibility gets seized upon as something with which one may concern oneself". To uncover and to will (to understand and to act) are clearly not the same here. In a similar way, it remains possible for Dasein not to appropriate in a proper way its ownmost possibility. E.gr., it is possible for Dasein to relate itself "unwillingly" (p. 193) to its existential possibilities. We can avoid the possibility of death and fight shy of its company by turning our eyes away from it. We can positively will not to see what we secretly understand. Although in *Being and Time*, understanding is never the kind of distant and purely theoretical understanding, but a practical kind, which projects a possibility by mentally anticipating it, this does not mean, however, that will or choice could themselves be reduced to such an anticipation by the mind. Understanding and willing (or choosing) do complement each other, but they are not the same. If this is so, how is it then possible to proceed from a unveiled disclosure of what we are, to that kind of resolute choice for, or willing of ourselves which is called by Heidegger "anticipatory resoluteness" ("vorlaufende Entschossenheit" – p. 325 sq.)? Or even more importantly, why should this uncovering of that what we really are, have any specific existential consequences at all? Why would it not be possible for our anticipation of death to remain a sheer hypothetical possibility which we can pass lightly over after glancing rapidly through it, because it is and remains after all, an aspect of our being which cannot but repel us and frighten us out of any idea of the appropriation of it as a true possibility of our own. How can we positively will to be the ground of a nothingness, as *Being and Time* explains the meaning of the voice of conscience (§58)? Moreover, by what means can our will be moved to defeat or to overturn its own tendency of falling which is characterized as a "Bewegtkeit" (a movement, a kind of motion) of Dasein (p. 178-180), yet without expressing any kind of negative evaluation, as Heidegger puts it on p.175? In other words, how can we be moved or brought back from everyday fallenness to existential authenticity that is also called "wanting to have a conscience" ("gewissen-haben-wollen" (288); or "letting itself be called forth" ("Sichvorrufenlassen" – p. 287)? The absence of a convincing answer to that crucial question is the true reason for the blind alley of *Being and Time*. I know that one might reply that it is precisely proper to the voice of conscience to call us into the truth of our being. This answer, however, is far from convincing in every respect. The problem is that, for Heidegger, the phenomenon of conscience should first of all be seen and analysed as a phenomenon of ontological understanding of the truth. It is a phenomenon which, in order to understand it in its original sense, must be abstracted from all its usual ethical connotations (p. 269, 282-3). Seen in that manner, the call of conscience is in fact the way in which the uncanniness of our being pursues us in the false quietude of everyday fallenness. It is the way in which Dasein can be reminded by itself of itself. It is the calling in us of the truth of the nothingness of our being[8]. Yet following the voice of conscience is even for Heidegger the result of a form of *hearing* which is formally constituted by a positive willingness *to* be recalled from everyday fallenness. In this way, the will is put again at the centre of the phenomenon of understanding as hearing. "Understanding the appeal" means "wanting to have a conscience" (p. 288)[9]. „It reaches him who wants to be brought back" (p. 271)[10]. The step towards a positive choice for the appropriation of the truth (the explicit appropriation of what has been disclosed – p. 307) is, therefore, not made by a mere unveiling or understanding of the "truth of existence" (308), but by the will[11]. But why could the self not judge at this point that the truth is far too absurd and abominable to be honoured by an act of appropriation by the will? Is, after all, my freedom not too precious to be commanded by the frightening absurdity of freeing myself for death, or as p. 310 puts it in an almost pseudo-religious sense: "to follow the call of conscience and to free for death the possibility of acquiring power over Dasein's existence ...?" How can a truth which I can in no way understand as the unveiling of a positive good to be strived for by the will, have any existential consequences at all? This is the question to which *Being and Time* could not find a convincing answer within the confines of its ontological reduction. This blind alley becomes very obvious when Heidegger, on p. 310, has to ask himself the crucial question whether, after all, his ontological interpretation of Dasein is not dependent on a *factical ideal*, on a definite ontical way of understanding authentic existence? His answer is "that this is so indeed". This fact, he continues, is not only not to be denied, but also to be conceived in its positive necessity for the object of the investigation. This means, in fact, that the question as to the concrete possibility of an appropriation of the existential truth cannot be

---

[8] It is characteristic that "Gewißheit" ("being-certain") p. 307, as "die ausdrückliche Zueignung des Erschlossenen", and hence as "Entschlossenheit", is said to be a "Für-wahr-halten" (taking for true) *before* it is also called a "Sich-frei-halten-für" (308).

[9] *Anrufverstehen* besagt: *Gewissen-haben-wollen*.

[10] "Vom Ruf getroffen wird, wer zurückgeholt sein will".

[11] Understanding cannot be reduced, therefore, to the more active side of Heidegger's "Verstehen" as "projection" and "appropriation" of what is understood. There is also the part of "Vernehmen" in it. Yet, here again, this "Vernehmen" cannot be separated from the will, since this "Vernehmen" is characterized as an *obeying* (hearing) to the truth of the being in which we are thrown. Being "speaks" in our obeying understanding of it.

solved within the limits of the "ontological reduction" operated by *Being and Time*. The question cannot be taken apart from the concretely lived self-consciousness or ideal of the will.

Are there, then, no other ideals possible to live by and by which to understand the reality of existence, its temporality and its finitude? Of course, there are. But this is not the right question. The right question is to know whether the acceptance of finitude and the banishing of all teleological explanation of the *movement* of the human being, are by necessity *one and the same*. It seems to me that they are not, that Heidegger's explanation of the movement of Dasein is itself a failure. Other existential principles will, therefore, have to be invoked at the root of authentic human experience before we will be in a position to think, on an existential level, the whole enigma of the living movement of Being-in-the-world; that is, before it will be possible to demonstrate the inadmissibility of Heidegger's attempt to push away human desire, and the longing and expectation which belong to it, into the sphere of the illusions and false certainties of everyday business with the "things of the world".

How can desire be thought in a manner which is not concealed from our human finitude? In order to find an answer to this question, we will have recourse to the *Eléments pour une éthique* of Jean Nabert.

III. HUMAN ACTION AND THE REGENERATION OF THE PAST

I agree with Heidegger in saying that the being of Dasein is being-possible, in such a way that Dasein "is" itself the disclosing of the future, from out of which this being can let itself come towards itself as possibility, and into which it can project-in-advance its possibilities as its own. Dasein is the being that, on the grounds of what it is, can withdraw from its being-thrown into immersion with the world of things (Aufgehen bei), in order to let itself approach itself from out of a future that remains formally distinguished from the ecstasy of the being-alongside. This implies that the being of Dasein, as being-possible, must be structured such that it makes our transcendence over and against things possible. That which has to be thought, therefore, is the manner in which Dasein's being free for its possibility, ultimately attunes this Dasein to something other than "the things of the world". That is why Heidegger introduces the idea of "Seinkonnen zu ihm selbst, umwillen seiner" (the being possible of being for itself for the sake of itself).

In the first part of *Being and Time*, "already-being-ahead-of-itself-alongside" (*Sich vorweg schon sein bei*) seems in the first instance to point to a movement of transcendence in which Dasein is ahead of itself in such a way, that it opens (discloses, projects) for itself a future in which it can project its own authentic factical, yet ontical possibilities as its own – and, in this way, also projects itself forwards in an ontic sense. We have seen, however, how, for Heidegger, this movement of transcendence becomes ultimately identified with the anticipation of death. Thus resolute anticipation enforces upon us a kind of cleavage between the authenticity of withdrawal and the inauthenticity of creative activity as a search for (ontical) novelty. Our question is whether Heidegger – regardless of the appearance to the contrary – has really succeeded in thinking the future as *future*; that means, as that from out of which a creative regeneration or renewal of the past becomes possible and meaningful. In other words, our question is whether that which he ultimately presents as authenticity, does not rather come down to a position in which history can endlessly repeat itself, from out of the past of thrownness, in what is presented as the history of the heroical acceptance of our mortal finitude – and precisely not an attitude of future-relatedness in which *novelty* through the *regeneration* of the past and the creation of human value become possible. What must we, as finite and mortal beings who know that they will die, be internally oriented towards, such that, despite the perspective of death, a creative and at the same time regenerative orientation toward the future can be the outcome of it that is, a directedness towards the new, in which the past can be reborn? Or still further: how would a recalling of the past be really meaningful if not in the name of a will to regeneration, to which we are innerly driven by our being inhabited and guided by a forceful principle of novelty, re-creation and hope at the heart of our existence? This is the way in which Nabert portrays the meaning of action: as a history of regeneration of the *past* of "nature" to which we belong, in the name and spiritual force of a principle of *transcending* nature; a principle which affirms itself in us (and which Nabert, in his rather idealistic terminology, defines as "the pure self", but also as the "God, who dwells in us"[12]) and whereby this regeneration is to be seen as the source of our creation of human value[13] and of all ethical refinement of man, up to the most sublime moral sanctity.

---

[12] I myself would not speak here immediately of the divine Absolute as immanent in the soul or the spirit, but rather of our openness to originary being as evoked under n° 1 of this paper. This is being as ontologically distinguished from beings (entities). It is being in its transcendental unity, fulness and perfection, dispersing itself in and over all what is, and for which we are opened in all our ontical relations and performances. It is in that transcendental openness for being, openness which is also an understanding of being *as such*, that this divine-like fulness can become for us the manifestation of our sharing, as finite beings, in the Being of God himself. In this sense, the indwelling of God in us is mediated by the gift or the "coming over us" of divine-like being as the inner ground of our ownmost Possibility. Our ultimate Possibility is as universal as transcendental being itself.

[13] Honesty, temperance, justice, fidelity, love ...

This desire for regeneration is not a disavowal or a forgetting of the past[14], on the contrary, it includes a relationship, unceasingly maintained, of the self to its past (p. 27). Such will to regeneration can only follow out of a deeply felt and at the same time mysterious experience of failure, fault and guilt with respect to our past actions; it is an effort to raise oneself up after a kind of fall. However, this history of regeneration is only possible, Nabert says, when a relation of the self to the God, who dwells in it, breaks into the distress of a self which understands itself as identified with a past which it condemns (p. 27). Living man is, therefore, to be understood as the cooperation, as well as the unsolvable discrepancy and rivalry, of the forces which have constituted this unacceptable past: of what belongs to nature and what belongs to an aspiration which transcends nature (p. 19), and which is ultimately grounded in something by which we ourselves are surpassed. It is precisely this unsolvable inadequacy between the two principles which make up our metaphysical constitution, and hence the undeletable *difference* between every historical action and that at which it inwardly aims. It is this difference which forbids any interpretation of moral regeneration in terms of a more complete or fulfilled and happy act of immanent self-realisation, resp. autonomous self-creation, of the Ego in the world. The "pure self" *is* not itself a possible end or a value "in" the world, nor is regeneration a spiral movement towards an ever greater and glorious self-fulfilment in the world. To the contrary, every truly regenerative action must install a kind of self-displacement[15] with respect to the more primitive "topos" or the kind of need, inclination and action in which a failed or guilty action, as will to immanent self-realisation actually occurred. Regeneration, therefore, does not result in the (re)discovery of our true *"self"*-realisation in the world. Through its aspiration towards that which transcends the finite capacities of man, hence towards the impossible, the effort of regeneration „sauve le monde de la plus redoutable suffisance (l'autopistie: croyance en soi-même; l'autorythmie: suffisance de soi-même; l'autolâtrie: adoration de soi-même)" (Paul Evdokimov[16]). The redemptive truth of regeneration is first of all *in* the ongoing displacement itself, and not just in the value-creation which may follow from it, for this value-creation is only a historical sign of the event of regeneration itself. (The limited scope of this paper does not allow us to enter into more detail with respect to this important point).

---

[14] Forgetting is the charge made by Heidegger against all craving for novelty in the world.

[15] Such a self-displacement happens e.g. in the acceptance of the moral law, in the opening of oneself for the other, in the opennes for the higher destination of man, etc.

[16] *Sacrement de l'amour*, Paris: Desclée de Brouwer, 1962, 1977, p. 103.

Seen in this way, the temporality of freedom finds her source in an a-temporal "beginning" that, as the giving principle of a regenerative and, *in a subordinated way*, also a creative future, is itself withdrawn (separated, ontologically distuinguished) from all human projection and thus from all historicity. At that moment the temporality of freedom can no longer be reduced to the generation of an existential movement consisting in a letting oneself be thrown back onto the historical past (the heritage), from out of a confrontation with ones own limit (death). Now, the meaning of time is not just the circular existential movement in which the past can be repeated in an "authentic" manner, but a movement of future-directed, and at the same time dislocating self-surmounting (transcendence) in the name of a calling Possibility which is first and foremost to be seen as a *gift*. It is a responsive self-surmounting, in which alone the human being is truely constituted as a person and out of which this human person can return freely to reality as it stands, in order to renew it. This free return to "reality here and now" presupposes a movement of transcendence, in which the human self internally relates itself to and resources itself in that a-temporal "Mystery" which envelopes all beings within itself, and from out of which the temporal regeneration of our lived reality is *both* granted *and* given as a task, as being our ownmost possibility. Such freedom and temporality lead to a re-creation of the world (although unfinishable and inconclusive), not to its de-creation like it seems to have been the case for the Heidegger of *Being and Time*[17]. Through regeneration, life and the world of action become the signifiers of our belonging to a discontinuous "elsewhere" irreducable to any possible immanent goal or value-creation *in* the world. The sense of a temporal life cannot be reduced, here, to a surrendering to the impersonality of thrownness, in order to retake it in our history as our own (as our ownmost "gewesen")[18]. Such a surrendering (trans-*des*cendence) is only humanly meaningful when it is innerly cautioned by the counterweight of a move-

---

[17] If the ascetic resignation proposed by Heidegger were to be taken strictly, it would serve no practical purpose for humanity, since it is only withdrawal from the field of any positive contribution to the world. Such an attitude is more interested in one's own authenticity than anything else, like Schopenhauer's ascetic. Yet for Heidegger, such a withdrawal also leads to what is called by him the modification of our everyday existence *in* the world, where it aims at something like a new "orientation" for all of our everyday business with the things of the world. However, Heidegger is not very clear as to what this new orientation can concretely mean. At one particular place (p. 326), he calls it "letting itself be encountered undisguisedly by that which it [resoluteness] seizes upon in taking action" ("das unverstellte Begegnenlassen dessen, was sie [die Entschlossenheit] handelnd ergreift").

[18] Neither can the sense of a temporal life be defined as the time of the completion of our self in the world.

ment of transcendence (trans-*as*cendence) which makes up the "moral" substance of our being human (as Nabert would say[19]) and which supplies us with the powerful leverage to overcome the distress of our self-centered past. We have first to revert to the atemporal source of ourselves, before returning again to the world. We have to listen to a wordless voice which speaks in us in the murmur of an impalpable silence, in a vibration which makes us vibrate in our turn. We have to rediscover our most inner well in order to find again a more authentic way of being-with-others-in-the-world. Then, we can discover our being-together as a co-responsivity, together with their free possibility to respond to their own in fact to our commonly shared transcendent dignity. Such a life of regenerative creativity coincides, in fact, with the generation of a movement which consists in submitting oneself towards the never ending moral endeavour of regeneration (displacement) of our past, individual and collective, and this in the name of a higher desire and hope which both transcend the horizon of the empirical self in the world. Here too, the past can return in a more "authentic" manner, but only in so far as it can be regenerated and appropriated in a new and *different* way, from out of our orientation towards the principle of the New, which remains transcendent *and different*[20] with respect to every historical situation, but which nevertheless *calls* us into our ownmost Possibility (and integral unity[21]) and which, by doing so, "opens" or "lends" itself to taking up history in itself. Our creation of value, then, and hence historicity is a living in the "middle" between nature and God, and so also between a past which we have left, and a future which is to be resourced again and again in what Nabert calls "the God, who dwells in us".

Thus, living in the "middle" (W.Desmond) becomes the hallmark of our finitude. The hope which inspires it, is not the kind of "hybris" proper to "modernity" which Heidegger seems to have had in mind (which he rightly rejects as an unbridled craving for novelty and which we designated in our turn as the appealing but thoroughly illusive movement towards an ever greater and glorious self-fulfilment in the world). It is the hope which says that human life is mysteriously opened from within to a transcendence, from which it derives its true sense of the future, of regenerative moral creativity, and of its desire as well. The same certainty in us, which gives ground and bottom to our hope, is the inner certainty which gives full scope to our desire in a context of relentless lack and finitude. This hope is the source of an

---

[19] Op. cit., p. 19.

[20] No historical action can be seen as a inner and necessary "mediation" of our transcendent aim.

[21] A unity which cannot be identified, however, with a purely immanent and self-sufficient or self-creative "self-integration" of a metaphysically unrelated and independent Ego.

inexhaustable expectation, but not the guarantee for any final achievement in the immanence of the world. Even here, our ownmost possibility remains an impossibility within the horizon of the world. „L'espérance dit qu'il y a de l'autre, au-delà du trait d'horizon, de la coupure interne"[22] (Daniel Sibony). True existential hope affirms that there is "an other" beyond the confines of the horizon, beyond the inner cut of the difference between the world and "the God who dwells in us", as Nabert would say.

A self living "in the middle" doesn't have its center of gravity in its outer power to freely realize itself through action in the world, but in its inner passibility[23] for the self-impression of "Another" in the heart of man, and correspondingly in man's response to this Other. This is the source from which the energy of regeneration is persistently flowing out. The time of freedom is the time-span of such a response, hence the time of a possible re-location of self as the "from where out" of the moral regeneration of our acting in the world. This is why King David could sing in Ps. 16,8-11: I have set the Lord always before me ... he will show me the path of life.

---

[22] In: *Les trois monothéismes. Juifs, Chrétiens, Musulmans entre leurs sources et leurs destins*, Paris: Seuil, 1992, p. 281.

[23] Passiveness is more radical in meaning than receptivity; such a stronger sense is needed here, because of the fact that we find ourselves already engaged in our desire before we can become consciously receptive to its ownmost source and meaning.

JOHN F. X. KNASAS
University of Saint Thomas
United States

THE POST-MODERN NOTION OF FREEDOM
AND AQUINAS' *RATIO ENTIS*

I have always been disturbed by the attitude that truly creative types cannot possibly live by a Judeo-Christian ethics. Rather, they must be Nietzschean supermen, Heideggarian poets, or Sartrean authentic *pour-soi*. These characters profess a freedom unfounded on truth and incompatible with the strictures of moral law. They are beyond good and evil. But it seems to me that these post-moderns and their followers ignore the public record of the Christian saints. As saints none were murders, adulterers, fornicators, liars, or thieves. Yet for all that conformity to the moral law, the parade of Christian sanctity presents a striking panorama of "different lifestyles" – viz., the learning of Aquinas, the missionary activity of Francis Xavier, the contemplation of Teresa of Avila, the "little way" of Theresa of Lisieux, etc.. Originality and novelty are rampant here because it is precisely within these differences that sanctity is expressed. And who can say that one has seen the end of it? We know now that one would have been grossly mistaken to have made that claim in the third, twelfth, fifteenth, or for that matter, any previous century. Sanctity continually bursts stereotypes. And yet among the saints one again finds no regret that the activities of murdering, theft, lying, etc., are differences off-limits to the realization of sanctity. Evidently you can be creative and moral at the same time.

Motivated by this religious data, I would like to try to show that on the metaphysical level a similar result obtains. I will argue that a natural law ethics can be thought through in the light of a moral agent informed by the *ratio entis*. While such an ethics has the traditional absolute norms, it will also have all the advantages of analogy and so will be home to creative and novel realizations of the moral good.

I

First, though, I must sketch in more detail what I mean by the post-modern sense of freedom. By it I mean a philosophical "hardening," or "taking to the extreme", of a common and ordinary enough phenomenon. I will call that phenomenon the "play of projection". By this phrase I refer to the fact that by the attitudes, e.g., hopes, wishes, desires, imaginings, with which we come at things we can invest them, charge them, with a look, an appearance, a "meaning", that they would otherwise not have. This phenomenon is as common as "Let's pretend" games played by children. During the summer vacation in which I was nine years old, my cousin spun us this story that underground an old barn in the neighboring woods, the U. S. armed forces had set up a massive base. All through the summer my cousin embellished the tale. We at least half believed him and when he finally confessed the fib, those woods and surroundings instantly lost the appearance of "depth", lost a sense of mystery and enchantment.

There is no doubt that this play of projection enlists the creative capacities of the human person and brings us the enjoyment of experiencing novelty. I do not think that these items should be denied and rendered anathema. But the best context for the healthy employment of the play of projection is another matter. I deny that the context is post-modernism. For what happens in post-modernism is that the play of projection becomes radically fundamental so that it is constitutive of our experience of things. The experience of things arises in and through the mediation of human projection. As situated on such a basic level, the play of projection takes no cues from things; rather, things take their cues for it. So conceived, the play of projection seems to be synonymous with an unparalleled freedom.

In *The Basic Problems of Phenomenology*[1], Martin Heidegger seems to express just such an extremism for projection. This point emerges in Heidegger's description of understanding (*verstehen*). He emphasizes that understanding is not at all primarily a cognition but a basic determination of existence itself: "To exist is essentially... to understand"[2]. Hence, what is it for *Dasein* to exist? In sum, for *Dasein* to exist is for *Dasein* to be free.

> This entity, the Dasein, has it own being in a certain way under control, as it comports itself in this or that way toward its capacity to be, as it has already

---

[1] Martin Heidegger, *The Basic Problems of Phenomenology*, trans. by Albert Hofstadter (Bloomington & Indianapolis: Indiana University Press, 1988). The book is the text of a course that Heidegger gave at the University of Marburg in the summer of 1927. It was published only in 1975. Its close philosophical relationship to *Being and Time* (1927) is explained by Hofstadter in his "Translator's Introduction".

[2] Heidegger, *Basic Problems*, p. 276.

decided in this or that way for or against it. 'The Dasein is occupied with its own being' means more precisely: it is occupied with its own *ability to be*. As existent, the Dasein is free for specific possibilities of its own self. It is its own most peculiar able-to-be. These possibilities of itself are not empty logical possibilities lying outside itself, in which it can engage or from which it could keep aloof; instead they are, as such, determinations of existence. If the Dasein is free for definite possibilities of itself, for its ability to be, then the Dasein is in this *being-free-for*; it *is* these possibilities themselves[3].

Heidegger then connects these thoughts on *Dasein's* freedom with the original existential concept of understanding.

To be one's own most peculiar ability to be, to take it over and keep oneself in the possibility, to understand oneself in one's own factual freedom, that is, *to understand oneself in the being of one's own most peculiar ability-to-be, is the original existential concept of understanding*[4].

As a basic determination of existence, understanding means our freedom, our being in control of, at the head of, and as such the meaning goes back to the etymology of the German *"vorstehen"* – to stand in front of, at the head of, to preside over. Heidegger identifies understanding in the sense of freedom with the condition of possibility for all of *Dasein's* particular manners of comportment, not only practical but also cognitive[5]. This remark, along with others[6], is important because it seems to exclude a rational basis for freedom.

The absolute and underivative character of understanding freedom comes out again in Heidegger's clarification of the structure of understanding. In a word, understanding is projection[7]. Yet what I project upon is a can-be of my own self and what I project is my own self. These remarks

---

[3] Ibid., p. 276.

[4] Ibid., p. 276.

[5] "If understanding is the basic determination of existence, it is as such the condition of possibility for all of *Dasein's* particular possible manners of comportment. It is the condition of possibility for all kinds of comportment, not only practical but also cognitive." Ibid., p. 276.

[6] "If, however, an understanding of being always already lies at the basis of all comportment of the *Dasein* toward beings, whether nature or history, whether theoretical, or practical, then plainly I cannot adequately define the concept of understanding if, in trying to make the definition, I look solely to specific types of cognitive comportment towards beings. Thus what is required is to find a sufficiently original concept of understanding from which alone not only all modes of cognition but every type of comportment that relates to beings by inspection and circumspection can be conceived in a fundamental way." Ibid., p. 275.

[7] "To understand means, more precisely, *to project oneself upon a possibility*." Ibid., p. 277.

confirm that understanding is self-contained. Nor should one think that the self contains some stable nature that controls or guides the exercise of freedom. Heidegger says that *Dasein* "[...] is always only that which it has chosen itself to be, that which it understands itself to be in the projection of its own most peculiar ability-to-be"[8].

Heidegger goes on to insist, however, that understanding is not so self-contained that it involves an "isolated punctual ego"[9]. *Dasein* is being-in-the-world. But again, the exercise of freedom remains what is prior so that intra-worldly being, including other *Daseins*, are taken up in the light of that free projection. He says, "[...] along with understanding there is always already projected a particular possible being with others and a particular possible being toward intraworldly beings"[10]. This talk of being in the world and being with others does not mean that *Dasein* ceases to be in the driver's seat. Heidegger says that authentic understanding consists in being determined primarily by oneself, not by things, circumstances, or others[11]. Finally, Heidegger insists that in every existential understanding, i.e., in every free projection, there is enclosed an understanding of being. We cannot understand without projecting a sense of being in virtue of which a world is disclosed[12].

Heidegger's notion of *verstehen* strikingly calls to mind Sartre's position on the absolute freedom of the human subject, the *pour-soi*. In *Being and Nothingness*, Sartre passionately argues that we are not limited by our place, past, surroundings, fellow-brethren, or death. In general, Sartre points out that the coefficient of adversity found in these items is always a factor of our freely chosen projects. The standard example is the boulder on the road. What it is, viz., a help or a hindrance, depends upon what I want to do. If I wish to travel to a town beyond, the boulder is a hindrance; if I wish to survey the countryside, the boulder becomes a help[13]. It is true that in his *Letter on Humanism*, Heidegger takes some pains to distinguish his position from Sartrean existentialism[14]. To Heidegger's mind, Sartre is still too metaphysical, viz., insufficiently attentive to the Being of beings. Sartrean projection is upon already present beings and so aligns itself with a subjectivity

---

[8] Ibid., p. 278.
[9] Ibid., p. 278.
[10] Ibid., p. 278.
[11] Ibid., p. 279.
[12] "An understanding of the being of existence in general is enclosed in every existential understanding." Ibid., p. 279.
[13] Jean-Paul Sartre, *Being and Nothingness*, trans. by Hazel E. Barnes, (New York: Washington Square Press, 1969), p. 620.
[14] Martin Heidegger, *Letter on Humanism*, edited by David Farrell Knell, *Martin Heidegger: Basic Writings* (New York: Harper & Row, Publishers, 1977), p. 208.

that exploits and manipulates beings. Heidegger appears to want to avoid this subjectivity by a more radical subjectivity that accounts for the very Being in the light of which beings themselves become present. From my perspective, this dispute Heidegger picks with Sartrean existentialism is a lover's quarrel, for common to both is the primacy of the play of projection. Even though Heidegger insists that "[...] man does not decide whether and how beings appear [...] the advent of beings lies in the destiny of Being"[15] and also remarks that "the sentence [from *Being and Time*: 'Only so long as *Dasein* is, is there Being.'] does not say that Being is the product of man"[16], it is not clear to me that the term "man" here means Heideggerian *Dasein*. Rather, it seems to mean "the Dasein of man in the traditional sense of *existentia* and thought in modern philosophy as the actuality of *ego cogito*". Already cited texts from *Basic Problems* indicate quite unmistakably that Heideggerian *Dasein* does decide how beings appear and does produces the Being of beings.

II

What is a metaphysician to say to all of this? Three comments come to my mind. First, the post-modern construal of the play of projection is not without cost. Some debits are the following. First is a loss of objectivity. From an experience with less fundamental projections, we know that projections can make a difference in the appearance of objects. How does the post-modern know that our most fundamental projections are not causing things to appear in ways other than they really are? This doubt seems irremovable. Second, in the wake of the first problem, one can ask if social communication is ever possible. Is there ever a true encounter with the genuinely other person and how would we know? In the perspective of post-modernism, one will simply just decide that one's projection is the appropriate way of dealing with others. This move gives human existence a tyrannous character. Third, can one "just decide"? Decision is usually understood to be a response to value? But does the post-modern ever encounter real value? Like everything else, value appears only subsequent to projection. As mentioned, however, the objectivity of projection is always doubtful. Hence, why choose?[17]

---

[15] Ibid., p. 210.

[16] Ibid., p. 216.

[17] In his *For an Ontology of Morals* (Evanston: Northwestern University Press, 1971), p. 93, Henry Veatch explains the inability of transcendental method to allow real ethical obligation.

My second comment is that the post-modern's radicalization of the play of projection seems to be obviously false. We are not always mediating the presence of things in and through our freely chosen projects. But Heidegger is sensitive to this charge. He says that the experience of things as non-handy means to experience things as "unfamiliar". This latter experience is in turn reduced to some free projection of *Dasein*. Only because a fit into my presently chosen project is lacking does the non-handy come across as the unfamiliar. So, for Heidegger, the facts seem to show that we never experience things apart from some freely chosen project. What Heidegger calls *Dasein's* "productive comportment" appears to be universal and enveloping[18].

In reply, Heidegger's analysis works only because it does not go far enough. True, we do experience the non-handy as the unfamiliar, as what lacks a fit in one's project. But by presenting itself as the unfamiliar, as *contra* my project, something can give us pause, something can bring our projecting to a halt. The noteworthy point is that the temporary suspension of projecting does not mean the non-presencing of the thing. The thing remains suspended before one without the mediation of some freely chosen project. The presence of things as what-I-do-not-know-what-to-do-with is an open invitation to consider things in terms of what they are doing for themselves, viz., existing. It is true, as Heidegger describes[19], that someone entering a shoemaker's shop with the preoccupations of a banker will experience the shop's contents as "unfamiliar". They will not mesh with the project of high finance and will appear with a screech of unfamiliarity. But is it that difficult to imagine the banker as dropping his project of banking and letting things just present themselves? I think not.

In sum, we can see that presencing outstrips productive comportment. Productive comportment has an ebb and flow that contrasts to the continued presence of things. The latter belies the former. As mentioned, the unfamiliar can stop the comporting in its tracks. But other factors can do the same. Exhaustion in the midst of a difficult task can lead us to place the projecting aside but without the loss of the presence of things. To return to Sartre's boulder on the road example, if I encounter the boulder at high noon, I may decide to put off what I want to make of it and break for lunch. Does the boulder cease to be present? No. But in virtue of what productive comportment is it present? None. Long ago Aristotle noted[20] that success in

---

[18] See *Basic Problems*, pp. 112-117 for Heidegger's case for the fundamentality of productive comportment.

[19] Ibid., p. 304.

[20] Aristotle, *Metaphysics* I, 2, 982b 11-27.

meeting practical needs and necessities meant a diminution of practical concern without a commensurate diminution in the presencing of things. In fact from this continued presencing, philosophy took its rise. Hence, I fail to see productive comportment as subsuming the presencing of things. Being does not mean producedness.

The post-modern will likely insist that things that I claim are still present apart from productive comportment remain present *as things present at hand*. In other words, their presence remains contextual. In this case the context is "presence at hand". This remark leads to my third comment. It is far from clear that this noted context must be taken as a projection, as a constitutive *apriori*. In fact, the context contains no features that would preempt an *aposteriori* source. Even the ineluctibility of the context is an indecisive feature for its projective nature. For the context may be ineluctible because it derives from an immediate and spontaneous abstraction from real things given in sensation[21].

What is said here is important for showing that the play of projection so lionized by post-modernism occurs against a larger sky. Our projections do not traject into the void. They occur within Reality, within Being understood as this ineluctible *aposteriori* context for our appreciations of beings as being. For all of his talk about a return to being, I think that Heidegger himself misses it[22].

III

Despite these criticisms, the post-modern will still balk at making the play of projection something less than fundamental. A major motivation appears to be a perceived incompatibility between human freedom and any cuing of the human person by reality itself. In other words, if human existence is not fundamentally projective, then it is fundamentally receptive; it is other-determined rather than self-determined. The opposition is starkly presented by Heidegger in contrasting authentic understanding with inauthentic understanding. He presents both in *Basic Problems* within a temporal interpretation of understanding. Authentic understanding he calls "resoluteness",

---

[21] For an extended elaboration of this reply, see John F. X. Knasas, *A Heideggerian Critique of Aquinas and a Gilsonian Reply*, "The Thomist", 58 (1994), 415-439.

[22] In *Basic Problems*, Heidegger is searching for the horizon against which being in the sense of a world view is projected; see p. 280. This horizon turns out to the temporality of *Dasein* (p. 302) which seems to be another gloss of *Dasein*'s cognitively ungrounded freedom. In my opinion, Heidegger seems to be oblivious to the analogon of the *ratio entis* that is in truth the horizon that profiles what he is calling being.

and resoluteness is said to have its own temporal structure. When *Dasein* goes for a freely chosen possibility, it is both going ahead of itself and returning to itself. It is going ahead of itself because the possibility as freely chosen becomes one with *Dasein*; it is returning to itself because again as freely chosen, the possibility embodies *Dasein* as free which *Dasein* was before the choice. There is a cycling here in which *Dasein*'s exercise of freedom returns *Dasein* to its own freedom. The "going ahead" is the future component of resoluteness, the "returning" is the past component. But resoluteness also includes a present called the instant. Characteristic of the instant is that something is enpresented. The enpresencing occurs according to the exigencies, or demands, of the free future projection[23].

Heidegger next turns to a temporal analysis of inauthentic understanding. As a word of introduction, one could say that the temporality of authentic understanding was shot through with an awareness of *Dasein*'s freedom. Resoluteness concerned a conscious holding on to this freedom. Resoluteness is to exist in this freedom. With inauthentic understanding the awareness of *Dasein*'s freedom is lost. Hence, the future of inauthentic understanding is determined by the possibilities of things, not by the can-be of *Dasein*. Heidegger's way of saying it is "*Dasein* comes toward itself from out of things"[24]. In short, *Dasein* identifies itself not with its own possibilities but with the possibilities of things. *Dasein*'s future, that towards which it moves, is non-*Dasein*. Furthermore, what *Dasein* returns to, i.e., its past, is not its own freedom but again the possibilities of things. *Dasein*'s inauthentic past is marked by a forgetfulness of itself and its own can-be, or freedom. The inauthentic present will be elaborated later. For the most part *Dasein* exists in the temporality of inauthentic understanding. Inauthenticity predominates because *Dasein*'s intentionality first bears upon things in themselves[25]. Such a focus inadvertently covers over the founding role for things as played by *Dasein*.

IV

In the remainder of my paper, I want to neutralize this last motivation for the post-modern radicalization of the play of projection. Does a cognitive link to reality chain and bind human activity? Does a fundamental aposteriorism kill the poets, the artists, and creative thinkers among us? One

---

[23] *Basic Problems*, p. 287.
[24] Ibid., p. 289.
[25] For Heidegger's analysis of perceptual intentionality and the projection of being contained within it, see ibid., pp. 55-72.

could say yes to these questions only in the light of a very impoverished understanding of what Aquinas calls the *ratio entis*. Humans would be reduced to robots of the real, would suffer a great diminution of freedom and creativity, if the *ratio entis* is taken as the greatest genus. A genus must not include the differences by which it is determined to its species. In other words, the differences of the genus must be viewed as extrinsic to, or outside of, the genus. The reason for saying this lies in the thought that otherwise the genus would be placed twice in the definition of the species. For example, if the genus "animal" included the difference "rational", then the definition of man would not be rational animal but rational animal animal[26].

Yet this extrinsicism of the difference to the genus must be understood in a nuanced fashion. If the difference is understood as simply extrinsic to the genus, then the genus would be only a portion of the species. Since only whole is predicated of whole, not part of whole, a pure extrinsicism for the difference would render the genus a mere part and make predication of the genus impossible. Consequently, Aquinas distinguishes abstraction with and without precision[27]. Abstracted with precision, a common nature like a generic notion is closed off to its very differences. The nature is rendered into merely a part of the instance from which it was abstracted. Hence, it cannot be predicated, i.e., identified, with the instance. If this was the only kind of abstraction of common natures, knowledge of anything would become impossible, for one could never say what anything is.

Abstracted without precision a common nature is understood to remain open to the very differences from which it abstracts. For example, human nature abstracted without precision as "man" does not include any definite complexion, but neither does it go on to exclude what it does not include. As such "man" is appreciated as what is able to be complected. Note that here the differences are outside in the sense that the commonality remains

---

[26] "If being were a genus we should have to find a difference through which to contract it to a species. But no difference shares in the genus in such a way that the genus is included in the notion of the difference, for thus the genus would be included twice in the definition of the species. Rather, the difference is outside what is understood in the nature of the genus. But there is nothing that is outside that which is understood by being (*ens*), if being is included in the concept of things of which it is predicated. Thus being cannot be contracted by any difference. Being is, therefore, not a genus." St. Thomas Aquinas, *Summa Contra Gentiles*, I, 25, *Quod autem*; trans. by Anton C. Pegis (Notre Dame: University of Notre Dame Press, 1975), I, p. 127.

[27] On these two kinds of abstraction, see Aquinas, *On Being and Essence*, ch. 2; for commentary, see Joseph Owens, *The Accidental and Essential Character of Being in the Doctrine of St. Thomas Aquinas*, edited by John R. Catan in *St. Thomas Aquinas on the Existence of God: Collected Papers of Joseph Owens, C.Ss.R.* (New York: State University of New York Press, 1980), pp. 84-90.

open to them. This "openness" keeps the differences present and permits prediction of the commonality, even while it understands the differences as extrinsic. In sum, in abstraction without precision of a genus the differences are rendered extrinsic but potentially contained.

Now if being is like a genus, then all the differences of being would have to be placed outside of being and so rendered nugatory. That would prevent any differentiation of being. Being would be frozen and static. Nothing new under the sun would have the foreboding sense of metaphysical necessity. By this genus-like understanding of being, aposteriorism would strike the intellect dumb. It would be the end of creativity.

But Aquinas contrasts the *ratio entis* from a generic notion. Being is differentiated but not in and through the addition of something extrinsic. Rather, being is differentiated into special modes[28]. These modes are the diverse genera of things, viz., substance and the various accidents. But the multiplication of being into these modes is not in and through something extrinsic like a difference of a genus, for as mentioned, only non-being is extrinsic to being and non-being cannot differentiate. Rather the multiplication is stated this way: the mode expresses something not expressed by the name being. Being provides for its own differentiation. Scholastics have formulated the situation of being vis-à-vis its diverse genera this way. Being contains them implicitly but actually. In contrast, the generic notion contains its differences implicitly but potentially[29].

Elsewhere Aquinas calls the community of *ens* analogous[30]. Neo-Thomists have fashioned some felicitous ways of expressing the nature of the analogous concept[31]. These philosophers reiterate the same point – an analogous concept is not picked out apart from the differences of its instances but *within* those very differences. In contrast, a univocal commonality is picked out apart from the differences of the instances. Hence, what makes the instances of the univocal commonality the same will not be what renders them different. For example, "triangle" expresses the commonality grasped in the

---

[28] Aquinas, *De Ver.* I, 1c.

[29] "The analogical concept is radically different: it has only a relative or proportional unity, and it does not include the diversity of its inferiors potentially. ... In order that it may not be univocal in any degree, therefore, the analogical concept must include diversity actually, without in any way rendering that diversity explicit." James F. Anderson, *The Bond of Being: An Essay on Analogy and Existence* (New York: Greenwood Press, Publishers: 1969), pp. 256-7.

[30] *In I Sent.*, d. 19, q. 5, a. 2, ad 1m; *In I Sent.*, prol. Q. 1, a. 2, ad 2m; *De Ver.* II, 11c.

[31] For remarks of Jacques Maritain, Gerald Phelan, and Joseph Owens, see John F. X. Knasas, *Aquinas, Analogy, and the Divine Infinity*, "Doctor Communis", 40 (1987), pp. 72-73. Also in Knasas, *The Preface to Thomistic Metaphysics: A Contribution to the Neo-Thomist Debate on the Start of Metaphysics* (New York: Peter Lang, 1990), pp. 100-103.

equilateral three-sided figure and the right angled three-sided figure. In this situation the equal sides of the first instance and the right angle of the second instance serve simply to differentiate the instances. They do not convey the sameness as it is witnessed by the right angle in a square. The instances are the same in virtue of something else. With the analogical concept, however, we have a commonality that is grasped within the very differences, they serve to render the instances the same. As Aquinas has been noted to say, "some things are said to be alike which communicate in the same form (*in eadem forma*), but not according to the same formality (*secundum eandem rationem*)"[32].

The analogous concept may sound beyond belief and brushed aside as the fanciful product of metaphysics. Common, non-metaphysical experience, though, provides many instances of analogy. Consider the way in which "great baseball player" is applied both to Willie Mays and Sandy Koufax. Mays was a great out-fielder and hitter, Koufax a great pitcher. Different as each of these things are, they nevertheless serve to make Mays and Koufax alike. In these cases, there is a sameness in the differences and differences in the sameness. The very thing that makes Mays the same as Koufax, viz., Mays' hitting, is also the very thing that makes him different from Koufax and vice versa.

Concerning the analogous concept, there are two further important points to note. First, one must not mentally attempt to pry the analagous commonality, or analogon, apart from its instances, or analogates[33]. Recall, the commonality is within the differences of the instances. Any attempt to separate the commonality from these differences results in the loss of the commonality. Hence, inappropriate is the Scotistic demand to specify in what respect the instances are the same and in what respect they are different[34]. The demand fails to understand the nature of the analogous concept. Here the sameness is in the differences. Hence, one does not wish to avoid the differences of the instances. They carry the sameness.

Second, the analogous notion carries an astonishing intelligible wealth and plentitude. Because it is grasped within the differences of its instances, the analogical concept manifests itself as an unparalleled source of novelty. Different as the great baseball playing of Mays is from Koufax's, it is still the same in both. Great baseball playing in itself is acknowledged to contain both styles and who knows what myriad others. At the time of Ruth and

---

[32] Aquinas, *Summa Theologiae* I, 4, 3c.

[33] On the terminology of "analogon" and "analogate", see George P. Klubertanz, *St. Thomas on Analogy* (Chicago: Loyola University Press, 1960), pp. 6-7.

[34] For the demand, see Patrick Lee, *Language about God and the Theory of Analogy*, "The New Scholasticism", 58 (1984), pp. 40-41.

Cobb who could have envisaged a Mays or Koufax? Today who can guess what further analogates great baseball player will assume? And if the great baseball playing of Mays, for example, is awesome to behold, then great baseball player in itself must be stupendous[35].

Returning to the *ratio entis*, Aquinas' understanding of the differentiation of the *ratio entis* into its modes is the crux for comprehending how, *pace* the post-moderns, a fundamentally *aposteriori* stance is compatibile with the free creative capacities of the human being. The diverse *modi entis* never transcend the *ratio*. Their diversity occurs within *ens*. In other words, *ens* manifests itself as a sameness within difference. Properly understood, being presents itself as the source and matrix of novelty. Its different modes precisely in their differences emerge from being. But the novelty continues beyond these modes. These modes cognitively engender an appreciation of analogons and new possibilities for analogates. For example, the modes of being that are Chopin's and Beethoven's different ways of playing the piano engender an appreciation of the analogon great musician. The Thomistic knower of being is guaranteed an education in novelty by these analogons that strike the mind through their various analogates. He is instructed in the fact that there are many different ways to do things and who would be so bold to say that we have seen the end of them. Would a sports caster in the 1930's have been wise to say that he had seen all there was to great baseball playing? As the Thomist sees it, reality is nothing other than an inspiration to creativity. If we can say Chopin and Beethoven and others are inspirations to aspiring musicians, why can we not say the same of the *ratio entis*? The former is contained in and made possible by the second.

V

The compatibility of aposteriorism and creative freedom in the light of the *ratio entis* is nevertheless not a license to run absolutely wild. Despite its ability to make its way into a startling array of differences, no analogon is a case of anything goes. For example, my way of playing the piano is not a difference that would ever permit the presence of the analogon "great pianist". Some differences cannot carry the sameness. At first thought *ens* might seem to be an exception, for as mentioned any difference is a being. Was not this the reason *ens* is not a genus? All this is true. But in a way I would like to sketch, *ens* creates its own norms.

---

[35] On Aquinas' distinction of analogy into its types on the basis of the various ways in which the analogon is found in the analogates, see Knasas, Aquinas, *Analogy, and the Divine Infinity*, pp. 75-76.

The first step in this development is to realize that being is the total good. At first thought, this characterization of being might seem farfetched. Up until now I have presented quite an intellectual appreciation of being. Its guise was that of an object of knowledge; it was a *ratio* and an analogical *concept*. But is not our experience more than just knowing something? What we know, we also want to possess, i.e., to have in its real existence[36]. Knowledge seems to be only part of the story of the human being. Hence, how can one broaden the appreciation of being to encompass the willing of the good?

This appreciation follows on the heels of the *ratio entis* actually including all differences. Hence the real existence of things, not simply their cognitional existence, is a mode of being actually but implicitly contained in being. In other words, because being implicitly but actually contains its differences, being is not only an object of knowledge that leaves the real existence of things outside its consideration. It also actually includes the real existence of those things that we so ardently will, e.g., moral rectitude, friendship, physical well-being[37]. This point about being reiterates what I understand to be being as it is object of the practical intellect[38]. So, as an analogical notion, being both abstracts and does not abstract from real existence. Being both gets away from real existence and stays enmeshed in it. Because being gets away from it, being is an object of the speculative intellect[39]. But be-

---

[36] On the will as related to things outside the soul, see Aquinas, *S.C.G.* I, 72, *Adhuc* and *De Ver.* 21, 1c (cited in n. 37).

[37] "The true and the good must therefore add to the concept of being (*intellectum entis*), a relationship of that which perfects. But in any being there are two aspects to be considered, the formal character of its species and the act of being (*esse ipsum*) by which it subsists in that species. And so a being can be perfective in two ways. (1) It can be so just according to its specific character. In this way the intellect is perfected by a being, for it perceives the formal character of the being. But the being is still not in it according to its natural existence (*esse naturale*). It is this mode of perfecting which the true adds to being [...]. (2) A being is perfective of another not only according to its specific character but also according to the existence (*esse*) which it has in reality. In this fashion the good is perfective; for the good is in things, [...]" Aquinas, *De Ver.* 21, 1c; trans. by Robert W. Schmidt, *The Disputed Questions on Truth* (Chicago: Henry Regnery Company, 1954) III, pp. 6-7.

[38] "Ita nec apprehensio veri sine ratione boni et appetibilis [non movet appetitum]. Unde intellectus speculativus non movet, sed intellectus practicus". *S.T.* I-II, 9, 1, ad 2m. At *S.T.* I, 79, 11c, Aquinas says that the practical intellect directs what it apprehends to operation. But operation terminates in the *esse* of its effect. For example, see efficient causality in the *secunda via* at *S.T.* I, 2, 3c. Hence, in its consideration of the *ratio entis* the practical intellect must both regard real existence and regard it as good.

[39] As making some abstraction from real existence, the Thomistic *ratio entis* is neither an item of ontological realism, like a Platonic Form, nor is it an item open to ontological reasoning. The *ratio entis* remains knowable only in and through its analogates.

cause the *ratio entis* also stays enmeshed in real existence, being is an object of the practical intellect.

Able to be grasped as the total good, being excites in the human will a necessary desire for it. This necessary desire is the desire for happiness, the possession of all good things, as Boethius says. But since being is an analogon seen in the differences of its analogates, each of the analogates make a claim on our love. Here, though, the claim is to a response that is free. Since the analogates manifest the analogon only through their differences, they imperfectly present the analogon. They remain necessarily *lovable* but not necessarily *loved*.

Among these analogates human persons are special. As intellectual they are analogates that through their intellection have the *ratio entis* present within them. Our reverence for the *ratio entis* should spill over into a reverence for these unique analogates. In a human person we meet and confront being in a special way. Being can speak to us, it can inform us of itself. With human beings the claim of the analogates of being to a free response of love is especially intense. It calls forth an ethics that accords a most high dignity to individual human persons. It is an ethics that has no place for treating humans as mere means to ends.

The above connections are seen in a text from Aquinas on divine providence. Aquinas argues that in God's providence over rational creatures, God governs them for their own sakes. One argument is as follows:

> [...] it is evident that all parts are ordered to the perfection of the whole, since a whole does not exist for the sake of its parts, but, rather, the parts are for the whole. Now, intellectual natures have a closer relationship to a whole than do other natures, indeed, each intellectual substance is in a way all things. For it may comprehend the entirety of being through its intellect [*inquantum totius entis comprehensiva est suo intellectu*][40].

The connection of created intellect with being places an obligation even upon God. This obligation is to treat the human as an end in itself. Only a part of a larger whole is appropriate for means-to-end thinking. But as intellector of being, the human is more the entirety than a part thereof.

If God must treat rational creatures with dignity, obviously so must we. A number of absolute negative ethical norms easily follow. First, innocent human life is inviolable. Neither the citizen nor ruler can directly take it. In other words, murder is wrong. Murder falsely reduces the human to a mere part of some purported larger whole. Neither is suicide moral. The men-

---

[40] *S.C.G.* III, 112, *Praeterea*; trans. by Vernon J. Bourke (Notre Dame: University of Notre Dame Press, 1975), 3: II, pp. 116-117.

tioned necessary desire for being as the good renders suicide profoundly unnatural.

This high dignity accorded the human as an intellector of being also excludes any deliberate depriving of what is materially necessary for one to exist. In short, stealing is wrong.

Also insofar as sexual intercourse is by its nature a most intimate physical union of persons, there is no place for means-to-ends thinking that would lead to transiency. The person is again an intellector of being. One should understand that participation in sexual activity must be accompanied with the absolute respect owing to being. If one does not wish to provide that respect, then one ought to refrain from sex. One cannot make sexual intercourse a portion of some larger totality. As involving intellectors of being, sexual union is already a totality. In a literal way, one sees stars in the eyes of the beloved. For the beloved is an entire universe. An encounter with an entire universe is not a passing one because it resists reduction to a means that would be dispensible once the end is achieved. In other words, given the human persons involved, human sexuality ought to be exercised within a permanent and exclusive context. Finally, any deliberate diminution of the sexual act, e.g., contraception, is also wrong. It is against the nature of the sexual act understood as the giving of a totality.

At this point it may seem that by these negative norms, I am isolating the human being from the creativity of which I spoke earlier. Am I now taking with one hand what I had given with the other? I do not think so. These negative norms delineate a field for a morality that is home to the creativity of being. The more we are sensitive to being's legitimate expressions in our fellows, the more creative and novel will be our response. Through residing in various individuals, being sets up its own data that calls forth new responses. A mother or father never knows what analogate of good parent will need to be realized on any day in solicitude to their children. Likewise, a teacher can never predict what form of excellence will be required to communicate effectively with each new class. In that vein, is not Aquinas' greatness as an intellectual comprehensible only as a response to the Aristotelian challenge to his Christian faith? Analogates feed on analogates. We should not be afraid to submit ourselves to our fellows, for being with all its resources for newness is found there. The most difficult part of ethics is not the negative norms but the positive ones. Each of us is left to figure out for ourselves what analogate of good person is appropriate for us in our circumstances.

VI

In conclusion, I have tried to show that the best matrix to accommodate what is true in the play of projection that post-moderns use to characterize freedom is what Aquinas calls the *ratio entis*. Even though this is not a *projectum* but an *abstractum* taken from real things, it does not render the human a mere reflex of reality. Because of its analogical nature, it is an education in the emergence of novelty and is an invitation to project further new and unheard of analogates of being. Moreover, its connection with the total good engenders an ethics of respect for our fellows in so far as they have being present to them by intellection. This respect is encapsulated not only within the negative norms of natural law but also within the positive ones. Regarding the latter, ethics is also a call to creativity as we left to craft analogates of moral living suitable to our circumstances.

ANDRZEJ MARYNIARCZYK
Catholic University of Lublin
Poland

FREEDOM AND TRUTH
(TRUTH AS A WAY TO FREEDOM)

Freedom, as a characteristic of a personal being, is indeed the natural space in which the man lives, acts and developes. The question which from age to age has bothered philosophers is; "is freedom inherent to the human being" or "does man simply become free"?

In fact, throughout history, freedom was treated as an absolute value or was denied. The interpretation, in which freedom was pointed out as "a task" for the human being, has been rejected and has been clamored down. We can observe the same process in modern thought.

The attitude of taking freedom as an absolute value (or its negation) comes from the identification of the personal lives of man with the freedom or from placing of freedom as an *idea* (a primary value) that exists before or behind the man. This leads, in effect, to ascribing to the individual conscience the right to proclaim what good is and what evil is. Moral judgement is right just because it comes from one's conscience. In dealing freely the need for truth disappeared and in its place came the criterium of sincerity, authencity, and self-correspondece. It brought about the disappearance of the transcendental truth of good of every being (and the moral being as well).

This originated the extreme individualism in the social life, the liberalism in politics and the arrogance of authorities.

Meanwhile, liberty cannot be higher and more perfect than the human being. Liberty cannot be identified with any undeterminate action and separated from being. Freedom is a way of acting for the humane person, as a person. Self-determination and self-control is a sign of one's personal life. This kind of freedom cannot be achieved behind and separated from the cognition of the *Truth and Good* of being. This is because "Nil est volitum quin praecognitum". Being is what becomes a reality of our willing life and determines the area of liberty.

For philosophers it is a task to consider the truth of human freedom, to undertake an effort to put together freedom and human being, and to show the truth as a way to true human liberty.

I. THE DISCOVERY FREEDOMCREATIVE POWER OF THE TRUTH

The Greek term *aletheia* used to describe "the truth" is derived from the adjective *lethe* which means "forgetfulness", or "to fall into oblivion", and from the prefix "a-" which indicates the negation or the different condition as the adjective indicates. In this context the term *aletheia* means "the liberation from the forgetfulness" or "return to primary knowledge". We propose to explain the term *aletheia* by derivation it from the adjective *ale* which means "a homelessness" or "losing" (to lose) and from the verb *theidzoo* which means "to inspire" or "to adore". This derivation of the meaning of the term *aletheia* indicates "the inspiration of the homelessness" or "the direction of homelessness in the right way"[1].

Both meanings of the term *aletheia* point out that truth has a power of liberation". Truth has divine features or reviles its divine origin.

We need to distinguish between the understanding of truth as a liberty and as a way to liberty. As a base for this interpretation there are two great philosophical traditions: the platonic and the aristotelian.

1. TRUTH AS FREEDOM

The source of identification of freedom with man and with the idea of feedom is platonic anthropology. According to this anthropology the soul-ghost is a perfect and free being. Its manner of acting is identical with the manner of existence. The soul existing as a *logos* redices all of its acts to the acts of cognition (Plato does not distinguish the soul's powers such as; the will and reason (mind)). The truth is the life of the soul-ghost, and in the acts of thinking it expresses its *freedom*.

In the Plato's dialogues the term *truth* is used mostly in two basic meanings; as a qualification of "divine reality" (the idea) and as a "realization of

---

[1] R. Bultman, *Uso Greco ed Ellenistico di aletheia*, in: *Grande Lessico del Nuovo Testamento*, vo. 1, ed. F. Montagnini e G. Scarpat, Brescia 1965, cl. 640nn; R. Popowski, *Wielki słownik grecko-polski Nowego Testamentu*, Warszawa 1995, k. 222nn.

humane freedom". Hence in the Plato's Dialogues we can find an expression that truth "describes something real", "something what is", "what must be", "something what never originates and perishes", "what cannot be changeable and remains always the same".

Plato speaks about "the true guard" and "the true state", "the true government"[2] as well. These indicate that truth is a characteristic of the real reality" because if we do not admit the truth to something else, it cannot truly originate, and exist[3].

We have to notice that in the platonic tradition freedom and truth (similarly like a good) is before and behind being.

In the platonic dialogues we can meet next to metaphysical meaning of the term "truth" the ethical meanings as well. As an example we can take the Dialogue Fileb, where Plato says that "truth has a room with every ghost"[4], or in another Dialogue he says that "true is a beginning of any good in the life of gods and of the people as well"[5]. Moreover, Plato encourages every one to "love the truth and to do everything according to the will of truth. Truth has a power of liberation and of purification.

According to the soteriological function of platonic philosophy truth is the liberation of the soul-ghost which is imprisoned in the body. The soul-ghost cannot be free without or out of truth[6].

In this way, as we see, the term "truth" in platonic philosphy means some "divine reality" and "state of liberation". Free acting and free behaving are both acting in the spirit of truth.

With such an understanding of freedom, the human being does not participate in it, because his "natural" state is in a state of violation. The state of violation (the soul in the body) is a natural space of life for the mortal being according to the platonic interpretation. Freedom belongs to gods and the divine part of human beings – the soul.

2. TRUTH AS A WAY TO FREEDOM

Another manner of discussing the problem of truth and freedom is seen in the tradition of the realistic philosophy initiated by Aristotle. In the realist philosophy of Aristotle human freedom is treated as "a task" that is given to man to make him learn it and develop it by reading the truth and good in being.

---

[2] Platon, *Państwo*, 347 D; 372 E.
[3] *Fileb*, 39 B.
[4] *Fileb*, 39 B.
[5] *Prawa*, 730 C; *Państwo*, 532 C.
[6] *Państwo*, VIII, 621 A-C.

The human being, according to the aristotelian interpretation, is composed from the soul and body and acts by will and intellect, powers of the soul. Hence the will cannot be being but only the accident (power) of the human being. Feerdom cannot be something higher and more perfect than the human being. The will cannot act by itself and becomes a reality owing to the truth and good of being.

It is evident that freedom is connected with the will and not with the intellect. However, the will which by it's nature is directed to good, is blind, in selecting the proper (right) good. Therefore truth, with reference to human freedom, plays a double roll: truth forms the right will (recta voluntas) and as a characteristic of being is the good that is the object of the desire of the will. That is why behind the truth-good there cannot exist true freedom and there cannot be any possible development of the human person.

In contrast to the platonic anthropology (in which the human being is treated as perfect in the soul-ghost) Aristotle insists that human beings "become free". Hence, the acting of the human being towards the "proper good" makes man really free. Truth and good are the ultimate reasons for the personal activity of human beings. Truth is the reason human activity conducts from the material world to the inner human being: the good, on the other hand, is the reason human activity runs outside the human being. In these activities there is expressed and formed the true freedom of the human being. These kinds of human activities are directed by the truth of being: "ordinatur in unum, scilicet ad hominis perfectionem, quae est eius beatitudo"[7].

In the realistic antopology freedom is understood as the task and space of human rationality and amability. The truth is *the way to human freedom*.

It is important to notice the peculiarity of the understanding of truth and of freedom in aristotelian anthropology. The truth is not behind or before being, the truth is an expression of the rationality of the existence of being. We can read in the metaphysics of Aristotle that "being in its simple meaning can be understood as the truth"[8]. The words "being" and "not-being" are used to express the truth and falsity. The truth is a result of cognition of the nature of being. The truth and falsity – Aristotle explains – "depends, in the case of the objects, upon their being united or divided; so that he who thinks that what is divided is divided, or that what is united is united, is right"[...] It is not because we are right in thinking that you are white that you are white; it is because you are white that we are right in saying so"[9].

---

[7] S. Thomae Aquinatis, *In XIII libros metaphysicorum commentarium. Proemium.*
[8] Met., 1026 a.
[9] Met., 1051 b.

We can observe that in the Aristotelian interpretation of freedom the truth is closely connected with it but is not identified with it (liberty). The truth is treated as a way to true human freedom.

St. Thomas Aquinas explains humane freedom in the aristotelian tradition. He indicates that the truth prefects the subject (is a causa cognitionis) and as a transcendental value of being it is a "sign post" for the rational activity in the behaviour of the human being[10].

In Thomas Aquinas' writings we can find the diverse definition of the truth. He says that "the truth is what the reason apprehends"[11], or that "the truth is the final end of the whole of the universe"[12], or that "every thing is connected with its truth as with its existence"[13].

St. Thomas characterizing the definition of the truth, which we can meet in philosophy, organizes them into three groups. There is the meaning of the truth as an "expression of the existence of being"; as a sign of value of judgement, as a perfection of the personal being[14].

According to St. Thomas Aqinas the term "truth" indicates first of all the deepest roots of the rational order whose base is a being. The real being is a carrier of the truth of good which is the way to the fulfillment of the personal being as a guarantee of true human freedom.

In the realistic interpretation given by Aristotle and St. Thomas the truth and the good are necessarily connected with being (they do not exist before, or behind, or instead of being). The being as a carrier of the truth and good is what "primum cadit in intellectum et in voluntas" as well. Hence humane freedom becomes real in acts of decision of choosing the good, directed by its cognition. In the face of cognition of the truth of being which is real good, beings realize their freedom.

The truth is the way to freedom.

II. WHY FREEDOM IS FOUND THROUGH THE TRUTH

The ancient philosophers, especially Aristotle, identified the free man with the wise man – sofos. They indicated the role of free thinking as a base

---

[10] "Ens est prefectivum alterius non solum secundum rationem speciei, sed etiam secundum esse quod habet in rerum natura [...] Verum et bonum super intellectum entis addant respectum perfectivi", De Ver., q.21, a.1, resp.

[11] "Verum est id in quod tendit intellecuts", STh 1, q.16, a.1.

[12] "Veritatem esse ultimum finem totius universi", SCG I, 1.

[13] "Unumquodque ita se habet ad veritatem scut ad esse", STh I, q.16, a.3.

[14] "Id quod praecedit rationem veritatis [...] quod formaliter rationem veri perficit [...] addant respectum perfectivi", De Ver., q.1, a.1; q.21, a.1.

for free activity and behavior. This is not a form of ethical intellectualism. The truth which has been discovered is the highest good and the final end of human activity.

According to Aristotle, the metaphysical cognition is the idea of free cognition. Freedom of the metaphysical cognition is realized by the subject of cognition(a), by the object(b), and by the final end(c).

a. Aristotle remarks that only the man who is not entangled in some inner or outer conflict and trouble can be truly free in cognition and in his activity. "As more and more arts – says Aristotle in Metaphysics – were discovered, some relating to the necessities and some to the pastimes of life, the inventors of the latter were always considered wiser than those of the former, because their branches of knowledge did not aim at utility. Hence when all the discoveries of these were fully developed, the sciences which related neither to pleasure nor to the necessities of life were invented, and first in those places here men had leisure time"[15].

To be free in one's cognition, activity and in behavior is to be a man who has wisdom. Wisdom is a source of human freedom. Aristotle indicates that the person independent in cognition is a person who has a "theoretical knowledge rather than a practical", "who understands the nature of things", "who has the ability to teach and to discover things", "who processes a theory and knows the causes"[16].

Furthermore, a free man is one "who knows all things, so far as it is possible, without having knowledge of each one of them individually", "who can comprehended difficult things, which are not easy for human comprehension", "who is more accurately informed and better able to expound the causes"[17].

We can assume that "what is called Wisdom is connected with cognition of the primary causes and principles, so that, as it has been already stated, the man of experience is held to be wiser than the mere possessors of any power of sensation, the artist than the man of experience, the master craftsman than the erasion; and the speculative sciences to be more learned than the productive. Thus it is clear that Wisdom is knowledge of certain principles and causes"[18] and this knowledge is a base of human freedom.

b. The freedom of cognition is also determinated by the object. To this kind of cognition belongs the investigation of the "first principles and causes". It is because "the things which are most knowable are first principles and

---

[15] Met., 981 b 20.
[16] Met., 981 a 15 - 981 b 30.
[17] Met., 982 a 10-15.
[18] Met., 981 b 25- 982 a 5.

causes; for it is through these and from these that other things come to be known, and not these through the particulars which fall under them"[19]. These first principle and causes "are perhaps the hardest for man to grasp – remarks Aristotle – because they are furthest removed from the senses. Again, the most exact of the sciences are those which are most concerned with the first principles; for those which are based on fewer principles are more exact than those which include additional principle [...] Moreover, the science which investigates causes is more instructive than one which does not, for it is those who tell us the causes of any particular thing which instruct us"[20].

c. For freedom of cognition the final end of our consideration is very important. Truly free cognition is that which tends to achieve the truth for itself.

The discovery of the intelligibility of being as a transcendental property of all the real things was very important in the process of understanding the world and human beings. That has signified in the practice that the man conducts the cognitional dialog not only with other human beings (another "I") but with the world of material things as well, and at the same time he becomes the owner of the truth and its co-originator. This dialogue is possible because the things which exist carry the truth in themselves. Hence being can be the proper object of intellectual cognition.

This "co-participation in the truth" and its "co-origination" takes a part in the personal life of a human being and is a step in the process of the development of the human person. The cognition of the truth helps the man in growing as a person. That understanding of the truth, as a transcendental property of the real being describes the field of human freedom and is a principle (base) of the right development of human freedom.

It was clear indeed for the ancient philosopher that the truth is a base of human freedom. Through the cognition of the truth of things man becomes truly free and wise. And "among the sciences we consider that science which is desirable in itself and for the sake of knowledge as more near Wisdom than that which is desirable for its results, and that the superior is more nearly Wisdom than the subsidiary; for the wise man should give orders, not receive them; nor should he obey others, but the less wise should obey him"[21].

Thus as a result of this consideration we have to indicate, that this science and cognition is truly free "which knows why each action is to be done"[22]. "The Good in each particular case, and in general the highest

---

[19] Met., 982 b 5.
[20] Met., 982 a 25-30.
[21] Met., 982 a15.
[22] Met., 982 a 5.

Good in the whole of nature" and as one of the causes is the final end of human action.

III. THE TRUE FREEDOM

The activity of the person which is not directed by the truth is irrational activity. Freedom which is not directed by the true good is self-denying. In the experience of the intelligibility of being there is included the whole area of human liberty. Therefore in the metaphysical cognition we can cross (go out) beyond rationalism and empiricism as well. We are going beyond the empiricism because the transcendental comprehension, which is the characteristic of metaphysical cognition, goes out beyond sensory experience (we do not have the sensory experience of God, or of the human soul, or of the cause). We are crossing beyond rationalism because we have knowledge which is not closed in by what is contained in the sensory experiences. In the metaphysical cognition we comprehend the transcendental features of being.

We must notice that discovered transcendental rationality of the world determines not only the understanding of the whole of reality but it determines especially the human being, including his life, activity and behavior.

Now we have to point out the main consequences of this evident connection between truth and freedom.

1. The being as a carrier of the truth has a power to perfect his intellect and will.

2. Potentially our will is not determinated but in reality it is determined by the truth and good of being.

3. The transcendality of the truth and good of being eliminates any irrationality in human cognition in the world and human activity. This attitude would be true if we agreed that man is the creator of the truth and of freedom as well.

4. Cognition and the truth are connected with the individually existing being. Every being has its own truth and good and is a base of the authentical space of human liberty.

It is indeed evident that we cannot put the truth in opposition to freedom because the truth of being shows us the world as full of sense and the space of human rationality. In this way the human being becomes truly free and finds fulfilment in freedom.

WŁADYSŁAW PABIASZ
Pedagogical College in Częstochowa
Poland

DIE FREIHEIT UND DER MORALISCHE WERT

Der belgische Theologe Servais Théodore Pinckaers, geb. 1925, Professor der Moral – theologie im Freiburg i. Br. und Mitglied der Internationalen Theologischen Komission, stellt die These auf, daß zwei Arten der Freiheit bestehen: die den Werten gegenüber gleichgültige Freiheit und die von den Werten geformte Freiheit[1].

Die Konzeption der Freiheit, die Vorstellungen vom Menschen und seinen Vermögen und der Begriff von Gott sind zusammen verbunden und bilden die Gründe der Ethik. Es gibt zwei Wege, die zu der Erkenntnis der Tatsache und der Natur der menschlichen Freiheit führen: 1) eine Reflexion über unseren Handlungen und Emotionen, die die unmittelbare Folgen dieser Freiheit sind, und 2) eine Reflexion über das System der Moralität, über ihre Struktur und ihre Haupteigenschaften. Der erste Weg weist auf die Induktionsmethode, der zweite Weg auf die Deduktionsmethode. In der Geschichte treffen wir zwei Arten der Systematisierung der Moralität. Die erste für Patristik und Scholastik charakteristische hat sich auf dem Begriff des Glückes und der moralischen Tugenden gegründet. Die zweite für die Neuzeit charakteristische hat sich auf dem Begriff der Pflicht gegründet. Im ersten und zweiten Fall wurde Freiheit als eine Wurzel, als eine Quelle des Systems begriffen. Die den Werten gegenüber gleichgültige Freiheit besteht in den Systemen, die die Moralität auf der Pflicht gründen. Die von den Werten geformte Freiheit besteht in den Systemen, die die Moralität auf der Idee des Glückes und der Tugenden gründen. Die erste Freiheit ist

---

[1] S. Th. Pinckaers OP, *Les sources de la morale chrétienne. Sa méthode, son contenu, son histoire*, Fribourg Suisse 1985, s. 211.

historisch später. Sie stammt von W. Ockham (1300-1349) und ist heute mehr populär. Die zweite Freiheit ist früher. Sie entstammt der Patristik (bis 8. Jahrhundert nach Chr.) und ist heute gleichsam „unterirdisch".

I. DIE DEN WERTEN GEGENÜBER GLEICHGÜLTIGE FREIHEIT

Peter Lombard (1100-1164), Bischof in Paris, Theologe und Philosoph, Verfasser der *Sententiae*, hat uns folgende Definition der freien Wahl gelassen: „Die freie Wahl ist die Fähigkeit der Vernunft und des Willens, mit der wir das Gute mit der Hilfe der Gnade wählen oder das Böse ohne Gnade" („Liberum vero arbitrium est facultas rationis et voluntatis, qua bonum eligitur gratia assistente, vel malum eadem desistente"[2]). Wir haben auch zwei verschiedene Interpretationen des ersten Teiles dieser Definition. Der hl. Thomas von Aquin (1225-1274) interpretiert die Freiheit als eine Fähigkeit, die aus der Vernunft und aus dem Willen ausfließt. Die Vernunft und der Wille vereinigen sich, um die freie Wahl zu vollbringen. Die Wirkung der Vernunft und des Willens ist ursprünglich, anfänglich. Die freie Wahl ist sekundär[3]. W. Ockham meinte, daß die freie Wahl der Vernunft und dem Willen vorangeht, daß sie eine ursprüngliche Fähigkeit sei[4]. Schon früher behauptete Johannes Fidanza, der sog. hl. Bonaventura (1221-1274), daß die freie Wahl der Vernunft und dem Willen befiehlt, daß die Vernunft den Willen regiert, daß die Vernunft auch den Willen bewegt. Die freie Wahl ist erster Akt, nicht Erkennen und nicht Wollen[5]. Die Freiheit hat den Primat und die Priorität. Die Freiheit ist eine Pflicht des Menschen, die der Mensch ohne Rücksicht auf das Diktat der Vernunft erfüllen soll. Die Freiheit liegt in dem Willen. Die Freiheit ist das Vermögen des Willens, das Vermögen der Wahl zwischen den Gegensätzen; zwischen dem Wollen und Nicht-Wollen; zwischen der Wirkung und Nicht-Wirkung; zwischen dem, was das Recht anordnet, und dem Gegensatz des Rechtes. Die Freiheit identifiziert sich mit dem Willen und ist eine Quelle der Taten und des Verlangens. Die Freiheit ist das reine Wollen oder Nichtwollen. Das Verlangen nach Glück ist auch der freien Wahl untergeordnet. Das Glück darf und kann man auswählen, man darf und man kann es auch ablehnen. Das

---

[2] P. Lombardus, *II Sententiarum*, dist. 24, c. 3, in: J. Migne (Hrsg), *Patrologiae Cursus Completus. Series Latina*, Bd. 191, Parisiis 1854, kol. 349.

[3] S. Thomas de Aquino, *Summa Theologiae*, I, qu. 79, 82, 83, in.: *Opera omnia iusu impensaque Leonis XIII edita*, Editio Leonina, vol. 2, Romae 1882, s. 112 ff.

[4] A. Kühtmann, *Zur Geschichte des Terminismus*, Barlin 1911, s. 97 ff; R. Guelluy, *Philosophie et théologie chez G. d'Ockham*, Paris 1947, s. 56 ff.

[5] Johannes Fidanza, *In II Sententiarum*, d. 25, p. 1, a. 1, q. 2, in: *Opera omnia*, vol. 8, Queracchi 1898, s. 48 ff.

Leben kann ich und darf ich auswählen; kann ich und darf ich ihn wegnehmen.

Die spontanen und naturellen Neigungen des Menschen zur Wahrheit und zum Guten sind nur Triebe niedrigeren Ranges. Diese Neigungen sind unter der Freiheit. Zwischen diesen Neigungen und der Freiheit gibt es einen Widerspruch. Diese Neigungen sind sogar eine Bedrohung der Freiheit. Moralität und das Verlangen nach Glück sind zwei verschiedene Sachen. Die Emotionen sind auch Triebe niedrigeren Ranges. Sie sind auch eine Bedrohung für die Freiheit. Sie vermindern die Freiheit des Menschen. Man soll die Emotionen bekämpfen. Dieser Kampf ist unumgänglich.

Sobald die naturellen Neigungen des Menschen zum Guten und zur Wahrheit hinter der Freiheit sind, sind hinter der Freiheit auch die Leistungen, d. h. Tugenden und Charakterfehler. Im Sinne der Leistung gibt sie eine Determination. Die Leistung ist nun ein Feind der Freiheit. Je größer die Leistung ist, desto minder ist die Freiheit. Die Leistungen sollen wir der Freiheit unterordnen. Die Freiheit soll die Leistungen ausnutzen. Die Tugend ist überflüsig, unnütz. Der Mensch soll die Tugend beseitigen.

Jede menschliche Tat ist ganz und gar abgesondert, isoliert; ist getrennt von den vorigen und den nachfolgenden Taten. Vorige Wirkung bezeichnet weder vorige noch nachfolgende Wirkung. Es gibt keine Kontinuität des Verhaltens. Das bedeutet Zerlegung in kleine Teile der moralischen Wirkung. Die Freiheit wird dem Menschen angegeben, sie drängt sich dem Menschen auf. Die Freiheit ist total. Sie braucht keine Entwicklung. Kein Faktor vereinigt das Verhalten des Menschen. Der Zweck der einzelnen Taten existiert, aber er ist einmalig, er ist von Umständen bezeichnet. Die Freiheit ist ein Vermögen, in jeder Weile das zu tun, was dem Menschen gefällt und so, wie es ihm gefällt. Jede Tat soll man separat einschätzen (Kasuistik). In dieser Konzeption der Freiheit kommt die Selbstbestimmung des Menschen zu Worte. Der Mensch wählt zwischen den Gegensätzen aus, aber er gründet sich ausschließlich auf sich selbst. Die Freiheit bedeutet hier eine gänzliche Unabhängigkeit. Das bedeutet weiter eine Autonomie, d. h. eine Ablehnung jeder Norm und jeden Rechts, jeden Arguments pro und contra. Die Freiheit ist eine unbeschränkte Willkürlichkeit zum Vergnügen. Die Werte, wie z. B.: die Treue gegen Gut, Ideal, Person, Lebensgestalt, irgendwas, wer es auch sei – sind nur eine Bedrohung für die Freiheit. Das Symptom der Freiheit ist ein Verrat des Gutes und nicht die Treue gegen das Gute. Die einzige Treue in dieser Konzeption ist die Treue gegen sich selbst (Subjektivismus).

Die Einheit der Vernunft und des Willens wird hier zerrissen. Die Vernunft beeinflußt nicht den Willen, dringt nicht in den Willen ein. Der Wille wirkt allein, ohne Vernunft. Zwischen dem Voluntarismus und Rationalismus entsteht eine tiefe Spannung. Das Wesen der Freiheit ist Reden der

Vernunft: „nein". Recht, Pflicht, jeder Wert verfällt nur dem Willen. Das Verständnis der moralischen Gebote und Verbote ist unwichtig, ist glatt überflüssig. Die Freiheit Gottes ist auch souverän. Gott ist der freie Wille. Das Moralgesetz ist eine Konsequenz des göttlichen Willens und nicht der göttlichen Weisheit. Auch in Gott geht die Freiheit der Vernunft voraus. Ganzes Recht fließt aus dem Willen aus. Der Mensch kann nicht den Willen Gottes erkennen. Gottes Wille bedeutet Pflicht und Beschränkung des Menschen. Der Begriff der Pflicht ereignet sich Hauptkategorie der Moralität. Es gibt keine innerlich böse Taten. Die Spannung zwischen Recht und Freiheit besteht weiter.

Die den Werten gegenüber gleichgültige Freiheit bewirkt viele Spannungen und Gegensätze, z. B.: entweder Freiheit oder Recht; entweder Freiheit oder Vernunft; entweder Freiheit oder vernünftige Menschennatur; entweder Freiheit oder Gottesgnade; entweder freier Mensch oder Gott; entweder menschliche Person oder äußerliche Welt; entweder Freiheit oder Sensualität; entweder meine Freiheit oder die Freiheit der anderen Menschen; entweder Individuum oder Gesellschaft[6].

Zusammenfassend darf man sagen: wir sind uns bewußt geworden, daß in uns Freiheit und Gleichgültigkeit besteht; es besteht ein Gegensatz zwischen irgendeinem moralischen Determinismus und Freiheit; Freiheit bedeutet Fähigkeit des Verhaltens ohne jede rationelle Ursache. Freiheit ist eine Fähigkeit des sich selbst Bezeichnens unabhängig von den Motiven. Solche Freiheit stellt sich die gleiche Möglichkeit der Gegensätze.

II. DIE VON DEN WERTEN GEFORMTE FREIHEIT

Die von den Werten geformte Freiheit ist entschieden anders. Die den Werten gegenüber gleichgültige Freiheit ist eine Freiheit des Tuns der Fehler. Die von den Werten geformte Freiheit gründet sich auf den sicheren Prinzipien; sie unterliegt dem Zwang der Prinzipien; sie identifiziert sich nicht mit der Ablehnung der Prinzipien und der Gesetze. Die naturellen Dispositionen, die in der geistigen Natur des Menschen verwurzelt sind, bilden einen Keim und eine Quelle dieser Freiheit. Jeder Mensch hat fundamentale moralische Dispositionen, solche wie z. B.: der Sinn der Wahrheit, des Guten, der Rechtlichkeit, der Liebe; die Sehnsucht nach dem Erkennen und nach dem Glück. Diese heißen die Samen der Tugenden (semina virtu-

---

[6] Siehe: S. Th. Pinckaers OP, *Der Sinn für die Freundschaftsliebe als Urtatsache der thomistischen Ethik*, in: *Sein und Ethos*, Mainz 1963, s. 229-235; *La quête du bonheur*, Paris 1979, s. 45 ff; *Le renouveau de la morale*, Paris 1964, s. 111 ff; *La morale catholique*, Paris 1991, s. 101 ff.

tum). Diese Prädispositionen bilden die wahre moralische Freiheit. Je heftiger der Mensch sie entwickelt, desto mehr wird er frei[7].

Die wichtigste Aufgabe ist hier die Erziehung zur Freiheit. Die Erziehung zur wahren Freiheit umfaßt drei Phasen: 1) die Stufe der Disziplin; 2) die Stufe des Anwachsens und 3) die Stufe der moralischen Reife. Die Stufe der Disziplin besteht in der Erkenntnis und in der Akzeptation der Prinzipien des moralischen Verhaltens. Die Disziplin umfaßt die Übung der Vernunft und des Willens, d. h. Übergeben des Wissens, Bildung der Vernunft und Härtung des Willens. Die Disziplin beschränkt sich nicht auf den Zwang. Authentische Disziplin gründet sich auf den naturellen Inklinationen zur Wahrheit und zum Guten, auf dem Gewissen und auf den Prinzipien, die mit der vernünftigen, geistig-leiblichen Natur des Menschen vereinbart sind. Sie ist kein Abdruck des fremden Willens, erst recht nicht fremder Willkür. Die Erziehung auf dieser Etappe ist kein Kampf, sondern Dienst und Mitarbeit. Wichtigste Aufgabe des Erziehers ist die Beschaffung der individuell überzeugenden Motivation, daß die Beschränkungen der Handlungsfreiheit die Vorbereitung zum wertvollen Verhalten, d.h. moralisch guten Verhalten als Aufgabe haben. Es gibt nämlich Taten, die von dem moralischen Standpunkt aus innerlich bösartig sind. Darin besteht die Koordination der Freiheit mit dem moralischen Recht. Niemand gibt Freiheit. Jeder Mensch soll und sich muß die Freiheit erarbeiten. Je besser in moralischer Rücksicht wir werden, desto größere Freiheit gewinnen wir. Das Wachsen in der wahren Freiheit ist unmöglich ohne die Befolgung der Werte, z. B. des Dekalogs, der die Zusammenfassung der fundamentalen Werte ist.

Die zweite Etappe der Erziehung zur wahren Freiheit ist die Bildung der Tugend, der Tugenden. Hier sollen wir uns klarmachen, was die Tugend ist. Die Tugend ist keine Gewohnheit und keine mechanische Routine. Die Tugend ist eine Fähigkeit, ein Wachsen, eine Vervollkommung, ein Erblicken der Werte, eine Modalität des Wachsens auf wertvoller Weise. Die Tugend ist ein Mensch, der auf wertvolle Weise handelt; der Mensch, der geduldig und tapfer immer neuere Bemühungen aufnimmt. Diese Bildung der Tugend besteht in der Erarbeitung der beständigen Disposition zum Verhalten, das Wert hat. Der Beweggrund ist hier weder Lohn noch Strafe, sondern Liebe zum Wert. Der Mensch lernt hier, die eigene Aufgabe sorgfältig auszufüllen; Gerechtigkeit, Rechtschaffenheit und Großherzigkeit verwirklichen; Wahrheit suchen; uneigennützig lieben; Tapferkeit, Geduld und Ausdauer vorlegen. Das Verzeichnis dieser Werte, die der Mensch auf der zweiten Stufe der Erziehung gewinnt, finden wir in Christi Bergpredigt (Mt 5-7; Lk 6, 17-49).

---

[7] Siehe: S. Th. Pinckaers OP, C. J. Pinto de Oliveira, *Universalité et permanence des lois morales*, Fribourg–Paris 1986, s. 41.

Die dritte Etappe dieser Erziehung ist das Reifen in der Freiheit. Charakteristische Züge dieser Phase sind zwei: die Selbstbeherrschung den Werten gemäß und die schöpferische Fruchtbarkeit. Der Mensch regiert die Ganzheit des Lebens; ordnet das Leben dem höchsten Zweck dem Plan gemäß unter; gibt dem Leben Sinn; der Mensch wird offen für die anderen Menschen; mit seinem Leben dient der Mensch der Familie, dem Volk und der Kirche. Der Mensch gewinnt das Prinzip des Lebens. Darin besteht die wahre Autonomie des Menschen.

Die Überlegungen von S. Th. Pinckaers sind sowohl in der Heiligen Schrift, der Lehre der Kirchenvätern sowie in der Lehre von Thomas von Aquin und des II. Vaticanum[8] stark ver – wurzelt.

Gaudium et spes gibt uns folgende Feststellungen: es gibt wahre und falsche Freiheit; die Ungebundenheit des Tuns von allem, was gefällt, auch des Bösen, bestimmt die Negation der wahren Freiheit; die wahre Freiheit bedeutet freie und bewußte Wahl des Gutes; diese Auswahl ist persönlich, d. h. daß der Mensch von innen und nicht von außen berührt und gelenkt wird; der Mensch gewinnt die Freiheit durch Selbstbefreiung aus der Gefangenschaft der Leidenschaften; die menschliche Freiheit ist verletzt durch die Erbsünde; die Gottesgnade ist notwendig zur Erreichung der wahren Freiheit[9].

Lumen gentium spricht von „der Königsfreiheit", von „der Befreiung aus der Gefangenschaft der Vergiftung", von „menschlicher und christlicher Freiheit"[10]. Die Deklaraton *Dignitatis humanae* stellt fest: die Freiheit bedeutet das Versichern vor dem Zwang und sich von moralischen Normen leiten lassen[11]. Diese Ausdrücke bedeuten die von den Werten geformte Freiheit. Zu diesem Ausdruck passen, der Reihe nach, die späteren Feststellungen *des Katechismus der Katholischen Kirche*: Akzeptation der Kundgebung des göttlichen Willens ist nicht gegen die Freiheit (Nr. 154); die Quelle der Freiheit ist die Anerkennung der Abhängigkeit von dem Schöpfer (Nr. 301); das Tun des Bösen bedeutet Mißbrauch der Freiheit (Nr. 387); die moralischen Normen regeln die Nutzung der Freiheit (Nr. 396); „der Mensch soll nicht auf absoluter Weise die eigene Freiheit der weltlichen

---

[8] Siehe: S. Th. Pinckaers OP, *Ce qu'on ne peut jamais faire. La question des actes intrinsèquement mauvais. Histoire et discussion*, Fribourg-Paris 1986, s. 66 ff; *Eudaimonismus und sittliche Verbindlichkeit in der Ethik des heiligen Thomas. Stellungnahme zum Beitrag Hans Reiners*, in: *Sein und Ethos*, Mainz 19 63, s. 267-305; *Habitude – Habitus*, in: *Dictionnaire de Spiritualité*, Bd. 7, Paris 1969, s. 2-11; *La justice évangelique*, Paris 1986, s. 15 ff; *L'Evangile et la morale*, Fribourg–Paris 1990, s. 99 ff; S. Th. Pinckaers, L. Rumpf, *Loi et Evangile*, Genève 1981, s. 28 ff.

[9] *Gaudium et spes*, nr 17, in: „Acta Apostolicae Sedis", 58 (1966), ks. 1094 ff.

[10] *Lumen gentium*, nr 36, in: AAS 57 (1965), s. 58 ff.

[11] *Dignitatis humanae*, nr 4, in: AAS 58 (1966), s. 233.

Macht unterordnen, sondern nur Gott" (Nr. 450); die wahre menschliche Freiheit ist „Freiheit des Herzens, des Leibes und des Geistes" (Nr. 922); die Freiheit bedeutet Forderung: 1) zur Verantwortung fürs eigenen Leben und 2) zur beharrlichen Bekehrung (Nr. 1036); viele Menschen verblenden sich „mit der trügerischen Freiheit" (Nr. 1439); das Mißbrauchen der Freiheit bewirkt: das Unterliegen gegenüber den Versuchungen und das Tun des Bösen, die ständige Neigung zum Bösen und die Empfänglichkeit für moralische Fehler, das innere Zerreißen und den inneren Kampf zwischen dem Guten und Bösen (Nr. 1707); „die Freiheit ist in der Vernunft und im Willen gewurzelt, sie ist eine Möglichkeit der Wirkung und Nichtwirkung, des Tuns entweder dieses oder jenes, d. h. der freiwilligen Übernahme von Tätigkeiten. Dank dem freien Willen entscheidet jeder über sich selbst. Die Freiheit ist im Menschen eine Kraft des Wachsens und des Ausreifens in der Wahrheit und im Guten; sie erreicht ihre Vollkommenheit, wenn sie auf Gott gelenkt ist" (Nr. 1731); „die Freiheit, so lange bis sich auf die Dauer befestigt in ihrem höchsten Gute, d. h. in Gott, beweist die Möglichkeit der Wahl zwischen Gut und Böse und nun enweder des Wachsens in der Vollkommenheit oder des Sturzes und des Sündigens. Sie charakterisiert die Taten, die dem Menschen angemessen sind. Sie wird zur Quelle des Lobes oder des Verweises" (Nr. 1732); „wahre Freiheit ist nur Freiheit in Dienst des Guten und der Gerechtigkeit. Die Wahl des Ungehorsams und des Bösen ist ein Mißbrauch der Freiheit und führt zur Knechtschaft der Sünden" (Nr. 1733); „die Freiheit gibt uns kein Recht zum Sprechen und Tun von allem. [...] Der Mensch, der sich von dem moralischen Recht entfernt, überfällt die eigene Freiheit, vergewaltigt sich selbst, reißt die Bruderschaft mit den anderen Menschen ab und empört sich gegen die göttliche Wahrheit" (Nr. 1740). Folgende Werten bilden das Fundament der gerechten Freiheit, der wahren Freiheit, der authentischen Freiheit, der geistigen Freiheit: die Gewandheit der Entsagung, die gesunde Einschätzung der Wirklichkeit und die Selbstbeherrschung (Nr. 2223). Die Freiheit bedeutet den bewußten und freiwilligen Gehorsam gegen das Gute und nur wegen der Liebe und nicht aus dem Grunde des Lohnes oder der Strafe[12].

Papst Johannes Paul II umfaßt in der Enzyklika *Veritatis splendor* die Relationen zwischen der Freiheit und den Werten folgenderweise: die Wahrheit beleuchtet die Vernunft und formt die Freiheit des Menschen (Nr. 1); die Freiheit des Menschen und das göttliche, moralische Recht, die die Werte schützen, sind nicht widerstreitend, aber sie berufen sich miteinander für sich (Nr. 17); es gibt einen integralen und unauflöslichen Zusammenhang zwischen der Freiheit und der Wahrheit, zwischen der Freiheit und dem moralischen Recht, zwischen der Freiheit und der menschlichen

---

[12] *Katechizm Kościoła katolickiego*, Pallotinum 1994.

Natur, zwischen der Freiheit und dem Gewissen; es gibt keine Moralität ohne die Freiheit; die wahre Freiheit ist von der Wahrheit abhängig[13].

Zusammenfassend lassen wir uns erinnern an die Worte des hl. Ambrosius († 397): Der, wer den eigenen Leib in Zucht hält und mit seiner Seele lenkt, wer nicht erlaubt, damit sie von Leidenschaften beunruhigt sei, der ist Herr für sich selbst; man darf ihn einen König nennen, weil er herrschen kann über sich selbst; er ist frei und unabhängig; er übergibt sich nicht der Knechtschaft der Sünde"[14].

---

[13] Joannes Paulus II., *Veritatis splendor*, in: AAS 55 (1993), s. 1133-1228.

[14] S. Ambrosius, *Expositio Psalmi CXVIII*, 14, 30, in: J. Migne (Hrsg.), *Patrologiae Cursus Completus. Series Latina*, Bd. 15, A, Parisiis 1850, kol. 1403.

STEFAN SWIEŻAWSKI
ROMUALD JAKUB WEKSLER-WASZKINEL
Catholic University of Lublin
Poland

LIBERTÉ EN PHILOSOPHIE

Kazimir Wójcik: Mesdames et Messieurs, je voudrais vous présenter Monsieur le Professeur Stefan Swieżawski, maître de la philosophie polonaise, cofondateur du milieu philosophique de l'Université Catholique de Lublin. C'est un de *venerabilibus inceptoribus nostrae Philosophicae Facultatis*. Il a aussi été auditeur laïque du Concile Vatican II. – Il va s'entretenir avec le père Romuald Jacques Weksler-Waszkinel, docteur en philosophie, qui enseigne l'anthropologie philosophique à la Faculté de Philosophie de l'Université Catholique de Lublin et s'occupe aussi de recherches sur la philosophie d'Henri Bergson.
Monsieur le Professeur, je vous prie de prendre la parole.

Stefan Swieżawski: Merci bien! – Je suis très heureux de pouvoir prendre la parole ici, au Congrès à l'Université de Lublin où j'ai travaillé pendant plus de trente ans. Je suis obligé de vous expliquer pourquoi je n'ai pas pu présenter une conférence: atteignant bientôt l'age de 90 ans, je n'ai plus la possibilité de lire des notes ou bien de garder en mémoire toute une conférence. Et c'est la cause pour laquelle le père Weksler-Waszkinel, mon ami, a bien voulu entreprendre une conversation avec moi. – Eh bien, ce sera une conversation au lieu d'une conférence. Merci.

K. W.: Je dois encore ajouter que le sujet de cet entretien est *La liberté en philosophie*.

Romuald Jacques Weksler-Waszkinel: Monsieur le Professeur, c'est avec une profonde émotion que j'entame cet entretien. Il est hors de doute que vous appartenez aux personnes à l'endroit desquelles la Providence a été tout particulièrement bienveillante. Vous avez beaucoup reçu et vous en avez beaucoup rendu. Je tâcherai de montrer, dans les questions que je me permettrai de formuler, le bien-fondé de cette constatation.

Pour nombre d'entre nous, la possibilité de suivre vos cours, de participer à vos travaux pratiques et séminaires a été un don de la Providence. A l'occasion de ce Congrès Philosophique International, c'est un bon moment, je pense, pour vous dire solennellement merci, merci notre Professeur, merci notre Maître!

Né en 1907, vous êtes un témoin sensible de notre siècle difficile. Permettez-moi de toucher dans les questions qui suivent, quelques événements qui, comme je l'ai remarqué, ont été des dons particuliers d'une grande importance. Tout cela va nous préparer à la question principale, qui résume pour ainsi dire le titre de cet entretien: *La liberté en philosophie*.

Alors ma première question: Dans l'histoire de la philosophie polonaise, une date très importante, est l'année 1895. A ce moment-là Kazimierz Twardowski reçut la chaire de philosophie à l'Université Jean-Casimir à Lwów. (Léopol: en Ukraine maintenant). On sait très bien ce que fut l'école de Lwów et puis l'école de Lwów-Varsowie.

Vous, Monsieur le Professeur, vous commencez vos études en 1925, justement à Lwów. Vous faites partie de ce groupe privilégié, peut-être pas très nombreux aujourd'hui, qui a assisté aux cours et même participé aux fameux proséminaires et séminaires dirigés par le professeur Twardowski.

Ce Lwów d'alors, qu'est-ce qu'il aurait à nous dire aujourd'hui?

S. Swieżawski: Alors, je répondrai en attirant surtout votre attention sur le caractère de Lwów. C'est une ville exceptionnelle. Elle est située non loin d'ici, une ville qui vraiment est exceptionnelle par la réunion d'un nombre considérable d'éléments très divers, réunion – depuis des siècles – de différentes cultures, de différentes religions, d'hommes de différentes provenance raciales. C'était magnifique, c'était un peu comme le Tolède du XIIe siècle. Naturellement, les ennemis, ceux qui ne voulaient pas qu'il y eût une coexistence pacifique et fructueuse des différents éléments, ont contribué à rendre difficile la collaboration intime de ces courants, de ces différents éléments. Du point du vue catholique, Lwów est une ville extraordinaire, parce qu'il y a là trois archevêchés depuis le Moyen Age: latin, grec uniate et arménien. Moi-même, j'ai des ancêtres arméniens et ruthènes, ukrainiens; dans notre sang, nous sommes tous un mélange, un mélange d'éléments polonais, ukrainiens, arméniens; il y avait beaucoup d'éléments juifs.

Eh bien, c'est justement dans cette ville que naquit la célèbre école philosophique de Lwów. J'ai eu la grande chance d'être étudiant chez Casimir Twardowski. Je veux brièvement rappeler qui était Twardowski. Il était collègue de Husserl, de Meinong, élève de Franz Brentano, puis maître des grands professeurs qui furent ensuite mes maîtres: des célèbres logiciens, orientés plutôt vers le néopositivisme, Casimir Ajdukiewicz et Roman Ingarden, élève de Husserl et ami, collègue, d'Edith Stein.

Voilà c'est cette ambiance que j'ai bien connue depuis ma jeunesse et c'est là que j'ai été formé formais dans un climat de pluralisme philosophiques, bien qu'il y eût naturellement certaines, disons, tendances idéologiques dans cette école, c'est-à-dire un certain ultrarationalisme, une certaine méfiance vis-à-vis des religions confessionelles. Mais – en fin de compte – c'était un centre très honnête du point de vue de la recherche de la vérité, et ce sont mes professeurs et la voie par laquelle ils m'ont conduit qui en témoignent.

R. J. W.-W.: En l'année 1929/30, vous êtes parti pour Paris où vous avez rencontré, et c'est le don suivant, le privilège suivant, Jacques Maritain et Etienne Gilson.

Cette rencontre, qu'est-ce que cela a été pour vous?

S. Swieżawski: Depuis le collège, j'étais fasciné par le Moyen Age. Ce n'était pas encore une fascination pour la philosophie médiévale, mais pour le Moyen Age, pour les grands problèmes religieux, philosophiques, culturels de cette époque. Et c'est déjà au collège que j'ai eu la possibilité de lire quelques travaux de Maritain. Ensuite, à l'Université, où j'ai commencé à étudier non seulement la philosophie en général, mais aussi les auteurs médiévaux, j'ai eu la conviction que le grand maître de la philosophie médiévale, c'était Etienne Gilson.

Eh bien, c'est aussi le médiéviste polonais, le Père Constantin Michalski, qui dirigeait dans un certain sens mes études – il était professeur à l'Université de Cracovie – qui m'encouragea à faire ce voyage et à rester une année à Paris pour pouvoir connaître Gilson. Naturellement, je voulais connaître les deux (Gilson et Maritain), et ça a réussi. C'est vraiment un don de la Providence que déjà comme tout jeune étudiant j'ai pu participer aux célèbres rencontres de Meudon, où chez Jacques et Raïssa Maritain se rencontraient des personnages vraiment formidables comme Berdiaev, comme le peintre Arp, etc. Naturellement, je regardais tout cela les yeux grand ouverts, mais je ne comprenais presque rien. Pourtant je voyais que de grandes choses se passaient là. Et alors ensuite, mon deuxième séjour à Paris, c'était déjà avant le doctorat. Avant mon doctorat, je préparais une thèse sur Jean Duns Scot, je dirai ensuite pourquoi ... ?

Eh bien, j'ai rencontré personnellement Gilson. C'était vraiment un maître, un maître de grande envergure. Sa connaissance très profonde des problèmes m'a permis de borner le sujet de mon doctorat, de connaître la façon d'étudier, du point de vue historique, ces grands textes. Eh bien, d'un côté le travail philosophique, le travail de réinterprétation, de compréhension très exacte de textes philosophiques – ce que nous avait donné Twardowski, cela c'est associé à cette nouvelle méthode de relire à nouveau les grands textes médiévaux – ce que nous donnait Gilson.

R. J. W.-W.: Elève des professeur Twardowski et Ajdukiewicz, dès le commencement à vrai dire attiré par la pensée du Moyen Age.

Ne pensez-vous pas que cela a de quoi étonner?

Après Duns Scot, vous vous êtes occupé de la philosophie d'Aristote et de saint Thomas. Qui vous a poussé vers une philosophie qui n'était guère à la mode à Lwów? D'ailleurs, parmi vos maîtres spirituels, il y a de grands enseignants de l'Université Catholique de Lublin: le Père Woroniecki, dominicain, ainsi que l'abbé Korniłowicz, aumônier à Laski.

S. Swieżawski: Alors, c'est vrai que c'était assez étonnant. Car le centre philosophique de Lwów ne s'occupait guère du Moyen Age sauf Twardowski toutefois, qui a écrit un petit livre sur la philosophie médiévale; Twardowski avait eu une bonne école de philosophie médiévale grâce à Brentano, qui, avant d'être professeur à l'Université de Vienne, avait été dominicain; il avait une très bonne formation intellectuelle dominicaine en philosophie et en théologie. Ensuite, il n'a pas voulu rester dans l'Eglise catholique après le concile Vatican I, ne pouvant pas admettre l'infaillibilité du pape, Brentano est devenu vieux-catholique. Mais il avait toujours une très grande vénération, si l'on peut dire, pour les grands maîtres classiques, antiques et médiévaux.

Mais l'histoire de mon approche de saint Thomas a été assez spéciale. Vous avez parlé de deux grands maîtres polonais: le père Woroniecki, dominicain, et le père Korniłowicz, grand ami personnel de Maritain, fondateur du célèbre centre de Laski. Eh bien, c'était assez extraordinaire que pendant mes études, étant engagé dans le mouvement de la jeunesse catholique „Odrodzenie" (Renaissance), j'ai déjà eu des maîtres qui m'ont montré l'importance de saint Thomas pour une vue générale de la réalité – employons plutôt le mot allemand *Weltanschaung* – pas philosophie dans le sens strict, ou théologie.

Le Père Woroniecki – l'homme dont le Père Bocheński a dit avec raison que c'était l'homme le plus sage qu'il eût rencontré durant sa vie; le Père Woroniecki – grand connaisseur de la morale de saint Thomas, un homme qui vivait de saint Thomas. Un homme aussi qui avait une magnifique culture de langue maternelle: il parlait admirablement le polonais. Ensuite le Père Korniłowicz. Disons, le premier prêtre d'importance qui ait fait *l'apertura verso la sinistra*, c'est-à-dire une certaine ouverture de l'Eglise vers la gauche, vers la gauche dans le sens général. Il attirait par sa grande culture et son ouverture d'esprit, il attirait beaucoup de gens incroyants, beaucoup d'écrivains, beaucoup de poètes. Un peu comme Meudon près de Paris, c'était Laski près de Varsovie: un centre formidable, où se rendaient beaucoup de Juifs, qui avaient vraiment goûté et vu la grandeur du christianisme. Et c'est grâce au Père Korniłowicz que ce centre magnifique a pu être créé à Laski, et c'était un de mes maîtres. Mais ce n'était pas une étude de saint Thomas.

J'ai terminé alors ma thèse de doctorat sur la notion d'intention (*intentio*), pas dans le sens moral, mais dans ses plusieurs sens chez Jean Duns Scot; cette thèse m'a d'ailleurs été suggéré par mes professeurs, Twardowski et ensuite Ajdukiewicz, parce que Twardowski était déjà en retraite. Cette thèse donc m'a été suggéré parce que Brentano dans son livre *Psychologie vom empirischen Standpunkt* écrit que le terme *intentio*, qui a une telle importance ensuite dans toute la phénoménologie, *Intentionalität*, n'est-ce pas, etc., est de provenance scolastique. Alors, on m'a dit à Lwów: vous vous intéressez au Moyen Age, nous nous intéressons à Brentano, alors écrivez une thèse sur cette provenance scolastique de l'*intentio*.

J'ai écrit cette thèse, Gilson en a publié une partie dans les "Archives d'Histoire Littéraire et Doctrinale du Moyen Age", mais je ne suis pas du tout en admiration devant cette thèse, c'était vraiment une dissertation d'école. Cependant ensuite, j'ai réuni une grande quantité de textes de Duns Scot pour écrire un ouvrage plus ample sur le problème de la connaissance chez Scot. Ajdukiewicz s'est chargé de la direction de cette recherche. Ensuite, c'est lui qui m'a dit ces mots significatifs (il n'était pas historien, il n'était pas médiéviste, il ne connaissait même pas bien le latin. Mais il m'a dit ces mots assez étranges): si vous voulez étudier à fond Duns Scot, vous devez absolument connaître ses grands prédécesseurs, surtout Thomas d'Aquin, et puis Aristote, puisque Thomas d'Aquin s'est appuyé sur la philosophie d'Aristote. N'ayant pas connu le grec au collège (c'est seulement le latin qui m'y avait été enseigné), j'ai étudié le grec pour pouvoir lire directement Aristote, et ensuite (j'ai fait) un petit travail sur le problème de l'âme dans la "Métaphysique" d'Aristote (*métaphysique* dans le sens «ouvrage», pas "métaphysique" discipline!) et je suis arrivé à connaître un peu la conception philosophique de l'homme dans l'anthropologie philosophique d'Aristote.

Et alors, j'étais devant le choix d'un sujet pour la thèse qu'on appelle chez nous – et en Allemagne – *habilitation*; c'est à vrai dire le grand doctorat d'Etat. Eh bien, ce sujet je l'ai eu grâce à Ajdukiewicz, qui était très, très loin de la religion, du christianisme, mais qui avait une soif métaphysique très profonde, Il voulait connaître, connaître, avec son esprit extrêmement subtil, comme celui de Scot. D'ailleurs, préparer une thèse de doctorat chez lui, c'était un petit martyre, parce qu'il me demandait d'expliquer toutes les phrases de Scot, c'était fort difficile. Alors, il m'a dit: je vous suggère de préparer un ouvrage sur un problème qui vous semblera essentiel en anthropologie philosophique de saint Thomas. Je me suis donc mis, pour la première fois, à une étude approfondie de saint Thomas; le résultat, a été ma thèse d'*habilitation*, qui s'intitule: "Le problème central de l'anthropologie thomasienne: commensuratio animae ad hoc corpus". C'est là un terme classique dans l'anthropologie de saint Thomas.

R. J. W.-W.: Et ainsi là la Providence vous préparait au travail dans notre Université.

S. Swieżawski: Eh oui!

R. J. W.-W.: En tout cas, en 1946, vous commencez votre travail au sein de notre Université Catholique. Dans une de vos interviews, vous constatez: "Les rencontres de Lublin ont eu un caractère tout à fait particulier. /.../. A l'Université Catholique de Lublin, s'est formé alors un groupe de quelques philosophes tout à fait unique en son genre /.../"[1]. C'est le don suivant, cette fois pour nous tous. Il est possible que, dans un certain sens, ce Congrès, auquel nous participons depuis mardi, ait été rendu possible grâce à ce groupe de personnes.

Qui constituait ce groupe? En quoi consistait son caractère absolument original, unique?

S. Swieżawski: Je dois dire que tout se passe au début de l'époque communiste. Ce sont les années quarante. En 1946, le professeur Ajdukiewicz, exilé de Lwów – parce qu'il y a déjà le partage de la Pologne et toute cette histoire – reçoit la chaire de philohophie à l'Université de Poznań. Et c'est là que mon habilitation a eu lieu en janvier 46.

Je dois vous faire une confidence. Ajdukiewicz m'a dit, après la discussion d'habilitation, qui avait été assez intéressante: oui, si vous n'étiez pas tellement influencé par différents „Pères de l'Eglise", je vous proposerais un poste à l'Université d'Etat: Poznań, Varsovie, etc. Mais vous êtes trop catholique et votre place est à Lublin. Je dois dire que cela m'a un peu chagriné, car mon idée était toujours plutôt de travailler dans une université d'Etat (Lwów, Gilson et Collège de France ....). Mais ça a été providentiel, parce que je n'aurais jamais pensé à cette époque, d'abord, que Lublin deviendrait vraiment un centre unique, non seulement dans la Pologne communiste, mais dans toute l'Europe envahie par le régime communiste. Nous étions la seule université, entre Berlin et Seoul disions-nous, où l'on enseignait librement la philosophie. Ailleurs, seulement le marxisme. Et c'est justement là, à l'époque la plus sombre, la plus difficile, époque des représailles staliniennes ou beaucoup d'anciens professeurs étaient chassés de l'université et devaient être renplacés par d'autres, jeunes, qu'à cause de toutes ces circonstances nous avons pu créer à Lublin, à la Faculté de Philosophie, nouvellement ouverte, un petit groupe vraiment assez extraordinaire.

---

[1] Cf. S. Swieżawski, *Dobro i tajemnica*, Warszawa 1995, p. 216.

Moi, je dois dire que je le compare avec Lwów; je ne peux pas dire lequel de ces centres était, disons, plus important, différents, naturellement, mais d'importance certainement égale.

Alors, les personnes qui se sont rencontrées dans ce petit groupe, qui était en dehors du Conseil de la Faculté, c'était un groupe non-formel: Notre doyen Georges Kalinowski, un grand logicien, philosophe du droit, de la morale; le Père Krąpiec, qui était alors vraiment une nouvelle étoile en philosophie, surtout en métaphysique; le Père Charles Wojtyła, qui était un prêtre de brillante intelligence (de Cracovie – nous vivions alors à Cracovie, il était parmi nos intimes amis pendant ces années où il était prêtre, puis évêque, etc.); le Père Stanislas Kamiński, hélas! décédé, excellent méthodologue et logicien; enfin, nous deux, historiens, à savoir le Père Kurdziałek, spécialiste de la philosophie médiévale, et moi, médiéviste aussi, attiré plus particulièrement par le XIIIe et XVe siècles.

Et voilà: ce centre était vraiment imbu d'un pluralisme exemplaire. Il y avait de grandes différences entre chacun de nous. Mais nous avions certains fondements qui étaient pour nous inébranlables. Le premier fondement, était la conviction que l'université, la carte de visite de l'université, est le niveau de recherches, du travail scientifique. La deuxième chose: en philosophie, la discipline centrale, c'est la métaphysique. Naturellement, nous sommes contre tout irrationalisme, mais le rationalisme doit être mitigé par l'intellectualisme. Il faut connaître toute l'histoire de la philosophie; on ne peut pas étudier que la philosophie contemporaine, que la philosophie ancienne ou médiévale. Tout est important parce que, en métaphysique et en anthropologie philosophique, les vérités auxquelles on arrive sont en dehors du temps. A vrai dire, ce que dit Platon, ce que dit Leibniz, ce que disent nos contemporains de vrai dans ces disciplines, est ultratemporel. Eh bien, nous étions vraiment unis autour de ces thèses, bien que chacun de nous restât soi-même.

R. J. W.-W.: Il est absolument certain que dans la vie de l'Eglise de notre siècle, le concile Vatican II a été l'événement le plus important, l'événement magistral. Vous en étiez un des 50 auditeurs laïques. Voici le don suivant.

Nous aimerions vous demander quelques souvenirs de ce moment-là; qu'est-ce qui vous reste le plus profondément gravé dans la mémoire?

S. Swieżawski: Je suis tout à fait d'accord avec le premier auditeur laïque, Jean Guitton, qui a écrit un jour que si quelqu'un se mettait à écrire une histoire universelle vers l'année 3 000 et à réfléchir sur le vingtième siècle, il devrait constater que l'événement le plus grand de cette époque – non seulement pour l'histoire ecclésiastique, mais pour l'histoire en général – avait été le deuxième Concile Vatican. Je suis certain que c'est un événement de très grande importance.

Eh bien, ce qui me reste surtout en mémoire ...? Hélas! je n'ai pas connu Jean XXIII, ce personnage tout à fait exceptionel -nous sommes allés à Rome après sa mort. Mais j'ai eu la possibilité de contacter plusieurs fois Paul VI; je le considère comme un très grand pape. Je n'oublierai jamais cette scène où Paul VI, agenouillé, a ôté la tiare de sa tête (nous avons pu assister de très près à cette scène), il l'a donnée pour les pauvres et a mis sur sa tête la mitre de l'évêque de Rome. De Paul VI, j'ai entendu plusieurs fois ce mots (ce n'était peut-être pas exprimé littéralement de cette façon, mais c'était souvent répété au Vatican II): l'Eglise a terminé – et Elle doit le constater – l'époque constantinienne, l'époque commencée par Constantin le Grand. L'Eglise a perdu, Dieu merci, le fardeau de l'Etat, du juridisme étatique, de l'absolutisme, de toutes ses conséquences. Et Paul VI en était très fortement convaincu. Ensuite, le deuxième problème, auquel nous reviendrons et qui sera le problème presque principal de notre rencontre, c'est le problème de la fin de l'époque d'une philosophie et d'une théologie changée en idéologie.

R. J. W.-W.: Justement, nous nous approchons du problème central de notre entretien. Pendant le Concile, dans bien des interventions perce nettement le problème de la place de la philosphie dans le christianisme, dans la doctrine catholique précisément. Avec une assez grande acuité, s'est alors posé la question de l'actualité et de la place de l'oeuvre de s. Thomas d'Aquin dans l'enseignement de l'Eglise catholique.

Ces sujets-là justement, vous les abordez dans l'ouvrage, écrit en français avec le professeur Jerzy Kalinowski: *La philosophie à l'heure du Concile*. Ce livre a paru en 1965[2]. Sa traduction polonaise a paru 30 ans plus tard: *Habent sua fata libelli...*

Or, dans cette traduction polonaise, il y a un petit texte de vous qui ne figure pas dans l'original français. Ce petit texte est intitulé: *Le deuxième Concile Vatican et la philosophie*. Il y a là une constatation frappante, la voici: "On se rendait au Concile parfaitement compte de ce que deux phases, deux époques dans la vie de l'Eglise comme institution se sont terminées: l'époque constantinienne et l'époque thomiste. Il faut bien comprendre de quoi il s'agit là[3]".

Eh bien, Monsieur le Professeur, *la fin de l'époque thomiste*! Cela choque quelque peu!

Alors, j'ai deux questions: quelle est la genèse de ce que vous appelez époque thomiste? Ce ne fut pas saint Thomas qui en est le point de départ;

---

[2] Paris (Societé d'Edition Internationales) 1995.
[3] Cf. S. Swieżawski, *Drugi Sobór Watykański a filozofia*, in: J. Kalinowski, *Filozofia w dobie soboru*, Warszawa 1995, pp. 9-14.

trois ans après sa mort – en 1277 – paraissent les fameux *Articuli Parisienses*, qui, s'en prenant à la doctrine d'Aristote, visaient – principalement – l'averroïsme, mais aussi la philosophie de saint Thomas. Il ne fut alors – au XIIIe siècle -question d'aucun thomisme. Cependant, la présence d'un thomisme officiel, imposé même par le Droit Canon[4], suscite des plaintes de Gilson lui-même dans les années soixante de notre siècle[5]. L'existence d'une époque thomiste est donc un fait; quand et pourquoi est-elle née? – c'est ma première question.

Et la deuxième: la fin de l'époque thomiste, signifie-t-elle du même coup la fin de la philosophie de saint Thomas?

S. Swieżawski: Voilà: le problème est très grave. Si je suis arrivé à une certaine solution de ce problème, c'est de nouveau grâce à la Providence. Nous avons entrepris des études approfondies sur les manuscrits médiévaux conservés dans nos bibliothèques. Je dois rendre hommage ici à tout un grand groupe de mes élèves, dont certains sont présents ici, qui ont consacré les plus belles années de leur vie à cette recherche de dépouillement, tellement difficile et tellement pleine – comment dirais-je – de surprises intellectuelles. Eh bien. voilà c'est ce qui m'a obligé à profiter de tout ce grand travail de recherche, qui avait été mené pendant une période de vingt, vingt cinq ans, et à écrire un ouvrage synthétique sur cette époque peu connue, parce que mal interprétée par les modernistes et un peu négligée par les médiévistes, notamment sur le XVe siècle philosophique[6]. Eh bien, j'ai consacré vingt années de notre vie, de notre vie de famille, de notre vie conjugale, de ma vie personnelle, à écrire ces huit volumes[7].

En poursuivant ces études, je me suis rendu compte que dans l'Eglise, surtout à partir de Boniface VIII déjà, progressait une certaine tendance vers un régime de plus en plus fort. Et ce n'est pas le problème de la primauté du pape, mais celui d'un absolutisme monarchique pontifical. Au XVe s., nous savons bien ce qui se passe. La terre tremble non seulement à Constantinople et aux confins de l'Europe, mais elle tremble dans l'Europe entière. Il y a les grandes suites du schisme occidental, il y a les terribles

---

[4] Cf: *Codex Iuris Canonici* (1917) canon 1366, paragraphe 2: "Philosophiae rationalis ac theologiae studia et alumnorum in his disciplinis [...] professores *omnino pertractent ad Angelici Doctoris rationem doctrinam et principia, eaque sancte teneant"*.

[5] Cf: E. Gilson, *Les tribulations de Sophie*, Paris (Vrin) 1967, p. 18.

[6] C:. S. Swieżawski, *Między średniowieczem, a czasami nowymi*, Warszawa 1983.

[7] Cf: S. Swieżawski, *Dzieje filozofii europejskiej XV wieku*, Warszawa (ATK), t. I, *Poznanie*, 1974; t. II, *Wiedza*, 1974; t. III, *Byt*, 1978; t. IV, *Bóg*, 1979; t. V, *Wszechświat*, 1980; t. VI, *Człowiek*, 1983; t. VII, *U źródeł nowożytnej etyki. Filozofia moralna w Europie XV wieku*, Kraków (Znak) 1987; t. VIII, *Eklezjologia późnośredniowieczna na rozdrożu*, Kraków (PTT) 1990.

conséquences de la peste noire de 1348, il y a des appréhensions devant tout ce qui arrive, devant ce qui vient d'Orient. Ensuite, la découverte d'autres continents, d'autres pays, etc. Et c'est alors avec l'arrivée en Italie d'un grand nombre de penseurs grecs – le monde hellénique – le monde qui n'est pas chrétien, Platon, etc., et on pense qu'il faut créer une vraiment grande idée, une idéologie si l'on peut dire, admise par tout le monde, qui puisse faire renaître la force de la Grèce. Et Rome pense de même. Ce sont là des problèmes très intéressants, mais on ne peut pas entrer dans les détails.

A un certain moment, sous le pontificat de Nicolas V (Thomas Parentucelli) on arrive à la conviction que dans toutes les écoles de la chrétienté doit être introduite une seule *ratio studiorum*, et qu'il faut choisir la théologie et la philosophie qui va être le contenu de cette *ratio studiorum*. Au début, on pense à Platon et à Aristote, on hésite entre eux. Il y a beaucoup de penseurs qui estiment qu'il faut unir les deux. Mais en fin de compte, c'est Aristote qu'on choisit. Mais Aristote ne peut être présenté, ne peut être enseigné dans les écoles s'il n'est pas interprété, même par force, d'une façon concordante avec les vérités de la foi. Et voilà né le célèbre courant – c'est un peu mon hypohèse que j'ai pu élaborer grâce à une suggestion de Gilson – qui s'appelle *l'aristotélisme chrétien*. Cet aristotélisme chrétien, il avait aussi besoin d'un maître, qui pourrait le représenter le mieux. On pensait à Scot, mais finalement, c'est saint Thomas qui fut considéré comme le maître idéal, qui représente ce qu'on a appelé l'idéologie de l'aristotélisme chrétien. Saint Thomas est alors représenté surtout comme celui qui a "baptisé" Aristote. On oublie beaucoup de ses thèses, centrales au point de vue philosophique, elles sont négligées, et c'est seulement dans le sens de la fidélité vis-à-vis d'Aristote que saint Thomas est développé et de plus en plus reconnu. C'est alors que naît le thomisme en tant que doctrine obligatoire pour les chrétiens. La grande difficulté, à laquelle – nous le savons tous – on est arrivé au courant des siècles, c'est qu'on a commencé à considérer certaines vérités philosophiques de la même manière, avec le même respect, que les vérités de la foi. Et ça, ça a été terrible. On est parvenu, par exemple, à la Sorbonne au XVIIe s. à cette ordonnance selon laquelle un professeur commentant la physique dans un autre esprit que celui d'Aristote, était passible de la peine de mort. Et ensuite, et c'était même actuel avant le Concile, dans les années trente: on regardait un ecclésiastique non thomiste comme suspect. Un chrétien qui n'est pas thomiste est suspect! Eh bien, c'était intenable. Et cette chose-là m'a beaucoup frappé alors.

C'est la raison pour laquelle Vatican II a voulu terminer l'époque thomiste. Ce n'est pas le thomisme, c'est saint Thomas qui doit revenir, dans toute sa splendeur. Et je dis toujours: c'est l'époque thomasienne qui doit remplacer l'époque thomiste.

R. J. W-W.: Mais pourquoi justement doit-on revenir à saint Thomas? Où est sa vrai grandeur?

S. Swieżawski: Sa grandeur c'est surtout sa conception de l'*esse*, comme l'élément essentiel de toutes les choses qui ont une existence, tandis que Dieu est le seul être qui soit l'existence. Cela, c'est le centre, le noyau de la pensée de saint Thomas. Ensuite, il y a ce grand problème qu'aucune philosophie qui veut être et rester philosophie et qu'aucune théologie qui veut vraiment être théologie, ne peut jamais être imposée, jamais imposée! Une philsophie imposée cesse d'être philosophie. Une philosophie ne peut vivre que comme fruit d'un choix libre; libre choix de celui qui cherche la vérité.

C'était tellement beau au Moyen Age, tous les problèmes étaient réunis dans la *questio*, "quête", c'est la recherche. Ce ne sont pas des thèses qu'on accepte, ce sont des vérités qu'on recherche et qu'on contemple. C'est ce que disaient Woroniecki ou Maritain, c'est l'intuition bergsonienne qui revient ici. C'est un grand mérite de Bergson d'avoir contribué à faire renaître la philosophie contemplative, et non pas une philosophie de manuel, ni une philosophie juridique.

R. J. W.-W.: Pour mettre le point final, ou plutôt un point d'exclamation, encore une question: quel est votre philosophe préféré, que vous aimeriez recommander?

S. Swieżawski: Mon philosophe préféré est certainement saint Thomas! Mais je ne le propose même pas à tout le monde. Je dis: cherchez! cherchez!

Moi, je propose à tout le monde de suivre une bonne histoire de la philosophie. L'histoire de la philosophie, c'est l'histoire des problèmes. Quand on fait l'histoire de la philosophie comme histoire des problèmes, on en vient aux grands problèmes métaphysiques. Et là, il faut voir, est-ce que c'est Heidegger ou est-ce que c'est saint Thomas qui a raison dans sa conception de l'*esse*? C'est un libre choix.

Pour moi, Thomas est le grand maître et je suis heureux d'avoir pu, grâce à mes maîtres dont nous avons parlé, passer des années et des dizaines d'années de ma vie en compagnie de ses ouvrages.

R. J. W.-W.: je voudrais seulement ajouter que *Le Catéchisme de l'Eglise Catholique* – le plus récent, postconciliaire, invoque 62 fois saint Thomas d'Aquin. Parmi les saints, seul s. Augustin est mentionné plus souvent.

Et maintenat le temps pour des questions. S'il vous plaît ...

S. Swieżawski: Seulement, j'entends très mal: ayez la bonté de parler distinctement et à haute voix!

Radu A. Duduica (Institut Catholique de Bucarest, Romania):

– Je voudrais remercier Monsieur le Professeur Swieżawski, qui a été mon maître dans le temps noir de l'idéologie – de l'autre idéologie, non du thomisme – qui était mon maître dans les trop rares moments où je venais à Varsovie. J'ai pu le rencontrer et c'est cela qui m'a permis d'enseigner aujourd'hui, non le thomisme, Dieu m'en garde, mais la philosophie médiévale, et dans un esprit thomasien. Pendant, je pense, presque 20 années, on s'est vu à des intervalles qui n'étaient pas assez pour moi, et il m'a donné beaucoup d'instructions et beaucoup de dont, parce que c'était surtout du courage dont j'avais besoin quand j'ai commencé à enseigner dans cet Institut, qui est tout à fait nouveau. J'avais reçu exactement l'année de la chute du mur de Berlin de la part de Monsieur le Professeur son livre, *Saint Thomas relu à nouveau*, en français[8], et que je l'ai utilisé pour commencer mes cours; il a été exceptionel, vraiment, et je veux en remercier l'Auteur. Je suis heureux d'avoir eu l'occasion de le revoir ici. Merci.

Chantal Delsol (Université de Marne la Vallée, France):

– Monsieur le Professeur, à propos de la genèse du thomisme au XIVe et XVe s. Est-ce que vous n'avez pas le sentiment que saint Thomas était finalement le philosophe tout désigné, puisque c'est quand même l'époque où commence la querelle des deux glaives; l'époque de Marsile de Padoue, où on cherche à séparer le temporel et le spirituel. Et finalement Thomas d'Aquin est le seul philosophe chrétien, dans la suite d'Aristote, mais le seul philosophe chrétien qui permette à l'ordre politique de persévérer dans son être, de chercher le bonheur par lui-même, en dehors de l'ordre spirituel. Donc, qui d'autre? Est-ce que vous pensez que ce n'est pas presque une obligation, à cette époque, de se tourner vers Thomas d'Aquin, à cause de cette querelle des deux glaives?

S. Swieżawski: Je crois qu'il y avait beaucoup de raisons pour accepter saint Thomas. Mais le fait que cette doctrine ait été imposée, l'a changée déjà en idole.

Ch. Delsol: Bien sûr, bien sûr, mais c'est pour le choix. Je veux dire pour le choix.

S. Swieżawski: Pour le choix, certainement!

Ch. Delsol: Ça tombe bien, si j'ose dire.

---

[8] Cf. S. Swieżawski, *Redécouvrir Thomas d'Aquin*, Paris (Nouvelle Cité) 1989.
[9] Cf. S. Swieżawski, *Wielki przełom: (1907-1945)*, Lublin (RW KUL) 1991, p. 22-25.

S. Swieżawski: Le grand philosphe, J. Maritain, dit que Thomas d'Aquin est un saint prophétique qui était dirigé vers l'avenir, alors il comprenait beaucoup de choses que d'autres ne comprenaient pas. Ça, c'est certain. Même en philosophie de la nature, qu'on ne peut plus suivre, parce qu'elle est tout à fait englobée par la physique aristotélicienne, il y a aussi des intuitions formidables. Alors, il y avait beaucoup de raisons.

Ch. Delsol: Merci beaucoup!

R. J. W.-W.: Hélas, nous devons finir.

Monsieur le Professeur, dans un de vos livres autobiographiques, vous racontez un songe d'enfant que vous avez eu. C'était un vol très haut, sous le ciel, dans une coquille d'oeuf ébréchée attelée à de magnifiques papillons. J'estime que ce songe a été vraiment prophétique.

Nous remercions la Providence pour cette coquille ébréchée, pour ces magnifiques papillons, et pour vous, Monsieur le Professeur. Et nous vous remercions. Nous vous remercions très, très cordialment pour votre présence parmi nous.

Merci de tout mon coeur!

HUGO OCHOA
Universidad Católica de Valparaiso
Chile

GRUNDLAGE DER FREIHEIT BEI SCHELLING

Es ist zunächst einmal notwendig, sich klar zu machen, daß Schelling die Errichtung eines Systems beabsichtigt, und deshalb ist hier als Hypothese das „*hen kai pan*" anzuwenden, denn jedes System ist nichts anderes als der Versuch, die Totalität als Einheit zu subsumieren und zu verstehen, und die Einheit als Totalität. Wie unser Philosoph ausführt, wird diese Philosophie von Descartes eingeführt[1], der als Grundlage von Wahrheit und Gewißheit, will heißen als Anfang eines Systems das Ich des *cogito* setzt, das zugleich im selben Seinsakt das denkende Ich ist. Eines der wesentlichen Ziele dieser neuen Denkrichtung ist es, die Mündigkeit, Souveränität und Autonomie des Menschen zu begründen, und damit die Emanzipation von jeder Autorität im Sinne einer Heteronomie. Insofern nur die Vernunft Wahrheit und Gewißheit vermittelt, darf als gültig nur dasjenige akzeptiert werden, was die Prüfung durch die Vernunft durchlaufen hat, die in der Entfaltung ihrer selbst in irgend einer Weise den gesamten möglichen Bereich des Objektiven konstituiert und errichtet.

Indem es unvermeidlich mit dieser Infragestellung des einfach Gegebenen belastet wird, entsteht aus sich heraus ein Konflikt mit der Geschichte und mit der Tradition. Die Tradition erscheint als die Quelle aller Vorurteile, Konventionen und Irrtümer, und auf diese Weise erscheint sie außerdem als ein Hindernis für die Freiheit. Die neue Grundlage der Philosophie verlangt also im wesentlichen die Kritik der Tradition. Damit entsteht ein Abgrund zwischen einerseits dem universell Gültigen, Ewigen, Notwendigen,

---

[1] Schelling, *Zur Geschichte der neueren Philosophie. Münchner Vorlesungen*, in: Schelling, *Ausgewählte Werke*; Wissenschaftliche Buchgesellschaft, Darmstadt, 1968. S. 286 [bei Schröter S. 4].

den stets einsehbaren Wahrheiten der Vernunft, und andererseits den tatsächlichen, empirischen Wahrheiten, die von der Tradition überliefert werden. Es ist deshalb nicht verwunderlich, daß der deutsche Idealismus in permanente Konflikte über den Atheismus verstrickt ist. Und dies ist kein Zufall, denn das Christentum baut auf einer emminent geschichtlichen Grundlage auf. Es gründet auf der Heilsgeschichte einer tatsächlich erfolgten Offenbarung, deren Wahrheit allen Menschen mittels einer mündlichen und schriftlichen Überlieferung sowie mittels transzendenter Zeichen vermittelt wird. Vom Standpunkt der aufgeklärten Vernunft aus entbehrt deshalb der Anspruch auf absolute Wahrheit, den das Christentum erhebt, der Berechtigung. Die Aufklärung ordnet sich auf diese Weise einer Vernunftreligion zu, die die Grundlage ihrer Wahrheit nicht in der Offenbarung, sondern in der Vernunft hat. Aber damit stehen nicht nur reine Vernunftwahrheit und geschichtliche Wahrheit in Opposition, sondern auch Wissen und Glaube.

In diesem Zusammenhang möchte ich mich kurz mit Kant beschäftigen. Die Philosophie Kants ist ein Selbstbeweis der Vernunft. Kant legt die Grenzen der menschlichen Vernunft fest und zeigt von da aus, daß eine theoretische Vernunfterkenntnis, die ein gesichertes und notwendiges Wissen erlaubt, nur ausgehend von der empirischen Tatsache möglich ist. Damit verbannt er nicht nur als Scheinwissen jede Metaphysik, die dogmatisch vorgeht, in dem Sinn, daß sie jenseits der Grenzen einer möglichen Erfahrung geht und ein unbedingtes Wissen und die Wahrheit für ihre Aussagen beansprucht, sondern er hat auch die Metaphysik der Gegenstände beraubt, die ihr nach Kant angestammt sind: Gott, Freiheit, Unsterblichkeit. Über das, was jenseits der Sinne liegt, kann die theoretische Vernunft weder bejahende noch verneinende Aussagen vorschlagen. Bei Kant wird also die Religion nicht auf einem theoretischen Wissen, sondern auf der praktischen Vernunft beruhen. Die Ideen von Gott, Freiheit und Unsterblichkeit können niemals ein theoretisches Wissen werden, sondern sie werden notwendigerweise aus der begründenden Erwägung der moralischen Tat heraus postuliert. Aber es ist notwendig, sich zu vergegenwärtigen, daß diese Ideen der Menschen nicht auf dem Wege geschichtlicher Offenbarung vermittelt werden, sondern daß sie implizite Voraussetzungen der praktischen Vernunft sind: sie stellen die Grundlagen einer reinen Vernunftreligion dar, die auf der Moral aufbaut. Außerdem unterscheidet Kant zwischen einer Vernunftreligion, die universell gültig ist, weil sie aus der Natur der (praktischen) menschlichen Vernunft entspringt, und einer positiven Religion, die auf einer geschichtlichen Tatsache beruht.

In diesem Zusammenhang muß deshalb der Entwurf Schellings betrachtet werden: dieser versucht eine neue Synthese dieser zwei Elemente, deren Gegensatz in der Tat seit langem besteht. Einerseits die Religion, die auf der geschichtlichen Tatsache einer Offenbarung beruht, und andererseits das autonome Denken, das auf der reinen Vernunft beruht. Wenn also ein Werk gemäß dem Problem verstanden wird, das es zu lösen versucht, so liegt hier der erste Schlüssel der Deutung: die Kluft zwischen der Vernunftwahrheit und der Tatsachenwahrheit, zwischen Wissen und Glauben zu überwinden.

Nun sucht aber Schelling diese Lösung, indem er die Vernunft versteht gemäß einer zeitlichen Dimension, die sich in der Geschichte verwirklicht. Das heißt, er versucht eine Rekonstruktion der Geschichte der Vernunft, deren jeweilige Erscheinung in der Zeit nicht von der Totalität losgelöst werden kann und die deshalb einer besonderen Autonomie entbehrt. Er entwirft also ein spekulatives Wissen, das dem Glauben nicht entgegengesetzt ist, sondern ihn vielmehr zu Bewußtsein bringt und in gewisser Weise das Fundament des reinen Vernunftdenkens darstellt. Dieser bewußte Glaube, der die kategoriale Struktur der Vernunft überschreitet und der das Tatsächliche in seiner Tatsächlichkeit begreift, ist die Kontemplation. Aber diese Kontemplation, die das Wissen über eine Tatsache ist und deshalb die Qualität einer Meinung hat, ist eine Vision dessen, was durch das Denken rekonstruiert wird, und weil es eine Rekonstruktion des Denkens ist, ist es authentisches und legitimes Vernunftwissen.

Es ist dies ein Angelpunkt, denn es handelt sich um ein Wissen, worin, ungeachtet seiner Tatsächlichkeit, im Maßstab dessen, was darin betrachtet wird, eben die Rekonstruktion der Offenbarung des Absoluten liegt; der Akt der Festlegung erreicht das Absolute nicht objektiv, sondern als Subjekt-Objekt, denn es betrachtet, und also objektiv, etwas, das in einem Akt der Selbstdarstellung als Subjekt in Erscheinung tritt. Aber daß es Subjekt-Objekt ist, bedeutet nicht, daß es diese Determinanten absolut überwinde.

Es geht darum, eine Metaphysik des Seins und nicht des *nous* zu rekonstruieren. Schelling versucht indes, das Sein als Existenz zu erreichen. Nun ist aber die Existenz eben dasjenige, was nicht gedacht werden kann. Sie kann jedoch, obzwar es den Bereich des Bewußtseins absolut überschreitet, auch nicht als Nicht-Ich bezeichnet werden; die Existenz, das Sein ist in der Tat älter als das Ich wie auch das Nicht-Ich, sie ist, wie Schelling in *Vom Ich*[2] darlegt, dasjenige, was nie Objekt, aber paradoxerweise ebensowenig Subjekt sein kann[3]. Das Sein ist genauer gesagt das Verhüllte, Versteckte,

---

[2] Schelling, *Vom Ich als Princip der Philosophie oder über das Unbedingte im menschlichen Wissen*, Historisch-kritische Ausgabe, I, 2. Fromann-Holzboog Verlag, Stuttgart, 1980, S. 89.

[3] Vgl. Loer B., *Das Absolute und die Wirklichkeit in Schellings Philosophie. Mit der Erstedition einer Handschrift aus dem Berliner Schelling-Nachlaß*. Walter Gruyter Verlag, Berlin/New York, 1974, S. 31: "Diese Überschwenglichkeit, dieses das weder Subject noch Object ist, ist also die Voraussetzung aller Philosophie..." Das Zitat ist von Schelling.

Bedrückte. Nur hier und da tauchen die Formen seiner Unterdrückung auf. Die Unterdrückung ist es, welche die Vielfalt erzeugt. Das Sein ist das Eingeschlossene, das Versteckte, die Nuß, das Samenkorn, woraus die Vielfalt, durch die Unterdrückung gezwungen, entspringt. In diesem Sinnne wird das Bewußtsein seiner selbst, will heißen das *cogito*, endlich zur eigentümlichsten Form der Unterdrückung, denn es versucht, etwas freizusetzen, das nicht frei sein kann. Es öffnet Türen, aber es erscheint nur Finsternis. Niemand kann das Sein befreien, dieses kann nur sich selbst befreien. So daß der Versuch, es von der Vernunft oder vom Denken her zu befreien, nur eine andere Form der Unterdrückung ist, welche es nur versteckt, statt es zu zeigen. Das Selbstbewußtsein ist also nichts als die Form, die jenes Mandat, das an sich selbst gerichtet ist, annimmt, aber der wahrhaft höhere Zustand wird in einem Willen des Nichtwollens, in einer Gelassenheit erreicht.

In diesem Sinne dürfte das *ego*, welches *cogito* und *sum* vereinigt, in Wirklichkeit die Funktion eines Bindegliedes ausüben, und dies gemäß der klassischen doppelten Bestimmung, denn es wird eine Verbindungsfunktion und eine Existentialfunktion erfüllen. Wenn das Denken ein Sein ist, und wenn das Sein ein Denken ist, so deswegen, weil dasjenige, was in Wirklichkeit denkt, das Ich ist. Dieses jedoch kann aus zwei Blickrichtungen heraus gedacht werden: entweder wohnt das Sein dem Denken inne, und dies war die Meinung des jungen Schelling, oder das Ich wohnt dem Sein inne, und diese Perspektive wählt Schelling in *Die Weltalter*. Aber wenn dem so ist, dann ist, wie wir sagten, die Bestimmtheit des Ich, in dem Maße, in dem es einen Ausdruck, eine Manifestation des Seins darstellt, eine Beschränkung. Es handelt sich also darum, die Identität des Absoluten zu erreichen, jenseits der dem Ich und dem Nicht-Ich eigentümlichen Beschränkungen, und zwar eben deswegen, weil das Absolute sich als dasjenige offenbart, was jenseits oder über allen Beschränkungen steht. Es geht eben darum, das Absolute zu denken, aber seit Kant scheint dies notwendigerweise ein Widerspruch in sich zu sein, weil Denken notwendigerweise heißt: zum Objekt machen. Jeder dialektische Versuch, das Unbedingte zu fassen, bedeutet, eben aufgrund der Dialektik, es den Bedingungen eines Denkens unterwerfen, das sich selbst setzt und ebendeswegen nur sich selbst finden kann. Verlangt ist also eine Form des Wissens, die jenseits des Denkens liegt, ein Wissen, das weiß, ein rein kontemplatives Wissen, das im ältesten Sinn lediglich schaut. Es geht darum, die Falle des *cogito* zu überwinden, die das Sein im Denken ansiedelt und nicht in der reinen Kontemplation, die im

---

[4] Schelling, *Darstellung des philosophischen Empirismus,* in: *Ausgewählte Werke, Schriften von 1813-1830*, Wissenschaftliche Buchgesellschaft, Darmstadt, 1968, S. 509 [227].

übrigen einen zwitterhaften Ursprung hat, denn sie ist eine Tochter des Zweifels und ist deswegen in gewisser Weise eine Frucht der Dialektik.

„Philosophie solle die Thatsache der Welt erklären"[4], und wenn die Welt nichts anderes ist als göttliche Offenbarung, so kann das Realfundament dieser Offenbarung nichts anderes als ein lebendiges Prinzip sein. Die dialektische Auffassung, sagt Schelling, kann nur dann wahrhaftig sein, wenn es sich um eine Ewigkeit ohne jede Außenwirkung handelt, aber dann ist sie wie ein Nichts[5]. Ein absolutes Prinzip, das keine andere Funktion erfüllt als eine dialektische, ist paradoxerweise kein Prinzip, denn indem seine rein logische Selbsterhaltung und Autarkie absolut nicht in der Lage ist, allein aus sich selbst zu entspringen, so bedeutet jeder Bezug auf ein reales und existentes Anderes unvermeidlich eine Relativierung des Prinzips. Darum stellt sich das Problem aus dialektischer Blickrichtung im Sinn eines Dilemmas: entweder ist es Prinzip oder es ist absolut.

Aber weil sie dieselbe Grundlage hat, geschieht dasselbe mit der Vernunftreligion wie mit der dialektischen Vernunft. „Aber wir wissen, wie Gründe der Wissenschaft im Augenblick wenig vermögen gegen eine eingewurzelte Sinnesart, besonders wenn sie mit Einbildungen hoher Geistigkeit verbunden ist, wie die jetzt herrschende sogenannte reine Vernunftreligion, die Gott um so höher zu stellen meint, je reiner sie alle lebendige Bewegungskraft, alle Natur von ihm hinweggenommen hat"[6]. Es handelt sich um einen lebendigen Gott[7], das einzige Prinzip, das Aufschluß bietet über eine geschichtliche Offenbarung und über eine Schöpfung, die gemäß der Lösung, die Schelling vorschlägt, nicht weniger geschichtlich ist. Was sich offenbart, ist eine Person, insofern ist die schöpferische Dimension die Kundgabe der göttlichen Persönlichkeit. Kein Gott, der ein reines *Es* ist, befriedigt die Vernunft und das Gefühl, die verlangen, daß es ein *Er* sei[8]. Und in der Schrift gegen Jacobi[9]: „Der Erste, dem auf dem Wege reiner Vernunftforschung als die alles versöhnende Lösung des großen Räthsels der Gedanke in die Seele sprang, daß ein persönliches Wesen Urheber und Lenker der Welt seyn möge, war davon unstreitig wie von einem Wunder gerührt und in das höchste Erstaunen versetzt. Es war nicht nur ein kühner, es war schlechthin der kühnste aller Gedanken".

Bis hierher kommt Schelling, denn er kann die Eindeutigkeit des Seins nicht überwinden, und er greift wieder auf, was ein Leitmotiv seiner Philo-

---

[5] Schelling, *Die Weltalter*, in Ausgewählte Werke, Darmstadt, 1968, S. 66, [260].
[6] Ibid., S. 75-76 [269-70].
[7] Ibid., S. 65 [259].
[8] Ibid., S. 61 [255].
[9] Schelling, *Denkmal des Schrift von den göttlichen Dingen etc. des Herrn F. H. Jacobi*, in: Ausgewählte Werke, Schriften von 1805-1813, S. 574 [54].

sophie gewesen ist. So stellt er im „*System der gesammten Philosophie und der Naturphilosophie insbesondere*" den Satz auf: „Alles, was ist, ist, insofern es ist, Gott"[10], und weiter oben: „Alles, was ist, ist, insofern es ist, Eins"[11]. Und ebenfalls: „Alles, was ist, ist, insofern es ist, die absolute Identität"[12]. Aber auch in den *Stuttgarter Privatvorlesungen* heißt es, daß „Alles, was ist, nur in Gott sein kann"[13]. So daß der lebendige und persönliche Gott Schellings als eine Aufhebung, im dialektischen Wortsinn, des Pantheismus und Theismus zu verstehen ist, denn nur die Natur und Gott vereint erzeugen ein authentisches lebendes Wesen[14]. Das Leben Gottes, seine Offenbarung ist also die Entwicklung, die Evolution des organischen Ganzen des Universums. Die Aufhebung des Pantheismus beruht dann lediglich auf der Unterscheidung zwischen dem lebenden Subjekt und seinem Leben selbst, nur daß das Subjekt am Ende steht, am Anfang steht reines Leben.

Die Persönlichkeit Gottes ist letztendlich nichts anderes als die Natur selbst, im Sinn von *Gesicht*, was ebensosehr das Antlitz Gottes wie seine Sichtbarkeit bedeutet. Es ist in dieser Hinsicht unvermeidlich, sich an die ethymologische Bedeutung des Begriffs Person zu erinnern, und wenn wir die Dinge etwas weiter führen als Schelling es wollte, so beruht der persönliche Charakter Gottes auf einem Willen, sich herabzubegeben, um in einer Offenbarung gegenwärtig zu werden. Von lediglich dialektischen Prinzipien her ist der Weg notwendigerweise ein fortschreitender. Wenn im übrigen die Schöpfung und die Offenbarung Gottes auch ein Mittel sind zum Erreichen eines höheren Zweckes, so kann dieser doch nur erreicht werden, wenn das Absolute vor sich selbst nachgibt, sich beherrscht und beschränkt, zu dem rein Seinshaften herabsteigt, wie wir heute sagen würden. Das persönliche Prinzip Schellings ist letztendlich immer ein Ich; nie erreicht es die Dimension eines Du, es ist nie jemandes Gesprächspartner, es ist schließlich die einzige Hauptperson einer Geschichte, die das Ich selber schreibt. Auf diese Weise kehrt das Problem wiederum zum Ausgangspunkt zurück, denn es handelt sich immer um die Kontemplation, die das Absolute sich selbst widmet, und nur deshalb vermengen sich Wissen und Glaube. Aber diese Identität ereignet sich außerdem strenggenommen nur in der Vergangenheit, das einzige Zeitalter, das Schelling „erzählt". Und es scheint, daß es solchermaßen keinen Weg gibt, zu einer Gegenwart zu gelangen, in der dieses Absolute sich selbst tatsächlich transzendiert.

---

[10] In: *Schellings ausgewählte Werke, Schriften von 1801-1804*, S. 681 [157].

[11] Ibid., S. 680 [156].

[12] Ibid.

[13] In: Schriften von 1806-1813, S. 382 [438].

[14] Schelling, *Zusammenhang der Natur mit der Geisterwelt. Ein Gespräch*, in: *Schriften von 1806-1813*, S. 498 [70].

Die Kontemplation andererseits bedeutet die absolute Annullierung des Abstands, der zwischen dialektischen Polen besteht; man möchte sagen, es denkt nicht, es weiß. Das Selbstbewußtsein ist auch nicht als der Akt zu verstehen, durch den das Ich sich selbst denkt, das heißt in der Form der Wahrnehmung, sondern in der Form der Kontemplation, die eine geschichtliche Identität verfolgt. Wenn die Zeit die Form des inneren Sinns ist, so darf dies nicht als die Präfiguration *a priori* einer Sensibilität verstanden werden, sondern als die tatsächliche Konfiguration einer Identität. Wenn auf diese Weise die Kontemplation weder dialektisch ist noch sein kann, so ist sie notwendigerweise geschichtlich. Wenn es sich indessen nicht um eine Verkettung eines Werdens handelt, das sich in der Form einer Idee (Ich) ereignet, so ist es doch auch nicht eine Verkettung in der Form des Wirklichen (Natur oder Nicht-Ich), sofern es als bestimmte Existenz verstanden wird. Es handelt sich um das, was wir die transzendentale Geschichte des Seins nennen könnten, das jenseits des Idealen und des Realen steht.

Der Angelpunkt des Problems im deutschen Idealismus[15] ist die Verknüpfung zwischen Freiheit und Notwendigkeit[16], Subjekt und Objekt, Ich und Natur. Wenn die Philosophie vollständig ein Werk der Freiheit ist[17], weil sie aus dem reflexiven Selbstbewußtsein entsteht, das sich absolut vom Bewußtseinsstrom und den Darstellungen jedweder Art trennt und entfernt, wie soll dann seine Hauptbeschäftigung das Notwendige sein? Auf diese Weise baut die Frage „Wie ist eine Welt außerhalb unserer selbst möglich?"[18] einen Widerspruch auf zwischen den Polen des Seins wie Ich und Nicht-Ich, Prinzip und Wirklichkeit. „Indem ich den Gegenstand vorstelle, ist Gegenstand und Vorstellung eins und dasselbe"[19], und nur in dieser Unmöglichkeit, das Eine vom Andern zu trennen, liegt die Überzeugung von der Wirklichkeit der Dinge der Außenwelt. Aber der Philosoph schafft diese Identität mit der Frage aus der Welt: Wie entstehen in uns die Darstellungen der Dinge der Außenwelt?

Eine Lösung, die sich sofort aufdrängt, ist, zu denken, daß zwischen den Darstellungen und den Dingen eine reale Verbindung besteht, und diese kann nur ein Ursache-Wirkung-Verhältnis sein. In diesem Sinne könnte

---

[15] Vgl. Heidegger, *Schellings Abhandlung. Über das Wesen der menschlichen Freiheit*. Max Niemeyer Verlag, Tübingen, 1971.

[16] Vgl. Schelling, *Philosophische Untersuchungen über das Wesen der menschlichen Freiheit und die damit zusammenhängenden Gegenstände*, in: *Schriften von 1806-1813*, S. 277 [333].

[17] Schelling, *Ideen zu einer Philosophie der Natur als Einleitung in das Studium dieser Wissenschaft*, in: *Schriften von 1794-1798*, S. 335 [11].

[18] Ibid. S. 336 [12].

[19] Ibid. S. 339 [15].

man sagen, daß die Dinge unabhängig von uns sind und unsere Darstellungen von den Objekten abhängig sind, und auf diese Weise sind unsere Darstellungen wirklich insofern, als wir gezwungen sind, eine Kausalkonkordanz zwischen Objekt und Darstellung zu akzeptieren.

Aber, „Ferner, indem ich frage: wie kommt es, daß ich vorstelle?, erhebe ich mich selbst *über* die Vorstellung; ich werde *durch* diese Frage selbst zu einem Wesen, das in Ansehung alles Vorstellens sich ursprünglich *frei* fühlt"[20]. Mit dieser Frage verlasse ich notwendigerweise die Reihe der Darstellungen, und insofern ich mich von ihnen entferne, unterwerfe ich mir die Begriffe von Ursache und Wirkung, denn beide entstehen nur in der notwendigen Abfolge von Darstellungen, von denen ich mich entfernt habe (in den Begriffen Kants sind es Kategorien der Subjektivität). Wenn ich der Reihe der Darstellungen absolut unterworfen wäre, hätte ich nie die Frage nach der Möglichkeit der Darstellungen bei mir stellen können. Das Ich ist absolut frei und offenbart seine Freiheit in der Frage; das Fragen ist zugleich befreiend und frei, wie die vollkommenen *Praxen* bei Aristoteles[21], sie setzt das Ich unmittelbar für sich und nicht für etwas anderes. Es ist in der Tat unmöglich zu verstehen, wie die Dinge aufeinander einwirken, aber ich bin nicht ein Ding, insofern ich mich über die Verknüpfungen der Dinge erhebe, wenn ich mich frage, wie diese Verknüpfung möglich geworden ist.

Wenn dem nicht so wäre, so wäre ich selbst ein Ding, das in der Kette von Ursachen und Wirkungen inbegriffen ist, ich und das ganze Sein meiner Darstellungen wären nichts als ein Ergebnis, wir wären das Produkt einer mechanischen Handlung. Aber was in der Mechanik enthalten ist, kann sie nicht einfach verlassen und fragen, wie all dieses in der Kette möglich gewesen ist. Deswegen muß, wer die Frage stellt, eben durch die Frage darauf verzichten, seine Darstellungen aus den Dingen der Außenwelt heraus zu erklären.

„Wer für sich selbst nichts ist als das, was Dinge und Umstände aus ihm gemacht haben; wer ohne Gewalt über seine eigenen Vorstellungen von Strom der Ursachen und Wirkungen ergriffen mit fortgerissen wird, wie will er doch wissen, woher er kommt, wohin er geht und wie er das geworden ist, was er ist? Weiß es denn die Woge, die im Strome daher treibt? Er hat nicht einmal das Recht, zu sagen, er sey ein Resultat der Zusammenwirkung äußerer Dinge; denn um dieß sagen zu können, muß er voraussetzen, daß er sich *selbst* kenne, daß er also auch etwas *für sich selbst* sey"[22].

---

[20] Ibid. S. 340 [16].
[21] Vgl. Aristoteles, *Metaphysik*, IX, 6, 1048 b 18-34.
[22] Schelling, *Ideen zu einer Philosophie...*, S. 342 [18].

Das menschliche Wesen ist kein Spiegel, denn der Spiegel selbst sieht nicht, sieht sich nicht; das Bewußtsein bedeutet einen Akt absoluter Freiheit, durch den das Subjekt sich notwendigerweise von der Kausalkette trennt, und nur so kann es die Kette als solche betrachten. Das Bewußtsein wendet sich zu sich selbst und setzt sich als absolutes *prius* der Frage nach dem Ich und nach der natürlichen Welt; das Bewußtsein ist Selbstbewußtsein im Akt der Freiheit, der die Notwendigkeit als etwas vollkommen Fremdes und dessen ungeachtet als ein gegebenes *positum* definiert, das notwendigerweise in die Darstellungen aufgenommen wird.

Aber nun handelt es sich um Notwendigkeit und Freiheit des Absoluten, das als solches nur notwendig sein kann in dem Maße, in dem es aus sich heraus eine einzigartige Totalität gründet, die, wie wir sahen, in ihrem Sein nicht definitiv von ihm unterschieden werden kann. Die innere Verbindung all dessen, was ist, die Entwicklung oder Entfaltung des ursprünglichen Samenkorns, die Explizitmachung des Impliziten usw. ereignet sich nicht ohne Gesetz[23], eben weil die Verbindung, die das Ganze durchläuft, ein und dieselbe ist, und zwar dermaßen, daß Schelling sich weigert, es einfach nur Verbindung zu nennen. Aber ein an sich notwendiges Absolutes, das nichts weiter als notwendig wäre, würde ein Absolutes bedeuten, das auf die Grenzen der Vernunft beschränkt wäre, das heißt es würde bedeuten, es auf ein dialektisches Prinzip zu reduzieren. Gott ist also, auch wenn es paradox klingt, notwendigerweise frei, in Gott ist ebenso viel Notwendigkeit wie Freiheit[24].

Notwendig ist also einerseits das, was im absoluten Sinn *ist*, was nicht nicht sein kann, so daß die Notwendigkeit Gottes, wenn man dies so nennen kann, seine absolute Selbstsetzung ist. Die Freiheit Gottes andererseits beruht ebenfalls auf seinem absoluten Charakter, denn es ist nicht möglich, sein Sein zu relativieren, in dem Sinne, daß sein Wirken von außen determiniert wäre. Frei sein heißt Herr seiner selbst sein, so daß die Freiheit Gottes auf seiner absoluten Selbstbesitzung beruht.

Selbstsetzung und Selbstbesitzung, Notwendigkeit und Freiheit stehen in Beziehung und fordern einander, und die eine kann nicht ohne die andere gedacht werden. Nur was sich absolut setzt, ist in der Lage, sich absolut zu bestimmen; nur was sich absolut selbst bestimmt, ist in der Lage, sich absolut zu setzen, was nichts anderes heißt als daß nur das absolut Notwendige absolut frei sein kann, und umgekehrt. Dies ist die Lösung Schellings, aber wie wir sehen werden, bedeutet dies nicht, den Gegensatz zwischen einem

---

[23] Schelling, *System der gesammten Philosophie und der Naturphilosophie insbesondere*, in: *Schriften von 1801-1804*, S. 723 [199].
[24] *Die Weltalter,* in: *Schriften von 1813-1830*, S. 15 [209].

und dem anderen abzuschaffen, ganz im Gegenteil, aber es bedeutet die unmittelbare Forderung, den Widerspruch aufzuheben.

Die Notwendigkeit ist die Natur Gottes, die Freiheit ist die Liebe Gottes. Die Notwendigkeit ist die Kraft des Selbstbewußtseins, die Einwohnung seiner selbst in sich selbst, es ist die Kraft, die im Akt der Selbstsetzung das Absolute auf sich selbst beschränkt, denn es kann nur sich selbst absolut setzen; es ist, in den Worten Schellings, die Kraft der Egoität. Die Freiheit dagegen ist eine expansive Kraft, die sich schenkt, durch die Freiheit öffnet sich das Eingeschlossene, sie ist eine quellende und öffnende Kraft, ist die Kraft der Liebe. Die These Schellings ist, daß in dieser Hinsicht der Akt der Selbstbestimmung des Absoluten, will heißen seine eigentliche Konstitution als absolute Freiheit sich in der Form einer Tätigkeit des Absoluten verwirklicht: die schöpferische Tätigkeit, durch die es sich offenbart. So daß die Offenbarung, die die Schöpfung selbst ist, zugleich die Freiheit des Absoluten ist, durch welche dieses in seiner Entfaltung sich absolut selbst erreicht.

Obwohl in diesem Sinn der Gott, der notwendig ist, derselbe ist, der frei ist, sind Freiheit und Notwendigkeit nicht ein und dasselbe. Und wenn auch die Wesentlichkeit beider entgegengesetzter Prinzipien[25], will heißen, die Kraft der Zusammenziehung und der Ausdehnung, anerkannt werden muß, so gibt es doch zwischen ihnen eine Ordnung des Vorrangs. In diesem Sinn steht die Notwendigkeit Gottes vor seiner Freiheit, denn ein Wesen muß zunächst existieren, damit es frei handeln kann[26]. Aber in einem andern Sinn beherrscht, wenn die Freiheit Selbstbesitzung, d.h. Selbstbestimmung ist, in der Schöpfung Gott die Notwendigkeit seiner Natur mittels der Freiheit, und dann ist es die Freiheit, die über die Notwendigkeit Vorrang hat, und nicht die Notwendigkeit über die Freiheit.

Gott ist gemäß der Freiheit die reinste Liebe, die unendliche Fähigkeit der Kommunikation und der Expansion. Aber die Liebe erreicht aus sich heraus nicht das Sein, denn Sein ist Eigenart, Isolation, Selbstsein. Lediglich kraft der Freiheit kann Gott nicht wirklich existent sein, denn darin sucht er nicht das Seinige. Lediglich kraft der Notwendigkeit gäbe es keine Geschöpfe, gäbe es keine Offenbarung, gäbe es auch keine Gegenwart Gottes vor sich selbst, er wäre ein reines Nichts. So daß diese beiden Prinzipien, einerseits das quellend expansive Sein, das sich verschenkt, und die Kraft des Selbstseins, der Rückkehr zu sich selbst, das An-sich-Sein andererseits, auch wenn sie sich gegenseitig bedingen als Selbstbesitzung und Selbstsetzung, doch zugleich entgegengesetzt sind.

---

[25] Ibid., S. 17 [211].
[26] Ibid., S. 15 [209].

Dieser Gegensatz in Gott selbst ist es, was ihn zu einem lebendigen und wirklichen Wesen macht, das in sich selbst lebt, wirklich, weil es sich verwirklicht, sich in der Welt entfaltet. Die Entfaltung selbst ist nichts als der Versuch, den Gegensatz zwischen Freiheit und Notwendigkeit zu überwinden, und er konstituiert die Geschichte des Absoluten. Der Gegensatz bedeutet, daß beide nicht gleichzeitig erscheinen können, d.h. sobald ein Prinzip aktiv ist, muß das andere notwendigerweise passiv werden, und umgekehrt. Aber daß sie nicht gleichzeitig in Erscheinung treten können und daß sie dennoch sichtbar werden müssen, weil beide dieselben Rechte haben, heißt unvermeidlich, in das Absolute eine gewiße Abfolge einzuführen, und auf diese Weise können sich sozusagen Momente des Göttlichen bilden, wie Zeitalter oder Äonen des Ganzen.

Andererseits sind diese Prinzipien in der Tat in den Begriffen Schellings Ausgangspunkte, Kräfte oder Mächte des Anfangs, die in ihrem Gegensatz darum kämpfen, übereinander zu herrschen (das Wort „Kampf" ist hier mehr als nur rhetorisch gemeint). Die ganze Welt, die Schöpfung und das Leben selbst sind nichts als ein unermüdlicher, ewiger Kampf, und ein Beispiel dessen ist, gemäß Schelling, der ewige Kampf im Reich der Natur. Die Prinzipien sind also Kräfte, aber dies erhellt nicht nur ihren dynamischen Charakter, sondern es muß verstanden werden, daß ihre konstitutive, oder, wenn man so will, substantielle Identität selbst reine Tätigkeit ist. Es gibt ursprünglich nicht eine Art Subjekt, auf dem die Kraft beruht und das irgendwie sich von dieser unterscheide. Das Absolute insgesamt ist dieser Gegensatz der Kräfte, und das Ergebnis der Einheit ist die Entfaltung und Aktion der Kräfte. Es handelt sich, wie Schelling schreibt, darum, das Absolute als absolute Tat zu verstehen, deshalb nennt er es gemäß Dionysos Areopagita das Über-Sein, denn gemäß der Blickrichtung von *Die Weltalter* ist der Akt des Seins notwendigerweise bestimmend und deswegen einem Seienden angemessen, und Gott ist durchaus kein Seiendes.

Die antagonistischen Kräfte bilden eine nicht-substantielle Einheit, weil in den Worten Schellings „das gerad' Entgegengesetzte nur wesentlich und so zu sagen persönlich eins sein kann"[27]. Es handelt sich um eine persönliche Form des Göttlichen, die einzige, in der die entgegengesetzten Prinzipien von Notwendigkeit und Freiheit statthaben. Nun ist aber die Freiheit Quelle dessen, was wir die Subjektivität Gottes nennen könnten, insofern als durch die Freiheit als bejahende Kraft Gott zum Bewußtsein seiner selbst gelangt. Die Notwendigkeit dagegen ist die Quelle der Objektivität Gottes, insofern die Notwendigkeit die Natur Gottes ist, die Setzung seiner selbst. Dessen ungeachtet ist es kraft der Notwendigkeit, daß das Geschaffene sei-

---

[27] Ibid., S. 19 [213].

end ist, was eine Herabsetzung bezüglich dem wesentlichen Sein der Gottheit darstellt.

Jedoch „Philosophie solle die Thatsache der Welt erklären"[28], und von *Die Weltalter* aus gesehen, hat die Tatsache Welt ihren Ursprung in der Freiheit Gottes, denn, wie wir gesehen haben, gäbe es keine Schöpfung, wenn Gott reine Notwendigkeit wäre: es ist die Freiheit, die Kraft der Öffnung, die die absolute Isolierung und Selbstversunkenheit Gottes durchbricht. Hingegen kann diese Durchbrechung nur geschehen, wenn in dem Kampf eines der Prinzipien das andere überwindet. Aber beide sind von sich aus stark, so daß die einzige Lösung ist, daß eines dem anderen frei und freiwillig nachgibt. „An sich klar ist, daß überhaupt nichts sich als Seyendes aufzugeben vermag, als nur gegen ein Höheres"[29]. Und es geht eben um dieses, die Ordnung der Weltalter ist eine umgekehrte Ordnung. Das heißt, die Gottheit erreicht, um es irgendwie auszudrücken, ihre wahre Fülle am Schluß. Der Anfang unter dem Schutz einer moralischen Instanz, eines intelligenten und von vorneherein freien Schöpfers, unter Ausschluß jeder Natur (will heißen Notwendigkeit), ist bei Schelling undenkbar. Es handelt sich um eine umgekehrte Ordnung, denn bis dahin verlangte die systematische Vorgehensweise nach einem absoluten Prinzip, bezüglich dessen die Ordnung absteigender Natur ist, insofern die Notwendigkeit, Wahrheit und Gewißheit jedes Gliedes des Systems absolut aus seiner Beziehung zu dem ersten Prinzip herrührt: in dieser Hinsicht gilt die Analogie mit der Geometrie, die Schelling in *Vom Ich* hergestellt hatte. „Wer es in einen demonstrirbaren Begriff verwandeln will, der muß es nimmer für das Unbedingte halten. Denn das Absolute kann nimmer vermittelt werden, also nimmer ins Gebiet erweisbarer Begriffe fallen. Denn alles demonstrirbare setzt etwas schon demonstrirtes, oder das höchste nicht mehr demonstrirbare voraus. Wer also das Absolute demonstriren will, hebt es eben dadurch auf, und mit ihm alle Freiheit, alle absolute Identität u.s.w."[30].

Nun steht aber in *Die Weltalter* das Prinzip in Wirklichkeit am Ende, denn die Kräfte geben nach, und es entstehen diese verschiedenen Weltalter jeweils in bezug auf etwas Höheres. (*Die Weltalter* bildet in diesem Sinne eine Erweiterung der These der *Naturphilosophie*, denn dort wurde die Natur als die Vorgeschichte des Bewusstseins verstanden, als eine Entfaltung, auf deren Gipfel die Natur mittels einer Evolution, einer Entwicklung, die eigene Subjektivität des Ich und das volle Selbstbewußtsein erreicht).

---

[28] Schelling, *Darstellung des philosophischen Empirismus*, in: Op. cit., S. 509 [227].
[29] *Die Weltalter*, S. 39 [233].
[30] Schelling, *Vom Ich als Princip...*, Frommann-Holzboog, Stuttgart 1980, S. 109.

Das Prinzip, das in *Die Weltalter* vorgeschlagen wird, ist reine Verschließung, es ist, wie Schelling sagt, wie ein Nichts, es ist Bewußtlosigkeit, fast möchte ich wagen zu sagen, reines Objekt, Notwendigkeit. Andererseits jedoch bedeutet die Schöpfung selbst einen „Abstieg", Absturz des eigenen Seins der Gottheit. Die Verwirklichung des Göttlichen in Kreaturen muß fast im platonischen Sinne verstanden werden, wo die Gegenstände Gegenbilder, das heißt Bilder dessen sind, was in der Gottheit selbst gegenwärtig ist.

In gewisser Weise bleibt *Die Weltalter* in dieser doppelten Ordnung verstrickt: einerseits die Forderung nach einer systematischen Struktur und andererseits die Absicht einer historischen Struktur. Und dies steht vom Anfang des Werkes an fest, in jenen Worten, die wie eine Litanei in allen Abwandlungen wiederholt werden. „Das Vergangene wird gewußt, das Gegenwärtige wird erkannt, das Zukünftige wird geahndet". Wenn die wahrhafte Totalisierung der Wirklichkeit, ihre vollständige Erklärung sich definitiv in der Zukunft findet, dann hat es keinen Sinn und ist es unmöglich, ein System zu konstruieren, es ist nur möglich, es zu erahnen, oder, wie wir sagten, es zu betrachten, aber dies ist, wie Schelling sagt, unmöglich, es ist notwendig, sich an die eigene Epoche zu halten, es ist nicht möglich, die Früchte zu ernten, bevor sie reif sind. Die Zeit ist nicht gekommen, wo das Wissen reine Erzählung sein könnte. Wenn Schelling versucht, eine umgekehrte systematische Ordnung zu bauen, so erweist sich diese Absicht bereits von vornherein, von den ersten Zeilen an, als zum Scheitern verurteilt. Wenn die Grundlage des Wissens, die Schelling vorschlägt, so etwas wie die platonische Anamnese ist, dann ist, da wir keine Erinnerung an die Zukunft besitzen, eine Erzählung nicht möglich, die aus einer historischen Rekonstruktion des Werdens des Absoluten besteht, aber ebensowenig ist die Erstellung eines Systems möglich, insofern das Prinzip, mit dem die Geschichte endet, auf dem Scheitelpunkt der Erklärung nicht erreichbar ist, weil es absolute Zukunft ist.

MACIEJ POTĘPA
University of Łódź
Poland

FREIHEIT IN DER RELIGIONSPHILOSOPHIE: KANT UND SCHLEIERMACHER

In der Vorrede zur *Kritik der reinen Vernunft* formuliert Kant den berühmten Satz: „Ich mußte also das Wissen aufheben, um zum Glauben Platz zu bekommen" (R VB XXX). Zweifelsohne, es besteht ein systematischer Zusammenhang sowohl zwischen der klassisch gewordenen Definition von Religion in der *Kritik der praktischen Vernunft* als auch der Ausgangsthese der Schrift *Die Religion innerhalb der Grenzen der bloßen Vernunft*. Die Definition von Religion in der *Kritik der praktischen Vernunft* lautet bekanntlich: „Religion ist Erkenntnis aller Pflichten als göttlicher Gebote" (PV 233). Und die Ausgangsthese der Religionsschrift verbindet gerade diese Definition rückblickend mit einer generellen Zielbestimmung der Moralphilosophie überhaupt, daß Moral „unumgänglich" zur Religion führe. Alle drei Formeln vermitteln auf den ersten Blick, daß sie problematisch auf die Konzeption einer Philosophie der Religion angelegt sind. (Sowohl die theoretische Philsophie als auch parallel dazu die praktische Philosophie).

Das Wissen, dessen Aufhebung notwendig sein soll, um zum Glauben Platz zu bekommen, ist angemaßtes Wissen, dem die Legitimation fehlt, weil es die Grenzen des endlichen Erkenntnisvermögens überschreitet. Die kantische Kritik der Gottesbeweise läßt sich im Lichte dieses Programms als Etappe eines Weges zur Begründung eines Vernunftglaubens verstehen, indem sie sich als Kritik an einer kognitiven Kompetenzüberschreitung der Vernunft vollzieht. Die Antinomienlehre der *Kritik der reinen Vernunft* demonstriert hier mehr noch, als die Widerlegungsstrategien der Gottesbeweise es zeigen, daß der apriorischen Urteilsgewißheit des Erkenntnissubjekts ein erklärter und konsequent durchgeführter Wissensverzicht entspricht, der sich direkt aus der Anschauungsangewiesenheit apriorischen Wissens ergibt.

Man könnte daraus den Schluß ziehen, daß sowohl die Kritik der Gottesbeweise als auch die Antinomienlehre der *Kritik der reinen Vernunft*, die sich als Kritik an einer kognitiven Kompetenzüberschreitung der Vernunft vollzieht, zur Begründung eines Vernunftglaubens führt. Was hier in der *Kritik der reinen Vernunft* in der Formel „Ich mußte das Wissen aufheben, um zum Glauben Platz zu bekommen" gemeint ist, findet in der *Kritik der praktischen Vernunft* eine Grundlegung und in der Religionsschrift eine „Durchführung". Wenn es Kant bereits in der *Kritik der praktischen Vernunft* und nicht erst in der Religionsschrift schreibt, daß Religion „Erkenntnis aller Pflichten als göttlicher Gebote" sei, dann meint er freilich keinesfalls, daß „göttliche Gebote" Gegenstände menschlicher Erkenntnis wären.

Schon die Erkenntnis unserer Pflichten sei nicht möglich, weil sie nicht die Erfahrungsgegenstände, d.h. raumzeitlich identifizierten Objekte sein könnten. In jener formalhaften Definition von Religion hingegen spricht Kant offensichtlich von Erkenntnis im Sinne von Anerkenntnis, von „als wahr anerkennen", allerdings verbunden mit dem Verbindlichkeitsanspruch objektiver Erkenntnis. Dieses Führwahrhalten entspringt einem natürlichen Bedürfnis der Vernunft, dessen Legitimität Kant grundsätzlich verteidigt, dessen Mißbrauch er in der transzendentalen Dialektik kritisiert und für dessen angemessene Entsprechung er plädiert.

Aber Kants Satz „Ich mußte das Wissen aufheben, um zum Glauben Platz zu bekommen" ließe noch die Frage unbeantwortet, wodurch eine solche These von der Dependenz der Selbstverpflichtung des moralischen Subjekts der Religion die Moral zusätzlich qualifiziert. Der Beantwortung eben dieser Frage scheint die Religionsschrift zu dienen. Erst diese Schrift und nicht die im engeren Sinne moralphilosophischen Schriften Kants zeigt, daß und warum eine ausschließlich aus dem „Faktum der Vernunft" begründete Autorität des Sittengesetzes zwar notwendig ist, um die Autonomie der Vernunft in der Sittlichen Gesetzgebung herzuleiten, aber nicht hinreicht, um die unbedingte Verbindlichkeit des Sittengesetzes im Sinne eines eindeutigen Vorranges vor anderen Freiheitsentscheidungen zu garantieren. Ohne eine solche Garantie aber kann nicht einleuchtend gemacht werden, warum die Vernunft sich selbst zum Gesetz werden soll. Freiheit kann widervernünftigen Gebrauch von sich machen. Sie kann die Überordnung der Selbstliebe über die Beförderung der eigenen sittlichen Vollkommenheit zum bewußten und absichtlichen Prinzip erheben: Freiheit hier freilich verstanden als die Fähigkeit der Vernunft, von sich selbst einen „perversen" Gebrauch zu machen.

Diese Tendenz zu dieser Perversion gehört aber ursprünglich zur Vernunft, ja gerade zu jener „Natur der Vernunft". Diese Ambivalenz der Vernunft wird gerade in der Religionsschrift anhand der Lehre vom „radikal Bösen" demonstriert. Kant kennzeichnet in dieser Lehre die Natürlichkeit und die Ursprünglichkeit des „radikal Bösen" im menschlichen Wesen. In der Religionsschrift haißt es vom bösen „Hang": „Dieses Böse ist radikal, weil es den Grund aller Maximen verdirbt; zugleich auch als natürlicher Hang durch menschliche Kräfte nicht zu vertilgen" (*Religion innerhalb ...*, Akad.-Ausg., VI, 37). Im Folgenden wird die These vertreten, daß entgegen allem Anschein keine unüberwindbare Kluft zwischen dem im Sittengesetz artikulierten moralischen Anspruch und der Behauptung eines unausrottbaren Hanges zum Bösen besteht, sondern daß vielmehr umgekehrt eine tiefe Einsicht in die Wirkmächtigkeit des Bösen Kant dazu motiviert hat, seine Morallehre in der bekannten rigorosen Form zu konzipieren.

Der Schlüsselbegriff für das Verständnis des Zusammenhanges von moralischem Anspruch und Ernstnahme des Bösen bei Kant ist der Begriff der Autonomie. Der Mensch hat die Möglichkeit, sich selbst als Vernunftwesen zu bestimmen. Das bedeutet einerseits, daß es sich bei dem Aktus der Selbstbestimmung um ein Prinzip, ein der Sache nach Ursprüngliches und Unableitbares handelt, andererseits ist damit der bewußte Abweis von Fremdbestimmung (Heteronomie) gemeint. Beide Momente, der Prinzipcharakter und der Abweis der Fremdbestimmung, sind konstitutiv für das Selbstverständnis des endlichen Vernunftwesens Mensch als eines autonomen Wesens. Die Kantische Definition der Autonomie des Willens bezeichnet diesen Sachverhalt. Das Prinzip der Autonomie ist also: „nichts anderes zu wählen als so, daß die Maximen seiner Wahl in demselben Wollen zugleich als allgemeines Gesetz mit begriffen seien" (*Grundlegung zur Metaphysik der Sitten* = GMS, IV, 440). Dies ist der positive Freiheitsbegriff, den Kant „Autonomie durch Vernunft" nennt: „Denn Freiheit und eigene Gesetzgebung des Willens sind beides Autonomie, mithin Wechselbegriffe" (GMS, IV, 450).

Kant hat keinen Zweifel daran gelassen, daß die Autonomie der Grund der Würde des Menschen als eines Vernunftwesens und zugleich das „echte Prinzip der Moral" ist. Den Menschen faßt Kant als Subjekt, d.h. als Willenswesen auf, das sich die Regeln seines Handelns selbst, mithin unabhängig von vorgegebenen Autoritäten gibt. Autonomie ist die Formulierung für das „Praktischwerden" der Vernunft, d.h. für die Fähigkeit des der Möglichkeit nach vernünftigen Wesens, dem Vernunftgesetz unter dem Namen des Sittengesetzes „Eingang" zu verschaffen (GMS, IV, 37). Der Mensch, der diesen Anspruch akzeptiert bzw. der willens ist, sich diese Leistung gegen die naturhafte Komponente in ihm abzuringen, ist „Subjekt der Moralität, Persönlichkeit". Von der so verstandenen Persönlichkeit spricht Kant als von einem Selbstzweck (*Kritik der Urteilskraft* = KU, V. 435 f.).

Aber für Kant hat der Mensch durchaus die Möglichkeit der Verfehlung seines „eigentlichen Selbst". Vor diesem Hintergrund kann nun angedeutet werden, was in Kants Sinne böse ist; böse wäre demnach, anderen, untergeordneten Zwecken den Vorzug vor dem „Endzweck" der Bestimmung des Menschen als eines „Dubjekts der Moralität" zu geben. Nach alledem ist klar, daß der Mensch nach Kant durchaus die Möglichkeit der Verfehlung seines „eigentlichen Selbst" d.h. der radikalen Verfehlung seiner „sittlichen Persönlichkeit" hat. Die in der Willkürfreiheit des Menschen beschlossene Möglichkeit der Entscheidung zum Bösen ist zutiefst „menschlich".

In den Kantischen Überlegungen zum Bösen, vor allem in der Religionsschrift, tritt das Spannungsverhältnis zwischen moralischem (Vernunft-) Anspruch und der Einsicht in die dem Menschen fundamental zukommende Möglichkeit der Entscheidung zum Bösen deutlich zutage. Der im Moment des moralischen Sollens gesetzte Appellationscharakter des Vernunftsanspruchs erweist sich, auf der Ebene des Autonomieprinzips gesprochen, als Appell des Vernunftswesens an sich selbst. Er hat die bekannte, der Figur des Selbstbewußtseins analoge Struktur: Ich gebe mir ein Gesetz, d.h. eine Richtlinie für mich, durch die ich allererst den Status der „moralischen Persönlichkeit" erlange. Der im imperativischen Modus auftretende Appell ist zwar nicht selbst die Vernunft in ihrer Vollstruktur, aber der Imperativ gibt eine „Anzeige" auf die vollendete Struktur der Vernunft. Als endliche Vernunftwesen sind wir gleichsam permanent appellationsbedürftig. Die Chancen der „Realisierung" des Vernunftsanspruchs schwanken freilich; das endliche Vernunftwesen ist als solches dauerhaft irritierbar durch das Böse.

Eine vollständige und andauernde Verwirklichung des moralischen Sollens würde das Ende des Sollenscharakters bedeuten. Praktische Vernunft ist vielmehr, unter dem Namen der Autonomie, ein Leitfaden, ein Orientierungsrahmen für die Bestimmung der Handlungen (bzw. Maximen) solcher Wesen, die der Irrtümer, der Fehler, auch der Perversion des Bösen fähig sind. Gerade angesichts der Möglichkeit einer universalen Verweigerung des Vernunftanspruchs fällt das Sittengesetz in seiner Formulierung als kategorischer Imperativ so rigoros aus. Die Übel wird bei Kant als in der Freiheit des Menschen wurzelnde Möglichkeit zum Bösen erkannt und anerkannt. Und sie wird nicht als Grund zur Resignation angesehen, sondern als in der Struktur des Menschen verankerte Potentialitäten und Gegebenheiten, mit denen er leben muß und kann. So besagt Autonomie keineswegs so etwas wie Omnipotenz des Ich, wohl aber artikuliert sich im Begriff der Autonomie das Gebot, die letzte und tiefgreifendste Degradierung unserer selbst, das Böse, nicht akzeptieren zu sollen.

Wir achten die sittliche Persönlichkeit aber nur deshalb, weil sie der permanenten Gefährdung durch das Böse widersteht. Aber hier entsteht die Frage: wenn Freiheit widervernünftigen Gebrauch von sich machen kann, welche Garantie besteht dafür, daß der Mensch die Überordnung der Selbstliebe über die Beförderung der eigenen sittlichen Vollkommenheit zum bewußten und absichtlichen Prinzip nicht erheben wird? Hier leistet die Religionschrift wesentliche Hilfe.

Zur wesentlichen Eigenschaft des Bösen gehört bekanntlich seine Unerkennbarkeit – das folgt schon aus Kants Willenstheorie heraus – böse kann ebensowenig ein empirisch überprüfbares Prädikat sein wie auch sein Gegenteil „gut".

Für Kant ist das Prädikat „sittlich gut" kein Handlungsprädikat, sondern ausschließlich nur Willenprädikat. Aus der Intelligibilität des Willens aber folgt, daß er – der Wille – sich der intersubjektiven (wenn nicht sogar der innersubjektiven) Beurteilung grundsätzlich entzieht. Und eben hier droht der Rigorismus des kantischen Moralismus ins Unverbindliche umzuschlagen; es sei denn, daß eine zusätzliche Qualifikation der Autorität des Sittengesetzes geliefert wird, die hinreichende Begründung dafür gibt, daß es der Freiheit der Vernunft angemessener ist, das Sittengesetz mehr zu achten, als sich selbst zu lieben. Diese zusätzliche Qualifikation bekommt die Vernunft durch die Religion. Schon dadurch zeigt sich, im übrigen, daß die Religionstheorie des Aufklärens keineswegs als bloßer Anhang zum moralphilosophischen Autonomismus zu verstehen ist, sondern eher als dessen Ermöglichungsbedingung, und daß Kant der Religion eine außergewöhnliche Rolle und neuartige Würde zuspricht.

Man könnte in der Sprache der Aufklärungsschrift sagen, daß die Aufklärung sich als der Eintritt der Vernunft in eine religiös begründete Mündigkeit definieren läßt. Kants religionsphilosophisches Programm scheint darin zu bestehen, zu beweisen. daß es im Interesse der Selbsterhaltung der Vernunft liegt, an ihre eigene religiöse Legitimation zu glauben. Kant begründet keine vernünftige Religion, sondern er begründet die Notwendigkeit einer Vernunftreligion. Es geht nicht allein um einen Burgfrieden zwischen Glauben und Wissen, sondern es geht um die Legitimationsgrundlage dafür, daß die Vernunft für sich selbst unbedingte Autorität ist. Nur dann besteht der Aussicht, ihr, der Vernunft, einen plausiblen Ausweg aus der Sackgasse des radikal Bösen anzubieten.

Die Konzeption der Autonomie des Willens ergibt sich bei Kant konsequent aus der Idee der Freiheit. Die Autonomieerklärung ist das Resultat eines Freiheitsaktes der Vernunft, durch den sich vernünftige Wesen die Freiheit selbst zum Gesetz machen. Nur aber stößt gerade mit diesem Freiheit und Gesetz versöhnenden Argument, mit dem der Gedanke der Autonomie als die Selbstgesetzgebung, die Moralphilosophie Kants an ihre Grenzen. Nicht allein, daß die Vernunft nicht gegen das Böse gesichert ist. Sondern wir stehen vor der tiefergreifenden Schwierigkeit, nämlich wir sind ebensowenig imstande, die Beurteilungskriterien dafür finden, ob Handlungen nur legal (d.h. nur bloße Gesetzmäßigkeit von Handlungen im Augenhaben) oder auch moralisch sind (d.h. daß die Achtung vor dem Gesetz, dem ich gehorche, die ausschließliche Triebfeder meines Handelns ausmacht), als auch nicht dafür, ob Handlungen dem sittlichkeitswidrigen Prinzip des Primats der Selbstliebe oder dem guten Willen (d.h. der Achtung vor dem Sittengesetz) entspringen.

Hier greift die Religionsschrift. Erst hier nämlich diskutiert Kant konsequent die qualitative Differenz zwischen Handlung und Gesinnung als eine Aporie, die von der praktischen Philosophie hinterlassen wurde. Kant diskutiert jetzt das Problem, daß es keineswegs ausreicht, sich auf den guten Willen zu verlassen, wenn es um den Endzweck der praktischen Vernunft geht. Es bedarf einer zusätzlichen Garantie, auf die sich die Vernunft gewissermaßen im eigenen Interesse verpflichtet. Hier knüpft Kant unmittelbar an den christlichen Sündenvergebungsgedanken an. Er erläutert diesen Gedanken dahingehend, daß der Mensch als ein Wesen, dessen Handlungen auf die Bedingungen der „Zeitlichkeit" eingeschränkt sind, ein moralisches Mängelwesen bleiben muß.

Es bedarf daher einer Sicherheit dafür, daß die moralische Gesinnung den grundsätzlichen Mangel ausgleicht. Kant sagt: „Nun besteht die Schwierigkeit darin, wie die Gesinnung für die Tat, welche jederzeit (nicht überhaupt, sondern in jedem Zeitpunkte) mangelhaft ist, gelten könne. Die Auflösung derselben aber beruht darauf, daß die letztere (die Tat) als ein kontinuierlicher Fortschritt von mangelhaftem Guten ins Unendliche [...] immer mangelhaft bleibt; so daß wir das Gute in der Erscheinung, d.h. der Tat nach, in uns jederzeit als unzulänglich für ein heiliges Gesetz ansehen müssen; seinen Fortschritt aber ins Unendliche zur Angemessenheit mit dem letzteren wegen der Gesinnung [...] von einem Herzenskündiger in seiner reinen intellektuellen Anschauung als ein vollendetes Ganze auch der Tat (dem Lebenswandel) nach beurteilt denken können; und so der Mensch unerachtet seiner beständigen Mangelhaftigkeit doch überhaupt Gott wohlgefällig zu sein erwarten könne, in welchem Zeitpunkte auch sein Dasein abgebrochen werden möge" (S. 70, 71).

Die gute Gesinnung wird hier als Erfüllung des Gesetzes verheißen. Das scheinbar unbedingte „Handle so" des ethischen Rigorismus wird eigentümlich relativiert. Und deshalb lautet auf die Frage, die in den moralphilosophischen Schriften unbeantwortet geblieben ist, warum der Mensch überhaupt noch handeln soll, wenn das Gute grundsätzlich nicht von der intelligiblen Vernunft auf unsere Handlungen übertragbar werden kann, um diese zu qualifizieren, Kants Antwort, daß es vernünftig ist zu glauben, was die christliche Idee anbietet, nämlich daß der Gott, den die praktische Vernunft bereits im Gefolge des Freiheitspostulats ohnehin zu postulieren hatte, nicht allein als Gewissensforscher, sondern auch als ausgleichender Vergeber unserer unhintergehbaren Defizienz zu interpretieren sei.

Wir sind also nach Kant jederzeit zum Scheitern verueteilt; dennoch wird dem Scheitern jederzeit ein Sinn vermittelt, in dem die Gesinnung für die Tat angerechnet wird. Die Ausgangsthese der *Grundlegung zur Metaphysik der Sitten*, daß in der Welt nur der Wille allein als gut bezeichnet werden kann, erhält eine religiöse Sinngebung, indem das Prinzip der Rechtfertigung Gottes aus der klassischen Theodizee konsequent in dasjenige der religiösen Rechtfertigung der endlichen Vernunft verwandelt wird. Es geht hier also mehr um eine religiöse Fundierung der Vernunftmoral als um eine Moralisierung der Religion. Derartiges zeigt auch Kants Jesusbild. Für Kant ist Jesus „menschliches Urbild" wie auch „Vorbild für unsere Nachfolge" deshalb, weil in Jesus religiöse und moralische Existenz zur Deckung kommen. Jesus ist nicht religiös – das heißt, er unterwirft sich gehorsam dem unbedingten Willen Gottes –, weil er moralisch gesonnen ist, sondern umgekehrt: er handelt moralisch, weil er Gott gehorcht. Für Jesus ist das Gottesliebesgebot die Entscheidungsgrundlage für das Nächstenliebesgebot. „Vorbild" ist Jesus daher, weil bei ihm die „Erkenntnis göttlicher Gebote als sittlicher Pflichten" unmittelbar zu einem vollkommenen moralischen Lebenswandel führte.

Kant fügt in der erwähnten Definition von Religion übrigens hinzu: „als göttlicher Gebote, nicht als Sanktionen". Das bedeutet nicht nur, daß es keinen Einbruch von Heteronomie in die Autonomie der Selbstverpflichtung geben darf. Hier wird vielmehr auch die unbedingte Verbindlichkeit unserer Pflichten mit der einzigen Idee des Unbedingten erläutert, die die Philosophie zusammen mit der Theologie anerkennt: mit der Idee Gottes. Deshalb führt Moral unumgänglich zur Religion.

Wenn Ernst Cassirer mit Recht darauf hingewiesen hat, daß die neue aufklärerische Universalisierung des moralischen Anspruchs der Vernunft tatsächlich als gemeines Erbe jener Humanisierung der Religion, die die Aufklärung der Renaissance verdankt, zu beschreiben ist, dann läßt sich die Vernunftreligion Kants als eine Wiederaufnahme der Idee einer „Religion innerhalb der Grenzen der Humanität" (Cassirer) begreifen. Damit hat die Aufklärung eine Wirkungsgeschichte eingeleitet, über deren Bedeutung wohl abschließend noch nicht entschieden werden kann. Man kann das anhand von Schleiermachers Kant-Abhängigkeit zeigen.

Es scheint, daß Schleiermacher und damit die wesentliche Entwicklung protestantischer Religionsphilosophie im 19. Jahrhundert Kant jedenfalls zu zweierlei Hinsicht beerbt hat. Zu einem ist dieses Erbe zu finden in der Bestimmung der Bedeutung des Gefühls für die Struktur des seiner selbst bewußten Subjekts als Focus des Gottesbewußtseins, und zum anderen ist es zu finden in der Würdigung der religiösen Grundlage der Humanität Jesu als sittliches Ideal.

„Gefühl" bei Kant bezeichnet eine besondere Selbstbeziehung des Bewußtseins und ist kein Gegenbegriff zu Bewußtsein. Und hierin ist Schleiermacher mehr als andere Romantiker Nachfolger Kants, indem er dem

Gefühl den Status von Bewußtsein und sogar von Bewußtsein *kat'exochen* verleiht. Die entsprechende Theorie findet sich bei Kant in der *Kritik der ästhetischen Urteilskraft*, die bekanntlich der erste Teil eines Werkes ist, das mit dem Entwurf einer transzendentalen Theologie abschließt.

Im „Gefühlsbegriff" bei Kant geht es nicht um Objektbestimmung, das heißt, nicht darum, eine gegebene unbestimmte Erscheinung dem Bewußtsein als Objekt der Erfahrung zu vermitteln. Es geht vielmehr um eine durch einen Gegenstand veranlaßte neuartige Selbstbeziehung, die sowohl von der den Gegenstand konstituierenden Funktion als auch von der normativ-zweckbestimmenden Funktion befreit ist. Es geht also um eine nichtgegenständliche Selbstbeziehung. Diese entsteht dadurch, daß etwas ohne Begriff gefällt. Das Gefühl bei Kant ist dementsprechend nicht reflexiv. Es wird erst im Geschmacksurteil zum Gegenstand von Reflexion. Diese nichtreflexive Struktur des Gefühls, das dennoch ein Bewußtsein seiner selbst ist, wird bei Schleiermacher zu Theorien des „unmittelbaren Selbstbewußtseins" ausgearbeitet und zudem theologisch qualifiziert.

Das Subjekt ist sich im unmittelbaren Selbstbewußtsein Schleiermacher zufolge bewußt, daß es eine Einheit ist, sieht aber zugleich ein, daß es weder Urheber dieser Einheit selbst noch des Wissens um diese Einheit sein kann. Anders gesagt: Schleiermacher expliziert in der Dialektik eine konstruktive Entfaltung des unmittelbaren Selbstbewußtseins als Abhängigkeitsgefühl des Subjekts. Die Aufhebung des Gegensatzes von Denken und Wollen im unmittelbaren Selbstbewußtsein kann sich nur dann als Selbstbewußtsein erfassen, wenn sich das Selbstbewußtsein in dieser Aufhebung als bedingt und bestimmt begreift. Die freie Selbsttätigkeit des unmittelbaren Selbstbewußtsein ist in ihrer Freiheit dadurch schlechthin abhängig, daß sie sich nicht ursprünglich selbst dazu gemacht hat, freie Selbsttätigkeit zu sein, sondern letztlich schlechthin gegeben ist. Schleiermacher „ergänzt" durch den Begriff „unmittelbares Selbstbewußtsein" – Gefühl – die „fehlende Einheit" des Bewußtseins, die die Vertrautheit eines individuellen Existierenden mit sich repräsentiert.

Der Begriff des unmittelbaren Selbstbewußtseins weist darauf hin, daß das Subjekt nicht imstande ist, sein Sein mit Hilfe von Reflexion zu vermitteln. Seine absolute Macht zerbricht an der Faktizität der ihm unzugänglichen Selbstvermittlung. Das Selbstbewußtsein ist für Schleiermacher im Gegensatz zu Fichte und Hegel kein Raum, in dem das für sich transparente Subjekt dank der Reflexion sich selbst und die Welt begründet. Für den Autor der Dialektik ist es nicht möglich, aus dem Selbstbewußtsein das Wissen um die Wirklichkeit zu deduzieren.

Schleiermacher spricht in der Glaubenslehre nicht von der vorreflexiven, subjektlosen Aktivität des Selbstbewußtseins, die von der realen Zeit absieht, wie es in der Dialektik der Fall ist, sondern faßt das Selbstbewußtsein als subjektive Realität auf, die mit einer konkreten Zeit und einem konkreten Raum verbunden ist. Es ist hier also die Rede von dem zeitlich bestimmten Bewußtsein, in dem die Selbstaktivität und Passivität, die Spontaneität und Rezeptivität miteinander verbunden sind. In einem so dargestellten Selbstbewußtsein setzen sich Aktivität und Passivität des Subjekts gegenseitig voraus.

Schleiermacher führt bei der Beschreibung der Struktur des Selbstbewußtseins zwei Begriffe ein, und zwar das Abhängigkeitsgefühl und das Freiheitsgefühl. Das Abhängigkeitsgefühl weist darauf hin, daß wir so sein können, wie wir sind, nur dank dem, was von uns anders ist. Das Freiheitsgefühl hingegen beruht darauf, daß das, was anders ist, von uns bestimmt wird. So werden das Abhängigkeitsgefühl und das Freiheitsgefühl aufeinander bezogen. Im Falle des Abhängigkeitsgefühls wird das Andere als aktive Grundlage aufgefaßt, von der das Abhängigkeitsgefühl herkommt; diese Grundlage ist also der aktive Pol, während das abhängige Selbstbewußtsein der passive Pol ist. Im Falle des Freiheitsgefühls hingegen haben wir es mit einer umgekehrten Relation zu tun, und zwar werden die freie Selbstaktivität als aktiver Pol und das, worauf sie gerichtet ist, als passiver Pol aufgefaßt.

Die Analyse des Bezugs des Selbstbewußtseins auf die Welt in der Glaubenslehre hat zum Ziel, sowohl das unbedingte Gefühl der absoluten Freiheit als auch das Gefühl der absoluten Abhängigkeit als Dimensionen abzulehnen, in denen sich das menschliche Selbstbewußtsein wirklich bewegt. Wir können eigentlich nur in einem Fall dem Selbstbewußtsein den Charakter einer absoluten Freiheit zuschreiben, und zwar dann, wenn es mit Hilfe des Begriffs *causa sui* beschrieben werden könnte, d.h. wenn es imstande wäre, sich selbst zu setzen. Auf diese Weise bereitet Schleiermacher den Grund für den Hauptbegriff seiner Glaubenslehre, und zwar für den Begriff „das schlechthinnige Anhängigkeitsgefühl" vor.

Die freie Selbsttätigkeit ist sich ihrer eigenen Voraussetzung im Bereich ihrer auf die Objekte der Welt bezogenen Aktivität nicht bewußt. Es ist eher so, daß das Selbstbewußtsein freie Selbsttätigkeit als gegeben vorfindet. Die Tatsache, daß die freie Selbsttätigkeit des Selbstbewußtseins ihm gegeben und nicht von ihm selbst gesetzt wird, läßt sich im Bereich der Gefühle der relativen Freiheit und der relativen Abhängigkeit, die den Bezug des Selbstbewußtseins auf die Objekte der Welt charakterisieren, nicht erklären. Am Ende erweist es sich, daß die relative Freiheit des Selbstbewußtseins, die darin zum Ausdruck kommt, daß das Subjekt auf die zur Welt gehörenden Objekte einwirken kann, im schlechthinnigen Abhängigkeitsgefühl begründet ist. Die freie Selbsttätigkeit des unmittelbaren Selbstbewußtseins ist in ihrer Freiheit davon abhängig, daß das Selbstbewußtsein sie nicht begründet hat. Anders gesagt, die freie Selbsttätigkeit des Selbstbewußtseins, die man als Grundlage der Einwirkung auf die Objekte der Welt voraussetzen muß, läßt sich nicht von diesen Objekten herleiten. Daraus ergibt sich die Schlußfolgerung – laut Schleiermacher – daß sie „woandersher" stammen muß.

Mit Hilfe des Abhängigkeitsgefühls wird das Moment entwickelt, das durch die Selbsttätigkeit des Selbstbewußtseins nicht gesetzt wird, und zwar die Unmöglichkeit der freien Selbsttätigkeit, sich selbst zu setzen. Das schlechthinnige Abhängigkeitsgefühl wird hier nicht deswegen eingeführt, um die freie Selbsttätigkeit zu negieren, sodern deshalb, um ihre Möglichkeitsbedingen zu zeigen. Anders gesagt: die freie Selbsttätigkeit des Selbstbewußtseins wird als ein solches Moment im Selbstbewußtsein erfaßt, das durch das Selbstbewußtsein nicht gesetzt worden ist.

Schleiermacher will auf die freie Selbsttätigkeit des Selbstbewußtseins nicht verzichten, weil es – wie er behauptet – „das Interesse der menschlichen Freiheit" verlangt.

Freie Selbsttätigkeit als Zentrum der Subjektivität ist sich selbst so gegeben, daß sie sich in ihrem Zentrum gleichzeitig außerhalb ihrer eigenen Subjektivität bestimmt. Wenn wir aus dieser Perspektive Schleiermachers Philosophie der Religion betrachten, so gewinnen wir noch ein wesentliches Argument mehr dafür, daß Hegels Polemik gegen den Autor der Glaubenslehre unbegründet ist, weil das Argument, daß das religiöse Gefühl sich ausschließlich auf das Abhängigkeitsgefühl stützen würde, wodurch dann „der Hund der beste Christ" wäre, nur dann sinnvoll ist, wenn wir im absoluten Abhängigkeitsgefühl von der freien Selbsttätigkeit des Selbstbewußtseins abstrahieren würden.

Das Abhängigkeitsgefühl läßt sich sinnvoll nur dann schildern, wenn es ein Gefühl der Abhängigkeit von etwas ist; es impliziert also das Vorhandensein von etwas, wovon wir abhängig sind. Schleiermacher spricht in diesem Zusammenhang von dem „Woher der Abhängigkeit".

Man muß nach ihm das im Selbstbewußtsein mitvorausgesetzte Moment des „Woher des Abhängigkeitsgefühls" mit dem Begriff Gottes bezeichnen. Gott darf man nicht mit der Welt identifizieren, weil das aktive Selbstbewußtsein sich seiner selbst bewußt wird als sich selbst samt der Natur gegeben.

Wir erinnern uns doch daran, daß Schleiermacher jegliche Bedingtheit des Abhängigkeitsgefühls durch das vorher vorausgesetzte Wissen um Gott ausschließt. Eben auf diese Weise will Schleiermacher den primären und direkten Charakter des religiösen Abhängigkeitsgefühl bewahren. Gemäß den Voraussetzungen der Glaubenslehre können wir uns nicht auf das vorher in der Dialektik erlangte Wissen um Gott berufen. Schleiermacher ist sich dessen bewußt, daß das Wort Gott die Vorstellung Gottes voraussetzt. Doch diese Vorstellung bedeutet nach ihm nichts anderes als den „Ausdruck des Abhängigkeitsgefühls". Auf diese Weise besteht er auf seiner These, nach der das Wissen um Gott keinen objektiven Charakter hat, und das Wort „Gott" primär nichts anderes bedeutet als das, woher das schlechthinnige Abhängigkeitsgefühl kommt.

Schleiermacher geht entscheidend in einem über Kant hinaus, daß er diesem unmittelbaren Selbstbewußtsein oder Gefühl eine fundamentale oder konstitutive Funktion für andere, nämlich für das gegenständliche Bewußtsein zuweist. Das unmittelbare Selbstbewußtsein wird in einer Weise zum Paradigma im Bewußtseinsakt überhaupt, als hätte schon Kant selbst die Figur des ästhetischen Gefühls zum Paradigma der transzendentalen Apperzeption gemacht. Zum anderen stellt Schleiermacher den Wirkungscharakter des Gefühls in den Vordergrund. (Das Gefühl bei Kant übernimmt die Vermittlungsfunktion der Erkenntnisvermögen.)

Das Gefühl als Wirkung verweist auf die Ursache – Schleiermacher sagt: auf ein „Woher", und diese nennt er Gott. Kurz gesagt wird – wenn gilt, daß das Gefühl bzw. das unmittelbare Selbstbewußtsein als Paradigma für alle anderen Bewußtseinsakte zu gelten hat – Gott zum Stifter des Selbstbewußtseins des Subjekts.

Für Schleiermachers Begriff des Selbstbewußtseins ist damit nicht mehr die Spontaneität des „Ich denke" im Sinne der Kantischen Verstandeskritik konstitutiv, sondern die Rezeptivität des Gefühls im Sinne der Kantischen Ästhetik. Bewußtsein ist primär Abhängigkeitsbewußtsein, das heißt, sich wissen heißt ursprünglich: sich abhängig fühlen. Die theologische Ausführung dieses Gedankens läßt sich bei Schleiermacher geeignet an seinem Jesusbild erläutern. Auch bei Schleiermacher wird Jesus als „Urbild" charakterisiert. Seine Urbildlichkeit besteht darin, durch jenes Abhängigkeitsbewußtsein in vollkommener Weise bestimmt zu sein. Jesus ist dasjenige Subjekt, an dem in seiner und uneigeschränkter Weise das Bewußtsein als Gefühl ausgebildet ist, uneingeschränkt durch alle sonstigen Weltbezüge des reflexiven Denkens (Wissens) bzw. des Handelns (Tuns). Schleiermacher knüpft damit faktisch unmittelbar an Kants Deutung von Jesus als Urbild religiöser Legitimation des moralischen Handelns und als Vorbild für unsere Nachfolge an.

Man könnte aber bei dieser Anknüpfung die Frage stellen, ob es sich hier um eine Radikalisierung des Mündigkeitsmanifestes – jetzt gütig für das individuelle Gefühl – im Paradigma aufgeklärter Religionsphilosophie handelt, oder aber um einen Rückgriff in eine neue verschuldete Abhängigkeit. Schleiermacher selbst hat sich verachtend über die transzendentalphilosophische Symbiose aus Religion und Moral geäußert: „Und was tut Eure Moral", ruft er aus. „Sie entwickelt aus der Natur des Menschen und seines Verhältnisses gegen das Universum ein System von Pflichten. [...].

Die Theoretiker in der Religion, die aufs Wissen über die Natur des Universums und eines höchsten Wesens, dessen Werk es ist, ausgehen, sind

Metaphysiker; aber artig genug, auch etwas Moral nicht zu verschmähen. Die Praktiker, denen der Wille Gottes Hauptsache ist, sind Moralisten; aber ein wenig im Stile der Metaphysik. Die Idee des Guten nehmt ihr und tragt sie in die Metaphysik als Naturgesetz eines unbeschränkten und unbedürftigen Wesens, und die Idee eines Urwesens nehmt Ihr aus der Metaphysik und tragt sie in die Moral, damit dieses große Werk nicht anonym bleibe [...]. Mengt aber und rührt, wie Ihr wollt, dies geht nie zusammen, Ihr treibt ein leeres Spiel mit Materien, die sich einander nicht aneignen. Ihr behaltet immer nur Metaphysik und Moral [...]. Warum habt Ihr es nicht längst aufgelöst in seine Teile und das schändliche Plagiat entdeckt"? (*Reden*, 43-45).

Es scheint mir, daß Schleiermachers Vorwurf gegen die religiöse Metaphysik der Transzendentalphilosophie, daß sie ein mißlungenes Plagiat sei, nicht berechtigt ist, weil es hier mehr um eine religiöse Fundierung der Vernunftsmoral als um eine Moralisierung der Religion geht. Eine ganz andere Frage ist dagegen, weshalb Schleiermachers und nicht Kants Ansatz in der Religionsphilosophie des 19. und 20. Jahrhunderts aufgenommen und modifiziert, fortgebildet und aktualisiert wird: Religion und religiöses Bewußtsein basieren nicht primär auf den durch die kirchliche Tradition und Autorität verbürgten Inhalten, sie verdanken sich vielmehr der Gottesbeziehung des religiösen Bewußtseins.

PATRICK DE LAUBIER
Université de Genève
Switzerland

LA PHILOSOPHIE MORALE DE VLADIMIR SOLOVIEV

INTRODUCTION

La Justification du bien, cette grande synthèse de philosophie morale que Soloviev publia 3 ans avant sa mort est probablement un de ses ouvrages les plus importants sinon le plus considérable. Lorsqu'on connaît les conditions de rédaction de ce volumineux traité écrit sans souci d'érudition, mais nourri d'une vaste culture, on reste impressionné par ce tour de force.

Soloviev a abordé à maintes reprises les questions éthiques, mais cette fois nous avons un traité qui se propose de *justifier le bien*. Cette vaste entreprise peut être mise en parallèle avec les thèses scolastiques sur l'éthique auxquelles Soloviev fait parfois allusion, mais de manière très discrète. Pour lui, la philosophie morale comme science commence avec Kant et c'est à partir des positions kantiennes qu'il développe ses propres thèses. Pourtant, Soloviev se rapproche des perspectives de la scolastique sur des points essentiels sans pour autant en adopter les méthodes ni toujours l'esprit. D'ores et déjà on peut dire que ce qui les unit c'est la Bible, mais ce qui les distingue est ce que Gilson appelait le *seul modernisme réussi*, à savoir l'utilisation de la philosophie d'Aristote, d'ailleurs profondément transformée dans une perspective chrétienne, pour faire de la théologie une science.

Les scolastiques mettent au service de la théologie une philosophie d'inspiration chrétienne et Soloviev élabore une philosophie morale en s'inspirant vitalement de la révélation biblique pour en faire une philosophie *d'affectivité chrétienne*. Dans les deux cas la raison et la Révélation concourent à l'établissement de philosophies morales qu'on pourrait qualifier, en utilisant la terminologie de Maritain, *d'adéquatement prises* (*Science et sagesse 1935*) en indiquant par là qu'un savoir purement philosophique serait incapable de constituer une science pratique de l'usage effectif de la liberté dans l'état actuel de la nature humaine. On est obligé en effet de constater que la raison et surtout la volonté humaines appellent des lumières et des énergies venant d'ailleurs pour s'orienter selon la raison et pour répondre aux aspirations les plus profondes du coeur de l'homme. Les scolastiques ont une réponse de théologiens qui usent de la philosophie, Soloviev propose une solution en tant que philosophe se référant à la théologie pour conforter un savoir qui devient une philosophie morale *adéquatement prise*.

Il faut cependant remarquer que cette approche n'est pas adoptée d'emblée par Soloviev qui commence par déclarer que sa philosophie morale est indépendante de la métaphysique et de la religion. On peut expliquer cette attitude par l'influence de Kant dont Soloviev admet d'abord le formalisme pour l'abandonner par réalisme lorsqu'il s'agit de la mise en oeuvre des impératifs moraux. Il admet alors que la plénitude du bien se trouve dans *l'unité du bien et du bonheur*, conception qui le rapproche des scolastiques entre les mains desquels l'eudémonisme grec devient *itinerarium mentis ad Deum* ou fin dernière béatifique chrétienne.

Soloviev développe plutôt une philosophie affectivement religieuse et chrétienne qu'une philosophie d'inspiration chrétienne clairement distinguée de la théologie. Il faudrait reprendre ici les débats mémorables des années 30 à propos de la philosophie chrétienne pour situer la position originale du philosophe russe entre Blondel, dont la pensée est *d'aspiration* chrétienne et celle de Maritain par exemple, que est *d'inspiration* chrétienne.

Successivement on examinera, dans une première partie, la classification des inclinations morales selon Soloviev et les scolastiques et ensuite, dans une seconde partie, l'adéquation de leurs philosophies morales pour tenir compte de la condition humaine telle qu'elle est.

I. LES INCLINATIONS MORALES ET LEURS CLASSIFICATIONS

Le témoignage de la conscience, affirme Soloviev, apporte une certitude qui suffit à légitimer la réflexion morale. La conscience morale est même, selon lui, indépendante de la réponse que l'on donne au libre arbitre, car la raison commandée par une nécessité morale, affirme Soloviev, ne laisse pas de place à un choix arbitraire:

Lorsque je choisis le bien, ce n'est point du tout parce que je le veux, mais parce que cela est bon, (chto ono karacho) pour sa valeur, et parce que je puis concevoir son importance (p. 22 de la traduction et p. 118 de l'édition russe 1988).

Notons tout de suite que Soloviev reconnaît que ce n'est pas l'obligation pure qui fonde la moralité, comme le soutient Kant, mais c'est au contraire le caractère objectif du bien, *bonum honestum*, qui fonde l'obligation.

Les scolastiques fondent la philosophie morale sur une métaphysique de l'être et, pour eux, le bien est précisément la plénitude de l'être. Le bien moral chez l'homme n'est pas un transcendental, comme semble le penser Soloviev, mais un *bien particularisé* (Maritain) qui passe par l'exercice de sa liberté capable de choisir entre le bien et le mal. Le choix, bon ou mauvais, est celui de la volonté conformément ou en contradiction avec les exigences de la raison pratique dont les premiers principes sont les préceptes de la loi naturelle qui est la loi éternelle participée en chaque homme. Selon les scolastiques, le bien moral est, dans son essence, une valeur objective, *bonum honestum*, et dans son exercice, une fin visant au bonheur dont la vision béatifique est le sommet. Soloviev pense que l'eudémonisme d'Aristote est un *hédonisme, prudent* (p. 123) mais ce n'est pas dans cet esprit que les scolastiques fondent leur éthique du bonheur en citant Aristote.

Soloviev avait déclaré que sa philosophie morale était indépendante de la métaphysique mais il adopte une position de semi-réalisme, phénoménologique, qui l'écarte de Kant et le rapproche des scolastiques. Les données primordiales de la moralité qu'il propose reposent sur des valeurs objectives qui rejoignent le *bonum honestum* des aristotéliciens.

En lieu et place de la classification des vertus dans la tradition grecque reprise et complétée par les docteurs chrétiens, Soloviev établit un classement qui est peut-être l'apport le plus original de son traité à savoir, trois exigences, principes ou sentiments réglant les rapports de la conscience avec ce qui est inférieur (pudeur), égal (pitié) et supérieur (piété). Le coeur de l'ouvrage tourne autour de ces trois pôles de l'agir moral. La pudeur (*tchousvto cstyda*) d'abord, qui est l'aspect le plus original de la synthèse de Soloviev, ne consiste nullement dans un mépris du corps, mais dans une exigence morale de subordination de la chair à l'esprit pour éviter que l'animalité ne puisse plus servir de matière ou de fondement à la vie spirituelle tant au point de vue proprement physique que psychologique. *L'éthique est l'hygiène non la thérapeutique de la vie spirituelle*, écrit Soloviev pour marquer qu'il s'agit d'une volonté de maîtrise de l'esprit sur la chair qui doit constamment sauvegarder la dignité de l'homme en préservant la vie de l'esprit toujours menacée par les passions qui échappent au contrôle de la raison. Cet ascétisme ne s'oppose pas au corps en lui-même, mais aux passions qui asservissent l'esprit. Si cet ascétisme était recherché pour lui-même, il pourrait fort bien être au service d'intentions spirituelles perverses, après tout remarque Soloviev, le Diable na mange pas, ne boit pas, ne dort pas et reste célibataire...

Le second principe moral est la pitié (*tchoustvo jalosti*): la seule base de toute relation morale envers autrui est, en principe, la pitié et la compassion affirme Soloviev qui se dissocie aussitôt de Schopenhauer ou de Hartmann en précisant que ce n'est pas le fait d'être associés pour la joie ou le plaisir. Nous ne ressentons pas ce qu'éprouve autrui comme si nous ne formions qu'un seul être, les personnes restent distinctes, mais la pitié peut aller très loin et Soloviev, après avoir exclu une perspective d'inspiration bouddhiste, cite un ascète, Isaac le Syrien, qui embrassait toute la création de sa compassion, sans supprimer les distinctions de personnes. Schopenhauer en faisant de la pitié la base unique de la moralité, se trompait, car la pitié peut très bien exister chez quelqu'un qui manque complètement de pudeur par exemple. En réalité un authentique altruisme exige non seulement d'aider tout le monde, mais aussi de n'offenser personne.

Le troisième principe est la piété (*tchoustvo blagotchestia*). Les manifestations de la pitié sont conditionnées par l'égalité, la piété, en revanche est associée à l'idée d'un être supérieur il naît au sein même de la famille et s'adresse aux parents. Cette attitude est la première base de la religion qui est celle des ancêtres. H. Spencer fait dériver la religion du culte des ancêtres, mais il ne sait pas reconnaître, selon Soloviev, la pure idée de la Providence qui est l'essence même de l'attitude vraiment religieuse, les ancêtres et plus généralement les héros et les saints ont laissé un héritage spirituel qui témoigne d'une paternité suprême, providentielle. La Providence n'est donc pas inventée, elle est découverte par ceux qui savent comprendre ces images visibles de l'invisible.

Les scolastiques, de leur côté, distinguent quatre vertus cardinales, justice, prudence, tempérance et force et trois vertus théologales foi, espérance, charité. Les premières sont empruntées aux Grecs, les secondes à la Bible. La raison suffit pour orienter les premières, il faut la grâce surnaturelle pour les secondes.

Il s'agit là des principes intérieurs des actions humaines. Les principes extérieurs sont exprimés par les lois dont St. Thomas a formulé l'architecture classique en distinguant, d'une part, la loi éternelle, la loi naturelle, la loi positive et d'autre part, la loi révélée. La loi naturelle, ou non écrite, par laquelle la raison participe à la loi éternelle est structurée selon trois niveaux qui peuvent être comparés aux trois principes primordiaux de Soloviev:

1. Il y a en premier lieu, inscrite en l'homme, un inclination au bien, selon ce qu'il a de commun avec toutes les autres substances, au sens où toute substance aspire à la conservation de son être suivant sa nature. En vertu de cette inclination, relèvera de la loi naturelle tout ce qui intéresse la conservation de la vie humaine et empêche ce qui lui est contraire.

2. Est inscrite en l'homme, en second lieu, une inclination à certains biens plus spéciaux, selon ce qu'il a en commun avec les autres animaux. En vertu de quoi, on dira que relève de la loi naturelle "ce que la nature a enseigné à tous les animaux" (Digeste de Ulpien), c'est à dire l'union des sexes, l'éducation des enfants et autres choses semblables.

3. En troisième lieu, est inscrite en l'homme une inclination conforme à la nature de la raison, laquelle lui est propre: ainsi l'homme aura-t-il une inclination naturelle à reconnaître la vérité sur Dieu et à vivre en société, et en vertu de cela, relèvera de la loi naturelle ce qui se rapporte à une inclination de cet ordre, par exemple: que l'homme évite l'ignorance, qu'il n'offense pas ceux dans la société desquels il vit, et les autres prescriptions que cela implique (I,II, 94 art. 2 tr. Jean de la Croix Kaelin).

Ces inclinations sont données par la nature à l'état de tendances vitales qui vont s'actualiser progressivement et que les vertus doivent ensuite stabiliser pour rendre possible un agir conforme à la raison. On a comparé (J. de Finance) ce processus à l'apprentissage du langage qui est une activité rationnelle greffée sur une inclination vitale.

On notera l'approche empirique de cette division qui n'est pas sans analogie avec celle de Soloviev, à propos de ses *données primordiales de la moralité* que l'on peut rapprocher des inclinations vitales de St. Thomas.

Le sentiment de la pudeur, d'une part, ne nous donnant aucune conception théorique sur le principe spirituel de l'homme nous démontre cependant indubitablement l'existence de ce principe; le sentiment de pitié, d'autre part, ne nous dit rien de défini sur la nature métaphysique de l'unité universelle, mais nous indique concrètement l'existence (na diele souchestvovanie) d'une certaine liaison fondamentale entre tous les individus distincts, ceci avant toute expérience, et bien que tous ces individus soient empiriquement séparés Les uns des autres, ils deviennent cependant unis de plus en plus intimement dans cette réalité empirique elle-même. Dans le troisième domaine des relations morales, déterminé par le sentiment religieux ou de révérence, le véritable objet de ce sentiment se révèle comme le bien suprême et parfait, réalisé totalement et absolument de toute éternité. Dans une véritable expérience religieuse, la réalité de ce que nous éprouvons nous est immédiatement donnée, nous avons le sentiment direct d'une présence réelle de la divinité, nous éprouvons en nous son action (p. 165-6 et p. 247-8).

Soloviev va intégrer dans sa division tripartite non seulement les inclinations, mais aussi les vertus, sans distinguer radicalement entre les vertus morales et les vertus théologales et il définit le principe absolu de moralité en ces termes:

En harmonie parfaite et interne avec la volonté supérieure et reconnaissant à toutes les autres personnes une valeur et une importance absolues, puisqu'elles aussi sont à l'image et à la ressemblance de Dieu, prends part, le plus complètement qu'il t'es possible. à l'oeuvre de perfectionnement de toi-même et des autres, afin que le Royaume de Dieu se révèle définitivement dans le monde (p. 178 et 261).

II. DES PHILOSOPHIES MORALES ADÉQUATEMENT PRISES

Lorsque Soloviev en vient à la mise en pratique effective de l'ordre moral, il renonce à la philosophie morale indépendante et fait intervenir la théologie:

L'homme naturel diffère de l'homme spirituel, non parce que l'élément spirituel supérieur lui manque, mais parce qu'il n'a pas lui-même la force de réaliser complètement cet élément; pour l'obtenir, il doit être fertilisé par un nouvel acte créateur, ou par l'effet de ce qu'en théologie on appelle grâce, laquelle donne aux fils des hommes "le pouvoir de devenir enfants de Dieu" (Jean 1,12). Selon la doctrine des théologiens orthodoxes, la grâce ne supprime pas la nature en général et la nature de l'homme moral en particulier, mais la perfectionne. La nature morale de l'homme est une condition nécessaire et une donnée préalable de la manifestation de Dieu en l'homme (p. 194 et 276).

Nous sommes loin de ce que la raison et la volonté laissées à leurs propres forces peuvent réaliser. La discussion est maintenant portée sur un terrain théologique. Le chapitre sur *la réalité de l'ordre moral* s'achève par une véritable déclaration de foi christocentrique qui va commander toute la troisième partie de l'ouvrage (3/5 du texte) consacrée au *bien à travers l'histoire de l'humanité.*

Le sens (rozoum) de l'histoire en son développement réel nous oblige à reconnaître en Jésus-Christ, non le dernier mot du règne humain, mais le premier, tout-unissant et tout unique Verbe du Royaume de Dieu, non l'homme-Dieu, mais le Dieu-homme, ou l'individualité absolue. de ce point de vue, on comprend bien pourquoi Il apparut au milieu de l'histoire et non pas à son terme. Comme la fin du développement du monde est la révélation du Royaume de Dieu ou de l'ordre moral parfait réalisé par la nouvelle humanité qui croît spirituellement ayant comme souche le Dieu-homme, il est évident que ce phénomène universel doit être précédé par l'apparition individuelle du

Dieu-homme lui-même comme la première moitié de l'histoire, jusqu'au Christ, préparait le milieu où les conditions externes de sa naissance personnelle, ainsi, la seconde moitié prépare les conditions externes de Sa révélation universelle ou de la venue du Royaume de Dieu (p. 197 et 279).

Soloviev prend soin de préciser qu'il n'entend par cette expression ni la chrétienté historique, ni l'Église visible (p. 198). Ce n'est pas non plus une réalité extraterrestre puisque qu'il va terminer son ouvrage par un long chapitre sur *L'organisation morale de l'humanité dans son ensemble* qui va envisager une humanité unie et sanctifiée à l'intérieur même de l'histoire.

Il va ensuite oublier ses réserves à propos de l'Église visible puisqu'il évoquera à son propos les quatre notes traditionnelles: l'unité, la sainteté, la catholicité et l'apostolicité qui font d'elle *la piété organisée*. Cette Église à la fois visible et invisible est appelée, selon Soloviev, à jouer un rôle décisif dans cet accomplissement du Royaume de Dieu à l'intérieur de l'histoire.

Le moraliste s'est fait prophète messianique dont l'espérance, apparemment si assurée, contraste avec le pessimisme de son dernier ouvrage, *Trois entretiens*, (1900), rédigé au printemps 1899, soit quelques mois après la parution de la deuxième édition du traité qu'il a pris la peine de relire à cinq reprises (décembre 1898). Cette dimension eschatologique, avec toutes les difficultés d'interprétation qu'elle pose, fait partie intégrante de la morale *adéquatement prise* de Soloviev. Ce qu'on peut retenir de ce changement de perspective c'est d'une part son attente d'une certaine forme de réalisation du Royaume de Dieu à l'intérieur de l'histoire n'excluant pas le caractère tragique de la vie de l'Église qui est appelée à triompher après avoir connu, comme le Christ lui-même, l'épreuve ultime.

Parmi les scolastiques médiévaux, Bonaventure est un des principaux représentants de la théologie de l'histoire dont on peut comparer les perspectives eschatologiques avec celles de Soloviev. Bonaventure, en effet, et contrairement à St. Augustin et à St. Thomas, esquisse une théologie de l'histoire future, qui comporte un parallèle entre le déroulement de la vie historique de l'Église et la vie terrestre du Christ.

Reprenant une tradition héritée des Pères apostoliques, antérieurs à Augustin, il suggère un *hosanna de l'histoire*, sorte de Dimanche des rameaux historique, réalisant temporairement une paix authentiquement chrétienne dans le monde. Il envisage une période privilégiée pour l'Église, considérée comme le germe du Royaume de Dieu, avant l'épreuve ultime correspondant à la passion du Christ dont St. Paul dit que l'Église est le Corps.

Cette tradition a été reprise à maintes reprises par des saints aussi bien catholiques qu'orthodoxes et a trouvé dans l'expression de *civilisation de l'amour utilisée* tant par Paul VI depuis 1970 que par Jean Paul II une sorte de consécration indissociable de la doctrine sociale de l'Église catholique.

CONCLUSION

Pour Soloviev, comme pour les scolastiques, la réflexion morale puise sa source dans la Révélation biblique qui ne rend pas vain l'exercice de la raison, mais au contraire le conforte. Soloviev pensait, en s'appuyant sur Kant, élaborer une philosophie morale indépendante de la religion, mais loin de tenir ses promesses il développe une philosophie morale *adéquatement prise* confortée par la Révélation qui éclaire la condition humaine concrète, confirme la loi naturelle (Décalogue) et annonce un Sauveur (Évangile) et un Royaume qui n'est autre que l'Église visible et invisible. Sa morale est structurée de manière originale autour de trois sentiments primordiaux de pudeur, de pitié et de piété qui sont fréquemment évoqués dans la tradition biblique. Les scolastiques, qui sont avant tout des théologiens, usent d'une philosophie morale dont les éléments sont principalement tirés d'Aristote, mais repris dans un contexte vitalement chrétien, pour en faire une morale *adéquatement prise* structurée autour de la loi naturelle, participant à la loi éternelle et confortée dans son ordre par la Révélation qu'il s'agisse du Décalogue ou des Béatitudes.

L'aspect eschatologique, qui est commun aux scolastiques et à Soloviev, est aussi d'inspiration biblique. Elle donne à la philosophie morale de Soloviev, comme à la théologie morale des scolastiques, toute sa dimension historique concrète autour d'un messianisme qui est l'objet d'attente chez les Juifs, tandis que les chrétiens croient à sa réalisation avec le Christ, mais attendent sa deuxième venue ou *Parousie* (présence), sans renoncer à organiser la cité temporelle conformément aux exigences de la Révélation.

Une *civilisation de l'amour* réalisant temporairement à l'intérieur de l'histoire, et avant la grande épreuve de la fin et du dernier jugement, les idéaux bibliques, telle pourrait être la perspective commune, à moyen terme, aux intuitions de Soloviev, à la tradition catholique et aux Juifs pour lesquels Soloviev eut ses dernières pensées.

BIBLIOGRAPHIE VLADIMIR SOLOVIEV

Crise de la philosophie occidentale, 1874 (Aubier 1947); *Leçons sur la divino-humanité* 1877-78 (Cerf 1991); *Le judaïsme et la question chrétienne* 1884 (1992 Desclée); *La Sophia et les autres écrits français*, 1876-1897 (1981 Age d'homme); *La grande controverse et la politique chrétienne – Orient/Occident* 1883 (Aubier 1953); *Le sens de l'amour 1892-94 et le drame de la vie de Platon* 1898 (OEIL 1985); *Opravdanie Dobra*, réédition (in *Oeuvres en deux volumes*, tome I, "La pensée", Moscou 1988); tr. *La justification du bien*, 1897 – (Aubier 1939), *Trois entretiens* 1900 (OEIL 1984).

Sur V. Soloviev

Mgr d'Herbigny, *Un Newman russe, Vladimir Soloviev* 1909 (Beauchesne 1934); Serge Soloviev, *Vie de Wladimir Solowiew par son neveu*, 1977 (SOS, 1982); Maxime Herman, introduction à *Crise de la philosophie occidentale* (1947); Basile Zenkovsky, *Histoire de la philosophie russe* 1955, Tome II (Gallimard 1992); Mgr Jean Rupp, *Message ecclésial de Solowiew 1974 (Lethielleux 1974)*; Frederick Copleston, *Philosophy in Russia from Herzen to Lenin and Berdyaev* 1986 (University of Notre-dame Press 1986) et *Russian Religious Philosophy, Selected aspects* 1988 (U. of ND Press 1988); Les trois premiers numéros d'*Istina* de l'année 1992 ont été consacrés en grande partie à l'oeuvre de V. Soloviev; Société Vladimir Soloviev, *Vladimir Soloviev, Oecuménisme et eschatologie*, édité par Patrick de Laubier et Igor Sogologorsky 1994 (X. de Guibert, Paris 1994).

Scolastiques

St. Thomas d'Auguin, *Summa Theologiae,* Edition Paulinae 1962; St. Bonaventure, *Hexaëmeron*, 1273 (Desclée/Cerf *Les six jours de la création*, 1991), *Breviloquium,* 1257 (Editions franciscaines 1967); *Itinéraire de l'esprit vers Dieu,* 1259 (Vrin 1986).

Sur les scolastiques et la philosophie morale

Jacques Chevalier, *Histoire de la pensée* 1955 (Editions Universitaires, vol 3 et 4 1992); Frederick Copleston, *A History of Philosophy* 1962-63 (Image, Book I 1985).

Etienne Gilson, *L'esprit de la philosophie médiévale*, 1932 (Vrin 1969); *Le thomisme sixième édition 1964 (Vrin 1965); La philosophie de Saint Bonaventure*, 1923 (Vrin 1984); *Jean Duns Scot*, 1952 (Vrin 1952); Jacques Maritain, *Science et Sagesse*, 1935 (Oeuvres complètes, Fribourg, vol. VI, 1984); *Neuf leçons sur les notions premières de philosophie morale*, 1949 (O.C.IX, 1990); *La philosophie morale*, 1960 (O.C. XI 1991); *La loi naturelle ou loi non écrite*, 1986 (Editions universitaires, Fribourg 1986); Yves Simon, *Critique de la connaissance morale*, 1934 (Desclée de Brouwer 1934); *The Tradition of Natural Law, A Philosopher's Reflecions*, 1967 (Fordham University Press 1967); Josef Pieper, *La fin des temps*, 1950 (Editions universitaires, Fribourg 1982); Joseph Ratzinger, *La théologie de l'histoire de Saint Bonaventure*, 1959 (PUF, 1988); Joseph de Finance, *Ethique Générale*, 1967 (Universita Gregoriana 1988); Servais Pinckaers, *Les sources de la morale chrétienne*, 1985 (Editions universitaires, Fribourg/Cerf 1990); Benedict T. Viviano, *Le Royaume de Dieu dans l'histoire* 1988 (Cerf 1992); André de Muralt, *L'enjeu de la philosophie médiévale*, 1991 (E. J. Brill 1991).

Voir aussi l'encyclique *Veritatis splendor*, 1993, notamment le chapitre qui présente la morale thomiste.

DALIA MARIJA STANČIENĖ
Lithuania

THE CONCEPTION OF FREEDOM IN THE WORKS OF LITHUANIAN CATHOLIC PHILOSOPHERS

In response to economic and political developments, sciences came to Lithuania during the late Middle Ages. Young nobles used to go abroad to study in universities. There they created their own brotherhoods and clubs. During the XIV-XVII centuries, Lithuanians studied in the universities of Prague, Krakow, Konigsberg, Jena, Tubingen, Heidelberg, Graz, Basel, Geneva, Louvain, Strasbourg, Paris, Bologna, and Padua. There are 2000 names of students from Lithuania in the matriculation lists of the above mentioned universities[1].

A great number of them graduated with the degree of Bachelor of Liberal arts or Master of Philosophy. Some of them became professors of their colleges and universities. For example, A Čirskis (1660) was a professor in Regensburg (Germany), P. Vaičiūnaććs taught physics in Antwerpen, A. Virvičius taught poetics in Viterbe and Macherala in Italy[2].

But in Lithuania itself there were no opportunities for development of philosophy because of the lack of a proper schools. The religious conflicts within Western Christianity changed this. In order to stop the spread of the Reformation and Arian heresy, the bishop of Vilnius, Valerijonas Protasevičius (1504-1579) invited the Jesuits to Vilnius in 1569. The next year the Jesuits established a college in Vilnius. There they started to teach scholastic philosophy in 1571.

---

[1] R. Plečkaitis, *Feodalizmo laikotarpio filosofija Lietuvoje (Philosophy in Medieval Lithuania)*, Vilnius, "Minitis", 1975, p. 18.
[2] Ibid., p. 19.

In 1579 the college was transformed into a university in which five departments of philosophy were established: the departments of metaphysics, logic, ethics, mathematics, and history.

Soon Vilnius University became one of the most important and influential schools in Northern Europe. Not only Lithuanians and Poles studied there, but also Latvians, Belorussians, Ukranians, Germans, Spaniards, Italians, Frenchmen, Swedes, Hungarians, Greeks, and Tatars. The teaching Faculty was also international.

For instance, Petrus Viana (1550-1609) was a Spaniard, Joannes Schwang (1637-1710) and Nicolaus Stadtfeld (1570-1612) were both Germans, Joannes Baptista Andriani (1604-1675) was an Italian, Gorgonius Ageison (1609-1665) was a Dane, and Žigymantas Liauksminas (1597-1670), Petras Kojalavičius (1622-1654), Kristupas P. Einoravičius (1644-1714), Adomas Abramavičius (1710-1780) were Lithuanians[3].

The first generation of professional philosophers in Lithuania was educated within the Thomistic tradition. Scholasticism thrived in Lithuania up until the middle of the 18th century.

As far back as the second part of the 16th century Lithuania had become a center of religious tolerance in Europe. In 1563, the Lithuanian parliament granted freedom to all religious denominations without exception. This religious freedom was the cause of differences among these donominations.

Not only the Catholics and Protestants were involved in polemics with each other but also the Orthodox and Jews. There were also small communities of Muslim Tartars and Karaims, who had their own separate religion, based on the Old Testament. Under those conditions of political and public tolerance, religious pluralism resulted with the flourishing of culture: the capital of Lithuania became a center of book printing: one of the printing pioneers, the eminent Belarussian thinker Francis Skoryna, printed his first books here; Ivan Fiodorow reestablished his printing business in Vilnius after his printing house was destroyed by fanatics in Moscow. Because of political and legislated religious tolerance, Vilnius became a center of Jewish culture in Northern Europe.

These and many other facts allow us to maintain that in the 16th century the political, legal, and cultural development of the state began, which led to granting human rights and respecting individual freedom. Unfortunately, the expansionism of Russian, Prussian and Austro-Hungarian monarchies put an end to the democratic aspirations of Lithuania. Also, it hindered the development of the Lithuanian national consciousness.

---

[3] M. Biržiška, *Senasis Vilniaus univrsitetas (The Old University of Vilnius)*, London "Nida press", 1955, p. 15 and also R., Plečkaitis, *Philosophy in Medieval Lithuania*, p. 404-490.

The written native language is one of the most important factors in the development of national consciousness. In 1547 in Konigsberg, a protestant priest, Martynas Mažvydas (1510-1563) wrote and printed the first book in Lithuanian "The Simple Words of the Catechism..."

Almost fifty years later Father Mikalojus Daukša (¯1527-1613) issued the Catholic catechism in Lithuanian. These events started the development of Lithuanian national consciousness. We can therefore say that this development was begun by the competition between Protestantism and Catholicism. The latter not only initiated but also provided the means for the preservation of the national identity. For example, after the incorporation of Lithuania into the Russian Empire the Russian authorities promoted the policy of russification along with the encouragement of Orthodoxy. In this case the competition between Orthodoxy and Catholicism was beneficial to the national development: Catholic clergy widely used the argument that, preserving Catholicism, often Lithuanian people preserved their national identity. So in the 19th century, the Catholic bishop Motiejus Valančius (1801-1875) urged Lithuanian peasants not only to remain faithful to the Catholic church, but also to live according to its high moral standards and to seek education in their native language. As a result, the ban on written Lithuanian, imposed by Tsar Alexander II in 1866, did not achieve its end. On the contrary, it stimulated the struggle of Lithuania for its own national school, at that time an underground school. Naturally this struggle strengthened the feeling of national identity and further developed national consciousness.

On the other hand, this struggle focused Lithuanian thought too strongly on political issues. Therefore, it was up to professional philosophers to correct this. Thanks to the above mentioned processes, Lithuania had a basis for cultural and political development when, after the revolution of 1905, the restrictions which had been imposed upon national development, were lifted. Soon after the revolution, Lithuanians established their own National Scientific Society, Opera, and Art institutions. On this basis, the modernization of national consciousness started, and a new generation of intellectuals was educated. Against the background of the experienced political and cultural opression, the conflict between freedom and tyranny was the most important problem for philosophical thought. As far back as 1912, Ignas Šeinius wrote: "People already feel the call of freedom within their own souls: that freedom, which is a source of creativity... Nevertheless, we are still not sure which way to go, as if we had just woken up. Some of us abuse freedom wounding ourselves and others. Others use it to unite all the disoriented people and enslave them again. But freedom is only the means for

for the improvement of ourselves and others. But only a few men know this truth"[4].

The Lithuanian Catholic thinker Antanas Maceina (1908-1987)[5] looks at freedom through the prism of the Christan faith. He maintains that, "[...] the essence of freedom could be grasped only within its relation to God, that is, only when the idea of freedom is treated as a religious one"[6]. God, according to Maceina, is the source and guarantor of human freedom. Religion starts at the moment when man as a person meets God the person..."[7] In this way, Maceina makes the distinction between the ontological and anthropological approaches to the analysis of freedom. This enables him to separate himself from Existentialism, especially in treating the opposition between necessity and freedom – the central problem of Western philosophy from Aristotle to Hume. Maceina makes attempts to rehabilitate necessity and to reconcile it with freedom. He sees necessity as belonging to nature: "Nature is a realm of necessity in which we are living as free entities and trying to realize our freedom. Since necessity is the negation of freedom, one who acts from necessity is not free. Then how is it possible to realize freedom within the realm of necessity?"[8] Defining necessity as a notion of nature, Maceina concludes that man prepares possibility of freedom by inquiring about and understanding nature and, at the same time, necessity. "Understanding necessity is the precondition of freedom, and transformed necessity is realized freedom[9]. At first man understands nature as necessity and then he masters it. Thus, nature understood, transformed and mastered is called "culture". As a process, culture is history. Or as Maceina puts it: "Culture includes all the space of man's existence, which expands in all directions and so the creation of culture becomes the chronological process of history"[10]. In its own turn, history becomes the uninterrupted process of the realization of freedom, or in other words: "The history of humankind is the history of freedom". This is the anthropological dimension of freedom. But in the ontological dimension freedom appears as openness[11]. Maceina

---

[4] Ignas Šeinius, *Vasaros vaišės/Kuprelis (The Summer East)*, Vilnius "Vaga", 1970, p. 294-296.

[5] The professor, PhD. (1534), studied in the Universities of Kaunas, Louvain, Freiburg, Strasburg and Bruxelles. In 1944, before the Soviet Army occupied Lithuania he left for the West. He was a professor at Freiburg and Münster Universities.

[6] Antanas Maceina, *Dievas ir laisvė (God and Freedom)*, Chicago, "Ateitis", 1985, p. vii.

[7] Antanas Maceina, *Jobo drama (Drama of Job)*, Freiburg, "Venta", 1950, p. 191.

[8] A. Maceina, *Dievas ir laisvė*, p. 42.

[9] Ibid., p. 48.

[10] Ibid., p. 48.

[11] Ibid., p. 37.

treats openness in a scholastic way. Man is free because he is "the image and likeness" of God[12]. In other words, freedom ontologically understood is the divine element in man and in his activity. Through creativity and sin man ressembles the creativity of the Creator. Maceina maintains that to create is to interpret. Interpretation is possible because created things are open. They are open since they came into being through freedom, and they express freedom. Maceina makes the distinction between a created thing and a thing which belongs to necessity: the latter is fully defined, completed, and closed. Therefore, the natural phenomenon can be only investigated. Whereas the created object, which came into being through freedom, is open for interpretation.

In his interpretation of the relation between freedom and necessity, Maceina shows that man is united with his own world, since both are created by God. Therefore, when abstracted from each other, both lose their meaning: the world of pure necessity has no meaning, since necessity is blind; and man, when thought of without the world, becomes powerless, since he has no place and means of the realization of his own freedom[13].

Lithuanian philosopher Juozas Girnius (1915-1994)[14], a contemporary of Maceina, devotes much attention to the same problem. "Freedom and Being" was his first published book (Brooklyn, 1953). But even as far back as 1938, while studying at the Sorbonne and the College de France, J. Girnius decided to pursue his PhD by an analysis of Karl Jaspers' philosophy. Perhaps for this reason he made a personal acquaintance with this famous philosopher, paid visits to his home and spent long hours conversing with him.

Girnius regards freedom as a human and personal value. He did not pay much attention to abstract free will. He was engaged in the analysis of freedom as a basis for humanism and personal dignity. This was the central problem of his thought. He asks: what has man to do in order to express and realize his own humanity? And he answers: to participate in the creation of culture, which is the expression and the embodiment of human freedom.

Following Karl Jaspers and Martin Heideger, Girnius asks the question of the meaning of life in connection with mortality. "When death calls, writes Girnius, one must leave behind not only this world but also all his

---

[12] Ibid., p. 33.
[13] Ibid., p. 50-51.
[14] PhD (1951, Montreal University, Canada). He also studied in the Universities of Kaunas, Louvain, Freiburg, and Paris. In 1944, before the Soviet Army occupied Lithuania he left Lithuania for Germany. There he worked as a teacher in a camp of Deported Persons. In 1949 he left for the USA. From 1953 to 1969 he was the editor of the Lithuanian Encyclopedia; from 1965-1980 editor of the jorunal "Aidai".

exploits and works"[15]. The question arises as: what is the ultimate meaning of human life?"[16] Girnius answers that even death cannot deprive man of what he was, therefore "the ultimate vocation of man is creation of his own self"[17]. "Creativity" is the category which makes it possible to reveal the meaning of freedom for Girnius as well as for Maceina.

At the beginning, speaking about freedom, both philosophers share the Christian creationistic view. Nevertheless they develop their conceptions differently. Girnius tires to reconcile the principles of the existential philosophy of Jaspers with Thomistic metaphysics. He maintains that independent human reason can reach the first cause, that is God. But, since human reason is limited, and God is beyond all limits, reason cannot comprehend Him but only confess Him. And so, even after the proof of God's existence is accepted as valid, one has still a need to find God for himself, that is he is still free to believe or not to believe. Or, as Girnius puts it: "In spite of the reliability of the proof of God's existence man can find God by means of faith alone".

Girnius looks at the freedom of choice through an ethical prism. He maintains that free choice presupposes the existence of moral values and rests on them. It is not only freedom that makes human acts valuable but, on the contrary, the realization of the values through free acts makes freedom itself valuable"[18]. Displaying freedom as the basis of humanity, Girnius reveals freedom as one of the fundamental conditions for a valuable human activity within the definite limits of space and time, that is within history.

He shows that there is no morality without freedom, but at the same time he maintains that "freedom itself has no moral value, since it can serve for good and for evil equally"[19]. It is possible to preserve the positive value of freedom only by conscious faithfulness to what is invariable and valuable. Hence it seems quite possible to maintain that Girnius develops his conception of freedom against the background of rational moral choice. Because of that, he was criticized by Maceina[20]. The latter argued that the problems of God and freedom are insoluble within the limits of human reason alone. Of course, Girnius does not reject the metaphysical proof of God's existence, nevertheless he concentrates his attempts upon man's choice and maintains in his "Man Without God" that the unbeliever also realizes man's

---

[15] Juozas Girnius, *Žmogus be Dievo (Man Without God)*, Chicago, "Į Laisvę Fondo lietuviškai kultūrai ugdyti", 1964, p. 346.

[16] Ibid., p. 346.

[17] Ibid., p. 346.

[18] Ibid., p. 307.

[19] Ibid., p. 308.

[20] See Antanas Maceina, Laiškas Aidų redaktoriui Juozui Girniui (The Letter to the Editor of "Aidai" Juozas Girnius)// "Aidai", 1965 Nr. 10, p. 445.

freedom, and in this, though negative, way, gives witness to God. In a sense Maceina agrees with this statement of Girnius, but at the same time he underlines that on this anthropological level we can observe only the appearance of freedom but not its essence. And so Maceina remains faithful to the traditional scholastic hierarchy of philosophical disciplines. In his conception there is no place for indifferent freedom, nothing to say about an evil one: whereas Girnius suggests that indifference can be overcome only by means of moral values.

On the basis of this comparison of the two Lithuanian philosophers we can infer that, perhaps, there is no real possibility to reconcile Existentialism with Thomistic philosophy.

LINA ŠULCIENĖ
Vytautas Magnus University
Lithuania

THOUGHT OVER THE MYSTERY OF FREEDOM ON THE BASIS OF THOMISTIC ONTOLOGICAL PRINCIPLES

This report is an attempt to discuss two senses of the concept of freedom. Both meanings are stated in the encyclical "Veritatis splendor" by John Paul II. It says: "In the Book of Genesis we read: «The Lord God commanded the man, saying» You may eat freely of every tree of the garden, but of the tree of the knowledge of good and evil you shall not eat, for the day that you eat of it you shall die»". "The man", it is written further, "possesses an extremely far-reaching freedom, since he can eat «of every tree of the garden»"[1].

1. I will give a deeper insight into the first part of the quoted encyclical to show freedom as a possibility to "eat freely of every tree of the garden". This is the first meaning of the concept of freedom. I will attempt to search for the ontical basis of power of the person's free will, referring to Thomistic ontology.

First of all, the power of freedom is characteristic only of the human being. According to Aristotle's tradition, Thomistic philosophy defines every being as a unity of primary matter and the substantial form. We describe this matter as an absolutely passive substantial substrat and the source of pure potentiality and individuality of substance, while the substantial form is the active power and principle that actualizes the substance and brings the being into existence, essential to it. It is obvious, that the power of freedom of the human being is essentially based on its substantial form. It includes different moments which enable the first sense of the power of freedom.

1. 1. In the complexity of things all the beings are related to one precise whole, where any activity of any member of the complex does not destroy

---

[1] John Paul II, Encyclical *Veritatis splendor*, "Origins", 18(1993).

the order of the whole, but on the contrary, participates in the process of creation of this order. Therefore, the power of freedom to choose one thing from a number of things has to be and actually is harmonious with such an order of things.

A being which has the power of freedom, as well as a being, which lacks it, is connected with other members of the complex of being; they all restrict one another. This fundamental relativity is determined by the internal essential structure, that is, by the hylomorphic structure of every being, or to be more precise, by the necessity existing in the substantial form of all beings to be related to other beings. The basis of the external relativity of beings, lying in the substantial form of every being, is the first condition of the power of freedom, understood in its first meaning. For, one can "eat freely of every tree of the garden" only if there is a possible relation between the "eater" and "the trees of the garden".

1. 2. But such a relation is not sufficient for the power of freedom to exist, as it is common to other beings, to which we do not ascribe this power. Determining the relativity of the being, the substantial form determines its degree and activity level. The more we go down the pyramid of beings, the more complicated their structure becomes; in the same measure they become more dependent on others, and their autonomy is so much the more diminished. The field of activity of an animal is wider than that of a plant. The field of activity of a man is wider than that of an animal. A man, having the highest degree of activity in the whole complex of being, has the lowest degree of relation to other beings, because he can act on his own, choosing any of the possible connections, to "eat freely of every tree of the garden".

These two moments, namely the highest level of activity and the lowest degree of dependence, is evidently the field of ontology which houses the roots of the power of freedom understood in this way.

1. 3. Both moments received their best reflexion in the thomistic concept of subsistence that I will seek to reveal by quoting Jacques Maritain's work "A Short Essay on the Existence and the Existent"[2].

In J. Maritain's opinion, this concept discloses those features of the substance, which enable it to exceed the whole universum of objects by its own depth. This concept means that every being is not only a consistent part of its relativity to other beings, forming the whole, but it explains as well that the being itself is the very whole. The concept of subsistence is applied not only to the human being, but also to other substances; however, the degree of subsistence of beings changes in every stage of the hierarchy of being.

---

[2] Maritain J., *Court Traité de l'existence et de l'existant*, 2 edition, Paris 1964.

What content does the concept of subsistence have?

Developing the ontological division between the essence and the existence, J. Maritain distinguishes the existence as given and the existence as fulfilled. The existence is not only given, but it is also fulfilled, or, speaking in above mentioned terms, the being does not only exist, but it is also active. The essence, supplied by subsisting, becomes a basement which fulfills the existence. By subsistence the essence is transferred into such a state of subject or basis that enables the being to fulfill its existence. This fulfilment must have a basis. Due to subsistence individual nature even acquires the power to transfer incommunicability, which characterised it on the level of essence, into the level of existence. Thomism views incommunicability as a sign of the individuality of being, which is the very ontological unity, comprising in itself the existence characteristic of it. The being, marked by such a sign, is called *suppositum* by scholastics.

Thus, subsistence allows the essence, turned to a basis, to exist *per se separatim* (by itself) through the fulfilment of existence. Subsistence creates a new metaphysical dimension, a positive improvement. Now the essence becomes the centre of activity which fulfills the substantial being, specific to it. The being acts, and that means it is a substantial being, *suppositum: actiones sunt suppositorum*.

Going up the pyramide of being, we come across the subjects of existence, the basements, *supposita*, richer and richer in their internal complexity. Their activity shows a still more perfect spontaneity, a still higher degree of subsistence, from simple transitive activity of lifeless things to unclearly immanent activity of the life of plants, and at last to the clearly immanent life of sense and the absolutely immanent life of intellect. After coming to the last stage of the hierarchy, to the stage of the human beings, the threshold of freedom and the threshold of person are crossed over. Because of such "metaphysical improvement" *suppositum* becomes *persona*. Then subsistence brings in the highest positive perfection, reaching the state of active and autonomous self-realization, which is characteristic of a self-sufficient, self-governed whole. The whole of this kind ascribes its existence and the actions accomplished in it to itself.

In this way, the person's peculiarity in the complex of beings, and the basement of his power of freedom, lie in the depth of the concept of subsistence. The roots of the mystery of freedom and of the existence of man, eating "freely from every tree of the garden", are hidden in this "metaphysical improvement".

1. 4. But the freedom of choosing is not unlimited. Thomistic ontology finds one more essential moment for the power of freedom, namely, the finality lying in the substantial form of all the members of the complex of beings, as well as of a person, characterised by this power. The Thomistic principle is: *Quidquid agit, agit propter finem*. The complex of being is an acting and a changing whole, that is, a purposefully acting whole. And every separate member of the complex of being participates in this developement of the whole complex. Such participation is determined by the substantial form of every member.

1. 4. 1. The Ontological Premises of Finality. Every being is a result of the Cause, which creates the order of being. This Cause is an effective principle, creating the consequence, which is new and independent reality, but not a part of the Cause. However, the consequence participates in the perfection of the Cause. Finality is understood in the sense of participation. This participation is determined by the nature of every being. Nature determines every being, either in one way or in other, it determines all its active existence in general as well. Thus, such determination, defined by nature, is also the internal finality of the being. Finality is the tendency that determines the way of the existence of a being.

What end does every being have, directed by the internal finality of its nature? First of all, it is the maintaining of the nature in being that corresponds to the purpose of keeping order of the entire complex of being. Virtually, since the Cause creating the order of being is seen by the Thomistic ontology as the End of the development of this order, it means that the internal finality of every being is oriented to this End, too.

1. 4. 2. The Expression of Finality. The finality of the being expresses itself in such a way that every action presupposes the desired object into which the action is directed. In the statement *"quidquid agit, agit propter finem"* the verb *"agere"* implicates the content of the verb *"appetere"*, and the End, which is sought by the being by a certain act, has the aspect of the desired purpose. Tending to an end and seeking it, the being satisfies the need necessary for its nature; it removes any insufficiency, lack or incompleteness, it completes itself.

So, the power of freedom, understood in its first sense, as the choice from a number of things, comes together with finality, lying in a person. The person is free within the limits of this finality. He is free to choose neither the very principle of finality, nor his nature. The person is not free to choose the final End into which he is necessarily directed. The person is free to choose the means for the search for the End, which implies the sense of "eating freely from any tree of the garden".

2. However, there is another sense of the concept of freedom. Let us return to the sentence at which we stopped while quoting the encyclical: "But his freedom is not unlimited: It must halt before the «tree of knowledge of good and evil»"[3]. The relation between the power of freedom and the concepts of the Good and the Evil is discussed here. This relation is the most important one when trying to describe the concept of freedom in its second sense. So, we should have a look at the content of the Good and the Evil in the Thomistic ontology.

2. 1. The concept of the Good is used as a synonym to the concept of the end we have just discussed. A Thomistic axiom states: *Bonum est quod omnia appetunt*[4]. The Good is that toward which everything tends. The end or the Good satisfies the tendency, completes it by setting its boundaries. The Good is the final boundary of the action. The Good, understood in this way, is a transcendental feature of being, which describes the aspect of its desirability. It is one of the three qualities of being (Unity/unum, Truth/verum, the Good/bonum) by which the transcendentality of being is defined[5]. Therefore, the power of free choice, determining the character of the actions of the human being, is always connected to the Good as the end of action, which in its turn influences the choice.

2. 2. And even more, the action called out by the power of free choice is always good in the ontological sense, because the Good is the basic category, the importance of which is expressed in the thesis: *Omne ens – est bonum*[6]. Everything that exists is good. Good and being are convertible. There is a logical but not real difference between being as being and being as something, that is the Good. Therefore, the human power of freedom should participate and unfold only in the Good.

2. 3. The above statement is explained by the fact that being is not connected to anything beyond it in the ontical level. It does not have any relation to non-being, it cannot be in relation to anything external to it, in any sense and on any level. Everything beyond being is pure nothing. It simply does not exist. So Evil as such does not have any ontological basis. Classical ontology states that it is not real. Everything that exists is good and perfect. Imperfection, the Evil (*malum*) is virtually a lack of being. We talk of the Evil only when we lack something, that should certainly exist (in the sense of the substantial form), Evil is considered as *privatio*, as the absence of something that has to be, as it is necessary for the substantial form.

---

[3] John Paul II, Encyclical *Veritatis splendor*, ibid.

[4] S. Thomas Aquinas, *Summa theologiae*, I, q.5, a.1.

[5] The word "transcendental" is used here in the sence, which is attached to it by scholasticism. The latin word "transcendere" is used by scholastics to define something that is superior to other things because of its belonging to a higher level. In this case we have the difference of the level, but not of the degree, so we cannot proceed from one to the other, developing consecutively the first one. In this sense God transcends the created whole, and the spirit transcends the matter. Further, the idea of being transcends spiecies, genus and every individual being, covering everything in one aspect – the aspect of being, every individual being and all the complex of being as well.

[6] *Summa theologiae*, I, q.5, a.3.

2. 4. Thus we can reveal a double possibility to look at things connected with the power of freedom. As sin, suffering and the reality of the evident Evil existing in the world leave no doubt for the reality of the Evil; meanwhile the Evil does not have the ontological basement in the sense of the level of being, it simply does not exist. Thus we have two view-points with the different contents of the concepts of the Good and the Evil.

Keeping to the ontological position, man reflecting upon himself as a member of the complexity of being gives priority to the aspect of being as the whole. As far as the second view-point is concerned, we can say that it emerged when man broke the order not to eat from "the tree of the knowledge of good and evil". The breach of order made man sensitive to the two opposites – Good and Evil. At the same it made man sensitive to another level, that is to the level of morals. This view-point gives priority to an incommunicable relation between the Cause, the Keeper, the End of the order of being and the person. This relation is considered to be more important than the relation between the Cause, the Keeper and the End of the order of being and the order of being itself. The second view-point speaks of the moral law given by the Creator Himself to the person. By obeying this law the person becomes really free. The second sense of the concept of freedom in Thomism is connected with the person's open-heartedness to the Word of the Lord. Therefore, we should look for the grounds of the sense of this concept in the field of religion.

LITERATURE

1. John Paul II, Encyclical *Veritatis splendor*, Origins, 18(1993).
2. Maritain J., *Court Traité de l'existence et de l'existant*, 2e edition, Paris 1964.
3. Maritain J., *The Person and the Common Good*, London 1948.
4. Maritain J., *Moral Philosophy*, New York 1964.
5. Meyer H., *The Philosophy of St.Thomas Aquinas*, London 1954.
6. Raeymaeker L., *The Philosophy of Being*, London 1966.
7. St. Thomas Aquinas, *Summa theologiae*, Pars Prima.

PETER VOLEK
Theologicky Inštitút Badin
Slovak Republic

BEGRÜNDUNG DER FREIHEIT BEI EDITH STEIN

Edith Stein (1891-1942) hat in ihrem Leben und in der wissenschaftlichen Tätigkeit mehrere Etappen durchgemacht. Ihre philosophische Tätigkeit kann man in drei Etappen einteilen: 1. Die Zeit ihrer Tätigkeit, vorherrschend bestimmt durch die phänomenologische Methode (1916-1921). Diese Zeit beginnt mit ihrem Abschluß des Studiums an der Universität Göttingen und setzt mit ihrer Tätigkeit als Husserls Assistentin (1916-1918) und freie Wissenschaftlerin fort. Ihre Taufe im Jahr 1921 bringt eine Zäsur in ihr Leben und Wirken. 2. Die Zeit geprägt durch ihre Mühe um die Verbindung der Phänomenologie mit dem Thomismus (1921-1933). In dieser Zeit beginnt Edith Stein, sich den Thomismus im Eigenstudium anzueignen und bei ihrer Tätigkeit in den Einklang mit der Phänomenologie zu bringen. 3. Die Zeit der Tätigkeit im Kloster (1933-1942). In dieser Zeit kommen auch die mystischen Züge in ihr Werk hinein.
Während all dieser Zeit hat Edith Stein im Zentrum ihrer Gedanken die menschliche Person gehabt. Viele ihrer Arbeiten kreisen um dieses Thema. Dabei hat sie auch die Frage nach der menschlichen Freiheit nicht ausgelassen. Mit der Lösung dieses Problems bei Edith Stein will ich mich in meinem Beitrag befassen.

I. EDITH STEINS METHODISCHES VORGEHEN

Zum Beginn werde ich die Methode untersuchen, mit welcher Edith Stein zu diesem Problem kommt und es anpackt. Edith Steins Zugang zu diesem Problem ist durch zwei wichtige Vorentscheidungen geprägt: 1. Durch ihre Bestimmung des Verhältnisses zwischen Philosophie und

Glauben. 2. Durch ihre Auffasung der phänomenologichen Methode, die sie stets in ihren Werken benutzt.

Jetzt werde ich kurz diese Vorbedingungen untersuchen. Über das Verhältnis zwischen Vernunft und Glauben berichtet Edith Stein besonders in ihrem Hauptwerk *Endliches und ewiges Sein* [1]. Es geht dabei darum, wie man eine christliche Philosophie betreiben kann. Nach der Darstellung mehrerer zeitgenössischer Lösungen entscheidet sich Edith Stein für die Lösung, die in die Philosophie auch die Offenbarung hineinnimmt, aber nur als Hypothesen ([1], 29-30). Darum ist der Vorwurf von K.-H. Lembeck, daß damit Edith Stein die Wissenschaftlichkeit der Philosophie verläßt, unbegründet ([3], 170). Damit entschärft sie ihre Position aus ihrem früherem Werk *Husserls Phänomenologie und die Philosophie des hl. Thomas von Aquino*, wo sie von der formalen aber auch materialen Abhängigkeit der Philosophie von der Theologie spricht ([2], 66-67), worin Lembecks Bedenken ihren Grundboden hatten. Nach Edith Stein ist nämlich die volle Wahrheit nicht wie bei Husserl nur als regulative Idee zu fassen, sondern die volle Wahrheit findet sich in der biblischen Offenbarung Gottes ([2], 64). Die materiale Abhängigkeit der Philosophie vom Glauben bedeutet für Edith Stein das Hineinnehmen des Glaubens in die Wahrheiten, die der Philosoph annimmt, was man auch als weltanschauliches Element bezeichnen kann. Die formale Abhängigkeit der Philosophie vom Glauben bedeutet, daß die Wahrheit der philosophischen Aussagen an dem Glaubensaussagen gemessen wird. Entscheidend ist dabei die Auffassung der Philosophie als der Weg zur Wahrheit, wobei die letzte Wahrheit in der Offenbarung Gottes in der Schrift liegt ([4], 147).

Diese Auffassung von Edith Stein muß man vor Augen haben, wenn man Edith Steins Werke beurteilt. Manchmal kann man nämlich bei ihr Einflüsse davon bemerken, wenn sie z.B. einige Fragen mit Hilfe der Offenbarung ergänzen und lösen will.

Edith Steins Lösungen sind auch von ihrer Auffassung von der phänomenologischen Methode bedingt. Edith Stein versucht in ihren Werken, besonders seit der zweiten Etappe ihrer wissenschaftlichen Tätigkeit, die phänomenologische Methode mit dem Thomismus zu verbinden. Ihre Benutzung der phänomenologische Methode ist dadurch gekennzeichnet, daß Edith Stein die transzendentale Reduktion Husserls thematisch nicht befolgt, nur unthematisch, aber in einem etwas veränderten Sinn. Die phänomenologische Methode bei Husserl ist durch die eidetische und durch die phänomenologische Reduktion bestimmt. Die eidetische Reduktion versucht zum Eidos der Sachen zu kommen durch die Ausschaltung von allem Subjektiven, von allem Theoretischen, von aller Tradition, von nicht denknotwendigen Elementen und auch von der Existenz dessen, was man erlebt ([5] I, 16-17. 42. 45; [6], 24-28). Die eidetische Reduktion führt zur Wesensschau. Die phänomenologische Reduktion schaltet den Seinsglauben aus und führt zum reinen Bewußtsein ([5], 6). Seit der intensiveren Beschäftigung mit Kant seit 1907 hat Husserl dann auch seine phänomenologische Reduktion transzendental vertieft ([7], 28). Das hat ihn dann dazu geführt, daß er das Sein des Bewußtseins für absolutes Sein und alles andere Sein nur für relatives Sein erklärt hat ([5], 103-107), woran sich er auch später gehalten hat. Das hat ihn zum transzendentalen Idealismus geführt, was Edith Stein und die anderen Göttinger Phänomenologen stets abgelehnt hatten. Edith Stein lehnt Husserls Auffassung des Begriffs „transzendental", die zum transzendentalen absoluten Sein führt, ab, und benutzt die transzendentale Reduktion nur unthematisch bei der Analyse der Bedingung der Möglichkeit der Erkenntnis, wo sie etwas als Horizont der Seienden ([1], 261) und als Horizont der Wissenschaft ([1], 17) enthüllt. Auch dieses Ergebnis muß man bei der Beurteilung von Edith Steins Positionen berücksichtigen.

Der Einfluß von Edith Steins Verständnis der Beziehung zwischen Philosophie und Glaube und von ihrer Benutzung der phänomenologischen Methode mit der Ablehnung des transzendentalen Idealismus bei Husserl zeigt sich auch bei ihrem Verständnis der menschlichen Person und ihrer Freiheit. Deutlich wird es sich bei der Behandlung der einzelnen Problemen zeigen. Bei Edith Stein kann man mehrere Zugänge zum Problem der Freiheit finden.

II. DER ZUGANG ZUR FREIHEIT

1. VON DER VERANTWORTUNG

Der eine Zugang führt von der Verantwortung her. Edith Stein geht davon aus, daß der Mensch von den anderen als verantwortlich beurteilt wird ([8], 105). Edith Stein geht dabei von der Umgangsprache aus, in der die Rede von der menschlichen Verantwortung oft verwendet wird. Zudem wird die Verantwortung auch in der juridischen Praxis vorausgesetzt. Die Verantwortung ist das spezifisch Menschliche, das ihn von den Tieren unterscheidet. Edith Stein formuliert diese Verantwortung als ethische Aufgabe für den Menschen: „Er kann und soll sich selbst formen". ([8], 105). Als Bedingung der Verantwortung zeigt sich nach Edith Stein die Freiheit einer geistigen Person. Das zeigt Edith Stein reduktiv in mehreren Schritten:

1. Nur ein selbstherrliches, waches Ich, das sich selbst bewußt beherrschen und steuern kann, kann verantwortlich sein. Der Mensch muß deshalb geistig sein. Geistig ist der Mensch, der um sich selbst und um anderes weiß. Es ist eine Aufgeschlossenheit nach außen und nach innen ([8], 106). Edith

Stein unterscheidet dabei zwischen Ich und Selbst. Das Ich bezeichnet sie in anderen Werken als Kern der Person ([9], 156-158) (als Herz, [1], 402), als Ort, von dem aus sich die Seele sammeln und Entscheidungen fällen kann ([8], 114). Das Selbst ist der ganze Mensch, also mit allen seinen leiblichseelischen Anlagen, die das Ich formen soll ([8], 111). Dabei zeigt sich der Einfluß eigener mystischer Erfahrungen und der Lektüre des Johannes des Kreuz ([1], 408). Als Bedingung der Möglichkeit, Entscheidungen zu fällen, zeigt sich nach Edith Stein die intellektuelle Erkenntnis, also die Tätigkeit des Verstandes. Bei der Entscheidung kommt auch die Tätigkeit des Willens dazu ([8], 108-109).

2. Die Geistigkeit des Menschen zeigt sich auch in der freien Wahl des Tuns, also in ihrer Möglichkeit ([8], 106-107). Diese Wahl zeigt sich darin, daß die freien Akte aus einem Vorsatz hervorgehen können und durch einen Entschluß und Befehl eingeleitet werden müssen ([10, 52]). Die Wahl des Tuns ist auch durch die Motivation beeinflußt, die Edith Stein als „ein Sinn- und Kraftvolles (...) zu einem sinn- und kraftvollen Verhalten" ([1], 403) bezeichnet. Die Motivation selbst bestimmt Edith Stein als Grundgesetz des geistigen Lebens. Die Motivation zielt auf das Ich, das einen Akt vollzieht, weil es den anderen Akt vollzogen hat ([10], 34-42). Dabei setzt Edith Stein voraus, daß es keine Wahrnehmung des Subjekts ohne seine Aktivität gibt. Edith Stein hebt die Wichtigkeit der Erkenntnis für die Möglichkeit der freien Entscheidung besonders in ihrem Manuskript *Potenz und Akt* hervor. Nur durch „intelligere" kann man nämlich sich selbst und andere in Bewegung setzen ([11], 133).

3. Die Verantwortung ist auch durch das „Sollen" mitbedingt, das sich in einem Ruf im Innersten des Menschen zeigt ([8], 107), also im Gewissen. Das Gewissen charakterisiert Edith Stein als Leistung des Verstandes, also als Erkenntnis, zu dem sich auch eine Wertschätzung, ein Wunsch und ein Willensentschluß gesellt, die zusammmen die Motivation zu einem Tun ausmachen ([8], 120). Nur durch die Möglichkeit des Sollens ist die Möglichkeit gewahrleistet, sich Ziele zu setzten und zu verfolgen ([8], 107). Edith Stein dabei beschreibt eher die eigenen Wahrnemungen über das Verlauf der ethischen Entscheidungen, und sie sucht nicht die adäquate theoretische Erklärung und Begründung der ethischen Normen.

Einen ähnlichen Zugang zur Freiheit des Menschen aus der Verantwortung versucht Václav Havel. Er ist dazu von seiner existentiellen Erfahrung angeleitet worden, wo er aus dem Untersuchungshaft ein Entlassungsgesuch an die Staatsanwalt geschrieben hat. In ihm schrieb er alles so, wie er es sich ausdachte, wo er nicht alle seine Intentionen beschrieben hat. Er übersah, daß die Wahrheit nicht nur das ist, was gesagt wird, sondern auch unter welchen Umständen. Das, was er in diesem Gesuch geschrieben hat, war dann „politisch verwendet", also für die Propagation der bürgerlichen Freiheit in der damaligen ÈSSR. Havel war davon innerlich beunruhigt und er hat bemerkt, daß er nicht in der Wahrheit gelebt hat. In seinen Briefen an Olga, wo er darüber reflektiert hatte, schrieb er seine Gedanken zur Freiheit und zur Identität des Menschen, die ihm aus der Verantwortung für sein Tun zukommt. Für Havel ist die Verantwortung sogar eine notwendige Bedingung der Kontinuität und damit Identität der menschlichen Person, oder, wie er selber schrieb, des „Ich" (vgl. [12], List. Nr. 138, Nr. 139, 339-342, [13], Brief Nr. 138 und 139, 282-291, [14], 28-29). Der Unterschied zwischen Edith Stein und Havel besteht darin, daß Edith Stein zur Verantwortung aus der Umgangsprache kommt, während Havel aus der eigenen existentiellen Erfahrung.

Auch E. Lévinas bestimmt die Freiheit des Subjekts in der Verantwortung, die der Freiheit zugrundeliegt. Im Unterschied zu Edith Stein geht es bei Lévinas nicht um die Verantwortung für sich selbst, sondern um die Verantwortung für den Anderen: „Ich bin vorgeladen ohne Möglichkeit des Einspruchs, heimatlos, schon an mich selbst zurückverwiesen, aber ohne dort Halt finden zu können – genötigt, bevor ich beginne. Nichts, was dem Selbstbewußtsein glückt, etwas das nur Sinn hat als überraschendes Auftauchen einer Verantwortung in mir, dem Engagement zuvor, das heißt einer Verantwortung für den Anderen. Darin bin ich Einer und unersetzbar – Einer als unersetzbar in der Verantwortung" ([15], 229). Die Verantwortung bestätigt nach Lévinas die Einzigkeit des Ich: „Die Einzigkeit des Ich, das ist die Tatsache, daß niemand an meiner Stelle antworten und verantwortlich sein kann" ([16], 43). Lévinas begründet die Verantwortung ähnlich wie Edith Stein auf der uns von Gott zukommenden Verpflichtung ([17], 21).

2. VON DER AKTUELLEN SEELENTÄTIGKEIT

Einen weiteren Zugang zum Problem der Freiheit stellt der operative Zugang von der aktuellen Seelentätigkeit her. Der operative Zugang bedeutet, daß er von einer Tätigkeit des Menschen ausgeht, die der Mensch faktisch täglich ausübt, die man also nicht leugnen kann. Die aktuelle Seelentätigkeit besteht im bewußten Empfinden und in den verschiedenen freien Taten des Ich, wie z.B. ein Fragen, Bitten, Befehlen, Gehorchen. Die aktuelle Seelentätigkeit ist getragen von der potentiellen Seelentätigkeit als ihrem Grund. Der Grund dieser Tätigkeit ist die Seele, deren Wesen darin besteht, die Einflüsse von außen aufzunehmen, zu bearbeiten und frei davon Entscheidungen zu treffen. Dabei wird der eigene Leib als Werkzeug gebraucht ([1], 342-345). Die Seele vergleicht Edith Stein mit Teresia von Avila mit der inneren Burg, „worin das Ich sich frei bewegen kann, bald nach außen gehend, bald sich mehr ins Innere zurückziehend." ([1], 345). Das Ich „wohnt" im Leib und in der Seele. Das Wesen der Seele versteht Edith

Stein als das Innerste im Menschen, als den Kern, die Substanz der Seele, vo der aus die Erkenntnis, aber auch die Entscheidungen ausgehen. Darum identifiziert Edith Stein Kern und Seele ([11], 275f.). Den Zugang zur Seele findet Edith Stein durch das Ichleben, besonders durch die Selbstwahrnehmung und innere Wahrnehmung ([1], 347). Edith Stein ist dabei von der Phänomenologie Husserl beeinflußt, der auch oft von der inneren Wahrnehmung ausgeht. Die Freiheit erreicht auf diesem Weg bestimmt sie als die freie Bestimmung des eigenen Lebens ([1], 347).

3. VON DER SELBSTERKENNTNIS

Den dritten Zugang zur Freiheit bei Edith Stein kann man in ihrem Ausgang von der Sich-Erkenntnis und dem bewußten Sich-Gegenübertreten finden. Dadurch wird der Mensch zuerst sich selber bewußt und dann auch dem anderen gegenüber offen ([11], 267). Edith Stein geht dabei von der Tätigkeit des menschlichen Geistes aus (Sich-Erkenntnis) und untersucht die Bedingungen ihrer Möglichkeit. Als entscheidend zeigt sich dabei die Intentionalität des Geistes. Bei der Intentionalität ist der Geist nämlich auf etwas außer ihm Liegendes ausgerichtet. Dadurch kann der Mensch das andere erkennen, wohin er mit seinem Tun eingreifen kann. Auf der Erkenntnis aufbauend ist auch die Entscheidungsmöglichkeit gegeben. Das Zentrum, von dem die Erkenntnis und die Entscheidung ausgeht, ist das Ich. Die Freiheit bedeutet dann, der Herr über sich zu sein ([11], 267-268, [1], 347). Das bedeutet, daß man dem eigenen Tun die Richtung geben kann, daß man etwas unterlassen oder ausführen kann. Es geht dabei um die ontologische Freiheit, die die freie Handlung des Menschen ermöglicht. Ohne der Möglichkeit der Wahl der Handlung wäre keine Freiheit möglich. Wenn der Mensch wirklich Herr über sich selbst ist, dann realisiert er diese Möglichkeit, und nach Edith Stein geht er zu einem höheren Seinsmodus über. Dann wächst sein Seinsmodus, weil er sich für das Gute entschieden hat ([11], 367). Hier beschreibt Edith Stein die moralische Freiheit. Bei diesen Überlegungen ist Edith Stein oft auch vom Glauben beeinflußt. Hier muß man an ihre Bestimmung des Verhältnisses zwischen Philosophie und Glaube denken und alles von dort her erklären. Nach Edith Stein erreicht der Mensch die höchste Freiheit, wenn er sich Gott und seiner Gnade erschließt ([11], 432). Dabei bleibt immer die moralische Freiheit, sich dem Guten zu erschließen oder zu verschließen. Dazu muß man zuerst das Gute erkennen. Das Gute kann man nach Edith Stein als Gut erkennen und danach erstreben. Beim bewußten Streben ist das Erkennen des Guten sogar die Voraussetzung des Strebens danach ([1], 290). Obwohl jedes Seiende gut ist, ist es nicht ein Gut für das anderen Seiende. Nur das höchste Gut, also Gott, ist ein Gut für alle andere Seienden. Die anderen Seinden sind ein Gut für andere Seienden, nur insofern sie ihnen Vollkomenheit verleihen ([1], 293-294). Edith Stein unterscheidet dadurch zwischen der ontologischen Gutheit, die jedem Seienden zukommt, und der moralischen Gutheit, die zur Vervollkommung des Seienden dient. Die ontologische Gutheit gehört zu den transzendentalen Bestimmungen des Seienden, die jedem Seienden zukommen.

III. DIE ERKENNTNIS ALS VORAUSSETZUNG DER FREIHEIT

Wie ich schon gesagt habe, gilt auch für Edith Stein, daß ohne Erkenntnis keine Freiheit möglich ist. Die Erkenntnis wird nach ihr wiederum durch den Sinnzusammenhang der Wirklichkeit ermöglicht ([1], 310), das man als *a priori*, als Bedingung der Möglichkeit der Erkenntnis fassen kann. Diesen Sinnzusammenhang erklärt Edith Stein als Gottes Ideen von der Welt ([1], 310). Bei der näheren Erörterung dieses Problems erklärt sie diese Ideen als Wesenheiten oder reine Formen ([1], 217). In den reinen Formen sind alle Einzelzüge und Möglichkeiten der Gestaltung der wirklichen oder dichterischen Gestalten beschlossen ([1], 155). Die reinen Formen kann man als Raumgestalten oder Zeitgestalten verstehen ([1], 152). Edith Stein drückt damit den Gedanken aus, den auch Thomas von Aquin ausspricht, nämlich, daß in Gott sich die Ideen der Dinge finden ([12], q.3, a.2, c), aber sie drückt es auf eigene Weise aus und mit der Benutzung der Terminologie von Husserl. Der Sinnzusammenhang der Wirklichkeit ist wiederum durch eine bestimmte Struktur des sinnlichen Materials, die Edith Stein als Kategorien bestimmt, und durch die Gegenstandsauffassung, also durch die Gesetzlichkeit, die die Konstitution des Gegenstandes im Bewußtsein bestimmt, ermöglicht. In der Auseinandersetzung mit Kant bestimmt Edith Stein die Kategorien als durch eine subjektive und eine objektive Deduktion erwiesen. Edith Stein bezeichnet die objektive Deduktion als „Bedingungen der Erfahrungsgegenstände" und die subjektive Deduktion als „Bedingungen möglicher Erfahrung" ([9], 109). Nach Edith Stein hat Husserl die subjektive Deduktion mit der objektiven vermischt und deshalb die Kategorien nur als rein formale Funktionen des Subjektes angesehen. Im Unterschied zu Kant begründet Edith Stein die Kategorien als logische und zugleich auch als ontologische Formen. Als logische Formen haben die Kategorien die Bedeutung von Aussageweisen und als ontologische die von Seinsweisen ([1], 196).

Diese Kritik Edith Steins an Kant zeigt sich als berechtigt, weil Kant wirklich die subjektive Deduktion mit der objektiven Deduktion vermischt, z.B. in diesem Argument: „Die Bedingungen a priori einer möglichen Erfahrung überhaupt sind zugleich Bedingungen der Möglichkeit der Gegenstände der Erfahrung" ([13], A 111).

Die Erkenntis zeigt sich bei Edith Stein als eine hinreichende, aber nicht genügende Bedingung der Freiheit des Menschen. Dazu muß noch die freie Entscheidung kommen, wie sie es über Gott und den Menschen bestimmt: „Vernunft und Freiheit sind aber die Wesensmerkmale der Person" ([1], 317). Die volle moralische Freiheit erlangt der Mensch, wenn er den Plan Gottes mit ihm verwirklicht, der in der Vereinigung mit Gott gipfelt ([1], 462f.).

IV. DER ZUGANG ZU GOTT

Wenn man zu Gott kommen will, muß man ihn zuerst erkennen. Edith Stein sucht die Gotteserkenntnis auch philosophisch zu begründen. Dafür findet sie zwei grundsätzliche Wege:

1. Den augustinischen Weg zu Gott aus dem Innenleben der Seele. Im Innenleben des Bewußtseins zeigt sich die Gewißheit des eigenen Ich ([1], 36). Der Ausgang dieses Weges gleicht dem Husserlschen Ansatz seiner phänomenologischen Methode und ähnelt der Analyse des Augustins. Von dort aus beginnt Edith Stein das eigene Sein phänomenologisch zu untersuchen. In ihren phänomenologischen Analysen des eigenen Seins im Bewußtsein kann man fünf Wege zum ewigen Sein finden. Sie selbst bezeichnet sie als verschiedene Möglichkeiten, die uns die Idee des reinen Seins enthüllen. a) Der erste Weg besteht darin, daß das Ich von der Eigentümlichkeit seines von Augenblick zu Augenblick gefristeten Seins her zur Idee des ewigen Seins gelangen kann ([1], 53-54). b) Der zweite Weg geht davon aus, daß das eigene Ich Potentialität zum künftigen aktuellen Sein zeigt, die nur von einer ewigen Aktualität getragen werden kann – vom actus purus, von Gott ([1], 40). c) Der dritte Weg steigt von der Beobachtung der Grade des Seins zur Idee der Fülle des Seins auf ([1], 54). Dieser Weg ist den Gottesbeweisen von Thomas formal ähnlich und inhaltlich ist er dem vierten Weg aus den Seinsstufen am nächsten. d) Auf dem vierten Weg findet sie Gott als Quelle des Lebens und des eigenen Seins, das ins Dasein geworfen ist ([1], 52). e) Der fünfte Weg geht aus der Angst des Ich vor dem eigenen Nichtsein aus, die aber in der Entdeckung des ewigen Seins überwunden wird ([1], 56).

2. Den aristotelisch-thomanischen Weg zu Gott aus der Natur, aus der Objektwelt. Auf diesem Weg findet sie die metaphysische Struktur der endlichen Seienden und ihre verschiedene Stufen. Dadurch kommt sie zu Gott als dem Urbild der geschaffenen Welt ([1], 310). In ihm sind die Urbilder aller Dinge als Wesenheiten, als reine Formen ([1], 316). Die Seele ist der

Lebenssteigerung fähig, und der Glaube lehrt uns nach Edith Stein, wie man dazu kommen kann. Der Mensch ist nach dem Glauben zum ewigen Leben berufen ([1], 461). Dadurch wird nach ihr Gott als Garant der vollen Freiheit des Menschen, weil er das beste für den Menschen will, erwiesen. Dieser Erweis ist aber theologisch, aufgrund des Glaubens. Hier benutzt Edith Stein den Glauben nicht nur als Hypothese, sondern auch als Beweismittel, als Erkenntnisquelle.

ZUSAMMENFASSUNG

Edith Steins Begründung der Freiheit des Menschen ist sicher interessant und in vielen Teilen auch überzeugend. Ihr Zugang zur Freiheit aus der Verantwortung ist ähnlich wie bei Havel und Lévinas. Ihre Gedankenführungen wurden durch ihren Meister Husserl, aber auch von Thomas von Aquin und anderen Philosophen, zum Teil auch durch eigene religiöse und mystische Erfahrungen beeinflußt.

Manchmal ist sie selber nicht methodich sauber geblieben, wenn sie z.B. theologische Erwägungen und Begründungen in die philosophische Untersuchungen hineinnimmt. Auch ihre philosophische Anthropologie ist von ihrer Bestimmung des Verhältnisses von Philosophie und Theologie gekennzeichnet, wo sie auch Offenbarung in der Philosophie als Erkenntnisquelle benutzt. Dem kann man nur bedingt zustimmen, also nur in dem Sinne, wenn man Offenbarungswahrheiten nur als Hypothesen annimmt, z.B. für die Untersuchung der Transsubstantiation.

LITERATUR:

1. Stein, E.: *Endliches und Ewiges Sein. Versuch einer Aufstieges zum Sinn des Seins*. Freiburg im Br., Herder, 1986³ (1950¹, geschrieben 1936, Edith Steins Werke II).

2. Stein, E.: *Husserls Phänomenologie und die Philosophie des hl. Thomas von Aquino. Festschrift Edmund Husserl zum 70. Geburtstag gewidmet*. In: Jahrbuch für Philosophie und phänomenologische Forschung, Ergänzungsheft, 1929, 315-338. Nachdruck in: Husserl, E.: *Wege der Forschung*, Bd. XL, hg. von H. Noack. Darmstadt, Wissenschaftliche Buchgesellschaft, 1973, 61-86.

3. Lembeck, K.-H.: *Glaube im Wissen? Zur aporetischen Grundstruktur der Spätphilosophie Edith Steins*. In: Herbstrith, W. (Hrsg.): *Denken im Dialog. Zur Philosophie Edith Steins.*Tübingen, Attempto, 1991, 156-175.

4. Stallmach, J.: *Das Werk Edith Steins im Spannungsfeld vom Wissen und Glauben*. In: In: Herbstrith, W. (Hrsg.): *Denken im Dialog. Zur Philosophie Edith Steins*. Tübingen, Attempto, 1991, s. 142-155.

5. Husserl, E.: *Ideen zu einer reinen Phänomenologie und phänomenologischen Philosophie*. Erstes Buch: *Allgemeine Einführung in die reine Phänomenologie*. Zwei Teile. Neu hrsg. von Karl Schuhmann. The Hague, Martinus Nijhoff 1976 (Husserliana III/1, III/2).

6. Husserl, E.: *Logische Untersuchungen*. Zweiter Band: *Untersuchungen zur Phänomenologie und Theorie der Erkenntnis*. Text der 1. und der 2. Aufl. mit Ergänzungen. Erster und zweiter Teil. Hrsg. und eingeleitet von Ursula Panzer. The Hague, Martinus Nijhoff, 1984 (Husserliana XIX/1, XIX/2).

7. Kern, I.: *Husserl und Kant. Eine Untersuchung über Husserls Verhältnis zu Kant und dem Neukantianismus*. The Hague, Martinus Nijhoff, 1964 (Phaenomenologica 16).

8. Stein, E.: *Der Aufbau der menschlichen Person*. Freiburg im Br., Herder, 1994. (Geschrieben 1932/33, Edith Steins Werke XVI).

9. Stein, E.: *Einführung in die Philosophie*. Freiburg im Br., Herder, 1991. (Geschrieben zwischen 1917-1932, Edith Steins Werke XIII).

10. Stein, E.: *Beiträge zur philosophischen Begründung der Psychologie und Geisteswissenschaften*. In: Jahrbuch für Philosophie und phänomenologische Forschung, Band V, 1922, 1-283. Nachdruck: Tübingen, Max Niemeyer, 1970.

11. Stein, E.: *Potenz und Akt. Studien zu einer Philosophie des Seins*. Unveröffentliches Manuskript (1931). Original imn Edith Stein Archiv Köln, Kopie, von mir benutzt, in der Bayerischen Staatsbibliothek München, Conrad-Martusiana F, I, 2, Maschinenschrift.

12. von Aquin, Thomas: *Quaestiones disputatae, T. I, De veritate*. Torino-Roma, Ed. Marietti, 1964.

13. Kant, I.: *Kritik der reinen Vernunft*. Nach der 1. und 2. Auflage hrsg. von Raymond Schmidt. Hamburg, Meiner 1990³.

LESZEK PYRA
Agricultural Academy in Cracow
Poland

A MAN IN DIALOGUE WITH HIMSELF AND OTHERS IN REINHOLD NIEBUHR'S INTERPRETATION

For Niebuhr the starting-point for discussion of a uniqueness of man is the oldest statement – which has quite a long tradition – that a man was made by God "after his image and in his likeness". This statement allowing the anthropological conclusions of the ancien philosophers (stressing the importance of reason and memory) tries to establish the way forward because – according to the American author – stresses the importance of human freedom, which cannot be questioned if a man is to resemble God (to a certain degree at least).

Niebuhr is strongly convinced that the Hebraic thought dominates the Hellenic one particularly when it accentuates the depth and and uniqueness of personality, showing at the same time the kinds of dialogue in which a man engages: in particular a dialogue with himself and the others. These two kinds of dialogues will be discussed below.

I. THE INNER DIALOGUE

The dialogue of man with himself, the so-called inner dialogue is, according to the author, almost an empirical fact. Personally, I think that the logical empiricism which would include it into metaphysics and behaviourism would certainly do the same, but at the same time each branch of psychology allowing introspective methods is inclined to accept the existence of the before mentioned phenomenon. According to the author, it is the empirical fact in the sense that every penetrating man must admit that such a dialogue, not necessarily characterised by the appearance of any external symptoms, leads with himself from time to time[1].

However, I doubt whether Niebuhr is right when saying that the inner dialogue is a much better proof of man's freedom than reason. Perhaps Niebuhr thinks about a situation when such a dialogue gives a man a possibility of taking different viewpoints (aspects of dialogue) whereas reason seems to fulfill only the cognitive function, the function of objectivization and unification of the reality which is actually being examined.

The dialogue has different aspects. A man engaged in it approves of his acting or dissaproves of it, is glad of himself or not, complains of himself or accuses himself of something, and his reason helps him in it. The notion "dialogue" brings to mind the engagement of the two sides and, according to Niebuhr, one of them is "I" appearing as subject and the other is "I" appearing as object at which personality looks as if from outside, as object about which personality thinks. However, in connection with the above mentioned Niebuhr's understanding of the dialogue there appear some doubts if one can sensibly talk about the dialogue of "subjective" with "objective" sphere. It certainly depends on the assumption accepted by a given thinker, for example: Martin Buber does not accept the existence of such inner dialogue.

According to Niebuhr the great mistake of the hitherto-existing philosophy has been the identifying of personality appearing in subjective aspect with the mind (e.g. Cartesian "res cogitans"), whereas personality appearing in the objective aspect has been often identified with a body or with some unidentified psychophysical unity. In this way Western philosophy has blocked itself the way to the philosophy of dialogue, which the Judeo-Christian tradition has not. Writing about inner dialogue the author does not think about the appearance of the "two personalities" in a man. He is interested in a man who is fully mentally healthy and therefore disregards all these pathological cases in which there appears the dissociation of personality as in case of schizophrenia or somnambulism, when there appear two personalities not knowing about each other. Mentally healthy personality engaged in dialogue reaims one and the same personality disregarding of how often it engages itself in dialogue. The American thinker distinguishes different levels of inner dialogue. Sometimes it is a dialogue of personality on which a burden of responsibility for something is placed with a personality which observes whether it meets an obligation. Sometimes it is a dialogue of a personality tempted by need of an immediate satisfaction of a desire with personality which tries to give up immediate satisfaction in the name of fulfillment of some distant plans. And at last it may be a dialogue

---

[1] Reinhold Niebuhr, *The Self and the Dramas of History*, London 1956, p. 16.

between "two personalities" trying to remain loyal to two sides of a conflict; in such case loyalty to one side excludes loyalty to the other side.

The author rightly notices that the inner dialogue is often used by artists – particularly writers – who use it because in such a way it is much easier to present the truth about a given man than by reporting the dialogue with others or the description of behaviour of a given hero. The author describing the inner dialogue of a man whom he met and knew in the past should not claim that he wholly understood his inner dialogue because he describes his experiences on the basis of an analogy to his own inner dialogical experiences and such analogy may only be similar but never the same. Besides, not all inner tendencies may be detected, because most often only these tendencies are manifested which actually have won and which manifest themselves in definite actions or in giving up of such actions.

I think that Niebuhr should have emphasized that such given up actions should be revealed in inner dialogue, most probably to the closest persons (not necessarily relatives); it is obviously possible only in such case when a man is fully conscious of such tendencies. The author however does not take such motifs up and then states that personality remains a mysery even to the closest friend "because so little is known about the strategams which produced the victory of the one over the other force"[2]. It is really very difficult not to agree with such a statement. We truly do not know not only our relatives but also ourselves. But Niebuhr's conciderations should be completed, because not only forces appearing in a man are unknown or not fully self-realised but the same refers to the mechanism contributing to the victory of the one over the other. It is well understood by psychoanalysis, particularly Freudian and its cognitive value is not questioned by Niebuhr because Freud's conciderations affirm some of his own remarks referring to inner dialogue.

It is certainly a great merit of the depth psychology that it payed attention to the fact that the inner structure of personality is much more complicated than it was thought of at the beginning of the twentieth century. Subsequently the division of personality into id, ego and superego refers, according to Niebuhr, to two kinds of dialogue: between ego and id (inner dialogue) and between ego and superego (the dialogue with others); in consequence it may leave lasting signs in human psyche[3].

---

[2] Ibidem, p. 19.

[3] *The Dictionary of Foreign Terms* accepts the understanding of the notion "dialogue" as a conversation of two or more persons. Therefore we can assume that although in the Freudian theory of personality there appear three components making it possible to talk about dialogue; regardlessly we deal in such a situation with the two pairs engaged in two separate dialogues: id – ego and ego – superego. *Słownik wyrazów obcych*, ed. Jan Tokarski, Warszawa 1980, p. 151.

According to the American author Freud's theory has also faults and the greatest of it seems to be refusing a man a right to freedom. The Freudian man is limited by neurotical anxieties which are the result of negative influence of social repressions especially in regard to the claims of "id". Although the protestant thinker appreciates cognitive and particularly therapeutic value of Freudism he accuses the man from Vienna that he subjugated the two other spheres of personality to ego, as if he thought that personality was ego first of all whereas in fact personality comprises all three spheres as relatively independent entities. Such a mistake made it extremely difficult to understand the inner dialogue which is led among all of the parties concerned: id, ego and superego. The redeformation of the real state of things is the identifying of superego with social pressure whereas in reality it is – at least Niebuhr thinks so – the autonomous part of personality.

Freud seems also not to notice that personality is able to resist social pressure, giving up an occasion of achieving immediate personal profits, in order to realize values higher than those demanded by society. On the other hand Freud seems to be aware that a man is only in a small degree susceptible to the influence of social pressure and therefore the society is unable to bring it up in such a way that he could be useful to it in the highest degree[4]. Besides, there is much aggression in a human being which cannot be fully controlled by society.

Niebuhr agrees with Freud that by no means can conflicts be eliminated from human life. However in his opinion the creator of psychoanalysis fails completely when he begins to wonder how to use his theory in therapy of greater social groups. The American author does not hide his sarcasm writing the following words: "Thus a discipline, which has proved itself therapeutically effective in dealing with pathological states of individuals, has been betrayed into the insanity of speculating whether the Germans, Russians, and Japanese could be cured of their 'aggressiveness' by a sufficiently wide application of psycho-therapy"[5].

Referring to the opinion of Ernst Jones expressed in the book "Life and Work of Sigmund Freud"[6] the theologian states, not without some satisfaction, that psychoanalysis happens to fail in some respects. Freud himself came to such a conclusion surprised when hearing too often from his patients about incest committed in their youth. Enquiring about the causes of anxiety neurosis Freud thought at the beginning that they were results of traumatic sexual experiences of his patients' youth, later on however he

---

[4] Niebuhr, op. cit. The author refers first of all to Freud's work – *Das Unbehangen in der Kultur*, Wien 1930.

[5] Niebuhr, op. cit., p. 22.

[6] Cited after Niebuhr, ibidem.

became convinced that the reports of the patients were only their invention and as such only their unrealised wishes. And so in such cases psychoanalitical examinations proved to be a failure. And whereafter the convincing of the patients of a need to cooperate with a psychoanalyst testifies unanimously against the fact that psychotherapy can be used under constraint and brings at the same time in relief the existence and meaning of human freedom. His conciderations about the relation of inner dialogue to psychoanalysis Niebuhr ends with a statement that within the area of psychoanalysis one can talk about such dialogue because certain psychoanalytical assumptions – particularly the division of personality into particular parts and their mutual interference – make it possible to construct such a theory, but in no way can the dialogue with others be explained on their basis[7].

In the next section of his conciderations the author discusses one of the aspects of dialogue connected with the mutual relation of conscience and will which both constitute two levels of transcendence of a person. The will is according to him "the result of the self's transcendence over the complex of its impulses and desires"[8]. It can be also defined as the self integrated to achieve short-range or long-range purposes. The will, similarly to reason, is operative on all levels, which means that in case of hierarchy of aims it encompasses all of them. The reason however, which is helpful in the evaluation of aims, is treated by personality in an instrumental way because the final decision certainly depends on personality.

When conscience is concidered the author disavows a common belief that every self-criticism of personality gives evidence of its activity. It may happen that even if a person accuses itself it may do it from the point of view of its own interests, accusing itself for example of too much benevolence and too extreme self-sacrifice.

The conscience is defined as a particular activity of personality, namely such in which it evaluates its own desires and behaviour, whereas about the conscience one can talk only when the duty the person is obliged to fulfill does not coincide with its inclinations, when it feels an internal imperative to behave in a way which does not coincide with its own desires.

According to the author the contents of conscience changes according to place and time although there exist certain ethical norms which seem to be pretty universal, for example forbidding killing people, stealing. However he does not claim that they are universal in absolute sense.

One should nevertheless be aware of the fact that this relative universality of the so called elementary moral norms serves the Christian apologist to prove that a personality has in its essential nature deeply encoded intui-

---

[7] Op. cit., p. 20-23.
[8] Op. cit., p. 24.

tions about good and evil. We should appreciate a certain progressiveness of the author whose viewpoint in this respect is much more up-to-date than the viewpoints of many other Christian thinkers, claiming that into human nature there was written "unchangeable moral law". The contents of conscience is – according to him – changeable to a certain extent, thanks to a great social influence upon the genesis of moral norms. A man is first of all the creature of God, but a historical and social creature as well. As such he undertakes no moral decisions in vacuum: numerous moral obligations are put upon him by society.

The author evaluates conscience much higher than reason because he thinks that reason contributes to the augmentation of good in the world whereas reason, trying to look objectively at the relation of one human being to other human beings, increases egoistic inclinations in man, making a human being more greedy.

I think that Niebuhr is not right when he says that man's reflection in regard to his own behaviour contributes to such modification of it that a man cares more about his own interests. He would be right if men would love their neighbours by means of the love "agape" and would therefore easily forget about their own needs. But it is certainly not so and I am inclined to think that it is quite opposite, that when a man looks at oneself and the others from some wider perspective he is more inclined to notice the needs of his neighbours, at least to a certain extent. The foregoing opinion is – in comparison to Niebuhr's views – much more strongly grounded in the tradition of rationalism, it refers to the views of Hume, Hobbes and Helvetius. Such thinkers claimed that human egoistic inclinations were primary to the influence of civilization. If one takes this tradition into concideration the Niebuhrian criticism of reason, conceived within the area of ethics, is rather weak.

Better well-founded seems to be the other of Niebuhr's accusation of reason and its role played in expansion of a desire for more money, power, possessions etc., than one needs. There is no doubt that human interests, different desires, ambitions and also fears show a tendency to increase, and it is just reason which causes this and which tries to change actual situation because it is able to imagine a far better way of satisfying all its needs. It is worthy of mentioning that the author ascribes this capacity of expanding not only to men but also to groups and whole societies.

To support his own discussions concerning inner dialogue Niebuhr refers not only to psychoanalysis but also pays attention to the fact that such a dialogue was on numerous occasions described in the autobiographical memoirs of different people who – what should be underlined – were neither writers nor scholars and this, claims Niebuhr, even more supports the existence of such dialogue. The author reminds the reader the autobiographical memoirs of the actress – Lucy Sprague Mitchell and the airman – Charles Lindbergh. According to Niebuhr such memoirs show the complexity of personality and prove undoubtedly the existence of inner dialogue; at the same time they seem to be superiour to many anthropological theories of numerous scholars, who either did not want to see – or were unable to notice the existence of such a phenomenon. Particularly valuable are the memoirs of Ch. Lindbergh because they show a man as consisting of three components: body, mind and spirit and stress their interdependence and mutual influence[9]. It is certainly worthy of notice that Niebuhr identifies the mind (after Lindbergh) with reason whereas spirit is supposed to be superior to other parts of personality, it is supposed to be personality itself or the will itself, the will which tries to control all actual needs; nevertheless it is not completely free because it is entangled both body and mind.

I think that this division pays attention to something very essential, namely: giving up a very simplified concept of a man as consisting of dualistic division into body and mind it underlines the higher level of its organization stressing well the fact that not only impulses determine the behaviour of man, and not only reason itself, but something that is their resultant, which adds in a man thus creating personality itself and what the author would willingly identify with the will, simplifying however the whole problem.

According to the author, a man is the only being leading continuous dialogue with himself. I am ready to polemize with this statement. Even if we assume that such dialogue exists it is very difficult to admit that it is continuous: there seem to be moments in the life of each man when he does not lead any dialogue at all.

II. THE DIALOGUE WITH OTHERS

The author many times stresses the fact that the personality engaged in dialogue with others is aware of its dependence on them but is also aware of its ability to oppose them. This dialogue initiates something called "dramatic actions". It is based on constant (within the limits of time and space of biological lasting of a given human being) or only temporary relations with others. The personality engaged in the dialogue with others, the so called external dialogue, meets certain "invariable conditions of self-fulfillment and self-giving"[10]. They are as follows:

a) Personality detects a mystery in the other which she can never fully understand. By way of analogy to its own dialogue it may try to guess what

---

[9] Charles A. Lindbergh, *The Spirit of St. Louis*, New York 1953, p. 353.
[10] Niebuhr, op. cit., p. 42.

his neighbour's psychical processes are but this method of knowing the other may be deceptive because only the forms of inner dialogue may be similar whereas the contents quite different.

b) Mutual love is not enough to sustain even the closest relationship for a longer period. In this respect something more is needed, first to initiate and then to sustain mutuality. This "something more" means in fact noncalculating, sacrificial love "agape". Without such love every relationship is going to disappear sooner or later, claims Niebuhr.

c) Personality treats the other as a means to achieve its own aims.

d) A man recognizes the other as a limit to its own expansiveness. It becomes aware that it cannot fully penetrate the other and its mystery, that there should be some amount of reserve between the two individuals.

e) The uniqueness of persons makes each particular relationship something quite unique although its basis may be of quite common, general character, e.g. heterosexuality. Subsequently each marriage is based on such common ground but still it is something quite original, unique.

f) Personality is "open" to others and it means that it is not limited by any spatial or time limits.

g) Some historical factors definitely condition the pattern of particular dialogues. For example: the old patriarchal model of a family changed during the last decades as to give a woman more freedom and independence than she had, let us say – fifty years ago. Also the relation of children to parents evolved from a high degree of obedience (on children's behalf) to a great amount of partnership.

Recapitulating this section I would like to add up some remarks referring to some of the foregoing points. In reference to the condition "c" it should be noticed that nature invented a mechanism of "falling in love" in order to take care not so much of individuals but rather of human race and therefore one should not be astonished by the fact that love has a tendency to disappear. That is why so many moral philosophers underline the importance of a friendship between a husband and a wife and the importance of sharing certain common hobbies (interests) which strengthen the relationship of a given marriage.

As far as condition "f" is concerned I think that the author should have underlined the role played in such kind of dialogue by imaginatio very important when the dialogue is led with those not present (e.g. absent lover), but unfortunately he does not mention it at all.

The concept of the external dialogue is extended by Niebuhr in the direction of the dialogue of personality with society. This dialogue, which can be called "external social dialogue" has two dimensions: vertical and horizontal. The dialogue in its vertical dimension is in turn divided into the dialogue in which personality looks at society from below and one in which it looks at society from above. The dialogue from "below" means that a person refers to society as to something which is the complement and enrichment of its individual life by values which cannot be supplied by any individual man. It refers to the satisfaction of various material needs, but also to those having psychical and moral nature.

The dialogue from "above" means that personality feels it is better than society because its personal moral ideals exceed those of the society. In comparison to a person a society is much more strongly connected with nature and because it does not hope for eternal life it strives desperately for survival. Niebuhr is convinced that the aims to which a person and a society tend are divergent and they never overlap, even in the most democratic societies. At this point once again comes into prominence the author's pessimism expressing itself in the deepest conviction as to the impossibility of getting rid of the tension between social and individual strivings. The above mentioned tension influences conscience to a great degree, the conscience which the philosophical tradition often understood as an indication of inherent moral sense, the most typical in this respect being Shaftsbury's theory. Such theories are mistaken because they negate social influences on the decisions taken by individuals; unfortunately – according to the author – many thinkers claim something opposite, preferring the so called collective conscience theory, according to which conscience is nothing more and nothing less than the result of social influence over individual. In reality the truth seems to lie in the middle – and the evaluations done by conscience are expressed in face of a tension of an ambivalent relation of an individual to a society, because society is its complement on the one hand, and the source of frustration on the other. Sometimes an individual who does not posess a high moral level is subdued to the positive influence of moral norms postulated by society; but it also happens that moral requirements of the society irritate an individual by their mediocrity and in such case it may oppose them, therefore shaking the sensibleness of all collective interpretations of conscience.

We deal with the external social dialogue in its horizontal dimension when the so-called society of primary loyalty happens to fall into conflict with another society. During intensive rivalry or open conflict between societies (war), an individual is inclined to accept as its own the pride and prestige of the society of which it is a member. It is worthy to mention that the pride and prestige constitute sometimes a compensation – of real or imagined only – lack of meaning of individual's life.

In reference to the above mentioned section of Niebuhrian considerations quite an important remark enters my head. Although the author does not formulate it explicitly in his views there is hidden an implicite formulation of a division into the dialogue led between an individual and a group and an individual and a society. Being fully conscious of the pluralistic structure of western societies he gives the reader to understand that particular individuals must define their position in society especially by supporting one of the parties participating in the rivalry for power. It appears unanimously that in such a situation they remain in a horizontal dimension of dialogue with regard to the other parties (groups). Niebuhr however does not analyse such a situation which means that he either does not notice such a possibility or does not attach much importance to it.

At last it seems that the author makes much of the dialogic, horizontal relation of man to his national community, which thanks to the integrating positive influence of geographic, ethnic and linguistic unity constitutes for an individual a very special community, a community of basic loyalty – with such a community a personality is inclined to lead a particularly frequent and vivid dialogue. I would add that in front of such community a man feels most free and able to develop all his potential abilities.

PAOLA PREMOLI DE MARCHI
Internationale Akademie für Philosophie
Fürstentum Liechtenstein

PHILOSOPHY OF FREEDOM IN DIETRICH VON HILDEBRAND:
Freedom as Related to Truth, Moral Goodness and Affectivity

I. THREE SPHERES OF HUMAN FREEDOM: FREEDOM AS "LORD OF ACTIONS", INDIRECT FREEDOM AND COOPERATIVE FREEDOM

Von Hildebrand published his first and more extensive analysis of human freedom in *Christian Ethics*, which is a keystone of the phenomenological-realist ethics. In this work Hildebrand introduces the notion of freedom as a mark of the human will, as Aristotle had already done in the *Nicomachean Ethics*. In *Christian Ethics* Hildebrand considers the will as that faculty which is the source of a particular kind of act, namely of that kind of volitional act which he calls the "volitional response".

1. THE VOLITIONAL RESPONSE

The volitional response is an intentional experience, namely a conscious and rational relation between the person and an object. Feeling tired is not an intentional experience, but only a state, whereas being happy about the visit of a friend is, because it presupposes a conscious relation with the fact which motivates happiness[1]. Only persons can have intentional experiences, because these presuppose a spiritual subject which is able to transcend his own instincts and immanent trends, and to pose a spiritual relation with an object, adequate to the object itself.

---

[1] *Christian Ethics*, New York 1952, p. 17. Although the German edition (*Ethik*, in *Dietrich von Hildebrand Gesammelte werke* II, Stuttgard 1973), contains some additions, I used the first American edition because the texts I quoted remained unaltered.

According to von Hildebrand, intentional experiences can involve all the three dimensions which characterize the human being: the theoretical, the volitional and the affective sphere. When the person not only apprehends an object, for example in taking cognizance of a political fact or in being affected by beautiful music, but is also motivated by it and gives it an answer, for example, with the choice of supporting a decision of the government or appreciating the quality of a musical performance, we have a special kind of intentional relation, which is the response. The response can be a) theoretical – when the answer is a cognitive act, directed to the object in its essence and existence (e.g. in conviction), b) volitional – when the person responds to the importance of the object with an act of will (i.e. the decision to do something), or c) affective – when the person responds to the importance of the object with his heart (e.g. with joy or sorrow).

In *Christian Ethics* von Hildebrand considers freedom primarily, although not solely, as related to the volitional response. Even though he admits that in a wider sense the will can be also extended to volitional responses which do not result in actions but remain immanent activities[2] and to affective responses (in contrast to the theoretical ones, which are not free, but engendered by the object which "moves" the intellect), he says that in a narrower sense of the word "the will means only that specific act, which grounds the action"[3]. According to this narrower meaning of willing, the proper object of volitional responses is constituted by the state of affairs, and by a specific kind of the state of affairs, namely, the not yet real, but realizable state of affairs[4].

---

[2] *Christian Ethics*, p. 343.

[3] *Christian Ethics*, [p. 210].

[4] In *Das Wesen der Liebe*, (Gesammelte Werke III, Regensburg 1971) von Hildebrand expresses in the clearest manner the definition of the will which he uses in *Christian Ethics* and in many of his other works: "Der Wille im positiven Sinn des Wortes ist immer auf einen noch nicht realen, aber realisierbaren Sachverhalt gerichtet. Ich kann nicht Dinge oder Personen wollen, sondern nur einen Tatbestand oder Sachverhalt. Ich will immer, daß etwas sei oder nicht sein. Wenn der Tatbestand aber schon real ist, kann er auch nicht mehr das Objekt meines Wollens werden. Andererseits muß der noch nicht realisierte Sachverhalt an sich realisierbar sein, um Objekt meines Willens zu werden. [...] Wir müssen aber noch weitergehen: Der Sachverhalt muß nicht nur an sich realisierbar sein, sondern er muß durch mich oder durch mein Mitwirken realisierbar sein." *Das Wesen der Liebe*, p. 66.

2. TWO PERFECTIONS OF FREE WILL

What is then the nature of the will as a faculty of the person? According to von Hildebrand, the will manifests itself in the volitional response as being endowed by two perfections.[5]

The first perfection of the will consists in the decision to give an answer to an object which, because of its importance, can motivate the person. This perfection implies two characters of the will: first, its intentionality, secondly, that the intentional relation is not necessitated, but free. According to von Hildebrand, if we deny the intentional character of the will, we fall into arbitrariness, but this but this means destruction of freedom as such.

3. CRITIQUE OF ARBITRARINESS

For the arbitrary deletes the will from the great dialogue between person and universe. It separates the will from the logos of being, and above all from the world of values. Willing would thus no longer be a position taken by man toward something, becoming a merely blind movement[6].

The will necessarily presupposes an object, which in itself is able to motivate in virtue of its importance: knowing the object, the person freely takes a stance toward it and, since the decision of the will originates from the spiritual center of the person, it constitutes a non-caused beginning, which cannot be destroyed by any external cause[7]. The first perfection of the will manifests this capacity of saying a free "yes" or "no" to the object, as well as its capacity of choosing between different motivating objects. For this reason, this is the deepest and most decisive dimension of freedom. Moreover, it manifests also the intrinsic relation between the volitional response and knowledge[8].

---

[5] "The volitional response, the act of willing in the strict sense of the term, possesses two outstanding perfections. It is first of all free, insofar as the spiritual center of the person can engender a free response to an object endowed with one or another kind of importance; secondly, it is capable of starting a new causal chain by freely initiating certain activities of our body and mind and by having the power to command them freely." *Christian Ethics*, p. 284. In the footnote von Hildebrand compares this with St. Thomas' distinction between *actus elicitus* and *actus imperatus* of the will, in S. Th., Ia-IIae, q. 6, a. 4.

[6] *Christian Ethics*, p. 290.

[7] In *Transformation in Christ,* Manchester 1990, p. 217:
"[freedom in the first dimension] is that of which no external power can rob us. Our range of power can be grievously restricted – by imprisonment, for instance, or bodily diseases like a paralysis of our limbs or a loss of our power of speech. Yet, no outward force nor any bodily ailment can ever take from us the capacity for the right response to value".

[8] This relation between the will and freedom has been recognized by classical philosophy. St. Thomas, for example, expresses it in his *Summa Theologiae*, I-II, Q. 6, art. 1.:

The second dimension of the will consists of the capacity for commanding external activities: it manifests the perfection of the will as "the lord of actions", its capacity for starting a new chain of causes.

The first perfection of the will is a necessary condition for the second, as much as it constitutes the moment of the choice of the end of the action, so that "the right use of the first of these freedoms is decisive for the value of the use of the second"[9]; on the other hand, in *Christian Ethics* von Hildebrand also affirms that the second perfection is somehow contained in the first, since the will in its primary sense is the volitional response which is at the basis of actions. Later, von Hildebrand recognized the critique that the first dimension of the will is by no means restricted to the states of affairs that are not yet real and realizable through me and that the inner free response of the will can also refer to God, to the world of values, to other persons when they lie completely outside the reach of the second perfection of freedom.[10] Nevertheless, already in *Christian Ethics* von Hildebrand introduces – in addition to the sphere of the will as lord of actions – some important new spheres in which human freedom plays a role: indirect freedom and cooperative freedom.

4. INDIRECT FREEDOM

In this work von Hildebrand argues that whereas the will in its first perfection cannot be obstructed by any external cause, the second perfection, i.e. the capacity for starting a new causal chain, can be hindered by essential or accidental limitations, with the former including all the attitudes and acts which we cannot directly command because they are totally or partially beyond the sphere of our influence. Even if freedom has no role in what is totally beyond the power of the will, man is responsible for everything on which he can have some influence, even indirectly, like the objects of the affective sphere or virtues.[11] Therefore, the human being possess indirect

---

"Unde, cum homo maxime cognoscat finem sui operis et moveat seipsum, in eius actibus maxime voluntarium invenitur".

[9] *Ibidem*.

[10] This critique is most of all contained in J. Seifert, *Was ist und was motiviert eine sittliche Handlung*, Salzburg 1972 .

[11] *Christian Ethics*, p. 314.

"This zone of our indirect influence includes our own affective responses as well as our virtues and even the responses and virtues of other persons [...] But our indirect influence refers especially to those things which by their value or disvalue call for zealuos interest in their existence or their destruction, but which are withdrown from our command, and whose realization cannot therefore become our aim, in the strict sense. Nevertheless we can do our share. There is a large scale as to the nature of this share. It may consist either in a removal of obstacles [...] or in creating favorable circumstances".

freedom, which is directed to those objects which are not yet real, but also are not directly commanded by the will, even though the person can have a role in bringing them into existence.

5. COOPERATIVE FREEDOM

Von Hildebrand, however, does not limit the sphere of freedom to what is not yet real: in *Christian Ethics,* he also introduces a third important dimension of freedom "which is even more decisive than our indirect influence, and in certain cases presupposed for the displaying of this indirect influence"[12]. which is "the freedom of taking a position toward experiences which have to come into existence without our free intervention, and which also cannot be dissipated by our free influence"[13]. This is "cooperative freedom", which manifests itself for instance in the way in which we endure bodily pains which are imposed on us, but which acquires its greatest moral significance in the sphere of virtues and and of human affectivity, and properly in the experience of *being affected*, namely of being moved by something endowed with a high value or disvalue, and in the *affective responses* which we already mentioned, such as joy, sorrow, love, hate etc. Both being affected and affective responses arise spontaneously, and we cannot control them as we control actions, "yet we can take a position toward them which greatly modifies the character of the experience, and which can also be of great moral significance in itself"[14]. With respect to being affected, freedom plays a cooperative role both a) in opening the soul to the influence of values and b) in making this experience fruitful for the soul. These two roles of cooperative freedom, which can be considered as prologue and epilogue of the being affected, are also present in affective responses, nevertheless these responses can be even more essentially permeated by freedom through two acts, which von Hildebrand calls "sanction" and "disavowal". When joy arises in us, we can freely identify ourselves with it (sanction) or we can emancipate ourselves from it (disavowal): in doing this we make use "of the very core of human freedom: the capacity of sanctioning and of disavowing our own spontaneous attitudes"[15] since "so long as our free spiritual center does not disavow them, the person implicitly identifies himself with them."[16] The morally unconscious man is not aware of this capacity of his will and therefore maintains an undisputed solidarity with his affectivity: in this way his

---

[12] *Christian Ethics*, p. 315.
[13] *Christian Ethics*, p. 316.
[14] *Ibidem*.
[15] *Christian Ethics*, p. 321.
[16] *Christian Ethics*, p. 325.

affective responses are not free, but only spontaneous. Furthermore, the faculty of sanctioning or disavowing is fully conscious and actual only in him who possesses a general will to be good, that is to say, who has made a superactual decision for moral values. Here we can already see something of the essential connection which, according to von Hildebrand, must be seen both between freedom and affectivity (the affective sphere in man is a high degree spiritual and free) and between freedom and moral good (freedom actualizes itself mainly in relation to this kind of good).

II. FREEDOM AND TRUTH

1. INTENTIONALITY SUCH AS THE BOND BETWEEN FREEDOM AND TRUTH

As we have seen, an essential feature of Hildebrand's notion of freedom is its intentional character. According to Hildebrand's realist position, this not only implies that any free decision or act is directed to an object, but also that this object transcends the acting person and is the measure for the act, so that not yet realized states of affairs are the proper object of the will as lord of actions; what is not under the direct power of the will can become the object of indirect freedom, and within affective sphere freedom can actualize itself as cooperative freedom, as the skeleton of the affective experiences, or as indirect freedom, which prepares the conditions for the rising of these experiences. Therefore, intentionality implies that freedom presupposes truth, both in the ontological and in the gnoseological sense.

2. ESSENTIAL LAWS AS LIMIT TO ARBITRARINESS

In *Moralia*, von Hildebrand explains that there are essential laws of being which are known either because of their evidence or through deduction; these are the object of that a-priori knowledge which von Hildebrand explains most thematically in *What is Philosophy?* and in the *Prolegomena of Christian Ethics*. This knowledge is evident, certain and necessary because of the evidence, certainty and necessity of its object. As regards to freedom, von Hildebrand points out in *Moralia* that essential laws constitute a necessary correlate of freedom, because they pose an ultimate limit to the arbitrariness which, as we have seen, is incompatible with freedom. Although these laws ask for a theoretical response, namely for conviction, which involves the intellect and not directly the will, this does not contradict the fact that they nevertheless have a great moral value and that the will can oppose itself to them, as in the case of relativism: these truths - being incompatible with any notion of freedom as arbitrariness - are a scandal to pride, so that he who intends freedom as arbitrariness in general denies them, calls them tautologies, because he cannot stand any "limit" to be placed on his freedom.

We could say that these necessary laws are the objective, metaphysical truth which must be recognized by man as the objective limit of his freedom, and must become the measure of the subjective use of freedom. This does not mean at all that truth is considered as something merely negative for human freedom: on the contrary, von Hildebrand says that "between the truth of the necessary essences and true freedom there is a deep bond", because truth makes man free, taking him out of the sphere of the probable, of appareance, and of immanence, and joining him to the certain, the absolute, the valid in itself[17].

3. FREEDOM AND VALUE-KNOWLEDGE

The second kind of relation between freedom and truth is grounded in the fact that since the proper object of freedom is always something important – something which is able to motivate the subject – the higher the important is (values instead of the agreeable; moral values compared with other kinds of values), the more freedom actualizes itself, so that the person must know the highest in the hierarchy of the important, values, and most of all what is the most important for him – moral values – in order to be authentically free. Here the problem of the relation between knowledge and freedom, between intellect and willing, is at stake, because the free will can hinder knowledge, most of all when the object deeply involves the person and requires a humble attitude as in the case of moral values. As we will see, according to von Hildebrand, the human person becomes fully free through moral freedom, when he adheres to the values, but this *adaequatio voluntatis et cordis ad valorem* is possible only when the value grasped is authentic: "only the spiritual person who has been "liberated" by the truth can rise from the ontological freedom of will to moral freedom"[18]. The person must be able to see values in order to freely give answer to them, and this seeing requires the conquest of pride and concupiscence.

---

[17] *Moralia*, (Dietrich von Hildebrand Gesammelte Werke, IX, Regensburg 1980) p. 176. "Erstens ist die Erkenntnis dieser absoluten Wahrheiten ein sieghaftes Transzendieren unseres Geistes, eine Befreiung einiger Art. Daß wir nicht länger in der Welt des uns erscheinenden verbleiben, daß wir in das Absolute, von uns Unabhängige, unbedingt Gültige eindringen dürfen, daß unser Geist gleichsam in und auf ihm ruhen darf, ist ein Triumph der Transzendenz und das Gegenteil des Gefangenseins in trostloser Immanenz."

[18] *Ibidem*. "Nur die durch die Wahrheit 'befreite' geistige Person kann sich von der ontologischen Freiheit des Willens zur moralischen Freiheit erheben." – translation mine.

III. FREEDOM AND MORALITY

1. FROM ONTOLOGICAL TO MORAL FREEDOM

The human person posseses freedom as an ontological perfection, as an essential mark of his personal being. According to von Hildebrand, however, freedom as an ontological dimension of man – which consists in the "not being compelled or necessitated" ("*das nicht Gezwungen oder Genötigt sein*") – does not only imply the consciousness of not being forced to decide in a certain way, but "reaches its highest point in the case of the obedience to a moral command"[19]. If we consider the role of importance in freedom, Hildebrand's analysis of the categories of importance, which have to be considered as one of the most relevant contributions of von Hildebrand's philosophy[20], manifests its significance. This analysis is based on the following fundamental distinction: an object can motivate the person either because it is important in itself – a value – or because it is subjectively satisfying for the subject – the agreeable – or because it is an objective good for the person (for example, a medicine).

Even though human freedom can actualize itself in relation to any category of importance, it is not neutral in what it chooses. The hierarchy existing among values, objective goods for the person and the subjectively satisfying is a measure for the will: the person reveals above all his dignity through its capacity for transcending his immanence and for conforming himself to values, and especially to moral values, which are within the power of his free will and the most specifically personal of all the values. Since moral values are the unum necessarium for the actualization of the person (who is indeed considered responsible for not possessing them, whereas he can lack other values, such as intellectual or aesthetical ones without being considered "good" or "bad" for this), freedom, responsibility and morality are linked by a necessary and essential relation. On the one hand, "if we seriously denied the freedom of will all morality immediately collapses and the notions of moral good and bad would lose all sense"[21]; on the other hand, morality gives to freedom its most authentic meaning and ontological freedom is by its nature called to be directed to moral values.

The fundamental choice which is the source of all the moral life of the person consists in the decision either for the mere subjectively satsfying

---

[19] *Das Wesen der Liebe*, in *Dietrich von Hildebrand Gesammelte Werke*, III, J. Habbel, Regensburg 1971, p. 59.

[20] See for instance J. Seifert, "Dietrich von Hildebrands philosophische Entdeckung der *Wertantwort* und die Grundlegung der Ethik", in *Aletheia* V (1992), p. 34-58.

[21] *Christian Ethics*, p. 289.

(*commodum*) or for the objectively morally relevant (*iustum*). This free decision is the border between ontological and moral freedom, which is "the freedom of he who makes the right use of his inner freedom, in whom the central attitude of value response has achieved a definitive victory over pride and concupiscence, and whose behaviour in general and in its significant details is actually adapted to the logos of value as it appears in the various situations and aspects of life" and implies, "not only the capacity to obey the demand of values accidentally, but a permanent and intimate conformity to their persuasion, sealed with the express sanction of the central personality. Moral freedom in this sense [...] is equivalent to freedom proper, freedom in its perfection; above all, it goes incomparabily deeper than the merely formal or technical freedom embodied in the controlling position of the will"[22]. Human freedom reaches its highest actualization in the saint, who, even though presupposing grace, implies the fulfilment of the human dimension. Here the dignity of the person as free being appears in its greatness[23].

Authentic freedom therefore implies self-possession, but it is very far from any will to power which imposes itself on being, because it is directed to self-donation, as well as is "the opposite of those stoic ideals of apathy and ataraxy which require us to become insensitive to all goods", since "because we are free from all irrelevant and illegitimate ties, everything that bears on true values has a far deeper and stronger impact on our hearts. [...] The comparative reserve we impose on ourselves in regard to all genuine goods of the natural order has no meaning but to make us completely free for integral allegiance to the highest good"[24].

2. FREEDOM AND HAPPINESS

One of the strongest criticisms von Hildebrand made of Aristotelian ethics is of its reduction of the sphere of human freedom to the choice of the means to become happy, happiness being the necessary end of the will. Von Hildebrand does not deny that man is ordained to being happy, but he re-

---

[22] *Transformation in Christ*, p. 219.

[23] *Transformation in Christ*, p. 296:
"To sum up - true inner freedom means that we have relinquished our natural standpoint and live through Him, with Him, and in Him. This implies an unequivocal renunciation of the basis that had formerly provided us with a sense of natural security. Egocentric biases, complexes of fear, psychic cramp as well as laxity and self-indulgence of every kind - in a word, all illegitimate preoccupations, all that is not rooted in the call of God or in the appeal of true values – must be dislodged and stripped of their empire over us."

[24] *Transformation in Christ*, p. 297.

jects the idea that happiness can be considered as the key to explaining the moral life of the person.

The first reason for this rejection is that true happiness cannot be reached directly, simply in aiming at it as an end, but is obtained by man only as a superabundant effect of moral goodness. Only he that looks for moral values will receive happiness as a gift, and only the false and empty happiness of the subjectively satisfying can be aimed at directly by man.

The second reason is that the moral life of the person does not develop itself only as a series of choices among different means to be happy: the starting point of any moral life is that general will to be good which we already mentioned, in which the person takes a decided stance toward the world of values, or, on the other hand, chooses to abandon himself to the merely subjectively satisfying.

Both these elements show us the role which freedom plays in relation to good and happiness. Human freedom is a means to becoming happy, but only in as much as moral values are the end of its acting, only in as much as it becomes a *moral* freedom. On the other hand, only when the person conforms himself freely to the moral good can he receive happiness as a superabundant gift.

I will also mention the third important role which freedom plays in morality. Human moral life is not limited to the sphere of singular acts, but presupposes the general and fundamental choice of the world of moral values (which von Hildebrand calls "general will to be good"), and finds its fulfilment in the aquiring of virtues. Both are superactual relations, namely, general and permanent attitudes which are situated beyond the punctual and temporary character of the singular acts, and deeply penetrate the personality. Freedom plays a role even in this superactual sphere, although indirectly, because through any singular act and response the person can influence his superactual attitudes, which in itself cannot be commanded by the will[25].

IV. FREEDOM AND AFFECTIVITY

The third essential aspect of Hildebrand's notion of freedom is related to the role of freedom in the affective sphere. The reevaluation of the affec-

---

[25] Von Hildebrand's theory of virtue involves a critique of the interpretation of virtue as "habit", namely as something which derives spontaneously from the person because it has become habitual. According to von Hildebrand, virtues are general superactual responses to a specific sphere of goods; in any act of virtue, freedom is actualized as a value response and the easiness which virtue can cause in the performance of the corresponding acts does not imply at all a lack of freedom: on the contrary, it is the manifestation of that freedom from pride and concupiscence which is the ultimate end of morality. (See *Christian Ethics*, cap 27).

tive sphere as not only linked to the instinctual dimension of man had already been initiated by Scheler, and is a frequently recurring element in Hildebrandian anthropology. The fundamental condition which allows the affective sphere to be permeated by freedom is that it contains levels which are endowed with the character of spirituality. As we have seen, there are some affective experiences - such as being affected and affective responses - which are intentional, that is to say, which are consituted by meaningful relations between the person and an object which is able to motivate in virtue of its importance. These affective intentional experiences are not volitional acts, in as much as they cannot be commanded by the will, and freedom nevertheless plays an important role in preparing the way for them, and most of all in sanctioning or disavowing the affective responses.

The disparity between the sphere of the direct influence of human freedom, which is in the power of the will, and the affective sphere which, although possessing a deep role in the existential and moral condition of the human person falls within the scope of indirect freedom, reveals, according to von Hildebrand, a deep feature of the metaphysical status of man. Since he is a creature, the human person has the power to bring into existence only that which is limited as regarding its ontological dignity, so that "the higher something is, the more it possesses the character of a gift, which we cannot simply give to ourselves"[26]. Whereas volitional responses posses freedom as their proper perfection, in the affective responses "the heart and the plenitude of a human personality are fully actualized": the character of creaturehood is revealed in the fact that "it is not granted to man to possess this affective plenitude and freedom in one and the same act"[27].

The importance of this insight of von Hildebrand's manifests itself above all in love. Love manifests in the highest degree the fact that the deepest dimension of the affective sphere both involves the fullness of the human person, his heart, and remains beyond the power of the direct influence of freedom: love is always a gift, something that man cannot *directly* command, but only sanction through his cooperative freedom. And at the same time, this does not mean that the will has no role in love. Nevertheless, the body of the response of love is a "word" pronounced by the heart, and this word can only be the object of indirect freedom[28].

The distinction between the role of freedom in the volitional and in the affective sphere enters also into the question of the role of freedom in ac-

---

[26] *Christian Ethics*, p. 319.
[27] *Christian Ethics*, p. 320.
[28] *Das Wesen der Liebe*, p. 83. "Wir können uns Liebe nicht geben, auch wenn wir es wollten. Es steht nicht in unserer Macht, eine solche Antwort des Herzens frei zu setzen wie eine Willensantwort, noch sie zu kommandieren wie eine Tat."

tion and in contempletion, since the field of action and decision is proper to the influence of the will, whereas the objects which can be contemplated but not commanded by man are object of the affective responses[29].

D. von Hildebrand's philosophy of freedom makes it possible to encompass the different aspects of human experience in which freedom actualizes itself, and it is most of all a very important investigation into the many spheres in which human freedom actualizes itself. Hildebrand's philosophy of freedom indeed enables us to comprehend the many aspects of human experiences, and at the same time takes into account the metaphysical situation of man as a created person, who is endowed with a body and a spiritual center constituted by the unity of intellect, will and affectivity, and ordered to truth, moral goodness and happiness.

---

[29] *Das Wesen der Liebe*, p. 132 ff.

LORELLA CONGIUNTI
Italy

THE "IN-SISTENCIA" AS METAPHYSICAL PRESUPPOSITION OF FREEDOM IN THE PHILOSOPHICAL THOUGHT OF ISMAEL QUILES

"The *in-sistencia*[1] is the indispensable metaphysical presupposition to the existence of freedom"[2]: this is one of the most significant statements from *La esencia del hombre* of Ismael Quiles[3].

In the course of my short writing, I am going to make just a few remarks about freedom in the context of the *"in-sistencial* philosophical thought" developed by Quiles[4].

---

[1] The translation of the common meaning of *"in-sistencia"* is "insistence" or "insistency", but Quiles gives a particular philosophical sense to this word – which I will explain below – so I prefer to use the Spanish word with the hyphen: *"in-sistencia"*.

[2] «La in-sistencia es el presupuesto metafísico necesario de la libertad» Ismael Quiles, *La esencia del hombre*, in *Antropología filosófica in-sistencial,* Depalma, Buenos Aires 1983, page 346.

[3] Ismael Quiles (Valencia, Spain 1906 – Buenos Aires, Argentina 1993), a philosopher born in Spain but who has lived most of his life in Argentina. He developed a particular philophical thought subdivided in three basic stages, "the rational stage" (1938-1948) constituting a deep examination of Scholastic philosophy , "the *in-sistencial* stage" (1946-1960), an original philosophical proposal and in the meantime a reply to Existentialism, and "the synthesis between Eastern and Western culture", the third stage (since 1960) constituting a development of the preceding reflection caused by a comparison with the Eastern philosophical thought known directly by Quiles during his long journeys there. I believe that the *in-sistencial* stage is the central one and not only as to his chronology. It constitutes actually the more original contribution of Quiles and is introduced by the first stage and implicit in the development of the third one.

[4] To get a critical description of the Quiles' thought I take the liberty to refer to Lorella Congiunti, *Soggettività ed ontologia. Introduzione alla filosofia "in-sistenziale" di Ismael Quiles,* edited by Abelardo, Ardea (Rome) to be published and to the synthetical description of Julio Raúl Méndez, *La ontología del hombre en el «insistencialismo» de Ismael Quiles,* "Studium", XXV, 1985, pages 139-154.

I consider such consideration highly justified above all by the relationship established by Quiles between his peculiar idea of the *"in-sistencia"* and the notion of freedom. Furthermore, as I will show, such a relationship is closely connected to the topic of this conference, based, as it is, on freedom.

I wish to develop this thopic, beginning with a short comment on Quiles' "quotation", following two equally feasable directions within the necessary relation linking "in-sistencia" and freedom: on the one hand, freedom as a means to discover "in-sistencia", on the other hand, freedom as an issue entailed by the richness of "in-sistencia".

First of all, the meaning of "in-sistencia" should be clarified.

The *"in-sistencia"* is the notion used by Quiles to refer to the ontological situation typical of the human being and, at the same time, the way to attain it as well. The significance of this notion is to be found in the meaning of the word itself, which is a philosophical neology.

"The philosophical meaning we attach, in this work [i.e. *Antropología filosófica in-sistencial*], to the term *"in-sistere"* and to its derivatives comes from its original etymology "to stand firmly upon something , or to be firmly in it" or, to express it in a more concise formula, "to stand in". However we add a shade of meaning to it, which cannot be found explicitly in the Latin etymology and use, that is, inwardness"[5].

On analysing the elements of the word, which are stressed by the hyphen, *"in"* clearly implies both a dynamism and a position[6], that is to say, the peculiar movement of internalization[7] which is only possible when a firm basis exists, whereas *"sistencia"* referes to "being" [8]. The *"in-sistencia"* is therefore the internalized position peculiar to the human being. It defines man in its true and inner essence.

According to Quiles, the *"in-sistencia"* is not a thoroughly new concept in the history of philosophy; being an original reality (i.e., an original word,

---

[5] «El sentido filosofico que damos en esta obra a los téerminos "in-sistir" y sus derivados retorna a su primitiva etimologia "estar firmemente sobre o en algo", o en fórmula concisa "estar en". Pero le agregamos un matiz que reconocemos no hallarse explicitamente en la etimologia y uso latino: la interioridad» Ismael Quiles, quoted, page XVIII (Presentación).

[6] In fact in the Latin language *"in"* can be construed both with the accusative (to indicate the movement) and the ablative (to indicate the position).

[7] In order to indicate the possibility of making inward proper of man, Quiles uses a Castilian word that is difficult to translate and that has already been used by Ortega y Gasset i.e. *"ensimismamiento"*.

[8] To obtain a comparison, in my opinion indispensable, to the notion of "rational substance", see Lorella Congiunti, *quoted*.

an original known reality[9]) it is implicitly present throughout the history of philosophy and it stands out in authors like Plato, Plotino, and Saint Augustine. Above all the *"in-sistencia"*, although not defined as such, derives from each human being's experience[10].

As a matter of fact, man's condition, his behaviour and his attributes show the presence of a firm and solid centre "inside" the man himself. Particularly "freedom" is very closely linked to the *"in-sistencia"* as, according to Quiles, freedom cannot exist in a being that is not *"in-sistencial"*. Owing to this peculiarity, this relationship can be, in my opinion, analysed in terms of a "demonstration": freedom is, as I said before, a means to the discovery of *"in-sistencia"*. On the one hand, this way reinforces the idea of *"in-sistencia"* as *"primum esse"* of man, whereas, on the other hand, it makes it into a problem as *"primum cognitum"*[11].

According to Quiles, freedom is for man the "innermost experience" of his being and "in the act of freedom we seem to touch the core of our being more than in any other act"[12].

Freedom therefore characterizes itself in action, an action intimately experienced by man.

An action is free only if it is not caused by an external necessity or by an internal instinctive automatism.

For these reasons, Quiles defines an action free depending on its direction: from the "inside" to the "outside". An action which is not free, on the contrary, characterizes itself by its coming from the "outside" into the "inside".

An action that does not come from "inside" is not "mine".

Therefore the mere fact that the human being is able to undertake free acts bears witness to the existence of an inside world. Furthermore, freedom

---

[9] «*La in-sistencia -y en ella la esencia originaria del hombre-, no sólo es la primera realidad* "primum esse", *sino también la primera palabra y el primer conocimiento* "primum cognitum" *del hombre*» («*"In-sistencia"* – and in it the primitive essence of man – not only is the first reality *"primum esse"*, but also the first word and first knowledge *"primum cognitum"* of man») Ismael Quiles, *La esencia del hombre*, quoted, page 360. For a clarification and some remarks related to *in-sistencia* as *"primum cognitum"*, see Lorella Congiunti, *quoted.*

[10] To indicate this experience Quiles uses the word *"vivencia"*, a term that Ortega y Gasset has rendered of common use in the philosophical language and that is a translation of the German word *"Erlebnis"*.

[11] It is necessary to underline that Quiles makes this aspect problematic by the comparison with the Thomasian affirmation «*Non ergo per essentiam suam, sed per actus suum se cognoscit intellectus noster*», *Summa Theologiae*, pars I, q. 87, I, c.. See what indicated at the footnote no. 9.

[12] «*La más íntima vivencia de su ser*», «*en el acto de libertad parece que tocamos el fondo de nuestro ser, más, tal vez, que in ningún otro acto*» Ismael Quiles, *La esencia del hombre*, quoted, page 346.

implies the knowledge of the possibilities, a previous "contemplation" which would not be possible without a rational and not merely sensory centre, where such contemplation occurs.

Therefore, as a necessary condition for freedom to exist, there has to be an inner rational centre. Thus, freedom requires an ontological centre as its own metaphysical presupposition[13], the condition of a being which stands in itself, that is, *"in-siste"*. There follows that freedom is only possible for an *"in-sistencial"* being and as man knows himself as free, he is also *"in-sistente"*.

The above is a brief development of the first point. In order to clarify it, I have slightly stretched Quiles's methodology giving it a rational bend starting from real experience and then developing it in a more theoretical way.

In order to develop the second point, I will clarify Quiles's most typical and original methodology, by which the term *"in-sistencia"* also refers to a method based on the analysis of real experience, i.e., an intuitive method rooted in Platonism and Saint Augustine, borrowing from phenomenology and from existencialism the capacity of grasping the concreteness of real human experience.

This phenomenological analysis of human life reveals man as endowed with some features that classical philosophical thought has already identified. These are rationality, personality, conscience and freedom. The latter enriches chiefly the existential aspect of *"in-sistencia"* as it controls man's relationship not only with himself but also with the surrounding world. Indeed, existence *(ex-sistencia)* is only authentic if it is based on "in-sistencia"[14]. A human relationship is authentic if it is free and therefore life is meaningful when it is freely directed. Vice-versa, in today's society man is forced to live in an alienating and anonymous condition, thus his freedom is limited and his dignity offended.

Therefore, freedom is a way leading to the discovery of *"in-sistencia"*, and *"in-sistencia"* in itself implies freedom. "We believe that no other hu-

---

[13] In reality Quiles would call it *"óntico"* as for him *"óntico"* directly refers to being, while *"ontológico"* refers to the science of being.

[14] «Al volverse el hombre sobre sí y hacerse patente el ser del hombre a sí mismo, lejos de encontrarse encerrado en la subjetividad aislada, se descubre y se vive como abierto en múltiples direcciones [...] Puede ahora salir a ester y actuar afuera, entre los entes, sin perderme a mí mismo, porque lo hago desde este centro e instalado en él y por él me siento seguro en el ser que explica y ordena todos los entes. Ésta es la autéentica salida de sí, "ec-sistencia", que en realidad non es un simple salir de sí, ya que sale de sí sin dejar de ester en sí y autoafirmándose»; «La existencia auténtica surge de la in-istencia y se finda ontológicamente en ella». Ismael Quiles, *La esencia del hombre*, quoted, pages 335-336 and page 348.

man experience enlightens the very essence of man's freedom as clearly and definitely as «*in-sistencia*»"[15].

Another aspect which, I believe, is worth stressing in Quiles' consideration on freedom, is the *risk* connected to the *responsibility* of freedom.

As a matter of fact, freedom implies responsibility when by this word we mean "man's capacity to answer for his own actions". Man exercises the greatest freedom towards being.

According to Quiles man reacts to the impact with the being, that is, with the existing things, by affirming "being is", i.e. with a metaphysical statement. But Quiles also believes that, thanks to his free thought, man may deny such an immediate answer either and state "being is not". Such a metaphysical denial reveals the range of freedom as well as its weakness and precariousness, since "with such a lacking freedom that I have, I may invalidate my first contact with the being"[16].

Quiles' statement shows how, in order to gain insight into freedom, the latter has to be linked to truth; in other words being and his knowledge must be confronted. Man may deny the truth, however such a denial is not the highest expression of his freedom but rather its peculiarly human limit. The highest expression of freedom does not contradict truth.

Quiles' philosophical reflection has the merit of bringing subjectivity back to the solidity of ontology. In other words he believes that the meaning of man is to be found in terms of being. Thus the phenomenology of real experience can only be rooted in the metaphysical necessity of a firm and stable ontological centre. Therefore, freedom cannot be defined without being referred to *"in-sistencia"*.

Quiles' reflection on freedom can help today's confused culture to recover the unique dignity of the human position. With deep-felt involvement, he denounces "the danger of a merely external life; a danger which is making itself felt in our century more than ever before. It is worth recalling that politics, technology, the abolition of distances, over-organization, one-sided propaganda can turn, and actually do turn, XX century man into a puppet using someone else's brain, a man who has lost the capacity of choosing. He cannot help behaving in a certain way as if he were a machine and, even worse, to the extent of loosing the awareness of having lost his conscience,

---

[15] «Nos parece que ninguna otra experiencia humana ilumina tan clara y decisivamente la esencia de la libertad en el hombre como la in-sistencia». Ismael Quiles, *Más allá del existencialismo,* in *Antropología filosófica in-sistencial,* quoted, page 50.

[16] «Con esta libertad deficiente que tengo, puedo llegar a invalidar mi primer contacto con el ser». Ismael Quiles, *Tres lecciones de metafísica in-sistencial,* in *Antropología filosófica in-sistencial,* quoted, page 286. Quiles underlines as such a sceptical attitude is "necessarily precarious", Ibidem.

and of persuading himself that that is how it has to be, just like as in bygone ages slavery seemed natural"[17].

Therefore we can read Quiles' ontological reflection on freedom just as Mondin reads all the in-sistencial philosophy, that is in terms of a "a cultural proposal against alienation"[18], which is the consequence of the lack of the real freedom, or, to quote the invitation to this Conference, as the everlasting "culture of freedom founded upon truth", the only one capable of opposing contemporary "culture of liberty without limits".

---

[17] «El peligro de la vida puramente exterior, peligro que en el siglo XX es más agudo que en otro cualquiera. Por qué volver a recordar que la política, la técnica, la supresión de distancias, el exceso de organización, la propaganda dirigida unilateral, etc. , etc., pueden convertir, y de hecho están convirtiendo, al hombre del siglo XX en un muñeco que piensa con la cabeza de otro, que ha perdido la capacidad de elección y que non tiene más recurso que actuar en una dirección determinada come si fuera una máquina, y, lo que es peor, llegando a perder conciencia de que ha perdido su conciencia, y a persuadirse de que así tiene que ser, come en los tiempos antiguos parecía natural para algunos hombres la esclavitud?». Ismael Quiles, *quoted*, page XV *(Presentación)*.

[18] «Una proposta culturale per combattere l'alienazione», Battista Mondin, *L'antropologia insistenziale di Padre I. Quiles: una proposta culturale per combattere l'alienazione,* in AA.VV., *III Coloquio Internacional filosofía in-sistencial y cultura (10, 11 y 12 de agosto de 1983),* Fundación "Ser y Saber", Buenos Aires, 1988, pages 111-128.

CONTENTS

Foreword (*Zofia J. Zdybicka*) 5
Avant-propos (*Zofia J. Zdybicka*) 7
His Holiness John Paul II 9
Stanisław Wielgus, The Opening Address 17
Józef Glemp, Homélie d'ouverture du Congrès 25
Bolesław Pylak 29
Zofia J. Zdybicka 31

PLENARY SESSIONS

Mieczysław A. Krąpiec, The Nature of Human Freedom 35
Peter van Inwagen, The Mystery of Metaphysical Freedom 45
Battista Mondin, Freedom, an Essential and Primary Constituent of the Human Person 57
Giovanni Reale, Messaggio filosofico mediante il mito e concetto di libertà in Platone 73
Julio Terán Dutari, Analogie der Freiheit als Kern einer christlischen Philosophie nach dem Werk Erich Przywaras 85
Rocco Buttiglione, Person and Society 95
Herman De Dijn, Freedom in Contemporary Culture 107
Angelo Scola, Libertà grazia destino 127
Josef Seifert, To Be a Person – to Be Free 145
Michel Schooyans, Liberté humaine et participation politique . 187
Tadeusz Styczeń, Freedom and Law. For or against Life? The Ethician Confronting the "Inefficiency" of Truth 195
Władysław Stróżewski, Freedom and Value 217

Vittorio Possenti, Dialectique de la liberté. Vers une philosophie intégrale de la liberté 225
Georges Cottier, Liberté crée. Liberté et obéissance – réflections philosophiques 235
George F. McLean, Freedom as the Basis of Civil Society: The Transformation of Christian Philosophy at the Dawn of the New Millennium 257
Lothar Kraft, "To Enjoy Freedom We Must Bear Responsibility". Freedom as Seen by the Christian Democratic Union of Germany ... 273
Anton Rauscher, Das Recht auf Religionsfreiheit in einer säkularen Gesellschaft 279
Francesca Rivetti Barbò, Liberté et vérité. Du savoir commun à la philosophie 289
Jean Ladrière, Liberté et événement 303
Jose A. Ibañez-Martin, About the European Cultural Conscience: Human Condition and the Divine Person 319

CONCEPTIONS OF FREEDOM

Edualdo Forment, Que es ser hombre? 335
Abelardo Lobato, La libertad y el futuro del hombre. La perspectiva tomistica 353
Anna-Teresa Tymieniecka, Freedom in Human Creative Condition . 375
Jan Van der Veken, Can There Be Freedom in a Determinist World? . 385
Stanisław Judycki, Freedom and Determination 393
Ryszard Legutko, Freedom of Thought and Inviolability of Conscience . 407
Andrius Valevičius, Freedom and Personal Autonomy 415
Alessandro Ghisalberti, Le rapport entre liberté et félicité dans la philosophie médiévale: relectures contemporaines 423
Philippe Capelle, Liberté philosophique et ontologie théologale 441
Andrzej Walicki, Marxist Communism as a Conception of Freedom .. 451
Rachel Gazolla de Andrade, Réflexions éthico-politiques sur les racines de la notion de liberté dans la philosophie grecque ancienne 461
Paul Richard Blum, Der Ort der Freiheit – Argumente aus der Renaissance-Philosophie 469
Anna Małecka, Freedom and Moral Act in Thomas Carlyle's Philosophical Thought 487
Ignace Verhack, The Temporality of Freedom 493

John F. X. Knasas, The Post-Modern Notion of Freedom and Aquinas'
   Ratio Entis 511
Andrzej Maryniarczyk, Freedom and Truth (Truth as a Way
   to Freedom) 527
Władysław Pabiasz, Die Freiheit und der Moralische Wert 535
Stefan Swieżawski, Liberté en philosophie 543
Hugo Ochoa, Grundlage der Freiheit bei Schelling 557
Maciej Potępa, Freiheit in der Religionsphilosophie: Kant und
   Schleiermacher 571
Patrick de Laubier, La philosophie morale de Vladimir Soloviev 583
Dalia Marija Stančienè, The Conception of Freedom in the Works
   of Lithuanian Catholic Philosophers 593
Lina Šulcienè, Thought Over the Mystery of Freedom on the Basis
   of Thomistic Ontological Principles 601
Peter Volek, Begründung der Freiheit bei Edith Stein 607
Leszek Pyra, A Man in Dialogue with Himself and Others in Reinhold
   Niebuhr's Interpretation 617
Paola Premoli de Marchi, Philosophy of Freedom in Dietrich
   von Hildebrand: Freedom as Related to Truth, Moral Goodness
   and Affectivity 627
Lorella Congiunti, The "In-sistencia" as Metaphisical Presupposition
   of Freedom in the Philosophical Thought of Ismacl Quiles 639